CADOGAN

Vene

& the Dolomites

Cadogan Guides
West End House, 11 Hills Place, London W1R 1AH
guides@morrispub.co.uk

The Globe Pequot Press
6 Business Park Road, PO Box 833, Old Saybrook,
Connecticut 06475–0833

Copyright © Dana Facaros and Michael Pauls 1999
Illustrations © Horatio Monteverde 1996

Book and cover design by Animage

Cover photographs © front: VA001400/1 (Corbis)
                        back: Irene Stupar
                        inside back: the Italian Tourist Board

Maps © Cadogan Guides, drawn by Map Creation Ltd

Editorial Director: Vicki Ingle
Series Editor: Linda McQueen

Editor: Linda McQueen
Proofreading: Kate Paice
Indexing: Ann Hall
Production: Book Production Services

A catalogue record for this book is available from the British Library
ISBN 1-86011-904-2

The author and publishers have made every effort to ensure the accuracy of the
information in this book at the time of going to press. However they cannot accept
any responsibility for any loss, injury or inconvenience resulting from the use of
information contained in this guide.

Printed and bound in Great Britain by The Cromwell Press Ltd.

About the Authors

Dana Facaros and Michael Pauls have now written over 20 Cadogan Guides. For three years they and their two children Jackson and Lily lived in a tiny Umbrian hilltop village, then an equally remote French village in the Lot. They now live in Ireland.

Acknowledgements

Thanks to Linda and Nico and Tania, who took care of Lily, and to Lily for being good and leaving some ice-cream at Krioneri for the other campers. Also thanks to Claudia for her Venetian updating, and to all the tourist offices who took the time to answer questions, even the stupid ones. And a big thank you to Linda at Cadogan for her fresh, young and sparkling editing.

The publishers would like to thank the Italian Tourist Board in London for permission to use their library photograph of Lago di Misurina near Belluno, and also Map Creation for pulling out all the stops.

Villa plans in the Veneto chapter are from Andrea Palladio, *The Four Books of Architecture* (Dover Publications Inc., 31 East 2nd Street, Mineola N.Y. 11501).

Please help us to keep this guide up to date

We have done our best to ensure that the information in this guide is correct at the time of going to press. But places and facilities are constantly changing, and standards and prices in hotels and restaurants fluctuate. We would be delighted to receive any comments concerning existing entries or omissions, as well as suggestions for new features. All contributors will be acknowledged in the next edition, and authors of the best letters will be offered a copy of the Cadogan Guide of their choice.

Contents

Maps and Plans

Introduction

'Something for everyone', the rusty old sales pitch goes—only in Venetia here many of the Somethings are 24-carat gold. The Dolomites aren't just mountains, they are the Most Beautiful Mountains. Venice is Most Beautiful City; Lake Garda, the Palladian villas, the Renaissance paintings, the frescoes by Giotto, all *i più belli del mondo*, as the Italians say. You want to argue, except that they're probably right. The region that gave the world Bellini, Giorgione, Titian and Tiepolo may not have that clear Mediterranean quality of places further south, but it has an extra dimension of atmosphere that no photograph of Piazza San Marco, or La Rotonda, or Lake Garda ever conveys; this region is sumptuous, sensuous, lush, worldly, at times magnificent.

Venetia has roughly the same borders it had as the Roman Tenth Augustine Region of *Venetia et Histria*. The Italians call it the *Tre Venezie* for its three modern regions: the Veneto, Trentino-Alto Adige, and Friuli-Venezia Giulia. The latter two only joined Italy after the First World War; the frontier at Trieste was settled only in 1972. This has left the northeast the most cosmopolitan pocket of Italy, by a long shot. German often prevails in the Alto Adige/Süd Tirol, Slovenian in eastern and northern Friuli, while languages you may never have heard of such as Ladin, Friul, and Cimbro, are still spoken and undergoing a revival. Even Italian is beginning to lose out to Venetic, its colourful cousin (use the word 'dialect' at the risk of starting an argument). Religious traditions, folk customs, music, cuisine and national dress have not been forgotten or homogenized. If Venetia is a melting pot, it's a pot full of polenta, 'dust as beautiful as gold', according to Goldoni, a dish that crosses all its cultures, but one that can be grilled, fried, sliced and served in a thousand different ways.

Variety may be in its genes. Venice, the leading player in these parts for over a thousand years, was always the most cosmopolitan state in Europe, and influenced Venetia economically and culturally even before it became part the Serenissima in the early 15th century. You can still sense her presence; memories of her industry, her *dolce vita*, her fears and dreams have seeped into the land. In Italo Calvino's *Invisible Cities*, Marco Polo tells Kublai Khan of the cities he has visited. After hearing countless places described, Kublai Khan asks him why he never speaks of one city—his own, Venice. Polo replies 'Every time I describe a city I am saying something about Venice.' For him, Venice was implicit in everything. And so too, in Venetia, like a gentle sigh...

Along with its beauty and the magnificent villas dotted around the country-side, be warned that Venetia also possesses some equally magnificent sprawl and industry. This is nothing new: in the *Inferno*, Dante vividly describes the proto-Industrial Revolution goings-on in Venice's Arsenale. Since the Second World War, Venetia has re-established its historic position as one of the wealthiest regions in Italy, a place where people grow and make things: wine, apples, cheese, maize (source of all that polenta), clothes, furniture, gold jewellery, ceramics, chandeliers. With the great exception of Venice, of course, where hosting the world has been a way of life for about three centuries now, tourism is only a sideline here.

Palladian Villas

Villas of the Veneto

Non-Palladian Villas 🏛

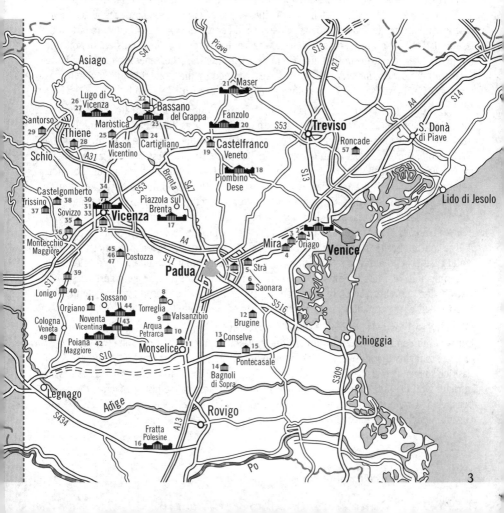

The best way to see Venetia is to travel leisurely, as free from timetables and schedules as possible. This is made easy because the region packs a lot into a small space. Venice and her pearly lagoon are only a few hours from the jagged, wind-clawed towers of the Dolomites. You can attend a ballet in Vicenza, in Europe's oldest theatre designed by Palladio, and the next night hear *Aida* in Verona's Roman arena. You can top off a lazy day on a sandy beach with a romantic evening in Àsolo. To see the highlights of the whole region, choose three or four bases—a perfect three-week holiday would include a few days in Venice, a week in the Veneto, a week in the Dolomites, and a few days in Friuli, perhaps on the seaside.

Visiting Venetia: A Little Orientation

As with Marco Polo, **Venice** is the place to start, not only for its intrinsically fascinating self, but to help understand the rest, especially the **Veneto**. Here Venice's sweet sisters, Padua, Vicenza, Verona and Treviso, are among Italy's richest art cities, each with a strong personality, each surrounded by a constellation of villas and smaller jewels—Monsèlice, Este, Àsolo, Maròstica, Bassano del Grappa, Rovigo, Oderzo, and Feltre. The south of the Veneto is defined by the flatlands and mystery-laden delta of the Po, interrupted by little clusters of volcanic bumps, the fabled Euganean Hills and Monti Bérici. To the west the Veneto is framed by **Lake Garda**, the most dramatic of the Italian Lakes, rimmed by the Dolomites and lovely towns Sirmione, Gardone, Salò, Malcesine, Riva, and Torri del Benaco.

The Veneto town of Belluno and its glittering resort of Cortina d'Ampezzo are the gateway to the strange and fabulous **Dolomites**. Each group of peaks is as different and beautiful as the next—if you have time for a short stay, you can see them at their most breathtaking along the Great Dolomites Road between Cortina and Bolzano. To the west lies the autonomous province of **Trentino**, where the delightful city of Trento hosted the famous Counter-Reformation council. It encompasses the westernmost Dolomites, the Brenta Group, lush valleys of orchards and vineyards, two resorts in gorgeous settings, Madonna di Campilgio and San Martino di Castrozza, as well as a score of beautifully preserved medieval castles with courtly frescoes. There are just as many fairytale castles up in bilingual **Süd Tirol/Alto Adige**, on the border of Austria and Switzerland, where strudel meets pasta head on. You could easily spend a day in and around Bolzano, the arty modern capital, or the celebrated watering hole of Merano; among its many secrets are some of Europe's best preserved Carolingian churches. Much of the western part of the province lies within the confines of Stelvio, Italy's largest national park, where you can ski year round.

Off to the east towards Slovenia, **Friuli-Venezia Giulia** may seem a bit off the beaten track, but was the centre of action in Roman times, when Aquileia was the capital of *Venetia et Histria*; today its the most important archaeological site in northern Italy. Cividale del Friuli has rich souvenirs of its days as the capital of a 8th-century Lombard duchy, while Trieste is an intriguing bit of Mitteleurope on the Med. Its other attractions are just as diverse: the sandy beaches at Grado, the Tuscan-like wine growing hills of the Collio, the karst and Grotta Gigante, Italy's largest forest around Tarvisio, and Ùdine, the city of Tiepolo.

Travel

By Air

From the UK and Ireland

There are direct flights to Venice, Verona and Trieste from several British airports, with good year-round services especially to Venice. Most scheduled flights are operated either by the Italian state airline **Alitalia**, ✆ (0171) 602 7111, or **British Airways**, ✆ (0345) 222 111. A few services to Venice only are operated by **Air UK**, ✆ (0990) 074074. The best-value deals are usually **Apex** or **SuperApex** fares, which you must book seven days ahead, and stay a Saturday night in Italy—no alterations or refunds are possible without high penalties. Return scheduled fares range typically from around £149 off-season; midsummer fares will probably be well over £249. **Sabena**, ✆(0181) 780 1444, and **Lufthansa**, ✆ (0345) 737 747, can offer cheaper fares (around £180 return) to Venice but these often have quite rigid restrictions and involve flying via another European destination such as Brussels.

Two companies currently offer extremely cheap scheduled flights: **Go** airlines, ✆ (0845) 605 4321, a branch of British Airways, operates flights between and Venice (7 times a week), which, if booked in advance, can cost as little as £80 return, although on a heavily booked flight this can rise to around £300. The starting prices for **Ryanair**, flights from Stansted to Treviso, ✆ (0541) 569 569, are around £59 and most prices are below £215; catch them when they have special offers, and a return flight can cost as little as £50. Early birds get the best seats in the airline business. A certain number of cheap seats are allotted for young people or bona fide students, and senior citizens, but once they're gone, that's it.

From Ireland, **Alitalia**, ✆ (00353 1) 844 6035, and **Aer Lingus**, Dublin ✆ (00 353 1) 705 3333, or Belfast, ✆ (0645) 737 747, operate direct flights to Rome and Milan only. The frequency depends on the time of year; you may well save money by flying to London and picking up a Go or Ryanair flight from there.

charter flights

Many inexpensive charter flights are available to Venice and Verona in summer, though you are unlikely to find rock-bottom bargains. One of the biggest UK operators is **Italy Sky Shuttle**, which uses a variety of carriers. You may find cheaper fares by combing the small ads in the travel pages, or from a specialist agent. Use a reputable ABTA-registered one, such as **Trailfinders** or **Campus Travel**. All these companies offer particularly good student and youth rates too. The main problems with cheaper flights tend to be inconvenient or unreliable flight schedules, and booking restrictions, i.e. you may have to make reservations far ahead, accept given dates and, if you miss your flight, there's no redress. Taking out good travel insurance, however cheap your ticket, is your only precaution.

> **Italy Sky Shuttle**, 227 Shepherd's Bush Rd, London W6 7AS, ✆ (0181) 748 1333.
>
> **Italflights**, 125 High Holborn, London WC1V 6QA, ✆ (0171) 405 6771.
>
> **Italia Nel Mondo**, 6 Palace Street, London SW1E 5HY, ✆ (0171) 828 9171.
>
> **Budget Travel**, 134 Lower Baggot Street, Dublin 2, ✆ (00353 1) 661 1866.
>
> **United Travel**, Stillorgan Bowl, Stillorgan, C. Dublin, ✆ (00353 1) 288 4346/7.

students and youth travel

Besides saving 25 per cent on regular flights, young people under 26 have the choice of flying on special discount charters.

Campus Travel, 52 Grosvenor Gardens, SW1W OAG, or 174 Kensington High Street, London W8 7RG, ✆ (0171) 730 3402, with branches at most UK universities, including Bristol, ✆ (0117) 929 2494; Manchester, ✆ (0161) 833 2046; Edinburgh, ✆ (0131) 668 3303; Birmingham, ✆ (0121) 414 1848; Oxford, ✆ (01865) 242 067; Cambridge, ✆ (01223) 324283, or find their website at *www.usitcampus.com*

STA, 74 and 86 Old Brompton Rd, London SW7 3LQ, or 117 Euston Rd, London NW1 2SX, ✆ (0171) 361 6161; Bristol, ✆ (0117) 929 4399; Leeds, ✆ (0113) 244 9212; Manchester, ✆ (0161) 834 0668; Oxford, ✆ (01865) 792800; Cambridge, ✆ (01223) 366966 and many other branches in the UK.

USIT, 19–21 Aston Quay, Dublin 2, ✆ (00353 1) 679 8833; Cork, ✆ (021) 270 900; Belfast, ✆ (01232) 324 073; Galway, ✆ (091) 565 177; Limerick ✆ (061) 415 064; Waterford, ✆ (051) 872 601. **Ireland**'s largest student travel agents.

From Mainland Europe

Air travel between Italy and other parts of Europe can be relatively expensive, especially for short hops, so check overland options unless you're in a great hurry. You may need to shop around a little for the best deals. Some airlines (**Alitalia, Qantas, Air France**, etc.) offer excellent rates on the European stages of intercontinental flights, and Italy is an important touchdown for many long-haul services to the Middle or Far East. Many of these may have inconvenient departure times and booking restrictions. Amsterdam, Paris and Athens are among the best centres for finding cheap flights.

From the USA and Canada

The main Italian air gateways for direct flights from North America are Rome and Milan, though, if you're doing a grand tour, check fares to other European destinations (Paris or Amsterdam, for example) which may well be cheaper. **Alitalia,** ✆ (800) 223 5730, Canada ✆ (800) 563 5954, the major carrier, may offer you a special deal if you're flying on to Verona, Venice or Trieste. **TWA**, ✆ (800) 892 4141, **British Airways**, ✆ (800) 247 9297 and **Delta,** ✆ (800) 241 414, also fly from a number of US cities to Italy. From Canada, **Air Canada**, ✆ (800) 776 3000, and **KLM** ✆ (800) 361 5330, operate from Toronto and Montreal. Summer round-trip fares from New York cost around US$1000–1300. British Airways sometimes run World Offers when prices may well drop under the $1000 mark. Otherwise, it may well be worth your while catching a cheap flight to London (New York–London fares are always very competitive) and then flying on from there. Prices are rather more from Canada, so you may prefer to fly from the States. As elsewhere, fares are very seasonal and much cheaper in winter, especially mid-week.

charters, discounts and special deals

From North America, standard scheduled flights on well-known airlines are expensive, but reassuringly reliable and convenient. Resilient, flexible and/or youthful travellers may be willing to shop around for budget deals on consolidated charters, stand-bys or perhaps even courier flights (remember you can usually only take hand luggage with you on the last). In the

USA, **Airhitch** and **Council Charter** are leading reputable cheap-flight specialists. Check the *Yellow Pages* for courier companies (**Now Voyager** is one of the largest USA ones, ✆ (212) 431 1616; **Board Courier Services** operates in several Canadian cities, ✆ (514) 633 0740). For discounted flights, try the small ads in newspaper travel pages (e.g. *New York Times*, *Chicago Tribune, Toronto Globe & Mail*). Firms like **STA** or Canada-based **Travel Cuts** are worth contacting for student fares. Numerous travel clubs and agencies also specialize in discount fares, but may require an annual membership fee.

Airhitch, 2641 Broadway, 3rd Floor, New York, NY 10025, ✆ (212) 864 2000.

Last Minute Travel Club, 100 Sylvan Road, Suite 600, Woburn, MA 01801, ✆ (800) 527 8646.

Now Voyager, 74 Varick St, Suite 307, New York, NY 10013, ✆ (212) 431 1616.

STA, 48 East 11th Street, New York, NY 10003, ✆ (800) 777 0112.

Travel CUTS, 187 College Street, Toronto, Ontario M5T 1P7, ✆ (416) 979 2406.

student and youth travel

STA Travel, New York City, ✆ (212) 627 3111, or toll-free, ✆ (800) 777 0112.

Travel Cuts, 187 College St, Toronto, Ontario M5T 1P7, ✆ (416) 979 2406. Canada's largest student travel specialists; branches in most provinces.

By Rail

From the UK and Europe

A train journey from London to Rome used to be something of a nightmare involving ferries and station changes and taking the best part of 24 hours. This experience can still be repeated, should you so desire it, and will cost you around £160 second class return plus an extra £14 for a couchette. There is, however, following the opening of the Channel Tunnel and the construction of new fast rail networks throughout Europe, an alternative. Take a Eurostar to Paris and a high-speed Eurocity train to Italy and your journey could be reduced by as much as 12 hours. Unfortunately the price will increase to around £500. Train travel, at whatever speed, has its benefits—the opportunity to watch the changing scenery, to acclimatise, and relax—but in an age of low-cost airlines, it is not much of an economy. For more information, contact either **Rail Europe Travel Centre**, 179 Piccadilly W1V OBA, ✆ (0990) 848 848, or **Eurostar**, EPS House, Waterloo Station, London SE1 8SE, ✆ (0990) 186 186, or, as a last resort, visit the **International Rail Centre** at Victoria Station, adjacent to Platform 2, ✆ (0990) 848 848—you can call this number but be warned, the operators cannot give out any information regarding prices, times, availability or anything vaguely useful.

One supremely luxurious way of reaching Italy by rail deserves a special mention: the **Orient Express** whirls you from London through Paris, Zurich, Innsbruck and Verona to Venice in a cocoon of traditional 20s and 30s glamour, with beautifully restored Pullman/*wagon-lits*. It's fiendishly expensive—and quite unforgettable for a once-in-a-lifetime treat. Current prices are about £1130 / $1900 per person (London–Venice one-way); prices include all meals. Several operators offer packages including smart Venice hotel accommodation and return flights home. Contact Venice-Simplon Orient Express, Suite 200, Hudson's Place, Victoria Station, London SW1V 1JL, ✆ (0171) 928 6000 for more information.

Interail (UK) or **Eurail** passes (USA/Canada) give unlimited travel for under-26s throughout Europe for one or two months. Various other cheap youth fares (BIJ tickets, etc.) are also available; organize these before you leave home. Useful addresses for rail travel include **Eurotrain**, 52 Grosvenor Gardens, London SW1W OAG, ✆ (0171) 730 8518); **Wasteels Travel**, Adjacent Platform 2, Victoria Station, London SW1V 1JT, ✆ (0171) 834 7066; any branch of **Thomas Cook**, or **CIT** (*see* addresses below).

If you are just planning to see Italy, inclusive rail passes may not be worthwhile. Fares on FS (*Ferrovie dello Stato*), the Italian State Railway, are among the lowest (kilometre for kilometre) in Europe. A month's under-26 full Interail pass costs £229, though you can now buy cheaper zonal passes covering three or four countries only. If you intend travelling extensively by train, one of the special Italian tourist passes may be a better bet (*see* below, p.14).

A convenient pocket-sized **timetable** detailing all the main and secondary Italian railway lines is now available in the UK, costing £7 (plus 50p postage). Contact **Accommodation Line Ltd**, 11–12 Hanover Square, London W1R 9PB, ✆ (0171) 409 1343; **Y Knot Travel**, Morley House, 1st Floor, 314/320 Regent Street, London W1, ✆ (0171) 436 0448; or **Italwings**, Travel & Accommodation, 87 Brewer Street, London W1R 5TB, ✆ (0171) 287 2117. If you wait until you arrive in Italy, however, you can pick up the Italian timetable (in two volumes) at any station for about L4500 each.

From USA and Canada, contact **Rail Europe**, central office at 226–230 Westchester Ave, White Plains, NY 10604, ✆ 914 682 2999 or ✆ (800) 438 7245. **Wasteels** also have a USA office at 5728 Major Boulevard, Suite 308, Orlando, 32819 Florida.

CIT Offices outside Italy

UK Marco Polo House, 3–5 Lansdowne Rd, Croydon, Surrey CR9 1LL, ✆ (0891) 71551 (50p a minute), ✆ (0181) 686 0677.

USA 15 W.44th St, 10th Floor, New York, NY 10036, ✆ (212) 730 2121, ✆ (888) FAX CIT.

Canada: 1450 City Councillors St. Suite 750, Montreal H3A 2E6, ✆ (514) 845 4310.

By Road
by bus and coach

Eurolines is the main international bus operator in Europe, with representatives in Italy and many other countries. In the UK, they can be found at Victoria Coach Station, London SW1W OAG, ✆ (01582) 404 511, and are booked through National Express. Regular services run to many northern Italian cities, but and needless to say, the journey is long and the relatively small savings on price (a return ticket from London to Rome costs £125; under-26 £112) make it a masochistic choice in comparison with a discounted air fare, or even rail travel. Within Italy, you can obtain more information on long-distance bus services from any CIT office.

by car

Driving to Venetia from the UK is a lengthy and expensive proposition. If you're only staying for a short period, check costs against airline fly-drive schemes. Plan for the best part of 30 hours' driving time, even if you stick to fast toll roads. The most scenic and hassle-free route is via the Alps, avoiding crowded Riviera roads in summer, but, if you take a route through Switzerland, expect to pay for the privilege (around £14 or SF30 for motorway use). In winter the passes may be closed and you will have to stick to those expensive tunnels (one-way tolls range from about L22,000 for a small car). You can avoid some of the driving by putting your car on the train, though this is scarcely a cheap option. **Express Sleeper Cars** run to Milan from Paris or Boulogne (infrequently in winter). Foreign-plated cars are no longer entitled to free breakdown assistance from the **Italian Auto Club** (ACI), but their prices are fair. Phone ACI on ✆ 00 39 06 44 77 to find out the current rates.

To bring a GB-registered car into Italy, you need a **vehicle registration document, full driving licence,** and **insurance papers**—these must be carried at all times when driving. Non-EU citizens should preferably have an **international driving licence** which has an Italian translation incorporated. Your vehicle should display a nationality plate indicating its country of registration. Before travelling, check everything is in perfect order. Minor infringements like worn tyres or burnt-out sidelights can cost you dear in any country. A **red triangular hazard sign** is obligatory; also recommended are a spare set of bulbs, a first-aid kit and a fire extinguisher. Spare parts for non-Italian cars can be difficult to find, especially Japanese models. Before crossing the Italian border, remember to fill up with petrol; *benzina* is still very expensive in Italy.

For more information on driving in Italy, *see* 'Getting Around By Car', pp.15–17, or contact the motoring organisations (**AA,** ✆ (0990) 500 600, or **RAC,** ✆ (0891) 347 333 in the UK, and **AAA,** ✆ (407) 444 4000 in the USA and (416) 221 4300 in Canada.

Entry Formalities

Passports and Visas

EU nationals with a valid passport can enter and stay in Italy as long as they like. Citizens of the USA, Canada, Australia and New Zealand need only a valid passport to stay up to three months in Italy, unless they get a visa in advance from an Italian embassy or consulate.

UK:	38 Eaton Place, London SW1X, ✆ (0171) 235 9371.
	32 Melville Street, Edinburgh EH3 7HA, ✆ (0131) 226 3631.
	111 Piccadilly, Manchester M1 2HY, ✆ (0161) 236 9024.
Ireland:	63–65 Northumberland Road, Dublin, ✆ (00353 1) 660 1744.
USA:	690 Park Avenue, New York, NY 10021, ✆ (212) 737 9100.
	12400 Wilshire Blvd, Suite 300, Los Angeles CA, ✆ (323) 8200622.
Canada:	136 Beverley Street, Toronto, ✆ (416) 977 1566.
Australia:	Level 45, The Gateway Building, Macquarie Place, Circular Quay, Sydney 2000, NSW, ✆ (2) 627 33 333.
New Zealand:	34 Grant Rd, Thorndon, Wellington, ✆ (4) 473 4339.
France:	47 Rue de Varennes, 73343 Paris, ✆ (1) 49 54 03 00.
Germany:	Karl Finkelnburgstrasse 49–51, 5300 Bonn 2, ✆ (228) 82 20.
Netherlands:	Herengracht 609, 1017 CE Amsterdam, ✆ (3120) 624 0043.

By law you should register with the police within eight days of your arrival in Italy. In practice this is done automatically for most visitors when they check in at their first hotel. Don't be alarmed if the owner of your self-catering property proposes to 'denounce' you to the police when you arrive—it's just a formality.

Customs

EU nationals over the age of 17 can now import a limitless amount of goods for personal use. Non-EU nationals have to pass through the Italian customs. How the frontier police manage to recruit such ugly, mean-looking characters to hold the submachine guns and dogs from such a good-looking population is a mystery, but they'll let you be if you don't look suspicious and haven't brought along more than 200 cigarettes or 100 cigars, or not more than a litre of hard drink or three bottles of wine, a couple of cameras, a movie camera, 10 rolls of film for each, a tape-recorder, radio, record-player, one canoe less than 5.5m, sports equipment for personal use, and one TV (though you'll have to pay for a licence for it at Customs). Pets must be accompanied by a bilingual Certificate of Health from your local Veterinary Inspector. You can take the same items listed above home with you without hassle—except of course your British pet. US citizens may return with $400 worth of merchandise—keep your receipts.

Currency

There are no limits to how much money you bring into Italy: legally you may not export more than L20,000 000 in Italian banknotes, a sum unlikely to trouble many of us, though officials rarely check.

Tour Operators and Special-interest Holidays

Dozens of general and specialist companies offer holidays in Italy. Some of the major ones are listed below. Not all of them are necesssarily ABTA-bonded; we recommend you check before booking.

UK general

Cosmos, Tourama House, 17 Holmesdale Rd, Bromley, Kent BR2 9LX, ✆ (0181) 464 3444.

Cresta Italy, Tabley Ct, Victoria St, Altringham, Cheshire WA14 1EZ, ✆ (0161) 927 7000.

Crystal Premier, Crystal House, The Courtyard, Arlington Rd, Surbiton, Surrey KT6 6BW, ✆ (0181) 390 5554.

First Choice PLC, Diamond House, 2 Peel Cross Road, Salford, Manchester M5 2AN, ✆ (0161) 745 7000.

Italian Escapades, 227 Shepherds Bush Road, London W6 7AS, ✆ (0181) 748 2661.

Italiatour, 9 Whyteleafe Business Village, Whyteleafe Hill, Whyteleafe, Surrey CR3 OAT, ✆ (01883) 623 363.

Magic of Italy, 227 Shepherds Bush Road, London W6 7AS, ✆ (0181) 748 7575.

Page & Moy, 136–140 London Road, Leicester LE2 1EN, ✆ (0116) 250 7979.

Sunvil, Sunvil House, 7–8 Upper Sq, Old Isleworth, Middx TW7 7BJ, ✆ (0181) 568 4499.

Thomson, Albert House, Tindal Bridge, Edward St, Birmingham B1 2RA, ✆ (0990) 502 555.

UK special-interest

Abercrombie & Kent (city breaks, country retreats and island-hopping cruises), Sloane Square House, Holbein Place, London SW1W 8NS, ✆ (0171) 730 9600.

Alternative Travel (walking and cycling tours), 69–71 Banbury Road, Oxford OX2 6PE, ✆ (01865) 310399.

Arblaster & Clarke (wine tours linked with opera), Clarke House, Farnham Road. West Liss, Hamps GU33 6JQ, ✆ (01730) 893 344.

Blair Travel for the Arts (opera and ballet), 117 Regent's Park Rd, London NW1 8UR, ✆ (0171) 483 4466.

British Museum Tours (guest lecturers, art and architecture), 46 Bloomsbury Street, London WC1B 3QQ, ✆ (0171) 323 8895.

Brompton Travel (tailor-made and opera), Brompton House, 64 Richmond Road, Kingston-upon-Thames, Surrey KT2 5EH, ✆ (0181) 549 3334.

Citalia (opera), Marco Polo House, 3–5 Lansdowne Road, Croydon CR9 1LL, ✆ (0181) 686 5533.

Italia 2000 (golf and sport), 8 Timperley Way, Up Hatherley, Cheltenham, Gloucestershire, GL51 5RH, ✆ (01242) 234 215.

JMB (opera), Rushwick, Worcester WR2 5SN, ✆ (01905) 425628.

Kirker (city breaks, tailor-made tours and trips to the Verona Opera), 3 New Concordia Wharf, Mill Street, London SE1 2BB, ✆ (0171) 231 3333.

Martin Randall Travel (cultural tours with expert guides: art and architecture, wines, gardens), 10 Barley Mow Passage, Chiswick, London W4 4PH, ✆ (0181) 742 3355.

Ramblers (walking tours), Box 43, Welwyn Garden City, Hertfordshire AL8 6PQ, ✆ (01707) 331133.

Saga (art and architecture—senior citizens), The Saga Building, Middelburg Square, Folkestone, Kent CT20 1AZ, ✆ (01303) 711 111.

Solo's (singles holidays), 54–8 High Street. Edgware, Middlesex HA8 7EJ, ✆ (0181) 951 2800.

Special Tours (escorted cultural tours: art, architecture, gardens), 81a Elizabeth St, London SW1W 9PG, ✆ (0171) 730 2297.

Swan Hellenic (cruises), 77 New Oxford Street, London WC1A 1PP, ✆ (0171) 800 2200.

Tasting Places (cookery courses near Verona), 40 Buspace Studios, Conlan Street, London W10 5AP, ✆ (0171) 460 0077.

Travelsphere (coach tours), Compass House, Rockingham Road, Market Harborough, Leicestershire LE16 7QD, ✆ (01858) 464818.

Venice Simplon-Orient Express (luxury rail tours), Sea Containers House, 20 Upper Ground, London SE1 9PF, ✆ (0171) 928 6000.

Wallace Arnold (coach tours), Gelderd Road, Leeds, LS12 6DH, ✆ (01132) 310739.

in the USA/Canada

American Express Vacations (prepacked or tailor-made tours), 300 Pinnacle Way, Norcross, GA 30093, ✆ (800) 241 1700.

CIT Tours (general and skiing) 342 Madison Ave, Suite 3207, New York, NY 10173, ✆ (212) 697 2100.

Dailey-Thorp Travel (music/opera), 330 West 58th Street, New York, NY 10019, ✆ (212) 307 1555.

Italiatour (fly-drive in conjunction with Alitalia), 666 5th Avenue, New York, NY 10103, © (212) 765 2183.

Maupintour, 1515 St Andrew's Drive, Lawrence, Kansas 66047, © (913) 843 1211.

Travel Concepts (wine/food), 62 Commonwealth Ave, Suite 3, Boston, MA 02116, © (617) 266 8450.

For self-catering and camping specialists *see* **Practical A–Z**, 'Where to Stay', pp.41–2.

Getting Around

Italy has an excellent network of airports, railways, highways and byways and you'll find getting around fairly easy—until one union or another takes it into its head to go on strike (to be fair they rarely do it during the high holiday season). There's plenty of talk about passing a law to regulate strikes, but it won't happen soon if ever. Instead, learn to recognize the word in Italian: *sciopero* (SHO-per-o), and do as the Romans do—quiver with resignation. There's always a day or two's notice, and strikes usually last only a day, just long enough to throw a spanner in the works if you have to catch a plane. Keep your ears open and watch for notices posted in the stations.

By Air

Air traffic within Italy is intense, with up to ten flights a day on popular routes. Domestic flights are handled by **Alitalia** © (0171) 602 7111, **ATI** (its internal arm) or **Avianova**. Air travel makes most sense when hopping between north and south. Shorter journeys are often just as quick (and much less expensive) by train or even bus if you take check-in and airport travelling times into account. Trieste, Venice and Verona all have direct flights to and from Rome and Milan.

Domestic flight **costs** are comparable to those in other European countries: a full-price return fare from Rome to Venice costs about £158 (one-way tickets are half-price). A complex system of discounts is available (some only at certain times of year) for night flights, weekend travel, senior (60 plus) and youth fares (12–26-year-olds; half-price or less for younger children). Family reductions are also available (up to 50%). Each airport has a bus terminal in the city; ask about schedules as you purchase your ticket to avoid hefty taxi fares. Baggage allowances vary between airlines. Tickets can be bought at CIT offices and other large travel agencies.

By Train

FS information from anywhere in Italy, © 1478 88088, open 7am–9pm,
www.fs-on-line.com

Italy's national railway, the **FS** (*Ferrovie dello Stato*) is well run, inexpensive (despite recent price rises) and often a pleasure to ride. On the FS, some of the trains are sleek and high-tech, but much of the rolling stock hasn't been changed for fifty years. Possible FS unpleasantnesses you may encounter, besides a strike, are delays, crowding (especially at weekends and in the summer), and crime on overnight trains, where someone rifles your bags while you sleep. The crowding, at least, becomes much less of a problem. Reserve a seat in advance (*fare una prenotazione*), the fee is small and can save you hours standing in some train corridor. On the more expensive trains, **reservations** are mandatory. Do check when you purchase your ticket in advance that the date is correct; tickets are only valid the day they're purchased unless you specify otherwise. A number on your reservation slip will indicate in which car your seat is— find it before you board rather than after. The same goes for sleepers and couchettes on overnight trains, which must also be reserved in advance. At sleepy rural train stations without information boards, the imminent arrival of a train is signalled by a platform bell.

Tickets may be purchased not only in the stations, but at many travel agents in the city centres. Fares are strictly determined by the kilometres travelled. The system is computerized and runs smoothly, at least until you try to get a reimbursement for an unused ticket (usually not worth the trouble). Be sure you ask which platform (*binario*) your train arrives at; the big permanent boards in the stations are not always correct. Always remember to stamp your ticket (*convalidare*) in the not very obvious yellow machines at the head of the platform before boarding the train, or else you may have to pay a fine. If you get on a train without a ticket you can buy one from the conductor, with an added 20% penalty. You can also pay a conductor to move up to first class or get a couchette, if there are places available.

There is a fairly straightforward **hierarchy of trains.** At the bottom of the pyramid is the humble *Locale* (also euphemistically known as an *Accelerato*) which often stops even where there's no station in sight; it can be excruciatingly slow. When you're checking the schedules, beware of what may look like the first train to your destination—if it's a *Locale*, it will be the last to arrive. A *Diretto* stops far less, an *Expresso* just at the main towns. *Intercity* trains whoosh between the big cities. *Eurocity* trains link Italian cities with major European centres. Both of these services require a supplement—some 30% more than a regular fare. Lording it above these are the *ETR 500 pendolino* trains, similar to the French TGV service, which can travel at up to 186mph. Reservations are free, but must be made at least five hours before the trip, and on some trains there are only first-class coaches. Sitting on the pinnacle are the true Kings of the Rails, the super-swish and super-fast *Eurostars.* These make very few stops, have both first and second class carriages, and carry a supplement which includes an obligatory seat reservation. So, the faster the train, the more you pay.

The FS offers several **passes.** A flexible option is the 'Flexi Card' (marketed as a 'Freedom Pass' in the UK) which allows unlimited travel for either four days within a month (L206,000), 8 days within a month (L287,000), 12 days within a month (L368,000) plus seat reservations and supplements on Eurostars. Another ticket, the *Kilometrico*, gives you 3000 kilometres of travel, made on a maximum of 20 journeys and is valid for two months (2nd Class L206,000, 1st Class 338,000); one advantage is that it can be used by up to five people at the same time. However, supplements are payable on *Intercity* trains. Other discounts, available only once you're in Italy, are 15 per cent on same-day return tickets and three-day returns (depending on the distance involved), and discounts for families of at least four travelling together. Senior citizens (men 65 and over, women 60) can also get a *Carta d'Argento* ('silver card') for L44,000 entitling them to a 20 per cent reduction in fares. A *Carta Verde* bestows a 20% discount on people under 26 and also costs L44,000.

Refreshments on routes of any great distance are provided by bar cars or trolleys; you can usually get sandwiches and coffee from vendors along the tracks at intermediary stops. Station bars often have a good variety of take-away travellers' fare; consider at least investing in a plastic bottle of mineral water, since there's no drinking water on the trains.

Besides trains and bars, Italy's stations offer other **facilities**. Most have a *Deposito*, where you can leave your bags for hours or days for a small fee. The larger ones have porters (who charge L1000–L1500 per piece) and some even have luggage trolleys; major stations have an *Albergo Diurno* ('Day Hotel', where you take a shower, get a shave and have a haircut, etc.), information offices, currency exchanges open at weekends (not at the most advantageous rates, however), hotel-finding and reservation services, kiosks with foreign papers, restaurants, etc. You can also arrange to have a **rental car** awaiting you at your destination—Avis, Hertz, Aurotrans and Maggiore are the firms most widespread in Italy, *see* p.17.

Beyond that, some words need to be said about riding the rails on the most serendipitous national line in Europe. The FS may have its strikes and delays, its petty crime and bureaucratic inconveniences, but when you catch it on its better side it will treat you to a dose of the real Italy before you even reach your destination. If there's a choice, try for one of the older cars, depressingly grey outside but fitted with comfortably upholstered seats, Art Deco lamps and old pictures of the towns and villages of the country. Best of all, the FS is relatively reliable, and even if there has been some delay you'll have an amenable station full of clocks to wait in; some of the station bars have astonishingly good food (some do not), but at any of them you may accept a well-brewed cappuccino and look blasé until the train comes in. Try to avoid travel on Friday evenings, when the major lines out of the big cities are packed. The FS is a lottery; you may find a train uncomfortably full of Italians (in which case stand by the doors, or impose on the salesmen in first class, where the conductor will be happy to change your ticket). Now and then, you may just have a beautiful 1920s compartment all to yourself for the night—even better if you're travelling with your beloved—and be serenaded on the platform.

By Coach and Bus

Inter-city coach travel is sometimes quicker than train travel, but also a bit more expensive. Coaches almost always depart from the vicinity of the train station, and tickets usually need to be purchased before you get on. In many regions they are the only means of public transport and well used, with frequent schedules. If you can't get a ticket before the coach leaves, get on anyway and pretend you can't speak a word of Italian; the worst that can happen is that someone will make you pay for a ticket. The base for all **country bus** lines will be the provincial capital.

City buses are the traveller's friend. Most cities (at least in the north) label routes well; all charge flat fees for rides within the city limits and immediate suburbs, at the time of writing around L1500. Bus tickets must always be purchased before you get on, either at a tobacconist's, a newspaper kiosk, in bars, or from ticket machines near the main stops. Once you get on, you must 'obliterate' your ticket in the machines in the front or back of the bus; controllers stage random checks to make sure you've punched your ticket. Fines for cheaters are about L50,000, and the odds are about 12 to 1 against a check, so many passengers take a chance. If you're good-hearted, you'll buy a ticket and help some overburdened municipal transit line meet its annual deficit.

By Car

The advantages of driving in Italy generally outweigh the disadvantages, but, before you bring your own car or hire one, consider the kind of holiday you're planning. For a tour of art cities or a few days lounging on the beach, you'd be better off not driving at all: parking is impossible, traffic impossible, deciphering one-way streets, signals and signs impossible. But for touring the countryside a car gives immeasurable freedom.

Third-party **insurance** is a minimum requirement in Italy (and you should be a lot more than minimally insured, as many of the locals have none whatever!). Obtain a Green Card from your insurer, which gives automatic proof that you are fully covered. Also get hold of a **European Accident Statement** form, which may simplify things if you are unlucky enough to have an accident. Always insist on a full translation of any statement you are asked to sign. Breakdown assistance insurance is obviously a sensible investment (e.g. AA's Five Star or RAC's Eurocover Motoring Assistance).

Petrol (*benzina*, unleaded is *benzina senza piombo*, and diesel *gasolio*) is still very expensive in Italy (around L1800 per litre; fill up before you cross the border). Many petrol stations close for lunch in the afternoon, and few stay open late at night, though you may find a 'self-service' where you feed a machine nice smooth L10,000 notes. Motorway (*autostrada*) tolls are quite high. Rest stops and petrol stations along the motorways stay open 24 hours. Other roads— *superstrade* on down through the Italian grading system—are free of charge.

Italians are famously anarchic behind a wheel. The only way to beat the locals is to join them by adopting an assertive and constantly alert driving style. Bear in mind that whoever hesitates is lost (especially at traffic lights, where the danger is less great of crashing into someone at the front than being rammed from behind). All drivers from boy racers to elderly nuns tempt prov-idence by overtaking at the most dangerous bend, and no matter how fast you are hammering along the *autostrada*, plenty will whizz past at apparently supersonic rates. North Americans used to leisurely speed limits and gentler road manners may find the Italian interpretation of the highway code somewhat stressful. Speed limits (generally ignored) are 130kph on motor-ways (110kph for cars under 1100cc or motorcycles), 110kph on main highways, 90kph on secondary roads, and 50kph in built-up areas. Speeding fines may be as much as L500,000, or L100,000 for jumping a red light (a popular Italian sport).

If you are undeterred by these caveats, you may actually enjoy driving in Italy, at least away from the congested tourist centres. Signposting is generally good, and roads are usually excel-lently maintained. Some of the roads are feats of engineering that the Romans themselves would have admired—bravura projects suspended on cliffs, crossing valleys on vast stilts and winding up hairpins.

Buy a good road map (the Italian Touring Club series is excellent). The **Automobile Club of Italy** (ACI) is a good friend to the foreign motorist. Besides having bushels of useful informa-tion and tips, they can be reached from anywhere by dialling **116**—also use this number if you have to find the nearest service station. If you need major repairs, the ACI can make sure the prices charged are according to their guidelines.

Hiring a Car

Hiring a car, *autonoleggio*, is simple but not particularly cheap—Italy has some of the highest rates in Europe. A small car (Fiat Punto or similar) with unlimited mileage and collision damage waiver, including tax, will set you back around L70,000–90,000 per day although if you hire for the car for over three days, this will decrease slightly pro rata. The minimum age limit is usually 25 (sometimes 23) and the driver must have held their licence for over a year—this will have to be produced, along with the driver's passport, when hiring the car.

Major rental companies have offices in airports or main stations, though it may be worthwhile checking prices of local firms. If you need a car for longer than three weeks, leasing may be a more economic alternative. The National Tourist Office has a list of firms that hire caravans (trailers) or camper vans. Non-residents are not allowed to buy cars in Italy.

Taking all things into account, it may make sense to arrange your car hire before leaving home and, in particular, to check-out fly-drive discounts. Notwithstanding the convenience of picking up the car when you arrive, it often works out cheaper. Prices tend towards the L70,000 per day mark, often with large discounts for a second week of hire.

Car Rental Agencies

UK and Ireland

Avis, ✆ 0990 900 500

Hertz, ✆ 0990 996 699

National Car Rental, ✆ 0990 365 365

Car Rental Direct, ✆ 0171 604 4688

Hertz, Dublin, ✆ (00353 1) 660 2255

USA and Canada

Avis, ✆ (800) 331 1084

Hertz, ✆ (800) 654 3131

Hertz, Canada (800) 263 0600

Hitchhiking

It is illegal to hitch on the *autostrade*, though you may pick up a lift near one of the toll booths. Don't hitch from the city centres; head for suburban exit routes. For the best chances of getting a lift, travel light, look respectable and take off your sunglasses. Hold a sign indicating your destination if you can. Never hitch at points which may cause an accident or obstruction; Italian traffic is bad enough already! Risks for women are lower in northern Italy than in the more macho south, but it is not advisable to hitch alone. Two or more men may encounter some reluctance.

By Motorcycle or Bicycle

Mopeds, Vespas and scooters are the vehicles of choice for a great many Italians. You will see them everywhere. In the traffic-congested towns this is a ubiquity born of necessity; when driving space is limited, two wheels are always better than one. However, in Italy, riding a two-wheeler often seems to be as much a form of cultural and social expression as it does a means of getting from A to B. Italian youths tend to prefer chic Italian lines, Vespas, Lambrettas and the like, which they parade self-consciously through the town's main drags. Older members of society, in the main, plump for mopeds, the type you can actually pedal should you feel so inclined. Choosing your machine, however, is only the first stage of this cultural process; it then becomes necessary to master the Italian way of riding. This means dispensing with a crash helmet, despite the fact that they are compulsory, in order to look as stylishly laid-back as possible while still achieving an alarming rate of speed: riding sidesaddle, or whilst on the phone, or smoking, or holding a dog or child under one arm; all of these methods have their determined and expert adherents.

Despite the obvious dangers of this means of transport (especially if you choose to do it Italian-style), there are clear benefits to moped-riding in Italy. For one thing it is cheaper than car hire—costs for a *motorino* range from about L30,000 per day, scooters somewhat more (up to L50,000), you must be at least 14—and can prove an excellent way of covering a town's sights in a limited space of time. Furthermore, because Italy is such a scooter-friendly place, car drivers are more conditioned to their presence and so are less likely to hurtle into them when taking corners. Nonetheless, you should only consider hiring a moped if you have ridden one before (Italy is no place to learn) and, despite local examples, you should wear a helmet. Also, be warned, some travel insurance policies exclude claims resulting from scooter or motorbike accidents.

Italians are keen cyclists, racing drivers straight up the Dolomites, but if you're not training for the Tour de France consider the topography well before planning a bicycling tour. Much of the Veneto and southern half of Friuli are fairly flat and prime cycling territory, but it can be sweltering in the summer. Prices begin at about L20,000 per day, which may make buying one interesting (L190,000–L300,000) if you plan to spend much time in the saddle, either in a bike shop or through the classified ad papers put out in nearly every city and region. If you bring your own bike, do check the airlines to see what their policies are on transporting them. Bikes can be transported by train in Italy, either with you or within a couple of days—apply at the baggage office (*ufficio bagagli*). Many towns in Venetia hire out bikes by the hour or day; ask at the tourist offices.

Practical A–Z

Climate and When to Go

Average temperatures in °C (°F)

	January	April	July	October
Trieste	5.3 (41)	12.9 (55)	24.0 (75)	15.6 (60)
Venice	3.8 (39)	12.6 (54)	23.6 (74)	15.1 (59)
Lake Garda	4.0 (39)	13.2 (55)	23.7 (74)	14.7 (58)
Cortina d'Ampezzo	−2.3 (29)	5.2 (41)	15.8 (60)	7.6 (45)
Merano	2.8 (37)	11.6 (52)	20.2 (68)	8.4 (47)
Treviso	−3.5 (26)	7.1 (44)	18.3 (64)	9.0 (48)

Average monthly rainfall in millimetres (inches)

	January	April	July	October
Trieste	57 (2)	104 (4)	57 (2)	112 (4)
Venice	58 (2)	77 (4)	37 (1)	66 (3)
Lake Garda	31 (1)	62 (3)	81 (3)	89 (3)
Cortina d'Ampezzo	51 (2)	138 (5)	148 (6)	119 (4)
Merano	10 (.5)	11 (.5)	6 (0)	90 (4)
Treviso	79 (3)	202 (8)	138 (5)	169 (6)

O Sole Mio notwithstanding, Italy isn't always sunny; it rains just as much in Rome every year as in London. Summer comes on humid and hot in Venetia, especially along the Po; the Dolomites stay fairly cool, though the valleys just below can be little ovens, and, while the coasts are often refreshed by breezes, Venice in its lagoon tends to swelter. You can get by without an umbrella, but take a light jacket for cool evenings. For average touring, August is probably the worst month. Transport facilities are jammed to capacity, prices are at their highest, and the large cities are abandoned to hordes of tourists while the locals take to the beach. As compensation, summer is prime festival time (*see* below).

Spring and autumn are the loveliest times to go. In spring the blossoming apple orchards around Trento and cherry orchards of Treviso and Modena rival the wild flowers of Italy's countryside and mountains; by May and June the gardens are at their peak. But in many ways the best and certainly the most soulful season of Venetia is autumn, when the landscapes match the colours of Venetian art; the Po Delta and lagoon are at their most haunting, the sumac on Trieste's karst bursts into scarlet flames, the vineyards are heavy with grapes. The weather is mild, places aren't crowded, and you won't need your umbrella too much, at least until November. During the winter the happiest visitors are either on skis, in the opera house, or at the table eating wild mushrooms and radicchio. It's the best time to go if you want the churches and museums to yourself, or want to meet Italians. Beware, though, that it can rain and rain, and mountain valleys can lie for days under banks of fog and mist.

Crime

Police or medical emergency number © 113

There is a fair amount of petty crime in Italy, although relatively little in Venetia—purse-snatchings, pickpocketing, minor thievery of the white-collar kind (always check your change) and car break-ins and theft—but violent crime is rare. Nearly all mishaps can be avoided with adequate precautions. Scooter-borne purse-snatchers can be foiled if you stay on the inside of the pavement and keep a firm hold on your property (sling your bag-strap across your body, not dangling from one shoulder); pickpockets strike in crowded buses or trams and gatherings: don't carry too much cash, and split it so you won't lose the lot at once. In cities and popular tourist sites, beware groups of scruffy-looking women or children with placards, apparently begging for money. They use distraction techniques to perfection. The smallest and most innocent-looking child is generally the most skilful pickpocket. If you are targeted, the best technique is to grab sharply hold of any vulnerable possessions or pockets and shout furiously. Be extra careful in train stations, don't leave valuables in hotel rooms, and always park your car in garages, guarded lots or on well-lit streets, with portable temptations out of sight. Purchasing small quantities of soft drugs for personal consumption is technically legal in Italy, though what constitutes a small quantity is unspecified, and if the police don't like you to begin with, it will probably be enough to get you into big trouble.

Political terrorism, once the scourge of Italy, has declined greatly in recent years, mainly thanks to special quasi-military squads of black-uniformed national police, the *Carabinieri*. Local matters are usually in the hands of the *Polizia Urbana*; the nattily dressed *Vigili Urbani* concern themselves with directing traffic, and handing out parking fines. If you need to summon any of them, dial ✆ 113.

Disabled Travellers

Italy has been relatively slow off the mark in its provision for disabled visitors. Cobblestones, uneven or non-existent pavements, appalling traffic conditions, crowded transport and endless flights of steps in many public places are all disincentives. Progress is gradually being made, however. Venice has added ramps to many bridges; the tourist office's Venice's-Lido map no.1 indicates the parts of the city accessible by wheelchair. A national support organization in your own country may have specific information on facilities in Venetia, and the Italian tourist office or CIT (travel agency) can also advise on hotels, museums with ramps and so on. If you book rail travel through CIT, you can request assistance. In Italy, a cooperative of disabled organizations, ✆ 167 179 179, dispenses advice on accommodation and travel.

In the UK, contact the **Royal Association for Disability & Rehabilitation** (RADAR), and ask for their guide *Getting There* (£5 inc p&p). They are based at 12 City Forum, 250 City Road, London EC1V 8AF, ✆ (0171) 250 3222. Americans should contact SATH (**Society for the Advancement of Travel for the Handicapped**), 347 Fifth Avenue, Suite 610, New York 10016, ✆ (212) 447 7284, ✆ 725 8253. Another useful organisation providing help on both sides of the Atlantic is **Mobility International**, at 45 Broadway West, Eugene, Oregon 97403, USA, ✆ (541) 343 1284. Australians could try **Australian Council for the Rehabilitation of the Disabled** (ACROD), 24 Cabarita Road, Ryde, New South Wales, ✆ (61) 297 432 699. If you need help while you are in Italy, contact the local tourist offices.

Embassies and Consulates

UK

Milan: Via San Paulo 7, ✆ 02 723 001.
Rome: Via XX Settembre 80/a, ✆ 06 482 5441.

Ireland

Rome: Largo Nazareno 3, ✆ 06 678 2541.

USA

Milan: Largo Donegani 1, ✆ 02 2900 1841.
Rome: Via V. Veneto 119/a, ✆ 06 46741.

Canada

Milan: Via Vittorio Pisani 19, ✆ 02 669 7451.
Rome: Via Zara 30, ✆ 06 440 3028.

Australia

Milan: Via Borgagna 2, ✆ 02 7601 1330.
Rome: Via Alessandria 215, ✆ 06 852 721.

New Zealand

Rome: Via Zara 28, ✆ 06 440 2928.

Festivals

There are literally thousands of festivals answering to every description in Venetia. Every *comune* has at least one or two, celebrating a patron saint; others are sponsored by the political parties (especially the Communists and Socialists), where everyone goes to meet their friends and enjoy the masses of cheap food. No matter where you are, look at the posters; Italy is swamped with culture, and best of all, remains refreshingly unsnobbish or élitist about it all. On the other hand, don't expect anything approaching uninhibited gaiety. Italy is a rather staid place these days, and festivals are largely occasions to dress up, hear some music, re-enact a historic event or have a pleasant outdoor supper. If, at a festival, you happen to notice Italians laughing too loudly, drinking too much, or singing extemporaneously, drop us a line; we would love to see it.

Below is a calendar of the most popular annual events in Venetia. Always check at the tourist offices for precise dates, which tend to change from year to year.

January

1	Parade of folk costumes and horse-drawn sleighs, at **Ortisei** (Bolzano).
5–6	Feast of the *pignarui*, **Tarcento** (Udine), 14th-century costumes in a torchlit parade of the Three Kings, followed by bonfires on all the surrounding hills.
6	Mass of the Sword, **Cividale del Friuli**, where the priest wears a sword in memory of the town's famous 14th-century patriarch; Taller Mass, at **Gemona del Friuli**, a re-enactment of an ancient ceremony, in which the mayor presents a coin (taller) to the priest, symbolizing homage to the Church's authority.
Mid-month	Gold and silver fair, **Vicenza**.

February

First week	Dobbiaco–Cortina Cross Country Ski race, ending at **Cortina d'Ampezzo**; *Padovantiquaria*, week-long antiques fair, **Padua**.
2nd week	Big agricultural fair, **Verona**.
2nd weekend	International Judo Tournament, **Vittorio Veneto**.

Carnival	**Venice** is the place to see the most beautiful masks and costumes, and to attend big-name events as the Lagoon city strives to recreate the old magic; **Sappada** (Belluno) celebrates with three weeks of parades and traditional events featuring a personage called *Rollate*, dressed in furs and hood, and wearing a carved wooden mask. On Carnival Friday, **Verona** celebrates the *Bacanal del gnocco*, a parade with the king of gnocchi and a feast, all in 15th century costume. Other traditional Carnival celebrations take place in **Arco** (Trento), **Muggia** (Trieste) and **Ora/Auer** (Bolzano).
25	*Festa della Renga*, feasting on local specialities, **Concordia Sagittaria** (Venice).

March

Second half	Wine fair, **Bolzano**.
19	*Lis cidulis*, at **Forni Avoltri** (Ùdine), in which burning logs of wood are rolled down the hillside.
Good Friday	Passion play, performed since 1600, at **Erto** (Pordenone).
Easter Mon	Parades in costume and horse races at **Merano**.
21	Trial of the *Vecia*, the old year, **Cavaso del Tomba** (Treviso).
25	Traditional horse fair, **Lonigo** (Vicenza).
29	*Antica Festa della Madonna Addolorata*, processions and spectacles draw some 50,000 to **Belluno**.

April

Mid-month	Sagra del Gnocco, eating and dancing, in **Teolo** (Padua); Flower festival, **Lignano Sabbiadoro** (Ùdine).
3rd week	Vinitaly, wine, spirits and olive oil fair, **Verona**; asparagus festival, **San Michele al Tagliamento-Bibione** (Venice); kite-flying festival, **Badia Polesine** (Padua).
End month	Giant antiques fair, and Città di Padova Rugby Tournament, both in **Padua**.

May

First week	Sagra di Sansonessa, country fair of food, games, and dancing, **Caorle** (Venice).
10	Palio della Valle dei Frassini, 19th-century fun and games at **Frassinelle Polesine** (Rovigo).
Ascension	La Sensa, or re-enactment of the Doge's Wedding of the Sea, **Venice**; Cross-kissing ceremony, at **Zuglio** (Udine), in which all the crosses from the countryside are decorated and brought to the church of S. Pietro.
Mid-month	Festa Medievale del Vino Bianco, **Soave**.
End month	Cherry festival, **Maróstica** (Vicenza); Fiera Maggio Arquatese, **Arquà Polesine** (Rovigo), with traditional costumes, races, parades, fireworks.

June

12–13	Sant'Antonio, Padua, the historic re-enactment of the transition of saint's relics from Arcella, and torchlight procession along the Bacchiglione.
Mid-month	Gold, silver, jewellery and watch fair, **Vicenza**.
19–21	Palio di **Noale** (Venice), with 14th-century costumes, market, games.
20	Migration of the flocks, at **Senales** (Bolzano), in which the sheep cross the glaciers to the Giogo Alto, with picnics, etc. Palio de la Marciliana, **Chioggia**, celebrating the 14th-century Battle of Chioggia.
Third week	San Vigilio, folklore, music, and stealing of the polenta pot at **Trento**.

24	San Giovanni Battista, with fireworks, **Lugo di Vicenza**.
June–July	Operetta festival, **Trieste**; Festival of Herbs, **Forni di Sopra** (Ùdine)
End of June	Flower markets, **Bolzano**. International Summer Curling competitions, **Cortina d'Ampezzo**.

July

July–Aug	Opera at the Arena, and Shakespeare in the Roman theatre, **Verona**; Festival delle Ville, theatre and other events in the villas along the Brenta Canal, **Mira** (Venice); Mura Sotto le Stelle, jazz and blues under the stars, **Cittadella**; Music festival at the Villa Manin, **Passariano** (Ùdine).
All month	International wood sculpture competition, **Recoaro Terme** (Vicenza); Mittelfest, celebrating Central Europe with music, theatre, etc. **Cividale del Friuli**; international choral singing competitions, **Gorizia**.
Full moon	Sardellata, midnight fishing and huge fireworks on Lake Garda, **Pal del Vò**.
First week	Toti del Monte International contest for aspiring opera singers, **Treviso**.
First Sun	Perdon de Barbana, nautical procession to the island monastery, **Grado**.
9	Historical pageant, **Palmanova** (Ùdine).
17–27	Fiera della Maddalena, thousand-year-old fair with events, songs, food and races, **Oderzo**.
3rd Sun	Feast of the Redentore, **Venice**, celebrating the end of the 1576 plague, with a tremendous fireworks show followed by a procession over a bridge of boats on the Giudecca Canal.
End month	Sagra del Pesce, seafood festival, folklore and fireworks, **Chioggia**.

August

All month	International Folk Festivals, **Gorizia** and **Aviano** (Pordenone); Agosto Medievale, costumes and performances evoke the Middle Ages, at **Gemona** (Ùdine).
1st weekend	Palio and pageant at **Feltre**, celebrating the city's gift of itself to Venice in 1404; fish festival, parades and food at **Porto Tolle** (Rovigo).
First week	Pavana d'Estate, festival of popular and ethnic music, **Teolo** (Padua); Aria Festa, ham and wine fest, San Daniele del Friuli.
15	Palio delle Contrade, at **Garda**, with fishing boat regatta and historical parade; songbird market, Vittorio Veneto.
Mid-Aug–Sept	International piano competitions at **Bolzano**; musical festival, **Portogruaro** (Venice).
19–21	Traditional festival of Santa Augusta, **Vittorio Veneto**, with fireworks.
Last Sat	Giro delle Mura, race around the walls of **Feltre**.
Last Sun	Medieval songbird festival, **Sacile** (Pordenone).
End Aug –early Sept	International Film Festival, Venice; Sagra di Santa Colomba, Piazzola sul Brenta (**Padua**), popular folk festival, with a donkey palio, dances, food, etc.

September

| Sept–Dec | *Autunno Musicale Trevigiano*, ballet, opera and concerts, **Treviso** |
| 1st Sun | Historical regatta in costume and gondola races in **Venice**; Palio in **Montagnana**; *Coppa d'Oro delle Dolomiti*, historic sportscar race, **Cortina d'Ampezzo**; *Preludio e Dama Castellana*, **Conegliano Veneto**, Renaissance costumes and checkers played with living pieces between the neighbourhoods, with penalties for the losers; *Gioco dell'Oca in Piazza*, playing of the medieval Goose Game, in costume, **Portogruaro** (Venice). |

2nd week	Human chess game at **Maróstica** (Vicenza), even-numbered years only; autumn festival at **Tirolo** (Bolzano); *Mestre/Treviso in Carrozza*, historic carriage procession along the Terraglio from **Mestre to Treviso**, stopping at villas along the way.
20 wedding	Re-enactment of 10th-century nabbing of the 12 Venetian brides by pirates on their night, **Caorle** (Venice).
3rd Sun	Gran Prix de **Merano** horse race and lottery; *Festa Regionale dell'Uva*, **Vò** (Padua), festival of grapes from around Italy, with a parade and plenty of wine; wine festival, **Gambellara** (Vicenza).

October

All month	International Silent Film Festival, **Pordenone**.
1st week	*Salone dell'Antiquariato*, antiques and old books, **Vicenza**; *Festa della Giuggiola*, food, medieval costumes, majorettes and flowers, **Arquà Petrarca**.
1st Sun	Feast of the Rosary, **Galzignano Terme** (Padua), procession in historical costume recalling the Battle of Lepanto, and a donkey race; *La Barcolana*, international sailing regatta, **Trieste**.
2nd Sun	Grape festival, **Merano**, local wines, costumes, and folklore events.
3rd Sun	Chestnut festival, **Drena** (Trento); pumpkin festival, **Salzano** (Venice).
20–29	Wine-tasting festival, **Ora** (Bolzano).

November

1st week	Art and antiques show, **Bolzano**.
Mid-month	*Fieracavalli*, major horse fair in **Verona** (since 1908); DOC wine and food fair, **Vicenza**; Fiera di San Martino, food and crafts' fair, **Belluno**.
21	Feast of the Madonna della Salute, **Venice**, pilgrimage on bridge of boats over the Grand Canal, in thanksgiving for deliverance from the 1630 plague.
28–mid Dec	*Fiera del Bestiame*, **Santa Lucia di Piave** (Treviso). Enormous traditional agricultural fair.
28–early Dec	International Ice Cream Fair, **Longarone**.

December

Throughout	Exhibition of *presepi* (Christmas cribs) in **Verona**.
First week	Fair of San Nicolò, traditional fair in **Trieste**; Fair of San Nicolò, with a Christmas parade at **Vipiteno** (Bolzano); Parade of St Nicholas and the Krampus, **Tarvisio**.
2nd week	Regional handicrafts fair, **Pordenone**; Festa del Mondorlato, in honour of nougat, at **Cologna Veneta**.
2nd–3rd week	Radicchio Fair, **Castelfranco Veneto** (Treviso).
20–31	Nocturnal floating nativity processions, **Adria** (Rovigo); giant traditional *presepio* and exhibition, **Soave**.
End Dec–Jan 6	Christmas market, **Bressanone**.

Food and Drink

There are those who eat to live and those who live to eat, and then there are the Italians, for whom food has an almost religious significance, unfathomably linked with love, La Mamma and tradition. In this singular country, where millions of otherwise sane people spend much of their waking hours worrying about their digestion, standards both at home and in the restaurants are understandably high. Few Italians are gluttons, but all are experts on what is what in the kitchen; to serve a meal that is not properly prepared and more than a little complex is tantamount to an insult. For the visitor this national culinary obsession comes as an extra bonus to the senses—along with Italy's remarkable sights, music and the warm sun on your back, you can enjoy some of the best tastes and smells the world can offer, prepared daily in Italy's kitchens and fermented in its countless wine cellars. Eating *all'Italiana* is not only delicious and wholesome, but now undeniably trendy. Foreigners flock here to learn the secrets of Italian cuisine and the even more elusive secret of how the Italians can live surrounded by such delights and still fit into their sleek Armani trousers.

Breakfast (*colazione*) in Italy is no lingering affair, but an early morning sugar and caffeine wake-up shot to the brain: a *cappuccino* (espresso with hot foamy milk, often sprinkled with chocolate—incidentally, first thing in the morning is the only time of day any self-respecting Italian will touch the stuff), a *caffè latte* (white coffee) or a *caffè lungo* (a generous portion of espresso), accompanied by a croissant-type roll, called a *cornetto* or *briosce*, or a fancy pastry. This repast can be consumed in any bar and repeated during the morning as often as necessary. Breakfast in Italian hotels is seldom worth the price.

Lunch (*pranzo*), generally served around 1pm, is traditionally the most important meal of the day, with a minimum of a first course (*primo piatto*—any kind of pasta dish, broth or soup, or rice dish or pizza), a second course (*secondo*—a meat dish, accompanied by a *contorno* or side dish—a vegetable, salad, or potatoes usually), followed by fruit or dessert and coffee. You can, however, begin with a platter of *antipasti*—the appetizers Italians do so brilliantly, ranging from warm seafood delicacies, to raw ham (*prosciutto crudo*), salami in a hundred varieties, lovely vegetables, savoury toasts, olives, pâté and many many more. There are restaurants that specialize in *antipasti*, and they usually don't take it amiss if you decide to forget the pasta and meat and just nibble on these scrumptious hors-d'œuvres (though in the end it will probably cost more than a full meal). Most Italians accompany their meal with wine and mineral water—*acqua minerale*, with or without bubbles (*con* or *senza gas*), which supposedly aids digestion—concluding their meals with a *digestivo* liqueur.

Cena, the **evening meal**, is usually eaten around 8pm. This is much the same as *pranzo* although lighter, without the pasta; a pizza and beer, eggs or a fish dish. In restaurants, however, they offer all the courses.

In Italy the various terms for types of **restaurants**—*ristorante, trattoria*, or *osteria*—have been confused. A *trattoria* or *osteria* can be just as elaborate as a restaurant, though rarely is a *ristorante* as informal as a traditional *trattoria*. Unfortunately the old habit of posting menus and prices in the windows has fallen from fashion, so it's often difficult to judge variety or prices. In general, the fancier the fittings, the fancier the **bill**, though neither of these points has anything at all to do with the quality of the food. If you're uncertain, do as you would at home—look for lots of locals. When you eat out, mentally add to the bill (*conto*) the bread and cover charge (*pane e coperto*, between L2000 and L4000), and a 15% service charge. This is often included in the bill (*servizio compreso*); if not, it will say *servizio non compreso*, and you'll have to do your own arithmetic. Additional tipping is at your own discretion, but not expected in family-owned and -run places.

People who haven't visited Italy for years and have fond memories of eating full meals for under a pound will be amazed at how much **prices** have risen; though in some respects eating out in Italy is still a bargain, especially when you figure out how much all that wine would have cost you at home. In many places you'll often find restaurants offering a *menu turistico*—

full, set meals of usually meagre inspiration for L20,000–30,000. More imaginative chefs often offer a *menu degustazione*—a set-price gourmet meal that allows you to taste their daily specialities and seasonal dishes. Both of these are cheaper than if you had ordered the same food à la carte.

Restaurant price categories

very expensive	over L80,000
expensive	L50,000–80,000
moderate	L30,000–50,000
inexpensive	below L30,000

When you leave a restaurant you will be given a receipt (*scontrino* or *ricevuto fiscale*) which according to Italian law you must take with you out of the door and carry for at least 60 metres. If you aren't given one, it means the restaurant is probably fudging on its taxes and thus offering you lower prices. There is a slim chance the tax police (*Guardia di Fianza*) may have their eye on you and the restaurant, and if you don't have a receipt they could slap you with a heavy fine.

As the pace of modern urban life militates against traditional lengthy home-cooked repasts with the family, followed by a siesta, alternatives to sit-down meals have mushroomed. Many office workers now behave much as their counterparts elsewhere in Europe and consume a rapid snack at lunchtime, returning home after a busy day to throw together some pasta and salad in the evenings. The original Italian fast food alternative, a buffet known as the 'hot table' (*tavola calda*) is becoming harder and harder to find among the international and made in Italy fast food franchises of various descriptions; bars often double as *panicotecas* (which make hot or cold sandwiches to order, or serve *tramezzini*, little sandwiches on plain, square white bread that are always much better than they look); outlets selling pizza by the slice (*al taglio*) are common in city centres. At any grocer's (*alimentari*) or market (*mercato*) you can buy the materials for countryside or hotel-room picnics; some will make sandwiches for you.

What comes as a suprise to many visitors is the tremendous regional diversity at the table; often next to nothing on the menu looks familiar, or is disguised by a local or dialect name. Expect further mystification, as many Italian chefs have wholeheartedly embraced the concept of *nouvelle cuisine*, or rather *nuova cucina*, and are constantly inventing dishes with even more names. If your waiter's English fails to elucidate, the menu decoder at the back of this book may help.

Regional Specialities in Venetia

Forget the Italian stereotypes; olives don't grow in Venetia (except around Lake Garda) so many dishes are prepared with butter. Tomatoes and oregano are used more sparingly here than in the south, and many dishes, for better or worse, are served with *polenta* (a pudding or cake of yellow maize flour), a brick-heavy substance to be approached with caution.

Venice

Venetian cuisine is delicious, although in Venice proper you'll have to pay way over the odds to have it done properly; you'll do much better, in quality and price, on the *terra firma*. In seaside or lagoonside restaurants, a typical meal might include oysters from Chioggia or *sarde in saor* (marinated sardines) for *antipasti*, followed by the classic *risi e bisi* (rice and peas, cooked with Parma ham and Parmesan) or the Veneto's favourite pasta, *bigoli in salsa* (thick spaghetti, served with a piquant onion, butter and anchovy sauce). Another favourite choice for primo are various types of *risotto*: *di mare*, with seafood, *in nero*, with cuttlefish cooked in its own ink, or *alla sbirraglia*, with vegetables, chicken and ham. For *secondo*, liver and onions (*fegato alla veneziana*) with polenta shares top billing with seafood dishes like scampi, cuttlefish in its own ink (*seppie alla veneziana*), *fritto* (Adriatic mixed fry) and lobster (*aragosta*), or the equally pricey large Venetian crab, the delicate *granceola*. Top it all off with a *tiramisù*, the traditional Veneto mascarpone, coffee and chocolate dessert.

Candied fruit has an important role in the sweet category, recalling Venice's long rule over the island that gave us both the name and Europe's first sugar cane—Candia (Crete). An enduring taste for sultanas and pine nuts was acquired from the Byzantines and Turks, studding not only pastries but dishes such as *stoccafisso* (salt cod) and fish prepared *in carpione* (fried or grilled, then marinated with vinegar, wine and fried onions—a favourite of Venetian sailors, as it lasted a long time at sea and helped to prevent scurvy).

The Veneto

Elsewhere along coastal areas look for fish soup, *brodetto di pesce*, often served with polenta. Catfish and other freshwater creatures are the speciality at Rovigo, served fried or in ragouts. Treviso's little river Sile yields the star ingredient of *anguilla* (or *bisato*) *in umido* (eel stew) while the province is renowned for its *radicchio*, red chicory, a favourite in winter salads. Since Roman times the Trevigiano was famous for its *soppressa* (salted meats) and spicy *divina lucanica tarvisiana*, a sausage better known these days as *luganeghe*. A traditional first course, *sopa coada*, is a rich chicken broth with pieces of meat and bread.

In springtime gastronomes flock to feast on white asparagus in Bassano del Grappa and the deep red cherries of Maróstica, while in the autumn wild mushrooms, especially from the hills of Montello, hold pride of place, along with game dishes served with *peverada* (a traditional sauce made of giblets, anchovies and lemons). Padua is the land of pumpkin dishes and poultry 'of the courtyard'—chicken and geese mainly, usually served roasted; if it's cooked *alla Padovana* it will be spit roast and very spicy. Vicenza is famous for its dried cod, *bacalà*, and tops its *bigoli* with duck sauce. Montagnana produces sweet hams, Verona is synonymous with gnocchi, tall golden Pandoro cakes, all kinds of fruit and peaches served in red wine; it also produces more cabbage than anywhere else in Italy. The latter features in the classic Veronese dish, *patissada de cavolo con gnocchi*. The Veneto's best known cheese is strong-flavoured Asiago, from the eponymous mountain plateau; another, Formaggio Monte Veronese DOC, is made at the Lessinia, above Verona, and hard to find outside the region.

Trentino-Alto Adige

In the Dolomites, look for hearty Austrian influences and plenty of calories (and polenta) to keep you warm in the mountains. Nearly every menu features gnocchi, various kinds of ravioli such as *alla trentina* (filled with meat or vegetables and curds), *Schlutzkrapfen* (little ravioli), *canederli* (Italianized *Knoderln*, gnocchi made with breadcrumbs, egg, cheese and bacon, served with a sauce or in a broth) and, biggest of all, *strangolapreti* ('priest stranglers'), a 16th-century tradition in the Trentino—gnocchi made of bread, eggs, and spinach topped with melted butter. Other first courses include the wine soup of the Val d'Isarco, *zuppa acida* (a soup of pickled tripe—an acquired taste), *risotto ai funghi* (with mushrooms) or *ai frutti di bosco* (with woodland berries—delicious but rather rare). Vegetable soups are usually based on barley, while others such as *patao* are based on yellow cornflour and *sauerkraut*. Speck, a cured ham, is found on pizzas, in tortellini, in sandwiches, or as *antipasti*, where it may share the plater with goose ham and various other meaty treats. Main courses range from goulash (often of game), fresh trout and grilled meats, omelettes packed with potatoes and meat, *lepre alla trentina* (jugged hare), *Würstel con crauti* (sausage and sauerkraut), *osei scampai* (veal 'birds' i.e. *involtini*, filled with bacon and sage), Wienerschnitzel (*cotoletta alla milanese*, in Italian), sweet and sour venison dishes, and the Trentino classic with a funny name, *smacafam*, a pie filled with game and salted meats and baked in a wood oven. A favourite snack is smoked or salted meats (*carne salata*) with rye bread and horseradish. Local cheeses include *Trentingrana*, a hard cheese similar to Parmesan, and ricotta, served fresh or smoked. *Apfelstrudel*, apple strudel, often with pine nuts and raisins, is everywhere. Also try *fortaies*, 'sweet snails' (not snails, really, but snail-shaped fritters with powdered sugar) and *torta de' fregoloti*, a pastry made with almonds and walnuts.

Friuli-Venezia Giulia

Little Friuli has one of the most cosmopolitan kitchens and most complicated menus in Italy, where you'll find the Austrian influences of Trentino and Alto Adige matched by dishes with a Slovene slant, which makes for an often surprising fusion cusine—where else in Italy can you find a poppyseed risotto or gnocchi with plums? On a more traditional level, polenta, 'the bread of the mountains', is by far the favourite stodge, often served hot and creamy with tomatoes and pepper, sausages, game, fish or garden vegetables, or with cheese (*toc in braide*). The single most famous Friulian comestible is *prosciutto di San Daniele*, a rival to Parma's famous hams. A special race of pigs supplies a delicious smoked ham, *affumicato di Sauris*, while the Carnia produces an array of salami and masses of mushrooms in the autumn. In Ùdine ravioli are called *cialsons*; also try *frico* (a fried cheese wafer) served with polenta and potatoes. Around Trieste, menus feature *jota* (a soup of sauerkraut, beans, potatoes, garlic, cumin and olive oil), potato gnocchi flavoured with herbs, goulash, tripe dishes, hot Prague ham, and *porzina* (pork) with mustard; also look for *blijeki alla carsolina* (the *alla carsolina* part means with rocket) and *palacinke* (crèpes) filled with ricotta. Grado takes a great deal of pride in its fish soup, or *boretto alla gradese*. Among the cheeses, Montasio is the best known, with the local *formai salat* from the Valcosa, Val d'Arzino and Valcellina.

The cosmopolitan pastries and desserts of Friuli-Venezia Giulia are a gastronomic epiphany, not at all your typical Italian afterthoughts, but proudly commanding equal status on the menu with the other courses. A shortlist of great expectations includes a wide choice of strudels (not only apple, but poppyseed, pear, grape, and cherry) and *krapfens*, Viennese-style Sachertorte, Hungarian *rigojanci* (all whipped cream and chocolate) and *dobos,* Slovenian filo pastry and cheese *presniz*, *gibanica* (full of ricotta, honey, poppyseeds and pinenuts), *strukliji kuhani* (filled with walnuts, raisins and rum), *putizza* (a flat Swiss roll type pastry, filled with nuts or poppyseeds) and *gubana*, laden with dried and candied fruit.

Venetia's Wines

If Italy has an infinite variety of regional dishes, there is an equally bewildering array of **regional wines**, many of which are rarely exported because they are best drunk young. Unless you're dining at a restaurant with an exceptional cellar, do as the Italians do and order a carafe of the local wine (*vino locale* or *vino della casa*). You won't often be wrong. Most

Italian wines are named after the grape and the district they come from. If the label says DOC (*Denominazione di Origine Controllata*) it means that the wine comes from a specially defined area and was produced according to a certain traditional method. DOCG (*Denominazione d'Origine Controllata e Garantia*) is allegedly a more rigorous classification, indicating that the wines not only conform to DOC standards, but are tested by government-appointed inspectors (who are now more in evidence since a hideous methanol scandal claimed 20 lives in 1986). *Classico* means that a wine comes from the oldest part of the zone of production, though is not necessarily better than a non-*Classico*. *Riserva*, *superiore* or *speciale* denotes a wine that has been aged longer and is more alcoholic; *Recioto*, a favourite in the Veneto, is a wine made from the outer clusters of grapes ('the ears') with a higher sugar and therefore alcohol, content. Other Italian wine words are *spumante* (sparkling); *frizzante* (pétillant), *amabile* (semi-sweet), *abboccato* (medium dry) and *passito* (strong sweet wine made from raisins). *Rosso* is red, *bianco* white; between the two extremes lie *rubiato* (ruby), *rosato*, *chiaretto* or *cerasuolo* (rose). *Secco* is dry, *dolce* sweet, *liquoroso* fortified and sweet. *Vendemmia* means vintage, a *cantina* is a cellar, and an *enoteca* is a wine-shop where you can taste and buy wines.

The **Veneto**, one of Italy's top three wine regions (along with Tuscany and Piedmont) has made massive strides in improving quality since the war. Verona's Valpolicella is now one of Italy's most prestigious red wines, followed in fame by its lesser cousin Bardolino, from the shores of Lake Garda. Other lesser known reds worth seeking out in the region include Pramaggiore Cabernet and Merlot, Venegazzu della Casa and Piave Raboso. Of the whites, Soave is the best known and most abundant, if not the most reputable, although small Soave estates have been producing wines of quality; dry white Bianco di Custoza is a more flavour-some bet with its mix of Tocai, while Tocai di Lison from the border of Friuli has an excellent reputation. Most of the house wine in Venice is Piave, and the favourite aperitif throughout the region is Prosecco, that charming sparkler from Conegliano. Then there's that famous wine by-product, *grappa*, a mighty, Schnapps-like aquavit drunk in black coffee after a meal (a *caffè corretto*) or for breakfast if it's chilly; Bassano del Grappa has Italy's oldest distillery.

Trentino-Alto Adige may have two personalities, one Italian and one Teutonic, but both make plenty of wine, predominately whites, nearly all from a single grape variety. The Chardonnays, Rhinerieslings, Sauvignons, Sylvaner, Pinot Bianco and Grigio, and Gewürztraminers are excellent; the various dry and sweet Moscaos are also worth a try. The most abundant red, Schiava/Vernatsch, isn't terribly compelling; you'll generally do better with a Cabernet Franc and Sauvignon, or seek out some of the more exotic reds, especially Trentino's Teroldego or Lagrein or rosé-scented Rosenmuskateller.

Similar to Trentino-Alto Adige, **Friuli-Venezia Giulia** abstains from blending and produces mono-grape wines from seven different DOC regions: Latisana, Isonzo, Grave del Friuli (the biggest), Aquileia, Carso, Collio Goriziano, and Colli Orientali (one of the best). The region's finest wines are Pinot Grigio, Riesling Renaro, Traminer, and the native Tocai, which appar-ently has nothing to do with the famous Hungarian or Alsatian grapes; Sauvignons and Chardonnays are now grown according to fashion and slip down a treat. The Colli Orientali also produce a notable sweet wine called Picolit, in tiny precious amounts, prized by connois-seurs. Friulian reds have mostly a French pedigree: Pinot Noir, Carbernet Franc and Merlot rule the roost, while the Colli Orientali produce an excellent wine from a local variety, Refosco. Rochi di Cialla and Giovanni Dri are just two of the best-known labels.

Health and Emergencies

You can insure yourself against almost any possible mishap—cancelled flights, stolen or lost baggage and illness. Check any current policies you hold to see if they cover you while abroad, and under what circumstances, and judge whether you need a special **traveller's insurance** policy for the journey. Travel agencies sell them, as well as insurance companies.

Citizens of EU countries are entitled to **reciprocal health care** in Italy's National Health Service and a 90% discount on prescriptions (bring **Form E111** with you). The E111 does not cover all medical expenses (no repatriation costs, for example, and no private treatment), and it is advisable to take out separate travel insurance for full cover. Citizens of non-EU countries should check carefully that they have adequate insurance for any medical expenses, and the cost of returning home. Australia has a reciprocal health care scheme with Italy, but New Zealand, Canada and the USA do not. If you already have health insurance, a student card, or a credit card, you may be entitled to some medical cover abroad.

In an **emergency**, dial **115** for fire (*incendio*) and **113** for an ambulance in Italy (*ambulanza*) or to find the nearest hospital (*ospedale*). Less serious problems can be treated at a *Pronto Soccorso* (casualty/first aid department) at any hospital clinic (*ambulatorio*) or at a local health unit (*Unita Sanitaria Locale*—USL). Airports and main railway stations also have **first-aid posts**. If you have to pay for any health treatment, make sure you get a receipt, so that you can make any claims for reimbursement later.

Dispensing **chemists** (*farmacia*) are generally open from 8.30am to 1pm and from 4 to 8pm. Pharmacists are trained to give advice for minor ills. Any large town will have a *farmacia* that stays open 24 hours; others take turns to stay open (the address rota is posted in the window).

No specific **vaccinations** are required or advised for citizens of most countries before visiting Italy; the main health risks are the usual travellers' woes of upset stomachs or the effects of too much sun. Take a supply of **medicaments** with you (insect repellent, anti-diarrhœal medicine, sun lotion and antiseptic cream), and any drugs you need regularly.

Most Italian doctors speak at least rudimentary English, but if you can't find one, contact your embassy or consulate for a list of English-speaking doctors.

Maps and Publications

The maps in this guide are for orientation only and, to explore in any detail, invest in a good, up-to-date regional map, produced by the **Touring Club Italiano**, and **Istituto Geografico de Agostini**. Get them in the UK at **Stanford's**, 12–14 Long Acre, London WC2 9LP, © (0171) 836 1321, or **The Travel Bookshop**, 13 Blenheim Crescent, London W11 2EE, © (0171) 229 5260. In the USA, try **The Complete Traveler**, 199 Madison Ave, New York, NY 10016, © (212) 685 9007. They are available at all major bookshops in Italy (e.g. Feltrinelli) or sometimes on news stands. Italian tourist offices are helpful and can often supply good area maps and town plans.

Money

It's a good idea to order a wad of lire from your home bank to have on hand when you arrive in the land of strikes, unforeseen delays and quirky banking hours (*see* below). Take great care how you carry it, however (don't keep it all in one place). Obtaining money is often a frustrating business involving much queueing and form-filling. The major banks and exchange bureaux licensed by the Bank of Italy give the best exchange rates for currency or traveller's cheques. Hotels, private exchanges in resorts and FS-run exchanges at railway stations usually have less advantageous rates, but are open outside normal banking hours. Weekend exchange offices can be found in most large cities, e.g. **Venice**: American Express, S. Moise 1471; CIT Piazza S. Marco. In addition there are exchange offices at most airports. Remember that Italians indicate decimals with commas and thousands with full points.

You can (for a significant commission) use your major credit card, Eurocheque card or British bank card (but check at your bank first) to take money out of Italian automatic tellers (*Bancomat*). You need a four-digit PIN number to use these. Make sure you read the instructions carefully, or your card may be retained by the machine. Besides traveller's cheques, most banks will give also you cash on a recognized credit card or Eurocheque with a Eurocheque card. Large hotels, resort area restaurants, most petrol stations, shops and car hire firms will accept plastic as well; many smaller places will not.

You can have money transferred to you through an Italian bank but this process may take over a week, even if it's sent urgent, *espressissimo*. You will need your passport as identification when you collect it.

Opening Hours and Museums

Although it varies from town to town, most of Venetia closes down at 1pm until 3 or 4pm to eat and properly digest the main meal of the day. Afternoon hours are from 4 to 7, often from 5 to 8 in the hot summer months. Bars are often the only places open during the early afternoon. Some cities close down completely during August when locals flee from the polluted frying pan to the hills, lakes or coast. In any case, don't be surprised if you find anywhere in Italy unexpectedly closed (or open for that matter), whatever its official stated hours.

Banks: Banking hours vary, but core times in large towns are usually Mon–Fri 8.30am–1pm and 3–4pm, closed weekends and on local and national holidays (*see* below). Outside normal hours, you will usually be able to find somewhere to change money (at disadvantageous rates).

Shops usually open Monday–Saturday from 8am to 1pm and 3.30pm to 7.30pm, though hours vary according to season and are shorter in smaller centres. In some large cities hours are longer. Some supermarkets and department stores stay open throughout the day.

Offices: Government-run dispensers of red tape (e.g. visa departments) often stay open for quite limited periods, usually during the mornings, Monday to Friday. It pays to get there as soon as they open (or before) to spare your nerves in an interminable queue. Anyway, take something to read, or write your memoirs.

Museums and galleries: Many of Italy's museums are magnificent, many are run with shameful neglect, and many have been closed for years for 'restoration' with slim prospects of reopening in the foreseeable future. With two works of art per inhabitant, Italy has a hard time financing the preservation of its heritage; ring the local tourist office to find out exactly what is open and what is 'temporarily' closed before setting off on a wild-goose chase.

Churches: Italy's churches have always been a prime target for art thieves and as a consequence are usually locked when there isn't a sacristan or caretaker to keep an eye on things.

All churches, except for the really important cathedrals and basilicas, close in the afternoon at the same hours as the shops, and the little ones tend to stay closed. Always have a pocketful of coins for the light machines in churches, or whatever work of art you came to inspect will remain clouded in ecclesiastical gloom. Don't do your visiting during services, and don't come to see paintings and statutes in churches the week preceding Easter—you will probably find them covered with mourning shrouds.

In general, Sunday afternoons and Mondays are dead periods for the sightseer—you may want to make them your travelling days. Places without specified opening hours can usually be visited on request, but it is best to go before 1pm. Entrance charges vary widely; major sights are fairly steep (L10,000 plus), but others may be completely free. EU citizens under 18 and over 65 get free admission to state museums, at least in theory.

National Holidays

Most museums, as well as banks and shops, are closed on the following national holidays.

1 January (New Year's Day)

6 January (Epiphany)

Easter Monday

25 April (Liberation Day)

1 May (Labour Day)

15 August (Assumption, also known as *Ferragosto*, the official start of the Italian holiday season)

1 November (All Saints' Day)

8 December (Immaculate Conception)

25 December (Christmas Day)

26 December (*Santo Stefano*, St Stephen's Day)

In addition to these general holidays, many towns also take their patron saint's day off.

Packing

You simply cannot overdress in Italy; whatever grand strides Italian designers have made on the international fashion merry-go-round, most of their clothes are purchased domestically, prices be damned. Now whether or not you want to try to keep up with the natives is your own affair and your own heavy suitcase—you may do well to compromise and just bring a couple of smart outfits for big nights out. It's not that the Italians are very formal; they simply like to dress up with a gorgeousness that adorns their cities just as much as those old Renaissance churches and palaces. The few places with dress codes are the major churches and basilicas (no shorts, sleeveless shirts or strappy sundresses—women should tuck a light silk scarf in a bag to throw over the shoulders), casinos, and a few posh restaurants.

After agonizing over fashion, remember to pack small and light: trans-Atlantic airlines limit baggage by size (two pieces are free up to 1.5m in height and width; in second-class you're allowed one of 1.5m and another up to 110cm). Within Europe limits are by weight; 20kg (44lbs) in second-class, 30kg (66lbs) in first. You may well be penalized for anything larger. If you're travelling mainly by train, you'll want to keep bags to a minimum: jamming big cases in overhead racks in a crowded compartment isn't much fun for anyone. Never take more than you can carry; but do bring the following: any prescription medicine you need, an extra pair of glasses or contact lenses if you wear them; a pocket knife and corkscrew (for picnics), a flash-light (for dark frescoed churches, caves and crypts), a travel alarm (for those early trains) and a pocket Italian-English dictionary (for flirting and other emergencies; outside the main tourist centres you may well have trouble finding someone who speaks English). If you're a light sleeper, you may want to invest in ear-plugs. Your electric appliances will work in Italy if you adapt and convert them to run on 220 AC with two round prongs on the plug.

Photography

Film and developing are much more expensive than they are in either the UK or the USA, though there are plenty of outlets where you can obtain them. Note that you are not allowed to take pictures in most museums and in some churches. Most cities now offer one-hour processing if you need your pics in a hurry.

Post Offices

Dealing with *la posta italiana*, the most expensive and slowest postal service in Europe, has always been a risky, frustrating, time-consuming affair. Even buying the right stamps requires dedicated research and saintly patience. One of the scandals that mesmerized Italy in recent years involved the minister of the post office, who disposed of literally tons of backlog mail by tossing it in the Tiber. When the news broke, he was replaced—the new minister, having learned his lesson, burned all the mail the post office was incapable of delivering. Not surprisingly, fed-up Italians view the invention of the fax machine as a gift from the Madonna.

Post offices in Italy are usually open from 8am until 1pm (Monday to Saturday), or until 6 or 7pm in a large city. To have your mail sent poste restante (general delivery), have it addressed to the central post office (*Fermo Posta*) and expect three to four weeks for it to arrive. Make sure your surname is very clearly written in block capitals. To pick up your mail you must present your passport and pay a nominal charge. Stamps (*francobolli*) may be purchased in post offices or at tobacconists (*tabacchi*, identified by their blue signs with a white T). Prices fluctuate. The rates for letters and postcards (depending how many words you write!) vary according to the whim of the tobacconist or postal clerk.

You can also have money telegraphed to you through the post office; if all goes well, this can happen in a mere three days, but expect a fair proportion of it to go into commission.

Shopping

'Made in Italy' has become a byword for style and quality, especially in fashion and leather, but also in home design, ceramics, kitchenware, jewellery, lace and linens, glassware and crystal, chocolates, bells, Christmas decorations, hats, straw work, art books, engravings, handmade stationery, gold and silverware, bicycles, sports cars, woodworking, a hundred kinds of liqueurs, aperitifs, coffee machines, gastronomic specialities, and antiques (both repro-ductions and the real thing). You'll find the best variety of goods in Verona and Venice—in other words, where the money is. Be sure to save receipts for Customs (or tax rebates, if you're not an EU resident) on the way home.

If you are looking for antiques, be sure to demand a certificate of authenticity—Venetia is Italy's top manufacturer of reproductions, and they can be very, very good. Monthly weekend antique markets are a thriving business, run on the following calendar:

First Sunday: Battaglia Terme, Vittorio Vèneto, Maròstica, Noventa Vicentina, Povegliano Veronese, Morgano-Badoere, Ùdine and Brugine

2nd Saturday: Àsolo, Adria

2nd Sunday: Cadoneghe, Noale, Portobuffolé, San Zenone degli Ezzelini, Roncade, and Montegrotto Terme

3rd Saturday and Sunday: Montagnana

3rd Sunday: Padua, Citadella, Mirano, Soave, Godega di Sant'Urbano, Paese, and Este

4th Saturday: Monsélice

4th Sunday: Treviso, Piazzola sul Brenta, Valeggio sul Mincio, and Dolo

To get your antique or modern art purchases home, you will have to apply to the Export Department of the Italian Ministry of Education—a possible hassle. You will have to pay an export tax as well; your seller should know the details.

Sports and Activities

Fishing: You don't need a permit for sea-fishing (without an aqualung), but Italy's coastal waters, polluted and over-exploited, may disappoint. Commercial fishing has depleted stocks to such an extent that the government has begun to declare two-and three-month moratoria on all fishing to give the fish a break. Many freshwater lakes and mountain streams are stocked, however, and if you're more interested in fresh fish than the sport of it, there are innumerable trout farms where you can practically pick the fish up out of the water with your hands. To fish in fresh water you need to purchase a year's membership card (currently L189,000) from the **Federazione Italiana della Pesca Sportiva**, which has an office in every province; they will inform you about local conditions and restrictions. Bait and equipment are readily available.

Football: Soccer (*il calcio*) is a national obsession. For many Italians its importance far outweighs tedious issues like the state of the nation, the government of the day, or any momentous international event—not least because of the weekly chance (slim but real) of becoming an instant lira billionaire in the Lotteria Sportiva. All major cities, and most minor ones, have at least one team of some sort. The sport was actually introduced by the English, but a Renaissance game, something like a cross between football and rugby, has existed in Italy for centuries. Modern Italian teams are known for their grace, precision, and coordination; rivalries are intense, scandals, especially involving bribery and cheating, are rife. The tempting rewards offered by such big-time entertainment attract all manner of corrupt practices, yet crowd violence is minimal compared with the havoc wreaked by Britain's lamentable fans. Big-league matches are played on Sunday afternoons from September to May. For information, contact the Federazione Italiana Giuoco Calcio, Via G Allegri 14, 00198 Rome, © 06 84911. Rugby and baseball are also played in most cities; even American football and basketball have their devotees.

Golf: Italians have been slower than some nationalities to appreciate the delights of biffing a small white ball into a hole in the ground, but they're catching on fast. New courses are now spawning all over the country. Write to or ring the local tourist offices or the Federazione Italiana Golf, Via Flaminia 388, 00196 Rome, ✆ 06 323 1825, to check details before turning up. Most take guests and hire equipment.

Hiking and mountaineering are becoming steadily more popular among native Italians every year. The Dolomites (*see* p.241) have a good system of waymarked trails and mountain refuges run by the Italian Alpine Club (CAI). If you are planning to use the more popular routes in summer, write beforehand to reserve beds in refuges. Walking is practicable between May and October, after most of the snow has melted; all the necessary gear—boots, packs, tents, etc.—are readily available in Italy but for more money than you'd pay at home.

The CAI can put you in touch with Alpine guides or climbing groups if you're up to some real adventure, or write to the Italian National Tourist Board for a list of operators offering mountaineering holidays. Some resorts have taken to offering *Settimane Verdi* (Green Weeks)—good-value accommodation and activity packages for summer visitors.

Hunting: Italy's most controversial sport pits avid enthusiasts against a growing number of environmentalists. The debate is fierce and the start of the season is marked by huge protests. Indiscriminate trapping, netting and shooting is responsible for the decimation of many migrant Mediterranean songbirds. Less controversial, at least from the conservation point of view, is duck, pigeon and wild-boar shooting.

Riding holidays are now available in many parts, particularly in the Dolomites, and there are stables in most seaside resorts as well. For more information, contact the the Associazione Nazionale per il Turismo Equestre, Via A Borelli 5, 00161 Rome, ✆ 06 444 1179.

Rowing andf canoeing: The annual regatta between the four ancient maritime republics of Venice, Amalfi, Genoa and Pisa (held in turn at each city) is a splendidly colourful event. The fast rivers of the mountain areas provide exciting white-water sport. For information contact Federazione Italiana Canoa e Kayak, Viale Tiziano 70, 00196 Rome, ✆ 06 368 58215.

Skiing and winter sports: Italy still lacks the cachet of neighbouring Switzerland or Austria among the skiing fraternity, but has caught up significantly and now has a better reputation for safety and efficiency than it once did, though erratic snow cover is always a problem. Downhill and cross-country (*sci di fondo*) skiing are available in the Dolomites, along with more exotic variants (for experts only) like helicopter skiing. The Sella Ronda links several resorts in an exhilarating day's circuit. The Marmolada glacier in Trentino-Adige, and the glacier above the Stelvio pass provide year-round sources of snowy runs. Prices are highest during Christmas and New Year holidays, in February and at Easter. Most resorts offer *Settimane Bianche* (White Weeks)—off-season packages at economical rates. Other winter sports such as ice-skating and bob-sleighing are available at larger resorts. For more, *see* p.241.

Tennis: If soccer is Italy's most popular spectator sport, tennis is probably the game most people actually play. Every *comune* has public courts for hourly hire, especially resorts. Private clubs may offer temporary membership to passing visitors, and hotel courts can often be used by non-residents for a reasonable fee. Contact local tourist offices for information.

Watersports: Despite Italy's notorious coastal pollution, watersports are immensely popular, especially sailing and windsurfing. Lake Garda has well-equipped sailing and windsurfing schools. Waterskiing is possible on all the major lakes, as well as at many coastal resorts. Boat and equipment hire tends to be quite expensive.

Venetia is not remarkable for its **beaches**, and although you'll find plenty of sand at major resorts—Venice's Lido, Lignano Sabbiadoro, Bibione, Grado, and Jesolo—much of the coast is disappointingly flat and dull and many seaside resorts are plagued by that peculiarly Italian phenomenon, the concessionaire, who parks ugly lines of sunbeds and brollies all the way along the best stretches of beach, and charges all comers handsomely for the privilege. During the winter you can see what happens when the beaches miss out on their manicures; many get depressingly rubbish-strewn. No one bats an eye at topless bathing, though nudism requires more discretion. For further information, write to the following organizations:

Federazione Italiana Vela (Italian Sailing Federation), Via Brigata Bisagno 2/17, Genoa, ℭ 010 56 57 23.

Federazione Italiana Motonautica (Italian Motorboat Federation), and **Federazione Italiana Sci Nautico** can both be found at Via Piranesi 44b, Milan, ℭ 02 76 10 50.

Telephones

Public telephones for international calls may be found in the offices of **Telecom Italia**, Italy's telephone company. They are the only places where you can make reverse-charge calls (*a erre*, collect calls) but be prepared for a wait, as all these calls go through the operator in Rome. Long-distance rates are among the highest in Europe. Calls within Italy are cheapest after 10pm; international calls after 11pm. Most phone booths now take either coins (L100, 200, 500 or 1000) or phone cards (*schede, telefoniche*) available in L5000, L10,000 and sometimes L15,000 amounts at tobacconists and news-stands—you will have to snap off the small perforated corner in order to use them. In smaller villages, you can usually find *telefoni a scatti*, with a meter on it, in at least one bar (a small commission is generally charged).

Direct calls may be made by dialling the international prefix (for the UK 0044, Ireland 00353, USA and Canada 001, Australia 0061, New Zealand 0064). If you're calling Italy from abroad, dial the country code 0039 and then the whole number, including the first zero.

Time

Italy is on Central European Time, one hour ahead of Greenwich Mean Time and six hours ahead of Eastern Standard Time. From the last weekend of March to the end of September, Italian Summer Time (daylight saving time) is in effect.

Toilets

They 'let down their breeches wherever and before whomsoever they please; according all St Mark's Place, and many parts of the sumptuous building, the Doge's Palace, are dedicated to Cloacina, and you may see Votaries at their devotions every hour of the day.' Thus Samuel Sharp in the 18th century. It's not so bad now, although don't expect Italy to makes its conveniences very convenient even in city centres—look for them in places like train and bus stations and bars. Ask for the *bagno, toilette,* or *gabinetto*; in stations and the smarter bars and cafes, there are washroom attendants who expect a few hundred lire for keeping the place decent. Don't confuse the Italian plurals; *signori* (gents), *signore* (ladies).

Tourist Offices

Known under various initials as EPT, APT or AAST, Italian tourist offices usually stay open from 8am to 12.30 or 1pm, and from 3 to 7pm, possibly longer in summer. Few open on Saturday afternoons or Sundays. Information booths can also be found at major railway stations and can provide hotel lists, town plans and terse information on local sights and transport. Queues can be maddeningly long. English is spoken in the main centres. If you're stuck, you may get more sense out of a friendly travel agency than an official tourist office. The Veneto regional government has a free phone tourist information number you can use while in Italy ✆ 167 853 040. Or contact your Italian State Tourist Office:

UK 1 Princes St, London W1R 8AY, ✆ (0171) 408 1254, ✉ (0171) 493 6695.

USA 630 Fifth Ave, Suite 1565, New York NY 10111, ✆ (212) 245 4822, ✉ (212) 586 9249.

12400 Wilshire Blvd, Suite 550, Los Angeles, CA 90025, ✆ (310) 820 0098, ✉ (310) 820 6357.

500 N. Michigan Ave, Suite 1046, Chicago IL 60611, ✆ (312) 644 0990/6, ✉ 644 3019.

Australia c/o Italian Embassy, 61–69 Macquerie St, Sydney 2000, NSW, ✆ (02) 9247 8442.

Canada 1 Place Ville Marie, Suite 1914, Montréal, Quebec H3B 3M9, ✆ (514) 866 7667.

Japan 2–7–14 Minimi, Aoyama, Minato-Ku, Tokyo 107, ✆ (813) 347 82 051.

France 23 Rue de la Paix, 75002 Paris, ✆ 01 42 66 66 68.

14 Avenue de Verdun, 06048 Nice, ✆ 04 93 87 75 81.

Germany Berliner Allee 26, 4 Düsseldorf, ✆ (211) 13 22 32.

Kaiserstrasse 65, 6000 Frankfurt/Main 1, ✆ (069) 2374.

Goethestrasse 20, 80336 München, ✆ (089) 53 03 69.

Netherlands Stadhouderskade 6, 1054 ES Amsterdam, ✆ (020) 616 8244.

N. Zealand c/o Italian Embassy, 36 Grant Road, Thomdon, Wellington, ✆ (04) 736 065.

Tourist and travel information may also be available from **Alitalia** (Italy's national airline) or **CIT** (Italy's state-run travel agency) offices in some countries. In the UK, contact the **Italian Travel Centre**, 30 St James's Street, London SW1A 1HB, ✆ (0171) 853 6464.

Where to Stay

All accommodation in Italy is classified by the Provincial Tourist Boards. Price control, however, has been deregulated since 1992. Hotels set their own tariffs from then on, which means that prices rocketed. After a period of rapid and erratic price fluctuation, tariffs are at last settling down again to more predictable levels under the influence of market forces. Good-value, interesting accommodation in cities can be very difficult to find.

The quality of furnishings and facilities has generally improved in all categories in recent years. Many hotels have installed smart bathrooms and electronic gadgetry. At the top end of the market, Italy has a number of exceptionally sybaritic hotels, furnished and decorated with real panache. But you can still find plenty of older-style hotels and *pensioni*, whose eccentricities of character and architecture (in some cases undeniably charming) may frequently be at odds with modern standards of comfort or even safety.

Accommodation prices

Category	Double with bath
luxury (*****)	L450–800,000
very expensive (****)	L300–450,000
expensive (***)	L200–300,000
moderate (**)	L120–200,000
cheap (*)	up to L120,000

Hotels and Guesthouses

Italian *alberghi* come in all shapes and sizes. They are rated from one to five stars, depending what facilities they offer (not their character, style or charm). The star ratings are some indication of price levels, but for tax reasons not all hotels choose to advertise themselves at the rating to which they are entitled, so you may find a modestly rated hotel just as comfortable (or more so) than a higher rated one. Conversely, you may find a hotel offers few stars in hopes of attracting budget-conscious travellers, but charges just as much as a higher-rated neighbour. *Pensioni* are generally more modest establishments, though nowadays the distinction between these and ordinary hotels is becoming blurred. *Locande* are traditionally an even more basic form of hostelry, but these days the term may denote somewhere fairly chic. Other inexpensive accommodation is sometimes known as *alloggi* or *affittacamere*. There are usually plenty of cheap dives around railway stations; for somewhere more salubrious, head for the historic quarters. Whatever the shortcomings of the décor, furnishings and fittings, you can usually rely at least on having clean sheets.

Price lists, by law, must be posted on the door of every room, along with meal prices and any extra charges (such as air-conditioning, or even a shower in cheap places). Many hotels display two or three different rates, depending on the season. Low-season rates may be about a third lower than peak-season tariffs. Some resort hotels close down altogether for several months a year. During high season you should always book ahead to be sure of a room (a fax reservation may be less frustrating to organize than one by post). If you have paid a deposit, your booking is valid under Italian law, but don't expect it to be refunded if you have to cancel. Tourist offices publish annual regional lists of hotels and pensions with current rates, but do not generally make reservations for visitors. Major city business hotels may offer significant discounts at weekends.

Main railway stations generally have accommodation booking desks; inevitably, a fee is charged. Chain hotels or motels are generally the easiest hotels to book, though not always the most interesting to stay in. Top of the list is CIGA (*Compagnia Grandi Alberghi*) with some of the most luxurious establishments in Italy, many of them grand, turn-of-the-century places that have been exquisitely restored. Venice's legendary Cipriani is one of its flagships. The French consortium *Relais et Châteaux* specializes in tastefully indulgent accommodation, often in historic buildings. At a more affordable level, one of the biggest chains in Italy is *Jolly Hotels*, always reliable if not all up to the same standard; these can generally be found near the centres of larger towns. Many motels are operated by the ACI (Italian Automobile Club) or by AGIP (the oil company) and usually located along major exit routes.

If you arrive without a reservation, begin looking or phoning round for accommodation early in the day. If possible, inspect the room (and bathroom facilities) before you book, and check the tariff carefully. Italian hoteliers may legally alter their rates twice during the year, so printed tariffs or tourist board lists (and prices quoted in this book!) may be out of date. Hoteliers who wilfully overcharge should be reported to the local tourist office. You will be asked for your passport for registration purposes.

Prices listed in this guide are for double rooms; you can expect to pay about two-thirds the rate for single occupancy, though in high season you may be charged the full double rate in a popular beach resort. Extra beds are usually charged at about a third more of the room rate. Rooms without private bathrooms generally charge 20–30% less, and most offer discounts for children sharing parents' rooms, or children's meals. A *camera singola* (single room) may cost anything from about L25,000 upwards. Double rooms (*camera doppia*) go from about L60,000 to L250,000 or more. If you want a double bed, specify a *camera matrimoniale*.

Breakfast is usually optional in hotels, though obligatory in *pensioni*. You can usually get better value by eating breakfast in a bar or café if you have any choice. In high season you may be expected to take half-board in resorts if the hotel has a restaurant, and one-night stays may be refused.

Hostels and Budget Accommodation

There aren't many youth hostels in Italy (where they are known as *alberghi* or *ostelli per la gioventù*), but they are generally pleasant and sometimes located in historic buildings. The **Associazione Italiana Alberghi per la Gioventù** (Italian Youth Hostel Association, or AIG) is affiliated to the International Youth Hostel Federation. For a full list of hostels, contact AIG at Via Cavour 44, 00184 Roma (✆ 06 487 1152; ✉ 06488 0492). An international membership card will enable you to stay in any of them. You can obtain these in advance from the following organizations.

UK   Youth Hostels Association of England and Wales, 14 Southampton
              Street, London, WC2, ✆ (0171) 836 1036.

USA   American Youth Hostels Inc., Box 37613, Washington DC 20013-7613,
              ✆ (202) 783 6161.

Australia Australian Youth Hostel Association, 60 Mary Street, Surry Hills, Sydney,
              NSW 2010, ✆ (02) 9621 1111.

Canada   Canadian Hostelling Association, 1600 James Naismith Drive, Suite 608,
              Gloucester, Ontario K1B 5N4, ✆ (613) 237 7884.

(Cards can usually be purchased on the spot in many hostels if you don't already have one.)

Religious institutions also run hostels; some are single sex, some will accept Catholics only. Rates are usually somewhere between L15,000 and L20,000, including breakfast. Discounts are available for senior citizens, and some family rooms are available. You generally have to check in after 5pm, and pay for your room before 9am. Hostels usually close for most of the daytime, and many operate a curfew. During the spring, noisy school parties cram hostels for field trips. In the summer, it's advisable to book ahead. Contact the hostels directly.

Villas, Flats and Chalets

If you're travelling in a group or with a family, self-catering can be the ideal way to experience Italy. The National Tourist Office has lists of agencies in the UK and USA which rent places on a weekly or fortnightly basis. CIT offices also rent flats and villas. If you have set your heart on a particular region, write ahead to its tourist office for a list of local agencies and owners, who will send brochures or particulars of their accommodation. Maid service is included in the more glamorous villas; ask whether bed linen and towels are provided. A few of the larger operators are listed below.

in the UK

Eurovillas, 36 East Street, Coggeshall, Essex CO6 1SH, ✆ (01376) 561156.

Inghams, 10–18 Putney Hill, London SW15 6AX, ✆ (0181) 780 4411.

Interhome, 383 Richmond Road, Twickenham, Middx TW1 2EF, ✆ (0181) 891 1294, website *www.interhome.co.uk*, e-mail *interhome.uk@ibm.net*

International Chapters, 47–51 St John's Wood High Street, London NW8 7NJ, ✆ (0171) 722 9560.

Magic of Italy, 227 Shepherds Bush Road, London W6 7AS, ✆ (0181) 748 7575.

Vacanze in Italia, Manor Courtyard, Bignor, Pulborough, West Sussex RH20 1QD, ✆ (01798) 869 461.

in the USA

At Home Abroad, 405 East 56th Street 6-H, New York, NY 10022-2466, ✆ (212) 421 9165, ✆ 752 1591, *athomabrod@aol.com*

Rentals for Italy (and Elsewhere!), Suzanne T. Pidduck, 1742 Calle Corva, Camarillo, CA 93010, ✆ (800) 726 6702/(805) 987 5278, ✆ (805) 482 7976, *mail@rentvillas. com*; they also offer car rentals schemes.

Hideaways International, 767 Islington Street, Portsmouth NH 03801, ✆ (617) 486 8955.

Hometours International, PO Box 11503, Knoxville, TN 37938, ✆ (423) 690 8484/(800) 367 4668.

RAVE, (Rent-a-Vacation Everywhere), 135 Meigs Street, Rochester, New York, NY 14607, ✆ (716) 256 0760.

Rural Self-catering

For a breath of rural seclusion, the normally gregarious Italians head for a spell on a **working farm**, in accommodation (usually self-catering) that often approximates to the French *gîte*. Often, however, the real pull is a restaurant in which you can sample some home-grown produce (olives, wine, etc.). Outdoor activities may also be on tap (riding, fishing, and so forth).

This branch of the Italian tourist industry is run by a special agency, **Agriturist**, and has boomed in recent years to include two other similar organizations, **Terranostra** and **Turismo Verde**. Prices of farmhouse accommodation are still reasonable (expect to pay around L40,000–60,000 for a cottage or double room). To make the most of your rural hosts, it's as well to have a little Italian under your belt. Local tourist offices will have information on this type of accommodation in their areas; otherwise you can obtain complete listings compiled by the regional centres.

Veneto: Agriturist Ufficio Regionale, Via Monteverdi 15, Mestre (VE), ℡ 041 987 400. Terranostra: Via Orsato 22, Marghera (VE), ℡ 041 930 033. Turismo Verde: Via Rizzardi 26, Marghera (VE), ℡ 041 929 900.

Trentino: Associazione Agriturismo Trentino, Via Jacopo Aconcio 13, Trento, ℡ 0461 235323; Trentino Verde, Sede Provinciale Turismo Rurale e Agriurismo di Qualità, Via Giusti 40, Trento, ℡ 0461 915 674.

Alto Adige: Alto Adige Promozione Turismo, Piazza Parocchia 11, 39100 Bolzano, ℡ 0471 307 000, ℮ 0471 993 889.

Friuli-Venezia Giulia: call ℡ 040 377 2491 for information.

Alpine Refuges

The Italian Alpine Club operates refuges (*rifugi*) on the main mountain trails (some accessible only by *funivie*). These may be predictably spartan, or surprisingly comfortable. Many have restaurants. For an up-to-date list, write to the Club Alpino Italiano, Via Fonseca Pimental 7, Milan, ℡ 02 2614 1378. Charges average L18,000–L25,000 per person per night, including breakfast. Most are open only from July to September, but those used by skiers are about 20% more expensive from December to April. Book ahead in August.

Camping

Life under canvas is not the fanatical craze it is in France, nor necessarily any great bargain, but there are over 2000 sites in Italy, particularly popular with holidaymaking families in August, when you can expect to find many sites at bursting point. Unofficial camping is generally frowned on and may attract a stern rebuke from the local police. Camper vans (and facilities for them) are increasingly popular. You can obtain a list of local sites from any regional tourist office. Campsite charges generally range from about L6–8000 per adult; tents and vehicles additionally cost about L7000 each. Small extra charges may also be levied for hot showers and electricity. A car-borne couple could therefore spend practically as much for a night at a well equipped campsite as in a cheap hotel. To obtain a camping carnet and to book ahead, write to the **Centro Internazionale Prenotazioni Campeggio**, Casella Postale 23, 50041, Calenzano, Firenze, ℡ 055882 381; ℮ 055 882 3918 (ask for their list of campsites as well as the booking form). The **Touring Club Italiano** (TCI) publishes a comprehensive annual guide to campsites and tourist villages throughout Italy which is available in bookshops for L29,5000. Write to TCI, Corso Italia 10, Milan, ℡ 02 85261/852 6245.

History

Prehistory, and the Rather Mysterious Paleoveneti (1100–3rd Century BC)

Some of the most creative cultures grow up from some of the messiest historical composts. The Mediterranean is a case in point, and Italy an extreme case, and its northeast corner as historically messy and creative as any place on this planet. Venetia's earliest inhabitants (5th–4th millennium BC) were peaceful shepherds, but little else was known about them until 1991 and the sensational discovery of the '**Ice Man**' who perished in an alpine storm 5300 years ago; his frozen, miraculously intact mummy is now on display in Bolzano, complete with all his gear and the stone statue steles carved by his Neolithic/early Copper Age contemporaries.

Many of the Ice Man's contemporaries were lake-dwellers, who built their houses on piles in the water—an art their descendants would one day perfect when they turned the mud flats in a lagoon into Venice. You can see how they lived at Lake Ledro, just above Lake Garda, where one of their lake houses has been reconstructed.

The Ice Man's world was invaded in the Bronze Age (2nd millennium BC) by proto-Celtic tribes from the Caucasus, some of whom settled on the Black Sea in Paphlagonia (now part of Turkey) and others in north-east Italy, settling in the fertile lands between the Alps and the Adriatic. These invaders seem to have been the first of the **Paleoveneti** (aka the ancient Veneti or even Heneti in some accounts). They maintained contact with their Veneti kinfolk back in Paphlogonia, and the Mycenaean Greeks traded with them and others along the Po near Adria.

Catastrophic floods, war, and migrations in the 12th–9th century, symptomatic of the great upheavals plaguing the entire Mediterranean at this time, brought the onset of the Western World's first Dark Age. According to Titus Livy, the great Roman historian from Padua, the Veneti living in Paphlagonia had fought as allies of the Trojans under their leader **Antenor**, and in the turmoil after the fall of Troy (c. 1180 BC) Antenor brought his tribes to the promised lands of their cousins, and founded Padua in the same way that Aeneas founded Rome. Livy, of course, wanted to give his folk a pedigree as good as the Romans, and whether or not Antenor and company ever fought at Troy, it is true the Veneti were long considered a race apart, of 'Illyrian' origin, different from the other Italic tribes; in their own myths they were raisers of horses from a place called 'Tessalia'. They were certainly more advanced than Venetia's natives, at least in an equine way: they had light, fast chariots, and knew how to ride.

By the 9th century BC, the Veneti of the coastal areas began to trade again with their old acquaintances across the Adriatic and Black Sea, most notably acting as agents between the Greek world and the wealthy Etruscans of Felsina (Bologna). The inland Veneti became known for their vineyards, cloth and bronze working. The intricate working and detail of their arte-facts places them firmly in the Celtic tradition, evidence of Polybius' description, that 'the Veneti differed only slightly from the Gauls in their customs and dress, but had a different language.'

This different language, the Indo-European-based **Venet** or **Venetic**, has been the subject of much debate. Once widespread in Venetia and eastern Lombardy, from Bergamo as far east as Istria and into the Dolomites, it was first written in the Etruscan alphabet in the 6th century BC. According to some linguists, its closest cousin is Latin prior to its infiltration by Etruscan. Pliny the Elder confirms a bond between the two, and cites the link between people of the Veneti and the ancient (pre-Rome) Latin league of Alba Longa. It makes sense, if Livy and Virgil are to be believed and the Veneti and Latins both washed ashore in Italy from the east, if not all as glorious descendants of Trojan warriors.

The original Veneti capital was **Ateste** (Este); by the time of their first contact with Rome in the 5th century BC, the Veneti had at least fifty towns, a population reck-oned at a million and a half, and a new capital at Padua. This was their golden age, enjoyed even as trouble appeared in this same century, in the shape of **Gauls** who came from over the Alps in wave after wave—and stayed, infiltrating south of Venetia into Etruscan lands north of the Apennines. Extremely talented in art and metalworking, they present the singular paradox of a nomadic people, caring little for the comforts of home, and everything for their freedom, yet culturally and tech-nologically up to date.

The Gauls invented one significant though overlooked military advance—horseshoes—and carried better swords than most of their foes. The native Veneti allied themselves with Rome against them, but got little thanks for it; on the Roman map, everything north of the Rubicon was lumped together as **Cisalpine Gaul**.

The Romans, Rise and Fall:
283 BC–475 AD

More rumblings came, this time from the south as **Rome** gradually subjugated the Etruscans, Latins, and neighbouring tribes. The little republic with the military camp ethic was successful on all fronts, and a sack by marauding Gauls in 390 BC proved only a brief interruption in Rome's march to conquest. Their arch-enemies, the Samnites, formed an alliance with the Northern Etruscans and Celts, leading to a general Italian commotion in which the Romans beat everybody, annexing almost all of Italy by 283 BC.

All the while, the Romans had been diabolically clever in managing their new demesne, maintaining most of the tribes and cities as nominally independent states (among them, Verona, Trieste, Oderzo, Este, Adria, Treviso, Vicenza, Feltre, Belluno, and Padua) while planting Latin colonies at important transport nodes (Aquileia, Chioggia, Concordia, Cividale del Friuli, Trento, and Altinum, which became the region's biggest port and something of a Roman holiday resort). A major Roman contribution was the great network of roads, beginning with the Via Postumia (148 BC) from Genoa to Verona and Aquileia, and the Via Popilia, linking the Adriatic coast as far south as Rimini, all of which made a truly united Italy seem close to reality.

The northeast, the Roman Tenth Augustine Region of *Venetia et Histria*, 'the flower of Italy, that ornament of the people of Rome,' as Cicero once flattered it, actually turned out to be one of the sleepier corners. The famous men it contributed (the poet Catullus, architect-author Vitruvius, the historian Livy) and the events it saw, such as the meeting of Augustus and Herod the Great in Aquileia, made their mark elsewhere. What the Romans loved best about Venetia was its lagoons, a major source of salt (an imperial monopoly). The Veneti preserved fish in salt to create those favourite Roman condiments, *garum* and *allec*, which must have tasted something like Vietnamese fish sauce; they produced it all along the coast from the Po to the River Timavo on an ancient industrial scale, and imported it all over the empire.

The sparsely populated northern section of what is now Alto Adige was conquered in 15 AD by Augustus' stepson Nero Drusus as a buffer between Italy and the hostile Germanic tribes. These mountains were divided into the Imperial provinces of **Raetia** (along with Switzerland) and **Norico** (along with Austria) which if anything were even sleepier than Venetia et Histria.

The Romans did however busy themselves with more roadworks in the Dolomites, laying out the originals of the modern *autostrade* that link Italy with the great alpine passes.

The 2nd century AD saw the emergence of the well known north-south economic divide in Italy. The south—the former lands of Magna Graecia—ruined by Hannibal, impoverished by the Roman Republic, now sank deeper into decline, wrecked by foreign competition. In the north, a sounder economy led to the growth of new centres; in Venetia Padua, Verona and Aquileia were among the most prominent. On balance, though, both politically and economically Italy was becoming an increasingly less significant part of the empire. Of the 2nd-century emperors, fewer came from Italy than from Spain, Illyria, or Africa.

By the 3rd century, the legions were no longer the formidable military machine of Augustus' day. In 256 the **Franks** and **Alemanni** invaded Gaul descending as far as the Adige, and in 268 much of the east detached itself from the empire under the leadership of Odenathus of Palmyra. Somehow Rome recovered and prevailed, under four soldier-emperors led by **Diocletian**, who completely revamped the structure of the state and economy, replacing it with a gigantic bureaucracy. Taxes reached new heights as people's ability to pay them declined, and society became increasingly militarized. The biggest change was the division of the empire into halves, each ruled by a co-emperor called 'Augustus'; the western emperors after Diocletian usually kept their court at army headquarters in Milan, and Rome itself became a marble-veneered backwater.

The confused politics of the 4th century are dominated by **Constantine** (306–337), who ruled both halves of the empire, and favoured Christianity, by now the majority religion in the East but largely identified with the ruling classes and urban populations in Italy and the West. But even the new faith wasn't able to stay the disasters that began in 406. Visigoths, Franks, Vandals, Alans and Suevi overran Gaul and Spain. Italy's turn came in 408, when Western Emperor **Honorius**, ruling from the empire's new capital of Ravenna, had his brilliant general Stilicho (who himself happened to be a Vandal) murdered. A Visigothic invasion followed, including Alaric's sack of Rome in 410. St Augustine, probably echoing the thoughts of most Romans, wrote that the end of the world must be near. Rome should have been so lucky; judgement was postponed long enough for **Attila the Hun** to pass through Italy in 451, decimating Venetia, uprooting its vineyards and burning Padua and Altinum to the ground.

So completely had things changed, it was scarcely possible to tell the Romans from the barbarians. By the 470s, the real ruler in Italy was a Goth general named **Odoacer**, who led a half-Romanized Germanic army and thought of himself as the genuine heir of the Caesars. In 476, he decided to dispense with the lingering charade of the Western Empire, and had himself crowned King of Italy at Pavia. In the confusion, Venetia was left as a province of the Eastern Empire, but a faraway, and fairly autonomous one. The fall of Rome was to prove its big chance; Attila in his rampage had indirectly founded a new city of refugees called **Venice**.

476–1000: The Dark Ages

In Italy, the Dark Ages were never as dark as common belief would have it. One key to understanding the period is that the Roman cities never entirely disappeared. A few expired totally, like Altinum, but most of the rest shrank to provincial market centres, their theatres, arenas and aqueducts abandoned. Amidst the confusion of Rome's fall, popes and monks and battling barons, Goths, Greeks and Lombards were weaving a strange cocoon for Roman Italy. From its silence, centuries later, would be born a new Italian people, suddenly bursting with talent and energy.

Odoacer's government was a peaceful parenthesis for Italy until Byzantine Emperor Zeno, in 488, commissioned young King **Theodoric of the Ostrogoths** to invade, a ploy meant to take Ostrogoth pressure off Constantinople. Odoacer's army was waiting, but the Goths defeated them decisively near Verona. Most of the peninsula was speedily occupied, though Odoacer held out in impregnable Ravenna for another three years. At last Theodoric tricked him out with a promise to share Italy with him, then performed the traditional murder at what was supposed to be a reconciliation banquet.

Despite that black mark, Theodoric—a strapping fellow with long Asterix moustaches, typical of the half-cultured, half-barbaric protagonists of the Roman twilight—reorganized his new dominions with remarkable sophistication. Inheriting a civil service that had come down from Odoacer, and before him the Empire, Theodoric used it well to stabilize his realm. The Church was a harder nut to crack. In the disorders of the first barbarian invasions, the Roman pope and scores of local bishops had achieved a great degree of temporal power, filling the vacuum left by the collapse of the Roman system. This temporal power gave the Church a diabolical incentive to oppose any strong government in Italy—especially one of heretical Arian Christians. Theodoric himself had no use for theological disputes, but his policy of religious tolerance proved as intolerable to the Church as his Arianism. Most of his subjects, at least, were thankful for it.

The old guard Romans and Veneti, however, continued to regard the Goths as usurpers; religious bigotry grew, and many looked towards Constantinople in hopes of a restoration of legitimate government. Embittered and increasily paranoid, Theodoric died in 526, leaving as heir a young grandson named Athalaric, who, with his good Gothic warrior's upbringing, drank himself to death. His mother Amalasuntha was then forced to marry her cousin Theodehad, who had her murdered. With no strong hand in control, the kingdom was ripe for mischief. There was no doubt in anyone's mind that the next move would come from Constantinople.

The Eastern Empire had just the right sort of emperor to take up the challenge: the great **Justinian**. Amalasuntha's murder in 536 gave him his excuse to invade Italy, in the person of his young and brilliant general **Belisarius**. The historical irony was profound; in the ancient homeland of the Roman Empire, Roman troops now came not as liberators, but as foreign, largely Greek-speaking conquerors. Belisarius, and his successor, the eunuch Narses, ultimately prevailed over the Goths in a series of terrible wars that lasted until 563, but the damage to an already stricken society and economy was incalculable.

Italy's total exhaustion was exposed a mere five years later, when the **Lombards**, a Germanic tribe who drank out of their enemies' skulls and otherwise worked hard to earn the title of barbarians, overran the north, setting up their capital at Cividale del Friuli. Although first sharing Italy with semi-independent Byzantine dukes, the Exarchs (Byzantine Viceroys) of Ravenna, and the remarkable new trading city of Venice, the Lombards, under the ruthless and crafty **King Aistulf**, saw their chance to go for the whole boot. Aistulf conquered almost all of the Byzantine Exarchate; in 753, even the old Imperial capital of Ravenna fell into his hands. If the Lombards' final solution were to be averted, the popes would need help from outside. The logical people to ask were the Franks.

At the time, the popes had something to offer in return. For years, the Mayors of the Palace had wanted to supplant the Merovingian dynasty, but lacked the appearance of legitimacy that only the mystic pageantry of the papacy could provide. At the beginning of Aistulf's campaigns, Pope Zacharias quickly gave his blessing to the change of dynasties, and **Pepin**, the new king of the Franks, sent his army over the Alps, in 753 and 756, to foil Aistulf's designs. His unsuccessful attempt to tame Venice, which refused to take sides, helped set that city on its idiosyncratic track.

By 773 the conflict remained the same, though with a different cast of characters. The new Lombard king was Desiderius, the Frankish, his cordially hostile son-in-law **Charlemagne**, who also invaded Italy twice, in 775 and 776, deposed his father-in-law and took the Iron Crown of Italy for himself. In 799, Pope Leo III set an imperial crown on his head, resuscitating not only the idea of empire, but of an empire that belonged to the successors of St Peter to dispose of as they wished. It changed the political face of Italy for ever, beginning the contorted *pas de deux* of pope and emperor that was to be the mainspring of Italian history throughout the Middle Ages.

With the disintegration of Charlemagne's empire, Italy reverted to a finely balanced anarchy. In Venetia, forests and marshes replaced the ravaged and abandoned farmland, creating a physical as well as a psychological barrier between the precocious maritime city of Venice and the people who remained on mainland. For the latter, the 9th and early 10th centuries were a bad time of endless wars of petty nobles and battling bishops, forcing many cities to look to their own resources, defending their interests against the Church and nobles alike. An invasion by the Magyars from Hungary in the early 10th century forced the cities to build their first walls and the rural nobles their first castles, which became a source of control over the populations who sought their shelter—hence the origins of the fabulous Este family, and the demonic Ezzelini.

A big break for the cities came in 961, with the invasion of the German **Otto the Great**, the conqueror of the Hungarians, at the request of the powerful Count of Tuscany at Canossa. Otto deposed the last feeble King of Italy, Berengar II, married his widow and was crowned Holy Roman Emperor in Rome the following year. Not that any of the Italians were happy to see him, but the strong government of Otto and his successors beat down the great nobles, gave more power to the bishops, and allowed the growing cities to expand their power and influence. A new pattern was established; the Germanic emperors would be meddling in Italian affairs for centuries, not powerful enough to establish total control, but at least usually able to keep out important rivals.

1000–1154: The Rise of the *Comuni*

Like the rest of Christendom, Italy looked ahead to the year 1000 fearing nothing but the worst—the old legends prophesied that this nice round number would bring with it the end of the world. Perhaps only historical hindsight could see the sprouts of new life and growth that were appearing everywhere on Italian soil at this time, perhaps most remarkably symbolized by the building of St Mark's in Venice. In the towns, business was very good, and the political prospects even brighter. The first mention of a truly independent *comune* (a term used throughout this book, meaning a free city state; the best translation might be 'commonwealth') was in Milan, in 1024; before long similar *comuni* appeared in Verona, Padua, Vicenza, and Treviso.

Throughout this period the papacy had declined greatly in power. In the 1050s, a remarkable monk named Hildebrand controlled papal policy, working behind the scenes to reassert the influence of the Church. When he became pope himself in 1073, **Gregory VII** immediately set himself in conflict with the emperors over the issue of investiture—whether the church or secular powers would appoint church officials. Fifty years of intermittent war followed, including the famous penance in the snow of **Emperor Henry IV** at Canossa (1077) and his donation, that same year, of the lands of Friuli, from the Cadore to Slovenia and Istria to the **Patriarchate of Aquileia**. Elsewhere, the cities of the north used the long struggle between pope and emperor as an opportunity to increase their influence, and in some cases achieve outright independence.

A different fate was in store for the Dolomites. Keen to keep the road to Rome open and well-disposed for their all-important papal coronations, the German emperors in the 1020s made powerful feudal princes of the bishops at the important crossroads towns of **Trento** and **Bressanone**. As time went on, the vassals of the bishop-princes were equally keen to escape their clutches, and littered the mountains with castles to defend their relatively autonmous fiefs.

1154–1300: Guelphs and Ghibellines

While all this was happening, of course, the **First Crusade** (1097-1130) occupied the headlines, partially a result of the new militancy of the papacy begin by Gregory VII. For Italy, and especially for Pisa and Genoa, with plenty of boats to help ship Crusaders, the affair meant nothing but pure profit. Venice sat this Crusade out, not wanting to disrupt its own trade in the East, but it quickly moved to get in on the new action. It also financed the continued independence of the *comuni*, with a big enough surplus for building projects like the Verona's San Zeno and Padua's Palazzo della Ragione. After a thousand years, Venetia and the other cities of the north were as prosperous as they had been in Roman times. Nor had those good old days ever been forgotten. Free *comuni* in the north called their elected leaders 'consuls' or 'senators', and artists and architects turned ancient Roman styles into the Romanesque.

Emperors and popes were still embroiled in the north. **Frederick I Barbarossa** of the Hohenstaufen, or Swabian dynasty, was strong enough back home in Germany, and he made it the cornerstone of his policy to reassert imperial power in Italy. Beginning in 1154, he crossed the Alps five times, molesting free cities that asked nothing more than the right to fight one another continually. After he brutally sacked and pillaged Lodi and Milan, the cities forgot their differences and formed a united front called the **Lombard League**, and joined up with **Pope Alexander III** (whom Frederick had exiled from Rome in favour of his antipope) to defeat him in 1176. Frederick was forced to recognize Italian freedoms, and equally galling, he was forced to kiss Alexander's foot in Venice. For all that, Frederick triumphed south of the Alps when he arranged a marriage that left his grandson **Frederick II** not only emperor but King of Sicily, thus giving him a strong power base in Italy itself.

The second Frederick's career dominated Italian politics for thirty years (1220–50). With his brilliant court, in which Italian was used for the first time (alongside Arabic and Latin), his half-Muslim army, his processions of dancing girls, eunuchs, and elephants, he provided Europe with a spectacle the like of which it had never seen. The popes excommunicated him at least twice, while all Italy divided into factions: the **Guelphs**, under the leadership of the popes, supported religious orthodoxy, the liberty of the *comuni*, and the interests of their emerging merchant class. The **Ghibellines** stood for the emperor, state economic control, the interests of the rural nobles, and religious and intellectual tolerance.

When fierce family feuds tore Verona apart (the germ of the Romeo and Juliet story), Frederick appointed his lieutenant in the region, **Ezzelino III da Romano,** as *podestà* to restore order. As he dragged the rebellious Guelph *comuni* of Padua, Vicenza and Treviso back into the imperial fold. Ezzelino, the first of the Italian self-made despots, or *signori,* was so wickedly effective that he earned the nickname 'the son of Satan' (*see* pp.65–6). Frederick's other campaigns and diplomacy in the north met with very limited success; nothing he gained was secure, revolts were frequent, and the Bolognese defeated and captured his son Enzo in 1249; Frederick died the next year.

To fight Frederick's other son Manfred, Pope Urban IV set an ultimately disastrous precedent by inviting in foreign assistance, in the person of **Charles of Anjou**, brother of the King of France. As protector of the Guelphs, Charles defeated Manfred (1266) and murdered the last of the Hohenstaufens, Conradin (1268). He held unchallenged sway over Italy until 1282, creating the perfect conditions to produce a whole new crop of Ezzelino wannabes in every town, until the revolt of the **Sicilian Vespers** started the wars up again. By now, however, the terms Guelph and Ghibelline had ceased to have much meaning; men and cities changed sides as they found expedient, and the old parties began to seem like the black and white squares on a chessboard. If your neighbour and enemy were Guelph, you became for the moment Ghibelline, and if he changed so would you.

Some real changes did come out of all this sound and fury. In 1208 Venice hit its all-time biggest jackpot when it diverted the **Fourth Crusade** to the sack of Constantinople, winning for itself a small empire of islands in the Adriatic and Levant. Other cities fell under the rule of military despots, the *signori*, whose descendants would be styling themselves counts and dukes—the da Carrara of Padua, the della Scala of Verona, the da Camino in Treviso. Everywhere the freedom of the *comuni* was in jeopardy; after so much useless strife the temptation to submit to a strong leader often proved overwhelming.. Still, trade and money flowed as never before; cities built new cathedrals and incredible skyscraper skylines, with the tall tower-fortresses of the now urbanized nobles. Above all, it was a great age of culture. The time of Guelphs and Ghibellines was also the time of Dante (b. 1265) and Giotto (b. 1266).

1300–1550: Renaissance Italy

This paradoxical Italy continued into the 14th century, with a golden age of culture and an opulent economy alongside continuous war and turmoil. With no serious threats from any other foreign power, the myriad Italian states were able to menace each other joyfully without interference. By now most wars had become a sort of game, conducted on behalf of cities by bands of paid mercenaries, led by a hired captain called a *condottiere*, who were never allowed to enter the cities themselves. The arrangement suited everyone well. The soldiers had lovely horses and armour, and no real desire to do each other serious harm. The cities were usually free from grand ambitions; everyone was making too much money to want to wreck the system. Best of all, the worst schemers and troublemakers on the Italian stage were fortuitously removed from the scene. With the election of the French Pope **Clement V** in 1303, the papacy moved to Avignon, a puppet of the French king and temporarily without influence in Italian affairs.

By far the biggest event of the 14th century was the **Black Death** of 1347–48, in which it is estimated that Italy lost one-third of its population. The shock brought a rude halt to what had been four hundred years of almost continuous growth, though its effects did not prove a permanent setback for the economy. In fact, the plague's grim joke was that it actually made life better for most who survived; working people in the cities, no longer overcrowded, found their rents lower and their labour worth more, while in the country farmers were able to increase their profits by tilling only the best land.

By now the peninsula was split up by long-established, cohesive states pursing different ends and often warring against each other. Italian statesmen well understood the idea of a balance of power long before political theorists invented the term, and most of them probably believed Italy was enjoying the best of all possible worlds. Foremost among the major states was Venice, the oldest and most glorious, with its oligarchic but singularly effective constitution, and its exotic career of trade and contacts with the East (see **Venice** 'History' pp.80–81). The Venetians waged a series of wars against arch-rival Genoa, finally exhausting her after the **War of Chioggia** in 1379. Once serenely aloof from Italian politics, Venice then added to her sea realms a small land empire, including by 1428 Ùdine, Treviso, Verona, Padua, Vicenza, Belluno, Brescia and Bergamo. One city she subdued but never captured was Adriatic rival Trieste, which in 1382 had come under the protection of the Austrian emperors. In the north the independent Bishop-Princes of Trento served to create a kind of demilitarized zone between Venice and their vassals who had managed to achieve real independence, the Counts of Tyrol, and their 14th-century successors, the up and coming **Habsburg** dynasty.

Meanwhile, the Renaissance—the new art and scholarship that began in Florence in the 1400s from a solid foundation of medieval accomplishment—found a happy home in northeast Italy. Masters like Giotto (back in 1309), Donatello, and Antonello da Messina spent time in the region, leaving seeds of the imagination for Venetia's artists. Àsolo, under the exiled Queen of Cyprus, became a courtly ideal of Renaissance art and literature and the University of Padua led Europe in the study of medicine.

1494–1529: The Wars of Italy

The Italians brought the trouble down on themselves, when Duke Lodovico of Milan invited the French King **Charles VIII** to cross the Alps and assert his claim to the throne of Milan's enemy, Naples. Charles did just that, and the failure of the combined Italian states to stop him (at the inconclusive Battle of Fornovo, 1485) showed just how helpless Italy was at the hands of emerging new nation-states like France or Spain. When the Spaniards saw how easy it was, they, too, marched in, and before long the German emperor and even the Swiss entered this new market for Italian real estate. The popes did as much as anyone to keep the pot boiling. Alexander VI and his son Cesare Borgia carried the war across central Italy in an attempt to found a new state for the Borgia family, and Julius II's madcap policy saw him unite the emperor and the Italian states in the **League of Cambrai**, which soundly defeated Venice in 1508, sapping her strength just when it was most needed to fight the Turks. Julius egged on the Swiss, French and Spaniards in turn, before finally crying 'Out with the barbarians!' when it was already too late.

By 1516, with the French ruling Milan and the Spanish in control of the south, it seemed as if a settlement would be possible. The worst possible luck for Italy, however, came with the accession in Spain of the insatiable Habsburg megalomaniac **Charles V** who got enough loans from the Fugger banks to buy himself the crown of the Holy Roman Empire in 1519, making him the most powerful ruler in Europe since Charlemagne. As soon as he had emptied Spain's treasury, driven her to revolt and plunged Germany into civil war, he turned his tender attentions to Italy. The wars began anew, bloodier than anything Italy had seen for centuries.

1529–1600: Italy in Chains, but Venice Recovers

Two years after the dramatic 1527 **Sack of Rome** by Imperial troops and German mercenaries, Charles V met Pope Clement VII in Bologna for his fateful coronation as Holy Roman Emperor (he was to be the last ever crowned by a pope) and to draw the map of Italy, which, save only the Republic of Venice, was at the mercy of the Spaniards.

It also marked the beginning of the bitter struggles of the **Counter-Reformation**. In Italy, the Spaniards found a perfect ally in the papacy. One had the difficult job of breaking the spirit of a nation that, though conquered, was still wealthy, culturally sophisticated and ready to resist; the other saw an opportunity to recapture by force the hearts and minds it had lost long before. The job of re-educating Italy was put in the hands of the new Jesuit order; their schools and propaganda machine bored the pope's message deeply into the Italian mind. The Church's **Council of Trent** (1545–63) provided long-needed reforms, and although it was too little too late to bring the Protestants back to the fold, it initiated the creation of sumptuous new churches, spectacles and dramatic sermons that helped redefine Catholicism. Protected by its lagoon, and clever enough to avoid the Spaniards and most of the Jesuits, Venice quickly recovered its conquered territories of the Veneto lost in the War of Cambrai and went about perfecting a way of life that came to be the envy of Italy (*see* pp.72–4). Venetian artists attained a brilliance and virtuosity never seen before, just in time to embellish the scores of new churches, palaces, and villas of the mid-16th-century building boom. In one issue, however, Venice combined with Spain: in turning back the Turkish threat at the **Battle of Lepanto** (1571), a victory that provided a tremendous boost to morale throughout Christendom.

1600–1796: The Age of Baroque

Palladio's country villas for the magnates of the Veneto are landmarks in architecture but were also an early symptom of decay. The old mercantile economy was failing, and the wealthy began to invest their money less productively in land instead of risking it in business. Despite Lepanto, Venice's position in the east continued to be eroded, damaged by the Portuguese discovery of the spice route to the Indies, by endless warfare with the Turks and the Austrian-backed pirates,

the Uskoks, in the north Adriatic. Yet when the chips were down, Venice had the spirit to stand up to Pope Paul V and his Spanish allies during the **Great Interdict** (1606), striking an irreversible blow to papal temporal authority while all Europe watched. It was her last starring role in European affairs, but the Venetians kept their head and made their decline remarkably serene and a great deal of fun.

Decline was not limited to Venice. After 1600 nearly everything started to go wrong for Italy across the board. The textiles and banking of the north, long the engines of the economy, both withered in the face of foreign competition; the popes soaked whomever they could for money to redecorate Rome. Bullied, humiliated and impoverished, 17th-century Italy tried hard to keep up its prominence in the arts and sciences. Galileo looked through telescopes and taught at Padua, Monteverdi wrote the first operas, and hundreds of talented though uninspired artists cranked out pretty pictures to meet the continuing high demand. Baroque art—the florid, expensive coloratura style that serves as a perfect symbol for the age itself—impressed everyone with the majesty of Church and State. Baroque impresarios managed the wonderful pageantry of Church holidays, state occasions and carnivals that kept the crowds amused; manners and clothing were decorously berserk.

By the 18th century, there were very few painters or scholars or scientists. There were no more heroic revolts either. Italy in this period hardly has any history at all; with Spain's increasing decadence, the great powers decided the futures of Italy's major states, and used the minor ones as a kind of overflow tank to hold surplus princes. Gambling revenues became one of the main props of the Venetian state. There carnival was exended to six months in order to bring in decadent aristocrats from around Europe; this was the age of blundering spies and scamps like Casanova, of the glittering brilliance of Vivaldi, of Grand Tourists, opera at La Fenice, and Canaletto.

1796–1830: Napoleon and Austrians

Napoleon (that greatest of Italian generals) arrived in 1796 on behalf of the French Revolutionary Directorate, winning at Rivoli north of Verona and sweeping away Austrians, Spaniards, the Pope, the bishop princes of the Dolomites and the Doge, replacing them with the '**Cisalpine Republic**' and '**Kingdom of Illyria**' in the east. Italy woke up with a start from its baroque slumbers, and local nobles gaily joined the French cause. In 1799, however, while Napoleon was off in Egypt, the advance through Italy by an Austro-Russian army, aided by Nelson's fleet, restored the status quo.

In 1800 Napoleon returned in a campaign that saw the great victory at Marengo, which gave him the opportunity once more to reorganize Italian affairs as the nation's self-crowned king. Napoleonic rule lasted only until 1814, but in that time important public works were begun and laws, education and everything else reformed after the French model; immense Church properties were expropriated, and medieval relics everywhere put to rest—including the Venetian Republic, which Napoleon for some reason took a special delight in liquidating. The French, however, soon outstayed their welcome. Besides hauling much of Italy's artistic heritage off to the Louvre, implementing high war taxes and conscription (some 25,000 Italians died on the Russian front), and brutally repressing a number of local revolts, they systematically exploited Italy for the benefit of the Napoleonic élite and the crowds of speculators who came flocking over the Alps. When the Austrians and English came to chase all the little Napoleons out, no one was sad to see them go.

But the experience had given Italians a taste of the opportunities offered by the modern world, as well as a sense of national feeling that had been suppressed for centuries. The 1815 **Congress of Vienna** put the clock back to 1796; indeed the Habsburgs and Bourbons thought they could pretend the Napoleonic upheavals had never happened, and the political reaction in the territories was fierce. The only major change from the *ancien régime* was that all of Venetia now unwillingly (except for the South Tyrol) belonged to **Austria**.

1848–1915: The Risorgimento and United Italy

Simmering discontent kindled into action across Italy in the revolutionary year of 1848. On 22 March, the fire spread to Venice. The Austrian authorities simply fled, and the Venetian Republic was back in business. Within a few days, a democratic assembly was elected; leadership passed to **Daniele Manin**, a lawyer who had distinguished himself in liberal struggles in Venice for a decade. A day after the events in Venice, **King Carlo Alberto** of Piedmont-Savoy declared war on Austria.

At first, the odds seemed to favour Piedmont, the strongest state and leading force in Italian unification. Austria's army was disorganized and outnumbered, and

for the time being it could expect little help from Vienna. The Piedmontese won early victories, but under the timid leadership of the King they failed to follow them up. The Austrians fell back to the firm base of their defences in Italy, the circuit of fortresses called the Quadrilateral (Peschiera, Verona, Mantua and Legnano, in the western Veneto). Here they won a resounding victory, at Custozza, on 25 July, that knocked Piedmont ingloriously out of the war.

Shutting out the disappointments of 1848, Venice put up a brave and determined resistance. Though blockaded by the Austrian fleet, the Venetians nevertheless had a large quantity of arms and men to complement the natural protection of their lagoon in withstanding a siege. The Austrians bombarded the city continuously from May of 1849. An outbreak of cholera, as much as a total absence of outside support, decided the issue. The city surrendered on 22 August.

Despite failure on a grand scale, at least the Italians knew they would get another chance. Unification was inevitable, but there were two irreconcilable contenders for the honour of accomplishing it. On one side, the democrats and radicals dreamed of a truly reborn, revolutionary Italy, and looked to the popular hero **Garibaldi** to deliver it; on the other, moderates wanted the Piedmontese to do the job, ensuring a stable future by making **Vittorio Emanuele II** King of Italy. Vittorio Emanuele's minister, the polished, clever Count Camillo Cavour, spent the 1850s getting Piedmont into shape for the struggle, building its economy and army, participating in the Crimean War to earn diplomatic support, and plotting with the French for an alliance against Austria.

War came in 1859, just as a rebellion chased the pope's troops out of Bologna. The French and Piedmontese defeated Austria in two inconclusive, extremely bloody battles, at Magenta and Solferino. Piedmont annexed Lombardy and the Marches, and the armistice of 1850 was arranged so that France picked up Nice and Savoy, while Tuscany, Emilia-Romagna, and the duchies of Parma and Modena went to Piedmont. These gains were increased in the next two year, when Garibaldi and his Thousand picked up Sicily and the south.

With Austria still in control of Venetia, most Italians felt that the first duty of the nation was to complete the work of unification. The logical place to look for an ally against Austria was with Bismarck and **Prussia**, then preparing for the climax of their own nation's struggle for unification. In April 1866, Italy and Prussia signed a treaty, proposing the Veneto as reward for Italian aid in the coming war with Austria. That war was not long in coming. Hostilities began in June, and before the year was out the Italians had been decisively defeated on land, at Custozza (again) and on sea, at Lissa. Fortunately for them, von Moltke's Prussian army was causing even greater embarrassments to the Austrians up north. The Veneto, and western Friuli joined Italy—a gift from Prussia.

Despite popular feeling, and its conquest by Garibaldi, Trentino remained a part of Austria, as did eastern Venezia Giulia. In these regions secret revolutionary committees for unity with Italy soon gave politics a new word: **irredentism**, from *irredenta* or 'unredeemed'. Unfortunately the price of their 'redemption' as part of Italy was to cost the country dear—its entrance into the First World War.

After 1900, with the rise of a strong socialist movement, strikes, riots and police repression often occupied centre stage in Italian politics. But at the same time new industries, at least in the north, made the country a fully integral part of the European economy. The fifteen years before the war, prosperous and contented ones for many, came to be known by the slightly derogatory term *Italietta,* the 'little Italy' of modest bourgeois happiness, an age of sweet Puccini operas, the first motorcars, blooming 'Liberty'-style architecture, and Sunday afternoons on the beach.

1915–1945: War, Fascism, and War

Besides the hope of gaining Trentino, Trieste, and Istria, Italy's entrance into **First World War** was influenced by a certain segment of the intelligentsia who found Italietta boring and disgraceful: followers of the artistic Futurists and the perverse, idolized poet **Gabriele D'Annunzio**. These helped Italy leap blindly into the war in 1915. Venetia saw the bulk of the fighting—especially along the Piave and Isonzo rivers, at Asiago and at Monte Grappa. Italian armies fought with their accustomed flair, masterminding an utter catastrophe at Caporetto (October 1917) that any other nation but Austria would have parlayed into a total victory. No thanks to their incompetent generals, the poorly armed and equipped Italians somehow held firm for another year, until the total exhaustion of Austria allowed them to prevail at **Vittorio Veneto**, capturing some 600,000 prisoners in November 1918.

In return for 650,000 dead, a million casualties, severe privation on the home front and a war debt higher than anyone could count, Italy received Trieste, Gorizia, Trentino, and the South Tyrol up to the natural frontier of the Brenner Pass, where many German-speakers who suddenly found themselves Italian began in turn a new Irredentist movement, yearning to be reunited with Austria.

Led somehow to expect much more, Italians felt they had been cheated, and nationalist sentiment increased, especially when D'Annunzio led a band of freebooters to seize the half-Italian city of Fiume in September 1919, after the peace conferences had promised it to Yugoslavia. The Italian economy was a shambles, and, at least in the north, revolution was in the air. The trouble had encouraged extremists of both right and left, and many Italians became convinced that the liberal state was finished.

Enter **Benito Mussolini**, a professional intriguer with bad manners and no fixed principles. Before the War he had found his real talent as editor of the Socialist Party paper *Avanti!*—the best it ever had, tripling the circulation in a year. When he decided that what Italy really needed was war, he left to found a new paper, and contributed mightily to the jingoist agitation of 1915. In the post-War confusion, he found his opportunity. A little bit at a time, he developed the idea of Fascism, at first less a philosophy than an astute use of mass propaganda and a sense of design. With a little discreet money supplied by frightened industrialists, Mussolini had no trouble finding recruits for his black-shirted gangs, who had their first successes bashing Slavs in the city of Trieste.

The basic principle, combing left- and right-wing extremism into something the ruling classes could live with, proved attractive to many Italians, and a series of weak governments chose to stand by while the fascist squadre cast their shadow over more and more of Italy. Mussolini's accession to power was the result of an improbable gamble. In the particularly anarchic month of October 1922, he announced that his followers would march on Rome. **King Vittorio Emanuele III** refused to sign a decree of martial law to disperse them, and there was nothing to do but offer Mussolini the post of prime minister. At first, he governed Italy with undeniable competence. Order was restored, and the economy and foreign policy handled intelligently by non-fascist professionals. Mussolini increased his popularity by singling out especially obnoxious unions and corrupt leftist local governments for punishment. In the 1924 elections, despite the flagrant rigging and intimidation, the Fascists won only a slight majority.

Mussolini evolved a new economic philosophy, the 'corporate state', where labour and capital were supposed to live in harmony under a syndicalist government control. But the longer Fascism lasted, the more unreal it seemed, a patchwork government of Mussolini and his ageing cronies, magnified and rendered heroic by cinematic technique—stirring rhetoric before oceanic crowds, colourful pageantry, magnificent, larger-than-life post offices and railway stations built of travertine and marble, dashing aviators and winsome gymnasts from the Fascist youth groups on parade. In a way it was the baroque all over again, and Italians tried not to think about the consequences. In the words of one of Mussolini's favourite slogans, painted on walls all over Italy, 'Whoever stops is lost.'

Mussolini couldn't stop, and the only possibility for new diversions lay with the chance of conquest and empire. His invasion of Ethiopia and his meddling in the Spanish Civil War, both in 1936, compromised Italy into a close alliance with Nazi Germany. Under Hitler's prodding, Mussolini invited all the unhappy German speakers in the Alto-Adige to leave, which they immediately did, in droves. Nevertheless, Mussolini's confidence and rhetoric never faltered as he led an entirely unprepared nation into the biggest war ever. The Allies invaded; the Germans poured in divisions to defend the peninsula. In 1943 they set Mussolini up in a puppet state called the Italian Social Republic at **Saló** on Lake Garda. In September, the Badoglio government finally signed an armistice with the Allies, too late to keep the War from dragging on another year and a half, as the Germans made good use of Italy's difficult terrain to slow the Allied advance. Meanwhile Italy finally gave itself something to be proud of, a determined, resourceful Resistance that established free zones in many areas, and harassed the Germans with sabotage and strikes. The *partigiani* caught Mussolini in April 1945, while he was trying to escape to Switzerland; after shooting him and his mistress, they hung him by the toes from the roof of a petrol station in Milan.

1945–the Present

Post-War Italy *cinema-verità*—Rossellini's *Rome, Open City,* or de Sica's *Bicycle Thieves*—captures the atmosphere better than words ever could. In a period of serious hardships that older Italians still remember, the nation slowly picked itself up and returned things to normal. The eastern border with Yugoslavia was the most lingering problem in the north—**Trieste**, as the major bone of contention, was made a neutral zone from 1947 to 1954, when it was finally given to Italy in exchange for what bits of Istria it still controlled.

A referendum in June 1946 made Italy a republic, but only by a narrow margin. The first governments fell to the new **Christian Democrats** under Alcide di Gasperi, the party that would run the show for decades in coalitions with a preposterous band of smaller parties. The main opposition was provided by the Communists, surely one of the most remarkable parties of modern European history. With the heritage of the only important socialist philosopher since Marx, Antonio Gramsci, and the democratic and broad-minded leaders Palmiere Togliatti and Enrico Berlinguer, Italian communism took the moral high ground and stayed there.

The economic miracle that began in the 1950s continues today, propelling the Italians into 6th place among the world's national economies. 'God made the world and Italy made everything in it,' was the slogan of the 60s. The rotten Christian Democratic corruption behind the glittering mask was revealed in the early 1990s, when a small group of judges and prosecutors in Milan took a minor political kickback scandal and from it unravelled the golden string that held together the whole tangle of Italian political depravity—what the Italians call the *tangentopoli*, or 'bribe city'. The Christian Democrats and the Socialists, the two leading parties, collapsed like a house of cards, leaving a vacuum filled by a jostling array of new parties and personalities, none of whom so far has been able to put the brakes on the merry-go-round of Italian politics: noisiest of all was media tycoon **Silvio Berlusconi**'s rightest Forza Italia, which won Mr Television a brief tenure as prime minister in 1994. Plagued by allegations of scandals and bribery, Berlusconi was soon forced out by the more enduring, middle-of-the-road Olive party of Romano **Prodi**, with the support of the former Communists. Prodi's stringent economic measures allowed Italy to squeak into Euroland in January 1999, but led to the Communists' withdrawing their support of his government in late 1998, and giving it to current prime minister **Massimo d'Alema**'s DS (Democrazia di Sinistra) party, Italy's 60th government since the Second World War.

One of the jokers in the Italian deck is the neo-fascist MSI party of Alberto Fini, and another is Milanese lawyer **Umberto Bossi**, the only Italian political figure to dress badly since the time of King Aistulf. Bossi's new Lombard League, or **Lega Lombarda**, was around even before *tangentopolis*, breaking though in the 1990 elections in Lombardy; by 1994 he had united with similar northern leagues to form the Lega Nord. Although many of the Lega's positions change by the hour, its basic tenet of federalism, to cut out the voracious politicians and bureaucrats of Rome and allow the wealthy north of Italy to keep more of its profits for itself, has understandably struck a deep chord in Venetia. In September 1996, Bossi attracted a lot of attention by declaring the north (as far south as Umbria and the Marches) as the independent Republic of Padania, and made a three-day march down the Po to Venice. Unlike Mussolini's march on Rome, the whole affair turned out to be a badly staged comedy, although it did put federalism, perhaps on the Spanish model, a little higher up on the politicians' agenda.

In Venetia, with its history of separateness from the rest of Italy, there is a growing interest in reviving the glories of the Serenissima. New groups such as the Società Filologica Veneta have sprouted up, with the goal of defending the Veneto language and culture, and there's a Liga Veneta for greater regional autonomy and greater recognition for the German speakers in the Sud Tirol. As of 1998, you can take classes in Venetic, and listen to long-winded arguments about how the Paleoveneti were Celts (one of Bossi's favourite topics), in the hopes of showing that they aren't like the rest of the Italians and should go their separate ways.

But, truer to the spirit of the once great cosmopolitan Republic of Venice, the natives seem rather more impressed with their economy. The Veneto has become a vast metropolis of four and a half million people, connected by the A4 highway. Its economy, with a gross domestic product of over $95 billion, is larger than that of Israel and Greece; its exports are worth more than those of Portugal and Argentina. People talk of the 'Veneto model' that has evolved since the war, creating a climate that encourages small, mainly family-run businesses (some 65 per cent are of recent origin) aimed towards the export market, employing a devoted workforce making something that is unique or at least better than foreign competition: Benetton is a case in point. Luxury goods (fashion, jewellery, housewares and everything else related to the cleverly promoted mystique of Italian design) are a mainstay, just as they were during the Renaissance and Middle Ages. Before the war, 60% of the work was in agriculture; today only 6% of the population are farmers, while the unemployment rate, at a measly 5%—microscopic in European terms—has brought emigrants from around the world in search of a job, restoring some of Venetia's old international feel, especially noticable the further east you go; if old Venice is cosmopolitan because of international tourism, Trieste is so because of its newfound status as Mitteleurope on the Med.

Venetia produced one of the three great schools of Italian art—not a spiritual or intellectual school like the Tuscan, or anything half as imposing or classical as the Roman, but an art of visual delight and sensuality. A love of decoration, of gold and glitter and gorgeous colours is the thread that links the glimmering richness of the 11th-century Byzantine style mosaics of St Mark with the effervescent sparkle of Tiepolo in the 18th century.

Art and Architecture

Architecture too was showy—you'll find little of that sombre, rusticated stone monumentality that characterizes Tuscany or Rome, but palaces meant to dazzle, and villas set like gems in the landscape.

Paleoveneti (8th–2nd centuries BC)

The mysterious Paleoveneti excelled in metal work, and many of their artefacts are indistinguishable from Celtic. The museums in Este and Adria have the most extensive collections of Paleoveneti and other pre-Roman artefacts, but all the archaeology museums in Venetia have evocative bits and bobs. Among their most striking works are the little metal plaques, or *laminette*, from the 5th century BC, engraved with warriors and women in the Santa Corona museum, in Vicenza.

Roman Art (3rd century BC– 5th century AD)

Roman art may have been derivative of Etruscan and Greek models, but it showed a special talent for mosaics, portraiture, wall paintings, and glasswork; architecturally, the Romans were brilliant engineers,

grand exponents of the arch and inventors of concrete. **Verona** is one of the best places in Italy to admire their ability to build large and well, in its Ponte della Pietra, the ancient theatre, Porta dei Borsari, and especially the Arena, a pink marble oval that rivals the Colosseum in size and grandeur. The city was the birthplace of Vitruvius, the only classical writer on architecture whose works have come down to us.

Aquileia was one of the few great Roman cities that died completely in the early Middle Ages. Although its marbles were pillaged by the Venetians and others, it remains the most evocative Roman and Early Christian archaeological site in the region, with beautifully preserved Roman and palaeochristian mosaics and a fine museum.

The so-called 'Villa of Catullus' (actually a bath complex) at **Sirmione** on Lake Garda is one of Italy's most poetic ruins. Other Roman odds and ends remain in **Trieste** (theatre, gate, museum), and in the museums of **Padua, Oderzo** and **Venice**. The latter has a fair share of Greek originals as well, donated by collectors, although none that can match Venice's finest Greek work—the four horses of St Mark, the only surviving bronze *quadriga* from antiquity.

Dark and Early Middle Ages (5th–10th centuries)

Artistically, at least, the decline of Rome was a bonus for Venetia, especially when Emperor Honorius transferred the capital of the Western Empire to nearby Ravenna. Although Roman sculpture and painting were already degraded, mosaics thrived, a decorative art patronized by the rich. It was a strange time; a 5th-century chronicle declares: 'Those who are alive perish from thirst, while corpses float in the water…priests practise usury and Syrians sing psalms… eunuchs learn the art of war and barbarian mercenaries study literature.'

The Greek artists working in Ravenna drifted into Venetia—the 7th-century frescoes in the cathedral crypt in **Adria** are a rare record of their migration. Their still, 'hieratic' art, really an inheritance from decadent Rome, was to remain prominent until the 13th century, and found its greatest expression in mosaics, where highly stylized, spiritual beings live in a gold-ground paradise, with no need of shadows or perspective or other such worldly tricks. Beautiful examples remain at **Aquileia** and **Grado**, and at **Torcello** in Venice, where the style lingered long enough to adorn St Mark's. In architecture, forms that originated in the time of Constantine prevailed—basilican churches, derived directly from Roman law courts and octagonal baptistries.

In the 7th–10th centuries, while Byzantine artists painted and mosaiced their ethereal almond-eyed creatures, the native population under the Lombards produced works in a vigorous style that had little use for Roman or Byzantine models. Instead of mosaics, the Lombards' talent lay in architecture, sculpture and metalwork. The churches and museum of **Cividale del Friuli**, the capital of a Lombard duchy, contain unique sculptures and reliefs from the 8th century. More art from the period awaits in the Castelvecchio museum in **Verona**, and in the Dolomites: rare 8th-century Lombard frescoes in the church of San Procolo at **Naturno**, along with rare Carolingian churches and frescoes in an excellent state of preservation, in the **Val Monastero** and in **Malles Venosta**, hugging the Swiss frontier.

Veneto-Byzantine & Romanesque (11th–12th centuries)

By the 11th century, **Venice** had taken over the artistic crown in northeast Italy from Ravenna, in a typically lavish if rather conservative way: the Veneto-Byzantine style of the magnificent mosaics and Pala d'Oro in St Mark's basilica is still 90% Byzantine. But influences from other parts of Italy were seeping into the heart of the lagoon: the vigorous reliefs of the Labours of the Months on St Mark's central portal, St Mark's Campanile and the church of SS. Maria e Donato in Murano are in the new Romanesque style from Lombardy.

Lombard Romanesque churches are characterized by broad, triangular façades, blind arcading, gabled porches, rib vaulting, and presbyteries raised above the nave and crypt. The best examples are in **Trento** (the Duomo) and in **Verona**, near the Lombard frontier (the Palazzo della Ragione, S. Fermo, S. Lorenzo, the Duomo and, most magnificently, San Zeno, with its superb Romanesque decoration and unique bronze doors, a 'poor man's Bible' that predates the church by a century). Other architects in 12th-century opted for a Veneto-Byzantine and Romanesque compromise, as in the Friulian abbey of Santa Maria in Sylvis in **Sesto al Reghena**, the hodge-podge S. Giusto, in **Trieste**, and Santa Sofia in **Padua**. In the next century Padua would witness the most amazing Veneto-Byzantine-Romanesque wedding of all, in the fabulous multi-domed Basilica of St Anthony.

The 11th and 12th centuries also saw the erection of urban skyscrapers by the nobility, family fortresses and towers built when the *comuni* forced the barons to move into the towns. Larger cities once had hundreds of them, and although municipal authorities gradually succeeded in having most of them demolished, **Rovigo** still has two of the oldest and crookedest. This same period is marked by an epidemic of castle building, especially in the Dolomites; some have charming courtly frescoes from medieval romances (Castel Sabbionara, at **Avio**; Castel Róncolo, **Bolzano**; Castel Rodengo, near **Rio di Pusteria**).

Gothic and Early Renaissance (13th–14th centuries)

The Italians never really appreciated Gothic; trapped in their Roman sensibilities and snobbishness, they looked on the soaring flying-buttressed cathedrals from the Ile-de-France as barbaric. Still, they weren't entirely immune to its charms. Bonino's ornately chivalric Scaliger tombs in **Verona** are a prime example of what they could do when they bothered. Most Italian Gothic, however, is austere, coinciding with back-to-basics Franciscan and Dominican religious revivals of the 13th century, resulting in piously plain Gothic-barn churches that loom over city rooftops like beached whales, among them S. Nicolò in **Treviso**, Santa Corona in **Vicenza**, the Frari and SS. Giovanni e Paolo in **Venice**, and the most beautiful, the Dominican Santa Anastasia in **Verona**.

At the same time the Venetians were rolling in swag from the Fourth Crusade (1204) and for their secular buildings they took Gothic and twisted it merrily around to suit their flamboyant, cosmopolitan tastes. Gothic arches took on Byzantine and Islamic designs, and plain walls were enlivened with coloured marbles in different shapes and patterns, reliefs, round *paterae* of semi-precious stones, and even gold. The resulting hybrid, Venetian Gothic, became the city's own distinct style, seen in scores of magnificent palaces from the Fondaco dei Turchi to the Ca' d'Oro, culminating in the Palazzo Ducale. Venetian Gothic became so closely identified with Venice that the style took on a second life in the 16th century, in public buildings designed to mark the Republic's presence on the *terra firma* (**Udine**'s Piazza della Libertà and **Belluno**'s Palazzo dei Rettori).

In painting, the colourful, decorative fairytale style called International Gothic also lingered longer in Venetia than elsewhere in Italy. The great Pisanello of Pisa and Stefano da Verona were its major exponents in **Verona**; in **Venice** painters like Paolo Veneziano, Jacobello del Fiore and Michele Giambono and the Vivarini family remained popular into the 15th century. Other jewels of the period to seek out include the delightful fresco cycles in **Trento**'s Castello di Buonconsiglio and the cathedral cloister at **Bressanone**.

The Gothic spirit endured for centuries in the Dolomites, especially in polychrome sculpture and ornate altarpieces that often combine a powerful expressiveness with a love of rich decoration; the two greatest masters, Michael Pacher and Hans Klocker, are represented in the excellent collections at **Bolzano** and **Bressanone**. In Trentino, the joys of Gothic were prolonged into the 16th century by the Bachenis family; Simone's striking *Dance of Death* on the cemetery church of **Pinzolo** is as memorable as it is retro, even by Venetia standards.

In Tuscany, the 14th century was one of the most exciting and vigorous phases in Italian art, when great imaginative leaps occurred in architecture, painting, and sculpture. In 1308, the most influential of all early Tuscans, Giotto, left the Veneto the seeds of the future in the Cappella degli Scrovegni or Arena Chapel in **Padua**, teaching local artists about forms in space, composition, and a new, more natural way to paint figures. His chief followers of the Paduan school, Altichiero and Menabuoi, frescoed Padua's Baptistry, Oratory of San Giorgio and the Ermitani church; another, Tommaso da Modena, left

beautiful works in **Treviso** and almost nowhere else. Other anonymous Giottoesque painters roamed as far afield as **Bolzano** (the Domenicani church) and **Feltre** (SS. Vittore e Corona).

The Renaissance of the Quattrocento

The visit to **Padua** by Giotto was followed up in the next century by a prolonged stay by another Tuscan genius, Donatello; the perfect harmony and classical calm of his great equestrian statue of Gattamelata and his complex reliefs in the Basilica of Sant'Antonio were formative influence on Venice's Lombardo and Bon families, as well as on Antonio Rizzo of Verona. The Lombardi and Bons went on to create an overwhelming share of **Venice**'s best Renaissance churches, palaces, sculptures, and tombs along with Mauro Codussi, who instilled a certain amount of Tuscan order and classicism into the Venetian imagination.

The great revolution in Venetian painting began in the mid 15th century, and owes much to the brothers-in-law, Andrea Mantegna and Giovanni Bellini. Mantegna influenced generations of artists and sculptors with his strong interest in antiquity, his scientific perspective, and his powerfully sculpted figures, while Giovanni Bellini (*see* pp.66–8) perfected a luminous oil painting technique to express natural light and rich, autumnal colours. Other major figures of the *quattrocento* include narrative masters Gentile Bellini and Vittore Carpaccio, the more rustic Cima da Conegliano, and the more elegant Carlo Crivelli.

The 16th Century: The Venetian High Renaissance and Mannerism

While the rest of Italy, increasingly oppressed by reaction and war, followed the artists of Rome in learning drawing and anatomy, the Venetians followed Giovanni Bellini and his obsession with the expressive qualities of atmosphere and colour. The shooting star among his many pupils was Giorgione of Castelfranco, a major if tragically short-lived figure in the new manner; his *Tempest* in the Accademia is a remarkable study in brooding tension. Giorgione is credited with inventing 'easel painting'—art that served neither Church nor State nor the vanity of a patron, but stood on its own for the pleasure of the viewer.

Another Bellini alumnus, Titian, the High Renaissance master of the Venetian school, was a revolutionary in his own right, one of the first painters to put the 'art' into art in his dramatic compositions and striking tonal effects produced by large brushstrokes, or even finger-painting. His contemporary, Tintoretto, took these Mannerist tendencies to extremes, while Paolo Veronese painted lavish canvases that are the culmination of all that Venice had to teach in decoration and magnificence. Veronese's followers, Zelotti, Battista Franco and others, laboured beaverishly across the Veneto, filling patrician villas with allegories, mythologies and virtues.

One of the greatest sculptors in *cinquecento* Venice was Jacopo Sansovino, who adapted his training in Tuscany and Rome to create a distinctive Venetian architectural style, richly decorated with sculpture and classical motifs. He was greatly admired by Andrea Palladio, whose creamy white temple-fronted villas—as characteristic of the rural Veneto as Venetian Gothic is of Venice—would inspire architects as far away as England and colonial America (*see* pp.69–72). Palladio's colleague and artistic heir, Vincenzo Scamozzi, added a Mannerist touch that became the rage for the next century in the Veneto, even when the more populist baroque style squashed Mannerism and its intellectual fancies elsewhere in Italy.

Baroque and Rococo (17th and 18th centuries)

> *Art shall move to devotion the heart of the beholder.*

> The Council of Trent

As an art designed to induce temporal obedience and psychological oblivion, baroque's effects are difficult to describe. On the whole, however, history saw that little of its most excessive moods (as in Rome or Naples) touched Venetia; the Venetians kicked the Jesuits out, and the Spaniards had little influence in the Republic. In short, the 17th century saw more of the same Palladian

villas, Venetian palaces, atmospheric painting and decorated churches, but squared into baroque. The age does provide some exceptions to the rule that in art, less is more: the churches of La Salute in **Venice** and the Inviolata in **Riva del Garda**, or the uncanny paintings of Francesco Maffei of **Vicenza**, the furniture of Andrea Brustalon (Ca' Rezzonico, in **Venice**) or the gardens of the Villa Barbarigo in **Valsanzibio**.

In the 18th century Venice bloomed like Camille on her death bed, when its charming, elegant school of painting was in demand across Europe, thanks almost entirely to one figure: Giambattista Tiepolo. Tiepolo's buoyant ceiling art and narrative frescoes, shimmering with light, added a fresh, scintillating rococo fizz to Veronese's grandeur. If Giotto's Cappella degli Scrovegni is the majestic overture in the art of Italian fresco, Tiepolo's Villa Valmara in **Vicenza** and the Palazzo Labia in **Venice** are the grand finale.

Less majestic but extremely popular 18th-century figures include Antonio Canaletto, who produced countless views of Venice snapped up by English and French travellers on the Grand Tour; another now famous painter of views, proto-Impressionist Francesco Guardi had to wait until the 19th century to gain recognition. Pietro Longhi, their contemporary, devoted himself to little genre scenes that offer an insight into the Venice of 200 years ago; Rosalba Carriera's pastel portraits were the rage of Europe's nobility. Meanwhile, Venetian architect Giorgio Massari translated their rococo sensibility into stone, specializing in churches that doubled as concert halls, while in the countryside neo-Palladian villas grew bigger and bigger in Venice's hectic Götterdämmerung: Villa Pisani on the **Brenta Canal** and Villa Manin near **Passariano** in Friuli are monsters of the genre.

Neoclassicism, Romanticism and Other -isms (19th and 20th centuries)

Whatever artistic spirit remained at the end of the 18th century evaporated with Napoleon and remained evaporated for a long time. Although Europe's greatest neoclassical sculptor, Antonio Canova, hailed from **Possagno** in the northern Veneto, he left very few of his pseudo-Greeks and Romans in the region. The Habsburgs built an entire new neoclassical quarter for **Trieste**, and Giuseppe Jappelli left his famous coffeehouse in **Padua** and designed romantic gardens for villas. Good collections of 19th-century art can be seen in Palazzo Pésaro (**Venice**) and the Museo Revoltella (**Trieste**).

Italians began to regain some of their artistic panache in the 20th century. The first years saw new grand hotels built on Venice's **Lido** and **Lake Garda**, many with a delightful Liberty-style (Italian Art Nouveau) touch. Other artistic trends also came from elsewhere. There was Futurism, an artistic movement that made dynamism, velocity, and modernity its creed (**Rovereto**'s museums) and at the same time, the so-called Metaphysical school led by Giorgio De Chirico and Carlo Carra, filled with a hallucinatory nostalgia and stillness; the Peggy Guggenheim museum in **Venice** has a good representative collection.

The Fascist style (Art Deco at the service of Mussolini's illusions of grandeur) often makes us smile, but as the only Italian school in the last two hundred years to achieve a consistent sense of design it presents a challenge to all modern Italian architects—one they have so far been unable to meet. Venetia has only a few examples: the Palazzo del Cinema on the Lido in **Venice**, war monuments in **Trieste, Trento** and **Rovereto. Bolzano** for its part got the very mixed blessing of a whole new Fascist quarter—Mussolini's way of asserting Italian domination over the German-speaking population.

In 1946, Renato Guttuso and Emile Vedova founded an avant-garde group in Venice, the Fronte Nuova, but without very noticeable improvement in the local art scene, then or now. Misplaced atavism prevented the construction of Frank Lloyd Wright's palace on the Grand Canal (although, when the same authorities vetoed a hospital designed by Le Corbusier, even Corby agreed they were right). But **Venice** does get its share of contemporary art, in special exhibitions and at the Biennale, although at times the latter has all the panache of a Eurovision art contest. Besides the Peggy Guggenheim, you'll find collections of modern and contemporary art—most notably in **Trento, Verona**, and **Ùdine**.

Artists' Directory

This short list of the principal architects, painters and sculptors of Venetia is bound to exasperate partisans of some artists and do scant justice to the rest, but we've tried to include the most representative works you'll find in the region.

Alticheiro (da Zevio, 1320–95): top Veronese painter of his day, and a talented follower of Giotto (S. Anastasia, S. Stefano, **Verona**; Oratorio de S. Giorgio, Padua).

Antonello da Messina (*c.* 1430–79): a Sicilian painter who visited Venice. Antonello became one of the first Italians to perfect the Van Eyckian oil painting techniques of Flanders; his compelling mastery of light, shadows, and the simplification of forms was a major influence on Giovanni Bellini (see the great but damaged *Pietà* in the Museo Correr, **Venice**).

Basaiti, Marco (1470–*c.* 1530): student and collaborator of Alvise Vivarini (Accademia, **Venice**).

Baschenis, Simone (? middle 16th century): precise, expressive Lombard painter with a Gothic sensibility; undeservedly obscure, only because he left his best work in tiny Alpine villages (*Dance of Death* at **Pinzolo** and **Carisolo** the Val di Non).

Bassano, Jacopo (da Ponte; 1510–92): son of village painter Francesco senior and head of a clan of artists working mainly from Bassano del Grappa, from whom they took their name. Jacopo began by painting in the monumental style of Parmigianino, but is better known for cranking out a succession of religious night scenes in rustic barnyards that became increasingly dramatic *à la* Tintoretto. Of his four painter sons, **Francesco the Younger** (1549–92) was his most skilled assistant and follower, until he jumped out a window; the more prolific **Leandro** less so (Palazzo Ducale, **Venice**; **Cartigliano**; also the museums in **Vicenza** and **Bassano**).

Bastiani, Lazzaro (*c.* 1420–1512): probably Carpaccio's master, and the painter responsible for the charming 'Baby Carpaccios' in **Venice**'s S. Alvise.

Bella, Gabriel (1730–99): painter of city scenes, a valuable source of information about 18th-century **Venice** despite their sublime ineptitude (Palazzo Querini-Stampalia).

Bellini, Gentile (1429–1507): elder son of Jacopo, famous for his meticulous depictions of Venetian ceremonies and narrative histories (*Miracles of the True Cross*, Accademia, **Venice**). Unfortunately, his histories painted for the Doge's Palace were lost in the fire.

Bellini, Giovanni (1435–1516): the greatest early Renaissance painter of Northern Italy. No artists before him painted with such sensitivity to light, atmosphere, colour, and nature; none since have approached the almost magical tenderness and empathy he conveyed in his Madonnas and other religious works (Accademia, San Zaccaria, and the Frari in **Venice**; S. Corona, **Vicenza**).

Bellini, Jacopo (1400–70): pupil of Gentile da Fabriano, father of Giovanni and Gentile, father-in-law of Mantegna, all of whom were influenced by Jacopo's beautiful drawings from nature (in the Louvre and British Museum); in Venetia his best works are his Madonnas, more natural and lifelike than others of his generation (Accademia, **Venice**; Castelvecchio, **Verona**).

Bon, Bartolomeo (d. 1464): prolific Venetian sculptor and architect, who worked with his brother Giovanni to produce some of **Venice**'s most lavishly decorative work (Porta della Carta and statues of the Ducal Palace, Ca' d'Oro).

Bonifazio Veronese (Bonifazio de' Pitati; 1487–1553): native of Verona who moved to Venice and fell under the spell of Titian and company; as he rarely signed anything, secondary paintings in their style have been so often attributed to him that he has become posthumously one of the most prolific painters of his generation.

Bonino (c. 1335–75): flamboyant Gothic sculptor from Campione (Lake Lugano), the cradle of northern builders and sculptors; in **Verona** he carved most of the Scaliger tombs.

Bordone, Paris (1500–1571): from Treviso, a pupil of Titian and follower of Giorgione, whose pastoral landscapes were a seminal influence on his work and earned him commissions from across Europe (The Presentation of the Ring of St Mark to the Doge, Accademia, **Venice**, is his masterpiece; also Scuola del Carmine, **Padua**).

Brustalon, Andrea (1662–1732) of Belluno: rococo sculptor and furniture maker of imagination and whimsy (Ca' Rezzonico, **Venice**; Museo Civico, **Belluno**).

Campagnola, Domenico (1500–1550s): adopted son and pupil of the great Paduan engraver Giulio Campagnola, a student of Mantegna; like Giulio he made bucolic landscapes a speciality (Scuola di S. Rocco and Scuola del Carmine, **Padua**).

Canaletto, Antonio (Giovanni Antonio Canal, 1697–1768): master of meticulous, colourful, and postcard-accurate Venetian vedute, or views, but go to England to see them—there is but one in the Accademia, and two in the Ca' Rezzonico (**Venice**).

Canova, Antonio (1757–1821): born in Possagno near Àsolo, a neoclassical celebrity sculptor—the favourite of Napoleon and Benjamin Franklin and everyone in between, including the popes, one of whom made him Marchese d'Ischia. The Museo Correr in **Venice** has a naturalistic early work, Daedalus and Icarus, but most of his sculptures went elsewhere; his studio in **Possagno** is now a museum of casts, while the village is crowned with a huge temple he built to hold his ashes.

Caroto, Giovanni (1480–1555): not the greatest Veronese artist, but an endearing one; the Big Carrot is best known for his portrait of a child in the Castelvecchio; also works in S. Fermo, both in **Verona**.

Carpaccio, Vittore (c. 1465–1525): a probable student of Gentile Bellini and the most charming of Venetian artists, with fairytale paintings full of documentary details from his life and times. The distinctive red tones he loved gave his name to paper-thin slices of raw beef fillet (major cycles at Scuola di S. Giorgio Schiavone and the Accademia; also the Two Courtesans, in the Museo Correr, all in **Venice**).

Carriera, Rosalba (1675–1757): a Venetian portraitist and miniaturist, and the first woman to make a good living as an artist; her soft, pastel portraits were the rage of the powdered wig set not only in Venice, but in Paris and Vienna, until she lost her eyesight in 1749 (**Venice**, Accademia and Ca' Rezzonico).

Castagno, Andrea del (1423–1457): a Tuscan master of striking form and composition, who visited Venice in 1445 and left the city some Renaissance food for thought in St Mark's and S. Zaccaria.

Catena, Vincenzo (1480–1531): a well-born Venetian merchant, humanist and friend of Giorgione who painted as a hobby, increasingly well as time went on (Judith, in the Palazzo Querini-Stampalia in **Venice**, is his masterpiece).

de Chirico, Giorgio (1888–1978): a Greek-Italian who was one of the founding fathers of the Metaphysical School (1916–18), best known for his enigmatic, often uncanny empty urban landscapes dotted with classical odds and ends and dressmakers' mannequins (Peggy Guggenheim, **Venice**).

Cima da Conegliano, Giovanni Battista (1459–1518): whose luminous autumnal colours and landscapes were inspired by Bellini—as Bellini was inspired by several of his compositions (Madonna del Orto and Accademia in **Venice**; Duomo, **Conegliano**).

Codussi, Mauro (c. 1420–1504): architect from Bergamo, who worked mainly in **Venice**; a genius at synthesizing traditional Venetian styles with the classical forms of the Renaissance (S. Michele in Isola, Venice's first Renaissance church; also S. Zaccaria, staircase at the Scuola di S. Giovanni Evangelista, Palazzo Vendramin-Calergi).

Crivelli, Carlo (*c.* 1435–1495): meticulous Venetian enamoured of luminous, perspective, crystalline forms, garlands, and cucumbers in his exclusively religious work; he spent most of his time in the Marches (Accademia, **Venice**; Castelvecchio, **Verona**).

Depero, Fortunato (1892–1960): a Futurist who moved to a colourful poster-like style (Museo Depero, **Rovereto**).

De Pisis, Filippo (1896–1956): a neo-Impressionist from Ferrara who spent a long period in Venice (Peggy Guggenheim, **Venice**).

Donatello (1386–1466), of Florence: the greatest European sculptor of the *quattrocento*, never equalled in technique, expressiveness, or imaginative content. He spent 1443–50 in **Padua**, casting his Gattamelata statue and sculptures and reliefs for the high altar for the Basilica di S. Antonio, a major inspiration to young Andrea Mantegna; also a statue in the Frari, **Venice**.

Falconetto, Giovanni Maria (1468–1534): Veronese architect who built in a charming antiquarian style that inspired Palladio, leading the way in the transformation of Gothic **Padua** (especially the Loggia della Gran Guardia and Loggia Cornaro) into a Renaissance city; he also designed the villa at **Luvigliano** in the Euganean Hills.

Fogolino, Marcello (1480–1550): a fine painter from Vicenza, who became court artist to Prince-bishop Bernardo Cles, introducing the Renaissance to Trento (Palazzo delle Albere and Castello di Buonconsiglio, **Trento**; Santa Corona, **Vicenza**).

Giambono, Michele (*c.* 1420–1462): one of the princes of Venetian retro; while everyone else moved on to the Renaissance, Giambono was still cranking out rich paintings in International Gothic (Accademia, altarpieces in St Mark's, **Venice**).

Gianfrancesco da Tolmezzo (*c.* 1450–1510): was the top quattrocento painter in his native Friuli (**Castel d'Aviano**, **San Giorgio della Richinvelda**, and **Forni di Sopra**—his masterpiece).

Giorgione (Giorgio da Castelfranco, *c.* 1478–1510): got his nickname 'Big George' not only for his height, but for the huge influence he had on Venetian painting. Although he barely lived past thirty and only several paintings are undisputedly by his hand, his poetic evocation of atmosphere and haunting, psychological ambiguity was echoed not only by Titian and Sebastiano del Piombo, his followers, but by his master Giovanni Bellini (paintings in the Accademia in **Venice** and **Castelfranco**).

Giotto di Bondone (*c.* 1267–1337): a Florentine, one of the most influential painters in history, the first Italian to break away from stylized Byzantine forms in favour of a more 'natural' and narrative style. Although associated with Florence and Assisi, he painted his masterpiece in **Padua**: the Cappella degli Scrovegni.

Giovanni da Ùdine (1487–1562): pupil and leading assistant of Raphael, as well as an architect and master of graceful stuccoes and grotesques. In 1552 he was made city architect of his native **Ùdine**, and designed the Torre dell'Orologio and fountain in Piazza Matteotti among other projects.

Giovanni da Verona (1457–1525): a Dominican friar and greatest marquetry artist of the century (S. Maria in Organo, **Verona**).

Guardi, Francesco (1712–1793): brother-in-law of Giambattista Tiepolo and younger brother of Gianantonio (1699–1760) with whom he worked, making early attributions difficult. Guardi's favourite subject was Venice, but his views, unlike Canaletto's, are suffused with light and atmosphere; many of canvases approach Impressionism in their handling—hence his revival in the 19th century, after a life of obscurity and poverty (Ca' d'Oro, Accademia, Angelo Raffaele, all in **Venice**).

Guariento (14th century): a follower of Giotto and founder of the Paduan school. His masterpiece, a massive fresco of Paradise in Venice's Ducal Palace, burned in a fire, though fragments hint at what was lost. His work has much of the same humane quality as Giotto (Ermitiani, **Padua**; Museo Civico, **Bassano del Grappa**).

Jacobello del Fiore (*c.* 1370–1439): Venetian master of Gothic International, fond of raised gold embossing (Accademia, **Venice**).

Jappelli, Giuseppe (1783–1852): stylish Paduan neoclassical/eclectic architect and romantic landscape gardener; designed the Caffè Pedrocchi and several other buildings around **Padua**; Villa Valmarana, **Saonara**; Villa Selvatico-Capodilista, **Rivella**; Grand Hotel Orologio in **Àbano Terme**).

Liberale da Verona (*c.* 1445–1529): genteel painter of frescoes, the Carpaccio of **Verona** (Duomo, Castelvecchio, S. Fermo).

Lombardo, Pietro (*c.* 1455–1516): native of Lombardy and founder of Venice's greatest family of sculptors and architects, strongly influenced by the Tuscan Renaissance and antique models (SS. Giovanni e Paolo, S. Giobbe, S. Francesco della Vigna, and his masterpiece, S. Maria dei Miracoli, all in **Venice**).

Lombardo, Tullio (*c.* 1455–1532): son of Pietro, with whom he often worked. Tullio was an exquisite marble-sculptor, best known for his tombs, especially the Vendramin tomb in Venice's SS. Giovanni e Paolo. His brother Antonio (c. 1458–1516) assisted him in the classical reliefs in the Basilica of S. Antonio, **Padua**.

Longhena, Baldassare (1598–1682): Venetian architect, a student of Scamozzi, whose best work was one of his first commissions: the church of the Salute (also Ca' Pesaro, both in **Venice**).

Longhi, Pietro (1702–1785): there weren't photographers in 18th-century Venice, but there was Pietro Longhi dutifully portraying society's foibles (Ca' Rezzonico, Accademia, Querini-Stampalia, all in **Venice**; also Palazzo Leoni Montanari, **Vicenza**). His son Alessandro (1733–1813) was official portrait painter of the Accademia, and in 1762 he published a biography of historical Venetian painters, with portraits of each.

Lorenzo Veneziano (active 1356–1379): disciple of Paolo Veneziano (no relation) and painter in a luxuriant, golden International Gothic style (Duomo, **Vicenza**; Accademia, **Venice**).

Lotto, Lorenzo (c. 1480–1556): a neurotic Venetian trained under Giovanni Bellini, best known for religious paintings—some great, some uninspired—and portraits that seem to catch their sitters off guard, capturing his own restless energy on canvas. Lotto was run out of Venice by Titian and Aretino and spent much his life in the Marches (Accademia, **Venice**; Santa Cristina at Quinto; Pinacoteca and S. Nicolò, **Treviso**).

Maffei, Francesco (c. 1600–60) of Vicenza: dissonant and unorthodox baroque painter, whose nervous brush often brings out the dark side of the age of curlicues (Museo Civico and Oratorio di S. Nicola, **Vicenza**; Castelvecchio, **Verona**).

Mansueti, Giovanni (c. 1465–1527): underrated student of Giovanni Bellini and a talented painter of narrative histories (Accademia, **Venice**; Museo Civico, **Vicenza**).

Mantegna, Andrea (c. 1420–1506): remarkable painter born near Padua, whose use of antiquity, sculptural forms as hard as coral and unusual perspectives dominated art in the Veneto until the rise of his brother-in-law Giambellini (Eremitani church, **Padua**; S. Zeno and Castelvecchio, **Verona**; Accademia, **Venice**).

dalle Masegne, Jacobello and Pier Paolo: 14th-century Venetian architects and sculptors, influenced by the works of the great Tuscan Nicolò Pisano, creator of a new realistic classically inspired style (S. Marco, **Venice**).

Massari, Giorgio (1687–1766): Venetian architect who collaborated with G. B. Tiepolo and Vivaldi to create some of the most delightful baroque churches in **Venice** (La Pietà and Gesuati; also Villa Cordellina-Lombardi in **Montecchio Maggiore**).

Mazzoni, Sebastiano (1611–78): irrepressible Florentine baroque master who loved to go over the top (Museo Civico, **Padua**; Pinacoteca, **Rovigo**).

Menabuoi, Giusto de' (d. 1397): Florentine painter who followed Giotto to **Padua**, where his masterpiece is the Baptistry (also frescoes in the Palazzo della Ragione).

Montagna, Bartolomeo (1450–1523): a painter of heavy dignity inspired by Antonello da Messina, founder of the Vicentine school (Monte Bérico, Museo Civico, **Vicenza**).

Morto da Feltre (Lorenzo Luzzo, 1467–1512): the Dead Man got his name from his pale complexion, but painted with Giorgione's colours (Museo Civico, **Feltre**).

Muttoni, Francesco (1668–1747): architect from Como and one of the most talented proponents of the Palladian revival in the Veneto (Palazzo Valmarano-Trento, **Vicenza**; Villa Da Porto, near **Lonigo**; Villa Fracanzan-Piovene, **Orgiano**).

Pacher, Michael (c. 1430–98): of Brunico, one of the leading late Gothic painters and sculptors of the day (Museo Diocesano, **Bressanone**; Nostra Signora at Gries, **Bolzano**).

Palladio (Andrea di Pietro della Gondola, 1508–80): the Veneto's most influential architect, not only for his buildings, but for his books and drawings that imaginatively reinterpreted the classics to fit the needs of the day (major buildings in **Vicenza**, **Venice**, **Piombino Dese**, **Masèr**, and on the **Brenta Canal**).

Palma Giovane (Jacopo Palma, 1544–1628): the most prolific painter of his day, the great-nephew of Palma Vecchio and a pupil of Titian, who specialized in large but usually vapid narrative paintings (every church in **Venice** seems to have at least one).

Palma Vecchio (Jacopo Negretti, c. 1480–1528): a student of Giovanni Bellini who successfully adopted the new sensuous style of Giorgione and young Titian, and is best known for his voluptuous Venetian blondes, often disguised as saints (S. Maria Formosa, **Venice**; S. Stefano, **Vicenza**).

Paolo Veneziano (c. 1290–1360): the leading painter of his day, a powerful Byzantine influence in Venetian art that would linger longer in the lagoon than elsewhere (**Venice**, Accademia; **Padua**, Museo Civico).

Pellegrino da San Daniele (Martin da Ùdine, 1467–1547): a little known Renaissance talent from

Ùdine, because he spent much of his life frescoing one church, S. Antonio, in **San Daniele del Friuli**; also an altarpiece in the basilica, **Aquileia**.

Piazzetta, Giambattista (1683–1754): Venetian baroque painter extraordinaire, who went to extremes in his use of light and dark, favouring the latter. An early influence on Giambattista Tiepolo, he became the first director of the Accademia (Accademia, SS. Giovanni e Paolo, and other churches, **Venice**).

Pisanello, Antonio (c. 1395–c. 1455): originator of the Renaissance medal and one of the leading and most graceful painters of the Gothic International school; he collaborated with Gentile da Fabriano on the lamented lost frescoes in the Doges' Palace (Castelvecchio, S. Fermo, and S. Anastasia, **Verona**; medals in Ca' d'Oro, **Venice**).

Pittoni, Giovanni Battista (1687–1767): one of the most popular painters of his day in Venice, who like many went from dark baroque to a lighter rococo mood under the influence of Tiepolo (S. Corona, **Vicenza**).

Pordenone (Giovanni de' Sacchis, 1484–1539): Titian's main rival, with a more monumental, Roman style inspired by Michelangelo, combined with quick brushstrokes and often bizarre iconography and expressions; Vasari claims that he was self-taught (S. Giovanni Elemosinario, **Venice**; Museo Civico, **Pordenone**; Duomo, **Treviso**).

Ricci, Sebastiano (1659–1734): decorative painter from Belluno inspired by the scenographic monumentality of Roman baroque; his work at its best is fresh and colourful, while other times it shows slapdash haste–Ricci was a terrible womanizer and often had to flee jealous husbands (S. Giustina, **Padua**; Museo Civico, **Vicenza**; S. Pietro, **Belluno**). He often worked with his nephew Marco Ricci (1670–1730; landscapes in the Accademia, **Venice**).

Il Riccio (Andrea Briosco, c. 1470–1532): High Renaissance sculptor and architect and great friend of Humanist scholars, famous for his intricate bronze work and statuettes (**Padua**, Museo Civico, S. Antonio— where the Pascal candelabrum is his masterpiece, also S. Giustina).

Rizzo, Antonio (c. 1445–1498): pure Renaissance sculptor and architect from Verona, who worked mostly in **Venice** (Tron monument, Frari; courtyard of the Palazzo Ducale).

Sammicheli, Michele (1484–1559): born in Verona, sometimes heavy-handed Renaissance architect and sculptor, as well as the Serenissima's masterbuilder of walls and fortifications (walls, **Padua**; also palaces in Treviso; walls, S. Bernardino and Palazzo Bevilacqua, **Verona**; Palazzo Grimani, **Venice**).

Sansovino, Jacopo (Jacopo Tatti, 1486–1570): sculptor and architect from Florence who took his name from his master Andrea Sansovino. Jacopo fled the Sack of Rome in 1527 and came to Venice, where he became chief architect to the Procurators of St Mark's and a good buddy of Titian and poison pen master Aretino. Sansovino created a new Venetian High Renaissance style–the rhythmic use of columns, arches, loggias, and reliefs, with sculpture playing an integral role (**Venice**, where he rebuilt St Mark's Square and designed the famous Library; sculptures in the Ducal Palace; also Villa Garzoni-Michiel, **Pontecasale**).

Scamozzi, Vincenzo (1552–1616): from Vicenza, Palladio's closest collaborator who completed many of his projects according to his own imagination, and a brilliant Mannerist architect in his own right (villas, palaces and Teatro Olimpico, **Vicenza**; Procuratie Nuove, **Venice**; Rocca Pisani, at **Lonigo**; Via Sacra, **Monsélice**).

Sebastiano del Piombo (Sebastiano Luciani, 1485–1547): a pupil of Giorgione, and a rich autumnal colourist. Sebastiano went to Rome when Giorgione died, and became the chief notary of the Vatican (hence his nickname, for the lead seals that still haunt the Posta Italiana); most works are in Rome, but see S. Giovanni Crisostomo, **Venice**.

Squarcione, Francesco (c. 1394–1474): a Paduan tailor who became a self taught painter, one of the first antique dealers, and teacher of Mantegna; not much of his documented work survives beyond a polyptych in the Museo Civico, **Padua**.

Stefano da Verona (or da Zevio, c. 1375–1450): delightful International Gothic master, lead painter in Verona in the generation after Turone (S. Fermo Maggiore, Castelvecchio, both in **Verona**).

Tiepolo, Giambattista (1691–1770): Venice's rococo wizard, generally considered the greatest European painter of the 18th century. He initially worked in the style of Piazzetta, but soon left all that gloomy *chiaroscuro* behind for one of the most colourful palettes in art; Tiepolo's subjects, many mythological, live in the delightful warm afterglow of Venice's decline (Palazzo Labia, Scuola dei Carmini, and Gesuati, **Venice**; Villa Valmarana, **Vicenza**; Oratorio della Purità and Museo Diocesano, **Ùdine**; Villa Pisani, **Stra**).

Tiepolo, Giandomenico (1727–1804): son of Giambattista, with whom he frescoed Villa Valmarana. While he could imitate his father's grand heroic manner to the point that attribution of some frescoes could go either way, Giandomenico's work tends to be more introspective and often wistful, especially his masquerades (Ca' Rezzonico, S. Polo, **Venice**; parish church, **Desenzano del Garda**).

Tintoretto (Jacopo Robusti, 1518–94): was given his name 'little dyer' because of his father's profession. A proud, ill-tempered workaholic, his ideal was to combine Michelangelo's drawing with the colouring of Titian, but his most amazing talent was in his visionary, unrestrained and original composition, often delighting in startling sleight-of-hand foreshortening. His most talented follower was a Greek who ended up in Spain—El Greco (Scuola di S. Rocco series; the world's largest painting, in the Palazzo Ducale; Accademia and S. Giorgio Maggiore, all in **Venice**; also Museo Civico, **Vicenza**).

Titian (Tiziano Vecellio, c. 1480s–1576): from Pieve di Cadore in the Dolomites; he became, with the death of Giovanni Bellini, official painter to the Venetian Republic. Generally regarded as the greatest painter of the Venetian school, Titian was a pupil of Giovanni Bellini at the same time as Giorgione, and followed the latter so closely that many of his early works have often been attributed to his colleague. Titian made his reputation with the monumental altarpiece of the *Assumption* in **Venice**'s Frari, a bold handling of form and colour that cast a spell on Tintoretto, Veronese and countless others. In his long career, his work evolved through several phases, influenced by Mannerism in the 1540s after a trip to Rome, and then in his last years, taking his revolutionary free brushwork to an extreme, most violently in his last unfinished work, the *Pietà* in the Accademia. Although Titian spent most of his life in Venice, his international reputation saw most of his canvases scattered across Europe: Emperor Charles V was such an admirer that he made Titian a Count Palatine, an extraordinary honour for a painter. Besides the Frari altarpieces, **Venice** keeps a few of his works in S. Salvatore, the Accademia, the Salute; also the cathedrals of **Treviso** and **Verona**.

Tommaso da Modena (c. 1325–1376): delightful, humane 14th-century painter, a follower of Giotto who worked for a long period in **Treviso** (church and seminary of S. Nicolò, also S. Caterina); also in Castelvecchio, **Verona**.

Troger, Paul (1698–1762): Tirolese rococo painter, trained by Giuseppe Maria Crespi in Bologna and Piazzetta in Venice, before he returned to decorate his native valleys with colourful airy frescoes (**Bressanone** cathedral, his masterpieces; also altars at **Monguelfo**, his birthplace).

Tura, Cosmè (c. 1430–1490): of the Ferrara school, whose singularly intense, craggy and weirdly tortured style is immediately recognizable and, for many, an acquired taste; Museo Correr, **Venice**).

Turone (active in the 1360s): Veronese master influenced by German miniaturists, teacher of Altichiero (Castelvecchio and S. Anastasia, **Verona**).

Veronese (Paulo Caliari, 1528–88): the most sumptuous and ravishingly decorative painter of the High Renaissance, fond of striking illusionism, shimmering colours, and curious perspectives set in Palladian architectural fancies (Villa Bàrbaro at **Masèr**; Accademia, Ducal Palace, and S. Sebastiano, **Venice**; S. Corona, **Vicenza**).

Verrocchio, Andrea del (Andrea di Cioni, 1435–88): painter, sculptor, and alchemist nicknamed 'true eye', Verrocchio was a follower of Donatello and teacher of Leonardo da Vinci. The greatest bronze sculptor of the day, he was hired by **Venice** to create the dynamic equestrian statue of Colleoni.

Vitale da Bologna (active 1330–59): a disarming and guileless fellow who set the tone for Bolognese painting, celebrated in part for the lack of mental effort it requires from the beholder (Museo del Duomo, **Ùdine**).

Vittoria, Alessandro (1525–1608): Venetian sculptor, a student of Sansovino famous for his elegant bronze statuettes and portrait busts (S. Francesco della Vigna, Frari, Ca' d'Oro, **Venice**).

Vivarini: 15th-century clan of painters from Murano, the chief rivals of the Bellini dynasty in Venice, noted for their rich, decorative and retro style. Antonio (c. 1415–76/84) collaborated with Giovanni d'Alemagna to paint altarpieces (S. Giobbe, **Venice**); brother Bartolomeo (1432–99) was more imaginative in his use of colour and rhythm (S. Maria Formosa, Frari, **Venice**); Alvise (1446–1503), son of Antonio, was influenced by Antonello da Messina (Frari, S. Giovanni in Brágora, **Venice**).

Zelotti, Giambattista (1526–78) of Verona: a collaborator of Veronese who became one of Palladio's chief and most interesting interior decorators (Villa Godi Malinverni, **Lonedo di Lugo**; Villa Emo, **Fanzolo**; La Malcontenta, on the **Brenta Canal**; Il Catajo, **Battaglia Terme**).

The Son of Satan

In stark contrast to the benign flock of winged lions left behind by Venice, in Venetia you'll find older, darker relics—walls, castles, towers, prisons and torture chambers—recalling one of the meanest hombres who ever lived. The very name Ezzelino still evokes a shiver in this part of the world, even though he's been frying in hell for over 700 years. Medieval Italy was precocious in so many ways, in banking, in trade, in art, in architecture, in literature—the list goes on and on. Ezzelino III da Romano was another first: Europe's first self-made tyrant.

He lived in interesting times. Two generations previously, in 1176, the Lombard League, including Verona, Vicenza, Padua, Belluno and Treviso, had battled to win

Tales of Tyranny and Harmony

the guarantee of their civic freedoms from the German Holy Roman Emperor, Frederick I Barbarossa. This came as a blow to the Ezzelini, the feudal lordlings of what is now northern Vicenza province and staunch members of the Emperor's Ghibelline party. Now the pro-papal Guelph *comuni* were open rivals, especially Vicenza, which had taken advantage of its new freedoms to snatch a chunk of Ezzelino turf.

Ezzelino hopes rose again with the advent of Barbarossa's grandson, Emperor Frederick II, Stupor Mundi, 'the Wonder of the World'. A man with a brilliant mind, a poet fluent in six languages, Frederick was the first 'Italian' emperor, having grown up in cosmopolitan Arab-Greek-Norman Sicily. This also made him singularly open-minded and tolerant. But these were the tub-thumping days of the Crusades, and the popes hated him from the start; when he regained Jerusalem by treaty in 1229, rather than by massacring the infidels, the popes excommunicated him.

Frederick hated the popes right back. They presented the biggest obstacle to his plans for a modern centralized empire, and it came as a major blow in 1230 when the *comuni* of northern Italy re-formed the Lombard League, declaring themselves the allies of Pope Gregory IX. It was an act that many *comuni* soon regretted, as Gregory made them prove their allegiance by accepting the Church's new weapon, the Inquisition, to roust out the Paterini and Cathar heretics they had hitherto tolerated. Many of these heretics belonged to the nobility, including Ezzelino II da Romano. Gregory demanded that his son, Ezzelino III, then serving as *podestà* (feudal mayor, or imperial representative) of Verona, turn his father over for burning. The younger Ezzelino refused; it was the only good deed of his life.

Ezzelino III was born 1194, the same year as Frederick. He was the most skilled military commander of his day, ruthless and ambitious, a bachelor who despised luxury and women. He was also completely devoted to the emperor. In 1234, when Frederick amassed a Saracen army from Sicily (immune from papal bans and excommunications) to attack the *comuni* of the Lombard League, he naturally chose Ezzelino as his lieutenant in Venetia, and, in Verona in 1236, put 3000 German cavalry and his Saracens under his command.

Ezzalino, advised by his astrologers, at once pounced on Vicenza and Padua, then the most powerful city on the *terra firma*. He did this with a brutality shocking even by the standards of the day, torturing his victims to death to extract names of other potential enemies, flinging others in dungeons to starve to death, then killing all their relatives. Stories of his cruelty dominate the literature of the 13th century and feature prominently in the *Cento Novelle Antiche*, gathered together in 1525. His subjects called him the 'Son of Satan'.

Although Frederick regained much of northern Italy, it was at the price of taking the blame for Ezzelino's atrocities and another excommunication. The emperor's colleagues, fearful for their own souls, began to abandon and betray him, and Frederick grew increasingly bitter. If he was alarmed by the monster he had created in the Veneto, he could at least trust him. In 1250, Stupor Mundi died of dysentery while preparing to crusade with St Louis in the hope of returning to the pope's good graces.

Ezzelino, for his part, was never bothered by remorse. In Padua alone he kept eight overflowing prisons 'notwithstanding the incessant toil of the executioner to empty them'. In 1256 Pope Alexander IV preached an anti-Ezzelino Crusade, offering all who fought him the same indulgences offered to Crusaders in the Holy Land. The offer attracted all the riffraff in Italy, who took Padua by sheer numbers; the gates were opened to welcome the 'liberators' who then raped and pillaged the city for a week. In revenge for that open gate, Ezzelino tortured and killed all but 200 of the 11,000 Paduans in his army.

The Pope's Crusaders were so incompetent that Ezzelino actually grew stronger and gained Brescia when the Ghibellines there delivered their *comune* to him, free of charge. This gave Ezzelino a bad case of hubris, and in 1259, aged 65, he decided to take all of Lombardy and Milan itself, believing the nobles there, as in Brescia, would hand their city to him. Off he marched with the most splendid army of his career, but the Brescians, by now disgusted by his cruelty, had secretly dealt with the Guelphs of Milan, Cremona, Ferrara and Mantua; when Ezzelino was well into Lombardy, at

Cassiano on the Adda, the Brescians abandoned him and his enemies closed in. Ezzelino fought until he was severely wounded in the foot. The Guelphs chained him up in the castle at Soncino, where he refused to speak or accept any aid, but furiously tore his bandages off with his teeth and died eleven days later.

His brother, the *podestà* of Treviso, and all his family were slain to make sure the family never plagued Venetia again. But in reality Ezzelino had more than his share of heirs: the mafia-like *signori*, the Carrara of Padua, the Scaligers of Verona, the Visconti of Milan, the Medici of Florence who would dominate Italian politics for centuries. In *The Civilization of the Renaissance in Italy* (1867) Jacob Burckhardt wrote Ezzelino's chilling epitaph:

> The conquests and usurpations which had hitherto taken place in the Middle Ages rested on real or pretended inheritance and other such claims... Here for the first time the attempt was openly made to found a throne by wholesale murder and endless barbarities, by the adoption, in short, of any means with a view to nothing but the end pursued. None of his successors, not even Cesare Borgia, rivalled the colossal guilt of Ezzelino; but the example once set was not forgotten, and his fall led to no return of justice among nations, and served as no warning to future transgressors.

Still the Best: Giovanni Bellini

Renaissance artists tended to be pernickety proud individualists, not averse to pulling a pistol on one another, and their lives often make for colourful reading. One great exception to the rule was Giovanni Bellini, who apparently never quarrelled, married, travelled, designed buildings, wrote letters or poetry, hobnobbed with princes, or in brief did anything at all except paint during a career that lasted for 65 years. In most art histories he gets a nod as the father of the Venetian school and master of Giorgione and Titian, but many visitors to the Veneto overlook him, bedazzled by the greater fireworks of the Three Ts (Titian, Tintoretto, and Tiepolo). Next to theirs, Bellini's work is very still, but like many quiet voices he often has more to say at the end of the day.

Giambellini, as our ancestors liked to call him, was born in Venice around 1430, with a paintbrush in his baby fist. His father Jacopo, a student of the great International Gothic master Gentile da Fabriano, was an innovator in his own way; one of the first artists to draw from nature, he also did a number of perspectivist studies in his notebooks. Giovanni and his older brother Gentile learned their craft at their father's knee, but early on they went separate ways: Gentile inherited Jacopo's workshop and style, while Giovanni inherited his love of the natural world. His heaven was on earth, in the Veneto; his saints were human, and his faith, while pure, was above all humane, and expressed itself not through halos and gold paint, but through a warm and sensuous empathy. Only Raphael, that other great painter of madonnas, had a similar gift. But while Raphael's are beautiful, tender loving mammas bursting with charm, Bellini's have the balance and measure of the *quattrocento*. They are women doing their bit in the divine scheme, brave yet wistful, perhaps knowing what's in store for their *bambino*. They never emote, or appeal for the viewer's sympathy, which makes them all the more poignant.

In 1453, family played another formative role in Bellini's development, when his older sister married Andrea Mantegna. Mantegna, already the top master of perspective in Italy, showed Giovanni how to place solid figures in three-dimensional settings, lessons revealed in a number of works now in Venice's Museo Correr: *Transfiguration,* the *Frizzoni Madonna*, *Crucifixion*, and the *Dead Christ Supported by Two Angels*. Some time around 1460, Andrea and Giovanni both produced paintings from a drawing of the *Agony in the Garden* in old Jacopo's notebooks. Both are in London's National Gallery: Mantegna's landscape is as precise as his figures, while Bellini has a more lyrical bent in his use of colour and light. His most important work of the period, the *Polyptych of S. Vincenzo Ferreri* in Venice's SS. Giovanni e Paolo (1464–8), shows his rapid progress—the pediment, which he painted first, is awkward, but the last figure he added, the Angel Gabriel, is exquisite.

The last key ingredient for Bellini came to Venice with Antonello da Messina in 1475. Antonello had just learned the art of oil painting from Jan Van Eyck, and among the Italians Bellini led the way in adopting the new medium, then mastering it to a degree that few painters since have ever equalled, painstakingly building up colour and depth in transparent glazes, enabling him to achieve a remarkable richness of tone and luminosity.

Critics call Bellini's mature style 'tonalism', for its emphasis on light and colour and atmosphere at the expense of design and line. In his experiments, the borders between solids and space begin to dissolve, replaced by melting transitions of light and shadow. Backgrounds and landscapes play a larger role in the composition than they ever had before, until they become as integral to the meaning as the central figures. An early example is the *Saint Francis* (1480, Frick Collection, New York City), while the *Pala Barbarigo* (1484, San Pietro Martire, Murano), the *Pala di San Giobbe* and *Madonna of the Little Trees* (1487, both in the Accademia) represent the culmination.

Bellini's splendid late style dates from around 1500, when he was seventy and could count nearly every young Venetian painter of distinction as a pupil. He was the Official Painter of Venice and had singlehandedly brought his hometown into the first ranks of the Renaissance alongside Florence and Rome. But he never stopped learning or innovating. His *Portrait of Doge Leonardo Loredan* (National Gallery, London, 1501) shows the first use of *impasto* (the building up of paint to produce texture)—the first individualist use of a brushstroke and the first step in the great revolution in western art that would separate art from the object represented. Other beautiful examples of Bellini's late style are the *Baptism of Christ* (Santa Corona, Vicenza) and the sublime *Sacra Conversazione* (San Zaccaria, Venice), where the complex shadings of colour and glazings are sheer wizardry—Leonardo da Vinci's famous *sfumato* technique but in colour, all merging to create a perfect lyrical unity.

And he still had time for young artists. Albrecht Dürer wrote home from Venice in 1507, 'Giambellino praised me in front of many gentlemen. He wanted something done by me, and he came in person to ask me, telling me he would pay me well. And everyone said that it really was very gracious of him to have favoured me in this way. He is very old, but he's still the best in painting.'

And he still had nine good years in him. He greatly admired the work of his pupil Giorgione, who had taken his tonalism a step further by emphasizing mood over matter, and painted for the delight of private patrons. Giambellini, after 60 years of painting for Church and State, was ready for a change. Five of his small mythologies remain in Venice's Accademia, while the others are abroad, including the *Feast of the Gods* (1514) in the National Gallery, Washington D.C. Perhaps most remarkable of all is his *Lady with a Mirror*

(1515) in Vienna's Kunsthistorisches Museum—perhaps the most touchingly optimistic and dreamily sensuous work ever painted by an artist in his late 80s, a year before his death.

The Council of Trent

In the 1520s Emperor Charles V, haughty ruler of much of Europe and the Americas, found his Germanic possessions in the throes of the Reformation, and his Catholic domains bracing themselves for a hysterical reaction. A staunch Catholic himself, Charles sought to heal the rift by asking the Pope to call a council—an idea first suggested by Luther himself—to look into some urgently needed reforms in the Church. Pope Clement VII refused point blank (the last thing any pope wanted was a revival of Counciliarism, with the threat that papal authority could be overruled in a general council), but after Charles V taught him a lesson by sacking Rome in 1527, Clement agreed that perhaps a council wasn't such a bad idea after all.

His successor, Paul III, let the uncongenial idea slide until 1538, when the Germans threatened to call a national council of their own, minus the Pope. But where to convoke it? Charles insisted that it take place on Imperial turf, while the Pope wanted an Italian city where he could influence the outcome. Eventually, Trento, an Italian city ruled by a prince-bishop under the Holy Roman Empire, proved to be the perfect compromise. After more delays, the Council finally convened in Trento on December 1545 to study the three goals Paul III had placed before it: to reunite Christendom, reform the Church's administration and procedures, and form a league of Christian princes against the Turks.

The council had hardly began when a typhus epidemic sent the prelates scurrying off to Bologna for safety, and it was another six years before a new pope, Julius III, ordered them back to Trent. Other events in Germany, such as the military advance of the Protestant princes, soon caused a new break-up. The last session of the Council, under Pius IV, met for two years, from January 1562 to December 1563, when a long list of decrees were promulgated and approved by the pope.

If the Council of Trent had signally failed to unite the Christians (after all the dithering, it was far too late for compromise) or unite their princes against the Turk, it did result in a new unified, clear-cut doctrine to confront the Protestant threat. This provided for vast improvements in pastoral care and the education of priests, and an end of clerical concubinage; there was to be a new edition of the Bible and a new catechism. In the face of Protestant doubt, the rites of the Seven Sacraments in themselves were confirmed as signs of grace (the spiritual state of the minister or recipient being incidental), and the Office of Propaganda was created to convert Protestant (and other) unbelievers.

The Council's last salvos, decided at the last minute during the last session, were aimed straight at the Protestants, confirming the existence of Purgatory, the veneration of saints, images and relics, and the value of indulgences. The Counter-Reformation had blasted off, and the 'Jesuit style', precursor of the baroque, incorporating all the richness, pomp and sensuality that the Protestants hated, inspired a wave of church-building to provide a visual symbol for the new Catholicism. It was a hothouse orchid that blossomed on a scorched and increasingly fearful Christendom.

In his famous *History of the Council of Trent* (first published in 1619, in London), Paolo Sarpi, the great Venetian monk and historian, called the controversies in Trent 'the *Iliad* of our age' and believed that the resulting Council's doctrines were an unmitigated disaster. According to Sarpi, the original goal of its well-meaning leaders—the restoration of the primitive Church, poor and democratic, to coax back the Protestants—had been distorted by the political intrigues of the Roman Curia, Jesuits and Spaniards.

> *This Council, which pious men desired and procured to reunite the Church (which was beginning to split apart), has, on the contrary, made the split a permanent one and the parties to it irreconcilable. It was planned by the princes to reform the Church; but it has brought about the greatest corruption of the Church since the name of 'Christian' was first heard.*
>
> Paolo Sarpi, *History of the Council of Trent*

Sarpi's *Iliad* analogy was certainly right in one respect. Instead of making peace, the Council of Trent turned out to be a Trojan horse for an ever grander, ever more militant Church, re-armed with its most fearful weapon, the Inquisition (reinstated by Paul III), an excess soon followed by the Wars of Religion and the even more horrific Thirty Years War—the worst Europe would see until the 20th century.

The Gentle Art of Building Villas: Palladio and his Heirs

The man who would change the face of Western architecture could not have had a more unlikely background. Andrea di Pietro della Gondola was born in 1508 into a poor family in Padua, who apprenticed him to a stonecutter at age 13. Treated harshly, he ran away 18 months later, taking refuge in Vicenza, where he found a job as an assistant with a kinder family of stonecutters. And so he would have remained, chiselling away, had not Dame Fortune smiled on him in 1537 and sent him to the humanist scholar Giangiorgio Trissino, to work on the villa he was redesigning at Crioli, just outside Vicenza.

Able to see a spark in Andrea that no one else had bothered to notice, Trissino became his fairy godfather, teaching him the essentials of a Renaissance education and the principles of classical architecture, especially *De Architectura* of Vitruvius, a treatise that had been rediscovered in the 1400s. The 30-year-old stonecutter blossomed. Trissino proudly introduced him to his humanist cronies in Vicenza, Padua, and Venice. He got him his first commission as an architect, designing the Villa Godi at Lonedo di Lugo (1538). At the same time Trissino was working on an epic poem, *L'Italia liberata dai Goti* (Italy freed from the Goths), with Justinian's General Belisarius and his guardian angel Palladio (from Pallas Athena, the goddess of wisdom) as the heroes. Trissino was so pleased with both the name he invented and his protégé that he united the two forever in 1540.

To complete Palladio's education, Trissino took him on a two-year study tour of Rome (1540-1), giving him first hand knowledge not only of the ancients, but of the pioneer architects of his day—Michele Sammicheli, Giulio Romano, Giovanni Maria Falconetto, and Sebastiano Serlio. Palladio would return to Rome four times, measuring and analyzing; he even wrote a bestselling guidebook to the ruins. Yet rather than direct inspiration, ancient Rome and Vitruvius would act primarily as emotional reference in all his work, as he created idylls that reflected an antiquity that was partly real (notably in Italy, where Roman ruins were everywhere), and partly the dream antiquity that infused the Renaissance. Palladio liked to flatter his villa clients by comparing them to Pliny and Seneca, philosophising in their country retreats.

But there was far more to Palladio than Roman play-acting; more then any other architect of that talented age, he was able to invent a style that was at once imposing yet sensuous, perfect for his time and place. Venetia's patrician élite, increasingly unable to risk their fortunes in new trade ventures or Middle Eastern derring-do, now sought to escape city business in the summer, seeking a life of balance and harmony in the country, enjoying the beauties of nature while supervising their new-found interests in agriculture. While they required the structures necessary for a working farm (*barchesse*), defence was no longer a consideration, even in the open country; by the time Palladio came on the scene, Venetia had recovered from the War of the Cambrai and was at peace. He led the way in abandoning the old fortified country residence in favour of light and comfort. His famous temple-fronts and airy double loggias, derived from his mistaken notions of Roman domestic architecture, were revolutionary in the 16th century and lend the villas an openness and serenity that feel at home in the surrounding countryside.

There are over three thousand of these villas in the Veneto alone. But why are Palladio's eighteen surviving houses the most satisfying? One lesson from Vitruvius that Palladio engraved on his heart was the ideal of harmony and proportion. According to his own writings, the elements of a building must correspond to the whole and to each other, the careful consonance of parts and dimensions that was the original meaning of the word *symmetry*. Within those restrictions, what he called 'the certain truth of mathematics which is final and unchangeable', he managed a subtle variation of size and shape according to each commission, although always with the idea that no matter where one stood inside a villa, the whole would be immediately comprehensible. Rudolph Wittkower, in his *Architectural Principles in the Age of Humanism* (1949) noted that Palladio's dimensions are based on the harmonic proportions of music, as in Pythagoras' musical scale. This was no accident—in the 16th century, music and architecture were praised as the most artificial of arts, based on science alone, and free from attempts to imitate or better nature. The country villa, more than any other building, was an isolated ideal that united the artificial and natural in perfect harmony (*see* over, p.70).

Because of the innate classical grandeur of his designs, Palladio didn't need to rely as much as past architects on expensive stone, marbles, reliefs, exterior frescoes and gilding for effect; his finest villas are endowed with a serene clarity and geometric simplicity, all white surfaces and columns, set against lush green lawns and gardens. And as buildings go they were bargains; what looks like stone is cheap brick coated with a sheen of stucco-like material called *intonaco* (one imagines Palladio had seen enough stone for a lifetime in his former career). Most of the capitals crowning the brick columns are made of terracotta, while other features that look like marble are nearly always wood, coated with straw and stucco. Because the villas were only for the summer, there was no need to worry about heating them and no need for expensive tapestries to insulate the walls; frescoes were the answer, a nice family allegory perhaps, or mythological allusions to suit the owner's private fancy.

Unlike Alberti, Michelangelo, Raphael, Sansovino, Giulio Romano and the other great architects of the Renaissance, Palladio was the first who did nothing but build. He was the first professional architect. But he also found the time to pass his knowledge on. Besides his very popular guide to Rome, he illustrated Daniele Barbaro's annotated edition of Vitruvius' *De Architectura*, and then, in 1570, published his own monumental *I Quattro Libri dell' Architettura*, offering practical advice for builders, illustrated with fine woodcuts of his own buildings. *I Quattro Libri* has never gone out of print, with good (and perhaps not so good) reason: 'With the touch of pedantry that suited the times and invested his writings with a fallacious air of scholarship, he was the very man to summarize and classify, and to save future generations of architects the labour of thinking for themselves,' as Sir Reginald Blomfield wrote in his *Studies in Architecture*.

These future generations would give Palladio a curious afterlife. The first foreign president of his fan club was Inigo Jones, who came to the Veneto in 1613, toured the villas and met Palladio's collaborator, Vincenzo Scamozzi. Smitten, Jones returned to England and designed stage sets in the Italian manner, collaborating on elaborate masques with Ben Jonson. By 1615, he

---

...in all works it is requisite that their parts should correspond together, and have such proportions, that there may be none whereby the whole cannot be measured, and likewise all the other parts.

I Quattro Libri dell'Archittura
Book IV, chapter 5,

Based on Pythagoras' musical scale, and the Renaissance concept that architecture can mirror music to reveal the universal harmonic ratios inherent in nature, Palladio proposes seven sets of beautiful and harmonious proportions for rooms:

1. Circular
2. Square (1:1)
3. The diagonal of the square for the room length (1:√2)
4. A square plus a third (3:4)
5. A square plus a half (2:3)
6. A square plus two-thirds (3:5)
7. Double square (1:2)

The double square is the *diapason*, or octave, as a lyre string of a given length will produce a note one octave above the note of a string half its size. Two strings of lengths in the ratio of 2 to 3 will produce harmony, a *diapente* or musical fifth. If the ratio is 3:4, you get a different harmony, a *diatesseron*, or fourth.

The ratio of 3:5 isn't musical, but it is extremely close to the famous proportion called the Golden Section, found throughout nature and in much ancient and medieval architecture. All of these relationships are commensurable—expressible in whole numbers, and easy for an architect to work with. The non-musical, incommensurable exception, the diagonal of a square, or √2, comes straight out of Vitruvius, and is believed to hark straight back to ancient Greek theories of proportions. The Romans never used it in building, and to tell the truth Palladio didn't either.

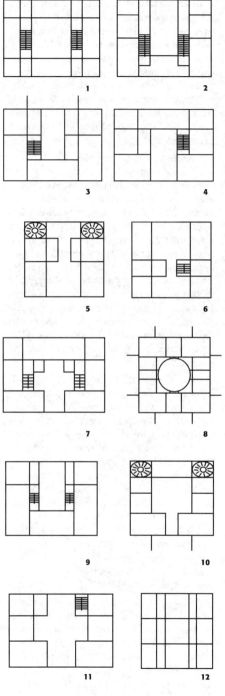

1. Villa Thiene
2. Villa Sarego
3. Villa Badoera, p.160
4. Villa Zeno
5. Villa Pisani, Montagnana
6. Villa Emo, p.164
7. Villa Pisani, Bagnolo
8. La Rotonda, p.187
9. Villa Pojana, p.192
10. Villa Cornaro, p.163
11. La Malcontenta, p.138
12. general pattern of villas

had worked his way up to the post of Surveyor of the King's Works, in effect the court architect. Even after that, he still had time for theatrical work. The very first masque he staged after gaining his royal post was called *The Golden Age Restored*, and this proved a fitting motto for what was to follow.

Jones may have brought the Renaissance in building to Britain, but he was hardly a slavish follower. His Banqueting House at Whitehall, the Queen's House at Greenwich and Covent Garden were highly original interpretations of the Palladian style. They induced a revolution in British tastes; Jones even had the effrontery to tack a Palladian façade on the old Gothic St. Paul's in London, which so embarrassed the old cathedral that it burned up along with the rest of London in 1666. After the fire, Jones's precocious Vitruvian visions were bumped aside for Christopher Wren's more genial mix of Renaissance and Continental baroque. For a whole century, British fashion would ignore Inigo Jones; even in the Veneto, Palladio's reputation took a nosedive in the 1600s, his fame entirely eclipsed by that of Scamozzi.

But in the early 18th century change was again in the air, and as John Charlton put it 'a new architectural religion was born, with Palladio as Mahomet, his *Four Books of Architecture* as the sacred text, and Inigo Jones as a major prophet. Of the new cult Lord Burlington was to be high priest and Chiswick House the temple.' After reading *Vitruvius Britannicus* by Colen Campbell (1715) and Venetian Giacomo Leoni's 'translation' of Palladio's *Four Books of Architecture* (1715), the young aristocrat-architect Burlington went to Vicenza in 1719 to study the master's works in person and to purchase every drawing by Palladio he could lay his hands on. The fresh interest by foreigners inspired a Palladian revival in Venetia itself, just when the booming economy ignited a veritable villa building spree. But while the architects of the *settecento* packed their houses with Palladian decorative elements and references, few even tried to follow the old master's recipes for harmonic proportions.

Neither did any of his foreign followers. Burlington, who loved Palladio for his re-interpretation of the ancients, was dogmatically more Palladian than Palladio (forgetting that Palladio himself often broke his own rules), and his greatest work, Chiswick House, seems cold compared to its model, La Rotonda. Burlington's strict interpretations influenced 18th-century domestic architecture in England more than Palladio himself, both through his own designs and the books he financed, especially *The Designs of Inigo Jones* by William Kent (1727).

Other influential works that followed, *Palladio Londinensis: Of the London Art of Building* by William Salmon (1738) and *The City and Country Builders and Workman's Treasury of Designs* by Batty Langley (1740), were sent to colonial America as pattern books, illustrated with Anglo-Palladian designs. There, in the more congenial climate and landscapes of Virginia and the Carolinas, Palladian architecture was to find its true home. The planters' houses and public buildings of the Old South in the 18th century are still revered as some of America's finest buildings, and Palladio's stamp is on most of them.

The northern colonies' first accomplished architect, Peter Harrison, carried the fashion up to Newport, Rhode Island, but the crowning achievement of Palladian architecture in America was to come courtesy of the copy of the *Quattro Libri* in the library of Thomas Jefferson. Jefferson once wrote to an architect friend, 'Palladio is the Bible. You should get it and stick close to it.' His three great works, the State Capitol at Richmond, his home at Monticello and the august rotunda of the University of Virginia, stand as reminders that, in architecture, America's first national style was a gift from Venice.

A Most Serene Civilization

Esto perpetua (May it last forever).

Paolo Sarpi's last words

There was nothing quite like the Serenissima, and there never will be again. The eight centuries in which the lagoon city kept her own counsel, plus the three and a half centuries when her government embraced the *terra firma* of Venetia, are marked by a way of life so distinct

and original as to be a civilization apart. It wasn't perfect, but the last two hundred years of Italian history would have been far different, and probably far happier, had Venice rather than Rome had been put in charge of the show. Of course the Italians themselves never considered any such thing; even today, in their national family, Venice is the quirky cousin born on the wrong side of the blanket who spent most of her life in exotic lands. She stands apart, proud and diffident and perhaps a little misunderstood. Modern Italians tend to find Rome far more beautiful.

Although Venetia was fragmented after the fall of Rome, and separated throughout the Middle Ages into two distinct camps, the precocious seagoing Republic and the more traditional states of the *terra firma*, there was always a close relationship between the sea Venetians and the land Venetians. They shared a common ancient history and language—Venet, the official language of the Serenissima until the Austrian occupation. And even though Venice remained aloof from mainland politics for centuries, avoiding the Ghibelline–Guelph gang rumbles that troubled the rest of the peninsula, her famous network of spies kept a close eye on potentially troublesome tyrants like Ezzelino da Romano and the Carrara of Padua. Protected by her impenetrable lagoon, Venice intervened only when it suited her interest or pleasure.

It was not exactly an attitude that won her many friends in Italy, but there wasn't much anyone could do about it, either—until the pincer-like siege by Genoa and its ally Padua cut off Venice's food supplies in the Battle of Chioggia (1379). This scared the pants off Venice, and changed her mind; holding her nose, she plunged into the murk of mainland affairs. By 1454 she had conquered (mostly by diplomacy) all of the present Veneto, Friuli, the Dolomites as far as Belluno, as well as Bergamo, Brescia and Istria. It proved to be an act of some prescience: as Venice's sway grew on the mainland, her traditional livelihood, trade in the East, was being drained away by Ottoman conquests, the opening of new markets in the Americas and, after Vasco da Gama, the opening up of alternative trade routes around the horn of Africa.

Unlike most empires, the *terra firma* cities were given the choice of whether or not they wanted to stay in or get out. Pope Julius II, who had the artistic foresight to muscle Michelangelo into painting the Sistine Chapel ceiling, was an imbecile at statecraft. Rather than support Venice as Europe's main bulwark against the Turks, he grew jealous and raised the international

League of the Cambrai against her in 1509. In face of the massive invasion, Venice released the *terra firma* from its oaths of allegiance. And as soon as the coast was clear, every last *comune* returned to St Mark's.

This hate and envy by outsiders gave the people of Venetia a strong sense of solidarity with one another—a bond strengthened by the law that compelled the mainlanders and overseas colonists to buy and sell with Venice alone. That this monopoly actually ran smoothly is testimony to the spirit of internal harmony in the Republic; outside conspirators and instigators notoriously found it difficult to latch on to a discontented citizen to work their schemes. People were happy and proud to be part of the Most Serene Republic. You can see it in the lions of St Mark that remain in place on gates and portals, columns and towers from Asiago to Ùdine. No two lions are alike; the symbol was never standardized, true to the Republic's unity in plurality. Veronese's banquet scenes are prototypes of UN cocktail parties. Even women, notoriously absent from Venetian life in the Middle Ages, increasingly distinguished themselves: Cassandra Fedele was one of Italy's first female poets, followed by Gaspara Stampa and Veronica Franco, while Elena Lucrezia Corner Piscopia became the first woman in Europe to earn a degree (a doctorate in philosophy, from Padua, in 1678).

Another source of solidarity arose from the sincere if quaint Venetian conviction that their destiny was mystical and divine. Like the Blues Brothers, they were on a mission from God. They had in Mark (never mind that they shanghaied him from Alexandria) a saint as good as Peter, not to mention all the other holy relics they swiped from Constantinople and elsewhere, in which they placed the most naïve and credulous belief. Other Italians commented in astonishment on the masses the Venetians held before going into battle; the Doge was not only a secular ruler but high priest, the Vicar of the Republic. The Venetians credited all their victories to heaven and all their defeats to the bungling of their leaders, whom more often than not they tossed in the clink. Failure was against the law.

Yet at the same time, religious fanaticism was as alien to their pragmatic nature as nationalism; throughout their history the Venetians would be condemned for doing business with Muslims. They bear the shame for having invented the Ghetto, yet Venetia was considered Europe's safest refuge for Jews. Under their spiritual leader Fra Paolo Sarpi, the Venetians hemmed and hawed over the Reformation, until many Protestants thought they would join them. The Jesuits were banned outright or strictly controlled. At the Council of Trent, it was Venetia's special ambassador who defended the rights of the Orthodox Christians in the west. Papal interference in the Republic was kept to a minimum, and the Venetians defied the Pope to keep it that way, even when he laid an Interdict on the whole Republic that lasted nearly two years (1606–1607).

For all their superstition, the Venetians didn't entirely rely on the bones of St Rocco to keep away the plague and epidemics (and they had perhaps more than their share, with 70 major outbreaks in 700 years). The Republic was famous for its hospitals—the University at Padua was the chief medical school of the Renaissance—and in times of war the Venetians astonished the world by caring not only for their own wounded, but the enemy's. In the 18th century, Venice was the first state in Europe to abolish torture.

The Venetians accumulated power and wealth with the aim of enjoying life, spending what they made on luxuries and spices and courtesans; they were besotted by music (a well-sung aria was about the only thing that could shut them up), and little bothered by intellectual debates, philosophical speculations or literature. They may have been proud that Petrarch, a Tuscan, had chosen to retire in the Euganean Hills south of Padua, but they absent-mindedly misplaced the great library he left them; they were far more interested in imitating his pioneering country villa lifestyle than reading any of his books.

But the Venetians also planned ahead for future generations in ways that shame modern democracies. Programmes such as diverting the River Brenta into canals to prevent the silting up of the lagoon took centuries to complete; special forests such as Cansiglio, deemed essential to future shipbuilding, were protected to the extent that it was death to chop down a tree. The Venetians put their considerable energy into land reclamation schemes and the draining of pestilent marshes; even in their decadent 18th century, when the State derived much of its income from gambling, they managed to find the money to build the wide quay of the Riva degli Schiavoni and the *Murazzi*, the great sea walls that shielded the lagoon from catastrophic floods, at least until 1966. Their villas were not just the pleasure domes most of them have become, but were working agricultural estates that fed the growing population of the cities. Although Columbus is a villain in Venetian eyes, they could thank him for a new crop—maize from the New World; Villa Emo, near Castelfranco, was one of the first places in Europe to sow it. Smart investments in silk and wool paid off with an economic boom in the late 17th and 18th century. Even in 1790, when the rest of the world looked at Venice as a non-stop party, it had the guts to teach the Barbary pirates a lesson, when even the English were paying them tribute.

All of this happened of course without the people having the slightest voice in politics. Yet they enjoyed more social justice than any one else in Italy, if not Europe. The mercantile oligarchy understood that the best way to maintain their exclusive grip on power and privilege was to keep the people happy and secure, and to that end, they, by their own strict laws, devoted themselves to the public good, paying heavy taxes and serving at the state's beck and call from age sixteen until the grave. Other aristocrats in Europe thought they were nuts. The Republic's biggest social problem was what to do with all the bankrupt noblemen.

As for the people, by contemporary standards they had it made. The government encouraged co-operative, independent guilds and confraternities (*scuole*): at the fall of the Republic, there were over 300 of these—either large religious charitable confraternities (the *scuole* connected to the churches), or guilds, from the arsenal workers on down to the greengrocers. These *scuole* were the backbone of society; each had its own constitution, senate and 'doge'; they regulated pay, set standards of craftsmanship, settled disputes and selected apprentices. Members paid dues to their *scuole* according to their earnings, and in return had access to the guild hospital and school, old age pensions, and the knowledge that the *scuola* would support their widows and orphans. Napoleon, busily melting the priceless treasure of St Mark's to pay his troops and stripping the Veneto of its art to beautify Paris, thought the whole system was a load of anachronistic rubbish, and he destroyed it along with everything else.

Venice

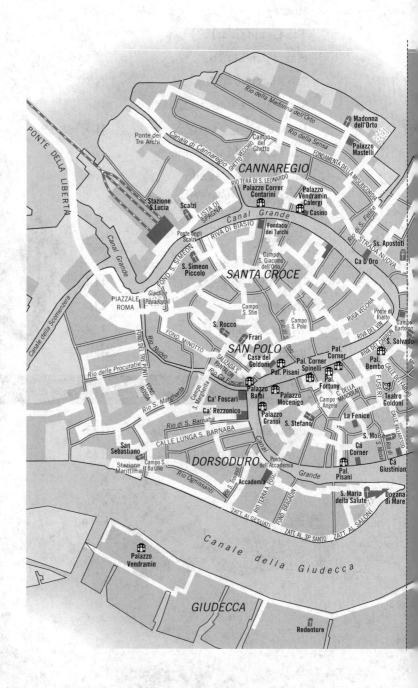

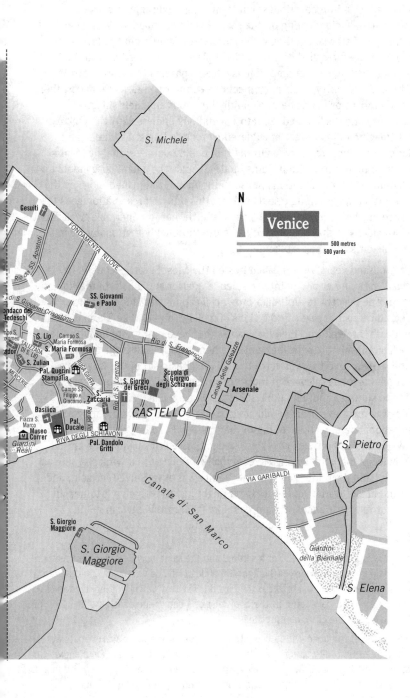

S. Michele

N

Venice

500 metres
500 yards

Gesuiti

FONDAMENTA NUOVE

Rio dei SS. Apostoli

di S Giovanni Crisostomo

SS. Giovanni
e Paolo

ndaco dei
Tedeschi

po S.
omeo
S. Lio   Campo S.
            Maria Formosa
SALIZZADA
DI S. LIO
ador
S. Maria Formosa

Rio di S. Francesco

S. Zulian

MERCERIE

Pal. Querini
Stampalia

CALLE GIUFFA

Campo SS
Filippo e
Giacomo

Rio di S. Lorenzo

S. Giorgio
dei Greci

Scuola di
S. Giorgio
degli Schiavoni

Canale delle Galeazze

Arsenale

S.
Zaccaria

CASTELLO

Basilica

Piazza S.
Marco

Museo
Correr

Pal.
Ducale

Rio del Vin

RIVA DEGLI SCHIAVONI

Giardini
Reali

RIVA DEGLI SCHIAVONI

Pal. Dandolo
Gritti

S. Pietro

VIA GARIBALDI

Canale di San Marco

S. Giorgio
Maggiore

S. Giorgio
Maggiore

Giardini
della Biennale

S. Elena

Venice seduces, Venice irritates, but Venice rarely disappoints. She is a golden fairy-tale city floating on the sea, a lovely mermaid with agate eyes and the gift of eternal youth. On the surface she is little changed from the days when Goethe called her the 'market-place of the Morning and the Evening lands', when her amphibious citizens dazzled the world with their wealth and pageantry, their magnificent fleet, their half-Oriental doges, their crafty merchant princes, their splendidly luminous art, their silken debauchery and decline and fall into a seemingly endless carnival. One can easily imagine Julius Caesar bewildered by today's Rome, or Romeo and Juliet missing their rendezvous in the traffic of modern Verona, but Marco Polo, were he to return from Cathay today, could take a familiar gondola up the familiar Grand Canal to his house in the Rialto, astonished more by the motor-boats than anything else. Credit for this unique preservation goes to the Lagoon, the amniotic fluid of Venice's birth, her impenetrable 'walls' and the formaldehyde that has pickled her more thoroughly than many far more venerable cities on the mainland.

For a thousand years Venice called herself the Most Serene Republic (*la Serenissima*), and at one point she ruled 'a quarter and a half' of the Roman Empire. The descent to an Italian provincial capital was steep and bitter-sweet; and sensitive souls find gallons of melancholy, or, like Thomas Mann, even death, brewed into the city's canals that have nothing to do with the more flagrant microbes. In the winter, when the streets are silent, Venice can be so evocative that you have to kick the ghosts out of the way to pass down the narrower alleys. But most people (some million or so a year) show up in the summer and, like their ancestors, have a jolly good time. For Venice is a most experienced old siren in her boudoir of watery mirrors. International organizations pump in the funds to keep her petticoats out of the water and smooth her wrinkles. Notices posted throughout the city acknowledge that she 'belongs to everybody', while with a wink she slides a knowing hand deep into your pocket. Venice has always lived for gold, and you can bet she wants yours—and you might just as well give it to her, in return for the most enchanting, dream-like favours any city can grant.

When to Go

Venice (Venezia) is as much a character as a setting, and the same may be said of its weather. In no other city will you be so aware of the light; on a clear, fine day no place could be more limpid and clear, no water as crystal bright as the Lagoon. The rosy dawn igniting the domes of St Mark's, the splash of an oar fading in the cool mist of a canal, the pearly twilit union of water and sky are among the city's oldest clichés.

If you seek solitude and romance with a capital R, go in **January**. Pack a warm coat, water-resistant shoes and an umbrella, and expect frequent fogs and mists. It may even snow—in 1987 you could even ski jump down the Rialto bridge. But there are also plenty of radiant diamond days, brilliant, sunny and chill; any time after October you take your chances.

As **spring** approaches there is Carnival, a game and beautiful but rather bland attempt to revive a piece of old Venice; Lent is fairly quiet, though in the undercurrent the Venetians are building up for their first major invasion of sightseers at Easter. By **April** the tourism industry is cranked up to full operational capacity; the gondolas are un-mothballed, the café tables have blossomed in the Piazza, the Casino has re-located to the Lido. In **June** even the Italians are considering a trip to the beach.

In **July** and **August** elbow-room is at a premium. Peripheral camping grounds are packed, queues at the tourist office's room-finding service stretch longer and longer, and the police are kept busy reminding the hordes that there's no picnicking in St Mark's Square. The heat can be sweltering, the ancient city gasping under a flood of cameras, shorts, sunglasses and rucksacks. Scores head off to the Lido for relief; a sudden thunderstorm over the Lagoon livens things up, as do the many festivals, especially the Redentore and its fireworks in July. In the **autumn** the city and the Venetians begin to unwind, the rains begin to fall, and you can watch them pack up the parasols and *cabanas* on the Lido with a wistful sigh.

History

Venice has always been so different, so improbable, that one can easily believe the legend that the original inhabitants sprang up from the dew and mists on the mud banks of the Lagoon. Historians who don't believe in fairies say that Venice was born of adversity: the islands and treacherous shallows of the Lagoon provided the citizens of the Veneto with a refuge from Attila the Hun and the Arian heresies sweeping the mainland. According to Venetians' own legends, the city was founded at exactly noon, 25 March 413, when the refugees laid the first stone on the Rialto. Twelve Lagoon townships grew up between modern Chioggia and Grado; when Theodoric the Great's secretary Cassiadorus visited them in 523 he wrote that they were 'scattered like sea-birds' nests over the face of the waters'.

In 697 the 12 townships united to elect their first duke, or Doge. Fishing, trading—in slaves, among other things—and their unique knowledge of the Lagoon brought the Venetians their first prosperity, but their key position in between the Byzantine empire and the 'barbarian' kings on the mainland also made them a bone of contention. In 810, the Franks, who had defeated the Lombards in the name of the Pope and claimed dominion over the whole of northern Italy, turned their attention to the last hold-out, Venice: Doge Obelario de'Antenori, engaged in a bitter internal feud with other Venetian factions, even invited Charlemagne's son Pepin to send his army into the city.

The quarrelling Venetians, until then undecided whether to support Rome or Constantinople, united at the approach of Pepin's fleet, deposed the Doge, declared for Byzantium, and entrenched themselves on the Rialto. The shallows and queer humours of the Lagoon confounded Pepin, and after a gruelling six-month siege he threw in the towel. A subsequent treaty between the Franks and the Eastern Emperor Nicephorus (814) recognized Venice as a subject of Byzantium, with important trading concessions. As Byzantine authority over the city was never more than words, it in effect marked the birth of an independent republic.

The Venetians lacked only a dynamic spiritual protector; their frumpy St Theodore with his crocodile was simply too low in the celestial hierarchy to fulfil the destiny they had in mind. In 829, Venetian merchants, supposedly on secret orders from the Doge, carried off one of the Republic's greatest coups when they purloined the body of St Mark from Alexandria, smuggling him past Egyptian customs by claiming that the saint was pickled pork. To acquire an Evangelist for themselves was, in itself, a demonstration of the Venetians' new ambition.

Marriage to the Sea

As the East–West trade expanded, the Venetians designed their domestic and external policies to accommodate it. At home they required peace and stability, and by the beginning of the 11th century had squelched all notions of an hereditary dogeship by exiling the most hyperactive families; Venice would never have the despotic *signori* who plagued the rest of Italy.

Raids by Dalmatian pirates spurred the Venetians to fight and win their first major war in 997, under Doge Pietro Orseolo, who captured the pirates' coastal strongholds. The Venetians were so pleased with themselves that they celebrated the event with a splendidly arrogant ritual every Ascension Day, the *Sensa* or 'Marriage of the Sea', in which the Doge would sail out to the Lido in his sumptuous barge, the *Bucintoro*, and cast a diamond ring into the sea, proclaiming 'We wed thee, O sea, in sign of our true and perpetual dominion'.

Venice, because of her location and fleet, supplied a great deal of the transport for the first three Crusades, and in return received her first important trading concessions in the Middle East. Arch-rival Genoa became increasingly envious, and in 1171 convinced the Byzantine Emperor to all but wipe out the Venetian merchants in Constantinople. Rashly, the Doge Vitale Michiel II set off in person to launch a revenge attack upon the Empire, and failed utterly, and on his return he was killed by an angry mob. The Venetians were always sore losers, but they learned from their mistakes: the Great Council, the *Maggior Consiglio*, was brought into being to check the power of the Doge and avert future calamities.

Vengeance stayed on the back-burner until the next Doge, the spry and crafty Enrico Dandolo, was contracted to provide transport for the Fourth Crusade. When the Crusaders turned up without their fare, Dandolo offered to forgo it in return for certain services: first, to reduce Venice's rebellious satellites in Dalmatia, and then, in 1204, to sail to Constantinople instead of Egypt. Aged 90 and almost blind, Dandolo personally led the attack; Christendom was scandalized, but Venice had gained, not only a glittering hoard of loot, but three-eighths of Constantinople and 'a quarter and a half' of the Roman Empire—enough islands and ports to control the trade routes in the Adriatic, Aegean, Asia Minor and the Black Sea.

To ensure their dominance at home, in 1297 the merchant élite limited membership in the *Maggior Consiglio* to themselves and their heirs (an event known in Venetian history as the *Serrata*, or Lock-out), their names inscribed in the famous *Golden Book*. The Doges were slowly reduced to honorary chairmen of the board, bound up by an increasingly complex web of laws and customs to curb any possible ambitions; for the patricians, fear of revolution from above was as powerful as fear of revolt from below.

A Rocky 14th Century

First the people (1300) and then the snubbed patricians (the 1310 Tiepolo Conspiracy) rose up against their disenfranchisement under the *Serrata*. Both were unsuccessful, but the latter threat was serious enough that a committee of public safety was formed to hunt down the conspirators, and in 1335 this committee became a permanent institution, the infamous Council of Ten. Because of its secrecy and speedy decisions, the Council of Ten (in later years it was streamlined into a Council of Three) was more truly executive than the figurehead

Doge: it guarded Venice's internal security, looked after foreign policy and, with its sumptuary laws, kept tabs on the Venetians' moral conduct as well.

Away from home the 14th century was marked by a fight to the death with Genoa over eastern trade routes. Each republic annihilated the other's fleet on more than one occasion before things came to a head in 1379, when the Genoese, fresh from a victory over the Venetian commander Vittor Pisani, captured Chioggia and waited for Venice to starve, boasting that they had come to 'bridle the horses of St Mark'. As was their custom, the Council of Ten had imprisoned Pisani for his defeat, but Venice was now in such a jam, with half of its fleet far away, that the people demanded his release to lead what remained of their navy. A brilliant commander, Pisani exploited his familiarity with the Lagoon and in turn blockaded the Genoese in Chioggia. When the other half of Venice's fleet came dramatically racing home, the Genoese surrendered (June 1380) and never recovered in the East.

Fresh Prey on the Mainland

Venice was determined never to feel hungry again, and set her sights on the mainland—not only for the sake of farmland, but to control her trade routes into the west that were being increasingly harried and taxed by the *signori* of the Veneto. Treviso came first, then opportunity knocked in 1402 with the sudden death of the Milanese duke Gian Galeazzo Visconti, whose conquests became the subject of a great land grab. Venice picked up Padua, Bassano, Verona and Belluno, and in 1454 added Ravenna, southern Trentino, Friuli, Crema and Bergamo. In 1489 the republic's overseas empire reached its greatest extent when it was presented with Cyprus, a somewhat reluctant 'gift' from the king's widow, a Venetian noblewoman named Caterina Cornaro who received the hilltown of Àsolo as compensation.

But just as Venice expanded, Fortune's wheel gave a creak and conspired to squeeze her back into her Lagoon. The Ottoman Turks captured Constantinople in 1453, and although the Venetians tried to negotiate trading terms with the sultans (as they had previously done with the infidel Saracens, to the opprobrium of the West), they would be spending the next three centuries fighting a losing battle for their eastern territories. The discovery of the New World was another blow, but gravest to the merchants of Venice was Vasco da Gama's voyage around the Cape of Good Hope to India in 1497, blazing a cheaper and easier route to Venice's prime markets that broke her monopoly of oriental luxuries; Western European merchants no longer had to pay Venice for safe passage to the East. In just 44 years nearly everything that Venice had worked for over 500 years was undermined.

On the mainland, Venice's rapid expansion had excited the fear and envy of Pope Julius, who rallied Italy's potentates and their foreign allies to form the League of Cambrai to humble the proud republic. They snatched her *terra firma* possessions after her defeat at Agnadello in 1509, but quarrelled amongst themselves afterwards, and before long all the territories they conquered voluntarily returned to Venice. Venice, however, never really recovered from this wound inflicted by the very people who should have rallied to her defence, and although her Arsenal produced a warship a day, and her captains helped to win a glorious victory over the Turks at Lepanto (1571), she was increasingly forced to retreat.

A Most Leisurely Collapse

The odds were stacked against her, but in her heyday Venice had accumulated enough wealth and verve to cushion her fall. Her noble families consoled themselves in the classical calm of

Palladio's villas, while the city found solace in masterpieces of Venice's golden age of art. Carnival, ever longer, ever more licentious, was sanctioned by the state to bring in moneyed visitors, like Lord Byron, who dubbed it 'the revel of the earth, the masque of Italy'. In the 1600s the city had 20,000 courtesans, many of them dressed as men to whet the Venetians' passion. It didn't suit everyone: 'Venice is a stink pot, charged with every virus of hell,' fumed one Dr Warner, in the 18th century.

In 1797, Napoleon, declaring he would be 'an Attila for the Venetian state', took it with scarcely a whimper, ending the story of the world's longest-enduring republic, in the reign of its 120th doge. Napoleon took the horses of St Mark to Paris as his trophy, and replaced the old *Pax tibi, Marce, Evangelista Meus* inscribed in the book the lion holds up on Venice's coat-of-arms with 'The Rights of Men and Citizens'. Reading it, a gondolier made the famous remark, 'At last he's turned the page'. Yet while many patricians danced merrily around his Liberty trees, freed at last from responsiblity, the people wept.

Napoleon gave Venice to Austria, whose rule was confirmed by the Congress of Vienna after the Emperor's defeat in 1815. The Austrians' main contribution was the railway causeway linking Venice irrevocably to the mainland (l846). Two years later, Venice gave its last gasp of independence, when a patriotic revolt led by Daniele Manin seized the city and re-established the republic, only to fall to the Austrian army once again after a heroic one-year siege.

Modern Venice

The former republic did, however, finally join the new kingdom of Italy in 1866, after Prussia had conveniently defeated the Austrians. Already better known as a magnet to visitors than for any activity of its own, Venice played a quiet role in the new state. Things changed under Mussolini, the industrial zones of Mestre and Marghera were begun on the mainland, and a road was added to the railway causeway. The city escaped damage in the two World Wars, despite heavy fighting in the environs; according to legend, when the Allies finally occupied Venice in 1945 they arrived in a fleet of gondolas.

But Venice was soon to engage in its own private battle with the sea. From the beginning the city had manipulated nature's waterways for her own survival, diverting a major outlet of the Po, the Brenta, the Piave, the Adige, and the Sile rivers to keep her Lagoon from silting up. In 1782, Venice completed the famous *murazzi*, the 4km-long, 20ft-high sea walls to protect the Lagoon. But on 4 November 1966 a deadly combination of wind, torrential storms, high tides and giant waves breached the *murazzi*, wrecked the Lido and left Venice under record *acque alte* (high waters) for 20 hours, with disastrous results to the city's architecture and art. The catastrophe galvanized the international community's efforts to save Venice. Even the Italian state, notorious for its indifference to Venice (historical grudges die slowly in Italy) passed a law in 1973 to preserve the city, and contributed to the construction of a new flood barricade similar to the one on the Thames.

This giant sea gate, known as 'Moses', has now been completed, but arguments continue over whether it will ever be effective if needed, and what its ecological consequences might be. Venice today is perennially in crisis, permanently under restoration, and seemingly threatened by a myriad potential disasters—the growth of algae in the Lagoon, the effects of the outpourings of Mestre on its foundations, the ageing of its native population, or perhaps most of all the sheer number of its tourists. Fears of an environmental catastrophe have, though, receded of late; somehow, the city contrives to survive, as unique as ever, and recent proposals to give it more of a function in the modern world, as, for example, a base for international organizations, may serve to give it new life as well.

The Face of Venice

Venice stands on 117 islets, divided by over 100 canals that are spanned by some 400 bridges. The longest bridges are the 4.2km rail and road causeways that link Venice to the mainland. The open sea is half that distance across the Lagoon, beyond the protective reefs or *lidi* formed by centuries of river silt and the Adriatic current. The Grand Canal, Venice's incomparable main street, was originally the bed of a river that fed the Lagoon; the other canals, its tributaries (called *rio*, singular, or *rii*, plural), were shallow channels meandering through the mud banks, and are nowhere as grand—some are merely glorified sewers.

A warren of 2300 alleys, or *calli*, handle Venice's pedestrian-only traffic, and they come with a colourful bouquet of names—a *rio terrà* is a filled-in canal; a *piscina* a filled-in pool; a *fondamenta* or *riva* a quay; a *salizzada* is a street that was paved in the 17th century; a *ruga* is one lined with shops; a *sottoportico* passes under a building. A Venetian square is a *campo*, recalling the days when they were open fields; the only square dignified with the title of 'piazza' is that of St Mark's, though the two smaller squares flanking the basilica are called *piazzette*, and there's one fume-filled *piazzale*, the dead end for buses and cars.

All the *rii* and *calli* have been divided into six quarters, or *sestieri*, since Venice's earliest days: **San Marco** (by the piazza), **Castello** (by the Arsenal) and **Cannaregio** (by the Ghetto), all on the northeast bank of the Grand Canal; and **San Polo** (by the church), **Santa Croce** (near the Piazzale Roma), and **Dorsoduro**, the 'hard-back' by the Accademia, all on the southwest bank. Besides these, the modern *comune* of Venice includes the towns on the Lagoon islands, the Lido, and the mainland *comuni* of Mestre and Marghera, Italy's version of the New Jersey Flats, where most Venetians live today. There is some concern that historic Venice (population around 79,000, down from 200,000 in its heyday) may soon become a city of second homes belonging to wealthy northern Italians and foreigners.

Signs, Directions, Piles and Hair

The Venetian language, Venetic or Venet, is still commonly heard—to the uninitiated it sounds like an Italian trying to speak Spanish with a numb mouth—and it turns up on the city's street signs. Your map may read 'San Giovanni e Paolo' but you should inquire for 'San Zanipolo'; 'San Giovanni Decollato' (decapitated John) is better known as 'San Zan Degola'. Still, despite the impossibility of giving comprehensible directions through the tangle of alleys (Venetians will invariably point you in the right direction, however, with a blithe *'sempre diritto!'*— 'straight ahead!'), it's hard to get hopelessly lost in Venice. It only measures about 1.5 by 3 kilometres, and there are helpful yellow signs at major crossings, pointing the way to San Marco, Rialto and the Accademia, or the Piazzale Roma and the Ferrovia if you despair and want to go home. When hunting for an address in Venice, make sure you're in the correct *sestiere*, as quite a few *calli* share names. Also, beware that houses in each *sestiere* are numbered consecutively in a system logical only to a postman from Mars; numbers up to 5000 are not unusual.

To support their houses the soft mud banks, the Venetians drove piles of Istrian pine 18ft into the solid clay—over a million posts hold up the church of Santa Maria della Salute alone. If Venice tends to lean and sink, it's due to erosion of these piles by the salty Adriatic, pollution, and the currents and wash caused by the deep channels dredged into the Lagoon for the large tankers sailing to Marghera. Or, as the Venetians explain, the city is a giant sponge.

Most Venetian houses are between four and six storeys high; some of the grander palazzi have gondola garages below. Others have wooden rooftop loggias, or *altane*, where the Renaissance ladies of Venice were wont to idle, bleaching their hair in the sun; they wore broad-brimmed hats to protect their complexions, and spread their tresses through a hole cut in the crown.

Getting There

by air

Venice's **Marco Polo Airport** is 13km north of the city near the Lagoon, and has regularly scheduled connections from London, New York (via Milan), Paris, Vienna, Nice, Zürich, Frankfurt, Düsseldorf, Rome, Milan, Palermo, and Naples. For flight information in Venice, ℰ 041 260 9260.

The airport is linked with Venice by water-taxi (ℰ 041 966 870 or ℰ 041 523 5775), the most expensive option (L140,000); or by *motoscafi* to San Marco (Zecca) roughly every hour (L17,000 per person), connecting with most flights from March to October, and if you're catching an early flight, you can reserve a departure (ℰ 041 541 5058). There is also an ATVO bus to the Piazzale Roma (L7000) or, cheapest of all, the ACTV city bus no.5 (L1500), which passes by twice an hour.

Some **charter flights** arrive at Treviso, 30km to the north. If a transfer is not included with your ticket, catch bus no.6 into Treviso, from where there are frequent trains and buses to Venice.

by sea

Adriatica lines (Zattere 1412, ℰ 041 520 4322 or ℰ 041 522 8018), has connections every 10 days June–Sept with Split (15 hours) and Dubrovnik (24 hours). There are also daily car-ferries between Venice, Corfu and Patras, Greece (2 days), and Alexandria (3½ days). An easier way to approach Venice on water is by taking the *Burchiello* from Padua along the Brenta Canal (*see* p.138).

by train

Venice's **Stazione Santa Lucia** (the **Ferrovia**) is the terminus of the *Venice Simplon-Orient Express* and less glamorous trains from the rest of Europe and Italy. All trains from Santa Lucia stop in Mestre, where you may have to change for some destinations. For rail information, ℰ 1478 88088.

Water-taxis, *vaporetti* and gondolas (*see* below) wait in front of the station to sweep you off into the city. If you've brought more luggage than you can carry, one of Venice's infamous porters (distinguished by their badges) will lug it to your choice of transport and, if you pay his fare on the water-taxi, will take it and you to your hotel (official price for one or two pieces of luggage is L30,000 between any two points in the historic centre, extra bags are L10,000). Sometimes you can track down a porter once you disembark at one of the main landings or the Lido. Since rates for baggage-handling are unregulated everywhere other than at the station, be sure to negotiate a price in advance.

by car

All roads to Venice end at the monstrous municipal parking towers in **Piazzale Roma** or its cheaper annexe, **Tronchetto**, © 041 520 7555, nothing less than the largest car park in Europe. You can leave your car there for L25,000 a day, or less for longer stays. In the summer, at Easter and Carnival, when the causeway turns into a solid conga-line of cars waiting to park, consider the Italian Auto Club's three alternative car parks (open to non-members): **Fusina**, © 041 547 0055, with a shady, year-round campsite, located at the mouth of the Brenta Canal south of Marghera (car park open summer only; *vaporetto* no.16 to Venice); **S. Giuliano**, in Mestre near the causeway (bus service to Venice), and **Punta Sabbioni**, © 041 530 0455, in between the Lido and Jesolo (ferry no.17 from Tronchetto).

Getting Around

vaporetti and motoscafi

Public transport in Venice means by water, by the grunting, canal-cutting **vaporetti** (the all-purpose water-buses), or the sleeker, faster *motoscafi*, run by the ACTV (© 041 528 7886). Note that the only canals served by public transport are the Grand Canal, the Rio Nuovo, the Canale di Cannaregio and the Rio dell'Arsenale; between them, you'll have to rely on your feet, which is not as gruelling as it sounds, as Venice is so small you can walk across it in an hour.

Single **tickets** (a flat rate of L6000) should be purchased and validated in the machines at the landing-stages (random inspections aren't very frequent, but if you get caught without a validated ticket you'll have to pay a L30,000 fine on the spot). As some landing stages don't sell tickets, it's best to stock up (most *tabacchi* sell them in blocks of ten). Or, if you intend being on a boat at least three times in a given day, purchase a **24-hour tourist pass**, for L18,000, valid for unlimited travel on all lines, or the **3-day pass**, for L35,000. If you plan to spend more than a few days in Venice, the cheapest option is to buy a *tesserino di abbonamento* from the ACTV office at Piazzale Roma (L10,000) and a passport photo—there's a machine at the Ferrovia) which is valid for three years and entitles you to buy monthly season tickets (L45,000) or single tickets at greatly reduced rates.

Lines of most interest to visitors are listed on p.88; most run until midnight. Precise schedules are listed in the tourist office's free monthly guide, *Un Ospite di Venezia*.

At San Marco you can also find a number of **excursion boats** to various points in the Lagoon; they are more expensive than public transport, but may be useful if you're pressed for time.

Venice Transport

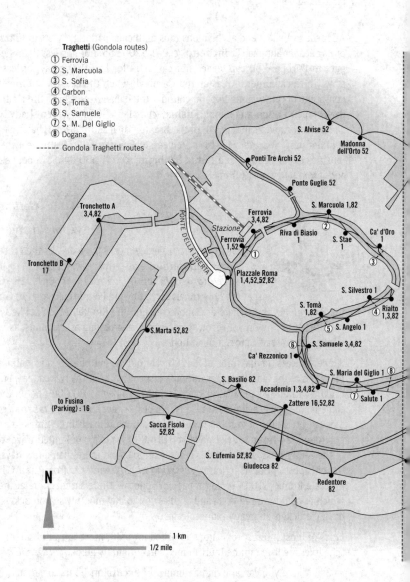

Traghetti (Gondola routes)
① Ferrovia
② S. Marcuola
③ S. Sofia
④ Carbon
⑤ S. Tomà
⑥ S. Samuele
⑦ S. M. Del Giglio
⑧ Dogana
------ Gondola Traghetti routes

S. Alvise 52

Madonna dell'Orto 52

Ponti Tre Archi 52

Ponte Guglie 52

S. Marcuola 1,82

Tronchetto A
3,4,82

Ferrovia
3,4,82

Stazione

Ferrovia
1,52
①

Riva di Biasio
1

②

S. Stae
1

Ca' d'Oro
1

③

Tronchetto B
17

Plazzale Roma
1,4,52,52,82

S. Silvestro 1

S.Marta 52,82

S. Tomà
1,82

④ Rialto
1,3,82

⑤ S. Angelo 1

⑥ S. Samuele 3,4,82

Ca' Rezzonico 1

S. Maria del Giglio 1 ⑧

S. Basilio 82

Accademia 1,3,4,82

⑦ Salute 1

to Fusina
(Parking) : 16

Zattere 16,52,82

Sacca Fisola
52,82

S. Eufemia 52,82

Giudecca 82

Redentore
82

N

1 km

1/2 mile

86

Regular Lines

1: *(accelerato)* Piazzale Roma–Ferrovia–Grand Canal–San Marco–Lido: stops every where; around the clock, every 10min (20mins after 9pm). The entire one-way journey takes an hour.

6: *(diretto motonave)* S. Zaccaria–Lido; every 20mins.

11: (the 'mixed' line) Lido–Alberoni (by bus)–Pellestrina (by boat)–Chioggia (by boat); about once an hour. (Not shown.)

12: Fondamente Nuove–Murano–Torcello–Burano–Treporti; about once an hour.

13: Fondamente Nuove–Murano–Vignole–S. Erasmo; about once an hour.

14: S. Zaccaria–Lido–Punta Sabbioni–Treporti–Burano–Torcello (every half-hour).

17: (car ferry) Tronchetto (Piazzale Roma)–Giudecca–Lido–Punta Sabbione; every 50mins.

52: (red 'barred') *(motoscafo)* Piazzale Roma–Giudecca–S. Zaccaria–Campo della Tana (the Arsenale)–Fondamente Nuove–Murano (all six stops)–S. Michele; every 20mins.

52: (green) *(motoscafo)* Lido–S. Zaccaria–Zattere–Piazzale Roma–Ferrovia–Fondamente Nuove–Murano; every 20mins.

82: (orange) *(diretto)* S. Zaccaria (S. Marco)–Lido–Giudecca–S. Giorgio Maggiore; a speedy circular tour; every 10min during the day, approx. once an hour at night.

82: (green) *(diretto)* S. Zaccaria–S. Giorgio Maggiore–Giudecca–Zattere–S. Marta; every 10mins.

N: *(servizio notturno)* Lido–S. Zaccaria–Accademia–S. Toma–Rialto–Piazzale Roma–Zattere–Zitelle–S. Giorgio Maggiore; every 20mins from about 11pm all night.

Summer only

3: Tronchetto–Grand Canal–S. Zaccaria–Tronchetto

4: S. Zaccaria–Grand Canal–Tronchetto–S. Zaccaria

16: (private service *L8000*) Zattere–Fusina car park; every 50mins.

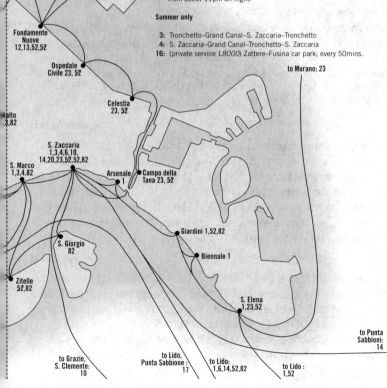

to Murano: 12,13,
to Mazzorbo, Burano,
Murano,Burano,Torcello: 12
to Vignole, S. Erasmo,
Treporti: 13

S. Michele
(Cimitero)
23, 52, 52̶

Fondamente
Nuove
12,13,52,52̶

Ospedale
Civile 23, 52̶

Celestia
23, 52̶

Rialto
3,82

to Murano: 23

S. Zaccaria
1,3,4,6,10,
14,20,23,52,52̶,82

S. Marco
1,3,4,82

Arsenale
1

Campo della
Tana 23, 52̶

Giardini 1,52̶,82

S. Giorgio
82

Biennale 1

Zitelle
52̶,82

S. Elena
1,23,52̶

to Punta
Sabbioni:
14

to Grazie,
S. Clemente:
10

to Lido,
Punta Sabbione :
17

to Lido:
1,6,14,52̶,82

to Lido :
1,52̶

Line 1	(*accelerato*, the Italian euphemism for slow-coach) runs in an hour from Piazzale Roma and the Ferrovia down the Grand Canal to San Marco and the Lido, and vice versa, stopping everywhere; every 10min (every 20mins after 9pm).
Line 82	(orange) (*diretto*) does a speedier circular tour from S. Zaccaria (S. Marco), including the extension to the Lido, the Giudecca and S. Giorgio Maggiore. Every 10mins during the day, approximately once an hour at night.
Line 82	(green) (*diretto*) has a smaller itinerary, beginning and ending at S. Zaccaria with stops at S. Giorgio Maggiore, all along the Giudecca, Zattere and S. Marta. Every 10mins.
Line 52	(red 'barred') a *motoscafo* linking various major landmarks (Piazzale Roma, Giudecca, S. Zaccaria, Campo della Tana and Fondamente Nuove) with the islands of Murano (all six stops) and S. Michele. Every 20mins.
Line 52	(green) a *motoscafo* between the Lido and all stops to S. Zaccaria, Zattere, Piazzale Roma, Ferrovia, Fondamente Nuove and Murano. Every 20mins.
Line 6	(*diretto motonave*) is the large steamer from S. Zaccaria to the Lido (every 20mins).
Line 11	(the 'mixed' line) begins at the Lido on a bus to Alberoni, from where you catch a boat for Pellestrina, then another for Chioggia, or vice versa (about once an hour, sometimes more).
Line 12	Fondamente Nuove to Murano, Burano, Torcello and Treporti (about once an hour).
Line 13	Fondamente Nuove to Murano, Vignole and S. Erasmo (about once an hour).
Line 14	S. Zaccaria to the Lido and Punta Sabbioni (every half-hour).
Line 16	(L8000) a private service, Zattere to the Fusina car park (summer only, every 50mins).
Line 17	car ferry from Tronchetto (Piazzale Roma) throught the Giudecca to the Lido and Punto Sabbione (every 50mins).
Line N	(*servizio notturno*) runs all night (every 20mins from about 11pm) doing a sweep which includes the Lido, S. Zaccaria, Accademia, S. Toma, Rialto, Piazzale Roma, Zattere, Zitelle and S. Giorgio Maggiore.

water-taxis

These are really more tourist excursion boats—they work like taxis, but their fares are de luxe. Stands are at the station, Piazzale Roma, Rialto, San Marco, Lido and the airport. These jaunty motor boats can hold up to 15 passengers, and fares are set for destinations beyond the historic centre, or you can pay L150,000 per hour. Within the centre the minimum fare for up to four people is L50,000; additional passengers are up to L10,000 each, and there are surcharges for baggage, holiday or nocturnal service (after 10pm), and for using a radio taxi (© 041 522 2303 or 041 240 6711).

gondolas

Gondolas, first mentioned in the city's annals in 1094, have a stately mystique that commands all other boats to give way. Shelley and many others have compared them to a funeral barque or the soul ferry to Hades, and not a few gondoliers share the infernal Charon's expectation of a solid gold tip for their services. Like Model Ts, gondolas come in any colour as long as it's black, still obeying the Sumptuary Law of 1562, though nowadays hardly any gondolas have cabins for clandestine trysts.

Once used by all and sundry, gondolas now operate frankly for tourists (and weddings). Official prices are L120,000 for a 50-minute ride (L150,000 after 8pm). Before setting out, agree with the gondolier on where you want to go and how long you expect it to take to avoid any unpleasantness later on.

In addition, gondolas retired from the tourist trade are used for **gondola traghetti** services across the Grand Canal at various points between its three bridges—your only chance to enjoy an economical, if brief, gondola ride for L700. *Traghetto* crossings are signposted in the streets nearby. For appearance's sake you'll have to stand up: only sissies ever sit down on *traghetti.*

hiring a boat

Perhaps the best way to spend a day in Venice is by bringing or hiring your own boat—a small motor boat or a rowing boat—though beware of the Venetian type of oar, which requires practice to use. It can be difficult to find a boat for hire, but ask in the Piazza San Marco tourist office for suggestions. *Motoscafi* for hire are easier to find, especially with chauffeurs: try Cooperativa San Marco, S. Marco 4267, ℂ 041 523 5775; Narduzzi & Solemar, S. Marco 2828, ℂ 041 716 000; or Serenissima Motoscafi, Castello 4545, ℂ 041 522 4281.

by bus

Piazzale Roma is Venice's bus terminus; there are frequent city buses from here to Mestre, Chioggia, Marghera and Malcontenta; regional buses every half-hour to Padua, and less frequently to other Veneto cities and Trieste. It has its own helpful tourist information office, ℂ 041 528 7886.

car hire

If you want to explore the mainland by car, several hire firms have offices at Piazzale Roma, the airports, or Mestre station: **Avis** (Marco Polo Airport) ℂ 041 541 5030; **Europcar** (Piazzale Roma) ℂ 041 523 8616, (Treviso Airport) ℂ 0422 23396; **Maggiore** (Marco Polo) ℂ 041 541 5040, (Mestre) ℂ 041 935 300.

Tourist Information

The main information office is in one corner of Piazza San Marco, to the far left as you face the square from the basilica (Ascensione 71/c, ℂ 041 522 6356). Branch offices at Palazzetto Selva, right by the S. Marco *vaporetto* stop (ℂ 041 529 8730), the railway station (ℂ 041 529 8727) and the bus station in Piazzale Roma (ℂ 041 522 7402) offer accommodation services. There are also offices on the Rotonda Marghera (ℂ 041 937 764), Marco Polo Airport (ℂ 041 541 5887) and on the Lido at Gran Viale 6 (ℂ 041 526 5721).

The main source in English on any current events is the fortnightly magazine *Un Ospite di Venezia,* distributed free at tourist offices. Otherwise, the two local papers *Il Gazzettino* and *Nuova Venezia* both have listings of films, concerts and so on in Venice and the *terra firma.* Another detailed source of information is the monthly city magazine *Marco Polo,* with articles written in Italian but summarized in English.

For L5000, people between the ages of 14 and 29 can buy a *Rolling Venice* card, which gives discounts on the city's attractions, from films at the Film Festival to museums, hostels, shops and restaurants (and access to the university canteen in Palazzo Badoer, Calle del Magazen 2840). It also allows you to buy a special reduced-price ticket for travelling on the *vaporetti.* Apply at one of these three associations: the Assessorato alla Gioventù, Corte Contarina 1529, San Marco, ℂ 041 274 7650/1 (*Mon–Fri 9.30–1, Tues and Thurs also 3–5*); Agenzia Arte e Storia, Corte Canal 659,

Santa Croce, ℂ 041 524 0232 (*Mon–Fri 9–1 and 3.30–7*); or Associazone Italiana Alberghi per la Gioventu, Calle del Castelforte 3101, San Polo, ℂ 041 520 4414 (*Mon–Sat 8–2*). Take a photo and your passport.

Practical A–Z

If you lose something in the city, try the Municipio, ℂ 041 274 8111; or if you lost it on a train, ℂ 041 785 238; or on a *vaporetto*, ℂ 041 780 310.

Ambulance, ℂ 041 523 000.

If you have an accident or become seriously ill, go to the *Pronto Soccorso* department of the **city hospital** in Campo Santi Giovanni e Paolo, Castello, or the **Ospedale del Mare**, 1 Lungomare d'Annunzio, Lido (ℂ 041 529 4111); if you need a doctor at night or on holidays ring the *Guardia Medica*, ℂ 041 529 4060.

Several *farmacie* are open all night on a rotating basis: the addresses are in the window of each, or you can ring ℂ 041 523 0573 for a list.

Places that exchange money outside normal banking hours include:

American Express: S. Moisè 1471, ℂ 041 520 0844, open April–Oct Mon–Sat 8–8; **CIT**: Piazza S. Marco 4850, ℂ 041 528 5480, open Mon–Sat 8–6; **INTRAS**: Piazza S. Marco, at the corner of the Procuratie Nuove and clock tower, open Mon–Sat 8.30–6; **World Vision**: (Thomas Cook), Calle delle Ostreghe 2457, S. Marco.

The **main post office** is in the Fóndaco dei Tedeschi, near the Ponte Rialto (open Mon–Sat 8.15–7.25). There are also smaller offices at the foot of Piazza San Marco (Calle dell'Ascensione) and at the western end of the Zattere, although you can buy stamps at any tobacco shop.

The Grand Canal

A ride down Venice's bustling and splendid main artery is most visitors' introduction to the city, and there's no finer one. The Grand Canal has always been Venice's status address, and along its looping banks the patricians of the Golden Book, or *Nobili Homini*, as they called themselves, built a hundred marble palaces with their front doors giving on to the water, framed by peppermint-stick posts where they moored their watery carriages.

The highlights, from Piazzale Roma to Piazza San Marco, include: the 12th-century **Fóndaco dei Turchi** (with rounded arches, on the right after the Station Bridge), the Ottoman merchants' headquarters until 1838, and now the Natural History Museum. Nearly opposite, Mauro Codussi's Renaissance **Palazzo Vendramin-Calergi**, where Richard Wagner died in 1883, is now the winter home of the casino. Back on the right bank, just after the San Stae landing, the Baroque **Palazzo Pésaro** is adorned with masks by Longhena. And then comes the loveliest palace of all, the **Ca' d'Oro**, with an florid Venetian Gothic facade, formerly etched in gold, now housing the Galleria Franchetti (*see* p.112).

After the Ca' d'Oro Europe's most famous bridge, the **Ponte di Rialto**, swings into view. 'Rialto' recalls the days when the canal was the Rio Alto; originally it was spanned here by a bridge of boats, then by a 13th-century wooden bridge. When that was on the verge of collapse, the republic held a competition for the design of a new stone structure. The winner, Antonio da Ponte, was the most audacious, proposing a single arch spanning 157ft; built in

1592, it has defied all the dire predictions of the day and still stands, even taking the additional weight of two rows of shops. The reliefs over the arch are of St Mark and St Theodore.

To the right stretch the extensive **Rialto Markets**, and on the left the **Fóndaco dei Tedeschi** (German Warehouse), once the busiest trading centre in Venice, where merchants from all over the north lived and traded. The building (now the post office) was remodelled in 1505 and adorned with exterior frescoes by Giorgione and Titian, of which only fragments survive (now in the Ca' d'Oro).

Beyond the Ponte di Rialto are two Renaissance masterpieces: across from the S. Silvestro landing, Sanmicheli's 1556 **Palazzo Grimani**, now the Appeals Court, and Mauro Codussi's **Palazzo Corner-Spinelli** (1510) just before Sant'Angelo landing stage. A short distance further along the left bank are the **Palazzi Mocenigo**, actually three palaces in one, where Byron lived for two years. A little way further on the same side, the wall of buildings gives way for the Campo San Samuele, dominated by the **Palazzo Grassi**, an 18th-century neoclassical residence, renovated by Fiat as a modern exhibition and cultural centre.

On the right bank, just after the bend in the canal, the lovely Gothic **Ca' Foscari** was built in 1437 for Doge Francesco Foscari: two doors down, by its own landing-stage, is Longhena's 1667 **Ca' Rezzonico**, where Browning died. Further on the canal is spanned by the wooden **Ponte dell'Accademia**, built in 1932 to replace the ungainly iron 'English bridge'.

On the left bank, before S. Maria del Giglio landing, the majestic Renaissance **Palazzo Corner** (Ca' Grande) was built by Sansovino in 1550. On the right bank, Longhena's Baroque master-piece **Santa Maria della Salute** is followed by the Customs House, or **Dogana di Mare**, crowned by a golden globe and weathervane of Fortune, guard the entrance to the Grand Canal. The next landing-stage is San Marco.

Byron Goes Swimming

Byron arrived in Venice in 1816, his heart full of romance as he rented a villa on the Brenta to compose the last canto of his *Childe Harolde's Pilgrimage*. The city's canals at least afforded him the personal advantage of being able to swim anywhere (his club foot made him shy of walking); on one occasion he swam a race from the Lido to the Rialto bridge and was the only man to finish.

It wasn't long before the emotional polish of *Childe Harolde* began to crack. To Byron's surprise, Venice didn't perfect his romantic temper, but cured him of it. He went to live in the Palazzo Mocenigo on the Grand Canal, in the company of 14 servants, a dog, a wolf, a fox, monkeys and a garlicky baker's wife, *La Fornarina*, who stabbed him in the hand with a fork—which so angered Byron that he ordered her out, whereupon she threw herself into the Grand Canal. Under such circumstances, all that had been breathless passion reeked of the ridiculous, as he himself admitted:

> *And the sad truth which hovers o'er my desk*
> *Turns what was once romantic to burlesque*

Venice, its women, its own ironic detachment and its love of liberty set Byron's mind free to write *Beppo: A Venetian Story*, spoofing Venice's *cavalieri serventi* (escort-

The Grand Canal

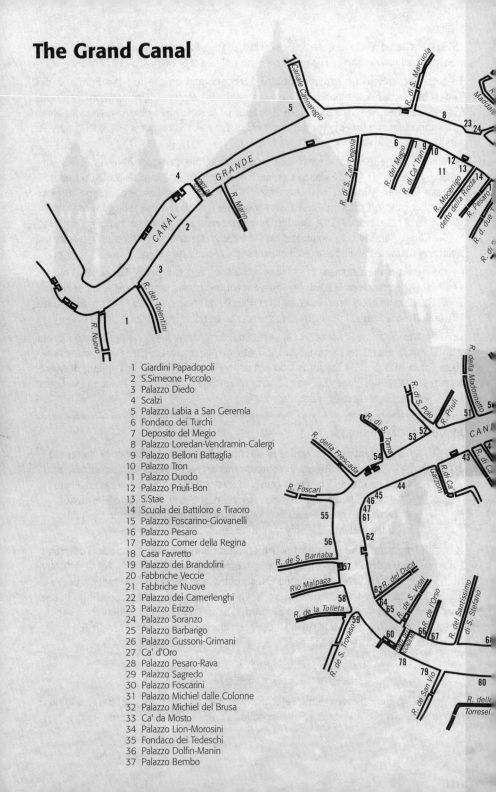

1 Giardini Papadopoli
2 S.Simeone Piccolo
3 Palazzo Diedo
4 Scalzi
5 Palazzo Labia a San Geremía
6 Fondaco dei Turchi
7 Deposito del Megio
8 Palazzo Loredan-Vendramin-Calergi
9 Palazzo Belloni Battaglia
10 Palazzo Tron
11 Palazzo Duodo
12 Palazzo Priuli-Bon
13 S.Stae
14 Scuola dei Battiloro e Tiraoro
15 Palazzo Foscarino-Giovanelli
16 Palazzo Pesaro
17 Palazzo Corner della Regina
18 Casa Favretto
19 Palazzo dei Brandolini
20 Fabbriche Veccie
21 Fabbriche Nuove
22 Palazzo dei Camerlenghi
23 Palazzo Erizzo
24 Palazzo Soranzo
25 Palazzo Barbarigo
26 Palazzo Gussoni-Grimani
27 Ca' d'Oro
28 Palazzo Pesaro-Rava
29 Palazzo Sagredo
30 Palazzo Foscarini
31 Palazzo Michiel dalle Colonne
32 Palazzo Michiel del Brusa
33 Ca' da Mosto
34 Palazzo Lion-Morosini
35 Fondaco dei Tedeschi
36 Palazzo Dolfin-Manin
37 Palazzo Bembo

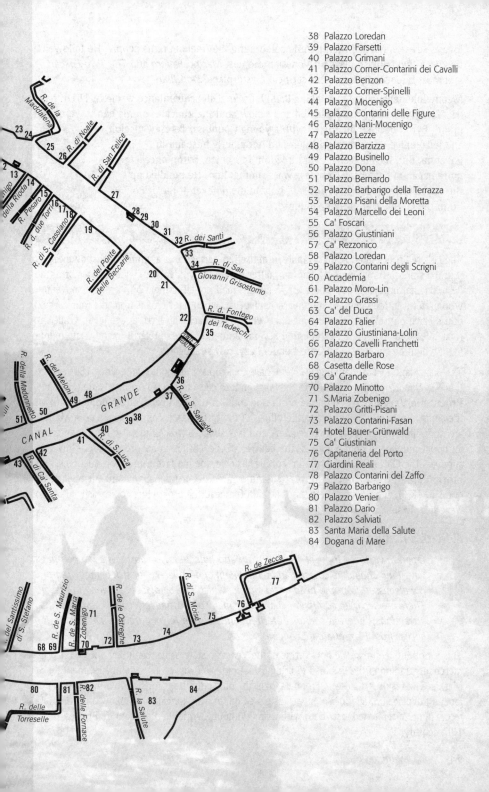

38 Palazzo Loredan
39 Palazzo Farsetti
40 Palazzo Grimani
41 Palazzo Corner-Contarini dei Cavalli
42 Palazzo Benzon
43 Palazzo Corner-Spinelli
44 Palazzo Mocenigo
45 Palazzo Contarini delle Figure
46 Palazzo Nani-Mocenigo
47 Palazzo Lezze
48 Palazzo Barzizza
49 Palazzo Businello
50 Palazzo Dona
51 Palazzo Bernardo
52 Palazzo Barbarigo della Terrazza
53 Palazzo Pisani della Moretta
54 Palazzo Marcello dei Leoni
55 Ca' Foscari
56 Palazzo Giustiniani
57 Ca' Rezzonico
58 Palazzo Loredan
59 Palazzo Contarini degli Scrigni
60 Accademia
61 Palazzo Moro-Lin
62 Palazzo Grassi
63 Ca' del Duca
64 Palazzo Falier
65 Palazzo Giustiniana-Lolin
66 Palazzo Cavelli Franchetti
67 Palazzo Barbaro
68 Casetta delle Rose
69 Ca' Grande
70 Palazzo Minotto
71 S.Maria Zobenigo
72 Palazzo Gritti-Pisani
73 Palazzo Contarini-Fasan
74 Hotel Bauer-Grünwald
75 Ca' Giustinian
76 Capitaneria del Porto
77 Giardini Reali
78 Palazzo Contarini del Zaffo
79 Palazzo Barbarigo
80 Palazzo Venier
81 Palazzo Dario
82 Palazzo Salviati
83 Santa Maria della Salute
84 Dogana di Mare

lovers—even nuns had them) while celebrating the freedom of its people. He followed this with two bookish plays on Venetian themes, *Marino Faliero* and *The Two Foscari*, and most importantly began his satirical masterpiece, *Don Juan*.

Meanwhile debauchery was taking its toll: an English acquaintance wrote in 1818 that 'His face had become pale, bloated and sallow, and the knuckles on his hands were lost in fat'. Byron became infatuated with a young Countess, Teresa Guiccioli, and left Venice to move in with her and her elderly husband in Ravenna. But, having tasted every freedom in Venice, Byron once more began to chafe; the Contessa was 'taming' him. He bundled up the manuscript of Don Juan and left, only to die of fever at the age of 36 in the Greek War of Independence.

Piazza San Marco

Venice's self-proclaimed Attila, Napoleon himself, described this asymmetrical showpiece as 'Europe's finest drawing-room', and no matter how often you've seen it in pictures or in the flesh, its charm never fades. There are Venetians (and not all of them purveyors of souvenirs) who prefer it in the height of summer at its liveliest, when Babylonians from the four corners of the earth outnumber even the pigeons, who swoop back and forth at eye level, while the rival café bands provide a Fellini-esque accompaniment. Others prefer it in the misty moonlight, when the familiar seems unreal under hazy, rosy streetlamps.

The piazza and its two flanking *piazzette* have looked essentially the same since 1810, when the 'Ala Napoleonica' was added to the west end, to close in Mauro Codussi's long, arcaded **Procuratie Vecchie** (1499) on the north side and Sansovino's **Procuratie Nuove** (1540) on the south. Both, originally used as the offices of the 'procurators' or caretakers of St Mark's, are now filled with jewellery, embroidery and lace shops. Two centuries ago they contained an equal number of coffee-houses, the centres of the 18th-century promenade. Only two survive—the **Caffè Quadri** in the Procuratie Vecchie, the old favourite of the Austrians, and **Florian's**, in the Procuratie Nuove, its hand-painted décor unchanged since it opened its doors in 1720, although with espressos at L7000 a head the proprietors could easily afford to remodel it in solid gold.

St Mark's Basilica

Open to visitors Mon–Sat 10–4.30, Sun and hols 2–5. No shorts, and women must have their shoulders covered and a minimum of décolletage, or risk being peremptorily dismissed from the head of the queue, which can be diabolically long in season. There are separate admission charges for many of the smaller chapels and individual attractions; different sections are frequently closed for restoration. Disabled ramp access from Piazzetta dei Leoncini.

This is nothing less than the holy shrine of the Venetian state. An ancient law decreed that all merchants trading in the East had to bring back from each voyage a new embellishment for St Mark's. The result is a glittering robbers' den, the only church in Christendom that would not look out of place in Xanadu. Yet it was dismissed out of hand for centuries. 'Low, impenetrable to the light, in wretched taste both within and without,' wrote the Président de Brosses in the 18th century.

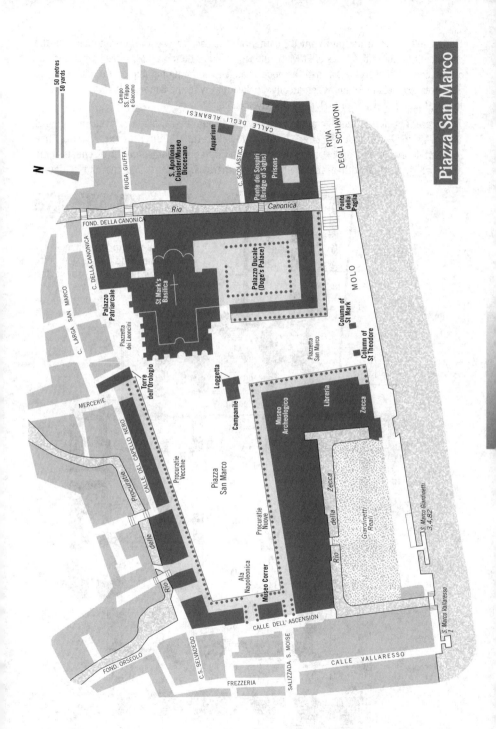

Until 1807, when it became Venice's cathedral, the basilica was the private chapel of the doge, built to house the relics of St Mark after their 'pious theft' in 828, a deed sanctioned by a tidy piece of apocrypha that had the good Evangelist mooring his ship on the Rialto on the way from Aquileia to Rome, when an angel hailed him with the famous *'Pax tibi...'* or 'Peace to you, Mark, my Evangelist. Here your body shall lie.'

The present structure, consecrated in 1094, was begun after a fire destroyed the original St Mark's in 976. Modelled after Constantinople's former Church of the Apostles, five rounded doorways, five upper arches and five round Byzantine domes are the essentials of the exterior, all frosted with a sheen of coloured marbles, ancient columns and sculpture

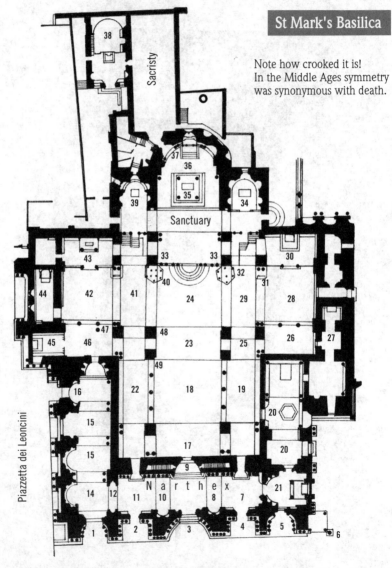

St Mark's Basilica

Note how crooked it is!
In the Middle Ages symmetry
was synonymous with death.

Names in *italics* refer to mosaics.

1   *Translation of the Body of St Mark* (1270)
2   *Venice Venerating the Relics of St Mark*
    (1718)
3   Central door, with magnificent
    13th-century carvings in arches
4   *Venice Welcoming the Relics of St Mark*
    (1700s)
5   *Removal of St Mark's Relics from Alexandria*
    (1700s)
6   Pietra del Bando, stone from which
    the Signoria's decrees were read
7   *Scenes from the Book of Genesis* (1200) and
    6th-century Byzantine door of
    S. Clemente
8   *Noah and the Flood* (1200s), tomb of
    Doge Vitale Falier (d. 1096)
9   *Madonna and Saints* (1060s); red marble slab
    where Emperor Barbarossa submitted to Pope
    Alexander III (1177); stair up to
    the Loggia and Museo Marciano
10 *Death of Noah and the Tower of Babel*
    (1200s)
11 *Story of Abraham* (1230s)
12 *Story of SS. Alipius and Simon, and Justice*
    (1200s)
14 Tomb of Doge Bartolomeo Gradenigo
    (d. 1342)
15 *Story of Joseph*, remade in 19th century
16 Porta dei Fiori (1200s); Manzù's bust of Pope
    John XXIII
17 *Christ with the Virgin and St Mark*
    (13th century, over the door)
18 Pentecost Dome (the earliest, 12th century)
19 On the wall: *Agony in the Garden and
    Madonna and Prophets* (13th century)
20 Baptistry, *Life of St John the Baptist* (14th
    century) and tomb of Doge Andrea Dandolo
21 Cappella Zen, by Tullio and Antonio Lombardo
    (1504–22)
22 On the wall: *Christ and Prophets*
    (13th century)
23 In arch: *Scenes of the Passion*
    (12th century)
24 Central Dome, the *Ascension*
    (12th century)
25 Tabernacle of the Madonna of the Kiss
    (12th century)
26 On wall: *Rediscovery of the Body of St Mark*
    (13th century)

27 Treasury
28 Dome of S. Leonardo; Gothic rose window
    (15th century)
29 In arch, *Scenes from the Life of Christ*
    (12th century)
30 Altar of the Sacrament; pilaster where
    St Mark's body was rediscovered,
    marked by marbles
31 Altar of St James (1462)
32 Pulpit where newly elected doge was shown
    to the people; entrance to the sanctuary
33 Rood screen (1394) by
    Jacopo di Marco Benato and Jacobello
    and Pier Paolo Dalle Masegne
34 Singing Gallery and Cappella di S. Lorenzo,
    sculptures by the Dalle Masegnes
    (14th century)
35 Dome, *Prophets Foretell the Religion of Christ*
    (12th century); Baldacchino, with Eastern
    alabaster columns (6th century?)
36 Pala d'Oro (10th–14th century)
37 Sacristy door, with reliefs by Sansovino
    (16th century)
38 Sacristy, with mosaics by Titian and
    Padovanino (16th century) and Church of
    St Theodore (15th century), once seat of the
    Inquisition, and now part of the sacristy: both
    are rarely open
39 Singing Gallery and Cappella di S. Pietro (14th
    century): note the Byzantine capitals
40 Two medieval pulpits stacked together
41 *Miracles of Christ* (16th century)
42 Dome, with *Life of St John the Evangelist*
    (12th century)
43 Cappella della Madonna di Nicopeia
    (miraculous 12th-century icon)
44 Cappella di S. Isidoro (14th-century mosaics
    and tomb of the Saint)
45 Cappella della Madonna dei Máscoli: *Life of
    the Virgin* by Andrea del Castagno, Michele
    Giambono, Jacopo Bellini
46 On wall: *Life of the Virgin* (13th century)
47 Finely carved Greek marble stoup
    (12th century)
48 *Virgin of the Gun* (13th century—rifle
    ex-voto from 1850s)
49 Il Capitello, altar topped with rare marble cibo-
    rium, with miraculous Byzantine Crucifixion
    panel

('As if in ecstasy,' wrote Ruskin, 'the crests of the arches break into marbly foam…'). The spandrils of the arches glitter with gaudy, Technicolor mosaics—the High Renaissance, dissatisfied with the 13th-century originals, saw fit to commission new painterly scenes, leaving intact only the *Translation of the Body of St Mark* on the extreme left, which includes the first historical depiction of the basilica itself. The three bands of 13th-century **reliefs** around the central portal, among Italy's finest Romanesque carvings, show Venetian trades, the Labours of the Months, and Chaos in the inner band.

Front and centre, seemingly ready to prance off the façade, the controversial 1979 copies of the bronze **horses of St Mark** masquerade well enough—from a distance. The ancient originals (cast some time between the 3rd century BC and 2nd century AD, and now inside the basilica's Museo Marciano) were one of the most powerful symbols of the Venetian Republic. Originally a 'triumphal quadriga' taken by Constantine the Great from Chios to grace the Hippodrome of his new city, it was carried off in turn by the artful Doge Dandolo in the 1204 Sack of Constantinople. Another prize from Byzantium are the four porphyry 'Moors' huddled in the corner of the south façade near the Doge's Palace; according to legend, they were changed into stone for daring to break into St Mark's treasury, though scholars prefer to believe that they are four chummy 3rd-century Roman Emperors, the Tetrarchs.

The Interior

The best mosaics, most of them from the 13th-century, cover the six domes of the **atrium**, or narthex, their old gold glimmering in the permanent twilight. The oldest mosaic in St Mark's is that of the *Madonna and Saints* above the central door, a survivor of the original 11th-century decoration of the basilica. A slab of red marble in the pavement marks the spot where the Emperor Barbarossa knelt and apologized to 'St Peter and his pope'—Alexander III, in 1177. This, a favourite subject of Venetian state art, is one of the few gold stars the republic ever earned with the papacy; mistrust and acrimony were far more common.

The interior, in the form of a Greek cross, dazzles the eye with the intricate splendour of a thousand details. The domes and upper vaults are adorned with golden mosaics on New Testament subjects, the oldest dating back to the 1090s, though there have been several restorations since. Ancient columns of rare marbles, alabaster, porphyry and verdantique, sawn into slices of rich colour, line the lower walls; the 12th-century pavement is a magnificent geometric mosaic of marble, glass, and porphyry. Like a mosque, the nave is covered with carpets.

The first door on the right leads to the 14th-century **baptistry**, much beloved by John Ruskin and famous for its mosaics on the life of John the Baptist, with a lovely Salome in red who could probably have had just as many heads as she pleased (*with luck this may have reopened by the time you visit*). Attached to the baptistry, the **Cappella Zen** was designed by Tullio Lombardo in 1504 to house the tomb of one Cardinal Zen, who had left a fortune to the Republic on condition he be buried in St Mark's. Further along the right transept you can visit the **treasury** (*open 9.45–5; adm*), containing the loot from Constantinople that Napoleon overlooked—golden bowls and crystal goblets studded with huge coloured gems, straight from the cavern of Ali Baba. Near the Altar of the Sacrament, at the end of the right transept, a lamp burns 'eternally' next to one pillar: after the 976 fire, the body of St Mark was lost, but in 1094 (after Bari had beaten Venice to the relics of St Nicolaus) the good Evangelist staged a miraculous reappearance, popping his hand out of the pillar during Mass. St Mark is now safely in place in a crypt under the high altar, in the **sanctuary** (*open 9.45–5; adm*). You can't visit his relics, but you can see the altar's retable, the fabulous, glowing **Pala d'Oro**, a masterpiece of medieval gold and jewel work. The upper section may originally have been in the Church of the Pantocrator in Constantinople, and the lower section was commissioned in that same city by Doge Pietro Orseolo I in 976. Over the years the Venetians added their own scenes, and the Pala took its present form in 1345.

In the left transept, the **Chapel of the Madonna of Nicopeia** shelters a venerated 10th-century icon hijacked from Constantinople, the *Protectress of Venice*, formerly carried into battle by the Byzantine Emperors. More fine mosaics are further to the left in the Chapel of St Isidore (the Venetian bodysnatchers kidnapped his relics from Chios—and in the mosaic he seems happy to go, grinning like a chimp). In the **Chapel of the Madonna dei Máscoli**, the mosaics on the *Life of the Virgin* by Tuscan Andrea Castagno and Michele Giambono (1453) were among the first harbingers of the Renaissance in Venice.

Before leaving, climb the steep stone stair near the west door of the narthex, to the **Museo Marciano, Galleria and Loggia dei Cavalli** (*open 9.45–5; adm*), for a closer look at the dome mosaics from the women's gallery and a visit to the loggia, where you can inspect the replica horses and compare them with the excellently restored, gilded, almost alive originals in the museum.

The Campanile

Open summer 9–7.30; winter 9.30–3.30; other months in between; adm.

St Mark's bell tower, to those uninitiated in the cult of Venice, seems like an alien presence, a Presbyterian brick sentinel in the otherwise delicately wrought piazza. But it has always been there, at least since 912; it was last altered in 1515, and when it gently collapsed into a pile of rubble on 14 July 1902 (the only casualty a cat) the Venetians felt its lack so acutely that they began to construct an exact replica, only a few hundred tons lighter and stronger, completed in 1912. It is 332ft tall, and you can take the lift up for a bird's-eye vision of Venice and its Lagoon; from up here the city seems amazingly compact. Though you have to pay for the view, misbehaving priests had it for free; the Council of Ten would suspend them in cages from the windows. Under the campanile, Sansovino's elegant **loggetta** adds a graceful note to the brick belfry. Its marbles and sculptures glorifying Venice took it on the nose when the campanile fell on top of them, but they have been carefully restored.

The Correr Museum and Clock Tower

At the far end of the piazza, in the Procuratie Nuove, the **Museo Correr** (*open 9–7, last tickets at 6; adm exp, but includes entrance to Palazzo Ducale*) contains an interesting collection of Venetian memorabilia—the robes, ducal bonnets and old-maidish nightcaps of the doges, the 20-inch-heeled *zoccoli*, once the rage among Venetian noblewomen, and a copy of the statue of Marco Polo from the temple of 500 Genies in Canton. Upstairs, the fine collection of Venetian paintings, includes two great works by Carpaccio, *The Courtesans* (or Ladies—in Venice it was notoriously hard to tell) and the *Young Man in a Red Beret*, with his archetypal Venetian face; Antonello da Messina's damaged but luminous *Pietà*, and others by Cosme Turà and a young Giovanni Bellini; a lively early sculpture by Canova *Daedalus and Icarus* (1779); and the Bosch-esque *Temptation of St Anthony* by Il Civetta (the little owl).

At the head of the Procuratie Vecchie two bronze wild men, called the 'Moors', sound the hours atop the clock tower, the **Torre dell'Orologio** (*due to re-open for its 500th anniversary in 1999*), built to a design by Mauro Codussi in 1499 above the entrance to Venice's main shopping street, the Merceria. The old Italians were fond of elaborate astronomical clocks, but none is as beautiful as this, with its richly coloured enamel and gilt face, its Madonna and obligatory lion. The Council of Ten (which actually encouraged fearsome false rumours about itself, to make its job easier) supposedly blinded the builders to prevent them from creating such a marvel for any other city. Below, flanking the basilica's north façade, a fountain and two porphyry lions just right for children to ride, stand in **Piazzetta Giovanni XXIII**, named after the beloved Venetian patriarch who became pope in 1959.

Piazzetta San Marco

To the south of the basilica, the Piazzetta San Marco was the republic's foyer, where ships would dock under the watchful eye of the doge. The view towards the Lagoon is framed by two tall Egyptian granite **columns**, trophies brought to Venice in the 1170s. The Venetians had a knack for converting their booty into self-serving symbols: atop one of the columns several Roman statues were pieced together to form their first patron saint, St Theodore with his crocodile (or dragon, or fish), while on the other stands an ancient Assyrian or Persian winged lion, under whose paw the Venetians slid a book, creating their symbol of St Mark.

Opposite the Doges' Palace stands the **Libreria**, built in 1536 by Sansovino and considered by Palladio to be the most beautiful building since antiquity, especially notable for the play of light and shadow in its sculpted arcades. Sansovino, trained as a sculptor, was notorious for paying scant attention to architectural details, and the library was scarcely completed when its ceiling collapsed. The goof-up cost him a trip to the Council of Ten's slammer, and he was only released on the pleading of Titian. Scholars with permission from the director can examine such treasures as the 1501 *Grimani breviary*, a masterwork of Flemish illuminators; Homeric *codices*, the 1459 world map of Fra Mauro, and Marco Polo's will. But not the famous library Petrarch willed to the Republic—the Venetians misplaced it.

Next to the library, at No.17, Venice's **Archaeology Museum** (*closed for restoration at the time of writing; due to re-open in 1999*) is one of the few museums in the city heated in the winter. It has an excellent collection of Greek sculpture, including a violent *Leda and the Swan* and ancient copies of the famous *Gallic Warriors of Pergamon*, all given to the city by collector Cardinal Grimani in 1523. On the other side of the Libreria, by the waterfront, is another fine building by Sansovino, the 1547 **Zecca**, or Old Mint, which once stamped out thousands of gold *zecchini*, and gave English a new word: 'sequin'.

The Palace of the Doges (Palazzo Ducale)

> *Open 15 April–Oct 9–7; winter 8.30–1; other months somewhere in between; adm exp—includes entry to the Museo Correr. Ticket office through Porta della Carta and in the courtyard.*

What St Mark's is to sacred architecture, the **Doges' Palace** is to the secular—unique and audacious, dreamlike in a half-light, an illuminated storybook of Venetian history and legend. Like the basilica, it was founded shortly after the city's consolidation on the Rialto, though it didn't begin to take its present form until 1309—with its delicate lower colonnade, its loggia of lacy Gothic tracery, and the massive top-heavy upper floor, like a cake held up by its own frosting. Its weight is partly relieved by the diamond pattern of white Istrian stone and red Verona marble on the façade, which from a distance gives the palace its wholesome peaches-and-cream complexion. Less benign are the two reddish pillars in the loggia (on the Piazzetta façade) said to have been dyed by the blood of Venice's enemies, whose tortured corpses were strung out between them.

Some of Italy's finest medieval sculpture crowns the 36 columns of the lower colonnade, depicting a few sacred and many profane subjects—animals, guildsmen, Turks, and Venetians. Beautiful sculptural groups adorn the corners, most notably the 13th-century *Judgement of Solomon*, near the palace's grand entrance, the 1443 **Porta della Carta** (Paper Door), a Gothic symphony in stone by Giovanni and Bartolomeo Bon.

Fires in 1574 and 1577 destroyed much of the palace, and at the time there were serious plans afoot to knock it down and let Palladio start again *à la* Renaissance. Fortunately, however, you can't teach an old doge new tricks, and the palace was rebuilt as it was, with Renaissance touches in the interior. Just within the Porta della Carta, don't miss Antonio Rizzo's delightful arcaded courtyard and his finely sculpted grand stairway, the **Scala dei Giganti**, named for its two Gargantuan statues of *Neptune* and *Mars* by Sansovino.

Visitors enter the palace via another grand stairway, Sansovino's **Scala d'Oro**. The first floor, once the private apartments of the doge, is now used for frequent special exhibitions (*separate adm*), while the golden stairway continues up to the *Secondo Piano Nobile*, from where the Venetian state was governed. After the fire that destroyed its great 15th-century frescoes, Veronese and Tintoretto were employed to paint the newly remodelled chambers with mytho-logical themes and scores of allegories and apotheoses of Venice—a smug, fleshy blonde in the eyes of these two. These paintings are the palace's chief glory, and signboards in each room identify them. Visiting ambassadors and other foreign official guests would be required to wait in the first room, the **Anticollegio**, so the frescoes (Tintoretto's *Bacchus and Ariadne* and Veronese's *Rape of Europa*) had to be especially impressive; in the next room, the **Sala del Collegio**, with several masterpieces by both artists, they would be presented to the hierarchy of the Venetian state.

Tintoretto's brush dominates in the **Sala del Senato**—less lavish, since only Venetians were admitted here—while the main work in the **Sala del Consiglio dei Dieci** is Veronese's ceiling, *Old Man in Eastern Costume with a Young Woman*. Under this the Council of Ten deliberated and pored over the accusations deposited in the *Bocche dei Leoni*—the lions' mouths spread over the Republic. To be considered, an accusation had to be signed and supported by two witnesses, and anyone found making a false accusation would suffer the punishment that would have been meted out to the accused had it been true. Next to the Ten's chamber, the old **Armoury** (Sala d'Armi) houses a fine collection of medieval and Renaissance arms and armour.

From here the visit continues downstairs, to the vast and magnificent **Sala del Maggior Consiglio**, built in 1340 and capable of holding the 2500 patricians of the Great Council. At the entrance hangs Tintoretto's crowded, and recently restored, *Paradiso*—the biggest oil painting in the world (23 by 72ft), all the Blessed looking up at Veronese's magnificent *Apotheosis of Venice* on the ceiling. The frieze along the upper wall portrays the first 76 doges, except for the space that would have held the portrait of Marin Falier (1355) had he not led a conspiracy to take sole power; instead, a black veil bears a dry note that he was decapitated for treason. The portraits of the last 44 doges, each painted by a contemporary painter, continue around the **Sala dello Scrutinio**, where the votes for office were counted. Elections for doge were Byzantine and elaborate—and frequent; the Maggior Consiglio preferred to choose doges who were old, and wouldn't last long enough to gain a following.

A Doge's Life: Gormenghast with Canals

Senator in Senate, Citizen in City were his titles, as well as Prince of Clothes, with a wardrobe of gold and silver damask robes, and scarlet silks. Once the Doge was dressed, the rest of his procession would fall in line, including all the paraphernalia of Byzantine royalty: a naked sword, six silver trumpets, a damask parasol, a chair, cushion, candle and eight standards bearing the Lion of St Mark in four colours symbolizing peace, war, truth and loyalty. Yet for all the pomp this was the only man in Venice not permitted to send a private note to his wife, or receive one from her, or from anyone else; nor could he accept any gift beyond flowers or rose-water, or go to a café or theatre, or engage in any money-making activity, while nevertheless having to meet the expenses of his office out of his own pocket. Nor could he abdicate, unless requested to do so.

The office was respected, but often not the man. When a Doge died he was privately buried in his family tomb before the state funeral—which used a dummy corpse with a wax mask. First, an 'Inquisition of the Defunct Doge' was held over the dummy, to discover if the Doge had kept to his Promissione (his oath of coronation), if his family owed the state any money, and if it were necessary to amend the Promissione to limit the powers of his successor still further. Then the dead Doge's dummy was taken to St Mark's to be hoisted in the air nine times by sailors, to the cry of 'Misericordia!' (Mercy), and then given a funeral service at Santi Giovanni e Paolo.

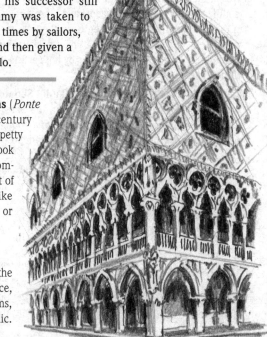

At the end of the tour the **Bridge of Sighs** (*Ponte dei Sospiri*) takes you to the 17th-century **Palazzo delle Prigioni**, mostly used for petty offenders. Those to whom the Republic took real exception were dumped into uncomfortable *pozzi*, or 'wells' in the lower part of the Palazzo Ducale, while celebrities like Casanova got to stay up in the *piombi* or 'leads' just under the roof (*see* below).

The Secret Itinerary

In 1984 the section of the palace where the real nitty-gritty business of state took place, a maze of narrow corridors and tiny rooms, was restored and opened to the public.

Because the rooms are so small the 1½-hour guided tour, the Itinerari Segreti ('Secret Itinerary') is limited to 20 people, and the reason why it's not better known is that it's only available in Italian (*mornings at 10 and 12; book at least a day in advance at the director's office on the first floor, or ring © 041 522 4951*).

The tour begins at the top of the Scala d'Oro, with the snug wood-panelled offices of the **Chancellery** and the 18th-century **Hall of the Chancellors**, lined with cupboards for holding treaties, each bearing the arms of a Chancellor. In the justice department is the **Torture Chamber**, where the three Signori della Notte dei Criminali (judges of the night criminals) would 'put to the question' anyone suspected of treason, hanging them by the wrists on a rope that is still in place. This ended in the early 1700s, when Venice, along with Tuscany, became one of the first states in Europe to abolish torture.

Next is the ornate **Sala dei Tre Capi**, the chamber of the three magistrates of the Council of Ten, who had to be present at all state meetings. As this chamber might be visited by foreign dignitaries, it was lavishly decorated with works by Veronese, Antonello da Messina and Hieronymus Bosch. From here it's up to the notorious **Piombi**, which despite their evil reputation appear downright cosy, as prisons go. Casanova's cell is pointed out, and there's an elaborate explanation of his famous escape through a hole in the roof.

Near the end of the tour comes one of Venice's marvels: the **attic of the Sala del Maggior Consiglio**, where you can see how the Arsenale's shipwrights made a vast ceiling float unsupported over the room below; built in 1577, it has yet to need any repairs.

San Marco to Rialto

The streets between the piazza and the market district of the Rialto are the busiest in Venice, especially the **Mercerie**, which begin under the clock tower and are lined with some of the city's smartest shops. It was down the Mercerie that Baiamonte Tiepolo, miffed at being excluded from the Golden Book, led his rebel aristocrats in 1310, when an old lady cried 'Death to tyrants!' from her window and hurled a brick at his standard-bearer, killing him on the spot, and causing such disarray that Tiepolo was forced to give up his attempted coup. It was a close call that the republic chose never to forget: the site, above the Sottoportego del Capello Nero, is marked by a stone relief of the heroine with her brick.

The Merceria continues to the church of **San Zulian**, redesigned in 1553 by Sansovino, with a façade most notable for Sansovino's statue of its pompous and scholarly benefactor, Tommaso Rangone. Sansovino also had a hand in **San Salvatore** in the next campo, adding the finishing touches to its noble Renaissance interior and designing the monument to Doge Francesco Venier. An 89-year-old Titian painted one of his more unusual works for this church, the *Annunciation*, which he signed with double emphasis *Titianus Fecit*—'*Fecit*' because his patrons refused to believe that he had painted it. In a chapel north of the altar is the *Supper at the House of Emmaus*, by the school of Giovanni Bellini.

Humming, bustling **Campo San Bartolomeo**, next on the Mercerie, has for centuries been one of the social hubs of Venice, and still gets packed with after-work crowds every evening. Its centre is graced by the **statue of Goldoni**, whose comedies in Venetian dialect still make the Venetians laugh; and by the look on his jolly face he still finds their antics amusing. Follow the crowds up to the **Ponte di Rialto** (*see* 'The Grand Canal', p.90), the geographical heart of Venice, and the principal node of its pedestrian and water traffic.

The city's central markets have been just across the bridge for a millennium, divided into sections for vegetables and for fish. Near the former you may pay your respects to Venice's oldest church, little **San Giacomo di Rialto**, founded perhaps as long ago as the 5th century and substantially reworked in 1071 and 1601. In the same campo stands a famous Venetian character, the 16th-century granite hunchback, **Gobbo di Rialto**, who supports a little stairway and marble podium from which the decrees of the Republic were proclaimed.

San Marco to the Accademia

Following the yellow signs 'To the Accademia' from the Piazza San Marco (starting by the tourist office), the first campo belongs to Baroque **San Moisè** (1668), Italy's most grotesque church, with a grimy opera-buffa façade, rockpile and altarpiece. For more opera and less buffa, take a detour up Calle Veste (the second right after Campo San Moisè) to monumental Campo San Fantin and **La Fenice** (1792), the Republic's last hurrah and one of Italy's most renowned opera houses, which saw the premieres of Verdi's *Rigoletto* and *La Traviata*. A fire set by a contractor during renovations ripped it apart in 1996, so expect to see only scaffolding for a long time to come. Venice has a venerable musical tradition, albeit one that had become more tradition than music by the time of the era of grand opera—although Mozart's great librettist, Lorenzo da Ponte, was a Venetian.

Back en route to the Accademia, in the next campo stands **Santa Maria Zobenigo** (or del Giglio), on which the Barbaro family stuck a fancy Baroque façade in 1680, not for God but for the glory of the Barbari; the façade is famous for its total lack of religious significance. The signs lead next to the Campo Francesco Morosini, named after the doge who recaptured the Morea from the Turks, but who is remembered everywhere else as the man who blew the top off the Parthenon. Better known as **Campo Santo Stefano**, it's one of the most elegant squares in Venice, a pleasant place to sit outside at a café table—particularly at **Paolin**, Venice's best *gelateria*. At one end, built directly over a canal, the Gothic church of **Santo Stefano** has the most gravity-defying campanile of all the leaning towers in Venice (most alarmingly viewed from the adjacent Campo Sant'Angelo). The interior is worth a look for its striking wood ceiling, soaring like a ship's keel, as well as its wooden choir stalls (1488).

The Accademia

Open daily; hours vary slightly throughout the year; summer Tues–Sat 9am–10pm, Sun 9am–8pm, Mon 9–2; closed 1 May, 25 Dec and 1 Jan; adm exp, free for under-18s and over-60s if members of the EU. It's a good idea to get there early since a maximum of 300 visitors are allowed at a time.

Just over the bridge and Grand Canal from Campo Santo Stefano stands the Galleria dell'Accademia, the grand cathedral of Venetian art, ablaze with light and colour. The collection is arranged chronologically, beginning in the former refectory of the Scuola (**Room I**): among them, 14th-century altarpieces by Paolo and Lorenzo Veneziano, whose half-Byzantine Madonnas look like fashion models for Venetian silks. Later altarpieces fill **Room II**, most importantly Giovanni Bellini's *Pala di San Giobbe*, one of the key works of the quattrocento: the architecture repeats its original setting in the church of San Giobbe; on the left St Francis invites the viewer into a scene made timeless by the music of the angels at the Madonna's feet. Other beautiful altarpieces in the room are by Carpaccio, Basaiti, and Cima da Conegliano (the subtle *Madonna of the Orange Tree*).

The next rooms are small but, like gifts, contain the best things: Mantegna's confidently aloof *St George*, the little allegories and a trio of Madonnas by Giovanni Bellini (including the lovely, softly coloured *Madonna of the Little Trees*) and Piero della Francesca's *St Jerome and Devotee*, a youthful study in perspective. In **Room V** you will find Giorgione's *La Vecchia*, with the warning '*Col Tempo*' ('With Time') in her hand, and the mysterious *The Tempest*, two of the few very paintings scholars accept as being indisputably by Big George, but how strange they are! It is said Giorgione invented easel painting for the pleasure of bored, purpose-less courtiers in Catherine Cornaro's Àsolo (*see* p.168) but the paintings seem to reflect rather than lighten their ennui and discontent.

Highlights of the next few rooms include Lorenzo Lotto's *Gentleman in his Study*, which catches its sitter off-guard before he could clear the nervously scattered scraps of paper from his table, and Paris Bordenone's masterpiece, *Fisherman Presenting St Mark's Ring to the Doge* (1554) celebrating a miracle of St Mark.

The climax of the Venetian High Renaissance comes in **Room X**, with Veronese's *Christ in the House of Levi* (1573), set in a Palladian loggia with a ghostly white imaginary background, in violent contrast to the rollicking feast of Turks, hounds, midgets, Germans and the artist himself (in the front, next to the pillar on the left). The painting was originally titled *The Last Supper*, and fell foul of the Inquisition, which took umbrage (especially at the Germans). Veronese was cross-examined, and ordered to make pious changes at his own expense; the artist, in true Venetian style, saved himself both the trouble and the money by simply giving it the title by which it has been known ever since.

Room X also contains Veronese's fine *Annunciation*, and some early masterworks by Tintoretto—*Translation of the Body of St Mark*, and *St Mark Freeing a Slave*, in which the Evangelist, in true Tintoretto-esque fashion, nosedives from the top of the canvas. The last great painting in the room was also the last ever by Titian, the sombre *La Pietà*, which he was working on when he died in 1576, aged about 90, from the plague; he intended it for his tomb, and smeared the paint on with his fingers.

Alongside several more Tintorettos, the following few rooms mainly contain work from the 17th and 18th centuries (Tiepolo, Sebatiano and Marco Ricci, Piazzetta, Longhi, Rosalba Carriera). Canaletto and Guardi, whose scenes of 18th-century Venice were the picture post-cards of the British aristocracy on their Grand Tour, are represented in **Room XVII**.

The final rooms of the Accademia were formerly part of the elegantly Gothic church of Santa Maria della Carità, and house more luminous 15th-century painting by Alvise Vivarini, Giovanni and Gentile Bellini, Marco Basaiti and Crivelli. **Room XX** has a fascinating series depicting the *Miracles of the True Cross* with Venetian backgrounds, painted by Gentile Bellini, Carpaccio and others. **Room XXI** contains the dreamily compelling and utterly charming *Cycle of S. Ursula* by Carpaccio, from the former Scuola di Sant'Orsola. Finally, the last room, **Room XXIV**, the former *albergo* of the church, contains two fine paintings that were originally made for it: Titian's striking *Presentation of the Virgin* (1538) and a triptych by Antonio Vivarini and Giovanni d'Alemagna (1446).

The Accademia lies in the *sestiere* of Dorsoduro, which can also boast the second-most-visited art gallery in Venice, the **Peggy Guggenheim Collection** (*open Easter–Oct Wed–Mon 11–6; closed Tues; adm exp*), just down the Grand Canal from the Accademia in her 18th-century Venetian palazzo. In her 30 years as a collector, until her death in 1979, Ms Guggenheim amassed an impressive quantity of brand-name 20th-century art—Bacon, Brancusi, Braque, Calder, Chagall, Dali, De Chirico, Duchamp, Dubuffet, Max Ernst (her second husband), Giacometti, Gris, Kandinsky, Klee, Magritte, Miró, Moore, Mondrian, Picasso, Pollock, Rothko and Smith. Administered by the Solomon R. Guggenheim Foundation in New York, the collection can come as a breath of fresh air after so much high Italian art, and also sponsors temporary exhibitions, even in winter; look out for posters.

From here it's a five-minute stroll down to the serene, octagonal basilica of **Santa Maria della Salute** 'of Health' (1631–81, *open 9–12, 3–6*), on the tip of Dorsoduro. One of five votive churches built after the passing of plagues (Venice, a busy international port, was particularly susceptible) La Salute is the masterpiece of Baldassare Longhena, its snow-white dome and marble jelly rolls dramatically set at the entrance of the Grand Canal. The interior is a relatively restrained white and grey Baroque, and the **sacristy** (*adm*) contains the *Marriage at Cana* by Tintoretto and several works by Titian, including his *St Mark Enthroned Between Saints*. Almost next to the basilica, on the point, stands the distinctive profile of the **Dogana di Mare**, the Customs House (*see* 'The Grand Canal', p.91).

The **Fondamenta delle Zattere**, facing away from the city towards the freighter-filled canal and the island of Giudecca, leads around to the **Gesuati**, the only church in Venice decorated by Umbrian artists. For a more elaborate feast, take the long stroll along the Fondamenta (or take *vaporetto* Line 5 to San Basegio) to Veronese's parish church of **San Sebastiano** on Rio di San Basilio. Veronese, it is said, murdered a man in Verona and took refuge in this neighbourhood, and over the next 10 years he and his brother Benedetto Caliari embellished San Sebastiano—beginning in 1555 with the ceiling frescoes of the sacristy and ending with the magnificent ceiling, *The Story of Esther*, and illusionistic paintings in the choir (*the custodian is usually there on weekday mornings or Sunday afternoons; tip him for turning on the lights*).

From San Sebastiano you head back towards the Grand Canal (Calle Avogaria and Calle Lunga S. Barnaba); turn left up Calle Pazienza to visit the 14th-century church of the **Carmini** with a landmark red campanile and lovely altars by Cima da Conegliano and Lorenzo Lotto. The **Scuola Grande dei Carmini** (*open Mon–Sat 9–12 and 3–6; adm; sometimes open for concerts*), next door, was designed by Longhena in the 1660s, and contains one of G. B. Tiepolo's best and brightest ceilings, *The Virgin in Glory*.

The Carmini is on the corner of the delightful **Campo Santa Margherita**. Traditionally the main marketplace of Dorsoduro, it's also a good spot to find relatively inexpensive pizzerias, restaurants and cafés that are not aimed primarily at tourists. It is also close to **Ca' Rezzonico** (Rio Terrà Canal down to the Fondamenta Rezzonico), home to the **Museo del Settecento Veneziano** (*open Oct–April 10–4, May–Sept 10–5; closed Fri; adm exp; at the time of writing only the first floor is open*), Venice's attic of 18th-century art, with bittersweet paintings by Giandomenico Tiepolo, some wild Rococo furniture by Andrea Brustolon, a pharmacy, genre scenes by Longhi (*The Lady and Hairdresser*), and a breathtaking view of the Grand

Canal. The house was owned in the last century by Robert Browning's son Pen, and the poet died there in 1889. One of the palaces you see opposite belonged to Doge Cristoforo Moro, whom the Venetians claim Shakespeare used as his model for Othello, confusing the doge's name with his race.

San Polo and Santa Croce

From the Ponte di Rialto, follow the yellow signs to Piazzale Roma, passing the pretty **Campo** and church of **San Polo** (*open Mon–Sat 7.10–5.30, Sun 3–5.30; adm*), with Giandomenico Tiepolo's dramatic *Stations of the Cross* in the Oratory of the Crucifix. The signs next take you before a venerable Venetian institution: the huge brick Gothic church of the **Frari** (*open Mon–Sat 9–6, Sun and hols 3–6; adm*), one of the most severe medieval buildings in the city, built between 1330 and 1469. Monteverdi, one of the founding fathers of opera and choir director at St Mark's, is buried here, as is Titian, whose tomb follows the Italian rule–the greater the artist, the worse the tomb (see Michelangelo's in Florence). The strange pyramid with a half-open door was intended by Antonio Canova to be Titian's tomb, but it eventually became the sculptor's own last resting place. The Frari is celebrated for its great art, and especially for the most overrated painting in Italy, Titian's *Assumption of the Virgin* (1516–18), in the centre of the Monk's Choir. Marvel at the art, at Titian's revolutionary Mannerist use of space and movement, but its big-eyed, heaven-gazing Virgin has as much artistic vision as a Sunday school holy card.

That, however, is not true of Giovanni Bellini's *Triptych of Madonna with Child and Saints* in the sacristy, or Donatello's rustic statue of *St John the Baptist* in the choir chapel. In the north aisle Titian's less theatrical *Madonna di Ca' Pésaro* was modelled on his wife Celia; the painting had a greater influence on Venetian composition than the *Assumption*. Also note the beautiful Renaissance **Tomb of Doge Nicolò Tron** by Antonio Rizzo in the sanctuary, from 1476.

The Scuola di San Rocco

Next to the Frari, the **Scuola di San Rocco** (*open summer 9–5.30; winter mornings only; adm*) was one of Venice's most important *scuole* (*see* p.74). San Rocco, renowned for his juju against the Black Death, was so popular among the Venetians that they stole his body from Montpelier and canonized him before the pope did, and his confraternity was one of the city's wealthiest. The *scuola* has a beautiful, lively façade by Scarpagnino, and inside it contains one of the wonders of Venice—or rather, 54 wonders—all painted by Tintoretto, who worked on the project from 1562 to 1585 without any assistance.

Tintoretto always managed to look at conventional subjects from a fresh point of view; while other artists of the High Renaissance composed their subjects with the epic vision of a Cecil B. de Mille, Tintoretto had the eye of a 16th-century Orson Welles, creating audacious, dynamic 'sets', often working out his compositions in his little box-stages, with wax figures and unusual lighting effects. In the *scuola*, especially in the upper floor, he was at the peak of his career, and painted what is considered by some to be the finest painting cycle in existence, culminating in the *Crucifixion*, where the event is the central drama of a busy human world. Vertigo is not an uncommon response—for an antidote, look at the funny carvings along the walls by Francesco Pianta. In the same room there are also several paintings on easels by Titian, and a *Christ* that some attribute to Titian, some to Giorgione.

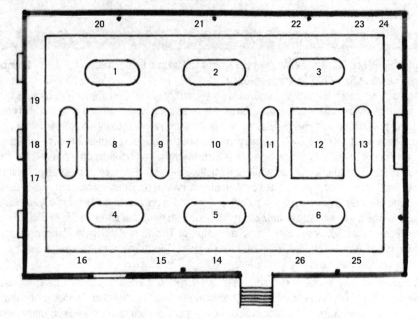

Tintoretto's Paintings

Ceiling:

1 God appearing to Moses
2 Vision of Ezekiel
3 Elisha Feeding the Multitude
4 Moses and the Pillar of Fire
5 Jacob's Ladder
6 Elisha Fed by an Angel in the Desert
7 Adam and Eve
8 Moses Bringing Forth Water from the Rock
9 Jonah Emerging from the Whale
10 The Miracle of the Brazen Serpent
11 The Sacrifice of Isaac
12 The Fall of Manna in the Desert
13 The Passover

Walls:

14 Ascension
15 Christ at Bethesda
16 The Temptation of Christ
17 San Rocco
18 Vision of San Rocco
19 San Sebastiano
20 Adoration of the Shepherds
21 Baptism of Christ
22 Resurrection
23 Christ in the Garden of Gethsemane
24 Last Supper
25 Miracle of the Loaves and Fishes
26 Resurrection of Lazarus

Just north, beyond Campo San Stin, the **Scuola Grande di San Giovanni Evangelista** (*open in theory if you ring the bell Mon–Fri 9.30–12.30, but it's best to call ahead, © 041 522 4134*) deserves a look for its beautiful Renaissance courtyard and double-ramp stairway (1498), Mauro Codussi's masterpiece, noted for the rhythms of its domes and barrel vaults.

From Campo San Stin, if you start along Calle Donà and keep as straight as possible, you should end up at **Ca' Pésaro** on the Grand Canal, a huge 17th-century pile by Longhena that is occupied by the **Galleria d'Arte Moderna** (*due to re-open in 1999; call © 041 721 127* *to check*), with a collection principally of works exhibited in the Biennale exhibitions. Italian contemporary art, much of it unfamiliar to a foreign audience, is the mainstay, but some international figures are also represented, such as Gustav Klimt. Ca' Pésaro also houses a **Museum of Oriental Art** (*open 9–2, Sat and Sun 9–1; closed Mon; adm*), with a higgledy-piggledy collection of Asian artefacts collected in the last century. If you really want to escape the crowds, however, head further up the canal to the stuffed Lagoon fowl in the **Natural History Museum** (*closed for restoration at the time of writing; due to re-open in 2000; call ✆ 041 524 0885 to check*) in the Venetian-Byzantine **Fóndaco dei Turchi**.

San Marco to Castello

From Piazzetta San Marco, the gracefully curving, ever-thronging **Riva degli Schiavoni** took its name from the Slavs of Dalmatia; in 1782, Venice was doing so much business here that the quay had to be widened. A few steps beyond the Palazzo Ducale, one of the city's finest Gothic palazzi was converted in 1822 to the famous **Hotel Danieli**, its name a corruption of the 'Dandolo' family who built it. The quay also has a robust **Memorial to Vittorio Emanuele II** (1887) where two of Venice's over 10,000 lions shelter—as often as not, with members of Venice's equally numerous if smaller feline population between their paws.

From Riva degli Schiavoni, the Sottoportico San Zaccaria leads back to the lovely Gothic-Renaissance **San Zaccaria** (*open 10–12 and 4–6*), begun by Antonio Gambello in 1444 and completed by Mauro Codussi in 1515. Inside, look for Bellini's extraordinary *Madonna and Saints* in the second chapel to the right, and the refined Florentine frescoes by Andrea del Castagno in the chapel of San Tarasio. Another church, back on the Riva itself, **La Pietà**, served the girls' orphanage which the red-headed priest Vivaldi made famous during his years as its concert master and composer (1704–38). The church was rebuilt shortly afterwards by Giorgio Massari with a remarkable oval interior, in luscious cream and gold with G. B. Tiepolo's extravagant *Triumph of Faith* on top. It has particularly fine acoustics—Vivaldi helped design it—and is still frequently used for concerts.

Due north of La Pietà stands the city's Greek Orthodox Church, the 16th-century **San Giorgio dei Greci**, with its tilting tower and *scuola*, now the **Museum of Byzantine Religious Painting** (*open Mon–Sat 9–1 and 2–5, Sun 9–1; adm*). Run by the Hellenic Centre for Byzantine Studies, many of its icons were painted in the 16th and 17th centuries by artists who fled the Turkish occupation. In Venice the Greeks came into contact with the Renaissance; the resulting Venetian-Cretan school nourished, most famously, El Greco.

Close by, another ethnic minority, the Dalmatians—present in Venice almost throughout the history of the Republic—began their tiny **Scuola di San Giorgio degli Schiavoni** in 1451 (*open 9.30–12.30 and 3.30–6.30; closed Mon; adm*). Its minute interior is decorated with the most beloved art in all Venice: Vittore Carpaccio's frescoes on the lives of the Dalmatia's patron saints—Augustine writing, watched by his patient little white dog; Jerome bringing his lion into the monastery, George charging a petticoat-munching dragon in a landscape strewn with maidenly leftovers from lunch, and more. Some of the greatest paintings by Carpaccio's more serious contemporaries, the Vivarini and Cima da Conegliano, hold pride of place in **San Giovanni in Brágora** (between San Giorgio degli Schiavoni and the Riva); the best work, Cima's *Baptism of Christ*, is in the sanctuary.

The Arsenale

From the Riva degli Schiavoni, the Fondamenta dell'Arsenale leads to the twin towers guarding the **Arsenale**. Founded in 1104, this, first of all arsenals, derived its name from the Venetian pronunciation of the Arabic *darsina'a*, or workshop, and up until the 17th century these were the greatest dockyards in the world, the very foundation of the Republic's wealth and power. In its heyday the Arsenale had a payroll of 16,000, and produced a ship a day to fight the Turks. Dante visited this great industrial complex twice, and as Blake would later do with his Dark Satanic Mills, found its imagery perfect for the *Inferno*.

Today the Arsenale is occupied by the Italian military, but you can look at the **Great Gateway** next to the towers, built in 1460—almost entirely from marble trophies nicked from Greece. Among the chorus line of lions is an ancient beast that Doge Francesco Morosini found in Piraeus, with 11th-century runes carved in its back in the name of Harold Hardrada, the member of the Byzantine Emperor's Varangian Guard who was later crowned king of Norway. Other very innocent-looking lions, eroded into lambs, were taken from the island of Delos in 1718 when the Turks weren't looking. The only way to get a look at the inside of the Arsenale is by taking the Line 52 *vaporetto*, which goes through the middle of it.

Venice's glorious maritime history is the subject of the fascinating artefacts and models in the **Museo Storico Navale** (*open Mon, Tues, Wed, Sat 8.45–1.30, Thurs 2.30–5; closed Fri, Sun and hols, adm*)—most dazzling of all is the model of the doge's barge, the *Bucintoro*. The museum is just past the gateway to the Arsenale, near the beginning of Via Garibaldi; in a neighbouring house lived two seafarers, originally from Genoa, who contributed more to the history Britain than that of Venice, Giovanni and Sebastiano Caboto.

Via Garibaldi and Fondamenta S. Anna continue to the Isola di San Pietro, site of the unmemorable **San Pietro di Castello** (*open Mon–Sat 10–5.30, Sun 3–5.30; adm*), until 1807 Venice's cathedral, its lonely, distant site a comment on the Republic's attitude towards the papacy. The attractive, detached campanile is by Codussi, and, inside, there is a marble throne incorporating a Moslem tombstone with verses from the Koran, which for centuries was said to have been the Throne of St Peter in Antioch. To the south are the refreshing pines and planes of the **Public Gardens**, where the International Exhibition of Modern Art, on Biennale, takes place in even-numbered years in the artsy pavilions. This, and the **Parco delle Rimembranze** further on, were a gift to this sometimes claustrophobic city of stone and water by Napoleon, who knocked down four extraneous churches to plant the trees. From here you can take Line 1 or 2 back to San Marco, or to the Lido.

San Marco to Santi Giovanni e Paolo

The *calli* that lead from the Piazzetta dei Leoncini around the back of San Marco and over the Rio di Palazzo will take you to the Romanesque cloister of Sant'Apollonia and one of Venice's newest museums, the **Museo Diocesano** (*open Mon–Sat 10.30–12.30*), containing an exceptional collection of trappings and art salvaged from the city's churches. Through a web of alleys to the north there's more art in the 16th-century Palazzo Querini-Stampalia, home of the **Fondazione Querini-Stampalia** (*open Tues, Wed, Thurs and Sun 10–1 and 3–6, Fri and Sat 10–1 and 3–10; closed Mon; adm exp*), which has an endearing assortment of genre paintings—scenes of 18th-century Venetian convents, dinner parties, music lessons, etc. by Pietro

Longhi and Gabriel Bella, as well as works by Bellini, Palma il Vecchio, Vincenzo Catena (a 16th-century merchant and the first known amateur to dabble in painting) and G. B. Tiepolo—all in a suitably furnished 18th-century patrician's *palazzo*.

Santa Maria Formosa *(open Mon–Sat 10–5.30, Sun 3–5.30; adm)*, in its charming campo just to the north, was rebuilt in 1492 by Codussi, who made creative use of its original Greek-cross plan. The head near the bottom of its campanile is notorious as being the most hideous thing in Venice, while, inside, Palma il Vecchio's *Santa Barbara* is famed as the loveliest of all Venetian blondes, modelled on the artist's own daughter. Another celebrated work, Bartolomeo Vivarini's *Madonna della Misericordia* (1473), is in the first chapel on the right; the parishioners shown under the protection of the Virgin's mantle earned their exalted position by paying for the painting.

The next campo to the north is dominated by **Santi Giovanni e Paolo** (or *San Zanipolo*), after St Mark's the most important church on the right bank *(open 7–12.30 and 3–7.15)*. A vast Gothic brick barn begun by the Dominicans in 1246, then almost entirely rebuilt after 1333, and finally completed in 1430, no one could accuse it of being beautiful, despite its fine front doorway. San Zanipolo was the pantheon of the doges; all their funerals were held here after the 1300s, and some 25 of them went no further, but lie in splendid Gothic and Renaissance tombs. Scattered among them are monuments to other honoured servants of the Venetian state, such as Marcantonio Bragadin, the commander who in 1571 was flayed alive by the Turks after he had surrendered Famagusta, in Cyprus, after a long siege; his bust sits on an urn holding his neatly folded skin. The adjacent chapel contains Giovanni Bellini's polyptych of *St Vincent Ferrer*, a fire-eating subject portrayed by the gentlest of painters; nearby there's a buoyand Baroque ceiling by Piazzetta in St Dominic's chapel, and a small shrine containing the foot of St Catherine of Siena. The right transept has paintings by Alvise Vivarini, Cima da Conegliano and Lorenzo Lotto; the finest tomb is in the chancel, that of Doge Andrea Vendramin, by Tullio and Antonio Lombardo (1478), while the **Chapel of the Rosary** in the north transept, which was severely damaged by fire in the last century, has a ceiling by Veronese from the church of the Umilità, long demolished.

Adjacent to San Zanipolo, the **Scuola Grande di San Marco** has one of the loveliest Renaissance façades in Italy, the fascinating *trompe-l'œil* lower half by Pietro and Tullio Lombardo, the upper floor by Mauro Codussi, and finished in 1495. The *scuola* is now used as Venice's municipal hospital, but it is possible to enter to see the lavish coffered ceiling in the library with the permission of the *Direttore di Sanità*.

Opposite stands the superbly dynamic **Equestrian Statue of Bartolomeo Colleoni**, the *condottiere* from Bergamo (1400–76) who had served the Republic so well on the mainland. In his lifetime proud of his emblem of *coglioni* (testicles—a play on his name), Colleoni envied Donatello's statue of his predecessor Gattamelata erected by the Venetians in Padua, and in his will he left the Republic 100,000 ducats if it would erect a similar statue of him in front of St Mark's. Greedy for the money but unable to countenance a monument to an individual in their sacred Piazza, the wily Venetians put the statue up before the *scuola* of St Mark. Verrocchio, the master of Leonardo and Botticelli, had only finished the plaster moulds when he died in 1488, leaving Alessandro Leopardi to do the casting. Verrocchio never saw a portrait of his subject, and all resemblances to Klaus Kinski are purely accidental.

Santa Maria dei Miracoli and the Ca' d'Oro

From Campo San Zanipolo, Largo G. Gallini leads to the perfect little Renaissance church of **Santa Maria dei Miracoli** (*open Mon–Sat 10–5.30, Sun and hols 3–5.30; adm*), built by Pietro Lombardo in the 1480s and often compared to an exquisite jewel box, elegant, graceful, and glowing with a soft marble sheen, inside and out. Just to the south are two enclosed courtyards, known as the **Corte Prima del Milion** and the **Corte Seconda del Milion**, where Marco Polo used to live. The latter in particular looks much as it did when the great traveller lived there; 'Million', his nickname in Venice, referred to the million, 'tall' tales he brought back with him from China. Nearby, Codussi's **San Giovanni Crisostomo** (1504) was his last work, a seminal piece of Renaissance architecture that contains Giovanni Bellini's last altar painting (*SS. Jerome, Christopher, and Augustine*), as well as a beautiful high altarpiece by Sebastiano del Piombo.

Further towards the railway station up the Grand Canal, signposted off the Strada Nuova (Via 28 Aprile), stands the enchanting Gothic **Ca' d'Oro**, finished in 1440 and currently housing the **Galleria Franchetti** (*open daily 9–2; adm*). In its collection are Mantegna's stern *St Sebastian*, Guardi's series of Venetian views, an excellent collection of Renaissance bronzes and medallions by Pisanello and Il Riccio, Tullio Lombardo's charming *Double Portrait*, and now sadly faded fragments of the famous frescoes by Giorgione and Titian from the Fóndaco dei Tedeschi. Also present are minor works by Titian, including a voluptuous *Venus*. The building itself is famous for the intricate traceries of its façade, best appreciated from the Grand Canal, and the courtyard, with a beautifully carved well-head by Bartolomeo Bon.

Due north, near the Fondamente Nuove, stands the unloved, unrestored church of the **Gesuiti** (*open daily 10–12 and 5–7*), built by the Jesuits when the republic relaxed its restrictions against them, in 1714–29: a Baroque extravaganza, full of *trompe l'œil* of white and green-grey marble draperies that would make a fitting memorial for Liberace. A previous church on this same site was the parish church of Titian, to which he contributed the *Martyrdom of St Lawrence*—the saint on a grill revered by Titian's patron, Philip II of Spain.

Cannaregio

Crumbling, piquant Cannaregio is the least visited *sestiere* in Venice, and here, perhaps, more than anywhere else in the city, you can begin to feel what everyday life is like behind the tourist glitz—children playing tag on the bridges, old men in shorts messing around in unglamorous, unpainted boats on murky canals, neighbourhood greasy spoons and bars, banners of laundry waving gaily overhead.

Northern Cannaregio was Tintoretto's home base, and he is buried in the beautiful Venetian Gothic **Madonna dell'Orto** (*open Mon–Sat 10–5.30, Sun and hols 3–5.30; adm*). It also contains several of his jumbo masterpieces, such as the *Sacrifice of the Golden Calf*, in which Tintoretto painted himself bearing the idol—though he refrained from predicting his place in the *Last Judgement*, which hangs opposite it. He also painted the highly original *Presentation of the Virgin* in the south aisle, near one of Cima da Conegliano's greatest works, *St John the Baptist*. The first chapel by the door has a *Madonna* by Giovanni Bellini.

From the Campo Madonna dell'Orto, take a short walk down the Fondamenta Contarini, where, across the canal, in the wall of the eccentric **Palazzo Mastelli** you can see one of Venice's curiosities: an old, stone relief of a Moor confronting a camel. There are three more 'Moors' in the **Campo dei Mori**, just in front of the Madonna dell'Orto. The original identities of these mysterious figures has long been forgotten, although a fourth one, embedded in one corner of the square and with a metal nose like Tycho Brahe, is named Signor Antonio Rioba. He featured in many Venetian pranks of yore: anonymous satires or denunciations would be signed in his name, and new arrivals in the city would be sent off to meet him.

Also in the area is another church, **Sant'Alvise** (*currently under restoration*), which must be the loneliest church in Venice. Its main features are a forceful *Calvary* by Giambattista Tiepolo and a set of charming tempera paintings that Ruskin called the 'Baby Carpaccios', but are now attributed to Carpaccio's master, Lazzaro Bastiani, as Carpaccio himself would only have been about eight years old when they were painted.

Three *rii* to the south of Sant'Alvise is the **Ghetto**—THE Ghetto, that is, for, like '*Arsenal*', the Venetians invented it: *ghetto* derives from the word '*getto*' meaning 'casting in metals', and there was an iron foundry here which preceded the establishment of a special quarter to which all Jews were ordered to move in 1516. The name is poignantly, coincidentally apt, for in Hebrew 'ghetto' comes from the root for 'cut off'. And cut off its residents were in Venice, for the Ghetto is an island, surrounded by a moat-like canal, and at night all Jews had to be within its windowless walls. Cramped for space, the houses are tall,with very low ceilings, which, as many people have noted, eerily presages ghetto tenements of centuries to come. But the Venetians did not invent the mentality behind the Ghetto; Spanish Jews in the Middle Ages were segregated, as were the Jews of ancient Rome. In fact, Venetian law specifically protected Jewish citizens and forbade preachers from inciting mobs against them—a common enough practice in the 16th century. Jewish refugees came to Venice from all over Europe; here they were relatively safe, even if they had to pay for it with high taxes and rents. When Napoleon threw open the gates of the Ghetto in 1797, it is said that the impoverished residents who remained were too weak to leave. The island of the **Ghetto Nuovo**, the oldest section, is a melancholy place, its small campo often empty and forlorn. The **Scuola Grande Tedesca** is the oldest of Venice's five synagogues, built by German Jews in 1528, and is in the same building as the small **Museo Comunità Israelitica/Ebraica** (*open 10.30–5; closed Sat and Jewish holidays; adm exp for the guided tour at 30mins past the hour*). The informative tours (in English) organized by the museum visit this synagogue and two others, the **Scuola Spagnola**—an opulent building by Longhena—and the **Scuola Levantina**.

Light years from the Ghetto in temperament, but only three minutes away on foot, the **Palazzo Labia** (next to the 1580 **Ponte delle Guglie**), has a ballroom with Giambattista Tiepolo's lavish, sensuous frescoes on the *Life of Cleopatra*. The palazzo is now owned by RAI, the Italian state broadcaster, and the ballroom is open for concerts (*or call © 041 524 812, well in advance to arrange an appointment between 3 and 4pm*). Away from the palazzo towards the railway station runs the garish, lively **Lista di Spagna**, Venice's tourist highway, lined with restaurants, bars, hotels and souvenir stands that are not always as cheap as they should be.

San Giorgio Maggiore and the Giudecca

The little islet of San Giorgio Maggiore, crowned by Palladio's church of **San Giorgio Maggiore** (*open daily 10–12.30 and 2.30–6.30; adm, including the campanile*), dominates the view of the Lagoon from the Piazzetta San Marco (*vaporetto* Line 82). Built according to his theories on harmony, with a temple front, it seems to hang between the water and the sky, bathed by light with as many variations as Monet's series on the Cathedral of Rouen. The austere white interior is relieved by Tintoretto's *Fall of Manna* and his celebrated *Last Supper* on the main altar, which is also notable for the fine carving on the Baroque choir stalls. A lift can whisk you to the top of the **Campanile** for a remarkable view over Venice and the Lagoon. The old monastery, partly designed by Palladio, is now the headquarters of the Giorgio Cini Foundation, dedicated to the arts and the sciences of the sea, and venue for frequent exhibitions and conferences.

La Giudecca (Lines 52 and 82) actually consists of eight islands that curve gracefully like a Spanish *tilde* just south of Venice; prominent among its buildings are a string of empty mills and factories—the product of a brief 19th-century flirtation with industry—and for the most part the atmosphere is relatively quiet and homely. Like Cannaregio, it's seldom visited, though a few people wander over to see Palladio's best church, **Il Redentore** (*open Mon–Sat 10–5.30, Sun 3–5.30; adm*). In 1576, during a plague that killed 46,000 Venetians, the doge and the senate vowed that if the catastrophe ended they would build a church and visit it once a year until the end of time. Palladio completed the Redentore in 1592, and on the third Sunday of each July a bridge of boats was constructed to take the authorities across from the Zattere. This event, the *Festa del Redentore*, is still one of the most exciting events on the Venetian calendar. The Redentore itself provides a fitting backdrop; Palladio's temple front, with its interlocking pediments, matches it basilican interior, with curving transpects and dome. The shadowy semi-circle of columns behind the altar adds a striking, mystical effect, all that survives of Palladio's desire to built a circular church, which he deemed most perfect to worship the essence of God.

Shopping

Venice is a fertile field for shoppers, whether you're looking for tacky bric-a-brac to brighten up the mantelpiece (just walk down the Lista di Spagna) or the latest in hand-crafted Italian design—but be warned that bargains are hard to find. Everything from fresh fish to lovely inlaid wooden boxes and huge quantities of tourist junk can be found at the **Rialto markets**. You will also come across food stalls in any number of squares and on barges along the smaller canals, but there is another large food and produce market in Castello, on **Via Garibaldi**. The main public auction house is **Franco Semezato**, Palazzo Giovanelli, Cannaregio 2292.

antiques

A flea market appears periodically in Campo San Maurizio, near Campo Santo Stefano, which is also the area with the largest concentration of antique shops. **Antonietta**

Santomanco della Toffola, Frezzeria 1504, S. Marco, has Russian and English silver, prints, and antique jewellery and glass, while the establishments of the print dealer **Pietro Scarpa** at Campo S. Moisè 1464 and Calle XXII Marzo 2089, S. Marco, are as much museums as shops. Away from the San Marco area, **Salizzada**, S. Lio 5672, in Castello, has old prints of Venice, clocks, and many other curious odds and ends, and **Xanthippe**, Dorsoduro 2773, near Ca' Rezzonico, is a highly eclectic shop specializing in the 19th century and Art Deco Venetian glass.

books

Venice has a good selection of bookshops. **Fantoni Libre Arte**, Salizzada di S. Luca 4121, S. Marco, has a monumental display of monumental art books, while **Sansovino**, Bacino Orseolo 84, S. Marco (just outside the Procuratie Vecchie), also has a large collection of art and coffee-table books combined with a huge stock of postcards. The best stock of books in Italian about every aspect of Venice, including some rare editions, is in **Filippi**, Calle del Paradiso 5763, Castello. If you're looking for books in English, try **Sangiorgio**, Calle Larga XXII Marzo 2087, S. Marco; **Alla Toletta**, Sacca della Toletta 1214, Dorsoduro, or **Serenissima**, Merceria dell'Orologio 739, San Marco.

fashion, fabrics and accessories

Most of Venice's high-fashion designer boutiques are located in the streets to the west of Piazza San Marco; fashion names like **Missoni**, with some of Italy's most beautiful knitwear, at Calle Vallaresso 1312, S. Marco, near Harry's Bar; **Krizia**, Mercerie del Capitello 4949, S. Marco, for more youth-oriented, colourful knits; **Laura Biagiotti**, Via XXII Marzo 2400/a, S. Marco; **Roberta di Camerino**, Lungomare Marconi 32, on the Lido, one of Venice's home-grown designers; and Giorgio Armani, at both **Giorgio Armani da Elysée**, Frezzeria 1693, S. Marco, and **Emporio Armani**, Calle dei Fabbri 989, S. Marco, with more accessible prices. For fashions by maverick Italian and French designers, try **La Coupole**, Via XXII Marzo or its sister shop, **La Fenice**, 1674, for more everyday-wear designers. Then there's **M. Antichità**, S. Marco 1691, offering velour dresses of Renaissance richness, and jewels to match.

Most Venetians, however, buy at least some of their clothes at the **COIN** department store, Salizzada San Giovanni Crisostomo, just north of Campo San Bartolomeo, part of a national chain, and a variety of cheap clothes stalls spread along Rio Terra San Leonardo, Cannaregio. Fashionable second-hand clothes are the mainstay at **Aldo Strausse**, Campo S. Giustina, in Castello, but **Emilio Ceccato**, Sottoportico di Rialto, S. Polo, is the place to find something very typically Venetian—gondoliers' shirts, jackets and tight trousers. Meanwhile, at the **Camiceria San Marco**, at Calle Vallaresso 1340, S. Marco, they will make up men's shirts and women's dresses to order for you within 24 hours.

For sensuous and expensive lingerie, visit **Jade Martine**, S. Marco 1645. The great place to find Venetian lace, whether for lingerie or tablecloths, is on Burano (*see* p.132), although beware that the bargains there are neither handmade nor even Buranese. Back in Venice itself, **Jesurum**, Piazza S. Marco 60/61, has a vast quantity of Venetian lace and linen of all kinds on display in a 12th-century former church behind St Mark's Basilica, as well as a selection of swimwear and summer clothes.

Not just lace but also other high-quality fabrics have figured equally among Venice's traditional specialities, using skills that in many cases have been reinvigorated in recent years. **Trois**, Campo S. Maurizio, S. Marco 2666, is an institution selling colourful pleated Fortuny silks, invented in Venice and made to traditional specifications on the Giudecca. More modern designs in silks and fabrics can be found at **Valli**, Merceria S. Zulian 783, S. Marco.

For posh shoes, **La Fenice**, Via XXII Marzo 2255, S. Marco, has a good selection by French and Italian designers. The greatest name in Venetian leather is **Vogini**, Via XXII Marzo 1300, S. Marco, which has a comprehensive selection of bags and luggage, and a complete range by Venetian designer Roberta di Camerino.

Jewellery in Venice tends to be expensive and conservative—particularly in the many shops in and around San Marco—and so may be of more interest for looking than buying. **Codognato**, S. Marco 1295, is one of the oldest jewellers in Venice, with some rare Tiffany, Cartier and Art Deco items; at **Missiaglia**, Piazza S. Marco 125, where you can see some of the most elegant pieces produced by Venetian gold and silversmiths working today.

food and drink

As well as in the markets (*see* above), other good places to pick up local specialities include **Pastificio Artigiano**, Strada Nuova 4292, Cannaregio, where Paolo Pavon has for fifty years created Venice's tastiest and most exotic pastas, among them *pasta al cacao* (chocolate pasta) and lemon, beetroot and curry varieties. Similarly, **Il Pastaio**, Calle del Varoteri 219, in the Rialto market, offers pastas in over a score of different colours. **Colussi**, Rugheta S. Apollonia 4325, near Campo Santi Filippo e Giacomo, is a *pasticceria* with an enormous range of unusual pastries.

If you do want to picnic as you make your way round Venice then **Rizzo Pane**, Calle delle Botteghe, S. Marco, just off Campo F. Morosini, is an *alimentari* where you'll find everything you need. For wines and spirits, **Cantinone Già Schiavi**, Fondamenta S. Trovaso 992, Dorsoduro, has plenty to choose from.

gifts

Anyone seeking unusual gifts will find plenty to look at in Venice, though, again, prices sometimes need to be handled with care. At **La Scialuppa**, Calle Seconda dei Saoneri 2695, S. Polo, you can buy the wares of woodworker Gilberto Penzo, who makes beautiful *forcole* (gondola oar locks, made of walnut), replicas of Venetian guild signs and many other things. **Calle Lunga 2137**, in Dorsoduro, is a workshop specializing in decorative wrought-iron, and **Fondamenta Minotto 154**, S. Croce, near S. Nicolò Tolentino and the railway station, has all sorts of gold and brass items, such as Venetian doorknockers. For children, **Signor Blum**, Calle Lunga S. Barnaba 2864, Dorsoduro, has beautiful jigsaw puzzles and brightly painted wooden toys. For an overview, the **Consorzio Artigianato Artistico Veneziano**, Calle Larga S. Marco 412, S. Marco, has a fair selection of all kinds of handmade Venetian crafts.

The most renowned of Venice's ancient crafts are, of course, an obvious choice. As Burano is the centre for lace, so too Murano (*see* below) is still the place to go for glassware, but in the city one of the grand names in Venetian glass is **Pauly**, at the end of Calle Larga, near Ponte Consorzi, S. Marco, which has 30 rooms of both traditional and contemporary designs in glass housed in a former doge's palazzo. At a less exalted level, **Paolo Rossi**, Campo S. Zaccaria 4685, S. Marco, has attractive reproductions of ancient glassware at still-reasonable prices, and **Arte Veneto**, Campo S. Zanipolo 6335, Castello, offers glass and ceramic trinkets that escape looking tacky or ridiculous. If you can contemplate carrying them home then mosaics, one of the oldest Venetian crafts, are also available, as individual *tessere* or larger items. Try **Arte del Mosaico**, Calle Erizzo 4002, Castello, or **Angelo Orsoni**, Campiello del Battello 1045, Cannaregio. For exquisite handmade paper, blank books and photo albums try **Paulo Olbi**, Calle della Mandorla 3653 (near Campo S. Angelo), and for paper designs, silk ties and masks made by Alberto Valese fusing Persian and Italian styles, visit **Alberto Valese-Ebrû**, Campo S. Stefano 3471, S. Marco (nearly opposite the church door).

Sports and Activities

Most of Venice's sporting facilities are found on the Lido or outer islands (*see* p.129).

Where to Stay

The rule of thumb in Venice is that whatever class of hotel you stay in, expect it to cost around a third more than it would on the mainland, even before the often outrageous charge for breakfast is added to the bill. Reservations are near-essential from about April to October and for Carnival; many hotels close in the winter, although many that do stay open offer substantial discounts at this time. Single rooms are always very hard to find. If you arrive at any time without reservations, tourist offices at the station and Piazzale Roma have a free room-finding service (a deposit is required, which is deducted from your hotel bill), though they get very busy in season. Also, the tourist office in Piazza San Marco has a list of agencies that rent self-catering flats.

luxury

★★★★★ **Cipriani**, Giudecca 10, ✆ 041 520 7744. Since 1963 this has been one of Italy's most luxurious hotels, a villa isolated in a lush garden at one end of the Giudecca that's so quiet and comfortable you could forget Venice exists, even though it's only a few minutes away by the hotel's 24-hour private launch service. An Olympic-size pool, sauna, jacuzzis in each room, tennis courts, and a superb restaurant are just some of its facilities, and no hotel anywhere could pamper you more.

★★★★★ **Danieli**, Riva degli Schiavoni 4196, ✆ 041 522 6480, 🖷 041 520 0208. The largest and most famous hotel in Venice, in what must be the most glorious location, overlooking the Lagoon and rubbing shoulders with the Palazzo Ducale. Formerly the Gothic palazzo of the Dandolo family, it has been a hotel since 1822; Dickens, Proust, George Sand and Wagner checked in here. Nearly every room has some story to tell, in a beautiful setting of silken walls, Gothic staircases, gilt mirrors and oriental rugs. The new wing, much vilified ever since it was built in the 1940s, is comfortable but lacks the charm and the stories.

★★★★★ **Gritti Palace**, S. Maria del Giglio 2467, S. Marco, ✆ 041 794 611. The 15th-century Grand Canal palace that once belonged to the dashing glutton and womanizer Doge

Andrea Gritti has been preserved as a true Venetian fantasy and elegant retreat, now part of the CIGA chain. All the rooms are furnished with Venetian antiques, but for a real splurge do as Somerset Maugham did and stay in the Ducal Suite. Another of its delights is the restaurant, the **Club del Doge**, on a terrace overlooking the canal.

very expensive

★★★★ **Concordia**, Calle Larga S. Marco 367, ✆ 041 520 6866, 🖷 041 520 6775. The only hotel overlooking Piazza S. Marco, the Concordia was swishly renovated in 1994 with a touch of Hollywood in some of its furnishings. Central air-conditioning is an added plus, as well as substanial off season discounts.

★★★★ **Londra Palace**, Riva degli Schiavoni 4171, Castello, ✆ 041 520 0533, 🖷 041 522 5032. Tchaikovsky wrote his *Fourth Symphony* in room 108 of this hotel, and it was also a favourite of Stravinsky. The hotel was created by linking two palaces together, and it has an elegant interior, over half the rooms with a stunning canal view, one of the cosiest lobbies in Venice, and exceptionally good service. There is also an excellent restaurant, **Les Deux Lions**.

★★★★ **Saturnia & International**, Via XXII Marzo 2398, S. Marco, ✆ 041 520 8377, 🖷 041 520 7131. A lovely hotel in a romantic quattrocento palazzo that has preserved centuries of accumulated decoration. Very near S. Marco, it has a garden court, faced by the nicest and quietest rooms. Off-season discounts.

expensive

★★★ **Accademia 'Villa Maravege'**, Fondamenta Bollani 1058, Dorsoduro, ✆ 041 521 0188, 🖷 041 523 9152. A hotel that offers a generous dollop of slightly faded charm in a 17th-century villa with a garden, just off the Grand Canal. Its 26 rooms are furnished with a menagerie of antiques, some of which look as if they were left behind by the villa's previous occupant—the Russian Embassy. The Accademia is a favourite of many, so book well in advance. Off-season discounts.

★★★ **La Fenice et Des Artistes**, Campiello de la Fenice 1936, S. Marco, ✆ 041 523 2333, 🖷 041 520 3721. A favourite of opera buffs in Venice (though that's not much use until La Fenice re-opens). Inside there are lots of mirrors, antiques and chandeliers to make artistes feel at home. Fully air-conditioned.

★★★ **Flora**, Calle Bergamaschi 2283/a, S. Marco, ✆ 041 520 5844. A small hotel on a little street that's remarkably quiet so near to the Piazza, with a charming garden and patio, spilling flowers. It's comfortably furnished, but ask for a large room. Air-conditioning and off-season discounts.

★★★ **Do Pozzi**, Corte do Pozzi 2373, S. Marco, ✆ 041 520 7855, 🖷 041 522 9413. With a bit of the look of an Italian country inn, this hotel has 29 quiet rooms on a charming little square, only a few minutes from Piazza San Marco. It's friendly and well run. Optional air-conditioning in all rooms.

★★★ **Malibran**, S. Giovanni Crisostomo 5864, Cannaregio, ✆ 041 522 8028. In the Corte del Milion, next to, or perhaps even incorporating, the house of Marco Polo.

★★★ **Sturion**, Calle del Sturion 679, San Polo, ✆ 041 523 6243, 🖷 041 522 8378. A popular choice, as it's one of the least expensive hotels actually on the Grand Canal. It's advisable to book well ahead for one of its eight large, finely furnished rooms.

★★★ **Agli Alboretti**, Rio Terrà Foscarini 884, Dorsoduro, ✆ 041 523 0058, ✉ 041 520 4048 A charming little hotel, recently refurbished, on a rare tree-lined lane near the Accademia; 19 rooms.

★★★ **La Calcina**, Zattere ai Gesuati 780, Dorsoduro, ✆ 041 520 6466. Near the Gesuati church and overlooking the Giudecca canal, this was Ruskin's *pensione* in 1877. Totally refurbished in 1996 with all mod cons. Book well ahead.

moderate

★★ **Falier**, Salizzada S. Pantalon 130, S. Croce, ✆ 041 710 882, ✉ 041 520 6554. A small hotel near Campo San Rocco. Elegantly furnished, it has two flower-filled terraces to lounge around on when your feet rebel; one room has its own terrace.

★★ **Messner**, Salute 216, Dorsoduro, ✆ 041 522 7443. A nicely modernized hotel only a hop from the Salute, and very suitable for families. Great showers, awful coffee.

★★ **Mignon**, SS. Apostoli 4535, Cannaregio, ✆ 041 523 7388, ✉ 041 520 8658. In a fairly quiet area, not far from the Ca' d'Oro, the Mignon boasts a little garden for leisurely breakfasts, though the rooms are rather plain. Has a loyal following.

★★ **La Residenza**, Campo Bandiera e Moro 3608, Castello, ✆ 041 528 5315, ✉ 041 588 5042. Located in a lovely 14th-century palace in a quiet square between San Marco and the Arsenale. The public rooms are flamboyantly decorated with 18th-century frescoes, paintings and antique furniture, though the bedrooms are simpler.

inexpensive

The largest concentration of cheaper hotels in Venice is around the Lista di Spagna, running eastwards into Cannaregio from the train station, though they can be pretty tacky and noisy. A more relaxed, pleasant and attractive area in which to find less expensive accommodation is in Dorsoduro, particularly around Campo S. Margherita.

★ **Antico Capon**, Campo S. Margherita 3004/b, Dorsoduro, ✆ 041 528 5292. Being refurbished by new management at the time of writing, this hotel has seven simple rooms, and, thankfully, no breakfast. It owes most of its charm to its sociable *Campo*.

★ **Casa Carettoni**, Lista di Spagna 130, Cannaregio, ✆ 041 716 231. The most pleasant and comfortable cheap hotel near the station; no breakfast is a plus, as you can do as Venetians do and take it in a nearby bar.

★ **Casa Petrarca**, Calle delle Fuseri 4393, S. Marco, ✆ 041 520 0430. Petrarch didn't really sleep in one of these six friendly rooms near the Piazza, but who cares?

★ **Casa Verardo**, Ruga Giuffa 4765, Castello, ✆ 041 528 6127, ✉ 041 523 2765. A classy, 9-room *locanda* with friendly owners.

★ **Sant'Anna**, Corte Bianco 269, Castello, ✆ 041 528 6466. A fine little hotel popular with those who want to escape tourist Venice, located just north of the Giardini Pubblici. Only eight rooms, including some triples.

★ **Silva**, Fondamenta Rimedio 4423, Castello, ✆ 041 522 7643. A bit hard to find—on one of the most photographed little canals in Venice, between the S. Zaccaria *vaporetto* stop and S. Maria Formosa. The rooms are fairly basic, but quiet, and the staff are friendly.

The tourist office has a list of all inexpensive hostel accommodation in Venice; as sleeping in the streets is now discouraged, schools are often pressed into use to take in the summer overflow, charging minimal rates to spread out a sleeping bag.

Camping is big business in the northeast corner of the Lagoon, around Cavallino, Jesolo and Punta Sabbioni, where there are any number of plushly appointed sites. The tourist office provides a complete list. Otherwise, the nearest campsite to Venice is **San Nicolò**, Riviera S. Nicolò 65, on the Lido, ✆ 041 526 7415 (International Camping Card required) (*closed at the time of writing; hoping to re-open in 1999*); another good site, open all year, is **Fusina**, Via Moranzani, Malcontenta, near Fusina, ✆ 041 547 0055, ✉ 041 547 0050. The *vaporetto* Line 16 from there to Venice runs every hour in summer, less frequently at other times.

Ostello Venezia, Fondamenta delle Zitelle 86, Giudecca, ✆ 041 523 8211. Venice's official youth hostel enjoys one of the most striking locations of any in Italy, with views across the Giudecca canal to San Marco. They don't take reservations over the phone, and to be assured of a place in July or August you have to write well in advance. At other times, you can chance it and book in person—the office opens as 6pm, but doors open at noon for waiting. IYHF cards required (but available at the hostel) and there's an 11.30pm curfew. Bed and breakfast L25,000; meals L14,000.

Foresteria Valdese, Calle della Madonnetta 5170, Castello, ✆ 041 528 6797. An old palazzo converted into a dormitory/*pensione* by the Waldensians. Check-in 9–1 and 6–8; beds in dorm L20,000, with breakfast; in rooms L24,000 per person.

Domus Cavanis, Rio Terrà Foscarini 912, Dorsoduro, ✆ 041 528 7374. A Catholic-run hostel open June–Sept only. Single (L45,000), double (L65,000) and triple (L90,000) rooms; students get about a 10% discount. Optional breakfast L7000.

Eating Out

The Venetians themselves are traditionally the worst cooks in Italy, and their beautiful city bears the ignominy of having a highest percentage of dud restaurants per capita. Not only is cooking in general well below the norm in Italy, but prices tend to be about 15% higher, and even the moderate ones can give you a nasty surprise at *conto* time with excessive service and cover charges. The cheap ones, serving up 500 tourist menus a day, are mere providers of calories to keep you on your feet; pizza is a good standby if you're on a budget. The restaurants listed here have a history of being decent or better, so chances are they still will be when you visit.

luxury

Antico Martini, Campo S. Fantin 1983, S. Marco, ✆ 041 522 4121. This is a Venetian classic, all Romance and elegance. It started out as a Turkish coffeehouse in the early 18th century, but nowadays is better known for seafood, a superb wine list and the best *pennette al pomodoro* in Venice. The intimate piano bar-restaurant stays open until 2am. Its romantic flavour is temporarily swallowed up by La Fenice's rebuilding operations directly outside. *Closed Tues, Wed midday, Dec and Feb.*

Danieli Terrace, in the Danieli Hotel, Riva degli Schiavoni 4196, Castello, ✆ 041 522 6480. The Danieli's rooftop restaurant is renowned for classic cuisine (try the *spaghetti alla Danieli*, prepared at your table) and perfect service in an incomparable setting overlooking Bacino San Marco.

very expensive

La Caravella, Calle Larga XXII Marzo 2397, S. Marco, ✆ 041 520 8901, in an annexe to the Saturnia Hotel (*see* above). For sheer variety of seasonal and local dishes, prepared by a master chef, few restaurants in Italy can top this merrily corny repro of a dining hall in a 16th-century Venetian galley. Try gilthead with thyme and fennel. Despite the décor, the atmosphere is fairly formal. *Open Oct–April, closed Wed.*

Do Forni, Calle dei Specchieri 468, S. Marco, ✆ 041 523 2148. For many Italians as well as foreigners, this is *the* place to eat in Venice. There are two dining rooms, one 'Orient Express'-style and the other rustic, and both are always filled with diners partaking of its excellent seafood *antipasti*, polenta, and seafood. *Closed Thurs* in winter.

Harry's Bar, Calle Vallaresso 1323, S. Marco, ✆ 041 523 6797. In a class by itself, a favourite of Hemingway and assorted other luminaries, this is as much a Venetian institution as the Doge's Palace, though food has become secondary to its celebrity atmosphere. Best to avoid the restaurant upstairs and just flit in for a quick hobnob while sampling a sandwich or the justly famous cocktails (a Bellini, Tiziano or Tiepolo—delectable fruit juices mixed with Prosecco), at a table downstairs near the bar. *Closed Mon.*

expensive

Dall'Amelia, Via Miranese 113, Mestre, ✆ 041 913 951. A restaurant that, despite its inconvenient mainland location, is of necessary inclusion, as all Italian gourmets cross the big bridge to dine here at least once. The oysters are delicious and there's a divine *tortelli di bronzino* (sea bass), plus wine from one of Italy's most renowned cellars.

Antica Besseta, Salizada da Ca'Zusto (at the end of Calle Savio), S. Croce, ✆ 041 524 0428. A family-run citadel of Venetian homecooking, where you can experience an authentic *risi e bisi*, or *bigoli in salsa*, scampi, and the family's own wine. *Closed Tues, Wed lunch, and part of July and Aug.*

Corte Sconta, Calle del Pestrin 3886, Castello, ✆ 041 522 7024. It may be off the beaten track, but the reputation of this trattoria rests solidly on its exquisite molluscs and crustaceans, served in a setting that's a breath of fresh air after the exposed beams and copper pots that dominate the typical Venetian restaurant. The Venetians claim the Corte Sconta is even better in the off-season; be sure to order the house wine. *Closed Sun, Mon, and most of July and Aug.*

Hostaria da Franz, Fondamenta San Isepo (or Giuseppe) 754, Castello, facing the side of the church, ✆ 041 522 7505. A restaurant well out of the way just north of the Giardini Pubblici, but it's well worth the trouble of getting lost *en route*. This is one of Venice's best: great oysters, *gnocchi* and seafood cooked the way it should be if all Venetians tried harder. The house wine is lovely. *Closed Tues.*

Antica Locanda Montin, Fondamenta di Borgo or Eremite 1147 (near S. Trovaso), Dorsoduro, ✆ 041 522 7151. This has long been Venice's most celebrated artists' eatery, with a vast garden, but the food can range erratically in quality from first to third division. *Closed Tues evening, Wed, and half of Aug.*

Trattoria Vini da Arturo, Calle degli Assassini 3656, S. Marco, ✆ 041 528 6974. In an infamous little street near La Fenice, this is a tiny trattoria that marches to a different drum from most Venetian restaurants, with not a speck of seafood on the menu. Instead, try the *papardelle al radicchio* or Venice's best steaks; its *tiramisù* is famous. *Closed Sun and half Aug.*

A La Vecia Cavana, Rio Terrà dei SS. Apostoli 4624, Cannaregio, ✆ 041 523 8644. Cannaregio's smartest restaurant; dine on Adriatic specialities. *Closed Tues.*

moderate

Altanella, Calle della Erbe 268, Giudecca, ✆ 041 522 7780. A delightful old seafood restaurant with an attractive setting on the Rio del Ponte Longo and a sideways glimpse of the Giudecca canal thrown in. Any of the grilled fish will be superb, and the *risotto di pesce* and *fritto* are worth the trip in themselves. *Closed Mon evening, Tues, and half of Aug. Reserve.*

Antica Mola, Fondamenta degli Ormesini 2800, Cannaregio (no tel), near the Ghetto. All the old favourites—fish, risotto, *zuppa di pesce*—and tables by the canal. *Closed Wed.*

Antico Giardinetto da Erasmo, S. Croce 2315, ✆ 041 721 301, behind the church of S. Cassiano. The star feature is delicious seafood cooked in a variety of styles. In good weather you can eat out in the little garden. *Closed Sat, Sun and Aug.*

Alla Madonna, Calle della Madonna 594, S. Polo (off Fond. del Vin, Rialto), ✆ 041 523 3824. A large, popular, and very Venetian fish restaurant. *Closed Wed and Jan.*

Ai Promessi Sposi, Calle dell'Oca 4367, Cannaregio, near Campo SS. Apostoli (no tel). Cheerful bar/trattoria with good basic fairly traditional food and a garden at the back. *Closed Wed.*

Da Remigio, Salizzada dei Greci 3416, Castello, ✆ 041 523 0089. A neighbourhood favourite, with solid Venetian cooking. Very popular with the locals. *Closed Mon, and Tues eve.*

Tre Spiedi, Salizzada S. Canciano 5906, Cannaregio, ✆ 041 528 0035, near the Campiello F. Corner and the central post office. A cosy atmosphere to go with local specialities like *spaghetti alla veneziana* and *braciola Bruno* (pork chops). *Closed Mon.*

cheap

Aciughetta, Campo SS. Filippo e Giacomo, Castello, ✆ 041 522 4292. One of the best cheap restaurants and bars near the Piazza San Marco, with good pizzas and atmosphere to boot. *Closed Tues.*

Pizzeria alle Oche, Calle del Tentor 1552, S. Croce, ✆ 041 524 1161, just before Ponte del Parucheta, south of S. Giacomo dell'Orio. Cheery, young atmosphere with 85 types of pizza, and take-away. *Closed Mon in winter.*

Rosticceria San Bartolomeo, Calle della Bissa 5424, San Marco, ✆ 041 522 3569. Honest cooking for honest prices, a no-frills trattoria with an cheaper snack bar downstairs.

San Tomà, Campo San Tomà 2864, San Polo, ✆ 041 523 8819. A good trattoria/pizzeria with convivial outdoor tables.

Da Crecola, S. Giacomo dell'Orio 1459, S. Croce, ✆ 041 524 1496. Set in a quiet corner by a canal wih outdoor tables. Good pasta dishes, like *tagliatelle alla gorgonzola*, and 50 different kinds of pizza, and a delightfully *pétillant* house wine.

Casa Mia, Calle dell'Oca 4430, Cannaregio, © 041 528 5590, near Campo SS. Apostoli. A lively pizzeria full of locals, and six courtyard tables. *Closed Tues.*

Vino Vino, Campo S. Fantin 1983, S. Marco, © 041 522 4121. A trendy offspring of the élite Antico Martini, where you can eat a well-cooked, filling dish (cooked by the same chefs!) with a glass of good wine at prices even students can afford. *Closed Tues, Wed midday, Dec and Feb.*

Entertainment and Nightlife

Sadly, in a city that's clearly made-to-order for pleasure, revelry and romance, life after dark is notoriously moribund. The locals take an evening stroll to their local *campo* for a chat with friends and an *aperitivo*, before heading home to dinner and the TV—the hotblooded may go on to bars and discos in Mestre, Marghera or the Lido. Visitors are left to become even poorer at the **Municipal Casino**, out on the Lido from April to October, and at other times in the Palazzo Vendramin on the Grand Canal (*hours are 3pm–2am, dress up and take your passport*). You might prefer to spend less more memorably on a moonlit gondola ride, or you can do as most people do—wander about. Venice is a different city at night, when the *bricole* lights in the Lagoon are a fitting backdrop for a mer-king's birthday pageant.

Even so, there are places to go among all this peace and quiet, and stacked against the absence of everyday nightlife there's Venice's packed calendar of special events. For an up-to-date calendar of current events, exhibitions, shows, films, and concerts in the city, consult *Un Ospite di Venezia*, free from tourist offices.

opera, classical music and theatre

Venice's music programme is heavily oriented to the classical. Opera (from December to May only), ballet, recitals and symphonic concerts, once at **La Fenice** are now perormed in a temporary pavillion at Tronchetto; tickets available through the Cassa di Risparmio, Campo S. Luca, © 041 529 1111. At Venice's main theatre **Teatro Goldoni**, Calle Goldoni 4650/b, S. Marco, © 041 520 5422, the Goldoni repertory holds pride of place, but there are other plays, as well as concerts; in summer performances are often moved ot Campo S. Polo.

Two other concert venues, worth visiting as much for the décor as the music, are the **Palazzo Labia**, Campo S. Geremia, Cannaregio (call ahead for tickets, © 041 524 2812), and Vivaldi's lovely rococo church of **La Pietà** (information and tickets, © 041 520 8711), where prices are usually high but the acoustics are well-nigh perfect.

cafés and bars

The classic cafés of Venice face each other across Piazza San Marco: **Florian's** and its great rival **Quadri**, both beautiful, and both correspondingly exorbitant. More fashionable with smart Venetians today, particularly on Sundays, is **Harry's Dolci**, Fondamenta S. Biagio 773 on the Giudecca, noted for its elegant teas, ice creams and cakes, as well as the Cipriani's **Cips**, which is now open for scrumptious sandwiches and cakes. **Caffè Costarica**, Rio Terrà di S. Leonardo, Cannaregio, brews Venice's most powerful *espresso* and great iced coffee (*frappé*), and also sells ground coffees and beans over the counter.

Throughout the day Venetians frequently drop into bars and wine bars (*bacaro*) for a 'shadow' (an *ombra*, a tiny glass of wine generally downed in one go) and *cichetti*, the Venetian equivalent of tapas. For the greatest variety of wines, try Venice's oldest wine bar, **Al Volta**, Calle Cavalli di S. Marco 4081, S. Marco, with over 2000 Italian and foreign labels to choose from and a sumptuous array of *cichetti*. *Open 9–2.30 and 5–9; closed Sun*. **Do Mori**, a resolutely traditional Rialto market bar, north of Ruga Vecchia San Giovanni, has delicious snacks (but no tables) to go with your *ombra*. *Open 8.30–9; closed Sun*.

Between 5pm and dinner is the time to indulge in a beer and *tramezzini*, finger sandwiches that come in a hundred varieties, and some of the best are to be found at eccentric **Bar alla Toletta**, Callle della Toletta 1191, Dorsoduro, run by a temperamental middle-aged couple with a voracious appetite for jazz.

The title of best *gelateria* in the city has by convention been accorded to **Paolin**, on the Campo Santo Stefano, S. Marco, above all for their divine pistachio. However, **Nico**, on the Zattere ai Gesuati, Dorsoduro, is also a must on anyone's ice cream tour, if the late night queues are anything to go by.

jazz, clubs and nightspots

Venice's few late-night bars and music venues can be fun, or just posy and dull, and what you find is pretty much a matter of pot luck. **Paradiso Perduto**, Fondamenta della Misericordia 2540, Cannaregio, ✆ 041 720 581, is the city's best-known and most popular late-night bar/restaurant with inexpensive though variable food, and a relaxed, bohemian atmosphere popular with a mix of locals and English visitors. Once known for live jazz, they now often have a bit of trouble with their late-night licence, so live events are rare. *Open 6pm–midnight, sometimes later; closed Wed*. A current favourite for young trendies is **Taverna l'Olandese Volante** (Flying Dutchman), Campo S. Lio 5658, Castello, ✆ 041 528 9349, Venice's answer to a pub, open late with snacks and simple food. The relaxed and informal wine bar **Osteria da Codroma**, Fondamenta Briati 2540, Dorsoduro, ✆ 041 520 4161, hosts a backgammon club, art shows and occasional live jazz. *Open 7pm–2am; closed Thurs*. Another restaurant/bar with music, dancing and sometimes live rock or jazz is **Ai Canottieri**, Ponte Tre Archi 690, Cannaregio, ✆ 041 715 408. *Open 7pm–2am; closed Sun*.

There are also quite a few fairly glitzy piano bars, such as **Linea d'Ombra**, Zattere ai Saloni, near the Salute, ✆ 041 528 5259. *Open 8pm–1am; closed Wed*. A favourite place for Venetians to make off to in Marghera is **Al Vapore**, Via Fratelli Bandiera 8, ✆ 041 930 796, which hosts live rock and jazz. In July and August there's a disco on the Lido: **Acropolis**, Lungomare Marconi 22, ✆ 041 526 0466. The Lido is also the place to hie for a late-night game of billiards, *chez* **Al Delfino**, an 'American Bar' with music and snacks at Lungomare Marconi 96, ✆ 041 526 8309. *Open until 2am*. Or **Villa Eva**, Gran Viale 49, ✆ 041 526 1884, with music and snacks from midnight until 4am. *Closed Thurs except in the summer*.

The main late-night drinking holes are **Harry's Bar** (*see* above, 'Eating Out'), especially if someone else is paying. **Osteria ai Assassini**, Calle degli Assassini, S. Marco, has wines, beers, and good *cichetti*. *Open till midnight; closed Sun*. For more filling victuals, try **Vino Vino** (*see* above, 'Eating Out'). *Open till 2am.* The **Creperia Poggi**, Cannaregio 2103, © 041 715 971, has music and also stays open till 2am, flipping crêpes until midnight. *Closed Sun.* The last chance for an ice cream is at 3am at the Lido's **Gelateria Bar Maleti**, Gran Viale 47. *Closed Wed.*

exhibitions and art festivals

Venice is one of Europe's top cities for exhibitions: major international shows fill the **Palazzo Grassi**, Campo S. Samuele, S. Marco, which Fiat has transformed into a lavishly equipped exhibition and cultural centre. High calibre art and photographic exhibitions also appear frequently at the **Palazzo Querini-Stampalia**, the **Peggy Guggenheim Collection**, and **Ca' Pésaro**.

Then there's the **Biennale**, the most famous contemporary art show in the world, founded in 1895 and now held, in principle, in even-numbered years. The main exhibits of the forty or so countries officially represented are set up in the permanent pavilions in the Giardini Pubblici, but there is also an open section for younger and less-established artists, in venues across the city.

The city's other great cultural junket is the **Venice Film Festival**, held in the Palazzo del Cinema and the Astra Cinema on the Lido every year in late August and September. As well as spotting the stars, you can sometimes get in to see films if you arrive at the cinemas really early—tickets are only sold on the same day as each showing.

traditional festivals

Venice's renowned **Carnival**, first held in the ten days preceding Lent in 1094, was revived in 1979 after several decades of dormancy. It attracts huge crowds, but faces an uphill battle against the inveterate Italian love of *bella figura*—getting dressed up in elaborate costumes, wandering down to San Marco and taking each other's picture is as much as most of the revellers get up to. Concerts and shows are put on all over Venice, with city and corporate sponsorship, but there's very little spontaneity or serious carousing, and certainly no trace of what Byron called the 'revel of the earth'.

Even so, a **Carnival mask** can still make a good souvenir, either in inexpensive papier mâché (*cartapesta*) or in leather. There are mask shops all over Venice, but for the real, traditionally crafted item, try **Giorgio Clanetti (Laboratorio Artigiano Maschere)**, Barbaria delle Tole 6657, Castello, near SS. Giovanni e Paolo.

In 1988 Venice revived another crowd pleaser, **La Sensa**, held on the first Sunday after Ascension Day, in which the doge married the sea (*see* p.80). Now the mayor plays the groom, in a replica of the state barge or *Bucintoro*. It's as corny and pretentious as it sounds, but on the same day you can watch the gondoliers race in the **Vogalonga**, or long row, from San Marco to Burano and back again.

Venice's most spectacular festival, **Il Redentore**, is held on the third Sunday of July, with its bridge of boats (*see* p.114). The greatest excitement happens the Saturday night before, when Venetians row out for an evening picnic on the water, manoeuvring for the best view of the fabulous fireworks display over the Lagoon. For landlubbers (and there are thousands of them) the prime viewing and picnicking spots are towards the eastern ends of either the Giudecca or the Zattere.

More perspiration is expended in the **Regata Storica** (first Sunday in September), a splendid pageant of historic vessels and crews in Renaissance costumes and hotly contested races by gondoliers and a variety of other rowers down the Grand Canal. Another bridge of boats is built on 21 November, this time across the Grand Canal to the Salute, for the feast of **Santa Maria della Salute**, which also commemorates the ending of another plague, in 1631. This event provides the only opportunity to see Longhena's unique basilica as it would have been when it was built, with its doors thrown open on to the Grand Canal.

The Lagoon and its Islands

Pearly and melting into the bright sky, iridescent blue or murky green, a sheet of glass yellow and pink in the dawn, or leaden, opaque grey: Venice's Lagoon is one of its wonders, a desolate, often melancholy and strange, often beautiful and seductive 'landscape' with a hundred personalities. It is 56km long and averages 8km across; half of it, the Laguna Morta ('Dead Lagoon'), where the tides never reach, consists of mud flats except in the spring, while the shallows of the Laguna Viva are always submerged, and cleansed by tides twice a day. To navigate this treacherous sea, the Venetians have developed an intricate network of channels, marked by *bricole*—wooden posts topped by orange lamps—that keep their craft from running aground. When threatened, the Venetians only had to pull out the *bricole* to confound their enemies; and as such the Lagoon was always known as 'the sacred walls of the nation'. Keeping the Brenta and other rivers from silting it up kept engineers busy for centuries.

> The city of the Venetians, by divine providence founded in the waters and protected by their environment, is defended by a wall of water. Therefore should anybody in any manner dare to infer damage to the public waters he shall be considered as an enemy of our country and shall be punished by no less pain that that committed to whomever violates the sacred border of the country. This act will be enforced forever.

16th-centuy edict of the Maistrato alle Acque

'Forever' unfortunately ended in the 20th century. New islands were made of landfill dredged up to deepen the shipping canals, upsetting the delicate balance of lagoon life; outboards and *vaporetti* churn up the gook from the Lagoon and canal beds, and send corroding waves against Venice's fragile buildings. These affect the tide, and increase both the number of *acque alte* and unnaturally low tides, that embarrrassingly expose Venice's underthings—and let air in where it was never supposed to go, accelerating the rot and the subsidence of its wooden piles and substructures.

Then there are the ingredients in the water itself. The Lagoon is a messy stew of 60 years' worth of organic waste, phosphates, agricultural and industrial by-products and sediments—a lethal mixture that ecologists warn will take a century to purify, even if by some miracle pollution is stopped now. It's a sobering thought, especially when many Venetians in their 50s remember when even the Grand Canal was clean enough to swim in.

And in recent years, the Lagoon has been sprouting the kind of blooms that break a girl's heart—algae, 'green pastures' of it, stinking and choking its fish. No one is sure if the algae epidemic isn't just part of a natural cycle; after all, there's an old church on one Lagoon island

to Treviso

to Trieste

to Castelfranco

Fiume Piave

A27

A4

13

245

Fiume Sile

Altino

Jesolo

14

A27

Mestre

Campalto

Aeroporto Marco Polo

Torcello

Lido di Jesolo

Mazzorbo

Burano

Cavallino

S.Francesco del Deserto

Treporti

Murano

Marghera

S. Giuliano

S. Erasmo

Litorale del Cavallino

A4

S. Michele

Mira

VENICE

La Certosa

Punta Sabbioni

Malcontenta

Fusina

S.Clemente

S. Lazzaro degli Armeni

Porto di Lido

Sacca Séssola

Lido

Povéglia

Litorale di Lido

Malamocco

Alberoni

Porto di Malamocco

S.Pietro in Volta

309

Valle di Millecampi

Adriatic

Litorale di Pellestrina Murazzi (Sea Walls)

Pellestrina

Sea

Porto di Chioggia

N

Chioggia

309

Sottomarin

Fiume Brenta

5 km

3 miles

Isola Verde

The Venetian Lagoon

127

called San Giorgio in Alga (St George in Algae). Crops of algae are on record in the 1700s and 1800s and at the beginning of this century, at times when water temperatures were abnormally high because of the weather. But other statistics are harder to reconcile with climatic cycles: since 1932, 78 species of algae have disappeared from the Lagoon, while 24 new ones have blossomed, these mostly microaglae thriving off the surplus of phosphates. These chemicals have now been banned in the Lagoon communities, leading to a noticeable fall in recent algae counts.

Once the largest of the 39 Lagoon islands were densely inhabited, each occupied by a town or at least a monastery. Now all but a few have been abandoned, many tiny ones with only a forlorn, vandalized shell of a building, overgrown with weeds. Occasionally one hears of plans to bring them back to life, only to wither on the vine of Italian bureaucracy. If you think you have a good idea, take it up with the Revenue Office (Intendenza di Finanza).

The Lido and South Lagoon

The Lido, one of the long spits of land that forms the protective outer edge of the Lagoon, is by far the most glamorous of the islands, one that has given its name to countless bathing establishments, bars, amusement arcades and cinemas all over the world. On its 12 kilometres of beach, poets, potentates and plutocrats at the turn of the century spent their holidays in palatial hotels and villas, making the Lido the pinnacle of Belle Epoque fashion, so brilliantly evoked in Thomas Mann's *Death in Venice*, and Visconti's subsequent film. The story was set and filmed in the **Grand Hotel des Bains**, just north of the Mussolini-style **Municipal Casino** and **Palazzo del Cinema**, where Venice hosts its Film Festival.

The Lido is still the playground of the Venetians and their visitors, with its bathing concessions, riding clubs, tennis courts, golf courses and shooting ranges. The free beach, the **Spiaggia Comunale**, is on the north part of the island, a 15-minute walk from the *vaporetto* stop at San Nicolò (go down the Gran Viale, and turn left on the Lungomare d'Annunzio), where you can hire a changing hut and frolic in the sand and sea.

Further north, beyond the private airfield, the **Porto di Lido** is maritime Venice's front door, the most important of the three entrances into the Lagoon, where you can watch the ships of the world sail by. This is where the Doge would sail to toss his ring into the waves, in the annual 'Marriage of the Sea'. It is stoutly defended by the mighty **Forte di Sant'Andrea** on the island of Le Vignole, built in 1543 by Venice's fortifications genius Sanmicheli. In times of danger, a great chain was extended from the fort across the channel.

One of the smaller Lagoon islands just off the Lido, with its landmark onion-domed campanile, is **San Lazzaro degli Armeni** (*vaporetto no.20 from Riva degli Schiavoni, open to visitors daily 3–5pm*). It was Venice's leper colony in the Middle Ages, but in 1715 the then-deserted island was given to the Mechitarist Fathers of the Armenian Catholic Church after they were expelled from Greece by the Turks. Today their monastery is still one of the world's major centres of Armenian culture and its monks, always noted as linguists, run a famous polyglot press able to print in 32 languages, one of the last survivors in a city once renowned for its publishing. Tours of San Lazzaro include a museum filled with relics of the ancient Christian history of Armenia, as well as memorabilia of Lord Byron, who spent a winter visiting the fathers and bruising his brain with Armenian. The fathers offer inexpensive prints of Venice for sale; or else they would appreciate a donation.

Despite dire reports about the state of the waters of the Adriatic, people still swim off the Lido without becoming mutants, but there is an alternative in the **swimming pool** on Sacca Fisola, at the west end of the Giudecca, ✆ 041 528 5430. If you're interested in **sailing**, enquire at the sailing club, the **Compagnia della Vela**, near the Giardinetti in S. Marco, ✆ 041 522 2593, for information on lessons and boat hire.

The Lido has the attractive 18-hole **Alberoni Golf Course**, Via del Forte Alberoni, ✆ 041 731 015, and two tennis clubs, the **Tennis Club Venezia**, Lungomare Marconi 41/d, ✆ 041 526 0335, and the **Campi Comunali di Tennis**, ✆ 041 526 5689. You can also ride along the Lido, like Byron and Shelley, although it's no longer a romantic hooves-in-the-surf affair—enquire at **Circolo Ippico Veneziano**, Ca' Bianco, Lido, ✆ 041 526 1820. If you prefer to **cycle** along the Lido, bikes can be hired at **Giorgio Barbieri**, Via Zara 5.

Where to Stay and Eat

luxury

★★★★★ **Excelsior Palace**, Lungomare Marconi 41, Lido di Venezia, ✆ 041 526 0201, ⊕ 041 526 7276. An immense confection, built in 1907 as the biggest and most luxurious resort hotel in the world and recently redesigned with as much flamboyance as ever. The outrageous exterior is part-Hollywood and part-Moorish neo-Gothic. Private beach, swimming pool, tennis courts, golf, nightclub and private launch service to Venice are some of its amenities. Ogling the stars at the film festival is another. The restaurant, ✆ 041 526 0201 (*very expensive*), offers the classic turn-of-the-century Lido experience, with everything you could desire—including a traditional Venetian meal. *Closed mid–Nov–mid-Mar.*

very expensive

★★★★ **Des Bains**, Lungomare Marconi 17, Lido di Venezia, ✆ 041 526 5921, ⊕ 041 526 0113. A grand old luxury hotel, now part of the Sheraton empire, that preserves much of its *Belle Epoque* revelries in its magnificent Liberty-style salon, private *cabanas*, and large garden designed for dalliance. Thomas Mann stayed here on several occasions, and has Aschenbach sigh his life away on the private beach. There's also a salt-water swimming pool, tennis courts, perfect service, and a launch service into Venice. *Closed Dec–mid-Mar.*

★★★★ **Quattro Fontane**, Via delle Quattro Fontane 16, Lido di Venezia, ✆ 041 526 0227, ⊕ 041 526 0726. The best of the smaller Lido hotels, it was formerly the seaside villa of a Venetian family. Its cool walled-in courtyard is inviting and tranquil, and the public and private rooms are furnished with antiques. Tennis court. Book well in advance. *Closed Nov–Mar.*

expensive

★★★ **Villa Parco**, Via Rodi 1, Lido di Venezia, ✆ 041 526 0015, ⊕ 041 526 7620. A recently renovated villa a short way from the beach with a fine little garden for a bit of privacy. Children are welcome.

From the Lido to Chioggia

Tourist Information

Chioggia: Viale Po 16, Lido di Sottomarina, ✆ 041 554 0466, ✆ 041 554 0855.

Buses/ferries from the Lido or quicker buses from Piazzale Roma will take you to Chioggia at the southermost end of the Lagoon. The seldom used bus/ferry route (leaving roughly every hour) allows you to take in **Malamocco**, a tranquil fishing village named after the first capital of the Lagoon townships, a nearby islet that lost its status after Pepin and his Franks nabbed it in 810. The capital moved to the Rialto, leaving the original Malamocco to sink poetically into the sea during a tremendous storm in 1106. Next to it, the small resort of **Alberoni** is home to the Lido Golf Course and the ferry to the next island reef, Pellestrina, which is even thinner. It has two sleepy villages, **San Pietro in Volta** and **Pellestrina**, where the *murazzi* or sea walls begin, the last great public works project of the Republic's Magistrato alle Acque. Built in response to to increased flooding in the 18th century, the 4km-long Murazzi are constructed of huge, white Istrian blocks and built, as their plaque proudly states: *Ausu Romano–Aere Veneto* ('With Roman audacity and Venetian money'). From 1782 until 4 November 1966 they succeeded in holding back the flood.

Dusty **Chioggia** is one of the most important fishing ports on the Adriatic, a kind of populist Venice where the streets and canals are arrow-straight and full of working craft, many with brightly painted sails. The morning **fish market**, brimming with exotic denizens of the deep is one of the wonders of Italy. On the map the town on its islands even resembles a fish, gutted and spread out flat, its straight narrow lanes lined up like bones.

The Venetians like to poke fun at Chioggia, which they consider a grumpy old place, and they like to wind it up by calling the little Lion of St Mark on its column in Piazzettta Vigo (where the ferry deposits you) the 'Cat of St Mark'. Goldoni was amused enough by it all to make the town the setting of one of his comedies, *Le Baruffe Chiozzotte*. Almost nothing remains of medieval Chioggia thanks to the blockade and siege by the Genoese in the 1380 Battle of Chioggia. But if you take the first bridge left from the port and continue straight, you will eventually reach the church of **San Domenico**, containing Carpaccio's last painting, *St Paul*, signed and dated 1520, and a beautiful quattrocento crucifix on the altar.

Chioggia's other monuments are strung along the main **Corso del Popolo** (the fish spine). The fish market is just beyond a large 14th-century grain warehouse, the **Granaio**, with a relief of the Madonna on the façade by Sansovino. Further up the Corso, past a couple of low-key churches, is the **Duomo**, built by Baldassare Longhena after the 14th-century original, except for the campanile, burned in 1623. In the chapel to the left of the altar are some murky, unpleasant 18th-century paintings of martyrdoms, one of which is attributed to Tiepolo, although it's hard to swallow. However, the Gothic chapel of San Martino has a lovely polyptych (1349) that really might be by Paolo Veneziano.

And when you've had your fill of fish and the locals, you can stroll along the long bridge (or catch the bus at the Duomo) for a swim among the vivacious Italian families at Chioggia's lido, **Sottomarina**, which attracts mainly Italian families; from here it's a short drive down into the Po Delta, now a natural park (*see* p.162).

Chioggia ✉ 30015

All the hotels are at Sottomarina, where you'll find typical family run seaside lodgings at the ★★★**Florida**, Viale Mediterraneo 9, ✆ 041 491 505, 🖷 041 496 6760 (*moderate; closed Nov–Jan*) or ★★★**Park**, Lungomare Adriatico, ✆ 041 496 5032, 🖷 041 490 111 (*moderate–inexpensive*). Seafood lovers flock to the cat—**El Gato**, right behind the fish market in Campo S. Andrea 653, ✆ 041401806 (*expensive*), where the chef prepares the freshest of fish in the tastiest of Venetian styles. *Closed Mon and Tues lunch, Jan and mid Feb.* At the old-fashioned **Trattoria Buon Pesce**, Stradale Ponte Caneva 625, ✆ 041 400 861 (*moderate*) start with *gnocchetti alla marinara* and follow it with oysters or crab. Prices are half what you'd pay in Venice.

Islands in the North Lagoon

San Michele

Most Venetian itineraries take in the islands of Murano, Burano and Torcello, all easily reached by inexpensive *vaporetti*. Lines 52 or 23 to Murano call at the cypress-studded cemetery island of **San Michele**, with its simple but elegant church of **San Michele in Isola** by Mauro Codussi (1469), his first-known work and Venice's first taste of the Florentine Renaissance, albeit with a Venetian twist in the tri-lobed front. It contains the tomb of Fra Paolo Sarpi, who led the ideological battle against the Pope when the republic was placed under the Great Interdict of 1607. Venice, considering St Mark the equal of St Peter, refused to be cowed and won the battle of will after two years, thanks mainly to Sarpi, whose *Treatise on the Interdict* proved it was illegal. In return, he was jumped and knifed by an assassin: '*Agnosco stylum romanae curiae,*' he quipped ('I recognize the method or the "dagger" of the Roman court'). His major work, the critical *History of the Council of Trent* (*see* p.68) didn't improve his standing in Rome, but made him a hero in Venice. Sarpi's main interest however, was science; he supported Copernicus and shared notes with Galileo, then lecturing at Padua, and 'discovered' the contraction of the iris.

The **cemetery** itself is entered through the cloister next to the church (*open daily 8.30–4*). The Protestant and Orthodox sections contain the tombs of some of the many foreigners who preferred to face eternity from Venice, among them Ezra Pound, Sergei Diaghilev, Frederick Rolfe (Baron Corvo) and Igor Stravinsky. The gate-keeper provides a basic map.

Murano, the Island of Glass

The island of Murano (*vaporetti nos.52, 52 or 23 from S. Zaccaria or nos.12 or 13 from Fondamente Nuove*) is synonymous with glass, the most celebrated of Venice's industries. The Venetians were the first in the Middle Ages to rediscover the secret of making crystal glass, and especially mirrors, and it was a secret they kept a monopoly on for centuries by using the most drastic measures: if ever a glassmaker let himself be coaxed abroad, the Council of Ten sent their assassins after him in hot pursuit. However, those who remained in Venice were treated with kid gloves. Because of the danger of fire, all the forges in Venice were relocated to Murano in 1291, and the little island became a kind of republic within a republic—minting its own coins, policing itself, even developing its own list of NHs (*nobili homini*—noblemen) in its own *Golden Book*—aristocrats of glass, who built solid palaces along Murano's own Grand Canal.

But glass-making declined like everything else in Venice, and only towards the end of the 19th century were the forges once more stoked up on Murano. Can you visit them? You betcha! After watching the glass being made, there's the inevitable tour of the 'Museum Show Rooms' with their American funeral parlour atmosphere, all solicitude, carpets and hush-hush—not unfitting, as some of the blooming chandeliers, befruited mirrors and poison-coloured chalices begin to make Death look good. There is no admission charge, and there's not even too much pressure to buy. It wasn't always so kitschy. The **Museo Vetrario** or Glass Museum (*open 10–5; closed Wed; adm*), in the 17th-century Palazzo Giustinian on Fondamenta Cavour has some simple pieces from Roman times, and a choice collection of 15th-century Murano glass, especially the delightful 1480 *Barovier Nuptial Cup*; later glass tends to prove that Murano's glassblowers have long had a wayward streak.

Nearby stands the another good reason to visit this rather dowdy island, the Veneto-Byzantine **Santi Maria e Donato** (*open daily 8–12 and 4–7*), a contemporary of St Mark's basilica, with a beautiful arcaded apse. The floor is paved with a marvellous 12th-century mosaic, incorporating coloured pieces of ancient Murano glass, and on the wall there's a fine Byzantine mosaic of the Virgin. The relics of Bishop Donato of Euboea were nabbed by Venetian body-snatchers, but in this case they outdid themselves, bringing home not only San Donato's bones but those of the dragon the good bishop slew with a gob of spit; you can see them hanging behind the altar. Back on the Fondamenta dei Vetrai, the 15th-century **San Pietro Martire** has one of Giovanni Bellini's best altarpieces, *Pala Barbarigo* (1484), a monumental *Sacra conversazione* of the Madonna enthroned with SS. Mark and Augustine, and Doge Barbarigo, that achieves a rare serenity that perfectly suits the subject.

Burano, the Island of Lace

Burano (*vaporetto no.12*) is the Legoland of the Lagoon, where everything is in brightly coloured miniature—the canals, the bridges, the leaning tower, and the houses, painted with a Fauvist sensibility in the deepest of colours. Traditionally on Burano the men fish and the women make Venetian point, 'the most Italian of all lace work', beautiful, intricate and murder on the eyesight. All over Burano you can find samples on sale (of which a great deal are machine-made or imported), or you can watch it being made at the **Scuola dei Merletti** in Piazza Galuppi (*open Tues–Sat 10–4; adm*). '*Scuola*' in this case is misleading; no young woman in Burano wants to learn such an excruciating art. The school itself was founded in 1872, when traditional lacemaking was already in decline. In the sacristy of the church of **San Martino** (with its tipsily leaning campanile) look for Giambattista Tiepolo's *Crucifixion*, which Mary McCarthy aptly described as 'a ghastly masquerade ball'.

From Burano you can hire a *sandola* (small gondola) to **San Francesco del Deserto**, some 20 minutes to the south. St Francis is said to have founded a chapel here in 1220, and the whole islet was subsequently given to his order for a **monastery** (*visitors welcome daily 9–11 and 3–5.30*). In true Franciscan fashion, it's not the buildings you'll remember (though there's a fine 14th-century cloister), but the love of nature evident in the beautiful gardens. Admission is free, but donations are appreciated.

Though fewer than 100 people remain on Torcello (*vaporetto no.12; no.14 takes twice as long*), this small island was once a serious rival to Venice herself. According to legend, its history began when God ordered the bishop of Roman *Altinum*, north of Mestre, to take his flock away from the heretical Lombards into the Lagoon. From a tower the bishop saw a star rise over Torcello, and so led the people of Altinum to this lonely island to set up their new home. It grew quickly, and for the first few centuries it seems to have been the real metropolis of the Lagoon, with 20,000 inhabitants, palaces, a mercantile fleet and five townships; but malaria decimated the population, the *Sile* silted up Torcello's corner of the Lagoon, and the bigger rising star of Venice drew its citizens to the Rialto.

Torcello is now a ghost island overgrown with weeds, its palaces either sunk into the marsh or quarried for their stone; narrow paths are all that remain of once bustling thoroughfares. One of these follows a canal from the landing stage past the picturesque Ponte del Diavolo to the grass-grown piazza in front of the magnificent Veneto-Byzantine **Cathedral of Santa Maria Assunta** with its lofty campanile, founded in 639 and rebuilt in the same Ravenna basilica-style in 1008. The interior (*no longer a cathedral, although mass is celebrated every Sunday during the summer; open daily 10.30–6; adm*) has the finest mosaics in Venice, all done by 11th- and 12th-century Greek artists, from the wonderful floor to the spectacular *Last Judgement* on the west wall and the unsettling, heart-rending *Teotoco*, the stark, gold-ground mosaic of the thin, weeping Virgin portrayed as the 'bearer of God'.

Next to the cathedral is the restored 11th-century octagonal church of **Santa Fosca**, surrounded by an attractive portico, a beautiful and rare late Byzantine work. Near here stands an ancient stone throne called the **Chair of Attila**, though its connection with the Hunnish supremo is nebulous. Across the square, the two surviving secular buildings of Torcello, the Palazzo del Consiglio and Palazzo dell'Archivio, contain the small **Museo dell'Estuario** (*open daily 10–12.30 and 2–4; closed Mon and hols; adm*), with an interesting collection of archaeological finds and artefacts from Torcello's former churches.

Where to Stay and Eating Out

Murano ✉ 30121

Après all those empty glasses, take comfort over a chilled bottle of Soave and a plate of *spaghetti al vongole* at **Ai Frati**, Fondamenta Venier 4, ✆ 041 736 694 (*expensive*), a classic Venetian seafood restaurant. *Closed Thurs, Feb.*

Burano ✉ 30121

No frills **Raspo de Ua**, Via Galuppi 560, ✆ 041 730 095, 🖷 041 730 397 (*inexpensive*) offers six rooms above a restaurant and a chance to get to know Burano after the tourists have melted back into the Lagoon.

Torcello ✉ 30012

★★★**Locanda Cipriani**, Piazza S. Fosca 29, ✆ 041 730 150, 🖷 041 735 433 (*very expensive*). There are only six rooms in this recently renovated and infamous country house hotel, basking in the most rural and tranquil spot of the whole *comune* of

Venice. Some have views over the hotel's blissful garden; you can sleep where Hemingway wrote his Venice novel, *Across the River and Into the Trees*—standing up because of haemorrhoids. All the rooms are spacious and fresh, and prices include half or full board. *Closed Jan.* The restaurant (*very expensive*) serves delicious seafood with all the Cipriani trimmings, in summer in the garden. *Closed Tues.*

Cavallino and Jesolo

One suspects these beach resorts closest to Venice owe part of their success to their total *lack* of any cultural 'obligations'. On the other hand, they have every facility for fun, Italian-style, from windsurfers and rollerblades to hire to water parks, horse-riding along the lagoon, bike trails and even covered *bocce* courts.

Tourist Information

Lido di Jesolo: Piazza Brescia 13, ℗ 042 137 0601, e-mail: *apt@marconinet.it*

There are two ports on the *litorale* linked to Venice: **Punta Sabbioni** (*vaporetto Line 14, from Riva degli Schiavoni and the Lido; car ferry Line 17, from Tronchetto*) and **Treporti** (*vaporetto Line 12*); frequent buses ply the strip between Jesolo with Punta Sabbioni. The **Litorale del Cavallino**, the 10km sliver of land that protects the northern part of the Lagoon, was long known as a semi-wild place of beach, dunes and pine forests. There's still some of that left, among its 28 camping grounds and umpteen hotels and restaurants. **Lido di Jesolo**, north from Punta Sabbioni, is a densely packed resort on a wide sandy beach, attracting some six million tourists a year.

Where to Stay and Eating Out

Because of the Adriatic's periodic pollution and algae problems, nearly all hoteliers have private pools as well as private beaches, including all those listed below.

Cavallino ✉ 30013

Quiet, out of the centre **★★★Fenix**, Via F. Baracca 45, ℗ 041 968 040, ✆ 041 968 831 (*moderate*) is convenient for the pines, beach, or trips into Venice. *Open mid May–Sept.* For lovely food, especially fresh, simply prepared seafood hot from the grill, book a table at the historic **Trattoria Laguna**, Via Pordelio 444, ℗ 041 968 058 (*expensive*), overlooking the lagoon, and save room for one of their famous desserts. *Closed Thurs out of season, and Jan–mid Feb.*

Lido di Jesolo ✉ 30017

An elegant construction from the 1930s, **★★★★Casa Bianca al Mare**, Piazzetta Casa Bianca 1, ℗ 042 137 0615, ✆ 042 137 1659 (*expensive*) is a lovely place to stay, set off by its own park. **★★★★Grand Hotel Las Vegas**, Via Mascagni 2, ℗ 042 197 1515, ✆ 042 138 0581 (*moderate*) is attractive, modern, and right on the sea; all rooms have balconies, and the restaurant is one of Jesolo's best. *Open May–Sept.* **★★★Christian**, Via Olanda 150, ℗/✆ 042 136 2264 (*moderate–inexpensive*) is similar, but simpler. *Closed Oct–Feb.*

The Veneto

The Veneto is lush and green, plush with art and architecture, and charged with the stuff that dreams are made on. The Bard may never have visited the cities where he set his plays, but there's something very Shakespearean about them—something gorgeous and poetic, full of character and Renaissance swagger. The literally thousands of villas and gardens, scattered from the foothills of the Dolomites to the plain of the Po, give the Veneto a uniquely rarefied if often daydreamy distinction; like Tuscany this is an eminently civilized land, but a much softer one, more sensuous, with less attitude.

The Veneto has always been one of the wealthiest corners of Italy, and since the war its beauty has often fallen victim to its own prosperity. While car-free in their historic centres, the cities are often engulfed by some mighty powerful sprawl, 'Venetopolis' as regional writer Carlo Pizzati dubbed it, a dragon with its tail dipped in Lake Garda, its body stretched over Verona, Vicenza and Padua, its neck resting on Mestre and Venice, its tongue licking Treviso and Belluno. Villas built in idyllic rural settings are often now on busy roads. As Pizzati writes, there is a fun side to Venetopolis and its highways: 'Someone from Treviso can have dinner in Venice and an hour later drive to Verona to go listen to *Rigoletto*. A Vicentino, after skiing in Cortina, can drive down to Padua to go to the movies and be back home only 20 minutes after showtime.' But you'd have to drive like an Italian nun to do it. The point is, in the Veneto you have to try a bit harder than in Tuscany to find the kind of landscapes immortalized by the great Venetian painters—they exist, and are never far away, although ironically the best way to find them is by joining the car crowd.

Venice to Padua: the Brenta Canal

Over the years, the river Brenta made itself universally detested by flooding the surrounding farmland and choking the Lagoon with silt, and in the 14th century the Venetians decided to control its antics once and for all. They raised its banks and dug a canal to divert its waters, and when all the hydraulic labours were completed in the 16th century they realized that the new canal was the ideal place for their summer *villeggiatura*; their gondoliers could conveniently row them straight to their doors, or, as Goethe and thousands of other visitors have done, they could travel there on the *Burchiello*, a water bus propelled by oars or horses. Over seventy villas and palaces sprouted up along this 'extension of the Grand Canal' and they were famous for their summer parties. Now, if only you could wave a magic wand and make the traffic disappear. The cars have replaced the fireflies that once made a summer's evening canal ride so magical, casting a glow bright enough to read by.

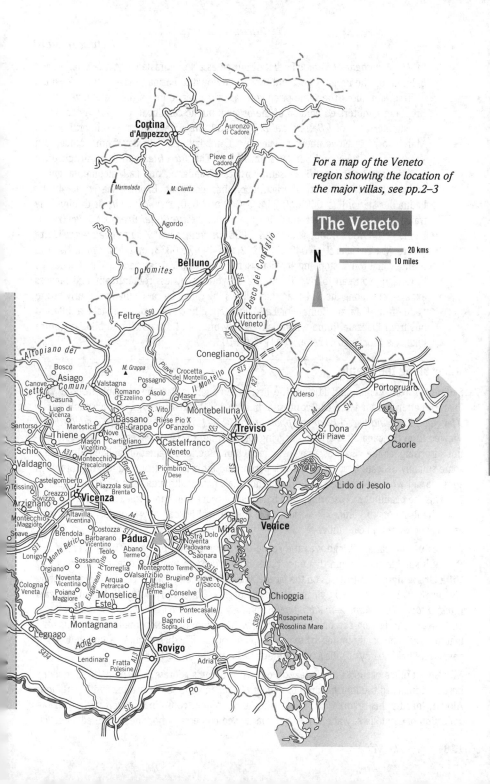

For a map of the Veneto
region showing the location of
the major villas, see pp.2–3

The Veneto

N

20 kms
10 miles

Cortina
d'Ampezzo

Auronzo
di Cadore

Pieve di
Cadore

Marmolada   M. Civetta

Agordo

Belluno

Dolomites

Bosco del Cansiglio

Feltre   S50

Vittorio
Veneto

Conegliano

Altopiano dei

Bosco

Asiago

M. Grappa

Possagno

Crocetta
del Montello

Canove
Sette
Comuni

Valstagna

Romano
d'Ezzelino

Asolo

Maser

Oderso

Portogruaro

Casuna

Lugo di
Vicenza

S. Vito

Montebelluna

Santorso

Maròstica

Bassano
del Grappa

Riese Pio X
O'Fanzolo

Treviso

S. Dona
di Piave

Caorle

Thiene

Nove

Mason
Vicentino

Cartigliano

Castelfranco
Veneto

Schio

Montecchio
Precalcino

Piombino
Dese

Valdagno

Castelgomberto

Piazzola sul
Brenta

Lido di Jesolo

Tissino

Sovizzo

Creazzo

Vicenza

Arzignano

Altavilla
Vicentina

Montecchio
Maggiore

Brendola

Costozza

Barbarano
Vicentino

Padua

Ongo

Mira

Venice

Spave

Lonigo

Sossano

Teolo

Abano
Terme

Stra Dolo

Noventa
Padovana

Saonara

Orgiano

Noventa
Vicentina

Torreglia

Montegrotto Terme

Valsanzibio

Brugine

Piove
di Sacco

Cologna
Veneta

Poiana
Maggiore

Arqua
Petrarca

Monselice

Battaglia
Terme

Conselve

Chioggia

Este

Pontecasale

Montagnana

Bagnoli di
Sopra

Rosapineta
Rosolina Mare

Legnago

Adige

Rovigo

Lendinara

Fratta
Polesine

Adria

Po

In *The Merchant of Venice* Portia, disguised as a young male lawyer, left her villa at Belmont on the Brenta Canal and proceeded down to Fusina to save Antonio's pound of flesh. For about the same price you can trace her route on the stately, villa-lined Brenta in a motorized version of the original public canalboat, the *Burchiello*, or on the simpler craft of *I Battelli del Brenta*; both lines make the day-long cruise from March to early November on Tuesday, Thursday and Saturday from Venice, and Wednesday, Friday and Sunday from Padua. The **Burchiello motor-launch** price includes admission into Villa Pisani, Barchessa Valmarana and La Malcontenta, guide, and coach back to the city of origin; book through Siamic Express, Via Trieste 42 (by Padua bus station), ✆ 049 660 944, ✉ 049 662 830, *siamic@tin.it*; or through any travel agent or CIT office abroad. For the similar *I Battelli del Brenta*: Via Pellizzo 1, Padua, ✆ 049 807 4340, ✉ 049 807 2830, *intercity.shiny.i/ battellidelbrenta*. **Delta Tours**, Via Toscana 2, ✆ 049 870 0232, ✉ 049 976 0833, *deltatour@tin.it* also run Brenta canal tours, stopping at Villa Pisana, Barchessa Valmarana and Villa Gradenigo in Oriago. You can follow the Brenta on your own, less romantically and far less expensively, along the S11 road that follows the canal, by car or the half-hourly bus to Padua from Piazzale Roma. For La Malcontenta, however, you must take a different bus from Piazzale Roma which leaves only once an hour. Or hire a bike at Centre Bike, Via Mocenigo 3, Mira, ✆ 041 420 110.

Villas along the Brenta

Sailing up from Venice and Fusina, the first grand sight is Palladio's temple-fronted Villa Foscari, better known as **La Malcontenta**, built in 1560 and as striking as it is simple (*open May–Oct, Tues and Sat 9–12 or by appointment, ✆ 041 520 3966; adm exp; guided tours*). Viewed from the canal, it is a vision begging for a Scarlett O'Hara to sweep down the steps— not surprising, as the villa was a favourite model for American plantation builders. Inside are some suitably delicate frescoes by Zelotti, Bernardino India and Battista Franco, one of which shows a sad woman—a possible source of the villa's name, although others say the unhappy one was the beautiful La Foscarina, who hated being cooped up here by her husband, far away from the fleshpots of Venice. Descendants of the original Foscari now own La Malcontenta, and have restored it beautifully.

Further up the canal, Oriago was the scene of early medieval battles between Venice and Padua. It still has the column that once marked their borders, as well as the late 16th-century **Villa Gradenigo**, with frescoes on the façade, which has recently been opened to canal-boating visitors. Mira Ponte, the next village, is the site of the 18th-century **Villa Widmann-Foscari** (*guided tours Tues–Sun, 9–6; adm exp*). If you only have time for one villa, don't make it this one—redone in French baroque soon after its construction, the villa contains some of its original furniture and gaudy murals by two of Tiepolo's pupils. The best parties, lasting up to eight days, were held nearby at Villa Corner, which had a facelift in the 1800s.

Mira's post office occupies the **Palazzo Foscarini**, Byron's address in 1817–19. While living here he composed the fourth Canto of *Childe Harold* and cut off his last links with perfidious Albion, through his divorce and sale of the family home, consoling himself with a rag-tag collection of gondoliers, waiters, pets and black-eyed contessas who, Shelley sniffed, 'smelled

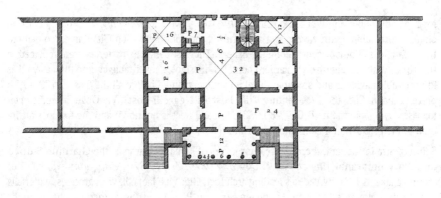

La Malcontenta, from
Palladio's Four Books of Architecture

so strongly of garlic that an ordinary Englishman cannot approach them'. You can visit the **Barchessa Valmarana** in Mira at Via Valmarana 11 (*open 9.30–12.30, 2.30–6, closed Mon*), the ornate wings of a demolished 18th-century villa belonging to one of Vicenza's most prominent families, decorated with baroque frescoes. In Dolo, on the other hand, 16th-century mills are a reminder that life wasn't all fun and games.

'If you've got it, flaunt it,' was the rule in Venice, especially in the 1700s, when one of the grandest villas in all Italy went up at Stra: the **Villa Nazionale** (or **Pisani**), enlarged by Alvise Pisani, scion of the fabulously wealthy banking family, to celebrate his election as doge in 1735 (© *049 502 074, hour-long guided tours June–Sept, Tues–Sun 9–6; until 7.30pm many days in Aug; Oct–May, Tues–Sun 9–1.30; adm*). The new doge had served as Venice's ambassador in Paris; he suggested that something in the Versailles mould might just do, complete with parterres and canals, and hired an architect with the delicious name of Frigimelica Preti to do the job. The villa was completed in 1760, but only after the original plans were scaled down (!). The Pisani sold their brick and mortar dream of grandeur to Napoleon, who gave it to his stepson and viceroy in Italy, Eugène Beauharnais. In June 1934 Mussolini chose it as the stage for his first meeting with Hitler, where he strutted about in full fig, offering the Führer tips on how to deal with Austria and those pesky socialists.

Although most of the villa has been stripped of its decoration, the ballroom makes up for the boredom with one of Tiepolo's most shimmering frescoes (the last he painted before leaving for Madrid), depicting, what else, the *Apotheosis of the Pisani Family*, who float about on clouds, hobnobbing with virtues and allegories of the continents. Son Giandomenico painted the *chiaroscuro* Roman scenes along the gallery. The vast park (the parterres were replaced in the 1800s with an English-style garden) contains the stables, a veritable equine Ritz, as well as innumerable pavilions and an expert-level box maze, planted before all the fuss, in 1721. Also on the canal in Strà, the 17th-century **Villa Foscari-Negrelli-Rossi**, Via Doge Pisani, is open for visits by appointment, ✆ 049 980 0335; the architect is unknown and the frescoes attributed to Pietro Liberi and Domenico de Bruni.

South of Stra in Saonara, there's a treat for lovers of Romantic gardens: the **Giardino Storico di Villa Valmarana** (*ring ahead, ✆ 049 879 0879, ✉ 049 879 1380; adm exp*) laid out around a lake in 1816 by Padua's leading architect, Giuseppe Jappelli, with grottoes, waterfalls and statues. Noventa Padovana, between Stra and Padua and the *autostrada*, has another collection of villas, notably the Palladian-style **Villa Giovanelli** with its statues and temple portico inscribed 'Villaggio S. Antonio'.

A Patrician's Life

In the 1540s the great humanist Luigi (Alvise) Cornaro wrote a philosophical treatise 'On the Sober Life'. Cornaro was 83 at the time, and he was sick and tired of hearing people knock old age. While defending the glories of the golden years, he incidentally left behind one of the best accounts of how a nobleman in the Veneto might expect to spend his time:

> *Let them come and see, and wonder at my good health, how I mount on horse-back without help, how I run upstairs and up hills, how cheerful, amusing, and contented I am, how free from care and disagreeable thoughts. Peace and joy never quit me... My friends are wise, learned, and distinguished people of good position, and when they are not with me I read and write, and try thereby as by all other means, to be useful to others. Each of these things I do at the proper time, and at my ease, in my dwelling, which is beautiful and lies in the best part of Padua, and is arranged both for summer and winter with all the resources of architecture, and provided with a garden by running water. In the spring and autumn, I go for a while to my hill in the most beautiful part of the Euganean mountains, where I have fountains and gardens, and a comfortable dwelling; and there I amuse myself with some easy and pleasant chase, which is suitable to my years. At other times I go to my villa on the plain. There all the paths lead to an open space, in the middle of which stands a pretty church; an arm of the Brenta flows through the plantations—fruitful, well-cultivated fields, now fully peopled, which the marshes and the foul air once made fitter for snakes than for men. It was I who drained the country; then the air became good, and people settled there and multiplied, and the land became cultivated as it now is, so that I can truly say: 'On this spot I gave to God an altar and a temple, and souls to worship Him.' This is my consolation and my happiness whenever I come here. In the spring and autumn, I also visit the neighbouring towns, to see and converse with*

my friends, through whom I make the acquaintance of other distinguished men, architects, painters, sculptors, musicians, and cultivators of the soil. I see what new things they have done, I look again at what I know already, and learn much that is of use to me... But what most of all delights me when I travel, is the beauty of the country and the palaces, lying now on the plain, now on the slopes of the hills, or on the banks of rivers and streams, surrounded by gardens and villas...

Cornaro goes on to say that he has just written his first comedy, then gives practical advice on draining marshlands and preserving lagoons, and writes of the joys of being a grandfather. When he turned 95, Cornaro added a postscript, saying that he owed part of his continued happiness to the fact that so many people had read his Treatise and were now enjoying their old age. He died, well over 100 years old, in 1565.

The Venetians were a notoriously long-lived race, and reading Cornaro one understands why: their lives were too delightful to give up easily. While other Italians mocked Venice for being a republic of old men, remember that they—the other Italians—were under the thumb of Spain, which wasn't half as much fun.

For a map of villas, along the Brenta and throughout the Veneto, see pp.2–3

Where to Stay and Eating Out

Dolo ✉ 30031

Sleep in an antique bed under the frescoes at the ★★★**Villa Ducale**, Riviera Martiri della Libertà 75, ✆/✉ 041 420 094 (*expensive*); another plus is the garden setting with fountains.

Locanda alla Posta, Via Cà Tron 33, ✆ 041 410 740 (*expensive*) has been around a long time, and now has a wonderful new chef to wake it from its hibernation: great fish, delicately prepared, and other dishes too. *Closed Mon.*

Mira ✉ 30034

★★★★**Villa Margherita**, Via Nazionale 416, ✆ 041 426 5800, ✉ 041 426 5838 (*expensive*) offers another chance to live like a patrician; some of its charming rooms have terraces, and breakfast is served on the garden patio, just as it should be. The restaurant, **Margherita**, in a Liberty villa down the road, specializes in seafood and is also one of the best in the area. *Closed Tues eve, Wed, Jan.*

A less elaborate,17th-century villa, ★★★**Riviera dei Dogi**, Via Don Minzoi 33, ✆ 041 424 466, ✉ 041 424 428 (*expensive–moderate*) has comfortable modernized rooms near the canal. One of the traditional places to round off a Brenta Canal excursion is the lovely poplar-shaded veranda at **Nalin**, Via Nuovissimo 29, ✆ 041 420 083 (*expensive–moderate*). In business since 1914, the emphasis is on Venetian seafood, finely grilled, and there are good Veneto wines as well. *Closed Sun eve, Mon, Aug.*

Padua

Although only half an hour from Venice, Padua (Padova) refuses to be overshadowed by the old dowager by the sea, and can rightly claim its own place among Italy's most interesting and historic cities. Nicknamed *La Dotta*, 'The Learned', Padua is the brain of the Veneto, once home of the great Roman historian Livy and, since 1221, to one of Europe's most celebrated universities, which counts Petrarch, Dante and Galileo among its alumni.

Padua's churches, under the brushes of Giotto, Guariento, Altichiero, Giusto de' Menabuoi and Mantegna, were virtually laboratories in the evolution of fresco. But most of all Padua attracts pilgrims; it is the last resting place of St Anthony of Padua, and his exotic, seven-domed mosque of a basilica is the city's most striking landmark. If that's not enough, Padua has more porticoed streets than any city in Italy except Bologna, some of which could easily serve as a setting for *The Taming of the Shrew*, which Shakespeare set in this lively, student-filled city.

History

According to Virgil, ancient Patavium was founded in 1185 BC by Antenor, a hero of the Trojan War, giving it a pedigree nearly as hallowed as Rome's. Unfortunately the archaeological record won't have it: Patavium was a simple Paleoveneto village on a branch of the Brenta river until the 4th century BC, when it became one of the Veneti's capitals. It sided with Rome against the Gauls in 45 BC, and grew into a prosperous Roman *municipium*. In 602 the Lombards burned it to the ground.

From the rubble Padua rose, a slow phoenix, to become an important *comune* by the 12th century. In the 13th century, it hosted one of the best characters of the day, St Anthony, and one of the worst, Ezzelino III da Romano, who robbed Padua of its independence while bleeding it white. In 1259 local *signori*, most importantly the Da Carrara, picked up where Ezzelino left off and fought over the pieces, then lost the city to the Scaligers of Verona in 1328. Doge Francesco Dandolo (after a deal reportedly made *under* his dining table) returned it to the Da Carrara in 1337, and as a bonus admitted them into Venice's Golden Book. For all the troubles, the 13th and 14th centuries were a golden age for Padua, in art, architecture and technology; it was the time of the famous Latin lecturer Vergerius, who made the university and Padua itself one of the earliest centres of Latin letters, and Giovanni Dondi (1320–89), who built Europe's first astronomical clocks (and whose descendants, after six centuries, still live just north of the cathedral, in Via Dondi dell'Orologio). The Da Carrara, however, had ambitions beyond an entry in the *Libro d'Oro*. Francesco da Carrara allied himself with the King of Hungary and raised himself against Venice; in 1373 the Paduans proudly hung the banner of St Mark as a war trophy in the Basilica of Sant'Antonio. After three more decades of the usual betrayals, scheming and conspiring on both sides, Venice besieged Padua, then raging with plague, in 1405; the last of the Da Carrara was heard shouting from the walls, inviting the devil 'to come and get him', as he was captured. He was later strangled in a Venetian prison.

Under the Venetians Padua continued to prosper; its university went on to become one of the chief medical schools in Europe. Many of Padua's students were involved in the Resistance in the Second World War, and the north part of the city was heavily bombed by the Americans (March 1944). But Padua is hardly one to forget its past—even long-gone buildings and streets are outlined on the pavement, giving the city a curious fourth dimension of time.

142   *The Veneto*

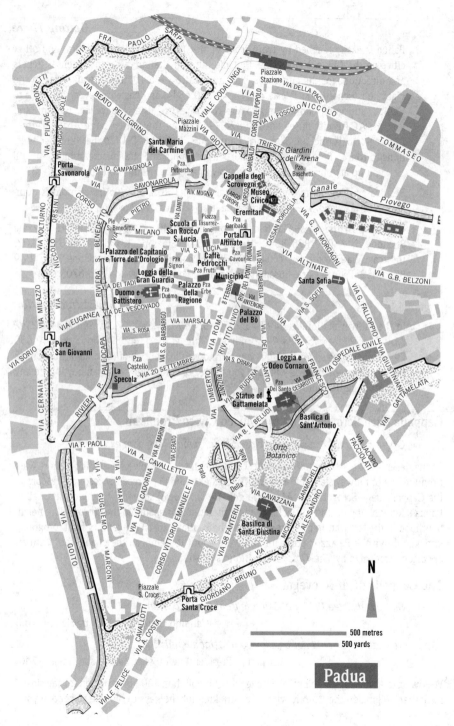

Padua

Padua is easily reached by **train** from Venice (40min), Vicenza (45min) and other cities on the Milan–Venice line. Outside the train station, a booth dispenses tickets and directions for the city buses. The **bus station** is a 10-minute walk away in the Piazzale Boschetti, Via Trieste 40, ✆ 049 820 6844, and has buses every half-hour to Venice, and good connections to Vicenza, Treviso, Este, Monsélice, Bassano and Rovigo; **ACAP** city buses (✆ 049 824 1111) from the station serve Àbano Terme, Montegrotto Terme and Torreglia. **Landomas**, ✆ 049 860 1426, has direct connections to Marco Polo or Treviso airports from Padua and the Euganean hills—they'll pick you up at your door if you book a day in advance. **Radio taxi**: ✆ 049 651 333.

Besides **cruises** along the Brenta Canal (*see* p.138) **Delta Tours** also offers mini-cruises on *La Padovanella* around Padua itself on the river Piovego.

Car hire firms: Avis: Piazzale Stazione 1, ✆ 049 664 198. Europcar: Piazzale Stazione 6, ✆ 049 875 8590. Hertz: Piazzale Stazione 1/VI, ✆ 049 875 2202. Intercar: Via Fistomba 8, ✆ 049 807 3957. Maggiore: Piazzale Stazione 15, ✆ 049 875 2852. Padova Car e Eurodollar: Corso del Popolo 77, ✆ 049 875 8703.

In the railway station, ✆ 049 875 2077 (*open Mon–Sat 9–7.30, Sun 8.30–12.30; Nov–Mar 9.20–5.45, Sun 9–12*); Riviera Mugnai 8, ✆ 049 875 0655, ✉ 049 650 794, e-mail *apt@padovanet.it*. If you plan to visit most or all of the main attractions in Padua, a **biglietto unico** will save you money on admissions; you can buy it from any one of the participating sites.

Cappella degli Scrovegni and the Museo Civico Eremitani

Open 9–6, until 7 in summer, closed Mon; same ticket, adm exp.

Padua deserves at least a whole day, but if you only have a couple of hours it's a short walk from the bus or railway station to its gem: Giotto's extraordinary, recently restored frescoes in the Cappella degli Scrovegni (or *Madonna dell'Arena*), a pearl sheltered by the crusty shell of Padua's Roman amphitheatre. It is lucky to be there; bombs shattered the surrounding neighbourhood in the last war. In another close call, the Paduans, in a 19th-century fit of 'progress', knocked down the Palazzo Scrovegni and were about to demolish the chapel too, until an opportune campaign by *The Times* saved Giotto's masterpiece.

The Cappella degli Scrovegni

Giotto translated the art of painting from Greek to Latin.

Cennino Cennini, *Il Libro dell'Arte* (1400)

Nowadays he would not be allowed to paint a tennis court.

Charles (Président) de Brosses, *Lettres sur l'Italie* (1740)

We owe the Arena Chapel to Enrico Scrovegni, who built it in 1303 in expiation for the sins of his father, Reginaldo the usurer, who died shrieking for the keys to his safe to keep anyone

Cappella degli Scrovegni

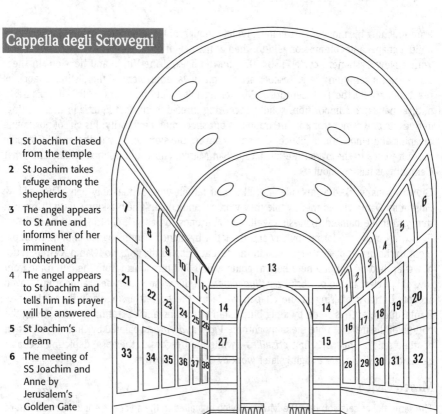

1 St Joachim chased from the temple
2 St Joachim takes refuge among the shepherds
3 The angel appears to St Anne and informs her of her imminent motherhood
4 The angel appears to St Joachim and tells him his prayer will be answered
5 St Joachim's dream
6 The meeting of SS Joachim and Anne by Jerusalem's Golden Gate
7 The birth of Mary
8 The Presentation of Mary at the Temple
9 Handing over the rod to St Simeone
10 The prayer for the blossoming of the rods
11 The wedding of Mary and Joseph
12 The Wedding Procession
13 God giving the Archangel Gabriel his orders
14 The Annunciation
15 The Visitation
16 The Nativity
17 The Adoration of the Magi

18 Presentation of Jesus at the Temple
19 The Flight into Egypt
20 The Massacre of the Innocents
21 Jesus among the Doctors of the Temple
22 The Baptism of Jesus
23 The Marriage at Cana

24 The Resurrection of Lazarus
25 The Entry of Jesus into Jerusalem
26 Chasing the Merchants from the Temple
27 Judas receiving the Thirty Pieces of Silver
28 The Last Supper
29 The Washing of the Feet

30 The Kiss of Judas
31 Jesus before Caiaphas
32 Jesus crowned with the Crown of Thorns
33 The Calvary
34 The Crucifixion
35 The Deposition
36 The Resurrection
37 The Ascension
38 Pentecost

from touching his money. Fortunately, he left enough of his filthy lucre behind for Enrico to build a chapel and commission Giotto, then at the height of his career, to fresco the interior with a New Testament cycle (1304–07), on the lives of the Virgin and her Son. In sheer power and inspiration these frescoes are the medieval equivalent of the Sistine Chapel, as revolutionary for the 14th century as Michelangelo's would be for the 16th. Giotto's fresh, natural narrative composition, solidly anchoring three-dimensional figures in their setting, derives its power not from divine trappings but sheer moral authority; his gift of portraying meaning and emotion in a glance or gesture conveys the story directly to the heart. Compare these frescoes to the Byzantine mosaics in San Marco, and you'll at once understand what Cennini was talking about.

Giotto's sons worked at his side and, like their father, were remarkably ugly. Their fellow Florentine Dante visited them while they worked, and couldn't help asking Giotto, 'How is it that you make painted figures so well, and real ones so badly?', Giotto returned at once, 'Because I make the former by day and the latter by night.' Dante laughed and, as a compliment to the artist, placed Reginaldo in the seventh ring of the *Inferno* (Canto XVII). Giotto, however, had no doubt where he was going; you'll find him fourth from the left in the front row of the elect in the powerful *Last Judgement* on the west wall. A delegation from heaven accepts Enrico's offering of the chapel, while on the far left a singularly harrowing pre-Dantesque Inferno is ruled by a big blue Satan munching and excreting sinners. Along the bottom of the frescoes note the monochrome *Vices and Virtues,* painted by Giotto in imitation of stone reliefs—history's first *grisailles*—while the frescoes in the apse, depicting the later career of the Virgin, are a slightly later work by Giotto's followers.

Museo Civico

The same ticket gets you into the Museo Civico, installed in the adjacent Augustine convent of the Eremitani, with its noteworthy **archaeological collection**: coins, vases and 14 funerary stelae from the 6th to 1st centuries BC, inscribed in bastard Etruscan. Padua is the only place in northern Italy where such stelae were discovered; apparently the local aristocracy wanted to put on airs by using the Greek alphabet.

The **painting section** houses literally acres of art, not always in chronological order, but a gold mine for connoisseurs of lesser-known painters, mingled among the greats—including Giotto, whose *Crucifixion* was designed for the altar of the Cappella Scrovegni. In the next rooms are works by his follower Guariento, founder of the Paduan school, who painted the lovely but rather odd series of *Angels*, weighing souls and fighting the devil, each slightly different, as if they were frames from a film.

The International Gothic style is represented by Lorenzo Veneziano, Jacopo Bellini (*Christ in Limbo*) and a charming but anonymous *millefleurs* Madonna (1408). The link in Padua from Giotto to the Renaissance was Francesco Squarcione, at least according to old art historians; a rather dry polyptych, one of only two documented works by his hand, is here. This is followed by a charming *Expedition of the Argonauts* by Lorenzo Costa of Ferrara, and then a number of 16th-century Paduan paintings showing the influence of Andrea Mantegna (including Bartolomeo Veneto's all-dwarfing *Madonna* and Pietro Paolo Agabiti's *Madonna with SS. Peter and Sebastian*, with the face of a Hollywood starlet—Sebastian, that is). Lombard painters check in with Madonnas by Da Vinci's follower Bernardo Luino and Andrea Previtali. In Italy, a bride brought her trousseau in an ornate wedding chest or *cassione*; Titian as a youth decorated two with mythological scenes, and other works in the room show his later influence.

In the next rooms you'll find Palma il Giovanni's rather bold *Santa Cristina*; portraits by Padua's leading female artist of the Renaissance, Chiara Varotari (1584–1663); a baroque *David and Goliath* by Pietro Muttoni della Vecchia (David, always so young and dashing in Renaissance paintings, has a grey beard here) and *Portraits of Philosophers* by the prolific Luca Giordano of Naples—his *Job* may be the best portrayal of a bad smell in Italian painting. In the 1600s, the nobility in the Veneto began to collect genre scenes and landscapes, bringing in artists from around Europe to cash in: especially represented here are Eismann and Philip Peter Roos, and the local painters they inspired, such as Antonio Marini of Venice, who specialized in battle scenes.

After these, the museum changes gear and returns to the 16th century with paintings by Domenico Campagnolo and Giampiero Silvio, both of whom worked in Padua; luminous Dutch paintings; and an enormous and fantastically detailed Brussels tapestry of *David Ordering Joab to Attack the Ammonites*. Il Romanino of Brescia weighs in with his master-piece, a huge altarpiece of the *Virgin and Saints* (originally in Santa Giustina) as well as a *Last Supper*, with Judas clutching his money under the table. Other paintings to look for: Tintoretto's *Crucifixion* (with a battle in the background); *Dinner at the House of Simon*; the *Martyrdom of SS. Primo and Feliciano*, and a small *Crucifixion* against a black sky by Veronese; and works by 17th-century painter Il Padovinino (Alessandro Varotari) and his followers. A portrait of Elena Lucrezia Cornaro Piscopia, painted in 1678 to honour her doctorate from Padua University, shares a room with what must be the campest portrait in all Italy: the 17th-century *Venetian Captain* by Sebastiano Mazzoni, matched only by its frame, carved with cupids, lions and a giant artichoke.

From the same century but from another world are the 'realist' works by Matteo di Pittocchi (Matteo of the Beggars); the paintings of tiny people being chased by snails and attacked by crabs by Faustino Bocchi (1659–1741); and the idyllic landscapes by Francesco Aviani (a Venetian proto-hippy, 1662–1715). There are striking 18th-century *trompe l'œil* by a brother and sister team, Pietro and Caterina Leopoldo della Santa, and G.B. Tiepolo's *St Patrick Bishop of Ireland*, in a very non-Irish setting; also genre scenes by Pietro Longhi and Rosalba Carrara's *Portrait of a Young Priest*.

Some of the finest paintings are part of the **Quadraria Emo Capodilista**, a private collection donated to the museum in 1864 that includes Giorgione's *Leda and the Swan* and *Country Idyll*; Giovanni Bellini's *A Young Senator* and *Christ's Descent From the Cross*, the latter painted with his father Jacopo; and a *Mythological Scene* by Titian. Another donation, the **Museo Bottacin**, has more from the 18th century, and a fabulous coin collection. The *bronzetti* from the 14th–17th centuries that fill the halls were a speciality of Padua, especially those by Andrea Briosco, better known as Il Riccio ('Curly'). His famous *Drinking Satyr* is here, as well as works by Alessandro Vittoria, Niccolò Roccatagliata and a certain Il Moderno, whose name was probably invented by his agent.

The Eremitani, Santa Sofia and the Carmine

Next to the museum, the church of the **Eremitani** (1306; *open Mon–Sat 8.15–12.15, 4–6; Sun 9.30–12, 4–6*) lacked the luck of the Cappella Scrovegni and was shattered in an air raid in 1944. What could be salvaged of the frescoes has been painstakingly pieced together—frescoes by Giusto de'Manabuoi and Guariento (his *Story of SS. Augustine, Philip and James* in the second chapel to the right of the altar), and most importantly the magnificent **Ovetari chapel**, begun by Andrea Mantegna in 1454 at the age of 23. Mantegna was a precocious young man: the pupil and adopted son of Squarcione, he took his master/father to court at age 17 for exploiting him. He also found his unique style at an early age, with its remarkable clarity of line and colour and fascination with antiquity—Squarcione had an archaeological collection, but another influence on Mantegna was Padua itself, with its university and Latin letters. Painted 150 years after Giotto, *The Martyrdom of St Christopher and St James* still astonishes, thanks to Mantegna's wizardly use of scientific perspective to foreshorten the action from below and his use of Roman architecture to depict the power of the state—massive, hard, polished and pitiless, populated by remorseless, indifferent men.

Padua's oldest church, the 9th-century **Santa Sofia**, is to the east, at the corner of Via S. Sofia and Via Altinate; much rebuilt in the 11th century, it has a lovely Veneto-Byzantine apse and a precious polychrome *Pietà* (1430) by Egidio da Wienerneustadt. The quarter to the west of the Ermitani, Borgo Molino, was once an 'island' cut off by the Bacchiglione. Its centrepiece, the **Carmine** church, was rebuilt as the headquarters of a confraternity by Lorenzo da Bologna in 1494. Although it was heavily damaged in the air raids, the shells somehow missed the Sacristy and **Scuola del Carmine** (1377), with its interior covered by elegant *cinquecento* frescoes by Domenico Campagnola and Stefano dall'Arzere. Near here, just off Piazza Petrarca, the **Porta di Ponte Molino** and Torre di Ezzelino are leftovers from the 13th-century walls.

To Caffè Pedrocchi and the University

A short walk south from the Eremitani leads into Piazza Garibaldi, site of Padua's oldest surviving gate, **Porta Altinate**, 'captured from Ezzelino da Romano in 1256' as the plaque boasts. The streets all around, however, were torn up in 1926 to create big squares for big buildings flaunting the might of the Corporate State. A whole neighbourhood, Borgo Santa Lucia, was bulldozed to create **Piazza Insurrezione**, sparing the **Scuola di San Rocco** (1525; *open 9.30–12.30 and 3.30–7.30, closed Mon; adm*) which, like the one in Venice, was built by a confraternity focused on plague prevention. Domenico Campagnola and Gualtiero Padovano frescoed it in 1537, although their work seems stale after Tintoretto's fireworks in Venice. Behind the Scuola, the church of **Santa Lucia** was also spared; founded in the 11th century, it has a fine painting of *San Luca* by G.B. Tiepolo on the left of the high altar. Via Santa Lucia still has a number of medieval houses; a remarkable one built over Via Marsilio da Padova is remembered as the **Casa di Ezzelino**.

South of Piazza Garibaldi and around the corner from another new square, **Piazza Cavour**, you'll find a stylish Egyptian-revival mausoleum with columned stone porches at either end. This is, in fact, the **Caffè Pedrocchi**, built in 1831 by Giuseppe Jappelli, and famous in its day for never closing (it couldn't—it had no doors) and for the intellectuals and students who came here to debate the revolutionary politics of Mazzini. When restorations are completed, you should be able to get a coffee again, as well as visit the upper floor (*open Tues–Sun 9.30–12.30, 3.30–7; adm*). In Jappelli's adjacent neo-Gothic **Pedrocchino** (built to contain the overflow of clients) students turned words into deeds in 1848, clashing with the Austrian police. Look carefully and you can still see the bullet-scars.

At the far end of the complex, the 16th-century **Municipio** (the former Palazzo Comunale) hides behind an uncomfortable façade of 1904. Opposite is the seat of the **University of Padua**, Andrea Moroni's 16th-century **Palazzo del Bo'** ('of the ox', a nickname derived from the sign of a tavern that stood on this site in 1221) (*guided tours Mar–Sept, Tues, Thurs 9, 10,11; Wed, Tues, Fri 3, 4, 5; adm*). The façade, attributed to Vincenzo Scamozzi, opens up to a handsome 16th-century courtyard. Galileo delivered his lectures on physics from an old wooden pulpit, still intact, and counted among his students Sweden's Gustavus Adolphus, who went on to mastermind the Protestant victories in the Thirty Years War. The golden Great Hall is covered with the armorial devices of its alumni; the steep claustrophobic **Anatomical Theatre** (1594) was the first permanent one anywhere, designed by Fabricius, tutor of William Harvey who went on to discover the circulation of blood—only one of scores of Renaissance Englishmen who earned degrees at Padua's School of Medicine. Other professors included Vesalius, author of the first original work on anatomy since Galen (1555), and Gabriello Fallopio, discoverer of the Fallopian tubes.

Before continuing to the Palazzo del Ragione, duck around the corner of the University to have a look at **Piazza Antenore**, with a pair of sarcophagi for a centrepiece. The one on columns supposedly contains what remains of Antenor, hero of the Trojan War and founder of ancient *Patavium*; the body was discovered in 1274, although modern scholars have had a peek and say Antenor was really a soldier from the 3rd century AD. The great Roman historian Livy was a son of the nearby Euganaen hills, and the other sarcophagus commemorates his 2000th birthday. Perhaps he'll get something nicer for his 3000th.

The Medieval Civic Centre: Palazzo della Ragione and Piazza dei Signori

Directly behind the Municipio (*see* above), the delightful medieval **Piazza delle Erbe** and **Piazza della Frutta** still host a bustling market every morning, divided by the massive, arcaded **Palazzo della Ragione** (*open 9–6, closed Mon; adm*). Constructed as Padua's law courts in 1218 and then rebuilt in 1306, its upper story or *Salone* is one of the largest medieval halls in existence, measuring 260 by 88ft, with an 85ft ceiling like a 'vaulting over a market square', as Goethe described it. Its great hull-shaped roof was rebuilt after a fire in 1756—an earlier blaze, in 1420, destroyed most of the frescoes by Giotto and his assistants, although some *Virtues* by Menabuoi survived. The rest were replaced with over 300 biblical and astrological scenes by Niccolò Miretto—one of the Renaissance's most important glorifications of astrology, which had had its own renaissance in the 13th century under Ezzelino's chief advisor and uncannily accurate astrologer, Guido Bonatto. Many of the later popes had astrologers; Petrarch roundly condemned them. Exhibitions are frequently staged under the eyes of Mars and Jupiter, but two exhibits never change: the *pietra del vituperio*, a cold stone block where the bankrupt had to sit bare-bottomed during three public meetings to absolve their debts, and a giant **wooden horse**, built for a joust in 1466, its fierce glance complemented by testicles the size of bowling balls.

Just to the west, the stately **Piazza dei Signori** saw many a joust in its day, and can boast Italy's oldest astronomical clock, built by Giovanni Dondi in 1344 and still ticking away, set in the tower of the **Palazzo del Capitaniato**. On the left is the fine Renaissance-style **Loggia della Gran Guardia** (or del Consiglio), completed by Giovanni Maria Falconetto in 1523; while behind Dondi's clock you'll find Padua University's Arts Faculty, the **Liviano**, built in 1939 by Gio Ponti. Ponti incorporated the upper floor of the old Da Carrara palace in the Liviano, with its remarkable **Sala dei Giganti** (*open Sept–June, Wed only, 9.30–12.30 and 3–6*), named after its huge 14th-century frescoes of ancient Romans and repainted by Domenico Campagnola in the 1530s; Altichiero added the more intimate 14th-century portrait of Petrarch sitting at his desk.

The Duomo and Baptistry

Around the corner from the square stands Padua's rather neglected **Duomo**, begun in the 12th century, but tampered with throughout the Renaissance—Michelangelo was only one of several cooks who spoiled the broth here before everyone lost interest and left the façade unfinished. The interior is neoclassical and serene, and the most memorable art is new, along the altar, where the smooth white figures of saints and trees melt into the stairs. In the 1370s Giusto de'Menabuoi frescoed the adjacent Romanesque **Baptistry** (*open 9.30–1 and 3–6, adm*), with over a hundred scenes; the dome, with its multitude of saints seated in the circles of paradise, is awesome but chilling.

The 15th-century bishop's palace to the left of the cathedral contains the **Pinacoteca dei Canonici** (entrance at Via Dietro Duomo 15) with portraits of the bishops by Bartolomeo Mantagnana, a portrait of Petrarch, probably from life, was transferred here from the house he lived in while he served as a canon (*open only by appointment, ☎ 049 662 814*). Stroll down Via del Vescovado, one of Padua's most characteristic porticoed streets; among the palazzi, No.32, the **Casa degli Specchi** (1502), is especially handsome.

Basilica di Sant'Antonio

One of the busiest and most beloved saints on the calendar, Anthony of Padua was a Portuguese missionary inspired by the teachings of St Francis. Sailing off to convert the infidels of the Middle East, he was shipwrecked in Italy, where he stayed, preached, and was canonized in 1232, only ten months after his death—an ecclesiastical speed record, which soon led to his nickname: in Padua Anthony isn't merely *a* saint, he is *The* Saint, Il Santo. A suitably unique basilica to shelter his mortal remains was begun the year of his death, according to legend, by a friar who accompanied St Francis to Egypt. For pure fantasy it is comparable only to St Mark's: a cluster of seven domes around a lofty, conical cupola, two octagonal *campanili* and two smaller minarets—perhaps not what a monk vowed to poverty might have ordered, but certainly a sign of the esteem in which his devotees held and continue to hold him; even Francis, the patron saint of Italy, doesn't have anything approaching Il Santo's organization. In an average year 341,810 masses are celebrated in the Basilica, with many more expected for the Millennium; even the 50 father confessors on duty are often hard pressed to keep up with demand.

Inside pilgrims queue patiently in the **Cappella del Santo** to pray, press a palm against his tomb and study the votive testimonials and photos (happy babies, wrecked cars, including insurance-style charts of the collision), proof of The Saint's interventions. One of Anthony's many tasks is running Heaven's Lost Property Office, and he doesn't appreciate insincere petitions; in 1780 William Beckford wrote that he prayed Anthony to relieve him of a crush he had on a young son of the Cornaro family, but was disappointed, and left the basilica a 'frail, infatuated mortal'. With all of the activity surrounding the tomb, no one pays much attention to the 16th-century marble reliefs lining St Anthony's chapel, although they are exquisite works of the Venetian Renaissance: the fourth and fifth are by Sansovino, the sixth and seventh by Tullio Lombardo, and the last by Antonio Lombardo. Behind the saint's chapel the **Cappella di Conti** has richly coloured frescoes on the life of SS. Philip and James by Florentine Giusto de'Menabuoi (1382).

The **high altar**, unfortunately dismantled and rearranged over the centuries, is mostly the work of Donatello (1443–50), crowned by his stone *Deposition*, over bronze statues of the Madonna and six patron saints of Padua and dramatic reliefs of the miracles of St Anthony below, each intricately crowded with figures in architectural perspectives that were to be a strong influence on Mantegna. The magnificent bronze **Paschal Candelabrum** (1519) is the masterpiece of Il Riccio, who spent nine years on the project; although it was designed for Easter, Christianity takes a backseat to the myriad satyrs, nymphs and other mythological creatures in relief, immersed in imaginative decorative motifs. Earlier in his career, Il Riccio helped his master Belluno (one of Donatello's assistants) cast the 12 bronze reliefs of Old Testament scenes on the choir walls. To the left of the altar, at the beginning of the ambulatory, note the **De Marchetti tomb** by Giovanni Comini (1690), an excellent example of the Hallowe'en-style tombs that were the rage in the baroque era—here a bust of dead man on a stack of books is topped by a skeleton blasting away on the trump of doom. Behind the high altar, in the ambulatory, don't miss the **Treasury** where one of a hundred glittering gold reliquaries holds the tongue and larynx of Il Santo, found perfectly intact when his tomb was opened in 1981, the 750th anniversary of his death. In the right transept, the **Cappella di San Felice** contains more beautiful frescoes and a remarkable *Crucifixion*, painted in the 1380s by Altichiero, the leading Giottoesque artist of the day. The basilica complex, big enough to require its own information office, includes several other exhibitions and museums in its cloisters. There's a free audio-visual (in Italian) on the saint's life, while the **Museo Antoniano** (*open 9–1 and 2–5, closed Mon; adm*) contains art made for the basilica over the centuries.

Sharing the large piazza in front of the basilica, a bit lost among the pigeons and exuberant souvenir stands, is one of the key works of the Renaissance, Donatello's **Statue of Gattamelata** (1453), the first large equestrian bronze since antiquity and Padua's answer to

Rome's Marcus Aurelius. The cool 'Honeyed Cat' was a *condottiere* who served Venice so well and honestly that the republic, in a rare moment of generosity, paid for this monument, which Donatello infused with a serene humanistic spirit, in marked contrast to Verrocchio's Colleoni statue in Venice. As a yardstick of taste, it is interesting to note that only 50 years after its completion the horse was being criticized for its realistic detail.

Flanking the piazza opposite Gattamelata, the **Oratorio di San Giorgio** (*closed for restoration*) was built in 1377, and beautifully frescoed by one of the leading heirs of Giotto, Altichiero of Verona, with help from Jacopo Avanzi. Until it reopens you can, however, visit the adjacent **Scuoletta del Santo**, an old confraternity with paintings on the *Life of St Anthony* by a variety of artists, some of which are winningly absurd; four, certainly not the best, are attributed to a teenage Titian (*open summer 9–1, 2.30–6.30, winter 10–1, 2–5, closed Mon; adm*).

Behind the basilica, on Via Cesarotti, the **Loggia and Odeo Cornaro** (1524 and 1530) are two Renaissance gems designed by Giovanni Maria Falconetto of Verona, whose refined use of ancient architectural orders exerted a major influence on Palladio. Built in the gardens of the humanist Alvise Cornaro (*see* pp.140–41) the Odeo was used for concerts and is decorated inside with exquisite stuccoes, while the Loggia saw performances of the plays of Ruzante (Angelo Beolco; *c.* 1496–1542), the Paduan dramatist who invented and played the role of Ruzante, 'the Joker', a satirically-minded peasant faced with one catastrophe after another; some of his works prefigure the *commedia dell'arte*.

Botanical Gardens, Europe's Biggest Square and La Specola

A few streets south of the Piazza del Santo, the **Orto Botanico** (*open April–Sept, Mon–Sat 9–1 and 3–6; Oct–Mar 9–1, adm*) was one of Europe's oldest botanical gardens, established in 1545; it retains the original layout, and even a few original specimens. At 'Goethe's palm', planted in 1585 and still flourishing, the great poet-scientist speculated on his Theory of the Ur-plant, that all plants evolved from one universal specimen.

Beyond, 'the largest piazza on the continent', **Prato della Valle**, was a swampy meadow converted into a square with a moat by the city's Venetian *procuratore* Andrea Memmo in 1775 to give Padua a new commercial centre. Today it does service as municipal car park, flea market, amusement park and 'theatre of acting statues' for 79 illustrious men associated with Padua (and one woman, the Renaissance poet Gaspara Stampa, who gets a bust at the foot of Il Riccio). One statue, of Alberto Azzo II, was erected by an outsider—the brother of King George III, in honour of their illustrious ancestor from Este (*see* p.157); the tourist office publishes a booklet in English giving the biography of each worthy.

On one side stands the 393ft **Basilica of Santa Giustina**, the 11th-largest church in all Christendom (*open daily, 7.30–12, 3.30–7.30*), designed by Il Riccio with an exotic cluster of domes echoing St Antony's, but the façade is unfinished and the interior stillborn baroque: best bits are an altarpiece by Sebastiano Ricci in the second chapel on the left, the large apse painting of the *Martydom of Santa Giustina* (1575) by Veronese and the 16th-century choir stalls. The left transept has a beautiful 14th-century tomb, the *Arca di S. Luca*, with alabaster reliefs made in Pisa. A door in the right transept leads to the original church, the 5th-century **Sacellum di San Prosdocimo**, burial place of Padua's first bishop, with a marble iconostasis; remains of the other previous churches lie beyond the monastery gate.

West of the basilicas, in Piazza Castello, Ezzelino da Romano rebuilt a castle in the medieval walls, now used as Padua's hoosegow. The tallest and oldest bit, the 144ft Torrelunga (1062) has had a rather more dignified career since 1767, when an astronomical observatory, **La Specola**, was added to the roof (*accessible round the back, off Riviera Tiso da Camposampiero; tickets for guided tours sold at Agenzia Next Tour, Via Bomporti 16, © 049 875 4949, on Tues, Wed, Fri 9pm–11pm*). Padua's massive and well-preserved Renaissance **walls**, considered impregnable in their day, were designed by Michele Sammicheli and finished in 1544. A few of the ornate gates, many in white Istrian stone, survive and are perhaps most easily seen from a bike saddle. The best are the **Porta Portello** (1519) to the northeast; the **Porta San Giovanni** and **Porta Savonarola** (1530, by Falconetto) to the west; and **Porta Santa Croce**, to the south.

Activities

Every summer a series of concerts, exhibitions, open-air films and shows takes place. The tourist office's *Padova Today* lists events. The Prato della Valle sees a large general market every Saturday, and an antique market every third Sunday of the month.

Padua ✉ *35100*

Where to Stay

expensive

By the basilica of Sant'Antonio, you can't miss the ★★★★**Donatello**, Via del Santo 102, © 049 875 0634, 🖷 049 8675 0829— Donatello's *Gattamelata* points right to it; rooms are air-conditioned and recently renovated. Also in the historic centre, the newer, more comfortable ★★★★**Majestic Toscanelli**, Via dell'Arco 2, © 049 663 244, 🖷 049 876 0025 has every luxury, and a popular restaurant, specializing in Brazilian dishes. ★★★★**Grande Italia**, Corso del Popolo 81, © 049 876 111, 🖷 049 875 0850, is in a beautiful Liberty building, conveniently opposite the railway station.

moderate

Small and cosy, ★★★**Leon Bianco**, Piazzetta Pedrocchi 12, © 049 875 0814, 🖷 049 875 6184, is right in the heart of Padua; from its roof terrace, where breakfast is served in summer, you can look down on the Caffè Pedrocchi. Cheaper and near the station, friendly ★★★**Al Cason**, Via Paolo Scarpi 40, © 049 66236, 🖷 049 875 4217, will make you feel at home, and fill you up with the classics in its restaurant.

inexpensive

★★**Sant'Antonio**, Via S. Fermo 118, © 049 875 1393, 🖷 049 875 2508, between the station and centre by the Porta Molino, has a friendly, family atmosphere. ★**Pavia**, Via del Papafava 11, © 049 661 558, is deservedly popular, clean, central and friendly. Near the station but on the wrong side of the tracks, ★★**Arcella**, Via J. D'Avanzo 7, © 049 605 581 has friendly owners, limited parking and a/c; another ten-minute walk from the station, in the same area, the homey ★**Junior**, Via L. Faggin 2, © 049 811 756 has no en suite baths, but easy parking. The large, pleasant, city-run **Ostello Città di Padova** is at Via Aleardi 30, © 049 875 2219, 🖷 049 654 210; IYHF cards required. Take bus 3, 8 or 11 from the station to the Prato della Valle.

La cucina padovana features what the Italians call 'courtyard meats' (*carni di cortile*)—chicken, duck, turkey, pheasant, capons, goose and pigeon. Pork, rabbit and freshwater fish are other favourites. Try one of the various *risotti* for *primo*.

expensive

Not far from the historic centre, **Antico Brolo**, Corso Milano 22, © 049 66455, occupies an elegant 15th-century building, with a garden for outdoor dining on its Veneto and Emilian specialities; try the chateaubriand with balsamic vinegar; tourist menu L50,000. *Closed Mon and Sun lunch, some of Aug.* There's a good pizzeria down in the old wine cellar where you'll spend a lot less.

moderate

In the suburb of Torre, 2km from the Padua-Est *autostrada* exit, **Dotto di Campagna**, Via Randaccio, © 049 625 469 offers elegant surroundings and inventive cookery based on the freshest of ingredients; for a first course try their famous *risotti* or *pasta fagioli*. Tourist menu L38,000. *Closed Sun eve, Mon, Aug.* For classic Paduan home cooking, featuring succulent boiled and roast meats, the crowds venture outside the city walls to **Da Giovanni**, Via Maroncelli 22, © 049 772 620 (bus 9 from the railway station). The home-made pasta is good, as are the locally raised capons. *Closed Sat lunch, Sun, Aug.*

inexpensive

For 150 years **Bertolini**, Via Antichiero 162, © 049 600 357, just north of the station, has been a favourite; go for the hearty vegetarian and seasonal dishes and homemade desserts. *Closed Sat.* Just outside Padua's western walls (take Corso Milano from the centre) **Bastioni del Moro**, Via Bronzetti 18, © 049 871 006, has had a recent facelift and serves up a delicious gnocchi with scallops and porcini mushrooms, indoors or in the summer garden; tourist menu L25,000, although prices soar if you order fish. *Closed Sun.*

South of Padua

The landscape south of Padua is as flat as any of the pancake prairies of the Po, with the exception of the lush Euganean hills: a retreat of poets and the world-weary since Roman times, dotted with villas, spas, trails and country restaurants where Paduans head on Sundays. South of the hills you'll find a handsome trio of medieval towns, Monsélice, Este and Montagnana, all 'with pasts', as people used to say of women who dared to have fun.

Getting Around

The spas and towns in the **Euganean Hills** are easily reached by **bus** from the main station in Padua. There are also regular **trains** from Padua to Monsélice (23km), Este (32km), Montagnana (52km) and Rovigo (45km), which take about the same time as the buses, although you may have to change trains at Monsélice. Buses from Monsélice go to Arquà Petrarca (10km).

Ábano Terme: Via Pietro d'Abano 18, ✆ 049 866 9055, ✉ 049 866 9053; **Montegrotto Terme**: Viale della Stazione 60, ✆ 049 793 384, ✉ 049 795 276. **Monsélice**: Piazza Mazzini, ✆ 042 972 380. **Este**: Piazza Maggiore, ✆ 042 93635 (with bikes to hire). **Montagnana**: Piazza V. Emanuele, ✆ 044 298 1320.

The Euganean Hills and Around

As soon as you leave Padua you'll spot them: the Euganean Hills or *Colli Euganei*, ancient volcanic islands, once surrounded by sea and now basking in the middle of the Veneto plain. Fertile, well watered by springs and defensible, they were settled early on in the Bronze Age by the Paleoveneti, who made Este their chief stronghold. Centuries later the Romans discovered the two key secrets of the Euganean Hills: wine (now DOC Colli Euganei) and hot mud. Livy, Suetonius and Martial all recommended the virtues of their mineral springs, which flow from the ground at 87°C, and they have been appreciated ever since: some 130 hotels built over thermal swimming pools provide health or beauty cures at **Ábano Terme** (from *Aponeus*, the Roman god of healing) and **Montegrotto Terme** (ancient *Mons Aegratorum*, 'mountain of the ill'), where the old Roman spa has been excavated. Children love Montegrotto's live butterfly zoo, the **Butterfly Arc**, with colourful species from around the world (*open April–Aug 9–12.30 and 2.30–5.30; adm*). In the same area, at Luvigliano near **Torréglia**, the vast **Villa dei Vescovi** (*open Mar–Nov, Mon, Wed and Fri 10.30–12.30 and 2–6; adm*) was designed by Giovanni Maria Falconetto (1579) for holidaying bishops: the interior has fine stuccoes, and the church houses a fine *Pala di San Martino* (1527) by Girolamo Santacroce of Bergamo.

From Torréglia, there's a road west to **Teolo**, Livy's birthplace. Here the **Museo di Arte Contemporanea** (*open daily exc Sat, 3–7*) in the Palazzetto dei Vicari was founded in honour of international art critic Dino Formaggio and houses works from many of Italy's finest living artists. Because of their unusual microclimate the Euganean hills are rich in flora, with over a thousand species, protected since 1989 under the auspices of a regional park. In Teolo you can join a 42km circular nature trail around the district or head north to visit the venerable Benedictine **Abbazia di Praglia** (*tours every half hour, 2.30–4.30 winter, 3.30–5.30 summer, closed Mon*), founded in 1117 but given the full Renaissance treatment, with a church by Tullio Lombardo and paintings by Bartolomeo Montagna, Giambattista Zelotti and others. The monks are famous for restoring old manuscripts and singing a mean Gregorian chant.

South of Torréglia, **Valsanzibio** was once the property of the Scrovegni money-bags and still maintains a quiet air of wealth, with an 18-hole golf course and the magnificent park and gardens at the **Villa Barbarigo** (*open 9–12, 2–7.30, until sunset in winter; adm exp*). Set in an enclosed valley, these are the grandest in the Veneto, laid out in the mid-1600s in the style of a Roman water garden (as at Tivoli) with fountains, waterfalls, nymphaea, pools, fish ponds, and a domed rabbits' island; it also has one of Italy's finest garden mazes, as devilish to get through as the one at Stra.

Arquà Petrarca

Beyond Valsanzibio lies **Arquà Petrarca**, a jewel of hilltown in a lovely setting. In 1370, the world-weary Petrarch chose Arquà as his last home, accompanied by his daughter Francesca and her husband and his stuffed cat, Laura II. His charming villa, the **Casa del Petrarca** (*open*

9–12.30, 3–7; adm), preserves much of its 14th-century structure and furnishings. Petrarch was *the* artsy trendsetter of the Middle Ages; his presence in Arquà attracted wealthy families from Padua and Venice, who built summer houses in the village—the first example of the lust for *villeggiatura* that would so transform the Veneto landscape over the next four centuries.

The house itself went through a number of owners, one of whom in the 16th century added delightful frescoes illustrating the sonnets (Petrarch chasing a goose, Petrarch being splashed...). With the exception of a radio mast, the view from the poet's study remains the same as it was over 600 years ago, and it isn't hard to imagine the plump old poet laureate sitting there, writing his *Letter to Posterity*, describing his life and career in some detail (he complains at having to wear spectacles after his 60th birthday). Famous signatures in the visitor's book are on display—Byron and his contessa, Teresa Guiccioli, came in 1818. Petrarch died here in 1374, while reading a book, and now occupies a huge Verona red marble sarcophagus in front of the church.

The fourth spa town in the Euganean Hills, **Battaglia Terme**, back on the SS16, is also a small industrial centre, with a severe villa-castle, **Il Catajo** (1570), the citadel of Venice's *condottiere* Pio Enea I degli Olbizzi. Sumptuous on the inside, with lively frescoes by Giambattista Zelotti, it has an English garden with a charming elephant fountain; you can even hire it out for a party (*© 049 526 541, otherwise open 15 Feb–Nov, Tues and Sun 2.30–6.30; adm*). East of Battaglia, two medieval Carrara properties merged to form a single *comune*, **Due Carrare**. The family citadel, **Castello di San Pelagio,** has a sumptuous interior and now a **Museo dell'Aria** (*open Tues–Sun 9–12.30, 2–6; summer 2.30–7; adm exp*) with exhibits dedicated to air travel, from mythology to space exploration. Carrara Santo Stefano is built around the Benedictine **Abbazia di Santo Stefano**, founded in 1027. Although the abbey was demolished in 1793 the church remains, with its beautiful 11th-century mosaic pavement and 14th-century marble tomb of Marsilio da Carrara (*open Sat 9–12, Sun 2–5, or by ringing ahead, © 049 911 5027*).

Where to Stay and Eating Out

Ábano Terme ✉ 35031

All of the spa hotels in the Euganean Hills have private mineral water pools, therapists and gardens, but none can match the class of Giuseppe Jappelli's 1825 ★★★★★**Grand Hotel Orologio**, Viale delle Terme 66, *© 049 866 9111, @ 049 866 9841 (very expensive)*, with a large park and landscaped pools that attract many guests seeking pampered tranquillity instead of magic mud. *Closed Dec–Feb.* Friendly ★★★**Verdi**, Via F. Busonera 200, *© 049 667 600, @ 049 667 025 (moderate)* offers more pools and mud for a quarter of the price. In nearby Torréglia, join the hungry Paduans at their favourite country restaurants: **Da Taparo**, Via Castelletto 42, *© 049 521 1060 (moderate)* with a beautiful terrace overlooking the hills to match its delicious Veneto cuisine (*closed Mon*); or **Antica Trattoria Ballotta**, Via Carromatto 2, *© 049 521 2970, @ 049 521 1385 (moderate)*, in business since 1605 and one of the oldest in Venetia, with fine dining inside or in the garden; or the panoramic **Rifugio Monte Rua**, Via Mone Rua 29, *© 049 521 1049 (moderate)*, where dishes change according to season. *Both closed Tues.*

Teolo ✉ 35037

In the centre of Teolo, ***Lussana**, V. Chiesa eolo 1, ✆ 049 992 5530, 📠 049 992 5530 (*moderate–inexpensive*) has bright rooms in a charming Liberty-style villa, with lovely views over a terraced garden and orchard. If you ring ahead and can behave yourself, you can sleep at **Praglia Abbey**, ✆ 049 990 0010 (a good way to make sure you catch a Gregorian Mass). There are two dormitories, one just for men inside the abbey, and another for both sexes on the grounds. It's free, but make a donation when you leave. In nearby Vò, stay in a delightful bed and breakfast in the middle of a vineyard, **Bacco e Arianna**, ✆ 049 994 0187 (*inexpensive*).

Arquà Petrarca ✉ 35032

A short drive north of Arquà, ****Villa Serena**, Via Bignago 90, ✆ 0429 718 044 (*inexpensive*) offers no-frills serenity. Nearer the centre of Arquà, at **La Montanella**, Via Costa 33, ✆ 0429 718 200 (*expensive–moderate*), you can enjoy not only the garden and views, but exquisite *risotti* and duck with fruit; select your wine, olive oil and vinegar from special menus. *Closed Tues eve, Wed, 2 weeks each in Aug and Jan.*

Monsélice, Este and Montagnana

Spilling like an opera set down the southern slopes of the Euganean Hills, the natural citadel of **Monsélice** (*Mons silicis*) was first fortified by the Romans. In its heyday it bristled with five rings of walls and 30 towers, built in 1239 by Ezzelino da Romano to control the road between Padua and Este. Most of the walls fell victim to medieval Italy's biggest enemy— 19th-century town planners. Nevertheless, the core of the citadel, Ezzelino's Ca' Marcello, was bought up in the early 1900s when it was on its last legs by industrialist and art patron Count Vittorio Cini, who beautifully restored it. Now part of the **Castello Cini** (*open April–11 Nov, guided tours at 9, 10, 11 and 2, 3, 4; summer 3, 4, 5; adm*), it houses the count's superb collection of medieval and Renaissance arms and antiques, and, they say, the ghost of Ezzelino's lover Avalda, who died here after a 17-year imprisonment.

The castle lies near the base of Vincenzo Scamozzi's striking **Via Sacra delle Sette Chiese** (1605), zigzagging up the hill passing the sumptuous **Villa Nani**, the Romanesque **Duomo** and seven **chapels** built by Scamozzi and frescoed by Palma Giovane (a mini-version of the Seven Churches of Rome, offering proportionately smaller indulgences). Near the top of the Via Sacra the elegant 16th-century **Villa Duodo and Esedra di San Francesco Saverio**, also by Scamozzi, is now a university centre of hydraulic studies. A path continues up to the **Rocca,** built by Frederick II, Ezzelino's boss, over a Lombard fort (*open Sat and Sun, book,* ✆ *042 972 931*). Just north of Monsélice in **Rivella**, the late *cinquecento* **Villa Selvatico-Capodilista** has an elegant, romantic garden designed by Jappelli in 1816. *Open April and October, Thurs–Sat 2–5, Sun 10–7.*

Monsélice's old rival, **Este** (ancient *Ateste*) is only 9km to the west. This was the capital of the Paleoveneti and, 2000 years later, of the powerful 11th-century Lombard lord, Marquess Alberto Azzo II, whose son Guelfo IV became Duke of Bavaria, and whose later descendants included the Electors of Hanover and George I of England (Queen Victoria was proud to say her roots went back to Este); another branch of the family, famous as art patrons in the Renaissance, moved on to Ferrara. Like Monsélice, medieval Este was a hotly contested piece of real estate, and bristles with the towers of the **Castello dei Carraresi**, built by the lords of Padua in 1339 and now put out to pasture in a public garden.

Abutting the garden, the 16th-century Palazzo Mocenigo houses the excellent **Museo Nazionale Atestino** (*open 9–7, adm*), its frescoed ceilings gazing down at artefacts from the first Veneto civilization in the 10th century BC up to Roman times: don't miss the vigorous 9th-century BC rams' heads; the 7th-century BC *Situla Benvenuti*, a bronze vase decorated with warrriors and fantastic animals; a superb collection of 6th–5th-century BC bronzes of warriors and horsemen; inscriptions in ancient Venetic, using the Etruscan alphabet; a rare gold medal issued by Augustus; and, a bit out of place, a luscious red-dressed *Madonna and Child* by Cima da Conegliano. Other highlights are the startlingly tilted 12th-century campanile of **San Martino**, the two grand clock towers in **Piazza Maggiore**, and Giambattista Tiepolo's altar-piece of *Santa Tecla vs. the Plague* in the **Duomo**. Behind the castle **Villa De Kunkler** was Byron's residence in 1817–18; here Shelley, his guest, wrote 'Lines Written among the Euganean Hills' after the death of his little daughter Clara:

> Many a green isle needs must be
> In the deep wide sea of Misery,
> Or the mariner, worn and wan,
> Never thus could voyage on...

Montagnana, 15km west, boasts some of the best-preserved medieval fortifications in Italy, the handiwork of Ezzelino da Romano and the Carrara family. The walls extend for two kilo-metres, defended by 24 intact towers—impressive but not effective; Venice lost and regained the town 13 times during the War of the Cambrai alone. Every September the walls form a picturesque backdrop to Montagnana's colourful Palio, inaugurated in 1259 to celebrate the liberation of the city from Ezzelino. Jutting out asymmetrically in the main piazza, the **Duomo** has a portal by Sansovino, a *Transfiguration* by Veronese, and a huge, anonymous painting of *The Battle of Lepanto*, to which the town contributed so generously with men and money that the Venetians paved the piazza in gratitude. The **Museo Civico A. Giacomelli** (*open Wed–Fri 10.30–12.30, Sat and Sun 10.30–1 and 3.30–6*), in the recently restored 12th-century **Castello di San Zeno**, has exhibits ranging from relics of prehistoric times to a whole room devoted to two native tenors, Giovanni Marinelli and Aureliano Pertile. Palladio mavens won't want to miss his **Palazzo Pisani**, by the Porto Padova.

Where to Stay and Eating Out

Monsélice ✉ 35043

Modern ★★★**Ceffri Villa Corner**, Via Orti 7, ✆ 0429 783 111, 🖷 0429 783 100 (*moderate*) has a pool and well-equipped rooms, and a good restaurant featuring homemade pasta with a L30,000 tourist menu; fungi fiends head to elegant **La Torre**, Piazza Mazzini 14, ✆ 0429 73752 (*moderate, expensive* for truffles) for gratification. *Closed Sun eve, Mon, and part of July and Aug.*

Montagnana ✉ 35044

★★★**Aldo Moro**, Via G. Marconi 27, ✆ 0429 81351, 🖷 0429 82842 (*moderate*) has fine rooms beside the Duomo, and a good restaurant serving the local *prosciutto dolce* *del montagnanese*. IYHF card-holders can stay in the best location in town, the magnificent **Rocca degli Alberi Youth Hostel** ('Tree Castle') at the Legnano Gate, built in 1362, ✆ 0429 81076, 📠 049 907 0266 (*inexpensive; closed mid-Oct–Mar*). For lunch or dinner, find **Da Stona**, Via Carrarese 51, ✆ 0429 81532 (*inexpensive*), an excellent trattoria with tasty homecooking, *pasta e fagioli, prosciutto dolce*, and a good local wine list; tourist menu L19,000. *Closed Mon*.

Southeast of Padua

Hardly any tourists make it into this flat country, but if you have a car it has treasures to seek out. In **Brugine**, just off the main Padua–Chioggia road, the 16th-century **Villa Roberti Bozzolato** designed by Andrea della Valle (now the Centro Internazionale di Storia dello Spazio e del Tempo) has delightful mythological frescoes by Paolo Veronese and Giambattista Zelotti; on the first Sunday of each month it hosts an antiques fair (*other times open by appointment only*, ✆ *049 580 6768*). **Conselve**, further south, was twice flattened in Venice's wars (1325, *vs*. Padua; 1508, *vs*. Europe) before it became an aristocratic retreat, as recalled in the elegant **Villa Sagredo**, built in the 1660s around a hunting lodge.

South, **Bagnoli di Sopra** has as its centrepiece Baldassare Longhena's **Villa Widmann-Borletti** (1656) a vast complex including a villa, a theatre, a church, set out in a green bordered by a party of statues by Antonio Bonazza, and a winery (*open Tues–Sat 9–12.30, 3–6.30*). Best of all, just east of Conselve in **Pontecasale** is Sansovino's **Villa Garzoni-Michiel** (1536–66), a landmark pre-Palladian work inspired by classical and Roman models (*plans to open it to the public*, ✆ *049 534 9602 for hours*). Another place to aim for is **Piove di Sacco** (it sounds like 'rain sack' but the name is really derived from *Plebs Sacci*, 'taxed people', from the Middle Ages, when this land was the personal property of the emperors). Piove's handsome, much remodelled **Duomo** has a *Madonna* by Giambattista Tiepolo, a polyptych by Paolo Veneziano and an altar by Sansovino (in the chapel to the left of the main altar), although the best picture in town is yet another *Madonna* in the 15th-century **Santuario della Madonna delle Grazie**, attributed to Giovanni Bellini.

Little Mesopotamia

About 20km south of Monsélice, Rovigo is the capital of the province wedged between Italy's two longest rivers, the mighty Adige and the mightier Po, known as the Polèsine or 'Little Mesopotamia'. Like ancient Mesopotamia it has been blessed and cursed by its rivers, which make it fertile but often spill over their banks. Six complete cycles of creation and destruction have molded the topography of Little Mesopotamia—miles of silt have left its ancient capital Adria high and dry. The main reason for a visit is to explore the Po Delta, a haunting landscape of water, dunes and trees, changing in mists of light and colour.

Getting Around

From **Rovigo** there are frequent buses to Adria and the Delta towns; trains also run from Rovigo to Adria and Chioggia (1hr 20mins), or south to Ferrara (30mins) and Bologna (1hr). Rovigo's **bus station** is on the Piazzale G. Di Vittorio; the **railway station** is on the Piazza Riconoscenza. Fratta Polèsine can be reached by bus from Rovigo (direction Trecenta).

Rovigo: Via J. H. Dunant 10, ✆ 0425 361 481, @ 0425 30416, *apt@gal.adigecolli.it*
Rosolina Mare: Via dei Ligustri 3, ✆ 0426 68012.

Rovigo

The other inhabitants of Venetia may sneer '*Rovigo no m'intrigo*' but this prosperous little provincial capital doesn't give a snap. For a landmark, Rovigo can match Bologna with its odd couple of leaning towers, the 11th-century **Torri Donà**, one tall, one stubby. Nearby (nothing is far), a lion of St Mark holds court with a statue of Vittorio Emanuele in central **Piazza Vittorio Emanuele II**, a handsome trapezoid dotted with palaces, one containing the **Pinacoteca dell'Accademia dei Concordi** (*open Mon–Fri 9.30–12 and 3.30–7, Sat 9.30–12; July and Aug, Mon–Sat 10–1; adm free*). Rovigo may be provincial, but it was hardly backward; founded by local scholars in 1580, the academy has over 600 paintings, including Giovanni Bellini's *Madonna* and *Christ Bearing the Cross*; Palma il Vecchio's *Flagellation*; Jan Gossaert's *Venus with a Mirror*; and a 17th-century *Cleopatra*, by Sebastiano Mazzoni, complete with a very realistic asp crawling along her languorous breast. Another section, the Count Silvestri collection, has excellent 17th–18th-century works by Sebastiano Bombelli, Pietro Longhi, Piazzetta, Luca Giordano and Bernardo Strozzi. The academy keeps its precious library adjacent, along with an Egyptian collection.

From adjacent Piazza Garibaldi and its equestrian bronze statue of Italy's most romantic hero, follow Via Silvestri back to Rovigo's most famous church, the octagonal **La Rotonda** with a detached tower by Longhena (*closed 11.30–4*). Built in 1603 by Francesco Zamberlan, a not entirely successful engineering pupil of Palladio (the dome had to be demolished the year after it was built), the interior is an art gallery of 17th-century Veneto painting: Pietro Liberi, Antonio Zanchi, Pietro Muttoni, Francesco Maffei and Giambattisa Pellizzari all contributed dramatic canvases to the greater glory of Rovigo's *podestàs*; the Virgin, angels, virtues and saints stream out of clouds and whirlwinds to pay homage to these robed representatives of Venetian officialdom. At the south end of town (take Corso del Popola down to Via S. Bellino), the monastery attached to S. Bartolomeo Apostolo is now the **Museo Civico della Civiltà in Polèsine** dedicated to archaeology, ethnography and local history (*closed for restoration at the time of writing*).

Up the Po: Fratta Polèsine and Lendinara

The villas of the Po flatlands, the Polèsine, are fairly simple compared to their counterparts in the northern Veneto, but have the advantage of being accessible by boat. The most important one, **Villa Badoera** (1570), is 18km southwest of Rovigo in the centre of **Fratta Polèsine** (*open daily exc Mon, April–Sept 10–12 and 3–7; Oct–Mar 10–12 and 2–5; adm*), a building stamped all over with Palladio's signature, from its Ionic temple front over a stately stair to the *barchesse*, perpendicular to the villa but united by curved arcades. Restorations have uncovered original frescoes of pseudo-Roman grotesques by Giallo Fiortino. In the Bronze Age, Mycenaean Greeks founded a trading counter here in Fratta, dealing with caravans that crossed over the Po plain; it thrived from the 11th–9th century BC, when it was wiped off the map in a cataclysmic flood.

The other main destination in these parts (although don't expect to see any other tourists!) is **Lendinara** on the left bank of the Adigetto, once property of the Este family of Ferrara. A miraculous spring flowed here, which is now channelled into the octagonal fountain in the centre of the church of the **Madonna del Pilastrello** (1581) in Piazza Alberto Mario, which has a vast collection of *ex votos*, including one by Paolo Veronese. A rich collection of Renaissance altars and statues fills the **Duomo**; and on Via Garibaldi the **Palazzo Dolfin-Marchiori**, built on a design by Scamozzi, has a garden by Giuseppe Jappelli. In central Piazza Risorgimento you'll find a pair of 14th-century towers left over from the Este castle, and a charming place to sip a *cappuccino*, the **Caffè Maggiore**, unchanged since 1915.

Adria

The deluge was on such a scale that only in the 6th century BC did people—beginning with the Paleoveneti and the Etruscans—return to the Po Delta, founding **Adria**, at the time 9km from the sea, but linked to it by an Etruscan canal, the Canale Bianca. They were soon followed by Greek merchants from Corinth, Corfu and Aegina, who lived with the Paleoveneti and Etruscans in wheeling and dealing harmony; it was praised as 'Shining Adria' by Strabo and 'noble city' by Pliny the Elder. As the Etruscan town of Felsina (Bologna) became the dominant regional power at the end of the 6th century, Adria lost out to Felsina's port of Spina, although not before Adria gave its name to the sea. The city remained an island of Greekness in the Veneto; in 385–350 BC Syracuse helped to defend it from the Gauls.

After decades of sporadic digging in search of the Etruscan and Greek necropolis, paydirt was struck in 1990 by accident during road work on Via Spolverin. The grave-goods—gold, swords and vases—are now in the **Museo Archeologico Nazionale** at Via G. Badini 59 (*open 9–7 daily, Thurs, Fri and Sat also 8.30–11pm; adm*). Further memories of Adria's glory days in this collection include excellent black-figure Corinthian vases (a beautiful one shows the apotheosis of Hercules); there's also a lovely collection of richly coloured Roman glass and a 3rd-century BC iron chariot of Gaulish workmanship, found entombed with two tiny horses, buried with either a Celtic or Paleoveneti warrior. Ancient Venetia was famous for its horses in antiquity, although the proof of their value was often demonstrated in the old-fashioned way—sacrificing them at funerals. In the courtyard, a Roman milestone from the Rimini-Aquileia Via Popilla (132 BC) carries the oldest Latin inscription in northern Italy.

The Venice of its day, Adria is now a rather dusty place with only one canal, dominated by a giant radio mast. But it kept its chin up for centuries even after the Romans. The **Duomo Nuovo** in Piazza Garibaldi has as its prize a Coptic relief from the 4th century, made just after the Council of Ephesus agreed on the divinity of the Virgin, showing her between the archangels Michael and Gabriel. The sacristy's lavish baroque wardrobes by Jacopo Piazzetta (1683) come from the Scuola della Carità in Venice, while a door in the left nave leads to the old Cathedral, with an octagonal baptismal font and remains of the 7th-century crypt that once formed part of the palaeochristian church, its walls decorated with early cartoon-like Byzantine frescoes. The baptismal font of another church, **S. Maria della Tomba**, in Via Angeli, once served in the Roman baths; it also has two fine terracottas, a 14th-century *Annunciation* and a 15th-century *Dormition of the Virgin* by Michele da Firenze.

The Po Delta

After travelling over 652km (405 miles), the Po ends its course in a 400-square-mile delta, a marshy fish-filled wonderland of a thousand islets, much appreciated by bitterns, coots, kingfishers, little egrets, herons, terns and migratory birds from the north. Before its current status as the **Parco del Po**, a few resorts mushroomed up along the sandy, pine-shaded shores— namely **Rosolina Mare**, a lovely beach for children, and the exclusive island 'club' **Isola di Albarella** with its golf course.

The Po, as it nears the Adriatic, splits into six major branches, each with its own character, including the navigable canal-like Po di Levante; the contorted, lushly overgrown Po di Maistra; and the majestic Po di Pila, which carries 60 per cent of the flow, and has most of the fisheries and birdlife, especially around **Rosapineta**. Dogged shepherds and their flocks, thatched houses with great chimneys called *casone* and gypsy shanty towns dot the lonesome shores. If you can, visit the delta in spring, when the colour are fiery and transparent, or at the end of summer, when mists hover over the pools and dunes, tinted scarlet with salicornia and violet with sea lavender, and the reeds and grasses turn to gold. There are several **boat cruises** to choose from which explore the delta and its bird life, most of them departing from **Porto Tolle** or **Taglio di Po**. One, Delta Tours in Padua, offers day-long cruises, with lunch on board; for schedules, ✆ 049 870 0232, 🖷 049 760 833.

Where to Stay and Eating Out

Rovigo ✉ 45100

A few steps from the centre, the Liberty-style ★★★★**Villa Regina Margherita**, Viale Regina Margherita 6, ✆ 0425 361540, 🖷 0425 31301 is the most stylish place to stay; bedrooms are well equipped, if lacking the tone of the public rooms. In a little villa in the pines, **Tre Pini**, Viale Porto Po 68, ✆ 0425 421111 (*moderate*) serves delightful homemade tortellini and fresh salmon. *Closed Sun, Aug.* At **Tavernetta Dante dai Trevisani**, Corso del Popolo 212, ✆ 0425 26386 (*moderate*) you can try that medieval Veneto favourite, *pappardelle all'anatra* (with duck sauce) as well as other treats. *Closed Sun.* The best place of all, however, is 8km south of Rovigo in Arquà Polèsine: **Degli Amici**, Via Quirina 4, ✆ 0425 91045 (*moderate*), where fresh- and salt-water fish share the menu with duck and goose, prepared in an old wood oven. *Closed Wed, and in summer Sat and Sun lunch.*

On the Delta ✉ 45010

East of Porto Tolle, at Scardovari, the seaside **Marina 70**, ✆ 0426 80080 (*expensive*) is devoted heart and soul to fresh seafood, prepared to traditional Italian methods and served on a pretty terrace. *Closed Mon.*

North of Padua

Some of the Veneto's best known sites are north of Padua, in the charmed foothills of the Dolomites: there's Castelfranco Veneto, birthplace of Giorgione, and Àsolo, where the Queen of Cyprus held her fabled Renaissance court; and outstanding villas, including Masèr, where Palladio and Veronese collaborated to create a unique work of art.

From Padua there are both **buses** and **trains** to Bassano del Grappa (40mins), via Castelfranco; from Vicenza change trains at Castelfranco, passing Cittadella on the way. From Venice, change in Treviso. Bassano's **bus station** is in the Piazzale Trento, near the tourist office, © 0424 30850, while the **train station** is at the top of Via Chilesotti.

Frequent buses from Montebelluna, Bassano or Treviso serve Àsolo (14km) and Masèr (6km further); others, from Bassano and Vicenza, run to Maròstica (20 buses daily), Lonedo di Lugo, Thiene (25km) and Asiago (36km).

Castelfranco Veneto: Via Francesco Maria Preti 39, © 0423 495 000.

Piazzola sul Brenta and Piombino Dese: Palladian Villas

There's a choice of roads north from Padua, and a choice of villas to see along the way. The SS47 follows the river Brenta to Cittadella, by way of **Piazzola sul Brenta** and the imposing **Villa Contarini** (*open 9–12 and 3–7, mid-Oct–Mar 9–12 and 2–5, closed Mon; adm*). Built in 1414, the villa was greatly enlarged in 1564 by Palladio for Marco Contarini, a Procurator of the Republic; later residents added the 17th-century *barchesse*, adorned with the full whack of Palladian statues and balustrades, on grounds that include an arcaded hemicycle, park and lake. The interior is more elaborate than the average villa as well, featuring special Music and Listening Rooms with excellent acoustics. Villa Contarini had an interesting career in the 19th century, when it was purchased by Silvestro Camerini, who made Piazzola into a model industrial/agricultural estate. One of its main products, jute, was still being processed in the 1960s.

The more easterly SS307 from Padua to Castelfranco Veneto passes near **Piombino Dese**, a sprawling rural *comune*, but a must-see detour for Palladiophiles, for its **Villa Cornaro** (1553) a block from the Piombino Dese train station (*open by appointment only, © 049 936 5017*), Built in 1553, this is among Palladio's most monumental and well-preserved villas, where he introduced one of his most original features—the two-storey projecting portico-loggia. It's also the only

Villa Cornaro, from Palladio's Four Books of Architecture

Palladian villa to preserve much of its original *intocato* cladding and tile floors; another unique feature is the grand Salon, where niches were designed to hold full-length statues of the Cornaro ancestors—a throwback to the ancient Romans, who liked to keep wax models and masks of their forebears around the place. The harmonious interior was only frescoed in 1716 (after the Cornari relocated their famous art collection), when Procurator Andrea Cornaro commissioned 21-year-old Mattia Bortoloni to execute 104 fresco panels in stucco frames, using the newly fashionable 'light manner'. The subjects were carefully chosen by Cornaro, who eschewed the usual mythologies or allegories for scenes from the Old and New Testaments. Not what one expects in a country house, although the Bible may have been merely a vehicle to smuggle in a forbidden Masonic message: the frescos on the eastern wall of the main room especially abound with Masonic symbols.

Castelfranco Veneto and Around

Square, walled **Castelfranco Veneto** was built by Treviso in 1199 to counter the ambitions of Padua, and basks in the glory of having given the world the romantic, enigmatic genius Giorgione, or Zorzon as the locals called him, born here in 1478. Zorzon in gratitude (it seems like a pleasant enough place to have grown up in) left Castelfranco the masterpiece now hanging in the neoclassical **Duomo**: the *Castelfranco Madonna* (1504), a triangular composition of the Virgin, St Francis and the soldier-saint Liberalis, their remote figures inhabiting the same ineffable, dreamlike world as his paintings in the Accademia. The *Castelfranco Madonna* was subject to one of the more spectacular art heists in the 1970s; the thieves' demands for a ransom were repeatedly refused, and the painting was abandoned after a shoot-out with the *carabinieri*.

Next to the Duomo, the **Casa del Giorgione** (*open Tues–Sun, 9–12 and 3–6; adm*) is decorated with a fascinating *chiaroscuro* frieze of scientific instruments and symbols of the liberal and mechanical arts, attributed to Giorgione (who, according to one interpretation of the frieze's allegory, must have been Jewish); it also has photos of all his known works. During Zorzon's brief life Castelfranco built its most elaborate gate, the **Porta di Treviso**, with its clock and Venetian lion (1499). From here Borgo Treviso leads to the charming gardens of 19th-century **Villa Revedin Bolasco** (*open Tues and Thurs 2–5, Sun 10–12.30, 2–5.30*). Just west of Castelfranco, near Castello di Godego, a series of prehistoric earthen walls standing between 6 and 13ft high form a partially visible rhomboid known as the **Motte**; most have been found to have precise astronomical alignments.

After Treviso built Castelfranco, the Paduans, tit for tat, founded the egg-shaped **Cittadella** 15km to the west. Its magnificent 13th-century **walls**, surrounded by a moat, are over a mile long and 40ft high; one of the 28 towers, the Torre di Malta, contained Ezzelino's infamous torture chamber ('...no man yet was ever sent to Malta/for treachery as foul as his shall be', *Paradiso* IX, 54). The Venetians added the fine lion with a kinky tail in the main square.

From Castelfranco you can also nip up to **Fanzolo**, 5km to the northeast, for another of Palladio's finest, **Villa Emo**, the only Palladian villa still owned by the family that commissioned it (*open April–Sept 3–7, Sun and hols 10–12.30 and 3–7; Oct–Mar, Sat and Sun only 2–6; adm exp*). Villa Emo has the typical Palladian five-part profile, with dovecotes surmounting the ends of the *barchesse* (now a hotel, *see* below); its temple front, with its tympanum stuccoed by Vittoria, was one of the first to have freestanding columns, not to mention a long ramp that enabled visitors to ride straight up to the door. Unlike many villas, this is still a working farm, and one with a famous pedigree—it was one of the first in Europe to grow maize (1536), used to fatten pigeons before it began to fatten the polenta-mad Venetians. The main rooms have brightly coloured mythologies by Giambattista Zelotti. Palladio also designed the long rows of brick farmworkers' cottages.

Close by, the little village of **Riese Pio X** is named for the Pontiff it produced, Pius X (Giuseppe Sarto, 1835–1914, canonized in 1951), whose home is now a museum. Although his policies were reactionary, he is remembered fondly in the Veneto. The story goes that his housekeeper took to wearing his old stockings, and found that they were not only holey but holy, and miraculously cured her bunions. When she told the pope, he laughed and said, 'They certainly don't do that for me!' Near Riese, **San Vito** has in its cemetery one of the most striking modern tombs in Italy, designed by Venetian architect Carlo Scarpa (1975) for himself and TV baron Giuseppe Brion. And although it's been abandoned since the 1700s, you can also have a look at what remains of the once-fabulous castle and gardens that Venice built in 1490 for Caterina Cornaro—the **Barco della Regina Cornaro**, in **Altìvole**.

Where to Stay and Eating Out

Scorzè (10km east of Piombino Dese) ✉ 30037

In the 17th century, the family of the Doge who built the Arsenale built themselves the ★★★**Villa Conestabile**, Via Roma 1, ✆ 041 445 027, ✇ 041 584 0088 (*expensive*). Rooms have kept their original parquet floors and marble-ized walls, and the park is lovely. An added bonus: buses to Venice, Padua and Treviso stop in front.

Castelfranco Veneto ✉ 31033

In the centre of Castelfranco a 17th-century palace houses ★★★**Al Moretto**, Via S. Pio X 10, ✆ 0423 721 313, ✇ 0423 721 066 (*moderate*; no restaurant). ★★★**Roma**, Via Fabio Filzi 39, ✆ 0423 721 616, ✇ 0423 721 515 (*moderate*) is outside the fortifications but offers a good view of them; all rooms have TV and air-conditioning. Next to the walls, **Alle Mura**, Via Preti 69, ✆ 0423 498 098 (*expensive–moderate*) is an elegant place, with well prepared seafood dishes and a garden. *Closed Thurs.*

Just above Castelfranco at Salvarosa, you can also stay at little old ★★★**Ca' delle Rose**, on the Circonvallazione Est, ✆ 0423 490 232, ✇ 0423 490 261 (*moderate*) and dine at its famous restaurant, **Barbesin**, ✆ 0423 490 446. The setting is as idyllic as the products of its kitchen, based entirely on fresh, seasonal ingredients; the veal with apples melts in your mouth. *Closed Wed eve and Thurs.* In the same area, ★★★★**Fior**, Via dei Carpani 18, ✆ 0423 721 212, ✇ 0423 498 771 (*expensive*) occupies an old villa and park, with tennis, pool, sauna and all the trimmings.

In Galliera Vèneto, midway between Castelfrano and Cittadella, a former patrician hunting lodge serves as a setting for **Palazzino**, Via Roma 29, ✆ 049 596 9224 (*expensive–moderate*), a great place to try Renaissance dishes such as pheasant stuffed with truffles, accompanied by vegetables just plucked from the restaurant's garden. *Closed Tues eve, Wed, and Aug.*

Fanzolo ✉ 31050

Stay in the wing of Palladio's ★★★**Villa Emo**, Via Stazione 5, ✆ 0423 476 414, ✉ 0423 487 043 (*expensive*): the handful of elegant rooms and suites come with a swimming pool on the grounds; peace and quiet guaranteed, and there's fine dining in the restaurant, open to non-guests (*expensive; closed Mon, Tues lunch*).

Montebelluna and il Montello

The Roman *Mons Bellonae*, Montebelluno is proud to be the world capital of ski and hiking boots, celebrated in all their glory in the **Museo dello Scarpone**, in one of a score of villas scattered about its hills above Piazza Garibaldi, the Villa Binetti-Zuccareda (Vicolo Zuccareda 1, *open 9–12 and 3–6*). Long before ski boots, however, what is now the centre of Montebelluno was an important medieval market; in Piazzetta di Mercato Vecchia a column erected by the Venetians in 1593 honours the commercial concessions Montebelluno enjoyed from the 9th century until 1872. Another country house, the Villa Biagi, houses the **Museo Civico**, Via Piave 41 (*open Tues–Sun 9–12.30 and 2.30–5.30, summer 3.30–6.30; adm*), with remains of a Paleoveneti necropolis discovered just to the north of Montebelluna.

The **Montello**, the beautiful hilly district between Montebelluno and the Piave, was once the main source of oak timber for Venetian galleys, yet was cut so carefully that 6000 hectares of primordial forest remained intact until the 19th century; in this century about a third of that has been reforested. Because of its strategic location on the Piave, the Montello saw heavy action in the First World War, when Austro-Hungarian shells flattened **Nervesa della Battaglia** and turned its 12th-century **Abbazia di S. Eustachio** (where Giovanni della Casa compiled the first Index of Prohibited Books for the Church, in 1555) into the striking ruins that stand to this day. From Nervesa 'La Panoramica' skirts the top of the hills, farms and villas en route to **Crocetta del Montello**, near Masèr.

Villa Barbaro at Masèr

Open Mar–Oct, Tues, Sat, Sun and hols 3–6; Nov–Feb, Sat, Sun, 2.30–5; adm exp.

This unique synthesis of two great talents, Palladio and Veronese, was created in 1568 for two great patrons, the Barbaro brothers, Daniele (Patriarch of Aquileia and humanistic scholar) and Marcantonio (Venetian ambassador and amateur sculptor). Palladio used the Temple of Fortuna Virilis in Rome as his inspiration for the central residence, while the *barchesse* are graceful wings with dovecotes rising at the ends, each with a sundial, forming the five-part profile that would inspire countless buildings (including the United States' Capitol). The horses frisking about the front lawn add to the patrician dignity, while the reliefs on the central pediment—the double-headed eagle of Byzantium (Aquileia, in this case) and two men astride dragons or sea monsters, each holding a woman in one arm and touching the horns of a central ox-head—add an air of mystery. Emblems like this were the rage in the Renaissance, full of puns and allegorical references for those in the know, which unfortunately doesn't include us.

Palladio taught Veronese about space and volume, and nowhere is this so evident as in these ravishing, architectonic *trompe-l'œil* frescoes, which repopulate the villa with the original owners and their pets, lingering as if the villa lay under the same spell as Sleeping Beauty's castle—an effect heightened by the slippers passed out to visitors at the door (to protect the

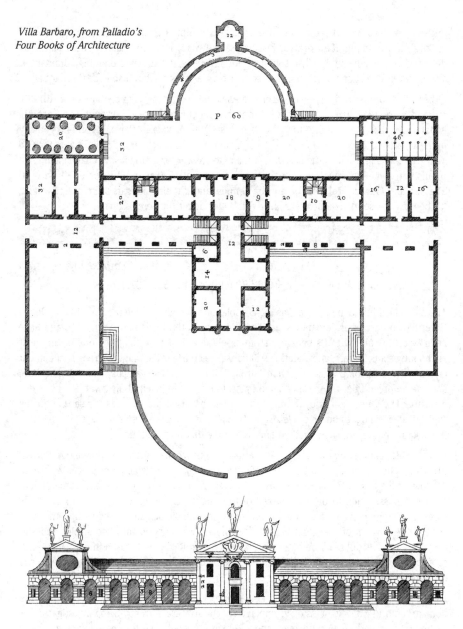

Villa Barbaro, from Palladio's Four Books of Architecture

original floors). Signora Barbaro and her sons gaze down from painted balconies; a little girl opens a door; a dog waits in a corner; painted windows offer views of imaginary landscapes; the huntsman in the far bedroom is Veronese, gazing across the row of rooms at his mistress. As delightful as these are, one tradition has it that Palladio was miffed that Veronese's *trompe-l'œil* detracted from the appreciation of the harmonic proportions of his rooms, and he punished the painter by completely snubbing him in the *Quattro Libri*. The back garden is taken up with a nymphaeum, guarded by giants sculpted by Marcantonio Barbaro. The striking, if crumbling, **Tempietto**, just across the road, is a miniature Barbaro pantheon designed by Palladio in 1580, inspired by his favourite Renaissance building, Bramante's Tempietto in Rome, and decorated with statues by Alessandro Vittoria and Orazio Marinali.

Other villas dot the road between Masèr and Àsolo, including the 17th-century **Villa Rinaldi**, a grand baroque stage set. Or there's a longer, enchanting route up through the **Forcella Mostaccin** (take the road into the mountains just south of Villa Barbaro). If you find yourself in these parts on 21 March, you can witness a curious old purification rite: the Trial of the Old Year ('*La Vecia*'), in which the past year is made to answer for all the ills that happened, in an Inquisition-style interrogation, and burned at the stake. **Masèr-Muliperte**, **Quinto di Treviso** and **Cavaso del Tomba** are the venues, and if their calendars seem out of whack, it's because the spring equinox was New Year's Day under the Serenissima.

Àsolo: 'Town of a Hundred Horizons'

Tourist Information

Piazza G. D'Annunzio 2, ✆ 0423 529 046, ✉ 0423 524 137.

The old walled hilltown of Àsolo was the consolation prize given by Venice in 1489 to Queen Caterina Cornaro after demanding her abdication from the throne of Cyprus. It could have been worse: Àsolo, with its benign lush microclimate, just happens to be one of the most enchanting spots in Italy, and Caterina's Renaissance court lent it a high degree of refinement and art. The handsome young Giorgione strolled through its rose gardens strumming his lute, and the enforced idleness that prevailed in Àsolo may have inspired his invention of art for pleasure. The Queen's friend, Cardinal Pietro Bembo, used her court as the setting for his sophisticated dialogues on love, *Gli Asolani* (1512), and created the verb *asolare* to describe the pleasant but meaningless method of passing time that prevailed here.

In the 19th century Àsolo came back into fashion when Robert and Elizabeth Barrett Browning chose it as a romantic retreat (Robert entitled his last volume of poems *Asolando* 'for love of the place'; *Pippa Passes* was set here as well). Their son Pen became something of the town boss, much to the disapproval of the English community who had followed his parents, buying up five houses in town and restarting the old silk and weaving industries. He invited the parents of the great English traveller Freya Stark to move to Àsolo, and she described an aspect of the little hill town that you may notice out of season in particular: 'The roofs of the town are red, darkened and mottled by centuries of sunlight and rain, for this is the dampest and greenest corner of Italy.'

Pliny wrote that Àsolo's Roman incarnation *Acelum* was one of the chief fortified *oppida* of the Roman Tenth Region. Remains of an Imperial-era **theatre** are currently being investigated not far from the car parks under the town, and a Roman aqueduct feeds the charming *cinquecento* **Fontana Maggiore**, nicknamed the *Ombelico del Mondo*, 'the navel of the world', the chief ornament in Àsolo's central Piazza Maggiore. The **Duomo** just below was built over the Roman baths, finally in 1747, and has fine works by Lotto (*Apparition of the Madonna*, 1506), Jacopo da Bassano and Vivarini. Just up from the piazza the **Castello della Regina** with its watch tower (in both senses of the word—it tells the time) encloses what little remains of the garden where Queen Caterina lived in 'lace and poetry'. Don't expect much: most of the garden is now privately owned as part of Browning's Villa Beach, and the courtyard hosts a lighted *bocce* court. In 1700 the castle's great hall was replaced with a theatre, but in 1930 the John Deere tractor heir bought it, dismantled it, and rebuilt it in Sarasota, Florida.

Near the castle, the frescoed **Loggia del Capitano** contains a museum dedicated to Queen Caterina, Browning, and La Duse (*but closed until kingdom come for restoration*). Most of the shops are down Via Browning, while next to the Porta Santa Caterina is the charming **Palazzetto di Eleonora Duse**, her last home; the poem engraved on the façade was written by Gabriele D'Annunzio in memory of their love. Continue through down narrow Via S. Caterina to the bizarre, rusticated 16th-century **Casa Longobarda**, built by a Lombard architect in the service of Queen Caterina and decorated with grotesques and mysterious reliefs. A lane on the left descends to the cemetery, last resting place of Eleonora Duse and Freya Stark. For the famous views of poet Giosuè Caducci's 'hundred horizons' of Àsolo, climb (or drive— the road is halfway down the hill) up to the **Rocca**, built over a Paleoveneti and Roman fort (*open Sat, Sun; adm*).

Possagno

North of Àsolo the foothills are known as the Colle degli Ezzelini for the tyrant's first base, a tower reconstructed at **Sopracastello**. The main town here, **Possagno**, was the birthplace of Antonio Canova (1757–1822), the ultimate neoclassical sculptor, favourite of Napoleon and several popes. You can visit his house, and his clay and plaster models in the **Gypsoteca** (*open daily exc Mon, 9–12 and 3–6; Oct–April 9–12 and 2–5; adm*). Most artists leave a work or two for their home towns to remember them by, but Canova designed nothing less than a full-scale model of the Pantheon with the Parthenon stuck on the front as his personal souvenir. The town itself describes the **Tempio** as 'one of the greatest monuments that man on earth has ever erected—in praise of God—to himself'. For L2000 you can climb up the dome (*open 9–12 and 2–5, closed Mon*); for free you can study the detached, leaning campanile and try to figure out if it was built that way.

Where to Stay and Eating Out

Montebelluna ✉ 31044

One of the town's many villas, ★★★**San Marco**, Via Buziol 19, ✆ 0423 300 766, ✉ 0423 22553 (*moderate*) makes a pleasant and peaceful place to sleep in the hills; no restaurant, but Montebelluna has a superb one just south on the road to Barcon: the **Enoteca Marchi**, Via Castellana 177, ✆ 0423 303 530 (*expensive*), a modern building in a pretty setting, with not only an excellent wine list but great asparagus and duck and other Veneto favourites. *Closed Tues eve, Wed, and part of Aug.*

Masèr and Around ✉ 31010

Just up the road from Palladio's villa, dine in enchanting surroundings at **Da Bastian**, Via Cornuda, ✆ 0423 565 400 (*moderate*), where the pâté, risotto, Venetian-style snails and desserts are renowned. *Closed Wed eve and Thurs, some of Aug.* Just north, in Cavaso del Tomba, you can also dine memorably at the romantic **Al**

Ringranziamento, Via S. Pio X 107, ✆ 0423 543271 (*expensive–moderate*) where the creative chef is a master at concocting delicious dishes, including some you won't see anywhere else in the Veneto. *Closed Mon, Tues lunch, some of Aug.*

Àsolo ✉ 31011

Àsolo can boast one of Italy's most charming and evocative hotels, ★★★★★**Villa Cipriani**, Via Canova 298, ✆ 0423 952 166, ✉ 0423 952 095 (*very expensive*), in a house dating from the 16th century that belonged to Robert Browning, decorated with Persian carpets owned by Eleonora Duse. Overlooking a paradise of hills and cypresses, the hotel has an enchanting garden filled with roses and songbirds; some of its 32 rooms are located in its garden houses. Also in the historic centre, the celebrated ★★★★**Al Sole**, Via Collegio 33, ✆ 0423 528 111, ✉ 0423 528 399 (*expensive*) has recently had a complete overhaul and is more comfortable than ever, but hasn't lost any of the charm. Along with memories of famous past guests, the present is catered for very well—the hotel has a special agreement with the local country club (but there's no restaurant). Overlooking Àsolo's central piazza, and with a little garden behind it, is ★★★**Duse**, Via Browning 190, ✆ 0423 55241, ✉ 0423 950 404 (*expensive*, but the cheapest in town).

One of Àsolo's oldest houses hosts the **Hosteria Ca' Derton**, Piazza D'Annunzio 11, ✆ 0423 52730 (*moderate*), featuring traditional specialities to match the setting. *Closed Mon.* Wood-panelled, intimate **Ai Due Archi**, Via Roma 55, ✆ 0423 952 201 (*moderate*) is elegant and antique like Àsolo itself, and serves up delicious polenta in various guises. *Closed Wed eve and Thurs.* Every celebrity that has passed through has had a drink at the historic **Caffé Centrale**, Via Roma 72; you should, too: it's a great place to watch the world go by.

Bassano del Grappa

Tourist Information

Bassano: Largo Corona d'Italia 35, ✆ 0424 524 351, ✉ 0424 525 301.

Sprawled over the foothills of the Alps where the Brenta begins its flow down the plain, the bustling town of Bassano celebrated its first millennium in 1998. Over the past 1000 years it has given the world lovely ceramics, white asparagus, fire-water, tenor Tito Gobbi (1913–84) and a dynasty of painters who adopted Bassano's name as their own and rather sombrely influenced 17th-century painting across Europe. In that same century, Bassano's Remondini family were pioneers in a phenomenon we take for granted—the mass media—churning out thousands of prints of Italian masterpieces, views and holy pictures that were sold around the world. With so many gold stars pasted on its forehead, it's not surprising that Bassano is a town of character, but one wearing a few patches after severe damage in the battles of 1917–18.

The first houses, back in 998, were clustered on a height overlooking the Brenta, around the **Castello Ezzelino**, which bears the name of the famous bad guy who rebuilt it (*guided tours of the walls, at 10.15, 11.15, 4.45, 5.45, also Sat 9.15 pm; closed Mon*). Most of the action these days happens in Bassano's three central squares: first, the medieval Piazzotto Montevecchio, where the old municipal pawn shop or **Monte di Pietà** is covered with the coats of arms of 120 Venetian *podestàs*. This is linked to piquant Piazza Libertà, hogged by the neoclassical façade of the mastodonic church of **San Giovanni**; while the next square, Piazza Garibaldi, is guarded physically and spiritually by the 13th-century **Torre Civica** (with 19th-century battlements) and the Gothic church of **San Francesco**. San Francesco's cloister contains Bassano's **Museo Civico** (*open 9–6.30, Tues–Sat; 3.30–6.30 Sun; adm; same ticket for the ceramics museum*), with the excellent Chini collection of vases from Magna Grecia, cartoons and studies by Canova, and paintings with an emphasis on the dark and stormy, especially by the Bassano family, and particularly Jacopo (see his masterpiece, the twilit *Baptism of St Lucia*). Alessandro Magnasco contributes the uncanny *Burial of a Trappist Monk* and *Franciscan Banquet*, full of racing, wraith-like friars. There are calmer works as well: Michele Giambono's *Madonna* and a beautiful, recently restored *Crucifix* by Guariento.

Palladio designed Bassano's landmark, the **Ponte degli Alpini**, the unique covered wooden bridge that spans the unruly Brenta. First constructed in 1599, the bridge has been rebuilt and repaired several times to the master's design—lastly in 1948 (when it was renamed in honour of Italy's alpine troops), with more repairs in 1969 after damage in a flood. At one end, in the Palazzo Beltrame-Menarola, the grappa distillery Poli operates a **Museo della Grappa** where you can taste and buy (*open 9–1 and 2.30–7.30; Mon am closed; adm free*).

A Grappa Digression

Although a lot of grappa does come from Bassano del Grappa, its name doesn't derive from the town or its mountains but from graspa, the residue left at the bottom of the wine vat after the must is removed; it can be drunk unaged and white, or aged in oak barrels, where it takes on a rich, amber tone. First mentioned in a 12th-century chronicle, grappa, or aqua vitae ('the water of life'), was chugged down as a miracle-working concoction of earth and fire to dispel ill humours. In 1601 the Doge created a University Confraternity of Aqua Vitae to control quality; during the First World War Italy's Alpine soldiers adopted Bassano's enduring bridge as their symbol and its grappa to keep them on their feet. One of their captains described it perfectly:

> Grappa is like a mule; it has no ancestors and no hope of descendants; it zigzags through you like a mule zigzags through the mountains; if you're tired you can hang on to it; if they shoot you can use it as a shield; if it's too sunny you can sleep under it; you can speak to it and it'll answer, cry and be consoled. And if you really have decided to die, it will take you off happily.

In our peaceful days grappa's fiery spirit is too potent for most: from 70 million litres guzzled in 1970, only 25 million were drunk in 1990, and most of that as a coffee 'corrector', as the Italians quaintly put it. The Veneto with its 20 distilleries is a leading producer, and Bassano is a good place to seek out some of the better, more elusive labels; besides Poli, look for Da Ponte, Folco Portinari, Jacopo de Poli, Maschio, Rino Dal Tosco or Carpenè Malvolti.

In the mid-17th century, Bassano and the nearby town of Nove became the Veneto's top ceramic manufacturers, a status they maintain to this day, thanks to 56 firms. In the 18th-century Palazzo Sturm, just up Via Ferracina from the bridge, the **Museo della Ceramica** *(open April–Oct 9–12.30 and 3.30–6.30, closed Mon; winter Fri 9–12, Sat, Sun 3–7; same adm as Museo Civico)* has a display of the local ware, porcelain knick-knacks and majolica.

Around Bassano, and the Brenta Canal

There are two villas worth seeking out in Bassano's suburbs. From the centre follow Via Roma/Via Beata Giovanna out to early 18th-century **Ca' Rezzonico**, attributed in part to Giorgio Massari. One of the few villas still isolated in the fields, the interior is lavishly stuccoed and decorated with paintings, some by Canova *(book to visit, © 0424 525880)*. Three kilometres southwest of Bassano in **Angarano**, Palladio designed **Villa Bianchi Michiel** with his usual lateral *barchesse*, although the 17th-century owners demolished the central body of the villa and replaced it with a loftier, more palatial house, crowned with a tympanum by Longhena *(visits by written request, Loc. S. Eusebio, Via Corte 15)*. Just south in **Cartigliano**, the striking 16th-century **Villa Morosini Cappello**, attributed to Palladio's disciple Francesco Zamberlan, is entirely wrapped in loggias and porticoes, and has recently been restored as the town hall *(open Mon–Fri 9–1, Wed 4.30–6.30, Sat 9–12, free)*. Stop, too, at Cartigliano's parish church for its excellent fresco cycle by Jacopo Bassano.

Angarano marks the beginning of Bassano's own **Brenta Canal**, dug in the last century to control the unpredictable river. Unlike its sister to the south, this canal has no villas, but it does have stalactite caves, the **Grotte di Oliero**, near **Valstagna**. There are four of these, excavated by waters thundering down from the Alpago, and one is open for visits by boat; admission includes a botanical park and speleological museum *(open Mar–May, Sept and Oct Sat and Sun; June–Aug daily exc Mon; adm)*.

This quiet corner of the Veneto wasn't always so peaceful. Among the nature trails in the area, one of the most beautiful is also one of the most vertical, the **Calà del Sasso**—4444 steps leading up to Sasso, on the Asiago plateau *(see below)* chiselled out of the rock in the 15th century by the Venetians. Alongside the steps, they hollowed a chute for the logs from the Asiago's forests; these would be floated down the Brenta to Venice's Arsenale and made into galleys. When they were cranking out a ship a day, the timber here was flying.

Romano d'Ezzelino and Monte Grappa

> *There in that part of sinful Italy*
> *which lies between Rialto's shores and where*
> *the Piave and the Brenta river spring*
> *rises a hill of no great height from which,*
> *some years ago, there plunged a flaming torch,*
> *who laid waste all the countryside round.*

Paradise IX, 25–30 (trans. by Mark Musa)

Dante is referring here to **Romano d'Ezzelino** and its infamous son, known as the 'flaming torch' from a dream his mother had before he was born. Dante already saw Ezzelino down in the Seventh Circle of hell with the other cruel tyrants—although his sister Cunizza, who went through four husbands and at least two lovers, retired in Florence and did good deeds, and met Dante in heaven. These days Romano d'Ezzelino is best known for its striking new car museum, the **Museo dell'Automobilie Bonfanti** (Via Torino 2, *open 10–12.30, 4.30–6.30; closed Mon; adm)*.

The 'Grappa' was added to Bassano's name in 1928, not for its firewater but in memory of the terrible fighting in the First World War at Cima Grappa, where the Italians held the line after Caporetto in 1917–18. The Strada Cadorna from Romano d'Ezzalino up to **Cima Grappa** (5824ft) was built during the conflict and ends in a gargantuan trench called **Galleria Vittorio Emanuele II**, dug by the Italians to shelter their battery of guns. Displays and a museum describe the conflict, while the monumental cemetery holds the remains of 12,615 Italians; the slightly smaller Austro-Hungarian cemetery contains 10,590 (*open mid-May–Sept 10–12 and 2–5; Oct–May 10–12 and 1–4*).

Where to Stay and Eating Out

Bassano del Grappa ✉ 36061

As you may have noticed wandering through town, dried mushrooms and honey as well as grappa are specialities of Bassano, but it's yet another treat that attracts droves of hungry gourmets every April: *Asparagi DOC di Bassano*, long fat white asparagus, delicate and full of flavour, and perfect for a spring-cleaning of one's internal plumbing. Anyone can grow white asparagus by shielding the stalks from the sun with mounds of dirt. But in Bassano they somehow do it better: try it the local way, *asparagi alla bassanese*, blanched and topped with a hollandaise-type sauce made with cooked eggs and olive oil, or simply *alla parmigiana*.

In the centre ★★★**Belvedere**, in a 15th-century house in Piazzale Gen. Giardino 14, ✆ 0424 529 845, 🖷 0424 529 849 (*expensive*) has the best rooms in town, convenient, if not always quiet; ask for one in the back. The elegant restaurant, at Viale delle Fosse 1, ✆ 0424 524 988, serves Bassano's finest gastronomic delights, both Veneto and Italian classics, with the promised view. *Closed Sun*. The traditional ★★★**Brennero**, near the station at Via Torino 7, ✆ 0424 228 538, 🖷 0424 227 921 (*moderate–inexpensive*) is comfortable for a short stay. Just east of Bassano, at Mussolente (✉ 36065), the lovely, award-winning ★★★★**Villa Palma**, Via Chemin Palma 30, ✆ 0424 577 407, 🖷 0424 87687 (*expensive*) occupies an elegant 17th-century villa, with plush rooms full of high-tech gizmos and a gourmet restaurant. Besides Bassano's hotel restaurants, there's the beautiful dining room of **Al Sole-Da Tiziano**, Via Vitorelli 41, ✆ 0424 523 206 (*moderate*), which offers a perfect risotto, delicious duck, and Bassano's favourite seasonal ingredients: mushrooms, white asparagus and radicchio. *Closed Mon, July*.

Nove, Maròstica, and West to Schio

Tourist Information

Marostica: Piazza Castello, ✆ 0424 72127, 🖷 0424 72800, e-mail: *proloco @telemar.it*. **Schio**: Palazzo Garbin, Piazza dello Statuto 16, ✆ 0445 691 212.

In a land rich in clay and water, **Nove** has been known since the 1600s for its majolica, a craft that graduated into fine porcelains in the 1700s. Budding potters learn the ropes at the national ceramics school: part of the complex includes the **Museo Istituto Statale d'Arte per la Ceramica**, Via Giove 1 (*open school hours*); the far larger **Museo Civico della**

Ceramica in the 19th-century Palazzo De Fabris (*open Tues–Sun, 9–1, adm*) has works from the last three centuries by local masters and foreign artists, including Picasso.

In contrast to workaday Nove, **Maròstica**, 7km west of Bassano, is a striking town enclosed in 13th-century walls, its upper castle sprawled over the hill, and a lower castle, once the abode of the Venetian lord, sitting like a giant rook in the main piazza. This provides the perfect setting for the storybook event that has put Maròstica on the map: the *Partita a Scacchi*, the human chess match, which takes place on even-numbered years, the second weekend in September. The game, played with its human (and horse) 'pieces' in medieval costume on a 72-square-foot board, commemorates the contest in 1454 for the fair hand of Lionora Parisio, disputed by Rinaldo d'Angarano and Vieri da Vallonara, whom Lionora loved. Her father, the Venetian *podestà*, refused to let the suitors fight the traditional duel for humanitarian reasons 'in sad memory of the unhappy lovers Madame Juliet Capuleti and Master Romeo Montecchio' and even offered the loser the hand of his younger daughter. The level of play matches the gorgeous costumes; each game is a reproduction of a famous grand masters' duel, although occasionally things go wrong when the pieces misunderstand their commands, announced in archaic Venetic, and move to the wrong square. If you feel like a round yourself, there's a smaller board under the loggia with 3ft chess pieces; if you come at the wrong time of year, all the Renaissance finery is on display in the lower castle in a small **Museo dei Costumi** (*open Sun 9–6, or by asking ahead at the Pro Loco; adm*).

West of Maròstica, in **Mason Vicentino**, the 18th-century **Villa Angaran delle Stelle** is one of the finest in the region, linked to a Gothic-Renaissance chapel and open for visits (*ring ahead, ✆ 0424 411456*). The vines you see growing here go into the bottles of DOC Breganze, produced in seven styles (the red, mostly Merlot, is good), which you can pursue along the scenic, signposted *Strada del Vino Breganze* through the hills.

Further west, Lonedo (part of **Lugo di Vicenza**, 6km north of Breganze) has two villas by Palladio. The **Villa Godi Valmarana Malinverni**, Via Palladio, 44 (*open Mar–May, Sept, Oct on Tues, Sat, Sun, and hols 2–6; June–Aug 3–7; adm*), was his very first (1540), noticeably predating his eye-opening visit to Rome. The central portion with its three-opening loggia, usually the most prominent and decorated part of his villas, is recessed behind two large wings, and the windows are asymmetrical, reminiscent of earlier fortress villas. But the loggia (inspired by Palladio's patron, Giangiorgio Trissino) is a first opening to the outside world; there had been no war for 30 years and Venetia was beginning to feel safe. The interior rooms, arranged symmetrically on a central axis, were frescoed by Zelotti, Padovano and assistants, and contain a fossil collection and a big collection of little-known Italian 19th-century painting. You can see Palladio's progress a couple of doors down, in the more classically elegant **Villa Piovene Porto Godi**, set in a neoclassical park; the stair, gate and *barchesse* were added in the 18th century (*gardens only, daily 2.30–7; adm*).

In the centre of pleasant **Thiene**, 10km to the west, the *quattrocento* **Villa de Porta Colleoni** (*open 15 Mar–Nov except July, Sun only for tours at 3, 4 and 5; adm*) is an attractive example of what Palladio was reacting against, with towers, battlements and Venetian Gothic windows; inside there are frescoes (some by Zelotti), antique ceramics and jumbo paintings of the former residents of the **stables**; these were especially designed in the 18th century by Francesco Muttoni and quaintly decorated with Cupids to encourage horsey love. Opposite, note the flamboyant little church of the **Natività**, its roofline studded with flames of curly kale. Continue west to **Santorso**, where the **Villa Bonifacio Rossi** was nearly completely redone in the 19th century, but has kept its beautiful park, with century-old trees, a little lake, and a quirky temple in the Pompeii style (*park open Mar–Oct, Sat, Sun and hols, 10–5; adm*).

Schio, west of Santorso, has been the Veneto's main textile manufacturer ever since it became part of the Serene Republic in 1406; 'Italy's Little Manchester' they called it in the late 18th century, after Niccolò Tron, Venetian ambassador to England, brought back the newfangled techniques of the Industrial Revolution. Schio's Lanificio Rossi, founded in 1817, was long the most important woollen manufacturer in the country—Rossi's enormous factory, the **Fabbrica Alta** in Via Pasubio, was finished in 1862 and can be visited on the tourist office's industrial archaeological tour. To house employees, a grid of houses called **Nuova Schio** was laid out with lofty intentions of mixing the various classes together. A project begun in 1990 is trying to bring the neighbourhood back to life. A monument to weavers stands in the main square, along with the **Duomo**, remodelled in the 18th century and containing a Palma Vecchia in the sacristy. Schio's finest church, however, is the early 16th-century **San Francesco**, located off Via Baratto and frescoed with the story of the Franciscan order.

Where to Stay and Eating Out

Maròstica ✉ 36063

Maròstica is famous for its cherries and a rather unusual dish, *paetarosta col magaragno*, young turkey roasted on a spit and served with pomegranate sauce. It just may appear on the menu of **Ristorante al Castello**, ✆ 0424 73315 (*moderate*), in the newly renovated upper castle; it has lovely views and lovely food, with an emphasis on fresh local ingredients. Top it off with a *caffè corretto*, 'corrected' with one of a score of different grappas. The restaurant is run by the talented chef of **★★★La Rosina**, in a superb hilltop setting 2km north in Valle San Florian, Contrà Narchetti 4, ✆ 0424 75839, ✉ 0424 470 290 (*moderate*); rooms are modern and comfortable. *Closed Aug*. In Maròstica proper, **★★★Europa**, Via Pizzamano 19, ✆ 0424 77842, ✉ 0424 72480 (*moderate*) is up to date, and serves not only Italian but Spanish dishes—one of your few chances for paella in the region—in its restaurant.

Lugo di Vicenza ✉ 36030

In the *foresteria* (guest house) of the Villa Godi Malinverni, **Taverna Torchio Antico**, Via Palladio 46, ✆ 0445 36030 (*moderate*) serves delicious Veneto cuisine. *Closed Mon, Tues eve exc in summer, and Jan*.

Asiago and the Altopiano dei Sette Comuni

Tourist Information

Asiago: Via Stazione 5, ✆ 0424 462 661 ✉ 0424 462 445.

When the inhabitants of Vicenza need a deep breath of fresh air, they head north of Thiene to the cool green mountain plateau of Asiago (3258ft). Although inhabited early on by the Paleoveneti, it was long isolated and cut off from the rest of the Veneto, not only physically but linguistically; later inhabitants were descendants of medieval Bavarian immigrants, and to this day they still speak a Germanic language called Cimbra. Between 1310 and 1807 the seven *comuni* of the plateau, Gallio, Lusiana, Conco, Enego, Fozo, Roana and Rotzo, constituted an autonomous confederated state, the *Spettabile reggenza dei sette comuni*, allied to the Republic of Venice. The Altopiano had the misfortune to find itself on the front lines of the First World War; nearly every building was blown to bits, and only swathes remain of the once-great forests harvested by Venice for her galleys (one of the loveliest walks in the area is the loggers' path down the **Calà del Sasso**, *see* p.172, from the hamlet of Sasso, south of Fozo).

Like the seven *comuni* that share its lofty pedestal, their capital **Asiago** was totally rebuilt after 1918. The focal point is a massive pink stone **Municipio** (1929), with an enormous tower bearing a winged lion. A delightful mossy fountain featuring Pan and all the animals of the forest splashes by the domed church, containing two mediocre Bassanos. A ghastly number of war dead—12,795 identified, 21,491 nameless, 19,999 Austro-Hungarians—lie in the hilltop Sacrario, which also houses a small **Museo Storico** (*open 9–12, 3–5*).

The *altopiano* has its share of ski resorts and mountain refuges, but on the whole its green meadows are uncannily quiet. Many *comuni* have their own souvenirs of the war to end all wars, most of all Roana and its hamlets west of Asiago; here in **Canove**, the **Museo Storico della Guerra 1915–1918**, Via Roma, 30 (*open mid-June–mid-Sept, 10–12, 3.30–7*) records the destruction of Canove, and contains materials gathered during its reconstruction—unexploded grenades, arms and other equipment left behind by various armies.

On a lighter note, in nearby **Cesuna**, the Valente family has set up part of their home in 1987 as a **Museo dei Cuchi** (Via XXV Aprile 16, ✆ 0424 694 283, *open daily 9–12.30, 3–7*). *Cuchi* are terracotta whistles, in hundreds of imaginative shapes and designs, whose local name is derived from their cuckoo-like sound. Traditionally made in various corners of the world (the oldest ever found were Greek, from the Bronze Age) they have had various uses—not only to imitate birds, but to keep away evil spirits or more mundane crop-stealers—before becoming toys. Whistle-makers, the *maestri cucari*, once thrived around Bassano and Maròstica, where they specialized in men riding chickens, referring to some convoluted legend involving Napoleon.

Cesuna is near the deep, steep, glacier-gouged **Val d'Assa**, 'the Sanctuary of Prehistory', rich in rock engravings from 5000 and 3000 BC, most abundantly at Canova di Roana and **Tunkelbald** and Bostel de Rotzo. Pick up a map at the Asiago tourist office; they also have information about visits to the University of Padua's astrophysical observatory.

Asiago ✉ *36012*   **Where to Stay and Eating Out**

Asiago is synonymous with its low-fat cow's milk cheese with a bit of a bite, one of the few in Italy to achieve DOC status. There are two kinds: fresh *asiago pressato*, delicate and soft, often used in cooking, fried or in salads, and *asiago d'allevo*, ripened like cheddar, and sold either *mezzano*, *vecchio* and *stravecchio* (middle-aged, old and extra old), becoming more intensely flavoured with age.

Long-established ★★★**Erica**, Via Garibaldi 55, ✆ 0424 462 113, 🖷 0424 462 861 (*moderate*) is a cosy bet for a summer or winter stay. *Open Dec–mid-April, June–mid-Sept.* In Kaberlaba, 5km from Asiago little ★★★**Da Barba**, ✆ 0424 463 363, 🖷 0424

462 888 (*moderate*) offers magnificent views, a warm welcome and good food not far from the pistes. *Closed May and mid-Oct–Nov.* Just northeast of Asiago in the *comune* of Gallio, the **Lepre Bianca da Pippo** (Phil's White Hare), at Camona, ✆ 0424 445 666, has not only cosy rooms (*moderate*) but memorable dining in an elegant English-style dining room; seasonal dishes, exquisitely fresh seafood (rare up in these hills) and delicate desserts (*restaurant expensive, closed Mon*).

Midway between Bassano del Grappa and Asiago, at Conco, ★★★**La Bocchetta**, ✆ 0424 704 117, ✆ 0424 700 024 (*moderate*) is an old mountain inn and restaurant from the early 18th century, rebuilt in over-the-top Tyrolean style, but with a handy indoor pool, sauna and mountain bike hire as well.

Vicenza

'The city of Palladio', prettily situated below the Monti Bérici, is an architectural pilgrimage shrine and knows it. Where other Italians grouse about being a nation of museum curators, the Vicentini glory in it: Vicenza, after all, is the best example of what a gentry immersed in humanistic thought and classical philosophy could achieve in bricks and mortar. Their pride in their unique city was recently vindicated when UNESCO placed Vicenza on its list of World Heritage Sites.

History

A Paleoveneto centre, Vicenza was made a Roman *municipium* in the year 49 BC, and later suffered, like all the towns in the region, invasions by the Eruli, Ostrogoths, Visigoths and the Lombards, who made the town one of their 36 duchies. Later ruled by count-bishops, Vicenza became a free *comune* in 1164, although it wasn't strong enough to fight the neighbourhood bullies—the Da Carrara of Padua, the Scaligers of Verona and the Visconti of Milan. On 28 April 1404 the city offered herself on a platter to Venice, which wasn't one to look a gift horse in the mouth.

Under the Republic, the splendour of Vicenza's architecture earned it the nickname 'the Venice of the *Terra Firma*'. The works by Palladio and his followers drew an impressive list of visitors—among them Montaigne, Inigo Jones, Montesquieu and De Brosses; Goethe wrote that he could easily spend 'a month, following a course of lessons on architecture with old Scamozzi'. During the Second World War, air raids severely damaged the old town centre; restorers repaired all the major monuments and now, in a second wave, are aiming at 'minor' buildings, for these days the roubles roll in Vicenza. The city (pop. 108,000) one of Italy's wealthiest, promotes itself as the *Città d'Oro*, thanks to its 800 gold-working firms (producing half of all Italy's goldwork); it was the birthplace of the inventor of the silicon chip, Federico Faggin, and produces machine tools, textiles, ceramics and shoes.

Getting There

Vicenza is on the main **rail** line between Verona (45mins) and Padua (35mins) and Venice (1hr); there is also a branch line up to Thiene. The station is on the south side of the town, at the end of Viale Roma. The FTV **bus station**, ✆ 0444 223115, is alongside it: buses depart from here for Bassano and Maròstica as well as to Asiago,

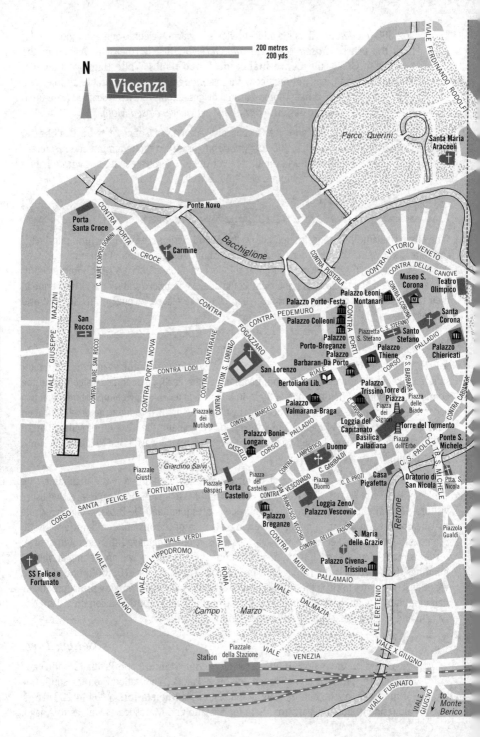

N

Vicenza

200 metres
200 yds

Parco Querini

Santa Maria
Aracoeli

Ponte Novo

Bacchiglione

Porta
Santa Croce

Carmine

CONTRA PORTA S. CROCE

C. MURE CORPUS DOMINI

CONTRA PLISTERIA

CONTRA VITTORIO VENETO

CONTRA DELLA CANOVE

Museo S.
Corona

Teatro
Olimpico

CONTRA PEDEMURO

Palazzo Leoni-
Montanari

CONTRA SCROGNA

Santa
Corona

Palazzo Porto-Festa

CONTRA PORTI

Palazzo Colleoni

Piazzetta C. S. STEFANO
S. Stefano

Santo
Stefano

San
Rocco

Viale GIUSEPPE MAZZINI

CONTRA MURE SAN ROCCO

CONTRA PORTA NOVA

CONTRA FOGAZZARO

CONTRA CANTARANE

CONTRA MOTTON S. LORENZO

Palazzo
Porto-Breganze

Palazzo
Barbaran-Da Porto

Palazzo
Thiene

Palazzo
Chiericati

PALLADIO

C. S. BARBARA

CORSO

San Lorenzo

C. RIALE

Bertoliana Lib.

CONTRA LODI

Palazzo
Trissino

Torre di
Piazza

C. CAVOUR

Piazza
delle
Biade

Piazzale
dei
Mutilato

CONTRA S. MARCELLO

Palazzo
Valmarana-Braga

Piazza dei
Signori

CORSO PALLADIO

Loggia del
Capitanato

Torre del Tormento

PTA. CASTELLO

Palazzo Bonin-
Longare

CORSO

C. LAMPERTICO

Basilica
Palladiana

Piazza
dell'Erbe

Ponte S.
Michele

Piazzale
Giusti

Giardino Salvi

CONTRA GARIBALDI

Duomo

C. GARIBALDI

C. S. PAOLO

C. P. B. S. MICHELE

Piazzale
Gaspari

Piazza
del
Castello

SAN FRANCESCO VECCHIO

Piazza
Duomo

C. D. PROTI

Casa
Pigafetta

Oratorio di
San Nicola

Ptta. S.
Nicola

Piazzola
Gualdi

CORSO SANTA FELICE E FORTUNATO

VIALE

Porta
Castello

CONTRA

C. D. PROTI

Loggia Zeno/
Palazzo Vescovile

S. Maria
delle Grazie

Retrone

MILANO

VIALE DELL'IPPODROMO

VIALE VERDI

VIALE ROMA

CONTRA MURE PALLAMAIO

CONTRA DELLA FASCINA

Palazzo
Breganze

Palazzo Civena-
Trissino

VLE. ERETENIO

SS Felice e
Fortunato

Campo   Marzo

VIALE DALMAZIA

Piazzale
della Stazione

Station

VIALE   VENEZIA

VIALE X GIUGNO

VIALE FUSINATO

VIALE X GIUGNO

to
Monte
Berico

VIALE FERDINANDO RODOLFI

Rovigo, Este, Lonigo and other destinations in the region. You can rent a **bike** at the train station's *deposito bagagli*—part of the deal includes a free map with bike routes.

Leave your car in one of the two attended car parks, one at the west end of the town by the Mercato Ortofrutticolo and the other to the east by the stadium. Both are linked to the centre by special bus service every five minutes.

Tourist Information

Piazza Matteotti, 12; also Piazza Duomo 5, © 0444 320 854, ✆ 0444 325 001.

Porta Castello to Piazza dei Signori

The Viale Roma, the main road up from the station, enters the city proper through the **Porta Castello**, with its powerful 11th-century tower. It also has one of the most startling palaces in Vicenza: the **Palazzo Breganze**, designed by Palladio and partly built by his pupil Scamozzi before the very monumentality of the design defeated him, leaving only two bays framed by three Corinthian columns the size of sequoias. Scamozzi also built the less exciting **Palazzo Bonin Longare** at No.13, in 1602, after his master's designs; the best part is the inner courtyard.

Contrà Vescovado begins by Palazzo Breganze and leads to the Gothic **Duomo**, its façade decorated with a diamond pattern that was carefully pieced together after the war. The side door on Contrà Lampertico is one of Palladio's few attempts at sacred architecture in Vicenza; he also designed the dome atop Lorenzo da Bologna's graceful tribune of 1482. Of the art, the most notable piece is a polyptych by Lorenzo Veneziano painted in 1356, in the fifth chapel on the right. Excavations have revealed remains of the Duomo's 8th-century ancestor, a stretch of Roman road in the crypt and, out in the square, a **cryptoportico**, a U-shaped subterranean passage under what must have been a very large 1st-century AD house.

Opposite the Duomo, slip into the courtyard of the neoclassical Bishop's Palace to see the exquisite **Zeno Loggia** (1494)

Map labels:
VIALE FERDINANDO RODOLFI
CONTRA PORTA S. LUCIA
VIA QUATTRO NOVEMBRE
VIA LEGIONE GALLIENO
Palazzo Angaran
Piazza XX Settembre
CONTRA S. DOMENICO
Palazzo Regaù
CONTRA XX SETTEMBRE
Ponte del Angeli
CONTRA PORTA PADOVA
ELEVA
D'ANGELI
Piazza Matteotti
C.S. ANDREA
Piazza S. Pietro
San Pietro
Palazzo Chiericati
Corte di Roda
VIA
CONTRA SAN PIETRO
VIA NAZARO
SAURO
CONTRA DELLE BARCHE
VIALE GIURIOLO
Bacchiglione
CONTRA DELLA PIARDA
Retrone
VIALE MARGHERITA
Santa Chiara
Santa Caterina
CONTRA S. CATERINA
Piazzale T. Fraccoli
VIA RISORGIMENTO NAZIONALE
BORGO BERGA
VIALE DANTE
to Villa Valmarana & La Rotonda

by Bernardino da Milano. Down Contrà Proti, turn at Via Pigafetta for the delightful Gothic **Casa Pigafetta** (1444), birthplace of Antonio Pigafetta, a local aristocrat who just happened to be in Spain in 1519 when Magellan was setting out on his world tour; Pigafetta went along and, unlike Magellan, survived; and wrote the definitive account of the voyage three years later. His motto '*Il n'est rose sans espine*' is inscribed on either side of the door. Beyond, to the left, lies the Piazza dei Signori.

Piazza dei Signori

This kingly square is the heart and soul of Vicenza, its public forum from Roman times to this day. In the 1540s the Vicentines decided that the piazza's crumbling Gothic Palazzo della Ragione no longer matched their new Renaissance-humanist aspirations and decided to give it a facelift. Having rejected new designs proposed by such luminaries as Sansovino and Giulio Romano, they surprisingly hired the still relatively unknown Palladio to give it a new look in 1549. It was his first big break, and Vicenza would never be the same. The marble loggias he added to the building, ever after known as the **Basilica** ('hall of justice', as in Latin; *open Tues–Sat 9.30–12, 2.15–5; Sun 9–12.30; free if there's no exhibition*) were to be his only work in stone in the Veneto and would painstakingly remain a work in progress for decades, showcasing Palladio's talents in the heart of his adopted city throughout his life—it was only completed in 1619. The result perfectly fulfils its aims, with two tiers of rounded arches interspersed with Doric and Ionic columns that give an appearance of Roman regularity, although Palladio had to vary the size of the arches to compensate for the irregularities in the trapezoidal structure. The great copper keel of a roof (rebuilt after the war, when it caught fire and collapsed) is concealed behind a balustrade lined with the life-size classical statues that would become a hallmark of Palladio's work; stare at them long enough and the urge to shoot them off like ducks in a penny arcade becomes almost irresistible.

To see what Palladio was disguising, go behind the Basilica to **Piazza delle Erbe**, home to Vicenza's daily food and produce market, and its pleasant-sounding **Torre del Tormento**, the medieval prison. In the adjacent piazzetta stands a **statue of Palladio**, contemplating the Basilica with a finger on his chin, as if trying to figure out what he forgot. The truth is it was his favourite work, and he didn't mind saying so himself.

The Basilica shares Piazza dei Signori with two columns, as in Piazzetta San Marco in Venice, one topped with the Redeemer (1640) and the other with St Mark's lion (1473), and the needle-like **Torre di Piazza** (or Torre Bissara, after the barons who raised it in the 12th century); in the 14th century the civic authorities tamed it with a mechanical clock and in 1444 added its headdress. Opposite, the 16th-century **Monte di Pietà**, built in two sections, was frescoed in the 1900s with Liberty-style pin-up girls, some of whom still faintly survive moral outrage, war damage and Father Time. Next to this stands Palladio's **Loggia del Capitanato**, now the seat of the town council, which was built to celebrate the great victory at Lepanto on October 7 1571; the Contrà del Monte façade is decorated with reliefs of trophies and statues of War (symbolized by Venice) and Peace (Vicenza). If its grand brick columns and arches seem confined in too narrow a space, it's because the loggia was meant to extend over several more bays; the building boom that made Palladio's fortune ended in the late 1560s, leaving most of his designs incomplete. Inside, ask to see the Camera Bernarda, decorated with frescoes transferred from Villa Porto at Torri di Quartesolo.

South of the Retone

From Piazza dei Signori, Via San Michele leads to the Retrone, one of Vicenza's two rivers, spanned here by the **Ponte San Michele** (1620). There are lovely views of the Retrone lapping the houses and, on the opposite bank, the **Oratorio di San Nicola**. This is remarkable for one of the creepiest altarpieces in Italy, *La Trinità* by the 17th-century Vicentine painter Francesco Maffei, whose feverish brush infected the Oratorio's walls as well with the assistance of Giulio Caprioni (*but unfortunately you have to find a guided tour to join to get in*).

Vicenza's Roman theatre, the 1st-century AD Teatro di Berga, was studied by Palladio but dismantled in the 1700s. Traces of it remain just south of S. Nicola, in and around picturesque **Piazzaola Gualdi**. Emperor Charles V stayed at the **Palazzo Gualdo** at No.10. Nearby, in Contrà Del Guanto, the octagonal **Oratorio di Santa Chiara e San Bernardino** (1451) is covered with a handsome wooden ceiling and has paintings by Giulio Carpioni. If it's closed, ring the bell at Via Burci 14.

Corso Palladio, Contrà Porti and Contrà Riale

Returning to the Piazza dei Signori, step behind the Loggia dei Capitanato to join **Corso Palladio**, the decumanus of ancient *Vicetia* and 'the most elegant street in Europe, not counting the Grand Canal in incomparable Venice'. This famous axis is lined with palaces, including, just to your right, Vincenzo Scamozzi's masterpiece, the **Palazzo Trissino**, with its Ionic portico and superb courtyard (begun in 1592, now the Municipio). A few doors down, the lovely late Gothic **Palazzo Da Schio** (1470s) is Vicenza's own 'Ca' d'Oro'.

Palladio himself is only dubiously linked to a couple of buildings on the street named after him; to find his work, turn up elegant **Contrà Porti**—the Roman *cardo*. One of his earlier works, **Palazzo Iseppo Da Porto** (1552) at No.21, is influenced by Raphael and contains frescoes by Giambattista Tiepolo. Next door, the sombre Gothic **Palazzo Porto-Colleoni** (No.19) hides an internal garden courtyard and an airy asymmetrical loggia; next to it, the late Gothic **Palazzo Porto-Breganze** (No.17), has a beautiful door added in 1481 and a precious mullioned window, the only one in Vicenza with Venetian reversed arches.

While building the Palazzo Porto-Festa, Palladio impressed the plutocrat Marc'Antonio Thiene, who hired him to redo his vast medieval **Palazzo Thiene** (now the Banca Popolare), a beauty treatment designed to create the most imposing residence in all Vicenza, although the project, like so many of Palladio's, was never completed. The Contrà Porti side of Palazzo Thiene is a fine work by Lorenzo da Bologna; around the corner is Palladio's part which, with its weighty sculpted windows, rustication and Mannerist classicizing, is his homage to Giulio Romano; Lord Burlington thought it was the most beautiful building in the world. Some of the interior retains its original and rather magnificent decoration; if the bank isn't too busy, ask to see the first floor's Rotonda with a domed vault and statues.

Opposite, on the corner of Contrà Riale, **Palazzo Barbaran-da Porto** was built from scratch by Palladio in 1570 and will hold the **Museo Palladiano** in 1999, coinciding with a big exhibit on Palladio's influences in Europe (*for more, contact the Institute for Palladian Studies, ✆ 0444 323 014*). Unlike the buildings he merely dressed in new clothes, the Palazzo Barbaran-da Porto is as symmetrical as pie, with two orders on the façade, Ionic on the ground level and Corinthian on the *piano nobile*; some of the frescoes inside are by Zelotti.

Continue down quiet Contrà Riale, where the convent of San Giacomo (1652) is now the **Bertoliana Civic Library**, repository of 400,000 volumes, 6000 manuscripts and rare incunabula dating from the 13th to the 19th century, including Francesco Colonna's novel *Hypnerotaumachia Polifilo*, published in 1499 by the famous Venetian press of Aldus. Widely read in Renaissance Vicenza, the *Hypnerotaumachia* was the first antiquity-worshipping hodgepodge fantasy, full of nostalgia for ancient architecture, hieroglyphs and pagan sacrifices; a number of architects based designs on the imaginary buildings in its woodcuts. Have a look down Stradella San Giacomo, with its view of a graceful 18th-century loggetta set amid ivy and a magnolia. Contrà Riale gives on to lively Corso Forgazzero, where at No.16 Palladio's **Palazzo Valmarana-Braga** (begun in 1566) is distinguished by gigantic pilasters crowned by an attic, framed by two armoured *telamones* in high relief, symbolically 'imprisoned' and specially designed to be seen in perspective in the narrow street.

Santa Corona, Santo Stefano and Pietro Longhi

In lower Corso Palladio, a square opens by the early Gothic church of **Santa Corona** (*open 8.30–12, 2.30–6*), built by the Dominicans in the 1260s to entice the many locals who strayed into the Paterene heresy back to the Catholic fold. In later centuries it was adorned with beautiful art, especially Veronese's *Adoration of the Magi* (1573), the three kings dressed in gorgeous reds and yellows; and Giovanni Bellini's *Baptism of Christ* (1502), a lovely example of his late style set in a rugged, rather un-Venetian landscape. The high altar (1670) is a massive bloom of inlaid marble and mother-of-pearl; the wooden choir stalls (1482–89) are lovely; and the altarpiece of the rococo Cappalla Thiene just to the right of the high altar has Giovanni Battista Pittoni's masterpiece *SS. Peter and Paul and Pius V Adoring Mary*. Palladio designed the Valmarana Chapel; note how the plan and the front view refer to his Redentore in Venice.

Alongside the church, the **Museo Santa Corona** contains natural history exhibits on the region, as well as Lombard relics, fine Roman mosaics, and Vicenza's oldest goldwork—a lamina embossed with Paleoveneti warriors, *c.* 1500 BC (*open Tues–Sat 9–12.30 and 2.15–5; Sun 9–12.30; adm*). The nearby **Palazzo Leoni Montanari**, built 1676–94 (now the Banco Ambrosiano) is one of Vicenza's few baroque palaces and contains, in the recently restored Sala dell'Antica Roma, 14 paintings by Venetian genre master Pietro Longhi and his school (*open April–Oct, Sat only 10–12, 4–7*). From S. Corona, take Contrà S. Stefano to the baroque **Santo Stefano** to see one of Palma Vecchio's most beautiful paintings, *Madonna with SS. George and Lucy and Musical Angel.*

Palazzo Chiericati: The Pinacoteca

In Piazza Matteotti, at the north end of the Corso, Palladio designed his masterful **Palazzo Chiericati** (1550, finished only in 1670). For once not constricted by a narrow street, he created the lightest and airiest palace of the century, extending the double loggias of his villas into a double colonnade of two different orders, playing with voids and solids; the rooms may fulfil his rules on harmonic proportions, but are topsy-turvy compared to previous palaces, running parallel to the façade. Since 1855, when a new wing was added, Palazzo Chiericati has been home to the *comune*'s **Pinacoteca** (*open Tues–Sat 9–12.30, 2.15–5; Sun and hols 9–12.30; adm*). The ground floor, containing a collection of contemporary Italian works (Carrà, De Pisis, Guidi, Lincini, Maccari, Oppi, Tancredi) retains its original stuccoes and frescoes, including a hilarious ceiling by Domenico Brusasorci, who took it upon himself to

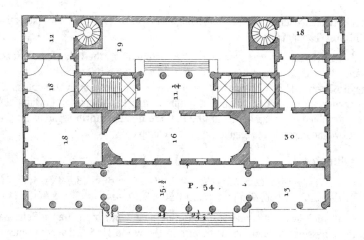

portray the sun god and his steeds in the position earthlings would see them at noon—all bums and bellies. The other paintings are in chronological order, with the oldest works in the 19th-century wing: there's a polyptych by Paolo Veneziano, a portrait of Pico della Mirandola by a follower of Bellini, a *Cavalry* by Hans Memling from a triptych, and works by the four top Vicentine painters of the *quattrocento*: Bartolomeo Montagna, Giovanni Buonconsiglio, Marcello Fogolino and Giovanni Speranza; Fogolino's *St Francis Receiving the Stigmata* incorporates another fine view of Vicenza..

The collection continues in the Palladian wing, with one of Bartolomeo Montagna's finest works, the *Madonna in Trono* with saints, and others by Cima da Conegliano and Veronese. The Flemish section includes Van Dyck's *Four Ages of Man* and Jan 'Velvet' Brueghel the Elder's *Madonna*. From the 17th century, there's the irrepressible Francesco Maffei (*Glorification of the Inquisitor Alvise Foscarini*) and Giulio Caprioni, along with Pietro and Marco Liberi and Francesco di Cairo; from the 18th century, Giambattista Piazzetta's *St Francis in Ecstasy*, landscapes by Marco Ricci, paintings by Francesco and Giambattista

Villa Chiericati, from Palladio's
Four Books of Architecture

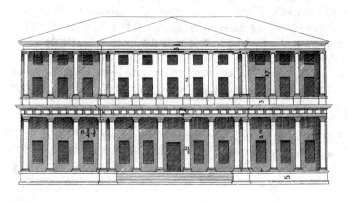

Pittoni, and two excellent Tiepolos (*Immacolata* and *Time Discovers Truth*) plus other paintings by his son Giandomenico.

Piazza Matteotti is the showcase for two more fine buildings: the **Palazzetto Giacomazzi-Trevisan**, the only rococo venture in this palazzo-ridden city, and **Palazzo Valmarano-Trento** (1718), a masterpiece by Francesco Muttoni, who kept up a regular correspondence with Lord Burlington to help him further Palladianism in England. Stretching along the north end of Piazza Matteotti, the **Palazzo del Territorio** began as a castle in the 13th century, and expanded to engulf the Teatro Olimpico.

Teatro Olimpico

Open 16 Mar–15 Oct, Mon–Sat, 9.30–12.20 and 3–5.30; Oct–Mar, Mon–Sat, 9.30–12.20, 2–4.30; Sun year round 9.30–12.20; adm.

This was Palladio's swansong, one of the most original works of the Italian Renaissance, as well as the oldest operational indoor theatre in the world (1580). Palladio himself was a member of the group of 25 literati, artists and dilettantes who founded the high-minded 'Olympic Academy' in 1555. The immediate inspiration for the Olimpico was a temporary wooden theatre that Palladio erected in the Basilica in 1561 for an opera, *L'Amor costante* by Alessandro Piccolomini, and a recital of his patron Giangiorgio Trissino's *Sofonisba*—monochrome frescoes in the Antiodeo show scenes from both works and document the ideas going through Palladio's mind. The architect's triumphant return to Vicenza from Venice in 1579 may have been the impetus to construct a permanent setting for the academy's plays and lectures, on the site of an old prison donated by the *comune*. For the seating and stage Palladio as always went back to his Vitruvius and the Roman works he had seen during his sojourns: his cavea has 13 rows of seats arranged in a semi-ellipse, topped by a Corinthian colonnade and a balustrade decorated with statues of members of the Academy.

Palladio died as the outer walls were going up, and the project was inherited by Vincenzo Scamozzi, who designed the rooms for academy use—the Odeo and Antiodeo—and, disregarding Palladio's plans for a stage screen with a triumphal arch and classical statues, built a stucco and wood stage set of a square and streets radiating out in flawless, fake perspective, representing Thebes, for the theatre's inaugural production in 1585, Sophocles' *Oedipus Rex*. But here Thebes has become a pure ideal, a Renaissance dream city, so perfect that no one ever thought to change the set, or bothered later, as the Council of Trent banned theatrical representations soon afterwards. Visitors over the centuries have adored it; William Beckford leapt on stage in 1780 and recited Aeschylus, feeling that he had at last 'penetrated into a real and perfect monument of antiquity.' Another perfect and memorable moment occurred in 1987 during a visit by the Queen Mother, when her bodyguard fell off the stage and penetrated the orchestra pit. Since the 1930s the theatre has slowly been brought back to life and now, between April and October, you may be able to catch a play or ballet on its venerable boards.

Over the Bacchiglione

Behind the theatre, Ponte degli Angeli crosses over the Bacchiglione to Piazza XX Settembre, site of **Palazzo Angaran** (1480), Vicenza's finest pre-Palladian Renaissance palace; the beautiful ornate late Gothic **Palazzo Regaù** stands nearby, at the beginning of Contrà XX Settembre. This neighbourhood, an old craftsmen's district, is locally known as the 'Republic of San Zulian': on Contrà Sant'Andrea, the **Corte dei Roda** is a traditional complex of artisans' houses and courtyards. Just to the right of the Ponte degli Angeli, Contrà San Pietro leads to **San Pietro** (*open 8–12, closed Fri*), the church of a Benedictine monastery from the Carolingian era, rebuilt in the Renaissance. The interior is a colourful gallery of late 16th-century works by the Maganza family of Vicenza, and there's a beautifully decorated cloister of 1427. Ask the sacristan to unlock the handsome **Oratorio dei Boccalotti** (1414).

From Palazzo Angaran, take Contrà Santa Lucia to Porta Santa Lucia (1369) and turn left for the church of **Santa Maria Aracœli** (1680; *ring ahead © 0444 514 438*), built on a design by the great baroque genius Guarino Guarini of Turin. The façade's several levels are adorned with statues; within is a mighty drum topped by a well-lit dome. The hyper-ornate High Altar (1696) explodes around a painting on that favourite Renaissance subject linking Christianity to classical Rome, *The Tiburtine Sibyl showing the Virgin and Child to Octavian*, attributed to Pietro Liberi. Just behind the church, Vicenza's prettiest public garden, the **Parco Querini**, is planted with pines and cedars of Lebanon; a statue-lined lane cuts through the lawns to a round island where the landscape designer Antonio Piovene built an elegant little Ionic temple (1820).

Outside the Historic Centre

North of the Duomo and Corso Palladio, **Corso Fogazzaro** is an ancient, atmospheric street where the porticoes have richly carved Gothic capitals and Vicenza holds a very popular antiques fair in spring and autumn. Here the Franciscan church of **San Lorenzo** (1280) has a grand façade and lovely marble portal, with a lunette of the *Madonna with Child and Saints* by Andriolo de Santi (1334). The interior is filled with sumptuous altars, frescoes and paintings dedicated by the noble families of Vicenza, notably the Pojana altar of 1474 in the right transept, and the chapel just left of the high altar, with a *Beheading of St Paul* by Bartolomeo Montagna. The 15th-century cloister is charming, and outside the apse you can see bits of Corso Fogazzaro's Roman predecessor. Further on, **Santa Maria del Carmine**, a Gothic church with a neo-Gothic façade, is decorated throughout with 15th-century bas-reliefs brought over from another church and altars by Veronese and Jacopo Bassano.

Beyond the Carmine, Contrà di Porta Santa Croce continues towards the gate of the same name, built during the Scaliger tenure. Following along Contrà Mure Corpus Domini, you come to the area where Alberto della Scala commissioned 'architect Giovanni' to lay out the walled district of **Porta Nuova**, a grid that had broad green spaces inside the blocks, defended by a little fort or **Rocchetta** (1365). **San Rocco** (1530), on Contrà Mure Corpus Domini, was, like the Duomo, designed by Lorenzo da Bologna. The walls and the altar are adorned with paintings by Giambattista Zelotti and Alessandro Maganza; don't miss the romantic cloister.

South, just outside Piazza Castello, the English-style **Giardino Salvi** contains a pair of loggias, one Palladian and one by Longhena (1649), reflected in the Seriola. Vicenza's oldest church, **SS. Felice e Fortunato** (*open Mon–Sat 9–12, 3.30–6.30*) is a ten-minute walk from here along Corso SS. Felice e Fortunato; built as a simple hall just after Constantine made Christianity the religion of the empire, it was remodelled in 398 with three naves and the Chapel of the Martyrium di Santa Maria Materdomini. Charlemagne visited the Benedictine monastery attached to the church; it was badly damaged by the Hungarians in 899 and rebuilt in the 1160s, with a battlemented bell tower and spire. In this century, the church has been un-restored as much as possible to its 4th-century appearance, revealing the original mosaics in the right aisle and the martyrium. The altarpiece, *St Valentine Healing the Sick* by Alessandro Maganza (1585), is the centre of the local celebrations on February 14.

Monte Bérico, Villa Valmarana and La Rotonda

Just to the south of the city rises Vicenza's holy hill, Monte Bérico. Buses make the ascent approximately every half-hour from the bus station, or you can walk up like a good pilgrim by way of Viale Eretenio, running parallel to the Retrone, stopping along the way to look at No.12, the elegant **Palazzo Civena-Trissino** (now the Eretenia Nursing Home), one of Palladio's earliest works (1540), showing the influence of Bramante and Raphael and an interest in their effects of *chiaroscuro* that would become a theme in his later work. Nearby, in Via delle Grazie, the church of **Santa Maria delle Grazie** (1494, rebuilt 1595) has recently been restored (*open Tues, Wed, Fri and Sat 9–12, Thurs 3–6, Mon and Sun closed*) and contains paintings by Maganza, De Pieri, Marinali and Jacopo and Leandro da Bassano.

At the end of Via Eretenio, turn left in Viale X Giugno and head up through the half-mile-long covered walkway or **Portici**, built in the 18th century to shelter pilgrims, with superb views along the way over the city and the Villa Rotonda, down in the 'Little Valley of Silence.' The baroque **Basilica di Monte Bérico** (*open Mon–Sat 7–12 and 2.30–7; Sun 7–7*) that crowns the hill commemorates two apparitions of the Virgin in the 1428, announcing the end of a plague that devastated Vicenza. It still does a brisk pilgrim trade, its polished, candle-flickering interior presided over by the painted marble statue of the Madonna of Monte Bérico, attributed to Antonino da Venezia; Vicenza's goldsmiths have crafted donations by the faithful into her fabulous necklace and a gold crown weighing eight pounds. The church possesses two first-class paintings: *La Pietà* by Bartolomeo Montagna, hanging near the altar, and the *Supper of St Gregory the Great* by Veronese, appropriately hung in the refectory (down the steps to the left), and carefully pieced together on Emperor Franz Joseph's orders after Austrian soldiers shredded it with their bayonets during the battle of Monte Bérico (10 June 1848), quashing Vicenza's popular revolt that had begun three months earlier.

Beyond the church, a pretty walk leads to Giovanni Antonio Selva's 18th-century **Villa Guiccioli**, the people's centre of resistance during the Battle of Monte Bérico. Now home to the **Museo del Risorgimento e della Resistanza** (*open Tues–Sat 9–12.30 and 2.15–5, Sun 9–12.30; April–Sept, Sun also 3.15–6; adm*) it houses documents on the city's history from the fall of Venice to 1945; the large garden that surrounds it is now a romantic public park.

Walk back down the Portici as far as Via M. D'Azeglio (alternatively, from the centre of Vicenza take AIM bus 8 or 13); from here the narrow Stradella S. Bastian leads to the **Villa Valmarana**, nicknamed 'dei Nani' after the stone dwarfs on the wall, arty ancestors of the modern garden gnome (*open mornings May–Sept, Wed, Thurs, Sat and Sun 10–12; afternoons 15 Mar–April, 2.30–5.30; May–Sept, 3–6, Oct–15 Nov, 2–5; adm exp*). The villa's main attraction, however, is its sumptuous decoration by the Tiepoli, father and son, in frameworks painted by Mengozzi Colonna, master of illusionary architectural perspectives. Giambattista based his frescoes on the *Iliad*, *Orlando Furioso*, the *Aeneid* and Tasso's *Jerusalem Delivered*, concentrating on the scenes where the heroes face the hard choice between duty and love. Duty, of course, always wins out, but Tiepolo's heart is on the side of the nearly sacrificed Iphigenia and the forlorn Angelica, Dido and Armida. Son Giandomenico contributed the ceiling and a landscape in the main villa, and painted his masterpiece in the *Foresteria* (guest house): intimate, gently ironical scenes of rural life that seem to undermine his father's Grand Manner right under his nose.

From there, a further five-minute walk along the Stradella Valmarana brings you to the celebrated Villa Almerico-Capra, better known as **La Rotonda** (*gardens open 15 Mar–early Nov, Tues–Sun 10–12 and 3–6; confirm for Fri, Sat, Sun, © 0444 321 793; adm. Interior open Wed only; adm exp*) designed by Palladio for a Monsignor Americo in 1567 and completed after his death by the faithful Scamozzi. Unlike Palladio's other villas which, under their classical skins, were functional farmhouses, the Villa Rotonda was built for sheer delight, for the

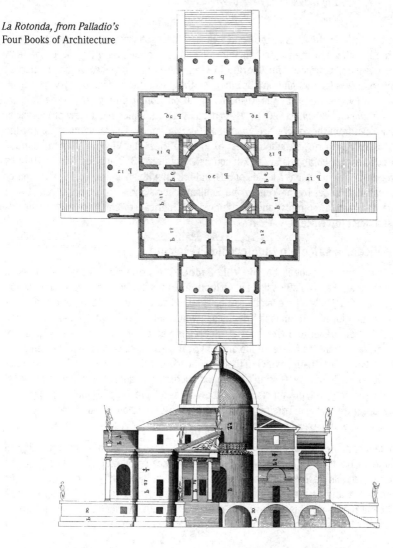

La Rotonda, from Palladio's Four Books of Architecture

Monsignor's garden parties and musical evenings, and, although no one knew it at the time, as the perfect setting for Joseph Losey's film *Don Giovanni*. One of the main interests of the Accademia Olimpica was mathematics, and La Rotonda is, if anything, an exercise in geometry—a circle in a cube, complemented by four symmetrical porches: its location is so perfect that one critic wrote that Palladio planned the hill before the villa. The round central hall has stucco decorations and rather overblown frescoes by Alessandro Maganza and Ludovico Dorigny; the four arms countain four identical suites of rooms. Alexander Pope, however, thought it ridiculous:

> 'tis very fine,
> But where d'ye sleep, or where d'ye dine?
> I find by all you have been telling
> That 'tis a house, but not a dwelling.

There are two historic churches in the same area, southwest of Vicenza, on the route of AIM bus 4 (although check at the tourist office for opening hours before setting out). The first, simple single-naved Franciscan **San Giorgio in Gogna** (982) is immersed in the greenery of Monte Bérico. It was far enough from the city to be the site of the *lazzaretto* or fever hospital, and to be used for executions by the Austrians. It has only one painting, *The Apparitions of the Virgin to Vincenza Pasini* (1620) by Alessandro Maganza, which has a view of Vicenza at the time, as seen from the exact place where San Giorgio stands. The same buses pass by the **Abbey of Sant'Agostino**, 5km southwest of Vicenza (near the Vicenza West *autostrada* exit). Founded by the Lombards in the 7th century, rebuilt in 1357 and restored in 1942 by the parish priest, the church has a façade of tufa and bricks, with an arched portal. The interior has 14th-century frescoes by the Veneto and Emilian schools and a golden polyptych (1404) by Battista da Vicenza, commissioned by Ludovico Chiericati to commemorate Vicenza's peaceful surrender to Venice.

North of Vicenza: Cricoli to Montecchio Precalcino

It's a pity you can't get inside it, but the **Villa Badoer-Trissino** where Giangiorgio Trissino met and christened Palladio still stands in **Cricoli**, just outside Vicenza on the Montecchio Precalcino road. Originally a little family castle, Trissino had the idea in 1537 to remodel it as the perfect setting for his 'Accademia Trissiniana', where all the young noblemen of Vicenza came to study from dawn to dusk under a strict regime based on Platonic rules, seeking to become 'universal men'. Moral rectitude and physical cleanliness were deemed essential to the study of Greek and Latin, which Trissino believed would lead his pupils to a proper mastery of Italian style (one of Trissino's goals was to create a national Italian language, based on Hellenic spelling and pronunciation); other classes were in philosophy, geography, astronomy and music, which Trissino considered the most important of all. As study aids, he covered the walls with Greek and Latin inscriptions extolling Study, Arts and Virtue.

Although neither noble nor young, Palladio attended the classes, but his most important lesson was Trissino's villa itself. In his remodelling Trissino, a keen student of Vitruvius, kept the towers of the original *castello*, linked them with a portico inspired by Falconetto's Loggia Cornaro in Padua and devised a ground plan of rooms according to Vitruvius' concepts of proportion and harmony. This arrangement of rooms was unprecedented, the archetype for Palladio's own villas (*see* pp.69–72).

Keen villa-fanciers will find plenty of less academic 18th-century examples littered along the road from Vicenza to **Montecchio Precalcino** (20km) where the charming Villino Forni Cerato is a fine late 16th-century work based on Serlio's treatises.

Montecchio Maggiore

Vicenza province alone has some 400 villas, and driving along the back roads between Vicenza and Montecchio Maggiore you can see quite a few of them. A few deserve special mention: the bright white *settecento* temple of **Villa Bonini**, near the western *autostrada* exit; in **Altavilla**, Francesco Muttoni's **Villa Valmarana Morosini** of 1724, a curious marriage of Palladian and baroque now owned by a university; in **Creazzo**, an eclectic 19th-century castle, and **Villa Fedinelli Seppiej**, Via Pozzetto, built in the 18th-century Palladian revival style (*open July–Oct, ✆ 0444 521 014*); and in **Sovizzo**, the large *cinquecento* **Villa Sale di San Damiano Curti**, Via Roma, expanded in the 19th century, when the owner added a little classical-style theatre to the garden (*ring ahead, ✆ 0444 551009, open Mon, Wed, Sat, Sun 10–12 and 3–6; free*). Sovizzo also has something far rarer than a villa in these parts: a **Copper Age megalithic tomb complex**, in a field at San Daniele.

Montecchio Maggiore, 13km west of Vicenza, is defended by two Scaliger castles standing side by side on a hill. In Luigi da Porto's 1529 tale of *Romeo and Juliet* they belonged to the rival clans the Montecchi and Cappelletti; the view of them from Da Porto's villa was an inspiration for the story. There's a car park by Castello della Villa or **Romeo's castle**, now used for summer performances, and a pretty walk from there to Castello di Bellaguardia or **Juliet's castle** (complete with balcony and the Ristorante d'Amore in the courtyard).

Just before Montecchio is the **Villa Cordellina-Lombardi** (*open April–Oct, Tues–Fri 9–1; Sat, Sun and hols 9–12, 3–6; adm*), built in the Palladian revival style in the 1730s by Giorgio Massari, which was frescoed by a young Giambattista Tiepolo with *The Family of Darius before Alexander* and *The Generosity of Scipio*; the sky Tiepolo painted on the ceiling glows with what would become his trademark luminosity. At Piazza Marconi 15, another villa houses the **Museo Civico G. Zannato** (*open Mon–Fri 9–12.30 and 2.30–6.30, Sat–Sun 9–12.30; free*), which includes a major collection of fossils (including 100 fossilized crabs), finds from the late Roman necropolis at Carpane near a section of the Via Postumia that linked Genoa to Aquileia, and a room of gems and semi-precious stones used in *pietra dura* inlays.

On the west end of Montecchio Maggiore you can pick up yet another wine road, the *Strada del vino* Recioto DOC Gambellara, which winds through Montorso, Montebello and Gambellara. Unlike the other Reciotos (natural sparkling dessert wines), Recioto di Gambellara is white; they also do a still white Gambellara and Vin Santo.

Vicenza ✉ *36100*   ***Where to Stay***

Vicenza has a limited selection of hotels. Near the railway station, ★★★★**Campo Marzo**, Viale Roma 21, ✆ 0444 545 700, ✎ 0444 320 495 (*expensive*) has modern, comfortable rooms, with air-conditioning, and a garage. For comfort in a central location, and a place to park, try ★★★**Cristina**, Corso B. Felice 32, ✆ 0444 323 751, ✎ 0444 543 656 (*moderate*). Up on the slopes of Monte Bérico, ★★**Casa Raffaele**, Viale X Giugno 10 (through an arch in the Portici), ✆ 0444 545 767,

@ 0444 542 2597 (*inexpensive*) offers good value, as well as tranquillity and great views. On a quiet street in the historic district are ★★**Due Mori**, Contrà da Rode 26 (near the Piazza dei Signori) © 0444 321 888, @ 0444 326 127 (*inexpensive*) and the more basic ★**Vicenza**, a few doors down, ©/@ 0444 321 512.

If you're driving, 6km west of town, in Altavilla (✉ 36077) towards Montecchio Maggiore, ★★★★**Genziana**, Via Mazzini 75, Selva, © 0444 572 398, @ 0444 574310 (*moderate*) is warm and welcoming and full of art; there's a pool too (*closed some of Aug*). Going in the other direction, Bolzano Vicentino (✉ 36050), in the hills above the Vicenza Nord *autostrada* exit, has ★★★**Locanda Grego,** Via Roma 24, © 0444 350 588, @ 0444 350 695 (*moderate*), occupying an old postal relay station, with well-furnished rooms and a good family-run restaurant. *Closed some of Aug.*

Eating Out

Whatever airs Vicenza puts on in the culture department become somewhat draughty in the kitchen—this is polenta and *baccalà* (salt cod) country, whose hearty and filling fare is not the most subtle on the stomach. But the locals beg to differ: their *baccalà alla vicentina*, made of top-quality cod endlessly pummelled with a wooden hammer, soaked for 36 hours, sprinkled with cheese and browned in a mix of butter, oil, anchovies and onions, then cooked over a slow flame, and seasoned with parsley, pepper and milk, is 'a whole refined civilization…simmering in the pot' according to writer Guido Piovene. A favourite way to eat polenta is sliced and grilled, accompanied with *sopressa* sausage from Valli del Pasubio and Recoaro, or pigeon roasted on embers. Other specialities include potato gnocchi made with cinnamon and raisins, and *bigoli con l'arna*, fat spaghetti with duck sauce, delicious with a glass of red Tocai. Montecchio Maggiore is known for its *mostarda*, a spicy condiment of fruit with mustard.

For perfectly prepared seafood, take a walk to Piazzetta Porta Padova, where **Nuovo Cinzia & Valerio**, © 0444 505 213 (*expensive*) serves tagliatelle with salmon, cuttle-fish risotto or grilled sole, followed by homemade ice cream and crisp biscuits. *Closed Sun eve, Mon, Aug.* Luigi Da Porto, author of the original version of *Romeo and Juliet*, was born in a 15th-century palace that was converted into an inn some 200 years ago: the **Antica Trattoria Tre Visi**, Corso Palladio 25, © 0444 324 868, (*moderate*) still serves food today and, with its fireplace and rustic fittings, is a charming place to enjoy good, basic Veneto cooking and homemade pasta dishes. *Closed Sun eve, Mon, July.* Just west of the city walls, at the family-run **Trattoria Framarin**, Via Battista Framarin 48, © 0444 570 407 (*moderate*) you'll also find delicious homemade pasta and a warm welcome. *Closed Sun, some of Aug. Inexpensive* choices include **Vecchia Guardia**, Contrà Pescherie Vecchie 11, © 0444 321 231, near Piazza dell'Erbe, for pizza and straightforward meals (*closed Thurs*) and the basic, lively and very popular **Antica Casa della Malvasia**, Contrà delle Morette 5, near Piazza dei Signori, © 0444 543 704, for real home cooking. A popular stop for a cheap lunch, **Righetti**'s bustling self-service canteen has seats spilling on to Piazza Duomo. *Closed Sat, Sun.* If you need something sweet and stylish, Vicenza has two historic *pasticcerias* near the

Basilica—**Antica Offelleria della Meneghi**, Contrà Cavour 18, and **Sorarù**, Piazzetta Palladio 17.

The real gastronomic fireworks await just east of Montecchio Maggiore at Arzignano's **Principe**, Via S. Caboto 16, © 0444 67131, @ 0444 675 921 (*expensive*), where one of Italy's top young chefs—trained in France—prepares superb, imaginative meals, accompanied by a selection of homemade breads, a chariot of French cheeses and delightful pastries. *Closed Sun some of Aug.* It's also a small hotel; *moderate*.

Up the Val d'Agno

From Montecchio Maggiore, what is now the SS246 to the Val d'Agno was a favourite Vicentine villa-building alley. One of the first, set in one of the most beautiful landscape gardens in the Veneto, **Villa Trissino** (1718) in the hamlet of **Trissino** was struck by lightning and left as a ruin, while the upper villa is by Francesco Muttoni, built over an old tower house. The same family still owns its first Villa Trissino, a Gothic-Renaissance palace on Via Paninsacco. Two kilometres up the road in **Castelgomberto**, the **Villa Piovene-Da Schio** (1666) has three large mythologies painted by a young Giambattista Tiepolo (1725) for the Palazzo Porto Sandi in Venice. You can't see them, but you can wander around the beautiful period park (*June–Sept, Sat 10–12, adm exp*).

Valdagno, the biggest town in the valley, is divided in two; its age-old textile industry on one side of the torrent, and on the other an ambitious 'ideal' industrial town, the **Città Sociale**, built between 1927–46, a mix of modernist architecture and traditional building material designed by Gaetano Marzotto, complete with a school, theatre and sports centre. At the head of the valley, the therapeutic virtues of the waters at **Recoaro Terme** were discovered in 1689; its mineral water, flavoured with *chinotto* (sour orange), is sold nationwide.

South of Vicenza: The Monti Bérici

With so many grander attractions on all sides, this clump of hills south of Vicenza is undeservedly neglected. Like Padua's Euganean Hills to the east, the Monti Bérici have volcanic origins under a hundred-million-year-old pile of marine sediment, and like the Euganean Hills, they also produce good wines, most famously a red Tocai, the 'pearl' of Bérici wines, introduced by a local carpenter drafted into the Austro-Hungarian army in the time of Maria Theresa. La Rotonda marks the beginning of the 78km Colli Bérici wine road that ends up at Montecchio Maggiore (*see* above).

Although wild and lonely in places, in certain spots the Monti Berici are as immaculate as Tuscany. One such place is **Brèndola** (12km southwest of Vicenza) where the historic centre hangs over an amphitheatre of garden terraces and the plain of San Valentino. Guarded by a ruined 11th-century bishops' citadel, the **Rocca dei Vescovi**, Brèndola's town hall occupies a 15th-century villa with a loggia. The 15th-century church, **Santa Maria dei Revese**, has a charming façade formed like a shell, and other villas look on to the prettiest square, **Piazzetta del Vicariato**. Others line the road south towards Lonigo, most theatrically the **Villa Da Porto** (or La Favorita) by Francesco Muttoni (1714), a Palladian revival showpiece located just north of Sarego (*currently under restoration*).

In the Veneto **Lonigo** is synonymous with horses and its Horse Fair, held every year since 1486 on 25 March, while its racetrack is used for racing brakeless motorcycles, which seems to be just as foolhardy as it sounds. Originally a possession of the Scaligers of Verona, Lonigo became the stamping ground of one of Venice's noblest families, the Pisani, after 1402. Along the porticoed streets and squares, look for the **Palazzo Pisani** by Sammicheli (1560; now the town hall) and the princely **Villa Giovanelli** with a scenic entrance (now a monastery). Strikingly set on a hill just above Lonigo is Vincenzo Scamozzi's loveliest work, the **Rocca Pisani** (1576), where he out-Palladios Palladio by perfecting the geometry of La Rotonda: the Rocca has a similar central plan and symmetrical façades (the main entrance distinguished by an Ionic porch), but omits all the stuccoes and frescoes that gild Palladio's lily; note how the Venetian windows were especially designed to frame the spectacular views (*open April–Nov daily, 9–12, 3–6; adm exp*). Nearby, the **Sanctuary of the Madonna degli Miracoli** has a charming shell-shaped façade sculpted in the soft stone quarried from the surrounding hills. Its miraculous Madonna has accumulated an impressive collection of *ex votos* dating back to the 15th century, now in an adjacent museum.

East of Lonigo stretches the **Val Liona**, the largest valley in the Monti Berici, known for its rich deposits of *nummulites* (Eocene fossils). The woods are dotted with medieval mills, stone quarries and the stone houses of stonecutters as well as more villas. **Sossano** to the south is the place to try Bérico-Euganean *prosciutto*, while just west in **Orgiano** Francesco Muttoni's centrally designed **Villa Fracanzan-Piovene** (1710) was one of the first examples of the Palladian revival in the Veneto and has lovely grounds. Unlike most, the family still maintains the villa's original vocation: an extensive collection of antique ploughs, tractors and other agricultural machines fills its **Museo della Civiltà Contadino**, and the kitchen has all of its original fittings (*guided tours Mar–15 Nov, Sun and hols only, 3–7; adm exp*).

Further south, **Poiana Maggiore**, named after the family that once owned it, has three of their villas all clustered together, most importantly Palladio's **Villa Pojana** (1550), Via Castello 41, with a façade and five round windows inspired by Serlio. The villa featured in his *Quattro Libri* although, like most of his illustrations, it was never completed to the design. **Noventa Vicentina** (from *Nova Entia,* a Benedictine foundation) has for its town hall the **Villa Barbarigo** (1588), with a double portico front, four pointy obelisques on the cornice and *barchesse* decorated with Tuscan porticoes; you can pop in to see the frescoes on weekday mornings, although the best art is nearby in the **Duomo** (1856): Giambattista Tiepolo's luminous *SS. Roch and Sebastian.* Two other charming villas await just north in **Agugliaro**. Palladio's recently restored **Villa Saraceno** (1549–68) on Via Finale was another one that featured in his writings, although one of the *barchesse* was never completed; frescoes inside are by the school of Veronese (now owned by the Landmark Trust, *open April–Oct Wed only, 2–4; adm*). Just up the road is the same family's former residence, the elegant **Palazzo delle Trombe** with its dovecote attributed to Michele Sammicheli.

North, in the heart of the hills on the ridge called the Riviera Berica, **Barbarano-Vicentino** is the centre of the DOC Colli Berici growing region and hosts a lively wine festival in September. Its Gothic **Palazzo dei Vicari** has a time-clobbered façade covered like a collage with coats of arms. From Barbarano you can visit the solitary **Scudelletta Gorge**, dominated by the church of San Giovanni in Monte, or follow the Riviera Berica to **Nanto**, famous for olive oil, truffles and *nantopietra*, the soft Vicenza stone prized by sculptors. **Lumignano**, in the centre of a group of palaeolithic caves, is celebrated for its delicate *bisi* (peas).

Returning towards Vicenza, **Costozza di Longare** was a favourite spot for summer villas, and with good reason: its name comes from its *covoli* (caves), which maintain a constant temperature of 13°C, a natural place to keep '*custodia*' wines in the Middle Ages, but also to provide air-conditioning to the villas, Renaissance-style. An ingenious system of air ducts links the cellars and rooms of the 17th-century **Villa Trento Carli** (*guided tours April–Oct, Thurs 8–6, Sat and Sun 10–12 and 3–6; adm*); the **Villa Eolia** (now a restaurant, *see* below), and the **Villa da Schio**, with a vast Italian garden and stone dwarfs. The Counts da Schio still use their cellars to store wine (*park and cellars open Tues–Sun 9.30–12.30, 3.30–7.30; adm exp*). Costozza's other caves were the home of the first mushroom-growing business in Italy, and they still sprout fungi today.

Where to Stay and Eating Out

Lonigo ✉ 36045

Folk drive down from Vicenza and further afield to eat at the ultramodern **La Peca**, with hilltop terrace, at Via Principe Giovanelli 2, ✆ 0444 830 214 (*very expensive*), owned and run by two young but gifted brother-chefs. You know you're in good hands as soon as you sit down and a basket full of warm homemade bread appears. Innovative recipes, with more than a passing nod at tradition. *Closed Sun eve and Mon, part of Jan and Aug.*

Costozza di Longare ✉ 36023

You can dine, and dine well, in a 16th-century villa frescoed by Zelotti, **Taverna Aeolia**, Piazza da Schio 1, ✆ 0444 555 036 (*moderate*), where the menu changes monthly; their *baccalà alla vicentina* is famous. *Closed Tues, and some of Nov.*

On the Road to Verona

After Montecchio Maggiore (*see* p.189) there's only one real reason to stop between Vicenza and Verona: **Soave**, where the vineyards of the archetype of Italian white wines literally engulf the old town, in a tender landscape that fits its name (the same as the English *suave*, even if it derives from a 6th-century Swabian encampment on the site). In contrast to all the green softness, Soave is crowned by the well-preserved and toothsomely crenellated **Castle of the Scaligers** (*open 9–12, 3–6, closed Mon; adm*), first built in the 10th century. *Après* castle, try a Soave Classico or the sweet Recioto di Soave, a dessert wine made from raisins, at the **Enoteca del Castello** on Via Roma.

Verona

> There is no world without Verona walls
> But purgatory, torture, hell itself
> Hence banished is banish'd from the world;
> And world's exile is death.
>
> *Romeo and Juliet*, Act III

Well, love does lead one to extremes, and although Verona isn't quite a world on its own, it is one of the choicest morsels on this planet. When Cupid's pilgrims alight here they sigh over

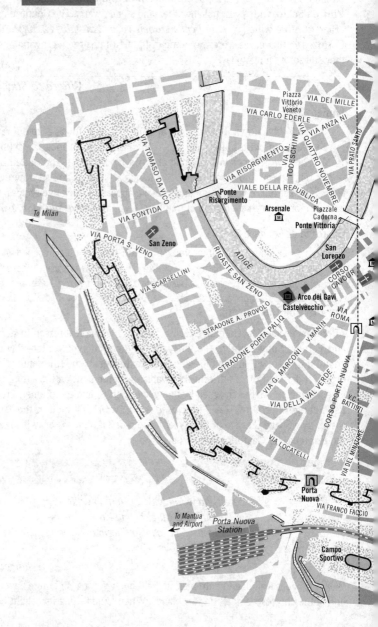

Verona

Piazza Vittorio Veneto

VIA DEI MILLE

VIA CARLO EDERLE

VIA ANZA NI

VIA QUATTRO NOVEMBRE

VIA M. TODESCHINI

VIA RISORGIMENTO

VIA PRATO SANTO

VIALE DELLA REPUBLICA

Ponte Risorgimento

VIA TOMASO DA VICO

VIA PONTIDA

To Milan

Arsenale

Piazzale Cadorna

Ponte Vittoria

San Zeno

VIA PORTA S. VENO

ADIGE

RIGASTE SAN ZENO

San Lorenzo

VIA SCARSELLINI

CORSO CAVOUR

Arco dei Gavi

Castelvecchio

VIA ROMA

STRADONE A. PROVOLO

STRADONE PORTA PALIO

V. MANIN

VIA G. MARCONI

VIA DELLA VAL VERDE

CORSO PORTA-NUOVA

V.C. BATTISTI

VIA DEL MINUZIONE

VIA LOCATELLI

Porta Nuova

VIA FRANCO FACCIO

To Mantua and Airport

Porta Nuova Station

Campo Sportivo

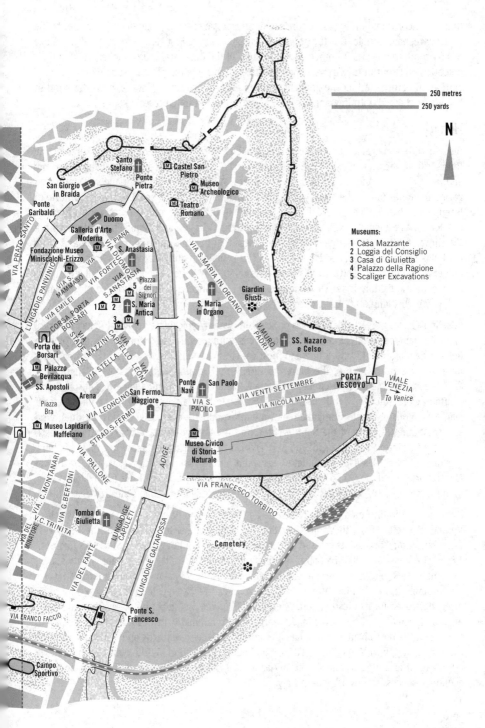

250 metres
250 yards

N

Santo Stefano
Ponte Pietra
Castel San Pietro
San Giorgio in Braida
Museo Archeologico
Ponte Garibaldi
Teatro Romano
Duomo
Galleria d'Arte Moderna
VIA PIANA
Fondazione Museo Miniscalchi-Erizzo
S. Anastasia
VIA S. MAMMASO
VIA DUOMO
VIA FORTE
VIA S. ANASTASIA
Piazza dei Signori
VIA PRATO SANTO
LUNGADIG. PANVINIO
VIA EMILEI
CORSA PORTA BORSARI
S. Maria Antica
VIA S. MARIA IN ORGANO
S. Maria in Organo
Giardini Giusti
Porta dei Borsari
VIA MAZZINI
VIA CAPPELLO
VIA STADE
V. MURO PADRI
SS. Nazaro e Celso
Palazzo Bevilacqua
SS. Apostoli
Arena
VIA STELLA
VIA LEONI
Ponte Navi
San Paolo
VIA LEONCINO
San Fermo Maggiore
PORTA VESCOVO
VIALE VENEZIA
To Venice
Piazza Bra
VIA S. PAOLO
VIA VENTI SETTEMBRE
VIA NICOLA MAZZA
Museo Lapidario Maffeiano
STRAD.S.FERMO
Museo Civico di Storia Naturale
ADIGE
VIA PALLONE
VIA C. MONTANARI
VIA G. BERTONI
Tomba di Giulietta
LUNGADIGE CAPULETI
VIA FRANCESCO TORBIDO
VIA DEL MINATORE
V.C. TRINITA
VIA DEL FANTE
LUNGADIGE GALTAROSSA
Cemetery
VIA FRANCO FACCIO
Ponte S. Francesco
Campo Sportivo

Museums:
1 Casa Mazzante
2 Loggia del Consiglio
3 Casa di Giulietta
4 Palazzo della Ragione
5 Scaliger Excavations

'Juliet's balcony' and other places concocted in response to a desperate need for shrines to the unlucky teenage couple. But the gorgeous rosy-pink city curling along the banks of the Adige has far more to offer than Romeo and Juliet and all the other star-crossed lovers singing their operatic hearts out in the Arena: evocative streets and romantic piazzas, sublime art, magnificent architecture, and all the gnocchi you can eat. According to Goethe, even the wind in Verona 'is charged with fragrance as if it had passed over a hill of roses'.

History

Blessed with a navigable river at the bottom of a busy Alpine pass, Verona was favoured by the Romans from the time of its colonization in 89 BC, and returned the favour by giving Rome the architect Vitruvius and the lyrical, lovesick poet Catullus. The city maintained its status as a regional capital under the Ostrogoths and Franks, and in 1107 became a free *comune* in league with Padua, Vicenza and Treviso. Freedom in the case of 12th-century Verona meant a free-for-all, as the city's nobility spiced up the national Guelph and Ghibelline rivalries with a sideshow of purely domestic feuds and vendettas that inspired the original *Romeo and Juliet* (by Luigi da Porto, 1529), and led to the *comune* actually inviting Ezzelino da Romano to take power as *podestà* in 1230. It was under his reign that Pope Gregory IX forced Verona to accept the Inquisition under Dominican Giovanni da Vincenza, who celebrated his arrival in 1233 by barbecuing 60 Cathars outside the Arena.

Ezzelino's successors, the della Scalas or Scaligeri, were a typical late medieval Italian family of exquisite gangsters, softening their lust for power with a refined taste for the arts. Bartolomeo della Scala was one of Dante's first and most generous patrons. His descendants' names were, however, uniquely canine, the better to terrify their opponents. 'Big Dog', Cangrande I (1311–29), was the greatest Ghibelline captain in Italy and gave such generous hospitality to Dante in exile that the poet dedicated his *Paradiso* to him (although one may well wonder if Dante's famous 'Letter to Cangrande' on how to read poetry ever arrived; most postmen who saw the name 'Big Dog of the Stair' written on the door would have walked straight past). Cangrande captured Vicenza, Padua and Treviso before dying suddenly aged 41; his heir, Mastino II (the Mastiff) consolidated his gains while his own successor, the fratricidal Cansignorio (Lord Dog, 1359–75) presided over the construction of the family's last great monuments. In 1387 Verona was seized by the Milanese warlord Gian Galeazzo Visconti.

By the time Visconti died in 1402, Verona had had enough of *signori* and annexed itself to Venice. Yet relations with Venice had their ups and downs. In the Wars of the League of Cambrai, Verona opened its gates to the German army and didn't return to St Mark's fold until 1517. The Venetians, who had absolved them of their oath of allegiance under enemy attack, took them back, but made Verona foot the bill for a vast new system of fortifications. However (and notably unlike Venice) Verona had the spunk to resist Napoleon in 1797—only to be partly destroyed for its presumption. There then followed a long period of Austrian rule, until most of the city joined the new Kingdom of Italy with Lombardy in 1859, although the part of Verona on the north bank of the Adige (the border between Lombardy and Venetia) remained Austrian along with Venice until 1866. Bombed in the Second World War, Verona quickly rebuilt itself as suited its rank, not only as a *città d'arte*, but as one of the great post-war economic success stories of modern Italy.

Verona's **airport** Valerio Catullo, to the southwest at Villafranca, has daily flights to London on British Airways, and direct flights to Rome, Naples and Bari. For information ✆ 045 809 5666. Every 20 minutes buses link the airport to Porta Nuova train station in Verona; there also three direct connections daily to the respective bus stations in Brescia, Mantua and Trento.

Verona is the junction of major **rail** lines from Venice (1hr 45min), Milan (2hrs), Bologna (1hr 40min), Trento (1hr) and Bolzano (1hr 40min). The station, **Porta Nuova**, is a 15-minute walk south of Piazza Brà, along Corso Porta Nuova; alternatively, city buses nos.71 or 72 link the railway station with Piazza delle Erbe and Piazza Brà. A machine dispenses bus tickets opposite the station. The provincial APT **bus depot** is across the street from Porta Nuova railway station (✆ 045 800 4129) and has frequent departures to Lake Garda and the mountains, and Mantua (1 hour). The historic centre is closed to traffic from 7.30 to 10am and from 1.30 to 4.30pm with the exception of cars going directly to hotels. There are **car parks** near the train station, Arena and Corso Porta Nuova, the main entry point if you are coming from the A4. **Bicycles** can be hired on the southeast corner of Piazza Brà, ✆ 045 504 901. **Taxis**: ✆ 045 532 666

Verona urban (ATM, ✆ 045 588 7111) and APT buses offer an *Invito a Verona* pass (available at the bus depot, tourist office or museums) from mid-June–Oct, a daily or weekly scheme that includes unlimited travel and museum admissions.

Tourist Information

In the side of Palazzo Barbiera, Via Leoncino 61, ✆ 045 806 8680 (next to the Arena) and Porta Nuova railway station, ✆ 045 800 861 (*both open daily, closed Sun in winter*). For the province: Piazza delle Erbe 38, ✆ 045 800 6997, ✉ 045 801 0682. Internet: *www.verona-apt.net*; e-mail: *veronapt@mbox.vol.it.* Youth information: Corso Porta Borsari 17, ✆ 045 801 0795.

Note: on the first Sunday of every month admission is free to the Arena, the Museo Castelvecchio, the Teatro Romano, Juliet's tomb and the Museo Lapidaro Maffeiano.

Porta Nuova to the Arena

The first thing most people see of Verona, whether arriving by rail or road, is Sammicheli's Renaissance gate, the **Porta Nuova**, now stranded on a traffic island at the head of the Corso Porta Nuova. This avenue leads straight under another gate, Gian Galeazzo Visconti's **Portoni della Brà**, and into the heart of tourist Verona: the large, irregular **Piazza Brà**, the favourite promenade of the Veronese and tourists, milling about a broad swathe of café-filled pavements (the Liston) curving around the **Arena** (*open 9–7, closed Mon; during opera season 8.15–3.30; adm; for opera information* see *p.206*). Built in the 1st century AD and, after the Colosseum, the best-preserved amphitheatre in Italy, the elliptical Arena measures 456 by 364ft and seats 25,000—the only substantial change was wrought by earthquakes, which shattered the outer arcade with the exception of the four arches of the wing or *ala*. Dressed in pink and white marble, the Arena is lovely enough to make one almost forget the brutal sports it was built to host. During the Middle Ages, Verona kept up Roman traditions by using it for public executions; in the Renaissance it hosted knightly tournaments, and in the baroque era it was used for bull-baiting. Since 1913, the death and mayhem has been purely operatic, with sets in Karnak proportions.

Opposite the Arena in Piazza Brà rises the 17th-century **Palazzo della Gran Guardia**, with a Visconti tower peeking over its shoulder; on the corner of Via Roma, at No.28, the **Museo Lapidario Maffeiano** (*open 9–3, Tues–Sun; adm*), established in 1714, was one of the first museums in the world dedicated to ancient inscriptions.

Piazza delle Erbe, Piazza dei Signori and the Scaliger Tombs

> *This is the vegetable market, and that day it was alive with delightful figures of women and girls, with faces from which gazed great languid eyes, with soft appetising bodies, marvellously golden and unashamedly dirty, made for the night far more than the day.*

> Heinrich Heine

From Piazza Brà, **Via Mazzini** (the first street in Italy to ban cars) is the most direct route to the core of medieval and Roman Verona, the **Piazza delle Erbe**. The market square that so entranced Heine occupies the old forum and still fulfils its original purpose, selling fast food, souvenirs and overpriced vegetables, although you'd be hard pressed these days to find an unashamedly dirty tomato of any kind. Four monuments on the piazza's spine poke their heads above the rainbow lake of parasols—a Lion of St Mark; a 1368 fountain built by Cansignorio topped by a Roman statue known as the 'Madonna Verona'; a 16th-century loggia called the 'Berlina' where malefactors were tied and pelted with rotten produce; and an elegant Gothic stone lantern.

A colourful panoply of buildings encases the square, including the charming **Casa Mazzanti**, formerly part of a Scaliger palace and brightened with 16th-century frescoes, and the 12th-century **Torre de Lamberti**, 275ft high, reached by a lift from the courtyard of the Palazzo della Ragione (*see below, open Tues–Sun 9–7; adm*). The shorter **Torre del Gardell** at the other end of the piazza was another work of Cansignorio. Six ancient gods blithely pose atop the adjacent yellow sandstone **Palazzo Maffei** (1668), while a battlemented red-brick palace, built in 1301 for a merchants' association, still does duty as Verona's Chamber of Commerce after 700 years.

From Piazza delle Erbe, the **Arco della Costa** ('of the rib'—named after a whalebone hung in the arch) leads into stately **Piazza dei Signori**, the civic centre of Verona, presided over by a grouchy statue of Dante (1865). The striped **Palazzo della Ragione** has a lovely Romanesque-Gothic courtyard, the Cortile del Mercato Vecchio, which forms a pretty setting for a series of free summer classical/jazz/blues concerts. Behind Dante, the **Loggia del Consiglio** (1493) is the city's finest Renaissance building, decorated with yellow and red frescoes and statues of five ancient celebrities of Verona (one of whom, Pliny the Elder, was pinched from Como). The adjacent crenellated **Tribunale** (law courts), formerly a Scaliger palace, has a portal by Sammicheli; in the courtyard, and in adjacent Via Dante, you can peer down through glass into Verona's Roman streets, revealed in the 1980s' **Scaliger excavations**. The underground corridors are used for photo exhibitions (*open 10–7, closed Mon*).

The arch adjoining the Tribunale leads to the grand Gothic pantheon of the della Scala, the **Scaliger Tombs** or *Arche Scaligere*, which Ruskin considered the crowning achievement of Veronese Gothic. The three major tombs portray their occupants in warlike, equestrian poses on top, and reposing in death below, although a copy replaces the best one, the horseman atop the Tomb of Cangrande (d. 1329), built into the wall of the 12th-century **Santa Maria Antica**. Don't miss the crowned dogs next to Cangrande's effigy, standing like firemen holding up ladders, the della Scala emblem. More ladders adorn the fantastical pinnacles of the tomb of 'Lord Dog' Cansignorio (d. 1375), the more sedate one of Mastino II (d. 1351), and the web of their wrought-iron enclosure. The rather plain 14th-century house in the same Via delle Arche Scaliger belonged to the Montecchi family (Shakespeare's Montagues), and has been known ever since as the **Casa di Romeo**.

The tour groups, however, are all over the **Casa di Giulietta**, near the Piazza delle Erbe at Via Cappello 23 (*open 9–7, closed Mon; adm*). Although the association is slim (the 13th-century house was once an inn called 'Il Cappello', reminiscent of the dal Cappello family, the original of the Capulets), it was restored on the outside in 1935 to fit the Shakespearian bill, with lovely windows and *de rigueur* balcony; inside you can peruse lovelorn graffiti of modern youth, ripe postcards, and photos of Italian girlhood's new Romeo, Leonardo di Caprio. The well fondled bronze statue of Juliet in the courtyard is a bit busty for a 13-year-old, but girls grew up faster back then.

Sant'Anastasia, Modern Art and the Duomo

North of the Scaliger Tombs, it's hard to miss Gothic **Sant'Anastasia**, Verona's largest church, begun in 1290 but never completed; in its woebegone façade only the fine portal, with frescoes and reliefs of St Peter Martyr, hints of its builders' good intentions. The interior, however, is beautiful, but, just coming in from the bright sun, many people start at what appears to be two men loitering under the holy water stoops; these are the *Gobbi*, or hunch-backs. The three naves are supported by massive marble columns and decorated by an all-star line-up of artists: there's the beautiful Fregoso altar by Sammicheli (the first on the right), and excellent frescoes by Verona native Altichiero from 1390, in the Cavalli Chapel in the right apse (note how the horse-head helmets that the worshippers wear on their backs resemble the dragon head on Cangrande's statue). The next chapel has 24 terracottas by Michele da Firenze on the *Life of Jesus*; paintings by the school of Mantegna fill the Pellegrini chapel, and, to the left of the high altar opposite a large 15th-century *Last Judgement*, the tomb of Cortesia Serego (1429) has an equestrian statue by Tuscan Nanni di Bartolo and frescoes by Michele Giambono. Best of all, in the sacristry, there's a fairytale fresco of *St George at Trebizond* (1438) by Pisanello, one of his finest works, although his watchful, calculating princess seems more formidable than any dragon. Nearby, in Via Piana, the medieval Palazzo Forti which once lodged Napoleon now houses the **Galleria d'Arte Moderna** (*open 9–7, closed Mon*) where frequent exhibitions share the walls with Italian masters (Hayez, Fattori, De Pisis, Boccioni, Vedova, Manzù) of the 19th and 20th centuries.

A few streets down Via Duomo, almost at the tip of the river's meander, stands Verona's **Duomo**, consecrated in 1187, Romanesque at the roots and Renaissance in its windows and octagonal crown. The portal, supported on the backs of griffons, was carved by the great 12th-century Master Nicolò of San Zeno (*see* below). Look for the chivalric figures of Roland and

Oliver guarding the west door and, on the south porch, a relief of Jonah being swallowed by the whale, and another of a dog biting a lion's buttocks; lastly, be sure to walk around to see the apse, made of volcanic tufa and one of the finest Romanesque works in the Veneto. Inside, there's the beautifully carved Tomb of St Agatha (1353) in the Cappella Mazzanti, and an *Assumption* by Titian in the first chapel on the left. Painted in 1540, it shows us a very different Virgin from Titian's famous goddess whirlwinding to heaven in Venice's Frari—this one looks down sympathetically at her friends on earth. In the second chapel on the right, Liberale da Verona contributed a delightful *Adoration of the Magi*, its foreground dominated by frolicking children, rabbits and dogs. A pope is buried in the choir—Lucius III, who preferred Verona to Rome, and made the city the papal seat from 1181 to 1185. The pretty cloister has a few remains of the Duomo's pre-Romanesque predecessor (victim of an earthquake), and in its ancient baptistry, **San Giovanni in Fonte**, there's an eight-sided font big enough to swim in, carved in 1200 from a single piece of marble and decorated with beautiful reliefs. The chapter library, the **Biblioteca Capitolare**, at Piazza del Duomo 10 (*open 9.30–12.30; also Tues, Fri 4–6; closed Thurs, Sun and July*) was founded in the 5th century as a *Scriptorium* and justifiably claims to be the oldest library still operating in Europe; it contains a magnificent collection of medieval manuscripts.

Head away from the cathedral, down Stradone Arcidiacono Pacifico/Via Sole to Via S. Mamaso 2A, for the **Fondazione Museo Miniscalchi-Erizzo**, a private, ecletic collection of furniture, paintings, weapons and more stored in a frescoed 15th-century palace (*open Tues–Sat 4–7, Sun 10.30–12.30 and 4–7; adm exp*).

North of the Adige: Veronetta

The north bank of the Adige, locally known as 'Veronetta', was that part of the city that remained in Austrian hands until 1866. It's due a whole morning unto itself: if you cross over the Ponte Garibaldi, just down from the Duomo, the first landmark is the large dome of **San Giorgio in Braida** (1477) to your right, worth a closer look inside to see Paolo Veronese's *Martyrdom of St George*. Follow the Adige down to **Santo Stefano**, an important palaeochristian church, pieced together in the 12th century from 5th–10th-century columns and capitals, and brightened with 14th-century frescoes, some by Altichiero. The bridge here, **Ponte Pietra**, was built by the Romans and blown up in the Second World War along with Verona's other bridges. The Veronese dredged up as much of its original stone as they could when they rebuilt it.

In ancient times, the citizens of Verona would trot over the Ponte Pietra to attend the latest plays at the picturesque **Teatro Romano** (*open 8–1.30 Tues–Sun; adm*). Actually, they still do: the cavea and arches, carved out of the cypress-clad hill of San Pietro in the time of Augustus, are in good enough nick to host a summer theatre season. A lift goes up to the **Archaeology Museum** (*same hours and ticket*), occupying a convent built on top of the theatre and containing a collection of small bronzes, portrait busts and a few mosaics. Further up still, the **Castel San Pietro** was built by the Austrians over Roman and Visconti-era fortifications, and has famous views over Verona at sunset.

South, on the Interato dell'Acqua Morta, **Santa Maria in Organo** has a façade (1533) by Fra Giovanni da Verona; the talented friar also made the extraordinary *intarsia* choir stalls, lectern and cupboards (in the sacristy) depicting scenes of old Verona, *trompe l'œil* birds, animals, musical instruments and flowers. Across the street that runs behind the church are the cool

Giardini Giusti (*open 9am–dusk; adm*) described by Thomas Coryate, the court jester of King James I's son Prince Henry, as 'a second paradise, and a passing delectable place of solace'. That was in 1611, the date of the enormous cypresses, formal box hedge parterres, fountains and grotto topped with a leering mask. The hillside was re-landscaped in the 19th century in the more romantic English style, making it a favourite setting for newlywed photos.

Continuing south, **Santi Nazaro e Celso** (1484) on Via Muro Padri contains 16th-century frescoes and a painting of the eponymous saints by Montagna, while **San Paolo** (rebuilt 1763), on Via San Paolo, boasts Veronese's beautiful *Madonna and Saints*, painted before he had to move to Venice, supposedly on the run after committing murder. On the river bank, at Lungadige Porta Vittoria 9, there's the elegant Palazzo Pompei, built in 1530 by Sammicheli and now housing the **Museo Civico di Storia Naturale** (*open 8–7, Sun 1.30–7; closed Fri; adm*), with an excellent fossil collection.

San Fermo Maggiore and Juliet's Tomb

From Piazza delle Erbe, Via Cappello/Leoni leads past the picturesque ruins of the 1st-century BC **Porta dei Leoni** (incorporated into a building), marking the beginning of the Roman *cardo maximus*. This leads to the splendid vertical apse of **San Fermo Maggiore**, an architectural club sandwich: it consists of two churches, one built on top of the other. The Romanesque bottom was begun in 1065 by the Benedictines, while the upper Gothic church, with its attractive red and white patterns, was added by the Franciscans in 1320, along with the façade. Walk around to see the apse, a harmonious *mélange* of both styles.

The upper church is covered with a lovely wooden ceiling of 1314 and fine 14th-century frescoes—the *Crucifixion* in the lunette over the door is by Turone. The first chapel on the right has a charming if mutilated fresco of scroll-bearing angels, by Stefano da Verona; in the right transept the Renaissance Cappella Alighieri has a pair of tombs by Sammicheli; and the left transept has good frescoes on the *Life of St Francis* by Liberale da Verona. The **Cappella delle Donne** contains one of Caroto's best altarpieces (*Madonna and Saints*, 1528) and a beautiful tomb, the *Monumento Brenzoni* (1439) by Florentine Nanni di Bartolo, with statues and a graceful fresco of the *Annunciation* and *Archangels* by Pisanello (1462). The lower church has more frescoes and columns and capitals inspired by classical models.

The so-called **Tomba di Giulietta** (*open 8.15–7; closed Mon; adm*) is back near the river on Via del Pontiere, not far from the Piazza Brà. Even the Veronese admit no connection with any tradition here, except that the Romanesque cloister and the 14th-century red marble sarcophagus would make a jolly good stage set for Shakespeare's last scene. A small **museum of frescoes** is an added attraction, including lovely 16th-century allegorical and mythological scenes by Paolo Farinati.

Piazza delle Erbe to Castelvecchio

From Piazza delle Erbe, Corso Porta Bórsari leads to an impressive Roman customs house, the twin-arched **Porta dei Bórsari** ('Gate of the Duty-collectors') built in the 1st century AD on the Via Postumia. A small temple to Jupiter stood nearby on Via Diaz, its foundation now traced in porphyry (the temple itself was relocated to Verona's Cimiterio Monumentale); bits of the Roman walls are just to the right. Back then, once you passed out of the Porta dei Bórsari, you'd find the Via Postumia chock-a-block with tombs, but now this is **Corso**

Cavour, one of Verona's most elegant thoroughfares, embellished with palaces from various epochs. The best is Sammicheli's refined if unfinished **Palazzo Bevilacqua** (1588, No.19), with its ornate, rhythmic alteration of large and small windows, columns and pediments; at No.44 his **Palazzo Canossa** is from the same period, but was finished only in 1675.

Opposite Palazzo Bevilacqua, the lovely Romanesque church of **San Lorenzo** (1117) preserves its upper, women's gallery (*matroneum*) reached by way of two cylindrical towers. To the left and a bit back from the Palazzo, another venerable church, **SS. Apostoli**, was founded in the 5th century and rebuilt several times since (especially after the Second World War); the oldest surviving bit is a votive chapel dedicated in the 6th century to Saints Teuteria and Tosca, modelled after the Mausoleum of Galla Placidia in Ravenna. Further down, Corso Cavour opens up into a small square with yet another Roman arch: the simple but elegant **Arco dei Gavi**, designed by Vitruvius in honour of a local family. The French demolished it in 1805, but in 1932 the local *fascisti* put it back together again.

Castelvecchio and its Museum of Art

Next to the arch, Cangrande II's fortress of **Castelvecchio** (1355) has weathered centuries of use by other top dogs, from the Venetians to Napoleon and the Nazis, to become Verona's excellent civic **museum of art** (*open Tues–Sun 9–7; adm*). Exhibits are arranged chronologically: among the oldest treasures in the first five rooms you'll find goldwork from the 4th–7th centuries, a sarcophagus (1179) carved with vivid reliefs of SS. Sergius and Bacchus, the *Archivolto di Peregrinus* (1120), and expressive 14th-century Veronese sculpture, especially a stark, painful *Crucifixion* by the Maestro di S. Anastasia. Two other statues are attributed to his circle, *St Catherine* and *St Cecilia*, patronesses of music, holding her invention—a portable organ—under her arm.

Beyond the collection of old town bells and detached frescoes wait excellent 14th-century paintings: *SS. James and Anthony* by Tommaso da Modena, a polyptych by Altichiero, and another by Turone, one of Verona's first documented painters. The museum is especially rich in lovely Madonnas, beginning with two straight out of fairytales, the *Madonna of the Quail* by Pisanello and the *Madonna of the Rose-garden* by Stefano da Verona; others are by Jacopo Bellini and Michele Giambono. A *Pietà* by Tuscan Filippo Lippi and early Flemish works offer a change of pace, before Room 15 returns to Venetian art with the *Madonna della Passione* by Carlo Crivelli and Andrea Mantegna's *Holy Family*. Local Renaissance painters Liberale da Verona, Francesco Morone and Francesco Bonsignori fill the next rooms, followed by another beautiful *Madonna* by Giovanni Bellini and Carpaccio's *SS. Caterina and Veneranda*.

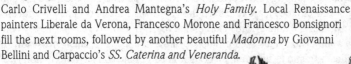

Next comes Verona's mascot, the striking 14th-century equestrian **statue of Cangrande I** from the Arche Scaligere, displayed outside the first-floor window of the Napoleonic wing. The pyjama-clad steed, complete with an equine hood ornament and deathly eyes, and the moronically grinning 'Big Dog' himself, with his ghastly dragon-helmet slung over his back, make an unforgettable pair, straight out of a malevolent pantomime. But this was the great Ghibelline captain to whom Dante dedicated his *Paradiso*; and, as with the Veneto's other great equestrian statues, of Gattamelata and Colleoni, a physical resemblance to the hero was irrelevant.

Behind the castle, Cangrande II's **Ponte Scaligero** spanning the Adige repeats the attractive 'swallowtail' battlements of the Castelvecchio; like the Ponte Pietra it was blown up in the war and meticulously reconstructed in the 1950s, in the indomitable Italian spirit of *dov'è era, comè era* ('where it was, as it was'), using the original stone.

Basilica of San Zeno Maggiore

A 15-minute walk west from the Castelvecchio, mostly along the riverbank, or bus 32 or 33 from Corso Porta Borsari, will take you to the superb **Basilica of San Zeno** (*open 7–12.30, 3.30–6.30*), one of the finest Romanesque buildings anywhere. First built in the 4th century next to a Benedictine monastery (of which only the massive brick tower on the left survives), the basilica took its present form between 1120 and 1398. Its magnificence demanded a legend: beneath its lofty campanile (finished in 1149) lies the tomb of a personage no less than Venice's old nemesis—Pepin the Short, king of the Franks. For centuries San Zeno was the symbol of Veronese liberty, the custodian of its *carroccio* or war wagon. All medieval Italian cities had them to take into battle, drawn by oxen and equipped with altars and priests to pray for their enemy's discomfort, and drums and trumpets to rally their own troops. Capturing another *comune*'s *carroccio* was the most devastating blow an army could inflict. Florence, for instance, got Fiesole's, and the mortified city never recovered.

The rich façade of San Zeno has a perfect centrepiece: a 12th-century rose window of the *Wheel of Fortune* by Maestro Brioloto. Below, the beautifully carved porch (1138) by Masters Nicolò and Guglielmo shows scenes from the months, the miracles of San Zeno, the *Hunt of Theodoric* (driving a stag straight to Hell) and other allegories. The **bronze doors** with their 48 panels are a 'poor man's Bible' and one of the wonders of 11th-century Italy. Even after a millennium, they have an unmatched freshness and vitality: in the Annunciation scene Mary covers her face in fear and anguish while the angel Gabriel does his best to comfort her; in the Descent into Hell Christ and a large, leering Satan fight a tug-of-war for souls. Other scenes seem strange to us, especially the one of two nursing mothers on the lower left-hand door, one suckling twin children, the other, what look to be twin crocodiles. In the 18th and 19th centuries, Grand Tourists found the doors appalling: 'To this low level did art fall during the Carlovingian decadence and the Hungarian invasions,' sniffed Hippolyte Taine; but Ruskin thought they beat any Renaissance work in Venice hands down.

The vast interior, divided into three naves by Roman columns and capitals, has a beautiful Gothic ceiling, 13th-and 14th-century frescoes and, on the altar, the magnificent triptych of the *Madonna, Angels and Saints* (1459) by Andrea Mantegna, a work that brilliantly combines the master's love of classical architecture and luminous colouring. Although the French returned the painting after Napoleon carted it off, they kept the predella, and the panels are copies of the originals in the Louvre and Tours. In the crypt below, the body of St Zeno glows in the dark. Also spare a glance for the handsome cloister, completed in 1313.

Just East of Verona: the Madonna di Campagna

Of the many surviving gates in Verona's walls, the furthest from the centre is the easterly 16th-century **Porta Vescovo** on the far side of monumental cemetery. Viale Venezia out from here leads to the suburb of **San Michele Extra**, built around a long-gone 8th-century Benedictine monastery. In the 1500s a fresco of the Madonna on a wall performed so many miracles that the bishop commissioned Michele Sammicheli to design a church to house it: this was the round and rather startling **Sanctuario della Madonna di Campagna** (1562), one of Longhena's inspirations for La Salute. It became the aim of a very popular all-night pilgrimage on the first Sunday of each May, until the authorities noticed that the pilgrims were having far too much May Day-style fun along the road, and abolished it all in 1804.

Verona ✉ *37100*   *Where to Stay*

There are plenty of soulless chain hotels on the fringes of the city, but not really enough nice places in the centre, especially during opera season in July or August, so do book. Rooms are also tight in March, when Verona hosts an agricultural fair.

very expensive

Goethe and Mozart slept at the ★★★★**Due Torri Baglioni**, Piazza Sant'Anastasia 4, ✆ 045 595 044, 🖷 045 800 4130, and would feel just at home today, at least in the rooms appointed with 18th-century antiques. The public rooms are equally resplendent, the ceilings adorned with 17th-century frescoes, the banquet rooms with circus scenes. In a quiet, traffic-free street near the Arena, ★★★★**Colomba d'Oro**, Via C. Cattaneo 10, ✆ 045 595 300, 🖷 045 594 974, offers very comfortable air-conditioned rooms behind its old stone façade, and secure parking, but no restaurant. A restored 16th-century palace houses the ★★★★**Accademia**, another excellent, atmospheric choice smack in the centre, at Via Scala 12, ✆/🖷 045 596 222.

expensive

Centrally located near the Arena, the recently renovated ★★★**Giulietta e Romeo**, Vicolo Tre Marchetti 3, ✆ 045 800 3554, 🖷 045 801 0862, is on a quiet street and offers fine rooms (and parking facilities), but no restaurant. Another good choice in the historic centre, ★★★**De' Capuleti**, Via del Pontiere, ✆ 045 800 0154, has air-conditioning and satellite TV for news junkies. If you're arriving by train, ★★★**Novo Hotel Rossi** is very convenient and simpatico, at Via delle Coste 2, ✆ 045 569 022, 🖷 045 578 297; some rooms fall in the *moderate* category. For tranquil rooms on the other side of the Adige, near the Roman Theatre, try ★★★**Italia**, Via Mameli 58, ✆ 045 918 088, 🖷 045 834 8028; rooms are modern and comfortable and priced right.

moderate

About 150 yards from the Arena, ★★**Sammicheli**, Via Valverde 2, ✆ 045 800 3749, 🖷 045 800 4508, is convenient for opera-goers, with easy parking, and colour TVs in each room. In the same area, the welcoming ★★**Torcolo**, Vicolo Listone 3, ✆ 045 800 7512, 🖷 045 800 4058, is convenient and not too noisy, on its quiet little square. Just south of the Castelvecchio, family-run ★★**Scalzi**, Via Scalzi 5, ✆ 045 590 422, 🖷 045 590 069, has similar amenities in a fairly quiet spot.

inexpensive

For cheaper rooms with or without bath in the centre, try ★**Catullo**, Via Valerio Catullo 1, ✆ 045 800 2786; some even have balconies. If you have an IYHF card, however, you can't beat the **Ostello Verona**, a 16th-century villa with frescoes in Via

Fontana del Ferro 15, ✆ 045 590 360, just beyond the Castel di San Pietro (take bus no.72 to the first stop across the river). Beds are up in the newer wing. The reception stays open year-round, 24 hours a day, but you won't be allowed in until 5pm; get there early in summer.

Eating Out

 The Veronese have long gastro-memories. They've been fond of potato gnocchi (served with melted butter and sage) since the late 16th century, when the ingredients were distributed after a great famine, and, like the Parisians, attribute their weakness for horsemeat to a siege when horses were all there was left to eat; it's served in stew called *pastissada de caval.* In summer look for Italy's finest peaches.

very expensive

The king of the Veronese restaurant scene is **Il Desco**, Via dietro San Sebastiano 7, ✆ 045 595 358, in a 15th-century palace, not far from the Ponte Nuovo. Expect exquisite dishes based on seasonal ingredients: gnocchi with ewe's milk cheese, red mullet with black olives and rosemary, goose liver in a sauce of sweet wine and grapes. *Closed Sun, hols, part of Jan and June.* Run by the same family for over a hundred years, **Arche**, Via delle Arche Scaligere 6, ✆ 045 800 7415, located near the Scaliger tombs, has long been the classic place to go for a special meal in an aristocratic setting. The freshest of fish is brought in daily from Chioggia and imaginatively prepared by the maestro in the kitchen. Excellent wine list. *Closed Sun, Mon lunch.*

expensive

An even older favourite, located a couple of streets from Piazza delle Erbe, **I Dodici Apostoli**, Corticella San Marco 3, ✆ 045 596 999, offers a traditional Renaissance setting—complete with frescoes of Romeo and Juliet. The name is derived from 12 18th-century 'apostles' of the kitchen who gathered here to dine. Some of the delicacies served today are adapted from Roman or Renaissance recipes; the *salmone in crosta* (marinated salmon in pastry) is famous. *Closed Sun eve, Mon, two weeks June and July.* For a glamorous gourmet experience, sit outside in Piazza dei Signori and have your every culinary care tended to by the elegant waiters of **Nuovo Marconi**, Via Fogge 4, ✆ 045 591 910. The food is as rooted in tradition as the surroundings: tagliolini with crab, gnocchi with pumpkin, and fine scampi and duck. *Closed Sun, part of June and July.* The century-old **Bottega del Vino**, Via Scudo di Francia 3 (off Via Mazzini), ✆ 045 800 4535, prepares traditional recipes using organically grown ingredients, with pasta made on the premises, customized to accompany a huge list of wine from around the world. *Closed Tues, except during opera season.* Another beauty, **Maffei**, Piazza delle Erbe 38, ✆ 045 801 0015, is both ancient and elegant and serves a melt-in-the-mouth cheese flan and risotto with pumpkin and *amarone.* *Closed Sun, Mon in July and Aug.*

moderate

Near Juliet's house, **Greppia**, Vicolo Samaritana 3, ✆ 045 800 4577, serves up traditional and Veronese favourites in a quiet little square. *Closed Mon, June.* Prices are lower over the Adige in Veronetta: **Alla Strueta**, Via Redentore 4 (near the Roman

Theatre), ✆ 045 803 2462, was an old workers' *osteria* now featuring delights on the order of smoked goose breast, gnocchi and, yes (or rather, neigh!), *pastissada de caval*. *Closed Mon and Tues lunch, Aug.* A deconsecrated medieval church off Via Garibaldi houses **Alla Pergola**, Piazzetta Santa Maria in Solaro 10, ✆ 045 800 4744, a traditional and reliable old favourite. *Closed Wed, Aug.*

inexpensive

You'll find a number of places around the Liston offer cheap, run-of-the-mill tourist menus, but for something special head north into the Borgo Trento quarter to **Giardino**, Via G. Giardino 2, ✆ 044 834 330, an exceptionally friendly trattoria serving delicious homemade *tortelli di formaggio*, grilled cutlets and Italian cheesecake (*tortine di ricotta*); tables are few, so book. In Veronetta **Osteria Morandin**, in Via XX Septembre 144 (just off Interrato dell'Acqua Morta) is another old standby, with a good choice of wines and a few dishes to go along. *Closed Sun*. Stop for a coffee at the historic **Antico Cafè Dante**, Via Fogge 1; for traditional Veronese pastries, **Cordioli**, Via Cappello 39, takes some beating. *Closed Wed.*

Entertainment and Nightlife

Verona bills itself as the 'city for all seasons' and offers a wide-ranging cultural programme throughout the year. Big events take place in the Arena, especially the Stagione Lirica, the **opera and ballet** festival founded in 1913, with performances almost daily in July and August. If you're travelling on a tight schedule, it's best to reserve your seat before coming to Italy: **Liaisons Abroad** in London ✆ 0171 376 4020, can arrange tickets before you go. Alternatively, for programme details and reservations, contact the **Ente Lirico Arena di Verona**, Piazza Brà 28, ✆ 045 8051811, *www.arena.it*; tickets sales are next to the Arena at Via Dietro Anfiteatro 6/b, ✆ 045 800 5151, ✉ 045 801 3287. If you get an unnumbered seat, plan on arriving an hour earlier to get yourself situated. And bring a cushion. At the same time Verona also hosts a **Shakespeare festival** (in Italian) in the Roman Theatre: same address as above for information and tickets.

From December to April there is **drama** in the Teatro Nuovo, and also more **opera and concerts** in the Teatro Filarmonico, sponsored by the Ente Lirico. From mid-December to mid-January Verona uses the arcades of the Arena for a massive show of Christmas cribs (*presepi*) from around the world. In the spring the city hosts one of Italy's oldest **carnivals**, first recorded in 1530; the last Friday of carnival is known as the 'Bacchanal of Gnocchi', presided over by the Papà dello Gnoco who walks about with a giant potato dumpling on a fork. All listings are in the tourist office's free *Passport Verona*. For discos, films and more casual artistic events, *Siri-Sera* is a broadsheet fly-posted weekly in cafés and around town. There are a number of **art galleries** around the Piazza delle Erbe, while the area between the Via Ponte Pietra, Via Duomo, Sottoriva, and Corso S. Anastasia is called the 'little city of antiques'. But buyer beware: the region is Italy's largest producer of reproductions.

Unlike the Venetians, the Veronese like to be out and about in the evening and have their own expression for pub-crawling, '*andar per goti*' (going Goth-ing), after a memorable binge by Theodoric's bunch back in the 5th century. The bars in Piazza

Brà and Piazza delle Erbe are the busiest. Old-fashioned **Al Carro Armato**, Via San Pietro Martire 2a, © 045 803 0175, near the Piazza de' Signori, is one of the most atmospheric; **Le Vecete,** near Piazza delle Erbe at Via Pellicciai 32, © 045 594 681, is a favourite wine bar (*closed Sun*).

South of Verona: La Pianura Veronese

Six hundred years ago, Verona's well-watered breadbasket (in this case, rice basket) was crossed by one of the wonders of Europe: the *Serraglio*, a mini-Great Wall of China, built in the mid-14th century by the Scaligers to defend Verona from Mantua and other bullies coming from the south. Stretching 16km, fortified with 200 towers, these thick walls, complete with moats and towers, were the most advanced fortifications of the day. But by the time the Venetians inherited the *Serraglio* in the 15th century they were not terribly impressed with its ability to stand up to the artillery of the day, and concentrated their defences at Legnano and Peschiera del Garda; now only traces of the great walls remain.

The *Serraglio*'s eastern hub was **Villafranca di Verona**, a town founded by Verona along the road to Mantua in 1185 as an agricultural colony and fortified camp. Laid out in an elongated grid, with an elevated **castle** on one end, its plan is reminiscent of the *bastides* or *ville-franches* ('free towns' with tax exemptions to attract settlers) founded by England and France during the Hundred Years War. There were a number of these in the Veneto, but this is the only one to keep its walls intact. Just as impressive, in its way, is the massive **Villa Canossa** at **Grezzano**, 4km southeast, a neo-Palladian ranch built in 1776, in the centre of an enormous rice plantation.

The source of all the moisture in these parts is the Adige and Lake Garda's main drain into the Po, the river Mincio. On its banks, **Valéggio sul Mincio** started out as another Veronese colony and was given a 14th-century castle and a bridge by the Visconti during their brazen attempt to seize all of Italy. Most of all they were interested in the possibilities of diverting the Mincio: they intended either to drain the lakes of Mantua downstream to make it easy to conquer, or to flood the plain inside the *Serraglio* in case Mantua attacked. In 1393 they invested an enormous sum in the project at **Borghetto** (a *frazione* of Valéggio), building at the end of the Scaliger's *Serraglio* the 1980ft-long **Ponte Rotta**, a cross between a fortified bridge and a dyke, with a system of portcullises that could be used to shut off the river's flow. It's still there, a bit overgrown but one of the surviving engineering marvels of the Middle Ages. Nearly six centuries later another Visconti, Luchino, found Borghetto's romantic, 19th-century atmosphere the perfect setting for his film *Senso*.

In fact, everything here is on a big scale. There's the **Cavour Parco Acquatico** south of town, a water fun park in a tropical garden with palms and sandy beaches, set in an enormous botanical park with lakes and beautiful old trees (© *045 795 0904, open May–Sept, 9.30am–7pm; adm L18,000 adults, L13,000 children*). In Valéggio itself, the old grounds of the Villa Maffe became in the early 19th century the **Sigurtà Gardens** (*open Mar–Nov daily 9–6; adm L30,000 per car*). This was the 40-year project of Dr Count Carlo Sigurtà, 'Italy's Capability Brown'—who, granted water rights from the Mincio, used them to transform a barren waste into 123 acres of Anglo-Italian gardens along a 7km lane; parking areas along the route allow you to get out and walk along the waterlily ponds, topiary gardens and valleys of roses.

One of the strangest encounters of any kind in Italian history occurred just north of Valéggio, in **Salionze**. Word had reached Pope Leo the Great that Attila the Hun had laid waste to the Veneto and was on his way to do the same to Rome. Leo rode forth to prevent Attila from coming any closer and met up with the Hunnish warlord in Salionze. Their meeting is faithfully recorded on Leo's tombstone in St Peter's: the Pope told Attila that he would get a fatal nosebleed if he came any closer. But there's a snag—Attila doesn't understand Latin. Fortunately SS Peter and Paul come down from the clouds to translate, and the Hun, suitably impressed, turns on his heel and retreats—it's as good an explanation as any for why Attila suddenly turned back from his stated goal.

The Eastern Plain: Legnano and Cologna Veneta

Halfway between Verona and Rovigo, **Legnano** is the biggest town and industrial centre of the Pianura. Two mighty floods of the Adige and Second World War bombardments have obliterated everything but a 16th-century tower, a last reminder that for a thousand years Legnano was a key in the Veneto's defences and a corner of the Austrian 'Quadrilateral'. It was also the birthplace of Antonio Salieri (1750–1825), the composer and director of the Viennese Opera, who did *not* poison Mozart, at least according to the locals (and most historians); Legnano's theatre is named in his honour.

Cologna Veneta, east of the Adige, was another agricultural colony, founded by the Romans this time, back in 170 BC; originally the main crop was hemp, although now the town specializes in *mandorlato* (nougat; try it at Rocco Garzotto & Figlio, Via Quari Destra 57). The historic centre is well preserved, around a picturesque 19th-century cathedral with an altarpiece of the *Nativity* by Bartolomeo Montagna. The neighbouring **Civico Museo Archaeologico** (*open Mon–Fri 9–12, exc Tues; Sat 4–6, Sun 9–12, 4–6*) has a good assortment of finds, not only from Roman times but also from the Paleoveneti and the Bronze Age (8th century BC). In nearby Pressana, **Villa Querini Stampalia** is an example of a villa that expanded over the years into a handsome mix of late Gothic and Renaissance elements.

Where to Stay and Eating Out

This is prime grazing land, for people, that is: Valéggio, famous for its homemade tortellini, has over 40 restaurants, and the Pianura has two gourmet shrines.

Valéggio sul Mincio ✉ 37067

A pretty country villa, **★★★Al Cacciatore**, Via Goito 31, ✆ 045 795 0500, 🖷 045 637 0375 (*moderate–inexpensive*) has recently been converted into a hotel with 19 rooms, with country-style furnishings and a restaurant. In the same price range, **★★★Eden**, Via Don G. Beltrame 10, ✆ 045 637 0850, 🖷 045 637 0860, is new and stylish, with very comfortable rooms in a quiet setting. Five kilometres from the centre, in the hills towards Custoza, **★★Belvedere**, Fraz. Santa Lucia ai Monti, ✆ 045 630 1019 (*moderate*) has fairly basic rooms but good solid traditional dishes to go with its lovely views; they make all their own sausages, as well as their tortellini and desserts. *Closed Wed and Thurs*. A charming 17th-century inn, the **Antica Locanda Minicio**, Via Michelangelo 12, Borghetto, ✆ 045 795 0059 (*expensive*) adds culinary expertise to a delightful setting—depending on the season you can dine by the fireplace or out on the banks of the Mincio. The dishes have a touch of Mantua in them, which isn't a bad thing. *Closed Wed eve, Thurs, some of Feb and Nov.* But many give the Tortellini de Valéggio crown to **Borsa**, Via Goito 2, ✆ 045 795 0093 (*moderate*) where the river and lake fish make a good *secondo*. *Closed Tues eve, Wed.*

Isola della Scala ✉ 37063

The 'Gilded Cage' or **Gabbia d'Oro**, 6km from Isola at Gabbia south of Verona, ✆ 045 733 0020, (*very expensive–expensive*) occupies an old inn, elegantly restored if not always easy to find on these arrow-straight country roads. The reward: Veronese regional cuisine at its finest, prepared with the best and freshest ingredients, although you may want to avoid some of the fussier dishes on the menu. *Closed Tues and Wed, Jan and Aug.*

Isola Rizza ✉ 37050

Lost in the middle of an ugly industrial area north of Legnano, next to a *panettoni* bakery, **Perbellini**, Via Muelle 10, ✆ 045 713 5352 (*very expensive–expensive*) is an island of classic refinement and masterful cuisine, every dish from *antipasti* to dessert a pure delight, with service to match. *Closed Sun eve and Mon, part of Jan, July and Aug.*

North of Verona: Lessinia Natural Park

Tourist Information

Bosco Chiesanuova : Piazza Chiesa, 34, ✆/📠 045 705 0088. For guided tours of Lessinia Natural Park: Via Ca' di Cozzi 41 (Verona) ✆ 045 915 155 📠 045 915 970.

North of Verona, the soft foothills of the Dolomites make up the Lessinia, now a Regional Natural Park, and one famous for rocks, in formations, fossils and flintstones. In the 13th century Lessinia was settled by Bavarians, whose descendants still speak a kind of medieval German, or Cimbra. Although traditionally a poor area, the inhabitants enjoyed a golden age in the 1600s manufacturing flintlocks. You can learn more about them, their folklore, costumes, and the huge *tromboni* (a kind of arquebus) that they blast on holidays at the small ethnographic museum (✆ 045 784 7026) in **Giazza**, one of Lessinia's prettiest villages with its medieval German houses. **Bolca**, southeast of Giazza, caused a sensation in the Renaissance when the discovery of a rich bed of fossilized fish was cited as proof of Noah's Flood. As well as interesting, they are also extremely beautiful and delicate, and in the local fossil museum (✆ 045 656 5111).

A winding road loops east to the next valley and **Bosco Chiesanuova**, Lessinia's modest winter sports centre. From here, follow the road to **Velo Veronese**, the starting point for a visit to **Camposilvano**, its fossil museum, and the **Valley of the Sphinxes** (*Valle delle Sfingi*), named for its striking chasms and landforms, made of layer upon layer of red ammonite. In recent years a beautiful stalactite cave was discovered in adjacent Roverè: **Grotta di Roverè 1000**, open for visits (✆ 045 783 5777).

Valpolicella

The cherry-scented prince of Veronese wines, Valpolicella was the *vino retico* quaffed by all the emperors from Augustus to Theodoric, and hails from 19 *comuni* west of Verona and south of Lessinia. The Molinara, Rondinella and Corvina grapes that grow so well here are vinified in different ways—the familiar stuff sold in your supermarket at home (*Superiore*), and three others, made from well-ripened grapes left to dry for several months: *Recioto della Valpolicella*, a fine dessert wine with a bittersweet aftertaste, not unlike port; DOCG *Amarone*, left longer in the vat to become a dry, powerful (16°) wine of great character that can be aged up to 20 years, one of the best and most distinctive wines in Italy; and *Ripasso*, wine fermented on the lees of the *Recioto* to take on some of nuances of *Armarone*.

Another pretty place to aim for is west, at **Molina**, where the Parco delle Cascate has paths along the waterfalls. North, beyond **Fosse**, the slopes of Corno d'Aquilio are pierced by the **Spluga della Preta**, one of the world's deepest chasms, its floor halfway to hell—2906ft down. Lessinia's wealth of flint first attracted people in the Lower Palaeolithic age (500,000 BC). Shelters and flint workshops have been discovered on the ridges and in the caves; some can be seen in the prehistory museum at **Sant'Anna d'Alfaedo**, along with a 20ft-long fossilized shark. South of Sant'Anna, not far off the road to Fane, don't miss the **Ponte di Veja**, a spectacular natural 170ft arch, the inspiration for the Malebolge bridge in Dante's *Inferno*.

The region of Valpolicella is sliced by torrents and dotted with Romanesque churches and villas. **Negràr**, one of the main centres, has a handsome 12th-century campanile and park at Villa Rizzardi. Just west in **Pedemonte**, Palladio's **Villa Serego poi Boccoli** was built in 1565–69, its two prominent wings bearing a continuous double portico of Ionic columns. West, in a hamlet of the same name, the 12th-century church of **San Floriano** is one of the prettiest in the area, with a frieze and an arcade on its tufa façade. **Fumane**, another important wine village to the north, has a number of stately homes and a landmark, the 16th-century **Villa della Torre** (on the road to Càvolo). The name of the architect has been forgotten, although the originality of the design suggests Giulio Romano; based on the concept of an ancient Roman villa, the rooms are off a peristyle court with a fountain. Other features include pools resembling Roman *piscinae*, a little octagonal temple, and towering dovecotes.

Further west, **Sant'Ambrogio** produces Verona's famous red marble in addition to red wine; nearby, in the lovely old hilltop hamlet of **San Giorgio**, the parish church was founded in the 7th century and expanded in the 1100s. The ciborium over the altar also dates from the 600s, and among the frescoes there's a fascinating 11th-century *Last Judgement*. In such ancient surroundings, perhaps it's not surprising that the parish maintains a custom long forgotten elsewhere in Italy: the distribution of fava beans after a funeral, symbolic of the afterlife. North of Sant'Ambrogio on the Adige, **Volargne** merits a detour for its riverside **Villa del Bene**, built in the 1400s and enlarged by Sammicheli in the next century. He enclosed the courtyard at the entrance, and added the portico and loggia to the façade, a second courtyard, and dovecotes; the interior has fine frescoes by Caroto and Domenico Brusasorci, including—rather bizarrely for a villa—scenes of the Apocalypse.

Up the Rear Slopes of Monte Baldo

Just west of Sant'Ambrogio (*see* above) is one of your last chances for a long time to cross the Adige and the A22 into the eastern valleys of Lake Garda's **Monte Baldo** (*see* below). Once over the Adige, turn north at **Affi**, a village made of rounded stones from the Adige, for **Rivoli Veronese**, a small village set in a morainic amphitheatre. This is the origin of the famous Rue de Rivoli in Paris, laid out by Napoleon to celebrate his great victory over the Austrians here on 14 January 1797.

Carry on north for **Caprino Veronese**, a medieval new town and later a favourite area for *villeggiatura*. One summer house, the 17th-century **Villa Carlotti**, is now the town hall and **Museo Civico** (*Tues, Wed, Fri, Sat 10–12*), where you can visit the 'Room of Dreams' with its caryatids and frescoes, and another containing a magnificent 14th-century statue group called *Il Compianto* ('The Lamented One'), where life-size figures of Joseph of Arimathea, St John, Nicodemus and the holy women mourn a strikingly dead cadaverous Christ.

From Caprino you can turn up the sometimes vertiginous road west for **San Zeno di Montagna**, with views over Lake Garda, or meander west towards **Platano**, where an enormous ancient plane tree predates even the 15th-century Palazzo Nichesola, with its high chimneys. The main road continues north by way of the striking **Santuario della Madonna della Corona**, set up on a nearly inaccessible rocky spur under a cliff, where a statue of Our Lady of Sorrows appeared in a blaze of light just as the Turks captured Rhodes from the Knights of St John in 1522, having apparently flown there to escape the infidels. The shrine was built in 1540 and 556 steps were dug out of the side of the mountain for pilgrims; thousands still come to pay their respects on 19 September, although most now drive up the paved road. Further north, **Ferrara di Monte Baldo** was an iron-mining centre and is now an excursion centre, with skiing and a botanical garden sheltering some of the many rare species that thrive in Monte Baldo's unique micro-climate. You won't, however, see the species the Italians like best—black truffles, which thrive under the big mountain's oaks.

Where to Stay and Eating Out

Bolca/Altissimo ✉ 36070

Just east of Bolca in Altissimo, dine superbly at **Casin del Gamba**, an old hunting lodge 2km from the centre at Via Pizzati 1, Roccolo, ✆ 0444 687 709 (*expensive*), where the chef prepares dishes entirely based on the season, accompanied by a great wine list and masterful desserts. *Closed Sun eve and Mon, part of Jan and Aug.*

Pedemonte ✉ 37020

Not far from Palladio's villa in Valpolicella, the lovely Relais & Chateau ★★★★**Villa del Quar**, Via Quar 12, ✆ 0456 800 681, ✉ 0456 800 604 (*very expensive*) has been beautifully restored, with 22 elegant rooms; the villa's restaurant, **Arquade**, occupies in part the villa's chapel and emphasizes the best of the region's cuisine, with the occasional French touch. *Closed Mon out of season, and Jan 6–mid-Mar.*

Sant'Ambrogio di Valpolicella ✉ 37010

Once you've looked at the vines, stop at **Groto de Corgnan**, Via Corgnano 41, ✆ 045 773 1372 (*expensive–moderate*) to sit around the fire and sip them with dishes specially concocted to bring out their best—the wine list includes the finest Amarones. *Closed Sun and Mon lunch.*

Lake Garda

Kennst du das Land wo die Citronen blühn?

Goethe

Garda is the largest of Italy's famous lakes (48km long, 16km across at its widest point) and the most dramatic, its 'Madonna-blue' waters, as Winston Churchill described them, lapping at the feet of the Dolomites. Shaped like the profile of a tall-hatted witch, its Latin name *Benacus* is of Celtic origin, a word similar to the Irish *bennach*, 'horned one', for its many headlands. Two of Italy's greatest poets of pure passion marked its shores: the ancient, tragic, lovelorn Catullus and that 20th-century Italian fire-hazard, Gabriele D'Annunzio.

The other Italian lakes are warm; Garda, Venice's 'little sea', has a genuine Mediterranean climate. Open to the south and blocked off from the cold winds of the north by the Dolomites, Garda's great volume (its average depth is 445ft) makes it a giant solar battery, warming the surrounding hills throughout the winter and keeping deadly frosts and clammy mists at bay. For Goethe and generations of chilblained travellers from Middle Europe, its olives, vines, citrus groves and palm trees have long signalled the beginning of their dream Italy. No tourist office could concoct a more scintillating oasis to stimulate what the Icelanders call 'a longing for figs', that urge to go south.

It does have its moods. Sailors and windsurfers come to test their mettle on the winds, first mentioned by Virgil: the *sover*, which blows from the north from midnight and through the morning, and the *ora*, which puffs from the south in the afternoon and evening. White caps and storms are not uncommon, but on the other hand the breezes are delightfully cool in the summer. Although services drop to a minimum, winter is a good time to visit, when the jagged peaks shimmer with snow and you can better take in the voluptuous charms that brought visitors to Garda in the first place.

Getting Around

There are two **train stations** at the southern end of Lake Garda, at Peschiera and Desenzano, both of which are also landings for the lake's **hydrofoils** (*aliscafi*) and **steamers**. APT **buses** from Verona go to their respective shores; others frequently link Peschiera, Sirmione and Desenzano. There are free buses from Peschiera to **Gardaland** and Caneva; Viaggi Taferner, ✆ 0474 555 757, runs buses directly to Gardaland from Brunico, Bressanone, Trento, Rovereto and Verona; Zani, ✆ 041 554 3400, has buses direct from Venice, Padua and Àbano Terme.

Local bus lines run up and down the road that winds around the lake shores—a marvel of Italian engineering called *La Gardesana, Occidentale* (SS45) on the west and *Orientale* (SS249) on the east. In summer, however, their scenic splendour sometimes pales before the sheer volume of holiday traffic.

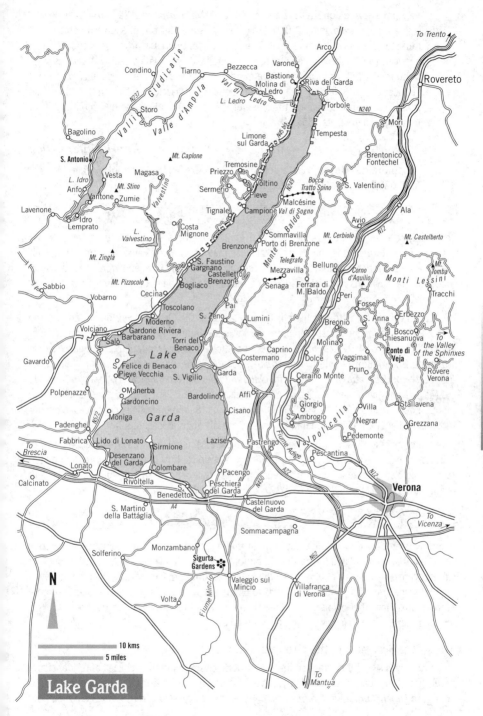

Lake Garda

All **boat services** on the lake are operated by *Navigazione sul Lago di Garda*, Piazza Matteotti 2, Desenzano, ℰ 030 9141 9511, where you can pick up a timetable; the tourist offices have them as well. The one **car ferry** crosses from Maderno to Torri; between Desenzano and Riva there are several hydrofoils a day, calling at various ports (2 hours the full trip), as well as the more frequent and leisurely steamers (4½ hours). Services are considerably reduced from October to March. Full fare on the 4-hour sail from Desenzano to Riva on the steamer is L15,400, and on the hydrofoil L20,700. Lunch on board costs L25,000.

Tourist Information

Peschiera del Garda, Piazza Bettelloni, ℰ 045 755 0381. **Sirmione**, Viale Marconi 2, ℰ 030 916 114, ✆ 030 916 222.

Peschiera del Garda and Gardaland

Peschiera, strategically set on the lake and River Mincio, is the gateway to Lake Garda, although from Roman times on its main role was that of a military camp. The imposing walls and moats were much repaired in the 16th century by the Venetians, and were in such a good state that the Austrians had little to do when they made Peschiera one of the corners of their 'Quadrilateral' defence.

What brings the crowds to Peschiera is its new status as the Orlando, Florida of Italy. It's the vortex for the nation's densest crop of theme parks, beginning with **Gardaland**, 3km north at Ronchi, ℰ 045 644 9777, Italy's largest and most massively popular Disneyland clone, attracting 2.5 million people a year (*open late Mar–June and Sept–Oct daily 9.30–6.30; July–mid-Sept daily 9am–midnight; adm; children under a metre high free*). Attractions include the Magic Mountain roller coaster, an African safari, some fairly scary space rides, a pirate ship, robots, a dolphin show and 'The World Of Barbie'. (Her Sublime Plasticity continues to exert a subliminal effect on Italian womanhood: every little girl owns at least ten Barbies.)

Two waterparks are just south of Peschiera along the Mincio (*see* p.207), while 5km east of Gardaland there's **Natura Viva**, a large safari park, tropical bird house and more, founded in 1969; they also operate a successful breeding programme for rare species such as pandas and lemurs (*open 15 Mar–Oct, 9–7; L12,000; L9000 for 3–12 year olds*).

Sirmione

Few towns enjoy the dramatic position of Sirmione, strung out along the narrow 4km-long peninsula that pierces Lake Garda's broad bottom like a pin. Lake views and a lush growth of palms, cypresses and parasol pines keep the medieval core from ever feeling claustrophic, even when it's heaving with people, as it tends to be in season: to find fewer daytrippers and more of the atmosphere that inspired Catullus, Dante, Goethe, Byron, and later Pound and Joyce, who met here, come before June or after September.

The Rocca Scaligera to the Grotte di Catullo

Large car parks signal the entrance into the historic centre; only the vehicles of residents and hotel guests are permitted into town over the bridge of the fairy-tale castle, the **Rocca Scaligera** (*open April–Oct 9–6 (may change summer 1999), Nov–Mar, 9–12.30; adm*). Built by Mastino I della Scala, *signore* of Verona in the 13th century, it is entirely surrounded by a moat where mallards and swans bob and float. Palms fill the courtyard; Dante slept here; but there's not much to see inside, though the views of lake and town from its swallowtail battlements and lofty tower are lovely. A second set of battlements protects the 15th-century church of **Santa Maria Maggiore**, overlooking a slender beach; note the reused Roman capital on the porticoed façade and the unusual pastel brick ceiling. Nearby begins the *passeggiata panoramica* that skirts the peninsula's east shore.

Rome's greatest lyric poet, Catullus, was born in Verona in 84 BC, only to die some 30 years later in the fever of a broken heart. In between passionate bouts at the Palatine home of his fickle mistress, 'Lesbia', he would cool his heels at the family villa at Sirmione. But chances are the great late 1st-century BC villa at the very tip of the rocky promontory known as the **Grotte di Catullo** wasn't it—only a millionaire could have afforded such an opulent pleasure dome. The superb site (*open daily Mar–Oct Tues–Sat 8.30–7, Sun 9–6; Nov–Feb Tues–Sat 8.30–4.30, Sun 9–4.30; adm exp*) is Romantic with a capital R, set among ancient olives and rosemary hedges. Rigidly rectangular, symmetrical and vast (551ft by 312ft), the villa was flanked by porticoes on the east and west (as well as a long underground crypto-porticus on the west), while a belvedere on the north end overlooked the lake. Of this only the supporting hall called the Aula dei Giganti survives, strewn with enormous chunks; some of the ceilings here once stood over 55ft high. A small **museum** on the site contains fragments of vases, lamps, spearheads and other bits salvaged from the ruins.

Near the Grotte di Catullo, standing alone on the peninsula's highest point, the Romanesque **San Pietro in Mavino** was built of scavenged Roman bricks; inside are frescoes from the 13th–16th century by the school of Verona. Also near here is the thermal **Stabilimento Termale Catullo**, where a pipe brings up steaming sulphuric water from the bottom of the lake, just the thing for respiratory ailments. The medieval lanes in the very centre have been given over to boutiques, bars, and pizzerias; if you want to escape, there are good places to swim off the rocks along the west shore.

Sirmione ✉ 25019

If you're driving, have the confirmation of your reservation handy to get past the castle guards.

A neoclassical villa built by an Austrian general and converted into a hotel in 1954, ★★★★★**Villa Cortine**, Via Grotte 12, ✆ 030 990 5890, ✆ 030 916 390 (*very expensive*) offers an immersion in romance, and perhaps the rarest amenity in the town—tranquillity. Its century-old garden occupies almost a third of the entire peninsula, with exotic flora, venerable trees, statues and fountains running down to the water's edge. Inside, all is plush and elegant under frescoed ceilings and perhaps a bit too exclusive, but it's ideal for a break from the real world, with private beach and dock, pool and tennis court. *Open April–Oct.* Another top choice, ★★★★★**Grand Hotel Terme**, Viale Marconi 7, ✆ 030 916 261, ✆ 030 916 568 (*very expensive*) has a private beach, pool, gym and a full health and beauty programme, as well as a lovely lakeside restaurant. *Open April–Oct.*

In the heart of the old town, ★★★**Catullo**, Piazza Flaminia 7, ✆ 030 990 5811, ✆ 030 916 444 (*expensive*) was refurbished in 1991, offering good-sized rooms with beautiful views and all modern amenities. *Open April–Nov.* Also in the centre, in a medieval building, ★★★★ **Eden**, Piazza Carducci 18, ✆ 030 916 481, ✆ 030 916 483 (*moderate*) has been beautifully remodelled with fine marbles, and has co-ordinated bedrooms with princely bathrooms, TV, and air-conditioning. Unusually, it does not have a restaurant. *Open Mar–Oct.*

Near the castle, ★★**Grifone**, Via Bocchio 4, ✆ 030 916 014, ✆ 030 916 548 (*inexpensive*) is more attractive on the outside than in the rooms, but has a great location. *Open April–Oct.* ★★**Speranza**, Via Casello 6, ✆ 030 916 116, ✆ 030 916 403 (*inexpensive*) has all the fittings of a three-star hotel, including air-conditioning and marble bathrooms, but at significantly lower prices. *Open Mar–Nov.*

One of Garda's finest restaurants is near the base of Sirmione's peninsula: the classy **Vecchia Lugana**, Via Verona 71, ✆ 030 919 012 (*expensive*). The menu changes to adapt with the seasons, and the food, based very much on lake fish, is exquisite, prepared with a light and wise touch—try the divine asparagus tagliatelle in a ragoût of lake fish, or the mixed grill of fish and meat; menus at L60,000 and L80,000. *Closed Mon eve and Tues.*

Near the Scaliger castle, **La Rucola**, Via Strentelle 7, ✆ 030 916 326 (*expensive*) has a great atmosphere to go with its particularly flavoursome specialities; many dishes judiciously prepared with fruit. *Closed Thurs.* **Marboré**, Via Vittorio Emanuele 71, ✆ 030 916 409 (*inexpensive*) serves tasty pizzas and simple L24,000 menus in a pretty garden by the lake. *Closed Mon.*

Desenzano del Garda: Via Porto Vecchio 27, ℗ 030 914 1510, ☏ 030 914 4209.

Lively, colourful and thoroughly pleasant **Desenzano del Garda**, on a wide gulf dotted with beaches, is Garda's largest town, built up in the 15th and 16th centuries (if you arrive by train, a bus will take you to the centre). Life centres around its busy portside cafés, presided over by a statue of Sant'Angela, foundress of the Ursuline Order, who seems appalled at all the carryings-on; another statue on the lake front, the whooshing **High Speed Monument**, celebrates an air speed record (709km per hour) set here in 1934 by Francesco Agello. On the lower end of the technological scale, Desenzano's Bronze Age (2200–1200 BC) inhabitants lived in pile dwellings, recently discovered in the peat bogs southwest of town and yielding the contents of the new **Museo Archeologico Rambotti**, in the cloister of Santa Maria de Senioribus, Via Anelli 7 (*open Tues, Fri, Sat, Sun and hols 3–7*). There are models of houses and, amongst the ornaments, little 'pearls' of amber: Desenzano was on the ancient trade route between the amber-rich Baltic and the Mediterranean, a route that endured until the end of the Roman period.

Desenzano, also on the Bergamo–Verona Via Gallica, became a popular resort (read refuge) of the Romans towards the end of the empire, when the rich and powerful retreated from the growing anarchy to their country estates. Incorporating vast agricultural lands, maintained by hundreds of slaves and retainers, these estates were the origins of feudalism. One of the most important was Desenzano's **Villa Romana**, just in from the Lungolago at Via Crocifisso 22 (*open Mar–Oct Tues–Fri 8.30–7, Sun 9–5.30; Oct–Feb Tues–Fri 8.30–4.30, Sun 9–4.30; adm*). Although begun in the 1st century BC, the villa was given its present form in the 4th century, fitted with sumptuous heated baths, a triclinium (dining hall) with three apses, and other rooms covered with the most extensive mosaic floors in northern Italy; pick up the free archaeological itinerary pamphlet in English. Nearby, along Via Roma, **Santa Maria Maddalena** has 27 huge canvases by a transplanted Venetian, Andrea Celesti (d. 1712) and a strikingly different *Last Supper* by Giandomenico Tiepolo.

Where to Stay and Eating Out

Desenzano del Garda ✉ 25015

One secret of Desenzano's success through the ages lies in a bottle, or rather bottles: a bewildering number of wines are grown on all sides of town. One, white Lugana DOC, from Trebbiano di Lugana grapes, was a favourite tipple of the Lombards when they weren't guzzling gore out of fresh skulls, today it goes better perhaps with *antipasti* and fish dishes, and is reputed for its joyous quality: '*Ubi Lugana ibi gaudium magnum*', or so they say.

Small, white ★★★★**Tripoli**, Piazza Matteotti 18, ℗ 030 914 1305, ☏ 030 914 4333 (*moderate*) has renovated, well-equipped rooms in the centre of the action and a garage, although ★★★**Il Veliero**, Via T. da Molin 33, ℗ 030 914 1318, ☏ 030 914

0322 (*moderate*) with its own beach and pier is only a short walk. Nearby, with its own olive grove, the ★★★**Piccola Vela**, Via T. dal Molin 36, ✆/✆ 030 991 4666 (*moderate*) has views over the lake from its balconies. The venerable ★★★**Mayer e Splendid**, right by the quay at Via U. Papa 10, ✆ 030 914 2253, ✆ 030 914 1409 (*inexpensive*) allows you to tumble out of bed and on to a steamer; not all rooms have bath, but there is parking. *Open Mar–Nov.*

Desenzano has a larger selection of good restaurants than any town on the lake. For an unforgettable feast, book a table at **Cavallino**, Via Murachette 21, ✆ 030 912 0217, where the chef creates imaginative seasonal dishes based on lake fish and seafood, duck, pigeon (the pigeon stuffed with foie gras is superb) and offal, followed by an excellent cheeseboard and desserts (*menu degustazione* L60,000 and L80,000). *Closed Mon and Tues lunch.* The equally delightful if rather formal **Esplanade**, Via Lario 10, ✆ 030 914 3361, has a lovely lakeside terrace where clients tuck into the likes of delicate lasagne with seafood infused with wine, or zucchini flowers stuffed with goats' cheese; excellent wine list and desserts; top-notch L70,000 *menu degustazione*, more *à la carte. Closed Wed.* Good home cooking is the draw at the picturesque **Trattoria Bicocca**, squeezed in a tight corner at Vic. Molini 6, ✆ 030 914 3658 (*moderate*) and offering a wide variety of lake fish—salmon trout, *coregone*, perch, sole, pike and gilt head, prepared with fresh herbs. *Closed Tues.*

Highlights of the Lombard Shore

The west or Lombard shore of Garda is its most prestigious, with the oldest villas (one, belonging to Gabriele D'Annunzio, is the lake's biggest attraction after Gardaland) and grandest hotels. The climate is especially benign between Gardone Riviera and Limone.

Tourist Information

Salò: Lungolago Zanardelli 39, ✆ 0365 21423. **Gardone Riviera**: Corso Repubblica, ✆ 0365 20347.

Salò

On the north edge of the Valtenesi, **Salò** (the Roman *Salodium*) is traditionally Garda's 'capital', the seat of the Venetian magistrates. It enjoys a privileged location, set on a deep bay with a grand promenade, lit by street lamps that resemble Minoan sacral horns. In 1901 an earthquake shook it hard, but architecturally, at least, it was an auspicious moment for a disaster, and when Saló was rebuilt it was with a Liberty-style flourish. Some fine older buildings survived the quake, including a late Gothic **Cathedral** with a Renaissance portal of 1509 stuck in its unfinished façade; among the paintings by Romanino and Moretto, there's a golden polyptych by Paolo Veneziano kept securely (but hard to see properly) under glass. The Venetian-style Loggia della Magnifica Patria at Lungolago Zanardelli 55 contains the tourist office and a small **Museo Civico Archeologico**, with items found in Salodium's necropolis. **L'Ateneo**, in the Renaissance Palazzo Fantoni, has a collection of 13th-century manuscripts and early printed books.

Salò ✉ 25087

One of loveliest places to stay on the lakes, ★★★★**Laurin**, Viale Landi 9, ✆ 0365 22022, 📧 0365 22382 (*expensive*) is an enchanting Liberty-style villa converted into a hotel in the 1960s, retaining the elegant period décor in the public rooms. The charming grounds include a swimming pool and beach access. *Closed Jan.* At the ★★★★**Duomo**, Lungolago Zanardelli 63, ✆ 0365 21026, 📧 0365 21028 (*expensive*) the first-floor rooms are the ones to request—all lead out to a huge geranium-laden balcony overlooking the lake. Rooms are big and modern, and there's a fine restaurant. For a good, reasonably priced and traditional meal, book a table at the **Osteria alla Campagnola**, Via Brunati 11, ✆ 0365 22153 (*moderate*). Garden-fresh vegetables are served with every dish, the pasta is homemade, and they make great use of wild mushrooms in season. Another extremely good-value place is the **Osteria dell'Orologio**, Via Butterini 26, ✆ 0365 290 158 (*inexpensive*), an old, beautifully restored inn where you can indulge in local dishes such as '*tonno del Garda*' (pork cooked in wine and spices), lake fish, and skewered wild birds. *Closed Wed.* The same family run the slightly more expensive **Antica Trattoria delle Rose**, Via Gasparo da Salò 33, ✆ 0365 43220 (*moderate*). Go for *pasta e fagioli*, or lake fish with fresh pasta. *Closed Wed.*

Gardone Riviera and D'Annunzio's Folly

North of Salò, sumptuous old villas, gardens and hotels line the lovely promenade at **Gardone Riviera**. Gardone became the most fashionable resort on Lake Garda in 1880, when a German scientist noted the almost uncanny consistency of its climate. One place that profits most from this mildness is the **Giardino Botanico Hruska** (*open Mar–Oct daily 9–6.30; adm*), a botanical garden with 8000 exotic blooms and plants (and just as many weeds!) growing between imported tufa cliffs and artificial streams.

Above the garden waits **Il Vittoriale degli Italiani**, the home of Gabriele D'Annunzio (1863–1938) (*open Oct–Mar Tues–Sun 9–12.30 (ticket office closes an hour earlier) and 2–6.30, Sat and Sun only until 6; April–Sept 8.30am–8pm; adm exp; you can buy a cheaper ticket for the museum and grounds only; expect queues*). This luxurious Liberty-style villa in an incomparable setting, designed for a German family by Giancarlo Maroni, was presented to the extravagant writer by Mussolini in 1925, ostensibly as a reward from a grateful nation for his patriotism and heroism during the First World War, but also as a sop to keep the volatile, unpredictable poet out of politics. D'Annunzio immediately dubbed his new home 'Il Vittoriale' after Italy's victory over Austria in 1918; with Maroni's help he recreated it in his own image, leaving posterity a remarkable mix of eccentric beauty and self-aggrandizing kitsch.

More Italian than Any Other Italian

Born Gaetano Rapagnetta into a very modest family in the Abruzzo, the self-styled Angel Gabriel of the Annunciation (one wonders what he would have thought of Madonna!) went on to become the greatest Italian poet of his generation, a leading figure in the *fin de siècle* Decadent school who managed to have nearly all of his works placed on the pope's Index. But Gabriele D'Annunzio scoffed at the idea that the pen is mightier than the sword. A fervent right-wing nationalist, he clamoured for Italy to enter the First World War and, when it was over, he was so furious that Fiume (Rijeka), a town promised as a prize to Italy, was actually to be ceded by the Allies to Yugoslavia, that he took matters into his own hands and invaded Fiume with a band of volunteers (September 1919). In Italy D'Annunzio was proclaimed a hero, stirring up a diplomatic furore before being forced to withdraw in January 1921.

Luigi Barzini has described D'Annunzio as 'perhaps more Italian than any other Italian' for his love of gesture, spectacle and theatre—what can you say about a man who would boast that he had once dined on roast baby? Yet for the Italians of his generation, no matter what their politics, he exerted a powerful influence in thought and fashion; he seemed a breath of fresh air, a new kind of 'superman', hard and passionate yet capable of writing exquisite, intoxicating verse; the spiritual father of the technology-infatuated Futurists, ready to destroy the old bourgeois *Italia vile* of museum curators and parish priests and create in its stead a great modern power, the 'New Italy'. He lived a life of total exhibitionism—extravagantly, decadently and beyond his means, at every moment the trend-setting, aristocratic aesthete, with his borzois and melodramatic affairs with the actress 'the Divine' Eleonora Duse and innumerable other loves (preferably duchesses). Apparently he thought the New Italians should all be as flamboyant and clever, and he disdained the corporate state of the Fascists. For Mussolini, the still-popular old nationalist was a loose cannon and an acute embarrassment, and he decided to pension him off into gilded retirement on Lake Garda, correctly calculating that the gift of the villa would appeal to his delusions of grandeur.

Where to Stay and Eating Out

Gardone Riviera ✉ 25083

Gardone Riviera and its suburb Fasano Riviera have competing Grand Hotels, both attractive old pleasure domes. In Gardone, the ★★★★**Grand Hotel**, Via Zanardelli 72, ✆ 0365 290 220, ✉ 0365 290 221 (*very expensive*), with its 180 rooms, was one of the largest resort hotels in Europe when built in 1881. It is still recognized as a landmark, and its countless chandeliers glitter as brightly as when Churchill stayed there in the late 1940s. The dining room and delicious food match the quality of the rooms. *Open mid-April–mid-Oct.* Fasano's alternative, ★★★★**Fasano Grand Hotel**, ✆ 0365 20261, ✉ 0365 22695 (*very expensive*) was built in the early 19th century as a Habsburg hunting palace and converted into a hotel around 1900. Surrounded by a large park, it's furnished with *belle époque* fittings; there are tennis courts, a heated pool and private beach, and the restaurant is one of Lake Garda's best. *Open May–Oct.* Another excellent choice, Fasano's ★★★★**Villa del Sogno**, Via Zanardelli 107, ✆ 0365 290 181, 🖅 0365 290 230 (*very expensive*) was its creator's neo-Renaissance 'Dream Villa' of the 1920s. Immersed in trees, there's a private beach five minutes' walk away and a pool in its flower-filled garden. *Open April–Oct.* A Liberty-style palace set in luxuriant gardens directly on the lake, ★★★**Villa Fiordaliso**, Corso Zanardelli 132, ✆ 0365 20158, 🖅 0365 290 011 (*very expensive*) has only seven rooms, all finely equipped. You can request (for a price) the suite where Mussolini and his mistress Clara Petacci spent their last few weeks. Located in a serene park, with a private beach and pier, it also boasts an elegant restaurant, the best in Gardone, featuring classic Lombard dishes; the *menu degustazione* goes for L65,000 and 90,000. *Closed Nov, Mon.*

Less pricey choices include lakeside ★★★**Monte Baldo**, Via Zanardelli 104, ✆ 0365 20951, 🖅 0365 20952 (*moderate*), where a well-aged outer appearance hides a fully refurbished and modern, stylish interior. The hotel also has a pool. *Open April–Oct.* Halfway up to Il Vittoriale, ★**Hohl**, Via dei Colli 4, ✆ 0365 20160 (*moderate–cheap*) is another atmospheric 19th-century villa in a pleasant garden. None of the rooms has a bath, but they're quiet.

Northern Lake Garda

North of Gardone Riviera and Gargnano the lake narrows, the cliffs plunge sheer into the water and the Gardesana road pierces tunnel after tunnel like a needle. In the morning, when the wind's up, windsurfers flit across the waves like a swarm of crazed one-winged butterflies.

Tourist Information

Limone sul Garda, Piazzale A. De Gaspari, ✆ 0365 954 070, 🖅 0365 954 355; **Riva del Garda**, Giardini di Porta Orientale 8, ✆ 0464 554 444, 🖅 0464 520 308; **Arco**, Viale delle Palme 1, ✆ 0464 532 155, 🖅 0464 532 353.

The inland route from Tremósine rejoins the lake and La Gardesana shore road at **Limone sul Garda**, a popular resort town with a teeny-tiny port and a beach over 3km long. Its name comes from the Latin *limen* (border), although by happy coincidence Limone was one of the main citrus-producing towns on Lake Garda, and to this day its lemon terraces with their white square pillars are a striking feature of the landscape: D.H. Lawrence, who lived south of Limone for a spell, liked to see them as the ruins of ancient temples.

Riva del Garda and Around

North of Limone the lake enters into the Trentino region, where the charming town of **Riva del Garda** sits snug beneath an amphitheatre formed by Monte Brione. An important commercial port for the bishops of Trento beginning in 1027, it was much sought and fought after through the centuries and ruled at various times by Verona, Milan and Venice before it was handed back to the bishop-princes of Trent in 1521. In 1703, during the War of the Spanish Succession, the French General Vendôme sacked it and all the surroundings, leaving only a ghost of the former town to be inherited by Napoleon in 1796.

With its long beaches and refreshing summer breezes, Riva revived as a resort during the days of Austrian rule (1813–1918), as the 'Southern Pearl on the Austro-Hungarian Riviera,' a pearl especially prized by writers: Stendhal, Thomas Mann, D.H. Lawrence and Kafka were among its habitués. The centre of town, Piazza III Novembre, has a plain **Torre Apponale** (1220) where salt and grain was stored (*adm with the same ticket as the Museo Civico*) and the Palazzo Pretorio, built by Verona's Cansignorio della Scala in 1376, while the lakefront was defended by the sombre grey bulk of the 12th-century castle, the **Rocca**, surrounded by a swan-filled moat. This now houses Riva's **Museo Civico** (*open Tues–Sun 9.30–6.30; July and Aug 9.30am–10.30pm, but hours change frequently*) with finds from the Bronze Age settlement at Lake Ledro, and six statue stelae with human features from the 4th–3rd millennium BC, recently discovered, and from Roman Riva, as well as paintings, detached frescoes and sculpture gleaned from the surroundings. Riva's best church, the **Inviolata** (1603), was commissioned by the princely Madruzzo family of Trento from an unknown but imaginative Portuguese architect, who was given a free hand with the gilt and stucco inside; it also has paintings by Palma Giovane.

Only 3km north, a dramatic 287ft waterfall, the **Cascata del Varone**, crashes down a tight grotto-like gorge by the village of Varone; walkways allow visitors to become mistily intimate with thundering water (*opening times according to season; adm*). From the west side of Riva the exciting Ponale Road (N240) rises to **Lake Ledro**, noted not only for its scenery but also the remains of a Bronze Age settlement (*c.* 2000 BC) of pile dwellings, discovered in 1929. One has been reconstructed near the ancient piles around **Molina di Ledro**, where the **Museo delle Palafitte** houses the pottery, axes, daggers and amber jewellery recovered from the site (*open June–Sept daily 9–1 and 2–6; Oct and Nov Tues–Sun 9–1 and 2–5; Dec Sat and Sun only 9–12 and 2–5; Mar–May Tues–Sun 9–1 and 2–5*); the visit includes the new prehistoric botanical garden, dedicated to the plants cultivated by northern Italian farmers in the Bronze Age. From here you can continue to Lake Idro, through the shadowy gorge of the **Valle d'Ampola**.

One of the most dramatic sights on Garda is just behind Riva, in a natural balcony of hills overlooking the lake: the jagged crag and **Castello d'Arco**, dramatically crowned with ancient, dagger-sharp cypresses and the swallowtail crenellations. Built to defend the Valle di Sarca, the main funnel of northern armies into Italy, it was controlled by the cultured Counts of Arco, who tugged their forelocks at various stages to Verona, Milan and Trento. The path up is lovely, if a bit tiring on a hot day, and despite the damage wrecked by Vêndome's troops there are a few frescoes left, including one of a courtly game of chess.

Arco itself, once heavily fortified and moated (the only surviving gate has a drawbridge) became, like Riva, a popular Austro-Hungarian resort in the 1800s, prized for its climate. In the centre, a baroque fountain dedicated to Moses splashes before the Palladian-inspired **Collegiata dell'Assunta** (1613), another Madruzzo project, this time by Trentino architect Giovanni Maria Filippi (*see* p.264). There's a pretty public garden full of Mediterranean plants near the pretty 19th-century **Casinò**, while on the edge of town, off Via Lomego, the park laid out at the end of the 19th century by the Habsburg Archduke Albrecht has recently been restored and opened as an **Arboretum** (*open winter 9–4, summer 8–7; free*). One kilometre south of Arco, the 15th century church of **San Rocco** at Càneve has fine frescoes from by the Veronese school from the early 16th century.

Dro, up the Sarca valley, is near the small lakes of Cavedine and Toblino, and **Le Sarche**, where an ancient glacier deposited the *marocche*, a remarkable field of enormous boulders. Olive trees, as well as enormous chestnuts, grow around **Drena** at the bottom of Val Cavedine. The landmark here is the stark **Castello**, its keep rising up like a finger accusing heaven (*open Nov–Mar, Sat, Sun 10–6; April–Oct daily exc Mon 10–6; adm*). Built by the Counts of Arco in 1175 and ruined by Vêndome in 1703, the lists, where knightly tournaments once took place, have been restored to host congresses and theatrical performances; the keep has splendid views, taking in the mighty *marocche*, and contains a museum of local artefacts, dating from the 18th century BC to the Renaissance.

Back on Garda's northeast shore, **Monte Baldo** looms over **Torbole**, an old fishing village and pleasant resort, and the mouth of the Sacra, the most important river feeding the lake.

Where to Stay and Eating Out

Limone ✉ 25010

★★★★**Le Palme**, ✆ 0365 954 681, 🖷 0365 954 120 (*moderate*) is housed in a pretty Venetian villa, preserving much of its original charm alongside modern amenities. Named after its two ancient palm trees, it has a fine terrace, tennis courts and a good fish restaurant. *Open April–Oct.* Above the centre ★★★**La Limonaia**, Via Sopino Alto 3, ✆ 0365 954 221, 🖷 0365 954 227 (*moderate*) enjoys a superb position, and has both an adult and a children's pool and a playground. *Open Mar–Oct.* Agreeable and small, ★★★**Sogno del Benaco**, ✆ 0365 954 026, 🖷 0365 954 357 (*moderate*) has fairly standard rooms. Above the lake in an olive grove, ★**Mercedes**, Via Nanzello 12, ✆ 0365 954 073 (*inexpensive*) has a pool and lovely views. *Open April–Nov.*

Riva del Garda ✉ 38066

When German intellectuals from Nietzsche to Günter Grass have needed a little rest and relaxation in Italy they have for many decades flocked to Riva del Garda to check in at ★★★★**Hotel du Lac et du Parc**, Viale Rovereto 44, ✆ 0464 551 500, 🖷 0464 555 200 (*very expensive*), modernized, spacious, airy and tranquil, and set in a large lakeside garden; facilities include indoor and outdoor pools, a beach, sailing school, gym, sauna and tennis courts. *Open April–Oct.* At the turn-of-the-century ★★★★**Grand Hotel Riva**, Piazza Garibaldi 10, ✆ 0464 521 800, 🖷 0464 552 293 (*expensive*), majestically positioned on the main square, 87 modern rooms look out over the lake; the rooftop restaurant combines fine food with incomparable views. It also has a private beach. *Open Mar–Oct.*

Right on the port in Riva's main square, ★★★★**Sole**, Piazza III Novembre, ✆ 0464 552 686, 🖷 0464 552 811 (*expensive*) has plenty of atmosphere and a beautiful terrace; most rooms have private baths and look out over the lake, though they vary widely in size and quality. Beside the harbour, ★★★**Centrale**, Piazza III Novembre 27, ✆ 0464 552 344, 🖷 0464 552 138 (*moderate*) has fully equipped spacious rooms and bathrooms; almost as good and slightly cheaper, ★★★**Portici**, Piazza III Novembre 19, ✆ 0464 555 400, 🖷 0464 555 453 (*moderate*) has been competely refurbished and has modern rooms, all with bathrooms. *Open April–Oct.* Built in 1400, ★**Restel de**

Fer, Via Restel de Fer 10, ✆ 0464 553 481, ✆ 0464 552 798 (*moderate–inexpensive*) has only five rooms and a good restaurant, with summer dining in the cloister. If you seek peace and quiet, a garden and pool in a panoramic spot, the family-run **★Villa Moretti**, 3km up in Varone, ✆ 0464 521 127, ✆ 0464 521 751(*inexpensive*) fits the bill. A good economy choice, **★Villa Minerva**, Viale Roma 40, ✆ 0464 553 031 (*inexpensive*) is very pleasant, and very popular. Riva's hostel, **Ostello Benacus**, Piazza Cavour 9, ✆ 0464 554 911, ✆ 0464 556 554, has beds for L19,000 per night. *Open Mar–Oct.*

Arco ✉ 38062

The modern **★★★★Palace Hotel Città**, Viale Roma 10, ✆ 0464 531 100, ✆ 0464 516 208 (*expensive in season*) has a balcony for every comfortable room, a pool, gym and slimming programme, and an optional vegetarian menu in the restaurant.

The best place to eat is the **Belvedere**, Via Serafini 2, ✆ 0464 516 144 (*inexpensive*), serving home-grown vegetables, local salami, fresh pasta and roast meats. *Closed Wed.* **★★★Al Sole**, Via Sant'Anna 35, ✆ 0464 516 676, ✆ 0464 518 585 (*moderate*) is a popular place to stay, and its restaurant also features local produce—try gnocchi with local prunes. *Closed Mon.*

Torbole ✉ 38069

Beautifully located on a spit of land with water on either side, the modern **★★★★Lido Blu**, Via Foci del Sarca 1, ✆ 0464 505 180, ✆ 0464 505 931 (*expensive*) is an excellent hotel for families, with a private beach, a gym, covered pool, windsurfing school and more. You can dine well and romantically in a 19th-century Austrian fort in nearby Coe, at **Da Sergio**, ✆ 0464 505 301 (*expensive*), with a menu based on fish, accompanied by a fine wine list. *Closed Wed except in summer.*

The East Shore: Malcésine to Bardolino

Garda's east shore belongs to the province of Verona, which likes to call it the Riviera degli Olivi—they are the only olives in the Veneto, so they make an impression—but its most outstanding feature is Monte Baldo, a massive ridge of limestone stretching 35km between Lake Garda and the Adige valley, cresting at 6989ft. Baldo is anything but bald: 'the botanical garden of Italy', it supports an astonishing variety of flora from Mediterranean palms to Arctic tundra; some 20 different flowers first discovered on Monte Baldo bear its name. The southern third of the Riviera degli Olivi is more grapey than olivey, the land of Bardolino.

Getting Around

APT buses run up the east coast from Verona and Peschiera as far as Riva, ✆ 045 800 4129. The car ferry crosses year-round from Torri del Benaco to Maderno.

Tourist Information

Malcésine, Via Capitanato 6/8, ✆ 045 740 0044, ✆ 045 740 1633. **Torri del Benaco**, Via Gardesana 5, ✆ 045 722 5120. **Garda**, Lungolago Regina Adelaide 3, ✆ 045 627 0384. **Bardolino**, at Piazza Matteotti 53, ✆ 045 721 0078.

Malcésine

South of Torbole, the forbidding cliffs of Monte di Nago hang perilously over the lake (but nevertheless attract scores of Lycra-bright human flies) before Malcésine, the loveliest town on the east shore. The Veronese lords always took care to protect this coast, and in the 13th century, over the old Lombard castle, they built their magnificent **Rocca Scaligero** (*open April–Oct daily 9.30–8; winter Sat, Sun and hols only; adm*) rising up on a sheer rock over the water; inside are natural history exhibits, prehistoric rock etchings and a room dedicated to Goethe, who was accused of spying while sketching the castle. As well as the Scaliger castle, note the 16th-century **Palazzo dei Capitani del Lago** in the centre of Malcésine's medieval web of streets.

Every half-hour a pair of cableways runs vertiginously up **Monte Baldo** (*L18,000 return; © 045 740 0206 for information*); the views are ravishing, and the ski slopes at the top are very popular with the Veronese. Malcésine has pretty walks through the olives, and the shore has lovely places to swim and sunbathe, especially around the cove called the Val di Sogno.

Torri del Benaco and Garda

Further south, past a steep, sparsely populated stretch of shore, laid-back **Torri del Benaco** and its lovely setting have been attracting pleasure tourists ever since the 15th century, when the great Medicean poet Poliziano came to stay; more recent fans have included André Gide and Stephen Spender. Its name comes from a rugged old tower in the centre which served as the headquarters of Berengario, the first king of Italy, in his 905 campaign against the Hungarians. Later it was defended by another **Scaliger castle** (1383), now a museum (*open April, May and Oct 9.30–12.30 and 2.30–6; June–Sept 9.30–1 and 4.30–7.30; adm*) with displays on olive oil, citrus, fishing, and the rock engravings found in the area from c. 2000 BC, similar to those in Asiago and illustrating the usual Bronze Age obsessions (solar discs, animals, warriors). The church of **Santa Trinità** has good 14th-century Giottoesque frescoes. There are some lovely paths to follow from Torri—one, up to the old village of **Albisano**, then over to Crer and Brancolino, takes in the largest patch of Torri's prehistoric graffiti, near Crer's church.

Other rock engravings lie along the scenic path laid out by the WWF, from Torri del Benaco to enchanting **Punta di San Vigilio**, immersed in old lemon groves and one of the prettiest places on the lake. Sirens' rocks along the point are occupied by the beautiful **Villa Guarienti** by Sammicheli, and its tiny port has the tiny old church of San Vigilio, and a 16th-century tavern, now an inn (*see* below). Sir Laurence Olivier was an old habitué.

On the other side of the Rocca del Garda, a green soufflé of a headland, lies **Garda** itself, a fine old town with Renaissance palazzi and villas. Source of the lake's modern name, from the Lombard *Warthe*, 'the watch', it became the capital of a county after Charlemagne defeated the Lombards. In its long-gone castle the wicked Count Berenguer secretly held Queen Adelaide of Italy prisoner in 960, after he murdered her husband Lotario and she refused to marry his son. After a year she was discovered by a monk, who spent another year plotting her escape. She then received the protection of Otto I of Germany, who defeated Berenguer along with the troublemaking Hungarians, married the widowed queen, and became Holy Roman Emperor.

Bardolino

To the south, Bardolino is synonymous with its lively red wine with a bitter cherry fragrance that goes so well with fishy *antipasti*; you can learn all you want to know about it at the Cantine Zeni's **Museo del Vino**, Via Costabella 9 (*open Mar–Oct daily 9–1 and 2–6*) or by following the wine route through the soft rolling hills, dotted with 19th-century villas. Originally the town was the property of the monks of San Zeno in Verona, who in the 8th century built **San Zeno**, one of the few surviving Carolingian buildings in Italy, with bits of its original decoration inside. **Cisano**, south of Bardolino, has a museum dedicated to the Riviera degli Olivi's other cash crop, the **Museo dell'Olio d'Oliva**, Via Peschiera 54, (*open 9–12.30 and 3–7, closed Sun and Wed pm*).

The next town, **Lazise**, was the main Venetian port, and near the harbour retains an ensemble of Venetian buildings as well as another castle, this one built in the 9th century by the Magyars and taken over and rebuilt by the Scaligers. As Peschiera is just down the road, Lazise has a theme park too, **Canevaworld**, quaintly combining a dinner with King Arthur in the 'Medieval Times' with a Caribbean island setting and waterslides (*open mid-May–Sept; separate adm, both very exp;* © *045 759 0622*).

Where to Stay and Eating Out

Malcésine ✉ 37018

★★★★**Val di Sogno**, © 045 740 0108, @ 045 740 1694 (*expensive*) is situated about 3 minutes out of town in a beautiful setting in its own grounds right on the lake shore. There is a pool, private beach, lakeside restaurant, and modern rooms with balconies. South of the centre, ★★★★**Park Hotel Querceto**, at Campiano, © 045 740 0344, @ 045 740 0848 (*expensive*) is a romantic place to stay, with a lovely views, a pool, garden, and one of the best restaurants in the area, where the cuisine is light and tasty, and adapted to the season. *Closed Nov–Mar.* The inviting ★★★**Vega**, Viale Roma, © 045 657 0355, @ 045 740 1604 (*moderate*) offers big, modern rooms, all with satellite TV, minibar, safe and air-conditioning, and a private beach. ★★★**Sailing Centre**, north of the centre at Molini Campagnola 3, © 045 740 0055, @ 045 740 0392 (*expensive–moderate*) has a beach, sailing and windsurf schools, sauna, pool, satellite TV and more. *Open end Mar–end Oct.*

The beautifully positioned ★★★**Malcésine**, Piazza Pallone, © 045 740 0173, @ 045 657 0073 (*moderate, with some rooms at cheap rates*) has a garden with swimming terrace, pleasant rooms, and an excellent value if average restaurant. Right in the centre, you can sleep where Goethe snoozed in 1786 at the simple ★★**San Marco**, Via Capitanato, © 045 740 0115 (*inexpensive*); all rooms have a bath. ★**Miralago**, Viale Roma, © 045 740 0111 (*inexpensive*) is a good budget option with lake view. By the Porto Vecchio, the **Trattoria da Pace** is a popular place with outdoor tables for seafood by the lake; around L40,000.

Torri del Benaco ✉ 37010

The comfortable ★★**Gardesana**, Piazza Calderini 20, © 045 722 5411, @ 045 722 5771 (*moderate*) is right on the harbour with splendid views of lake and castle. All rooms have baths, and breakfast and meals are served on the harbour patio when the weather is good. Near the lake, the plain and simple ★★★**Al Caval**, Via Gardesana 186, ✆ 045 722 5666, ✉ 045 629 6570 (*moderate*) has a park and windsurf rentals, and the best restaurant in town (*moderate*), where the usual lake fish get special treatment in terrines and pasta dishes. *Closed Jan–Mar.*

Punta San Virgilio/Garda ✉ 37016

★★★★**Locanda San Vigilio**, the little inn hidden out by Sammicheli's villa on Punta San Vigilio, ✆ 045 725 6688, ✉ 045 725 6551 (*very expensive*) has seven romantic rooms, a beach and delicious food. *Open mid-Mar–mid-Oct.* A lakeside villa, ★★★★**Du Parc**, Via Marconi 3, ✆ 045 725 5343, ✉ 045 725 5642 (*expensive*) has recently been entirely refurbished and upgraded. *Open July–Aug.* The large, modern and quite luxurious ★★★★**Eurotel**, ✆ 0456 270 3333, ✉ 045 725 6640 (*moderate*) has a fine garden and pool. *Open Easter–Oct.*

An exceptionally well-priced hotel, ★★★**Flora**, Via Giorgione 22 and 27, ✆/✉ 045 725 5348 (*moderate*) is situated slightly above the town in its own grounds, and slick and modern with pine fittings, spacious rooms, all with balcony, and fantastic amenities— tennis, mini-golf and *two* pools. *Open Easter–Oct.* Next door to the Flora, ★★★**Continental**, Via Giorgione 14, ✆ 045 725 5100, ✉ 045 725 6288 (*moderate*) is also in its own grounds and well-priced, but not quite as modern or comfortable—and with only one swimming pool. *Open Easter–Oct.* ★**Vittoria**, Lungolago Regina Adelaide, ✆ 045 725 5065, ✉ 045 627 0752 (*inexpensive*) is the best cheap hotel in Garda, at the end of the lakefront walk. The rooms are big, and service is very friendly. *Open Easter–Oct.* On the landward side of Garda, **Stafolet**, Via Poiano 12, ✆ 045 725 5427 (*moderate*) is worth asking directions to, for its wild duck and plump, spinach-filled *strangolopreti* ('priest stranglers'). Less distinguished, but good and cheap, **Al Pontesel**, Via Monte Baldo 71, ✆ 045 725 5419, features stout local cooking.

Bardolino ✉ 37011

You can dine well at **Aurora**, Via San Severo 18, ✆ 045 721 0038 (*moderate*) near the landmark church of San Zeno. Specialities include the produce of the lake, especially trout prepared in a variety of styles. *Closed Mon.*

The Eastern Veneto

While the western frontier of the Veneto is defined by Lake Garda, the eastern Veneto incorporates the two provinces north of Venice, Treviso and Belluno. The hills get bigger as you head north; much of Belluno province is in the Dolomites (*see* next chapter).

Treviso

Famous for radicchio, cherries and Benetton clothes, Treviso is one of the Veneto's best kept secrets, a 'Venice in miniature' laced with little canals (*canagi*) diverted from the river Sile, languorous with willow trees, lazy water wheels, swans, mossy walls, yet all humming with more than a little discreet prosperity. Roman *Tarvisium*, it enjoyed a fairly robust and riotous Middle Ages under its *signori*, the da Camino, some of whom were benign, such as the 'good'

Gherard, and some not nice, such as Riccardo, who was murdered while playing chess in 1312. Despite flirtations with anarchy, the 14th century saw the arrival of one of Giotto's greatest pupils, Tommaso da Modena, who spent most of his life painting in Treviso. After a brief period under the Scaligers, the city and its surrounding Marca were annexed by Venice in 1339, the first of its *terra firma* acquisitions.

Colours were an obsession in Treviso long before Benetton united them. Attractive building stone was scarce, so it became the custom to cover the humble bricks walls with plaster and frescoes, in the 1300s with simple colours and patterns, and by the 1500s with heroic mythologies and allegories. Although faded and fragmented since then—Treviso endured 35 air raids during the last war, including a fierce one on Good Friday 1944 that destroyed half of the city in five minutes—one of the delights is to pick out frescoes under the eaves, or hidden in the shadows of an arcade. Another is to take a stroll along the outside of the city walls, along the Sile to the south, and along the various Corsos and moats.

Getting Around

Treviso **airport** (© 0422 230 393) is southwest of the town; bus no.6 runs from there to the railway station; Ryan Air links it several times a week to London Stansted. Both the train and bus stations (© 0422 412 222) are in Via Roma south of the centre. **Trains** run from Venice or Mestre to Treviso (30min) and Belluno (2 hours), either directly or by changing at Padua or Conegliano. One line to Belluno goes via Conegliano and Vittòrio Vèneto; the other, longer but more scenic, via Montebelluna (also a getting-off point for Masèr and Àsolo; *see* pp.166 and 168) and Feltre (p.235).

Tourist Information

Piazza Monte di Pietà 8, © 0422 547 632, ✆ 0422 419 092, *tvapt@sevenonline.it*.

Piazza dei Signori and the Duomo

From the bus or train station, it's a 10-minute walk over the Sile along the Corso del Popolo and Via XX Settembre to the Piazza dei Signori, the heart of Treviso. Here stands the only surviving palace of the old *comune*, the enormous brick **Palazzo dei Trecento**, 'Of the Three Hundred', built in the 1200s and rebuilt after it took a bomb on the nose in the war; Treviso café society shelters underneath its loggia. Adjacent, the **Palazzo del Podestà** was rebuilt in 1877, along with the Torre Civica which looms over its shoulder. Behind the Palazzo dei Trecento, the **Monte di Pietà** (municipal pawn shop) contains the lovely Renaissance **Sala dei Reggitori** (*visits free, by appointment only:* © *0422 654 320*), with walls of gilt leather, a painted, beamed ceiling and canvases by Sebastiano Ricci and Luca Giordano. Just up and around the back of the Palazzo dei Trecento, the church of **Santa Lucia** (1389) has a detached fresco by Tommaso da Modena, the *Madonna delle Carceri*, 'of the prisons', recalling the building that once stood nearby.

The elegant and arcaded main street, the **Calmaggiore**, was Tarvisium's *decumanus*. It leads from the square to the **Duomo**, a Venetian Romanesque building with a cluster of domes, founded in the 12th century; the adjacent baptistry gives an idea of what the cathedral looked like before its many alterations. Besides fine Renaissance tombs of local prelates, much of the cathedral's name brand art is concentrated in the **Cappella Malchiostro**, just right of the altar, designed by Tullio and Antonio Lombardo, with works by Paris Bordone (*Adoration of the Shepherds*) and Girolamo da Treviso the elder (*Madonna del Fiore*). The frescoes are by Pordenone, while his mortal enemy Titian contributed *The Annunciation* on the altar; Vasari wrote that Pordenone always painted with his sword at his hip in case Titian showed up while he was working. Behind the cathedral, the **Museo Diocesano** (*open Mon–Thurs 9–12, Sat 9–12 and 3–6*) contains one of Tommaso da Modena's masterpieces, the detached fresco *Cristo Passo*, and fine marble reliefs from the 1200s.

Museo Civico and San Nicolò

From the Piazza Duomo, Via Canova leads past the 15th-century **Casa Trevigiana** (or Casa da Noal) (*open only for special exhibitions*), a reliquary of the city's architecture containing bits and pieces salvaged from her ruins. Via Canova meets Borgo Cavour near the **Museo Civico Luigi Bailo** (*open Tues–Sat 9–12.30, 2.30–5; Sun 9–12; adm*): the archaeological collection on the first floor includes Bronze Age swords (*c.* 1000 BC) and unusual 5th-century BC bronze discs from Montebelluna. Upstairs there's an excellent collection of masters from the Veneto.

Borgo Cavour makes a grandiose exit through the great Venetian gate, the **Porta dei Santi Quaranta** (1517), encompassed by an impressive stretch of the ramparts. However, if you turn instead down Via S. Liberale and turn right in Via Absidi, you'll come to Treviso's best church, the enormous Gothic **San Nicolò** with its attractive polygonal apse. The interior is a treasure house of lovely frescoes—from a huge *St Christopher* on the south wall to the charming pages by Lorenzo Lotto on the monument of Senator Agostino d'Onigo, sculpted by Giovanni Buora. Tommaso da Modena contributed the saints standing at attention on the columns, but even better are his perceptive portraits of 40 Dominicans (1352), some using medieval reading glasses, in the **Capitolo dei Domenicani** in the adjacent Seminario (*open April–Sept 8–6; Oct–Mar 8–12.30, 3–5.30; ring the bell*).

San Francesco

Treviso's east end, the Oltrecagnanàn, is separated from the rest of the city by one of its wider streams, the Cagnàn; on a little islet (take Via Trevisi-Via Pescheria from the Monte di Pietà) the lively **Pescheria**, or fish market, built in 1851 is a colourful, appetizing delight, and open every morning except Sunday. Just up Via S. Parisio from here is San Nicolò's near twin, the tall brick, Romanesque-Gothic **San Francesco**. This was once the great pantheon and art gallery of Treviso, but the masterpieces have been relocated to the Accademia, leaving only a fresco of the *Madonna and Saints* by Tomaso da Modena, to the left of the high altar, as well as the tombs of Francesca Petrarch (d. 1384) and Pietro Alighieri (d. 1364), the children of Italy's two greatest poets, whose final meeting-place here in Treviso is mostly a coincidence— Pietro's body was moved here when his original church was knocked over.

Back along the walls to the east, Viale Burchiellati leads shortly to the city's other great gate, Guglielmo Bergamasco's exotic **Porta San Tomaso** (1518), with its inscription 'The Lord protect you while you go in and out'. From here follow Borgo Mazzini to the ill-starred church of **Santa Caterina**, built in 1346 on the site of a da Camino palace that was razed in a popular revolt. Closed on the order of the Serenissima in 1772, badly bombed in the war, Santa

Caterina was pieced together after the war to house Tommaso da Modena's detached frescoes on *The Life of St Ursula*, a cycle that's just as delightful as Carpaccio's St Ursulas in the Accademia; other beautiful paintings, the *Madonna and Saints* and the *Story of Sant'Eligio*, are attributed to Pisanello. But guess what—it's closed for restoration. The other big church in these parts, **Santa Maria Maggiore**, has an attractive late Gothic façade (1473) and a Renaissance *tempietto* in the left nave, sheltering a miracle-working Madonna.

Along the Sile

Treviso's meandering Sile is the longest resurgent river in Italy, and its leafy banks have been made into a park: the **Oasi Naturalistica di Cervara**. In Santa Cristina, just west of Quinto, the parish church houses a *Madonna in Trono* by Lorenzo Lotto. On the other (east) side of Treviso in **Roncade**, the late 15th-century **Villa Giustinian** (attributed to the circle of Mauro Codussi) is a key work in the evolution of villa before Palladio: although built with defence in mind, it is the first case of a secular building decorated with classical elements—in this case a loggia and pediment. The villa is still a working farm after 500 years.

Treviso ✉ *31100*   ***Where to Stay***

There's not a lot of choice. Best Western's ★★★**Al Foghèr**, Viale della Repubblica 10, ✆ 0422 432 950, 🖷 0422 430 391 (*expensive–moderate*) is the pick of the bunch, outside the walls but in walking distance of the centre, with parking, well-equipped rooms, a warm welcome, and a good restaurant. Near the station, modern ★★★★**Continental**, Via Roma 16, ✆ 0422 411 662, 🖷 0422 411 620 (*expensive*) is convenient and air-conditioned, and has a garage, although if you're driving you may prefer one of the 20 rooms just north of town in the attractive patrician ★★★**Scala**, Viale Felissent 1, near the exit for Conegliano, ✆ 0422 307 600, 🖷 0422 305 048 (*expensive*) set in a pretty park. Smack in the historical centre, the hospitable and long-established ★★**Campeol**, Piazza Ancillotto 8, ✆ 0422 56601, 🖷 0422 540 871 (*moderate*) has good views. Near the Treviso Sud exchange on the A27 in Silèa, ★★★**La Fattoria**, Via Callalta 83, ✆ 0422 361 770, 🖷 0422 460 150 (*moderate*) offers cosy rooms in a restored farmhouse. *Closed part of Aug.*

Eating Out

Cichorium intybus, otherwise known as *radicchio trevignana*, is not only a local obsession, but a salad vegetable that has the same quality control as wine; to be DOC *radicchio trevignana* it must have sprouted up in one of eight *comuni* and grown under certain organic conditions. You can taste the difference (or so they claim!), especially in December, when it's at its best. Another speciality is *sopa coada*, a baked pigeon casserole. If money's no object, try it at **Alfredo**, Via Collalto 26, ✆ 0422 540 275 (*expensive*), long Treviso's most acclaimed restaurant, in a lovely, elegant *belle époque* setting. The imaginative menu has an emphasis on seafood. *Closed Sun eve, Mon, Aug; reserve.* In a beautiful 12th-century building, **Al Bersagliere**, Via Barberia 21, ✆ 0422 579 902 (*moderate*) offers a full selection of delicious *antipasti*, *sopa coada* and other Venetian specialities such as squid in its own ink, risotto, and liver Venetian-style. *Closed Sun, Sat lunch, Aug.* **Beccherie**, Piazza Anchillotto 10, ✆ 0422 540 871 (*moderate*) is one of Treviso's bastions of local atmosphere and cooking—a great place to try *pasta e fagioli* with radicchio. *Closed Sun eve, Mon and July.* **Toni del Spin**, Via Inferiore 7, ✆ 0422 543 829 (*moderate–inexpensive*) remains an old favourite for its Veneto dishes (*bigoli, risi e bisi*, etc.) topped off with American apple pie. *Closed Sun and Mon lunch.* If you have a car, it's a very short drive north to Ponzano Veneto and charming **Il Dominicale**, Via Postumia 51, ✆ 0422 969 360 (*moderate*), where you can linger in the garden over delicious renditions of the Italian classics. *Closed Sun, Mon, some of Aug.*

North of Treviso: the Marca Trevigniana

You can drive straight up to the Dolomites in less than two hours from Treviso, or spend a day exploring the fine towns of its province, the 'Joyous' Marca Trevigniana, along the way. At the grave risk of offending local pride, you'll find the Marca's most famous bits—Àsolo, Masèr and Castelfranco—in the section 'North of Padua' (*see* pp.164–9).

Tourist Information

Oderzo: Piazza Castello 1, ✆ 0422 815 251, ✉ 0422 814 081. **Conegliano**: Via Colombo 1, ✆/✉ 0438 21230. **Vittòrio Vèneto**: Piazza del Popolo 18, ✆ 0438 57243, ✉ 0438 53629.

Oderzo and Conegliano

A delightful mini-miniature Venice crisscrossed by canals and devoted to wine making, **Oderzo** may not be a household name, but in its Roman heyday as *Opitergium* it was recorded as far away as Egypt. The main square, Piazza Vittorio Emanuele II, marks its old forum, overlooked by the late Gothic **Duomo**, which contains some intriguing fresco fragments; in Via Garibaldi, Roman finds and mosaics fill the **Museo Civico Opitergino** (*open 9–12.30, 3–5.30, Sun 3–6.30; closed Mon, Thurs; adm*). Nearby, the **Pinacoteca Alberto Martini**, Via Garibaldi 63 (*open Mon–Fri 3–7, Sun 3–7*) has works by Oderzo-born surrealist painter Alberto Martini, as well as other contemporary Italians, mostly from Oderzo. Make the short detour north of Oderzo to **Portobuffolè**, a picturesque village of frescoed buildings and three funny Venetian lions (especially the spooked one with a pie pan face sticking out its tongue on the 15th-century Monte della Pietà, now the Cassa Marca). The oldest house, 13th-century **Casa di Gaia da Camino**, has a bicycling museum and hosts special exhibitions. A popular antiques market takes place on the second Sunday of each month.

West, **Conegliano** is a town neatly divided into old and new, with the grandiose neoclassical Accademia cinema and its giant sphinxes in the centre. It was the birthplace of Giambattista Cima (1460–1518)—'the sweet shepherd among Venetian painters' as Mary McCarthy called him—the son of a seller of hides, who often painted his native countryside in his backgrounds. If you haven't seen the originals, reproductions are displayed at his birthplace, the **Casa di Cima**, on quiet Via Cima 24 (*ring ahead, ✆ 0438 21660*). An original and beautiful Cima, a *Sacra Conversazione* in an architectural setting (1493), is the altarpiece of the 14th-century **Duomo**; also look out for Francesco Beccaruzzi's recently restored *SS. Marco, Leonardo and Caterina*. In the 16th century two non-Venetians, Ludovico Pozzoserrato of Belgium and

Francesco da Milano, collaborated on the 27 Old and New Testament scenes in the adjacent **Sala dei Battuti**, 'the Hall of the Beaten', i.e. a confraternity of flagellants (*open Sun 3–7, other days exc Wed 9–12 if you ring ahead;* © *0438 22606*). Be sure to stroll down arcaded **Via Venti Settembre**, lined with old frescoed palaces; the **castle** on the hill, begun in the 10th century, has a small **Museo Civico**.

Conegliano has a wine-making school, and produces a delightful Prosecco which you can go a-tasting along the pretty 42km **Strada del Prosecco**—between Conegliano's castle and **Valdobbiadene** to the west, then back east to Vittòrio Vèneto. On the way have a look at **San Pietro di Feletto**, its exterior richly frescoed in the 15th-century by an unknown painter, who pictures Jesus in a unique fashion: lines from his wounds are connected to chickens, wine, people lying in bed, and farm tools.

Vittòrio Vèneto

The Venetian Pre-Alps saw heavy action in the First World War, and the hills around Asiago, Monte Grappa and the Piave are often crowned with dispiritingly huge war cemeteries. Vittòrio Vèneto, north of Conegliano, was the site of Italy's final victorious battle (October 1918). The name, however, predates the war; in 1866, to celebrate the birth of Italy, the two rival towns Cèneda and Serravalle united and took the name of their royal godfather Vittorio Emanuele II. Since then they've united in sprawl in their valley.

The **Castello di San Martino**, dating back to the Lombards, overlooks Cèneda. The central square, Piazza Giovanni Paolo I, holds the **Loggia del Cenedese**, designed by Sansovino in 1538, now home to a museum of the Battle of 1918 (*open May–Sept 10–12, 4–6.30; Oct–April 10–12, 2–5; closed Mon; adm*); Albino Luciani (the 'smiling pope', John Paul I), long-time bishop of the diocese, founded the **Museo Diocesano** in the seminary, with works by Palma Giovane and Titian (*open by request*). Another church, **Santa Maria del Meschio**, has a beautiful altarpiece of the *Annunciation* by Andrea Previtali of Bergamo.

A poetic street (Via Dante/Virgilio/Petrarca) links the two halves of Vittòrio Vèneto. A clock tower announces **Serravalle**, with its old palaces and houses—the setting for Richard Attenborough's film *In Love and War* (1996). The 15th-century **Loggia Serravallese** houses, rather confusingly, the **Museo del Cenedese** (*open April–Sept 10–12 and 4.30–6.30; Oct–Mar 10–12, 3–5; closed Tues; same ticket as the Museo della Battaglia*), with a collection of Roman finds, sculpture, and minor paintings; admission also includes the beautifully frescoed (mid-1400s) church of San Lorenzo. Over the bridge, Serravalle's **Duomo** has a fine *Madonna col Bambino* by Titian. A woodsy path leads up to Serravalle's oldest church, hilltop **Santa Augusta**, where, the legend goes, the saint used to distribute bread to the poor until her disapproving father ran her through with his sword. Others say the church marks the site of an old Roman temple dedicated to Octavian Augustus. On 22–23 August the place is packed with pilgrims.

Vittòrio Vèneto's playground, the lovely **Bosco del Cansiglio**, a vast forest of fir, larch and beech on a lofty karstic plateau, was set aside by Venice in 1548 as its 'Forest of St Mark's Oars'; Mt Cansiglio itself offers the closest downhill skiing to Venice.

Oderzo ✉ 31046

The nicest place to sleep near Oderzo is 5km east at Gorgo al Monitcano: the 15th-century ★★★**Villa Revedin**, Via Palazzi 4, ✆/@ 0422 800 033 (*moderate*) set in a park; rooms are well equipped and the breakfasts superb. In the centre, **Gellius,** Calle Pretoria 6, ✆ 0422 713 577 (*moderate*) offers the chance to dine in an atmospheric Roman prison, but the food has improved dramatically in the last 2000 years. *Closed Mon, Tues lunch.* In Portobuffolè (✉ 31019) you can sleep in a beautiful villa once belonging to a doge, ★★★★**Villa Giustinian**, Via Giustiniani 11, ✆ 0422 850 244, @ 0422 850 260 (*expensive*); built in 1695 and elegantly furnished, the villa is encompassed by a large park. *Closed part of Aug.*

Conegliano ✉ 31015

Behind an exterior frescoed in the 1500s, ★★★**Canon d'Oro**, Via XX Settembre 129, ✆/@ 0438 34246 (*moderate*) has a warm welcome and plush modern rooms overlooking the town's main street. For an alternative, the ★★★**Sporting Hotel Ragno d'Oro**, Via Diaz 37, ✆ 0438 412 300, @ 0438 412 310 (*moderate*), set in parkland on Conegliano's outskirts, boasts tennis courts, a sizeable pool, sauna and satellite TV.

Just outside Conegliano, the lovely **Tre Panoce**, Via Vecchia Trevigiana 50, ✆ 0438 60071 (*expensive–moderate*) occupies a *seicento* farmhouse crowning a hill of vineyards, with outdoor tables in summer (if you're not driving, bus no.1 stops outside). You can try a number of little dishes by ordering the *menu veneto*, followed by delicious desserts. *Closed Sun evenings, Mon, Aug.* In a 13th-century building, **Al Salisà**, Via XX Settembre 2, ✆ 0438 24288 (*expensive–moderate*) is elegant, featuring succulent snails (*lumache*) and game specialities in season, especially venison. There's also a good local wine list, and special menus for lunch. *Closed Tues evenings, Wed, Aug.*

On the Strada del Prosecco between Valdobbiadene and Vittorio Veneto in Follina (✉ 31051) the elegant, prize-winning ★★★**Romantik Hotel Abbazia**, Via IV Novembre, ✆ 0438 971 277, @ 0438 970 001 (*expensive*) has lovely modern rooms, including jacuzzis in the baths, in a 17th-century estate. They even hire out bikes or cars for excursions. No restaurant; but a hop away in Miane, **Gigetto**, Via De Gasperi 4, ✆ 0438 960 020 (*expensive*) will treat you in the same manner, featuring the finest dishes the Marca Trevignana can offer, including lovely mushrooms; fantastic list of wines. *Closed Mon eve and Tues, some of Jan and Aug.*

Vittòrio Vèneto ✉ 31029

Not too many choices here: the best is ★★★**Hotel Terme**, Via della Terme 4, ✆ 0438 554 345, @ 0438 554 347 (*moderate*) with good, comfortable rooms near the station. Dine on hearty mountain specialities at the popular **Postiglione**, in an old post house at Via Cavour 39, ✆ 0438 556 924 (*moderate*). *Closed Tues and two weeks in July–Aug.* The finest dining in the region, however, is west in Tarzo: **Il Capitello**, Via S. Francesco, Cobranese, ✆ 0485 564 279 (*moderate*) featuring all that's exquisite, with a modern flair. *Closed Wed, Thurs lunch, Jan and Aug.*

Towards the Dolomites: Belluno and Feltre

A provincial capital, strategically located at the junction of the Piave and Ardo rivers, Belluno is one of those small perfectly proportioned Italian cities: urban, urbane and yet never far from magnificent views over the countryside—in this case, of the Venetian Dolomites.

Tourist Information

Belluno: Via Rodolfo Pesaro 21 © 0437 940 083, ◉ 0437 94 0073. **Feltre:** Piazza Trento-Trieste 9, © 043 92540, ◉ 043 92839.

Belluno

Inhabited since Paleoveneto time, the Romans made *Belunum* an important outpost at the foot of the Dolomites, a status continued under the Byzantines. In the late 10th century it came under the rule of prince-bishops and various *signori*; the arrival of Venice in 1404 brought Belluno the peace it needed to thrive. The Bellunesi can be tough, though; when the Nazis invaded in 1943, they put up a stiff fight—564 were killed in the conflict.

The latter are remembered in the large main square with a fountain that grew up outside the old walls, the Piazza dei Martiri, perhaps still better known as the Campedél. It's a short walk from here to the civic and religious centre of town, **Piazza del Duomo**, site of Belluno's finest buildings, the ornate **Palazzo dei Rettori** (1491), residence of the Venetian governors, and the **Duomo**, which for over 20 years was the home church of Pope John Paul I. Founded in the 7th century, and last redesigned by Pietro Lombardo, work on the cathedral dragged on until the 1600s, and tends to be overshadowed by the magnificent detached **campanile**, designed by Filippo Juvarra (1742); once restoration work is completed, you may be able to go up again for the bird's-eye views. Around the corner, the Art Deco post office is decorated with reliefs of Hermes and Isis winging letters to their destination (as the Italians say, *magari!*—if it were only true!)

In Via Duomo, the **Museo Civico** (*open 10–12, 3–6; Sun 10–12; closed Mon*) is a treat for fans of extrovert baroque painter and inveterate womanizer Sebastiano Ricci, who chased commissions and skirts as far as England; his *Hercules and Omphale* and *The Fall of Phaeton* are among his best work. You can also learn about some interesting if obscure local painters from the 1300–1800s, and there are good sculptures by Il Riccio and native Andrea Brustolon; the antiquities section has finds from the Paleoveneti necropoli at Mel, which yielded grave goods from the 8th–2nd century BC. Via Mezzaterra/Via Rialto follow the ancient Roman *castrum* by way of atmospheric **Piazza del Mercato**, a picture-perfect little square with arcades and a fountain from 1410. To the south Via Mezzaterra ends at the 12th-century **Porta Ruga** and a postcard view of the Piave valley and the mountains. Also have a look at the Gothic **Santo Stefano** (1468) in Via Roma, where a 15th-century relief of the Madonna in her merciful umbrella pose guards the door, leading into a handsome striped interior.

If you don't have time for a foray into the Dolomites, take the bus to the **Alpe del Nevegàl**, 12km south of Belluno, for gorgeous views, skiing in the winter and a chairlift to the Rifugio Brigata Alpina Cadore (5250ft), with an alpine garden. From the refuge it's an easy three-hour walk up to the **Col Visentin**, site of another refuge that commands a unique panorama: north across the sea of Dolomite peaks and south to the Venetian Lagoon. The hills of the **Alpago** are another popular weekend destination, especially the **Lago di Santa Croce**, a popular windsurfing venue, the focal point for its small villages: aim for **Pieve d'Alpago** in a lovely setting or **Tambre**, on the edge of the forest of Cansiglio (*see* above).

Feltre: the Dead Man and SS. Vittore e Corona

West from Belluno the SS50 skirts the Piave and the southern flank of the Dolomites on its way to hilltop Feltre. Sacked by the troops of Emperor Maximilian in during the War of the League of Cambrai, Feltre was immediately rebuilt and has changed little since, especially the houses along **Via Mezzaterra**, with their faded frescoes and dozens of marble plaques, all hammered into illegibility by someone who had it in for Feltre's memories. The jewel on Via Mezzaterra is the picturesque **Piazza Maggiore**, where a very quizzical Lion of St Mark stands vigil over the castle, the church of **San Rocco** has a fountain by Tullio Lombardo, and the superb 16th-century **Palazzo dei Rettori** (now the Municipio) is decked out with a Palladian portico. Inside, a small wooden theatre built in 1684 saw the production of Goldoni's first plays. In the centre of Piazza Maggiore, a statue honours the great Renaissance educator Vittorino da Feltre, whose famous school in Mantua taught the sons and daughters of the nobility sent from all over Italy and Europe, as well as the gifted poor. Vittoriano was the first in modern times to elevate gymnastics to the status it held in ancient Greek times, as an equal to languages, arithmetic and logic.

The Palazzo Villabuono, by the town's east gate on Via L. Luzzo 23, houses the **Museo Civico** (*closed for restoration at time of writing*) which has among its archaeological collection an altar to the *anna perrena* (the year), and among its paintings works by Gentile Bellini, Cima da Conegliano and Feltre's own contribution to the Renaissance, Lorenzo Luzzo, better known by his punk nickname *Il Morto da Feltre*, the Dead Man, given to him because of his unusual pallor. The *Transfiguration*, the Dead Man's most acclaimed work, is nearby in the sacristy of the church of **Ognissanti**. Back towards the centre, on Via del Paradiso 8, the **Galleria d'Arte Moderna Carlo Rizzarda** (*open June–Sept, Tues–Sun 10–1 and 4–7; adm*) features a collection of beautiful works in wrought iron, much of it from the forge of the local master Carlo Rizzarda (1883–1931).

Five kilometres from Feltre, signposted off the Treviso road (SS473), the Romanesque **Sanctuary of SS. Vittore e Corona** (*open April–Sept 8–12 and 3–7; Oct–Mar 9–12 and 3–6*) sits on Monte Miesna, up a steep little road. Built in 1100 and almost unchanged since, it shelters the remains of Vittore, a Roman soldier martyred in Syria in 171, and Corona (Stephania), who converted at the sight of his martyrdom and got the same herself. For such early saints, their story is very well documented and is illustrated by the frescoes in the cloister; their bodies spent a few centuries on Cyprus before the Venetians brought the relics here in 1096. The little apse is filled with their elevated sarcophagus, decorated with wind-blown acanthus (note the relief of Vittore on the underside); behind, look for the capitals inscribed with red Kufic script, reading 'The Universe is God'. The bishop's throne was carved from a single block; the frescoes go back to the 1200s, by the schools of Tommaso da Modena and Giotto. A number of figures are copied directly from Padua's Scrovegni Chapel—Giotto himself sold the reproduction rights. Don't miss the *Last Supper*, where the artist tried to paint prawns but drew scorpions instead.

Belluno ✉ 32100

Most people head up into the mountains, but if you want to stay, there are a few choices. Just west of the centre, the well-run ★★★★**Villa Carpenada**, Via Mier 158, ✆ 0437 948 343, @ 0437 948 345 (*expensive*) offers quiet rooms in an 18th-century villa. ★★★**Astor**, Piazza dei Martiri 26-E, ✆ 0437 942 094, @ 0437 942 493 (*moderate*) offers good value and comfortable, central rooms. Within walking distance of the station, ★★★**Delle Alpi**, Via J. Tasso 13, ✆ 0437 940 545, @ 0437 940 565, (*moderate–inexpensive*) has welcoming rooms and one of the best restaurants in town, specializing in seafood ferried up from the coast. *Closed Sun, some of Aug.* **Al Borgo**, in an 18th-century villa south of the Piave, Via Anconetta 8, ✆ 0437 926 755 (*moderate*) is another favourite place to eat, serving traditional favourites. *Closed Mon eve and Tues.*

Pieve d'Alpago ✉ 32010

Just outside Pieve in the hamlet of Plois, you'll find one of the top restaurants in all Venetia: **Dolada**, Via Dolada 9, ✆ 0437 479 141, @ 0437 478 068 (*very expensive*), overlooking Lago di Santa Croce and its surroundings. Wood panelling, candlelight and romance accompany inspired dishes in the best Italian tradition: homemade pasta, the celebrated *zuppa dolada*, superb fish, duck and lamb dishes and an exceptional wine list. *Closed Mon lunch and Tues, exc in July and Aug.* It also has rooms.

Feltre ✉ 32032

For all modern facilities, from parking to a private park, the place to go in Feltre is the ★★★★**Doriguzzi**, Viale del Piave 2, ✆ 043 92902, @ 043 983 660 (*expensive*), in a historic palazzo near the station.

The Dolomites

The Dolomites

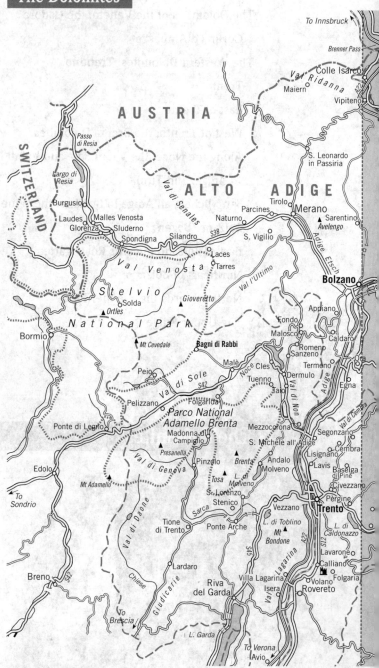

For Beauty's nothing
but beginning of Terror we're still just able to bear

Rilke, *The Duino Elegies*

There are mountains, and then there are the Dolomites. 'The most beautiful *construction* in the world', Le Corbusier called the range, made by the tiniest of architects—corals, billions upon billions of them, labouring in the primordial ocean 250 million years ago. Their masterpiece was thrust up from the sea bed 60 million years ago, to be honed and sharpened by aeons of ice and storms. Otherworldly peaks claw at the sky, each monumental sculpted range a petrified tempest of jagged needles, cloud-stabbing pinnacles and tremendous sheer walls, dyed a glowing rose by the dawn and blood-red by the setting sun.

These most romantic of mountains were named after a wandering French mineralogist with a fantastical name, Dieudonné Sylvain Guy Tancrède de Gratet de Dolomieu, who in 1789 was the first to describe their mineral content. Marmolada (10,961ft) is the highest peak in a range that has glaciers even in summer (17 other peaks top 10,000ft), but elsewhere the snow fields convert in July to a massive bouquet of wild flowers, streaked with blue gentians, yellow alpine poppies and buttercups, edelweiss, and pink rhododendron. The air and light in autumn are so sharp and fine they can break your heart.

Getting Around the Dolomites

Even the heirs of the Romans can only make the **trains** go so far in the mountains. The line north from Venice, Treviso and Belluno passes through Pieve di Cadore before petering out in Calalzo di Cadore, 35km from Cortina d'Ampezzo (2½ hours from Venice). The western Dolomites are linked by the main line between Verona and Munich, by way of Trento (1½ hours) and Bolzano (2½ hours) to the Brenner Pass (4 hours). Branch lines run from Bolzano to Merano and Malles Venosta, to the west, and from near Bressanone to Brunico and San Candido to the east.

To make up for the lack of trains, the Dolomites are exceptionally well served by two **bus** companies—*Dolomiti-Bus* in the east (for example, with daily routes to Agordo, Arabba, Falcade, and Colle S. Lucia from Venice) and the cheerful but still *SAD Buses* in the west. Besides their normal runs, the companies add special scenic tours in July and August from the major centres.

When to Go

Prices skyrocket in the Dolomites during their high-season periods (Christmas holidays, end of January to Easter, mid-July to mid-September). To avoid high prices and the crowds, try to go in June, early July or late September–October, when the alpine refuges are open but not packed to the gills, or immediately after the New Year holidays for skiing, when everyone else has to go back to work and the resorts offer big discounts. May and November are dead.

Mountain Sports

hiking

One is tempted to lapse into Italian hyperbole about hiking in the Dolomites—but suffice it to say it's as close as some of us will ever get to heaven. There are routes for everyone from semi-couch-potatoes to the rock-grappling daredevils, and eight **High Trails of the Dolomites** (*Alte Vie delle Dolomiti*) designed for those 'vagabonds of the path' who fall in between the two extremes. The trails range from 120–180km in length, and are designed to take the average walker two weeks.

Equipment: The High Trails have the virtue of keeping you on top of mountains and plateaux for most of their length. While they do not require special climbing skill, they do demand a stout pair of hiking boots with good rubber soles (80 per cent of accidents are caused by slipping) and protection against sudden storms, even in the middle of summer. A telescopic walking stick for descents and a mobile phone in case of emergencies are also recommended.

Maps: There are two good sets of maps that include the *Alte Vie* and other paths as well, and point out the location of the Alpine refuges: *Carta dei Sentieri e Rifugi*, Edizioni Tabacco Udine, and *Maps Kompass-Wanderkarten*, Edizioni Fleishmann-Starnberg. Both are scale 1:50,000, and are readily available at news-stands in the region. The relevant tourist offices have booklets on each trail in English that contain all the basic information, including phone numbers of the refuges. They also give a good idea of the level of difficulty of each trail.

Refuges: Strategically placed *rifugi alpini* provide shelter, but if you come when they are closed you'll need to carry camping gear. The refuges are open from the end of June to the end of September; in July and August it's wise to book a bed in advance to avoid disappointment. They vary dramatically. Many are owned by the Italian Alpine Club; others are privately owned, primarily by ski resorts. Some are along trails; others may be reached via cable car. All offer bed and board; nearly all now require that you bring a sleeping sheet, or buy one on the site. Prices vary mainly by altitude: the higher up and more difficult of access, the more expensive. Besides these refuges, there are the *baite* (wooden huts), *casere* (stone huts) and bivouacs (beds but no food) found along some of the higher trails: they generally have no custodians but offer shelter.

Write to the tourist offices in Belluno, Trento, and Bolzano for more information, or the **Italian Alpine Club** (CAI, Via Fonseca Pimental 7, 20121 Milan, ✆ 02 2614 1378, ✉ 02 2614 1395. Many of the 200 alpine refuges in Trentino are operated by the *Società degli Alpinisti Tridentini* (SAT), a branch of the CAI, at Via Manci 57, 38100 Trento, ✆ 04 6198 1871, ✉ 04 6198 6462. In the Alto Adige, the address is CAI, Piazza dell'Erbe 46, 39100 Bolzano, ✆ 0471 971 694.

skiing

The Dolomites are like a candy shop for winter sports junkies. As the sunny side of the Alps they enjoy good clear weather, and when it snows, it falls delightfully dry and powdery. There is a variety of slopes of all levels of difficulty, and country trails, toboggan and bobsled runs, ice rinks and speed-skating courses; if all of the ski runs were ironed out flat they would stretch from the Brenner Pass to Reggio Calabria. There are other bonuses as well: ski schools in July, and indoor heated pools in the middle of winter. Write ahead to the tourist offices in Belluno, Trento or Bolzano, or book a week's *Settimana Bianca* package (a week's room and board at a hotel, ski-pass and instruction) from CIT (Citalia) or other travel offices all over Italy. If you want to try as many resorts as possible, the *Dolomiti Superski* pass, 'the world's most extensive ski pass', gives unlimited access (for about $50/£35 a day) to 464 lifts and 1180km of ski runs for periods of one, two, or three weeks. For the latest information and prices, contact *www.DolomitiSuperski.com*, ✆ 04 7179 5397, ✉ 04 7179 4282.

The Dolomites of the Veneto: the Cadore

Although mostly Italian-speaking, much of the Cadore, the district north of Belluno along the upper Piave, was incorporated into Italy only after the First World War. Its somewhat overripe, fashionable, but beautifully positioned heart is Cortina d'Ampezzo, host of the 1956 Winter Olympics, which did much to introduce the Dolomites to the world.

Tourist Information

Pieve di Cadore: Via XX Settembre 18, in Tai, ✆ 0437 31644, 🖷 0435 31645.
Santo Stefano di Cadore: Via Venezia 40, ✆ 0435 62230, 🖷 0435 62077.
Sappada: Borgata Bach 20, ✆ 0435 469 131, 🖷 0435 66233.
San Vito di Cadore: Via Nazionale 9, ✆ 0436 9119, 🖷 0436 99345.

The Piave Valley

The roads north along the river Piave from Belluno (SS50) and Treviso (SS51) meet at the junction of Ponte nelle Alpi before continuing up through scenery marked by the steep pyramids of **Monte Dolada** and **Piz Gallina**. A less benign mountain, **Toc** (6303ft), looms over the town of **Longarone**. In 1963 a landslide from its slopes crashed into the local reservoir, Lake Vaiont, creating a tidal wave that killed nearly two thousand people in Longarone; a memorial church, unfortunately resembling a parking garage, has photos, scale models and a few poignant bits salvaged from the mud. A road runs along the path of the disaster, the lofty and narrow **Gola del Vaiont**, to the lake, 6km to the east.

From Longarone there's also the option of turning west on the SS251 for the **Val Zoldana**, a lovely valley lining the River Maè, on its way past the stunning peaks of Civetta and Pelmo to Selva di Cadore (*see* p.244). Dotted with hamlets in wood and stone and huge barns under rusting corrugated roofs, the Val Zoldana is Italy's *gelato* centre; nearly all of Europe's great homemade ice cream makers are natives, and every November they return for the annual International Ice Cream Fair at Longarone to compare notes, techniques and new flavours.

The main road from Longarone skirts the high banks of the Piave north to the foothills of the Antelao range, 'the King of Cadore', en route to **Pieve di Cadore**. *Pieve* means parish, and from Roman times on this was the most important one in the Cadore, a status that grew with the reputation of that mighty wielder of brush, Tiziano Vecellio (Titian), born here *c.* 1483. His statue stands in the main piazza, and his birthplace, the **Casa Natale di Tiziano** (*open 9.30–12.30 and 4–7; closed Mon; adm*), contains drawings, studies, and some original furnishings. In the church of **Santa Maria Nascente**, the last chapel on the left holds his *Madonna with SS. Andrew and Titian*, starring his own family—his daughter as the Virgin, his son as Titian the Bishop, his brother as St Andrew, while Titian himself looks in from the left, holding a staff. The most important building in Pieve doesn't leave room for any false modesty: the **Palazzo della Magnifica Comunità Cadorina** (*same hours as Titian's birthplace*). Built in 1525, it now houses the local historical museum, with pre-Roman weapons, 2nd-century BC bronze figurines, and more. Towards Tai, at the crossroads, the **Museo degli Occhiaia** (*open 9.30–12 and 3.30–7; adm*) contains a rare collection of antique spectacles. But what Pieve is proudest of these days is Babbo Natale (the Italian Santa Claus), who has made the town his home, with a Christmas-letter answering service for the *bambini*.

The road follows the Piave north past the end of the rail line at **Calalzo**, with buses for **Santo Stefano di Cadore**, the old capital of the federated Cadore villages, now thoroughly converted to its new tourism vocation. Just up from Santo Stefano, in **San Pietro di Cadore**, you'll find something unique in the mountains: a Veneto-style villa, **Palazzo Poli-de Pol** (1665), designed by Longhena and now the town hall; you can step in to see the frescoes. At San Pietro you can make a detour up the charming wooded **Valle Visdende**, or continue up the Piave to the popular if a bit overbuilt resort of **Sappada**; **Cimasappada**, another 4km up the road, has retained more of its traditional mountain character. A road from Cimasappada follows the Piave up to its source, marked by a monument.

From Pieve di Cadore there is also a direct road to Cortina d'Ampezzo, the SS51, which winds through the **Valle del Boite** with its many rustic wooden chalets, between the Antelao massif and **Monte Pelmo**, one of the most unusual and striking peaks in the Dolomites. The road passes through **Borca di Cadore** and the more important resort of **San Vito di Cadore** with its lake, an excellent base for ascending Pelmo.

Where to Stay and Eating Out

Sappada ✉ 32047

One reason for Sappada's popularity is its abundance of reasonably priced accommodation. At little ★★★**Haus Michaela**, Borgata Fontana 40, ✆ 0435 469 377, ✉ 0435 66131 (*moderate*) the emphasis is on fitness, with an indoor pool, sauna and gym (*open Dec–Easter and June–Sept*). Cheaper choices are ★★**Corona Ferrea**, Borgata Kratten 17, ✆ 0435 469 103, ✉ 0435 469 103 (*inexpensive*), which has comfortable rooms, all with bath (*open July–20 Sept, 20 Dec–15 April*), and the small ★★★**Sierra Hof**, Borgata Soravia 110, ✆ 0435 469 110, ✉ 0435 469 647 (*inexpensive*) near the centre of the village. Tiny and romantic **Keisn**, Borgata Kratten 8, ✆ 0435 469 070 (*expensive*) has the best food in the area (try the delicious *sformatino di zucchine* if it's on the menu) and wonderful desserts. *Closed Wed, Thurs lunch, June and Oct.*

In Cima Sappada, 4km away, ★★★**Belvedere**, Piazza Cima 93, ✆/✉ 0435 469 112 (*moderate*) has only 14 rooms, but does have its own sauna and a good restaurant (*open to non-residents*): mountain specialities include variations on venison and tasty desserts. *Open Dec–Mar, mid-June–Sept.* ★★★**Bellavista**, Via Cima, ✆ 0435 469 175, ✉ 0435 66194 (*moderate*) has had a recent remodelling; lovely views and mountain bike hire. *Open Dec–Easter, mid-June–Sept.*

San Vito di Cadore ✉ 32046

There are a number of comfortable hotels here: the best is ★★★★**Marcora**, Via Roma 28, ✆ 0436 9101, ✉ 0436 99156 (*very expensive*), in a fine setting with a pool. *Open 20 June–10 Sept, 20 Dec–20 Mar.* ★★★**Cima Belprá**, Via Calvi 1, at Chiapuzza, ✆ 0436 890 441, ✉ 0436 890 418 (*moderate–inexpensive*) is a welcoming place with the best restaurant in the whole area, **La Scaletta** (open to non-guests) with beautiful views, and traditional polenta and beef dishes. *Closed Mon out of season, and Nov.*

Cortina is the sort of place where David Niven and Audrey Hepburn would sit about in a café in turtlenecks and sunglasses, but it also enjoys the best location in the Dolomites: a lofty (1224–3243m), sunny, cross-shaped meadow at the junction of the Boite and Bigontina valleys, in the centre of a ring of extraordinary mountains—Tofane, the great 'mount owl' (scene of the 1997 World Championship); Cristallo, the 'crystal' mountain; Sorapis, licked by stony flames; and the Cinque Torri, the 'five towers'.

Devoted heart and soul to the sporting life, Cortina is almost as well known for its night-time activities in winter, when the *après ski* crowd fills its clubs to trip the light fantastic until the wee hours of dawn. But whatever worldly pleasure and delight this snowy fleshpot offers, it comes at a price, rating right up there with Venice herself on the bottom line of the tab.

Getting Around

Cortina's **bus** station is just off Via Marconi, and is served by SAD (℗ 1678 46047) and Dolomiti buses (℗ 0435 332 155). Services are greatly augmented in June–Sept, when buses serve virtually every paved road in the region; SAD buses make the Great Dolomites Road once a day (*see* p.278). There's one bus a day direct from Venice or Treviso (℗ 042 15944). The nearest **train** stations are Dobbiaco, 32km north (on the Bolzano–Lienz line), or Calalzo di Cadore, 35km south; both have regular bus connections to Cortina.

Tourist Information

Piazzetta S. Francesco 8, near the central Piazza Venezia, ℗ 0436 3231, ℗ 0436 3235, e-mail: *apt1@sunrise.it*. They have an accommodation service, good trail maps, and information about excursions and the *Dolomiti Superski* pass. The local alpine guides are next door, open in July, August and September, ℗ 0436 868505.

The Sporting Life

The 1956 Olympics endowed Cortina with superb winter sports facilities; here you can ski-jump, speed-skate, fly down bobsled and luge runs, and cut figures of eight in the ice stadium, not to mention the thousand and one downhill and cross-country ski runs in the vicinity. In the summer, it's an excellent base for hikers, rock climbing, delta planing, torrentialism and more, while in town there's a riding school, tennis, summer/winter swimming pools, and activities like the Ice Disco Dance in the Olympic Ice Stadium.

Cortina has its share of trendy shops, and a museum of contemporary art you can take in if it rains—the **Museo Ciasa de Ra Regoles**, Via del Parco, on the corner of Corso d'Italia, (*open 10.30–12.30, 4–7.30, closed Mon; adm*) has sections on palaeontology and ethnography, and art by De Pisis, Morandi, De Chirico and others. Two cable cars from Cortina wait to whisk you up to the mountains, both at the end of the town bus lines: in the north, near the Olympic stadium, to **Tofana di Mezzo** (10,640ft) where there are privately run alpine refuges, and in the west, to **Tondi di Faloria** (7687ft).

Expect to run up against the full-or half-board requirement nearly everywhere in Cortina in its high season (it's an old tradition in these parts: the ancient Greek writer Polybius wrote that in Cisalpine Gaul travellers at inns always requested the price for their whole stay, rather than have itemized accounts as elsewhere—history's first full-board arrangements). It may be mortifying to the pocketbook, but not to the flesh; the local cuisine is usually as *haute* as the price.

luxury–very expensive

If you're putting on the dog in Cortina, the place to do it is the ★★★★★**Miramonti Majestic**, Via Miramonti 103, ✆ 0436 4201, @ 0436 867 019. Warm, traditional and rustic, it has pretty wooden balconies affording magnificent views. The well-designed rooms have all imaginable creature comforts, and there's an indoor pool, tennis courts, golf, exercise facilities and sauna. *Open July–Aug, Christmas–Mar.*

If you'd rather be in the centre of action, the historic ★★★★**De La Poste**, Piazza Roma 14, ✆ 0436 4271, @ 0436 868 435, is a large alpine chalet with classy rooms and balconies; the Poste's terrace and bar see much of Cortina's social round, especially in the evening; half-pension mandatory in high season.

expensive

Ten minutes' walk from the centre, down at the bottom of the valley beside the river, another alpine chalet, ★★★★**Corona**, Via Val di Sotto 10, ✆ 0436 3251, @ 0436 867 339, is memorable for a modern art collection even more extensive than the one in the museum; it's also more convenient than most for the ski lift. *Open June–Sept, Dec–Mar.* Award-winning ★★★**Da Beppe Sello**, Via Ronco 68, ✆ 0436 3236, @ 0436 3237, is warm and welcoming, and serves some of the best food in Cortina, with game specialities in season. *Open Nov–Easter, mid-May–mid-Sept.*

moderate

The charmer in this price category is an 800-year-old farmhouse that's been run as an inn by the same family for the past century, ★★★**Menardi**, Via Majon 110, ✆ 0436 2400, @ 0436 862 183, furnished with antiques and bedecked with fresh flowers. *Open 20 June–20 Sept, 20 Dec–10 April.* Small, friendly and, by Cortina standards, cheap, is the ★★**Cavallino**, Corso d'Italia 142, ✆/@ 0436 2614.

inexpensive

★★★**Imperio**, Via C. Battisti 66, ✆ 0436 4246, @ 0436 4248, is an unpretentious hotel with no restaurant but adequate rooms, all with bath (*closed May*); as a second choice try the ★★**Montana**, Corso Italia 94, ✆ 0436 860 498, @ 0436 868 211. The tourist office issues lists of self-catering flats and rooms in private houses.

Eating Out

Elegant **El Toulà**, Via Ronco 123, ✆ 0436 3339, near Pocol (*expensive*), in a refurbished wooden farmhouse, specializes in perfect grilled meats, roast lamb, and desserts with a Tyrolean touch, accompanied by a renowned wine list. *Open Christmas–Easter, 15 July–30 Aug only; closed Mon.* Its rival, **Tivoli**, northeast of the centre at Via Lacedel 34, ℂ 0436 866 400 (*expensive*) offers lovely views and innovative, ultra-refined cuisine. *Closed Mon.* A brief walk up the hill behind town brings you to **Al Camin**, Via Alverà 99, ℂ 0436 862 010 (*moderate*), cosy with lots of wood and a fireplace, serving local versions of polenta and goulash. *Closed Mon.*

Excursions from Cortina

At a major crossroads, Cortina offers numerous forays into the surrounding mountains. For the classic Great Dolomites Road between Cortina and Bolzano, *see* p.278.

Tourist Information

Auronzo: Via Roma 10, ℂ 0435 9359, ✉ 0435 400 161.
Dobbiaco: Via delle Dolomiti 3, ℂ 0474 72132, ✉ 0474 72730.
Alleghe: Piazza Kennedy 17, ℂ 0437 523 333, ✉ 0437 723 881.
Agordo: Via Sommariva 10, ℂ 0437 62105, ✉ 0437 65205.

Lake Misurina and Around

For a beautiful short trip from Cortina, take the SS48 and SS48b over the lofty **Tre Croci pass** to **Lake Misurina**, shimmering below the jagged peaks of Sorapis and the remarkable triple-spired **Tre Cime di Lavaredo**, 15km northeast of Cortina. The colours of Misurina are so brilliant they look touched-up on the postcards; as a resort it makes a quiet alternative to Cortina, especially if ice skating is your sport. From Misurina it's a magnificent 7km drive up to the **Rifugio Auronzo**, located just beneath the Tre Cime di Lavaredo, where you can make the easy walk to the 1916 **Bersaglieri Memorial**, honouring Italy's famous sharpshooters.

Circular Routes from Misurina to Cortina

There are two possible circular routes from Misurina back to Cortina that make rewarding, full-day excursions. Both begin to the east on the SS48 via **Auronzo di Cadore**, past a peak known as the **Corno del Doge** for its resemblance to the Doge's horned bonnet. Auronzo, on the shores of an artificial lake, surrounded by fragrant spruce forests, makes another good alternative base, and has a cable car and chairlifts up **Monte Agudo**.

From Auronzo you can circle south around Pieve di Cadore and the Valle di Boite (161km altogether; *see* above, pp.242–3) or take the longer route around to the north (224km) through **Comelico** and the beautiful **Val di Sesto**, noted for its traditional wooden houses. Just south of the modern village of **Sesto** a short branch valley, the **Val Fiscalina/Fischleintal** is one of the most dramatic in all the Dolomites, skirting the edge of the **Parco Naturale Dolomiti di Sesto**. The Val Fiscalina is nicknamed 'Sesto's Sundial'; from here the peaks—from One to Nine—are divinely arranged to catch the sun and tell the hour.

At Sesto the route passes into the Alto Adige, passing by way of **San Candido/Innichen**, a pretty resort on the river Drava; it has a Benedictine monastery and a lovely Romanesque church, the early 13th-century **Collegiata SS. Candidus e Corbinian**, decorated with works from the period: a superb *Crucifixion* in polychrome wood, Gothic frescoes in the tribune, and sculptures in the recently restored crypt. The Collegiate's treasure and manuscripts are in an adjacent museum (*open June–mid-Oct, Thurs–Sat 5–5, Sun 10–11; mid-July–Aug, Tues–Sun 10–11, 5–7*). Another museum in San Candido, the **Museo Mineralogico Dolomythos**, in the Villa Wachtler, Via Peter Paul Rainer 9 (*open Mon–Sat 10–12, 4–7, adm*), is devoted to the bizarre geological and mythical history of the Dolomites.

The turn back to Cortina (SS51) is at **Dobbiaco/Toblach**, one of the original Dolomite resorts thanks to its magnificent setting, a lake, and a railway station built by the Habsburgs. The large **castle** in the old town was built for Venice's arch-enemy Emperor Maximilian in 1500. In July Dobbiaco holds a series of concerts in honour of Mahler, who spent his summers here; in summer, too, you can visit the little **Museo Gustav Mahler**, 4km from the centre at Casa Trenker (*ring the tourist office for hours*). From Dobbiaco, the road heads south to Cortina past the wooded Lago di Dobbiaco, then enters the dramatic **Val di Landro**, with the Cristallo group looming ahead over **Carbonin/Schluderbach**. Beyond are a pair of little lakes, the Black and the White, and the lonely ruins of the **Castel Sant'Umberto**. The road then circles around castle-crowned **Podestagno**, before descending into the Ampezzo with the Le Tofane group storming up to the right.

Cortina to Colle Santa Lucia and Agordo

There are two routes to these mountains southwest of Cortina: the main one follows the Great Dolomites Road (*see* p.278) through the Falzarego Pass before taking the SS203 southwards at Andraz, while an alternative, lesser-known but equally pretty route takes the smaller SS638 road through the **Passo di Giau**, where in recent years some of the most important mesolithic tombs in Europe (5000 BC) were discovered. The remains and artefacts of 'Mondeval man' can now be seen down in **Selva di Cadore**, in the **Museo Storico** (*open July and Aug, 4–6.30*) along with a reconstruction of the tombs. Selva is a growing resort in the lovely Val Fiorentina, where a road crosses into the Valle di Zoldana and ends up at Longarone (*see* p.242). Above Selva, **Colle Santa Lucia** is a pretty place with its old agricultural hamlets and a beautiful belvedere (31km from Cortina).

Continuing south from Colle Santa Lucia, the road passes **Caprile** and the mighty north wall of Civetta en route to **Àlleghe** with its lovely lake, formed in 1771 by a landslide from Civetta. At **Cencenighe** you have the option of turning off for Falcade and San Martino di Castrozza (*see* p.259), or continuing on to **Àgordo** (45km), an attractive town and resort along one of the principal branches of the Piave. The Passo Duran above Agordo leads back to Cortina via the Valle di Zoldo and the village of **Dont** (another 21km)—where, in spite of its name, you *do* have splendid views of Civetta and Pelmo, and do have the chance to buy local woodcrafts.

Where to Stay and Eating Out

Misurina ✉ 32040

★★★**Lavaredo**, Via Monte Piana 11, ℂ 0436 39227, ℮ 0436 39127 (*moderate*) has tennis courts and a good restaurant (*closed Nov–mid-Dec*), while ★★**Dolomiti des Alpes**, Via Monte Piana, ℂ 0436 39031, ℮ 0436 39216 (*inexpensive*), just above the lake, has a sauna-solarium. *Closed Oct–mid-Dec.* Overlooking Lake Misurina ★**Sport**, Via Monte Piana 18, ℂ/℮ 0436 39125 (*inexpensive*) has simple rooms.

Auronzo di Cadore ✉ 32041

Auronzo has far more choices: ★★★**Auronzo**, Via Roma 30, ✆ 0435 400 202, ⓔ 0435 99879 (*moderate*) is a cosy old place with tennis and a park on the lake shore. *Open Dec–Mar and June–Sept.* ★★**Vienna**, Via Verona 2, ✆ 0435 9394 (*inexpensive*) is near the lake with good views of the mountains. On the road east of Auronzo at Cima Gogna, **Cavaliere**, ✆ 0435 9834 (*moderate*) serves delicious sucking pig and risotto with herbs or mushrooms, amid traditional, wood-panelled décor. *Closed Wed.*

San Candido/Innichen ✉ 39038

The award-winning ★★★**Orso Grigio**, Via Rainer 2, ✆ 0474 913 115, ⓔ 0474 914 182 (*expensive–moderate*) has charming modern rooms in a handsome 18th-century building. *Open Jan–April, mid-June–mid-Oct.* Central, traditional ★★★**Posthotel**, Via Sesto 1, ✆ 0474 913 133, ⓔ 0474 913 635 (*expensive–moderate*) offers plenty of activities, including a games room for children, a Turkish bath, pool and solarium, and excellent local and international dishes in its restaurant. **Uhrmacher's Weinstube**, Via Tintori 1, ✆ 0474 913 158, is a special treat for wine or spirit lovers; visit the cellar and choose a wine to go with a snack, or try a glass from one of the thirty or so bottles they open every day. *Closed Wed, exc summer.*

Dobbiaco/Toblach ✉ 39034

Since 1911, the same family has run the recently renovated ★★★★**Cristallo**, Via S. Giovanni 37, ✆ 0474 972 138, ⓔ 0474 972 755 (*expensive*), a fine resort hotel in a beautiful setting, with an indoor pool and sauna. *Open Christmas–Easter, Jun–mid-Oct.* Dine at **Winkelkeller**, Via Conte Künigi 8, ✆ 0474 972 022 (*moderate*) on refined mountain cuisine. *Closed Wed, June and part of Oct.*

Selva di Cadore ✉ 32020

A fine place both to stay and to eat is ★★★**Giglio Rosso**, at Pescul, ✆ 0437 720 310, ⓔ 0437 521 110 (*moderate*), the kitchen does a fine mulberry risotto and turkey in beer. *Open Dec–Mar, June–Sept.*

Àlleghe/Caprile ✉ 32022

★★★**Coldai**, Via Coldai 13, ✆ 0437 523 305, ⓔ 0437 523 438 (*moderate–inexpensive*) has lovely views over the lake and pleasant rooms. *Closed May–mid-June, Oct, Nov.* The 130-year-old ★★★★**Alla Posta**, Piazza Dogliani 19, in Caprile ✆ 0437 721 171, ⓔ 0437 721 677 (*expensive*) is the most prestigious hotel, with TVs in each of its comfortable rooms, indoor pool, sauna and good restaurant. *Open 20 Dec–15 April, 15 June–30 Sept.* ★★**Marmolada**, Corso Veneto 27, ✆ 0437 721 107 (*inexpensive*) is simple but adequate—who wants to be indoors anyway? *Closed May, Oct.*

The Western Dolomites: Trentino

The autonomous, exceptionally well-organized and beautiful province of Trentino encompasses the western Dolomites, including the stunning Val di Fassa and the Brenta Group, majestically isolated from its sisters west of the Adige. Unlike the Alto Adige/Süd Tirol further north, Trentino is mostly Italian in language and heritage, sprinkled with a Ladin minority in the valleys. And Trento itself is a fine little art city, worth a day on its own.

Getting Around

Frequent trains and buses follow the Adige from Verona to Trento, stopping at the main towns. Getting off at the station in Rovereto is more fun than it used to be, with three life-size dinosaurs as a welcoming committee.

Tourist Information

Rovereto: Via Dante 63, ☎ 0464 430 363, ✆ 0464 435 528.
Lavarone: Municipio, ☎ 0464 784 151, *aptlavarone@seldati.it.*

From Verona to Trento: Up the Val Lagarina

From Verona, the A22 and SS12 follow the Adige up through the Valpolicella and the Monti Lessini, and enter Trentino near **Avio**, dominated by the proud 14th-century **Castello di Sabbionara** (*open Tues–Sun 10–1 and 2–6, until 5 in winter; closed Jan; adm*). This is only one of 29 castles that guarded the Val Lagarina, one of the main routes from the Mediterranean to northern Europe. Its owners, the Counts of Castelbarco, gave it to Venice in 1411, but after the Republic enlarged and decorated it, Emperor Maximilian snatched it in 1509, in the War of the Cambrai. The guardhouse preserves a wonderful 14th-century fresco of battling knights, the *Parata dei Combattenti*, perhaps painted to inspire the soldiers, while the keep has frescoes of courtly love, divided by painted fur hangings, attributed to an International Gothic master from Verona.

Rovereto, the 'Athens of the Trentino'

Further up the Adige, Rovereto is an evocative old place swimming in a sea of vineyards. It has a hallowed scholarly tradition: in the 1750s it had its own Academy, with a funny name, *degli Agiati*, 'of the slow coaches' and in 1769 it became the first city in Italy to hear the young Mozart play; in 1797 it was the birthplace of philospher Antonio Rosmini. Piled on top of the town, its landmark **Castello** was first built by the Castelbarco family, then rebuilt with its fat towers in 1416–87 by the Venetians, when Rovereto formed the northern extent of the Serenissima; they lost it after a 40-day siege by the Austrian Archduke. This area was also hotly contested in the First World War, as remembered in the castle's extensive **War Museum** (*open Mar–Nov, Tues–Sun 8.30–12.30 and 2–6; July–Sept 8.30–6.30; adm*). Below the castle in Piazza del Podestà, there's a spooky Fascist memorial to the Legione Trentini and local war heroes, as well as a handsome Venetian Municipio, originally the Palazzo Pretorio (1417). The other thing the Venetians did for Rovereto was introduce silk worms and mulberry trees into the economy; it was especially big in the 16th–18th centuries, when Italy had its own 'silk routes' just like China; picturesque **silk houses**, which provided the power to run the mills, overhang the river Leno below the castle.

A native of Rovereto, the Futurist Fortunato Depero (1892–1960) worked for many years in the town, and bequeathed it to the **Museo Depero**, Via della Terra 53, in the medieval centre (*open 9–12.30, 2.30–6; closed Mon; adm*). This perfect and rather striking little museum was designed by the artist himself as a showcase for his tapestries, puppets and paintings, dedicated to 'the Futurist reconstruction of the Universe'. This uniquely Italian school of the 20th century, which blindly believed in progress and speed and wanted to blow up St Mark's and ban spaghetti, produced some memorable works in spite of itself, the focus of Rovereto's **Archivio del '900**, on Corso A. Rosmini 58 (*open Oct–Mar 9–12.30 and 2.30–6; summer 2.30–7; closed Mon; adm*).

Another native, the great archaeologist Paolo Orsi, willed his private collection of statues, busts and vases from Magna Graecia to the city's **Museo Civico** in the Palazzo Parolari at Borgo S. Caterina 43 (*open Tues–Sat 9–12 and 3–6*). Now installed in its new headquarters, this is the third oldest museum in Italy, founded in 1851. Besides archaeology, other exhibits are on the natural sciences and the old silk industry, and the stars—in the new planetarium.

Cannons from each of the 19 belligerents in the First World War were melted down to make the largest ringing bell in the world, the **Campana dei Caduti**, or *Maria Dolens*. Located on the Colle di Miravalle in the southern quarter of Rovereto, it rings in memory of the victims of all wars every day at sundown. Just southeast of Rovereto, at **Lavini di Marco**, near the cylindrical First World War ossuary and ruined Castle Dante (where the poet sojourned in 1303) you can follow the '**Path of the Dinosaurs**', marked by Jurassic footprints planted 200 million years ago but discovered only by accident in 1991.

Up the Val Lagarina from Rovereto

Across the Adige from Rovereto, **Isera** is the centre for the production of Marzemino, one of Trentino's finest red wines—Mozart found it 'excellent' and the Romans liked it too—a 1st-century AD winemaking villa is currently being excavated. Nearby, the little town of **Villa Lagarina** has a surprisingly rich baroque chapel in its parish church, and a road up to two pretty woodland lakes and the picturesque 13th–15th century **Castel Noarna**, decorated with frescoes glorifying the owners, victories over the Turks, and views of other Trentino castles by a follower of Michelangelo; in the 17th century the castle was the rather nasty scene of numerous witchcraft trials (*to visit, ring ahead, ✆ 0464 435 222*).

Just north of Rovereto, on the right bank of the Adige, **Volano** repays a halt for its Gothic church of **San Rocco**, every square inch brightly frescoed by painters from Verona in the 15th and 16th centuries. Visible from the road, the imposing **Castel Beseno** (*open April–Oct 9–12 and 2–5.30, closed Mon; adm*) is the largest castle in the Trentino, built by the Counts of Castelbarco and inherited by the Tyrolean von Trapp family in 1460, who were responsible for most of the Renaissance improvements and the large space devoted to knightly tournaments. It has a number of well preserved military features, exhibits, and a room frescoed with scenes of the months. In nearby **Calliano**, the atmospheric 13th-century **Castelpietra** was a bulwark of Beseno; it once had a great wall along the Adige and controlled the road by means of an enormous iron door, which impressed Machiavelli but not Napoleon, who knocked it all down. The main Sala del Giudizio has some fascinating frescoes on hunting scenes and the Judgement of Solomon, and one of a man and a magpie—the former in a cage, much to the bird's amusement (*to visit, ring the owners, ✆ 0464 835 044*).

Two small resorts on a 3280ft meadowland below Monte Cornetto can be reached by the SS350 from Calliano: **Folgaria**, with its 17th-century Maso Spilzi, restored to its original appearance (*open June–Sept*) and **Lavarone**, near the crystal-clear Lago di Lavarone, where Freud spent three summers. The Austro-Hungarians heavily fortified this frontier with Italy between 1908–14. Their 'iron curtain of the highlands' had seven forts: one, **Forte Belvedere**, built around a huge three-storey pillbox with enough storage space to support 200 people for three months, has been restored as a museum—only the domes that once housed the three 100mm howitzers have been replaced. The interior has documents and photos relating to the war; according to some historians, the first artillery shots were fired from here against the Italians in 1915 (*open Easter–Oct, 9–6; closed Mon exc in July and Aug; adm*). The '**Path of Peace**' (*Sentiero della Pace*), a long-distance walk along the front lines of the First World War, begins near here and continues to the Stelvio pass.

Where to Stay and Eating Out

Rovereto ✉ 38068

> ★★★**Rovereto**, Corso Rosmini 82/d, ✆ 0464 435 522, ✉ 0464 439 644 (*expensive*) is a fine central hotel, with comfortable air-conditioned rooms in a variety of styles, and an excellent restaurant, **Novecento** (*moderate*), featuring regional dishes, delicious homemade pasta, and a vegetarian menu. *Closed Sun*. There's also a fine, modern **youth hostel**, Via della Scuola 16, ✆ 0464 433 707 (*inexpensive*) near the railway station. The best place to eat is **Al Borgo**, Via Garibaldi 13, ✆ 0464 436 300 (*expensive*), a surprisingly sophisticated little restaurant in the heart of town. The menu features delicious dishes like ham and spinach in puff pastry, risotto with lemon, or turbot with artichokes, followed by fantastic desserts, all accompanied by piano music in the evening. Unusually in Italy, they even bake their own bread. *Closed Sun eve and Mon, part of Feb and July.*

Lavarone/Folgaria ✉ 38046

> Freud stayed at the ★★★**Hotel du Lac** in Frazione Chiesa, ✆ 0464 783 112 ✉ 0464 783 255 (*moderate*). An indoor swimming pool and tennis courts in addition to its pretty setting on the lake make it a fine place to forget your neuroses. Lots of wood and flowers give ★★★**Camminetto**, near the chairlift Bertoldi, ✆/✉ 0464 783 214 (*inexpensive*), its cosy charm. *Open Dec–mid-April, mid-June–Sept*. Dine at Folgaria's **L'Antico Pineta**, Via de Gasperi 66, ✆ 0464 720 327 (*moderate*), a good place to try polenta laden with melted Asiago cheese.

Trento

Lying at the foot of Monte Bondone, between the banks of the Adige and the Fersina, the friendly capital of the Trentino owes much of its charm to the powerful prince-bishops who ruled it for centuries, most notably art patron Bernardo Cles (1514–39). The heritage they left behind is a delightful art city, perhaps in the second division in Italy, but one that would be near the top in any other country in the world. The prince-bishop's Castello di Buonsiglio has a fresco cycle of the months that is worth the trip alone, while the *centro storico*'s gently winding streets are merry with colourful *al fresco* frescoes.

Bernardo Cles was also behind the event that put Trento on the map, when he lobbied for it to become the venue of the great Counter-Reformation council of the Church (*see* p.68). His successor, Prince-Bishop Cristoforo Madruzzo (1539–67), nearly bankrupted his wealthy self in entertaining the dignitaries, but his hard work paid off in other ways, especially in promoting Madruzzo interests throughout Trentino and making the office of prince-bishop a private preserve of his own family for the next three generations.

Getting Around

The **bus** and FS **railway** station are almost next to each other on the Piazza Dante. Atestina buses go up all the valleys in the Trentino, ✆ 0461 983 627. For the Trento-Malè station, with trains up the Val di Non to Cles, turn left out of the main station, and walk 500m to Via Seconda da Trento 7, ✆ 0461 238 350.

Tourist Information

Via Alfieri 4, across the Piazza Dante from the station, ✆ 0461 983 880, ✉ 0461 984 508. **Trentino** regional information: Via Romagnosi 3, ✆ 0461 839 000, ✉ 0461 260 245; *apt@provincia.tn.it*. Free phone information in Italy, ✆ 1678 45034.

To the Duomo

Trento's points of interest can easily be seen on foot. **Piazza Dante**, in front of the station, is a convenient place to start (and find a place to park); the statues of the eponymous poet and other Italian celebrities were erected here, amid the public gardens in 1896 by Trento's irredentist societies in defiance of their Austrian rulers. Next to the station itself, the attractive 12th-century collegiate church of **San Lorenzo** stands in a sunken lawn.

From San Lorenzo, Via Andrea Pozzo and Via D. Orfane lead to pink **Santa Maria Maggiore** (1520), an elegant barrel-vaulted Renaissance church commissioned by Bernardo Cles who had seen Leon Battista Alberti's famous S. Andrea in Mantua, and wanted one for Trento. It was large enough to be used for several sittings of the Council of Trent, and has a beautiful organ gallery by Vincenzo Grandi (1534) and, among the paintings, the *Dispute with the Doctors* by Giambattista Moroni, the 16th-century master from Bergamo.

One block over to the east of S. Maria Maggiore runs Trento's most important street, **Via Belenzani**, forced through the old medieval quarters by Bernardo Cles who wanted a proper straight street to the cathedral. It is lined with fine palaces: the best, **Palazzo Pona Geremia**, was one of the first built in Trento; the façade is entirely covered with recently restored 16th-century frescoes of the locals receiving Emperor Maximilian and mythological subjects. Opposite, the **Palazzo Thun** (now the Municipio) is a far more severe work from the same century, while further down there's the luxurious **Palazzo Quetta**, actually two palaces linked behind a single 16th-century façade, and the elegant late baroque **Palazzo Malfatti Ferrari** with its graceful balconies.

Via Belenzani ends by the handsome porticoed **Case Cazuffi-Rella**, decorated with monochrome frescoes from the 1530s. These overlook **Piazza Duomo** and the 18th-century **fountain of Neptune**, the sea-god symbol of the region—not an obvious mascot until you focus on the trident he wields and recall the city's Roman name, *Tridentum*.

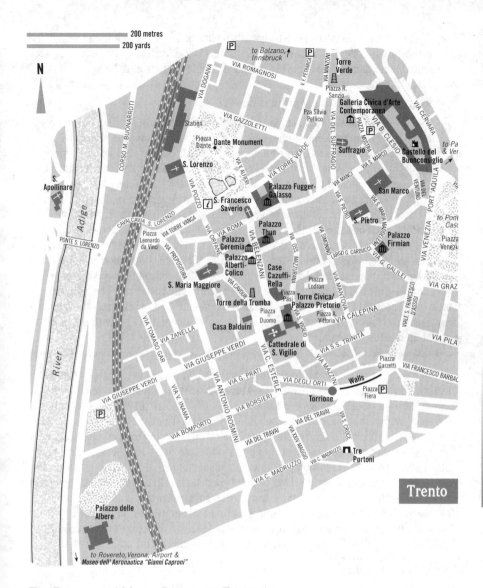

The Duomo and Museo Diocesano Tridentino

Trento's majestic cathedral was designed in the 13th century by Maestro Adamo d'Arogno but completed only in 1515. Although it took 300 years to build (the builders, rather unusually, stuck to the original plans); the style is pure monumental Romanesque, richly decorated with galleries along its three apses and dome. The whole is more impressive than any of the details, but look at the main door, with a Christ Pantocrator in the lunette, the rose window in the transept shaped like the Wheel of Fortune, and the apse door, with a lion porch and three huddled figures called the 'sons of Maestro Adamo'. The Council of Trent held its major sessions here, and its decrees were promulgated before the huge crucifix in a right-hand chapel. The baldacchino over the high altar is a replica of St Peter's, and to the right is the Renaissance tomb of Bernardo Cles. Excavations in 1977 unearthed a 6th-century basilica under the Duomo, the original home of the relics of Trento's patron saint Vigilio.

Vigilio and the Ciusi-Gobj Masquerade

Vigilio was a Roman patrician who studied in Athens, then moved to Trent with his family, where he was made bishop. His persuasive powers were good enough to convert his diocese, but when he went further afield to the Val Rendena and tipped over a statue of Saturn he was stoned to death. He is celebrated every 20–26 June with an enthusiastic Palio dell'Oca, in which teams from each of the city's districts don 17th-century costumes and race down the Adige on rafts, trying to slip a ring over the neck of a papier-mâché goose suspended over the river. The climactic moment comes on 26 June, commemorating the same day back in the Middle Ages when Trento hired workers from Feltre to reinforce the town walls. Food supplies being low, Trento's bishop realized that the city could not afford to feed the workers and sent them home—only the Feltrese returned in the night to raid the stores. The ensuing battle is re-enacted in costume in the Piazza Duomo—the Ciusi are from Feltre, and they have five chances to break the ranks of Trento's Gobj to make off with the prize: a pot of hot, bubbling polenta.

Next to the cathedral, the **Palazzo Pretorio**, crowned with swallowtail battlements and a medieval Torre Civica, houses the excellent **Museo Diocesano Tridentino** (*open 9–12.30, 2.30–6, closed Sun; adm*), renovated and opened by John Paul II in 1995. This contains the Duomo's Treasure and items from churches throughout Trentino. The paintings of the Council of Trent look like class photos; also note a 16th-century portrayal of a *Mass of St Gregory*, its nonchalant congregation sitting next to a band of pious skeletons; three pretty 12th-century ivory caskets made by Islamic craftsmen; an unusual 12th-century enamelled reliquary case, and four charming 15th-century wooden altarpieces from the church of San Zeno in the Val di Non, portraying three martyrs in scenes watched by a man in a beaver hat. The museum's greatest treasure, a cycle of six early 15th-century Flemish tapestries by Peter Van Aelst, woven masterpieces of portraiture and detail, were purchased and brought to Trento by Bernard Cles. The ticket also includes the excavations of the 6th-century basilica.

East of the Cathedral

In the 12th century, this was the first extension of Trent beyond the walls, and it's still called Borgo Nuovo today. Its main attraction is the mannerist-baroque **Palazzo Sardagna** on Via Calepina 14, frescoed inside with a zodiac by Marcello Fogolino, court painter to Bernardo Cles, visible along with the **Museo Tridentino di Scienze Naturali** (*open 9–12.30, 2.30–6, closed Mon*). Its collections date back to the 16th century 'Room of wonders' accumulated by the Madruzzo prince-bishops; newest exhibits contain fossils of the little *Tridentinosaurus antiquus*, a 260-million-year-old reptile that once stalked the Trentino.

Castello del Buonconsiglio and its Museums

Beginning at Via Belenzani (*see* above) Via Manci was the *decumanus* of Tridentium and is graced with another conspicuous house, the late Mannerist **Palazzo Fugger Galasso**, locally known as the Devil's palace; the story goes that the Fuggers enlisted Satan's aid and had it built in a single day. Via Manci leads straight to the residence of the prince-bishops, the **Castello del Buonconsiglio** (*open daily exc Mon, 10–6; winter 9–12 and 4–5.30; adm exp*). Because of Trento's location on the road to Rome, the medieval German Emperors courted the bishops by granting them a regal status that they retained until Napoleon. Originally their home was known as Malconsiglio (from the German *mahl*, or meeting), but as this means 'Bad Council' in Italian it engendered too many jokes and was discreetly changed.

Buonconsiglio is one of the finest castle-residences in Italy. It consists of two buildings—the 13th-century Castelvecchio that once guarded the road, with its Venetian Gothic loggia, and the Magno Palazzo, added by Bernardo Cles in 1528–36. Today both house the provincial museum of art: a fine collection of medieval manuscripts, music codices, wooden sculptures from the 15th and 16th centuries, and paintings, although these are overshadowed by the castle's own decoration commissioned by Bishop Cles: excellent 16th-century frescoes by Marcello Fogolino, Gerolamo Romanino and Dosso Dossi. The latter painted the Olympian gods on the vault, who had to conform to Counter-Reformation modesty levels—gods model turn-of-the-century bathing costumes, and the goddesses look like Tarzan's Jane. Best of all are the ravishing, detailed **Frescoes of the Months** in the Torre dell'Aquila, painted around the year 1400. While the nobility sports and flirts in the foreground, peasants perform their month-by-month labours, tending their flocks, making cheese, planting and harvesting, making wine. One scene has the oldest-known depiction of Trento, dominated by the castle itself. Another tower, the Torre Falco, was frescoed with elaborate hunting scenes (1530–39).

Buonconsiglio also has a historical collection from the Napoleonic era to the Second World War, including a startling Art Deco painting commemorating that important event, the *Allegory of the Annexation of Trentino to Italy* by Luigi Bonazzo. The idea for this museum was suggested back in 1903 by local patriot Cesare Battisti, who had no idea that 13 years later he would be imprisoned, tried and executed for high treason in this same castle by the Austrians, along with his companions Fabio Filzi and Damiano Chiesa. Their cells, the court-room where they were tried and the ditch where they were executed are shrines. You've probably already noticed Battisti's prominent memorial, a marble circle of columns on the hill of Doss Trento just across the Adige. The present is served by the new **Galleria Civica d'Arte Contemporanea** (*open 10–12 and 4–7, closed Mon; adm*), hosting changing exhibitions.

More Museums: Art, Planes and Saucepans

Cles' successor, Prince-Bishop Cristoforo Madruzzo, did not feel quite at ease at Buonconsiglio, and built himself a suburban residence on the Adige where he could get away from it all. This, the **Palazzo delle Albere**, 'of the poplars', named for the trees that once lined the road (now replaced by a Michelin factory and stadium), has some not very serious towers and a moat, and the **Museo d'Arte Moderna e Contemporanea** (*Via R. da Sansoverino 45, open 10–6, closed Mon; adm*). The 19th–20th-century art, mostly Italian and with a high concentration of Futurists, offers a stark contrast to the Renaissance frescoes by Marcello Fogolino on the Months, the Ages of Man, the Seven Liberal Arts, and the Virtues.

The **Museo dell'Aeronautica Gianni Caproni**, by Trento's airport at Via Lidorno 3 (*open 9–1 and 4–6, closed Mon; adm*), began in 1929 as the private collection of Gianni Caproni, a native of Trentino and one of Italy's leading aviation engineers in the 1910s and '20s; the museum contains a number of unique planes, as well as a model of Leonardo da Vinci's flying machine. Lastly, in the suburb of Ravina—head southwest, over the river and under the highways—the **Museo del Rame** (*Via Val Gola 22, open Mon–Sat by ringing ahead, ✆ 0461 923 330; adm free*) is a 'Milky Way of Copper' in a 16th-century farmhouse, the private collection of Signor Navarini, supplier of copper saucepans to Italy's master chefs. The collection goes back to the Renaissance, and among the pudding moulds includes one with Pope Pius IX's face on it, which must have made for an appetizing dessert. You can order a replica of this (or one with your own features) from the adjacent shop.

Around Trento: Monte Bondone

The slopes of Trento's own mountain, **Bondone**, can be easily reached by mountain road or cable car (*Mon–Sat 7am–9pm; Sun 9am–6pm*), departing from the Ponte di San Lorenzo in Trento (behind the bus station) and climbing as far as **Sardagna**. At least three buses a day continue from here up to **Vaneze** and **Vason**, Monte Bondone's ski resorts; from Vason another cable car ascends to one of Bondone's three summits (6884ft). Further along, **Viotte** is the site of an alpine refuge and excellent **Botanical Garden** (*open June–Sept, 9–12 and 2–5*), one of the richest in Europe, founded in 1938 on the banks of two artificial lakes, and planted with over two thousand species of high-altitude flora from around the world. Keep your eyes peeled for the pair of golden eagles who have recently nested nearby.

Trento ✉ 38100   ***Where to Stay***

expensive

Some of the cardinals attending the Council of Trent are said to have slept at the predecessor of the ★★★★**Accademia**, near Santa Maria Maggiore at Vicolo Collico 4/6, ✆ 0461 233 600, ✆ 0461 230 174. The panelled rooms are comfortable and air-conditioned; the restaurant is excellent, with a menu that changes monthly. ★★★★**Buonconsiglio**, Via Romagnosi 16/18, ✆ 0461 272 888, ✆ 0461 272 889, is another fine, recently totally revamped choice in the historic centre.

moderate

★★★**America**, Via Torre Verde 50, ✆ 0461 983 010, ✆ 0461 230 603, is a very comfortable choice from the 1920s, within walking distance of the train station. Right in the centre, ★★★**Aquila d'Oro**, Via Belenzani 76, ✆/✆ 0461 986 282, has extremely comfortable rooms, as well as café tables spilling out into the street. If you have a car, one of the nicest places to stay is the ★★★**Villa Madruzzo**, 3km east of Trento in Cognola, Via Ponte Alto 26, ✆ 0461 986 220, ✆ 0461 986 361. In a charming 19th-century villa located in a leafy park, it has modern, comfortable rooms, fine views and a very good traditional restaurant.

inexpensive

Two hotels with the same name offer chances for cheap sleeps in the centre: ★★**Venezia**, on Trento's prettiest street, Via Belenzani 70, ✆ 0461 234 559; and

Venezia, Piazza Duomo 45, ☎/✆ 0461 234 144, which has small, basic rooms with bath; ask for one overlooking the Duomo and fountain of Neptune.

Eating Out

Trentino cuisine is basically alpine: popular dishes include *canederli*, gnocchi made from breadcrumbs, egg, cheese and bacon; *patao*, a minestrone of yellow flour and sauerkraut, and *osei scampadi*, veal 'birds' cooked with sage.

expensive

Trento's most celebrated restaurant, **Chiesa**, in the 17th-century Palazzo Wolkenstein, Parco San Marco (near the Castello di Buonconsiglio) ☎ 0461 238 766, is famous for its 'Apple Party Menu' in which Trentino's favourite fruit appears in every course; other choices include smoked trout and a tempting cheese strudel, or even a 1500s menu based on the preferred dishes of Bernardo Cles, accompanied by an extensive wine list and scrumptious desserts. Reservations essential. *Closed Sun, Mon lunch, Aug.* **Osteria a Le Due Spade**, Via Don Rizzi 11, ☎ 0461 234 343, in business since 1545, serves refined dishes in a delightful dining room, decorated with mosaics. *Closed Sun, Mon lunch.*

moderate

Right under the Castello di Buonconsiglio, the retro **Port'Aquila**, Via Cervara 66, ☎ 0461 230 420, serves good *canederli*, polenta and other traditional dishes, served with well-aged Trentino vintages. *Closed Sun and Aug.*

inexpensive

The popular **Forst**, located in the middle of Trento in the 16th-century palace on Oss Mazzurana 38, ☎ 0461 235 590, is the place to drink beer and Trentino's wines, eat a pizza *tirolese* (with mushrooms and *speck*) or a *piatta trentino* (a mixture of local specialities). *Closed Mon, July.* **Al Vo'**, Vicolo del Vo' 11 (off Via Torre Verde) ☎ 0461 985 374, serves good regional dishes and unusual specialities, but can creep into the *moderate* category if you aren't careful. *Closed Sun, two weeks in July.*

East of Trento

The magic mountains wait, whether you turn east, west or north of Trento. San Martino di Castrozza and Paneveggio National Park are the main attractions in the Dolomites to the east, but there's plenty to see along the way.

Tourist Information

Baselga di Pinè: Via C. Battista 98, ☎ 0461 557 028, ✆ 0461 557 577.
Levico Terme: Via V. Emanuele 3, ☎ 0461 706 101, ✆ 0461 706 004.

The Val Sugana

The emerald Val Sugana follows the course of the Brenta, and was a busy place even in prehistoric times, as the main road from the Adriatic to the Danube. The Romans, of course, paved it (the Via Claudia Augusta Altinate), and the prince-bishops built along it. At **Civezzano**, within easy striking distance from Trento, Bernard Cles commissioned Antonio Medaglia, architect of

Santa Maria Maggiore, to rebuild the **Pieve del'Assunta** in an elegant late Gothic–early Renaissance style, while the Madruzzos commissioned the stained glass and paintings by Jacopo and Francesco Bassano. The fancy houses nearby were built to lodge dignitaries attending the Council of Trent. Above Civezzano rises the high plateau of **Pinè**, with its glacial lakes that turn into skating rinks in the winter; in 1995 they hosted the world speed-skate championships. There's some exceptionally lively German and Italian Renaissance frescoes in **San Mauro** south of the main town, **Baselga di Pinè**; it also has a beautiful late Gothic triptych, with doors, and a fancypants baroque high altar.

Pèrgine, the capital of the Val Sugana and one of the largest towns in the province, owes its elegant streets, especially Via Maier, to money made in the surrounding mines. A stiff walk (or drive) will take you up the **castle**, with views taking in the whole valley—a lovely sight in spring, when the cherries are in blossom. You can visit the pretty Gothic chapel, the prison infamous for its water torture, and even hang about for lunch (*see* below).

From Pèrgine, you can take a detour north into the **Valle dei Mòcheni**, a linguistic island, settled in the 16th and 17th century by Germans who worked the silver and copper mines, and over the centuries developed their own language, Mòcheno. At **Palù del Fersina** you can see their traditional houses; one, at Tolleri, is now a museum and cultural institute (*open Mon–Fri, 8–12, 2.30–5.30*). The *comune* has set up one of the mines by the lake at Erdemolo as a museum, the **Grua va Hardömbl** (*allow a 40min walk from Erdemolo; open weekends from May–Oct, daily exc Mon in July and Aug; book a tour © 0461 550 053; adm*).

A few kilometres from Pèrgine, **Lago di Caldonazzo** has been 'Trento's Lido' since the 1950s (it's surprisingly warm for an alpine lake, averaging 24°C in the summer) and fine for sailing and windsurfing. From **Vetriolo Terme** by the lake you can hike up to the summit of Panarotta for splendid views over Caldonazzo, as well over neighbouring (and equally warm) **Lake Levico**. This was long a favoured place, with its own aristocratic spa, **Levico Terme**, and ruined castle, where the prince-bishops once lodged in grandeur, with 60 horses parked in their stable. Just above Levico Terme, the ruins of an ancient Rhaetian walled village lie near the church of **San Biagio,** with fine frescoes from the 14th–16th centuries.

The eastern Valsugana is decidedly more arid. **Borgo Valsugana** (the Roman *Ausugum*) was a prize fought over by every Tom, Dick and Harry who passed through, from the Bishops of Feltre to the Scaligers, Counts of Tyrol, the da Carrara, the Visconti and Venetians before passing to Trento after the War of Cambrai. Many buildings in the *centro storico* have a Venetian touch; the 11th-century church, **Natività di Maria**, has a lavish baroque interior, while **San Rocco**, like every church dedicated to the saint in Trentino, was frescoed in the early 16th century. Above Borgo, the 13th-century **Castel Telvana** has spectacular views, on a site first fortified by the Romans and conquered by the Lombards in 590 (the precious Lombard 'prince's tomb' was excavated nearby); it is now the town council chambers and you can have a nose about. From Borgo you can head north into the wild Lagorai range, where Italian and Austrian trenches from the war are still visible, or south into the pretty **Valle di Sella**. Here a pagan temple underlies **San Lorenzo all'Armentèra,** its interior frescoed from the 12th century with scenes of Lawrence's life and martyrdom on the grill.

Further up the Val Sugana, the picturesque **Castel d'Ivano Fracena** guarded the Via Claudia Augusta Alinate in the Middle Ages, and has had more than its share of history; most recently, in 1984, it saw the wedding of Carlo Alberto Dalla Chiesa, whose battles against the Mafia in Palermo earned him a brutal assassination. Now a Cultural Institute, it is often open for concerts and exhibitions.

North, the gentle wooded Tesino valley has two fine old towns, whose enterprising natives travelled the world in the 1600s, from Russia to America, selling prints of Italian masterpieces from the Remondini Press in Bassano del Grappa (*see* p.170). **Pieve Tesino**, set in a green amphitheatre, has a number of 15th-century buildings, and a grand 18th-century fountain. The second town, **Castello Tesino**, has ruins of its Roman predecessor, next to the *quattro-cento* church of **S. Ipolito**, with frescoes on the story of St Julian, who beheaded his parents when he found them in his bed, thinking they were his wife and a lover. Two kilometres away, along the Brocòn road, the **Grotta di Castello Tesino** is one of the largest stalactite caverns in Italy; the Pro Loco (✆ 0461 594 136) can arrange guided tours.

Where to Stay and Eating Out

Pèrgine Valsugana ✉ 38057

There are two places to stay and/or eat here: modern, up-to-date ★★★**Al Ponte**, at Maso Grillo 4, ✆ 0461 531 317, ✆ 0461 531 288 (*moderate*), with its glass gallery, pool, and a good restaurant; or the **Castel Pèrgine**, ✆ 0461 531 158 (*moderate*), not as comfortable and haunted by a 'white lady', but with an innovative chef who knows what's what in the kitchen, and bases his dishes on regional ingredients (*open April–Oct, restaurant closed Mon*).

San Martino di Castrozza and Around

Tourist Information

San Martino: Via Passo Rolle 165, ✆ 0439 768 867, ✆ 0439 768 814.
Fiera di Primiero: ✆ 0439 62407, ✆ 0439 62992.

The stunning, pinnacle-crowned **Pale di San Martino** (10,470ft), the natural Gothic 'altars of St Martin', is the principal mountain group of the southern Dolomites, and **San Martino di Castrozza**, dramatically lying at its foot, is the biggest and best equipped winter resort south of Cortina d'Ampezzo (complete with helicopters up to the more difficult slopes, skating, and a bobsled run). The village is of recent construction—the Austrians demolished the medieval town in the First World War, leaving only the ancient church.

San Martino also makes a superb base for summer climbing and walking. Among the most popular excursions (be sure to pick up the map at the tourist office) is the ascent by cable car and chairlift to the summit of **Rosetta**. Most of the Pale is for experienced climbers; if you're not among them, the less demanding walks in the area include the path up Monte Cavallazza, facing the Pale (3hrs); or, closer at hand, to the Col Fosco or, more ambitiously, to Paneveggio.

Paneveggio National Park and the 'Forest of Violins'

Much of the best scenery around San Martino lies within the Parco Naturale Paneveggio–Pale di San Martino, a superb wilderness of venerable woods, emerald meadows, rushing streams, wild flowers and wildlife. Access to the park is from the visitors' centre in **Paneveggio**, a few kilometres north of San Martino, beyond the **Passo di Rolle**. There are two splendid paths that take in tremendous vistas, not only of the Pale di San Martino, but also the distinctive peaks of Marmolada, Pelmo, and Civetta. In past centuries the forests here provided Venice with the timber for its fleet; the Venetians not only replanted the trees a certain distance apart, to make sure the trunks were tall and straight for masts, but punished tree poachers with death. Another source of income came from Stradivarius, Amati, Guarneri and other violin makers in Cremona, who insisted on resonant Paneveggio spruce for their instruments. Rules are still strict: there are only a few campsites and no one may stay longer than 24 hours.

The Pale di San Martino is encircled by a road of scenic grandeur. The northern part of the route (SS346 and SS203) on the way to Agordo (*see* p.247) passes through the villages of **Canale d'Agordo** and **Falcade**, with ski facilities. The southern route, also via Agordo (SS347), passes through **Frassene**, a summer resort, then climbs through the forests of Gosaldo to the **Passo di Cereda** and 15th-century town of **Fiera di Primiero**. Like Cortina, Fiera stands at the crossing of two valleys, the Cismon and the Canali, and has good skiing; in the summer a popular outing is the hour's walk up to the sinister ruined **Castel di Pietra**, precariously balancing on a jagged rock with the Pale di S. Martino as a backdrop— built, according to legend, to withstand Attila the Hun.

Where to Stay and Eating Out

San Martino di Castrozza ✉ 38058

Soak up turn-of-the-century Dolomite atmosphere at ★★★★**Des Alpes**, Via Passo Rolle, ✆ 0439 769 069, @ 0439 769 068 (*expensive*). *Open Christmas–Mar, July–mid Sept.* ★★★**San Martino**, Via Passo Rolle 277 ✆ 0439 68011, @ 0439 68550 (*moderate*) also has an indoor pool, tennis courts and sauna.

Astride the Passo di Rolle north of San Martino, ★★★**Venezia**, ✆ 0439 68315, @ 0439 769 159 (*moderate*) has fantastic views stretching across the valley, and provides a great base for the National Park. Five minutes' walk up the hill behind San Martino brings you to the ★★**Suisse**, Via Dolomiti 1, ✆/@ 0439 68087 (*inexpensive*), a simple but comfortable bed and breakfast. The best dining around is at **Malga Ces**, at Loc. Malga Ces, ✆ 0439 68223 (*moderate*); specialities include *canederli*, polenta with venison, village cheeses and fruits of the forest. *Open Dec–mid-April, mid-June–Sept.*

Fiera di Primiero ✉ 38054

★★★★**Park Hotel Iris**, Via Roma 26, ✆ 0439 762 000, @ 0439 762 204 (*expensive–moderate*) is tranquil and rather grand, with one of the best restaurants in the area, serving not only Trentino's traditional cusine (*gnocchetti* in venison sauce) but some more exotic recipes such as goose breast with kiwi and Primiero's speciality, *tosèla*, slices of fresh cow's-milk cheese fried in melted butter, served piping hot with polenta or mushrooms. *Open Christmas–mid-April, June–Sept.*

Val di Fassa and Val di Fiemme

These two northeasternmost valleys of Trentino, running between the Pale di San Martino, Rosengarten and the western slopes of Marmolada, are among the most stunning and most independent-minded, and well loved by the cross-country-skiing fraternity.

Tourist Infomation

Canazei: Via Costa 79, Alba, ℭ 0462 601 113, ✆ 0462 602 502.
Cavalese: Via F.lli Bronzetti 60, ℭ 0462 241 111, ✆ 0462 230 649.

Val di Fassa

If you're approaching from San Martino, you can join the Val di Fassa by way of the SS346 from Falcade to **Moena**. Moena is the valley's capital and winter sports centre, and the 'boundary' between the Fassa and Fiemme valleys. It has two churches of note, the large 12th-century **San Vigilio**, with paintings by local artist Valentino Rovisi, a pupil of Tiepolo; and small **San Volfango**, richly decorated with 15th-century frescoes by one of the anonymous, itinerant artists who travelled around the Trentino. A path above Moena takes in not only majestic scenery, but traces of the First World War.

Seven *comuni* in the valley preserve their Ladin language and culture, especially **Vigo di Fassa**, 6km north of Moena, site of the Majon di Fashegn (Ladin Cultural Institute) and several *tabià*—the Ladini's traditional wooden cabins. A 20-minute walk leads up to the pretty Gothic church of **Santa Giuliana a Vigo**, with frescoes from the 1400s honouring the valley's patron saint. In the nearby hamlet of **San Giovanni**, dominated by the large Gothic church of the same name, the **Museo Ladino di Fassa**, dedicated to archaeology and ethnography, is due to reopen in 2000. While in San Giovanni, seek out the **Casa Soldà**, built in the 1500s by a soldier who made a fortune in the Turkish wars and invested his swag on decorating his house with frescoes. For a big thrill, take the three chairlifts from nearby Pozzo di Fassa up the flanks of Rosengarten, leaving you at the path to the **Torri del Vaiolet,** a strikingly sheer triple pinnacle.

Campitello di Fassa, the next town up the Val di Fassa, has a pretty church frescoed inside and out, and a funivia to the **Col Rodella** (8153ft), a famous viewpoint and winter sports wonderland; the lower station's **Museo degli Sci** (*open Dec–April, daily 8–6.30; adm free*) has a collection of ski gear and accessories from the early 20th century. Campitello has two frescoed churches from the 1400s, one devoted to the subject of Sabbath-breaking. Further up the valley, **Canazei** is the main base for exploring the other magnificent peaks in the area— Marmolada, Sassolungo and Sella. Canazei was rebuilt after 1912, after it was destroyed by fire, but the church in the nearby hamlet of Gries escaped, along with its paintings by Valentino Rovisi of Moena. The passes above Canazei lead towards Arabba and Cortina (*see* p.244) or north into the Val Gardena in the Alto Adige (*see* p.279).

Val di Fiemme

The Val di Fiemme begins west of Moena (*see* above). Less densely Ladin than the Val di Fassa, it was nevertheless virtually independent for centuries, a 'Magnifica Comunità' under the auspices of the prince-bishops of Trent. The lake-spangled mountains south of the valley, the **Catena dei Lagorai**, are one of the least developed areas in the Dolomites, and for the most part accessible only by foot. In **Predazzo**, the **Civico Museo di Geologia** was founded in 1899 (*under restoration at the time of writing*) and takes the subject of Dolomitic rocks and marine fossils in hand; the museum has set up a marked half- or full-day geological path at Doss Cappèl, reached by the Predazzo chair lift.

Down the valley, **Panchià** has a pretty covered bridge spanning the Avisio while another, from the 15th century, does the same work in **Tesero**, a delightful village that hasn't surrendered its soul to tourism, where furniture- and instrument-makers still ply their old trades. Perhaps too well. The chapel of **San Rocco** (1528) is frescoed with yet another 'Sunday Christ', surrounded by all the tools that are taboo on the Sabbath, which makes one wonder: were the Trentini of old inveterate workaholics or merely avoiding the collection plate?

At **Cavalese**, the capital of the Val di Fiemme, the *Regolani* elected to govern the valley held their parliament in the park of the parish church; you can still see their circle of stone benches, the **Banc de la Reson**. The *Magnifica Comunità* of Cavalese still has considerable local say, governing the Val di Fiemme from the grand old **Palazzo della Comunità**, rebuilt in the 1500s by Prince-Bishops Bernardo Cles and Cristoforo Madruzzo and frescoed with scenes dominated by the central figure of St Vigil. On the second floor a **museum** charts Fiemme's proud past and has works by the 17th–18th-century Fiemme school, a group of harmless painters who travelled about the smaller courts of Europe, led by Giuseppe Alberti, Orazio Giovannelli and the Unterpergers (*open July, Aug, Christmas, daily 4.30–7.30*). Local rule had its disadvantages for some: in nearby **Doss delle Strie**, 11 witches were burnt alive in 1505. A cable car from Cavalese ascends to **Mt Cermis** (7313ft).

Towards Trento: the Val di Cembra and its Pyramids

From Cavalese, the road follows the river Avisio through the steep, vine-terraced Val di Cembra, a valley where the inhabitants have always struggled to make a living. One of the main sources of income is porphyry, quarried with less than environmental correctness since the Second World War. The road then passes through a striking region of rocks eroded into spiky 'pyramids' near **Segonzano**. The highest ones stand over 150ft tall, and many are crowned with porphyry boulders, like natural umbrellas. Students of Dürer might recognize the medieval 'Roman' tower that inspired a pair of his watercolours, made during the artist's first trip to Venice. **Cembra** to the south on the other bank of the Avisio has two frescoed churches: **San Pietro** is especially interesting for its *Life of Jesus* (1500s) and a grand if rather unthreatening *Last Judgement* by Valentino Rovisi. Other frescoes, *quattrocentro* this time, are in little San Leonardo, in **Lisignano**, just south of Cembra: here the artist used his licence to include St Paul at the Last Supper, joining the other apostles at a feast of fish and pretzels (Tyrolean *Brezeln* bread) and to create a weird three-headed figure of the Trinity.

Where to Stay and Eating Out

Moena ✉ 38035

Moena is famous for its *puzzone* or 'stinky cheese' which in spite of its name tastes pretty good with toasted polenta. Near the centre, ★★★**Catinaccio Rosengarten**, Via Someda 6, ✆ 0462 573 235, ✆ 0462 574 474 (*expensive*) has an indoor pool and plenty of mountain atmosphere. *Open Christmas–mid-April, July–mid-Sept.* A sure, classy bet, ★★★**Post Hotel**, Piazza Italia, ✆ 0462 573 760, ✉ 0462 573 281 (*moderate*) has fine rooms and a good restaurant, **Tyrol**. *Open Dec–Easter, mid-June–mid-Sept.* Long one of the best restaurants in the region, **Malga Panna**, Via Costalunga 29, ✆ 0462 573 489 (*expensive*) offers a variety of menus, stretching from polenta with a selection of local cheeses and cold meats to the *menu degustazione* of trout, rabbit, *tortelli ai porcini*, speck, venison and strawberries. *Open Dec–April, July–Sept; closed Mon.*

Up above Moena at Passo di San Pelligrino, ★★★★**Monzoni**, ✆ 0462 573 352, ✉ 0462 574 490 (*expensive*) is a great place to stay: an old mountain refuge converted into a splendid hotel, with an emphasis on nightlife and fun. *Open Christmas–mid-April, mid-July–Aug.*

Canazei ✉ 38032

In a panoramic spot near the ski slopes, ★★★**La Perla**, Via Pareda 103, ✆ 0462 602 453, ✉ 0462 602 501 (*expensive*) is a comfortable spot, with a gym, indoor pool and sauna. *Closed Nov.* The little ★★**Dolomites Inn**, Via Arntersies 35, at Penia, ✆ 0462 602 212, ✉ 0462 602 474 (*moderate*) also has a fitness centre and two squash courts. *Open Dec–April, mid-June–mid-Sept.* ★★★**Bellevue**, ✆ 0462 601 104, ✉ 0462 601 527 (*moderate*) has great mountain views and pleasant rooms. *Open all year.* If you have yet to try *strangolopreti* ('priest-stranglers'), they're one of the specialities at **El Ciasel**, ✆ 0462 62190 (*moderate*) along with game dishes and polenta.

Cavalese ✉ 38033

★★★**San Valier**, ✆ 0462 341 285, ✉ 0462 231 020 (*moderate*) is in a pretty setting and has an indoor pool, fitness centre and sauna. *Closed Nov.* One of the nicest hotels has the funniest name, ★★★**Villa Trunka Lunka**, Via Degasperi 4, ✆ 0462 340 233, ✉ 0462 231 433 (*moderate*) with only 24 rooms, and a sauna and solarium. Right on the pistes of Mt Cermis, superbly positioned at 6562ft, ★★★**Sporting-Club Grand Chalet des Neiges** ✆/✉ 0462 341 650, also has a pool and sauna to go with its magnificent views. *Open mid-Dec–mid-Apr.* Restaurants sometimes have *caronzèi*, the valley's unique ravioli, filled with potatoes, *puzzone* cheese, nutmeg and chives, topped with cheese, sage and poppyseeds; try **Cantuccio**, Via Unterberger 14, ✆ 0462 340 140 (*expensive–moderate*) where mushrooms are king, and they make a mean rabbit in garlic cream and artichokes. *Closed Mon eve and Tues out of season.*

West of Trento: the Brenta Dolomites

The Brenta Group, separate from the other Dolomites, is just as marvellous and strange, and a challenge for experienced alpinists. The Adamello-Brenta Park is the last refuge of brown bears in the Alps, but you'd have to be very lucky to see one: there are only about a dozen. The following section circles the park clockwise—a 175km round trip from Trento.

Tourist Information

Fai della Paganella: ✆ 0461 583 130, ✉ 0461 583 410.
Molveno: ✆ 0461 586 924, ✉ 0461 586 221.
Pinzolo: ✆ 0465 51007, ✉ 0465 502 778.

Around Monte Paganella

To reach Monte Paganella, the eastern flank of the Brenta group facing Trento, first head north along the Adige to **San Michele all'Adige**, home to the **Museo degli Usi e Costumi della Gente Trentina**, a fascinating ethnographic collection occupying 40 rooms in a former Augustinian monastery (*open 9–12.30 and 2.30–6, closed Mon, adm*). Nearby **Mezzocorona** is the producer of the 'prince of Trentino wines', Teròldego, as well as spumante; it also lies at the beginning of the wine road to Bolzano (*see* p.271). Stop at **Cantine Mezzacorona** in Via IV Novembre, not only for tastings but to see the remains of a Roman farm of the first century AD, discovered during the excavations of the modern wine cellars (*open Mon–Fri, but ring ahead, © 0461 605 163, closed part of Aug*).

From Mezzocorona, follow the signs to the Paganella high plateau, the 'green island' in the mountains. Its three well-equipped resorts are served by four buses a day from Trento: **Fai della Paganella**, **Andalo** (both with cable cars to the summit of Monte Paganella—6972ft) and **Molveno**, near Lago di Molveno. Fai has beautiful views over the Adige valley, while Andalo is known for its traditional farmhouses (*masi*); a pretty hour and a half's walking trail, the *giro dei masi*, will take you past many of them. Lake Molveno is a favourite for wind-surfers, swimmers and sailors. An hour's path from its shore leads to a 16th-century Venetian sawmill (**Segheria Veneziana**), still remarkably intact, next to its old water-wheel. From Molveno the road continues south to **Ponte Arche**, passing Fiavé, where a 5000-year-old settlement of lake dwellers was discovered. East of Ponte Arche is picture postcard **Lake Toblino**, with its 12th-century **castle** (now an excellent restaurant) beautifully set on a tiny peninsula amid trees planted by Attila the Hun. Or so they say.

The Valli Giudicarie

The Brenta Group's southern peaks rise over Giudicarie Valleys, a network encompassing several rivers and torrents, running from lake to lake—from Molveno down to Idro. Just south of Molveno, **San Lorenzo in Banale** has a road rising north up the **Val d'Ambiez** and the Rifigio al Cacciatore, providing a quick route for hikers to approach the highest peaks of the Brenta group. Further along, the Giudicarie is defended by the lovely **Castel Stenico**, founded in the 12th century and an administrative centre for the prince-bishops. It retains some faded but good Renaissance frescoes; part of it now houses the archaeological collections of the Trentino provincial museum (*guided tours, daily except Mon 9–12 and 2–5; adm*). South of Stenico, in one of the Giudicarie's branch valleys, there's a surprise: the parish church of **Dasindo**, rebuilt in 1596 by hometown boy Giovanni Maria Filippi, who went to study Palladio's churches in Venice and incorporated the hemispherical dome and other things he learned in this, his first project; Filippi later became court architect to Emperor Rudolph in Prague. The main valley road next passes Lake Ponte Pia, where a detour leads to the narrow, unpopulated **Val d'Algone**, with a waterfall near Airone and another track into the Brenta.

Just outside **Tione**, the rather dull capital of the valley, the cemetery church of **San Vigilio** was frescoed with a giant St Christopher in 1474, the only authenticated work by Cristoforo Baschenis, member of a large clan of itinerant painters from Bergamo. Tione stands at the crossroads to the **Valle del Chiese**, where the river flows south into one of the smaller Italian lakes, Idro; Trentino's most rugged scenery lies along the upper Chiese in the **Val di Daone**, by the artificial lakes of Malga Boazzo and Malga Bissina under lofty Mount Fumo (11,215ft).

The Valle Rendena

The main road around the Brenta group, the SS239, heads north of Tione into the Valle Rendena along the river Sacra, one of the favourite stamping grounds of the Baschenis family. The attractive town of **Pinzolo** makes a good base for exploring the glacier-clad Brenta and Adamello mountains, with their scores of lakes. The exterior of its cemetery church, **San Vigilio**, was frescoed in 1539 by the most accomplished of all the Baschenis, Simone, portraying a vividly eerie medieval-style *Dance of Death*. Placid, business-like skeletons conduct princes, popes, soldiers and everyone else to their end, with a couplet of elegant poetry for each. More of Simone Baschenis' precise, luminous work (on the life of St Vigil) can be seen inside the church. Twenty years before, Simone had his go at a *Danse Macabre* on the façade of Santo Stefano at **Carisolo**, 2km up the road; inside are frescoes on Charlemagne's (probably legendary) visit to the Valle Rendena.

Carisolo stands at the entrance to the lovely **Val di Genova**, one of the most beautiful in the entire Alps, once the haunt of ogres and witches, all of whom were turned to stone after the Council of Trent. Now part of the **Parco Naturale Adamello-Brenta**, the Val di Genova is graced by the lofty **Cascate di Nardis** (4km from Carisolo), a woodland waterfall flowing from the glacier on **Presanella** (10,676ft)—in Pinzolo you can find a guide to make the ascent. To the east a chair-lift (the world's fastest, they claim, so hold on to your hat) rises to the lower slopes of **Cima Tosa**, the highest peak of the Brenta Dolomites.

Where to Stay and Eating Out

San Michele all'Adige ✉ 38010

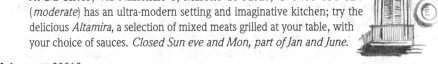

At **Da Silvio**, Via Nazionale 1, Masetto de Faedo, ✆ 0461 650 324 (*moderate*) has an ultra-modern setting and imaginative kitchen; try the delicious *Altamira*, a selection of mixed meats grilled at your table, with your choice of sauces. *Closed Sun eve and Mon, part of Jan and June.*

Molveno ✉ 38018

★★★**Belvedere**, Via Nazionale 9, ✆ 0461 586 933, ✆ 0461 586 044 (*expensive*) has fine rooms with exquisite views over the lake and mountains, an indoor pool, fitness centre and solarium. *Open Christmas, Feb, April–Oct.* An older hotel, the ★★★**Miralago**, Piazza Scuole 3, ✆ 0461 586 935, ✆ 0451 586 268 (*moderate*) offers an outdoor heated pool, garden and superb terrace among its amenities. For good Trentino homecooking, try **Alpotel Venezia** in the *centro storico*, Via Nazionale 8, ✆ 0461 586 920 (*inexpensive*); they do a good *strangolopreti alla trentina*.

Castel Toblino ✉ 38070

Dine in the romantic 12th-century **Castel Toblino**, on its little peninsula in the lake ✆ 0461 864 036 (*moderate*), amid frescoes and medieval weapons; it has been run for over 30 years by the same family, and the menu is based on trout, mushrooms and other Trentino treats. *Open Mar–Oct, closed Tues.*

Pinzolo ✉ 38086

***Centro Pineta**, Via Matteotti 43, ✆ 0465 502 758, ✉ 0465 502 311 (*moderate*) is a pleasant, medium-sized hotel, warm in the winter and cool in the summer, and pine-scented year-round, with good home cooking. *Open Dec–April and June–Sept.*

Madonna di Campiglio

From Pinzolo the SS289 zigzags up to the most important resort in the Brenta Dolomites, the superbly sited **Madonna di Campiglio**, 'the Empress' gardens' where Emperor Franz Josef brought his beloved Sissi to pick herbs and wildflowers in 1890, a memory Madonna di Campiglio evokes each year with its 'Habsburg Carnival' and costume ball.

Getting Around and Tourist Information

Besides the usual efficient Dolomiti and SAD buses, Madonna runs a special *pista a pista* shuttle bus service for skiers arriving at Verona or Milan Linate airport; ✆ 0465 442 000 for schedules.

Tourist offices: **Madonna di Campiglio**: Via Pradalago 4, ✆ 0465 442 000, ✉ 0465 540 404; **Folgarida**: ✆ 0463 986 113, ✉ 0463 986 594.

Madonna is more than ready for visitors the rest of the year as well; its winter sports facilities include a ski jump, 31 lifts, speed-skating, a regular skating rink and an indoor pool; in the summer it offers experienced climbers the chance to try their mettle on ice and wild, rocky terrain; for inexperienced walkers it has the most scenic trails in the group—the walk to the **Cascate Valesinelle** is especially lovely. Even if you only have enough spunk to get into a chair lift and a funicular, you can enjoy the marvellous views from the **Passo del Grostè**, some 7415ft above Madonna to the east, or from **Pradalago** to the west. Get the tourist office's footpath map to take Madonna's classic walk through the beautiful Val di Brenta and Valsinella just to the south. A more difficult path, the fabulous **Via Bocchette**, takes in the region's most bizarre naked pinnacles and fantastic cliffs, but should only be attempted with proper equipment by seasoned mountain maniacs.

North of Madonna the road passes through **Passo Campo Carlo Magno**, named after Charlemagne who supposedly stopped here on his way to Rome to receive the Emperor's crown. **Folgarida**, beyond the pass, is another well-endowed winter resort.

Where to Stay and Eating Out

Madonna di Campiglio ✉ 38084

Madonna di Campiglio is the one resort in the Brenta Dolomites with accommodation and facilities to please the most demanding customers, and prices are correspondingly high. You can shoot high-altitude drives while staying at the ****Golf Hotel**, up at the Passo Carlo Magno, ✆ 0465 441 003, ✉ 0465 440 294 (*very expensive*), one-time summer residence of the Habsburg emperors, now beautifully converted into a hotel. *Open mid-Dec–Mar and mid-June–mid-Sept.* Down in Madonna di Campiglio itself, the very attractive ****Spinale Club Hotel**, Via Monte Spinale 39, ✆ 0465 441 116,

@ 0465 442 189 (*very expensive–expensive*) is elegantly appointed, and has a large indoor pool and other sporting facilities; they also take special care of children. *Open Dec–Apr and June–Sept.* ***Palù**, Via Vallesinella 4, ℗ 0465 441 695, @ 0465 443 183 (*expensive*), an older hotel, has a/c in summer and a blazing fireplace to sit around in the winter. *Open Dec–Easter, July–Sept.* Small and cosy, **★★Hermitage**, Via Castelletto 65, ℗ 0465 441 558, @ 0465 441 618 (*moderate*) has a fine panoramic terrace and good food. *Open Dec–mid-April, July–Sept.* **★★Gianna**, Via Vallesinella 16, ℗ 0465 41106, @ 0465 40775 (*moderate*) is a family-run bargain, with a bus every half hour to town and the ski lifts. *Open Dec–Easter and July–Sept.*

Dine on venison with redcurrant compote or risotto with mushrooms at **Malga Montagnoli** at Spinale, ℗ 0465 42141 (*moderate*); or at **La Fontanella**, Via Dolomiti del Brenta 127, ℗ 0465 41398 (*moderate*) on filling polenta dishes or tagliatelle with hare sauce. For a special meal, there's **Artini**, Via Cima Tosa 47, ℗ 0465 440 122 (*expensive–moderate*), modern and luminous, and specializing in lovely mushroom dishes. *Open Dec–April, July–Sept.*

Along the Noce: the Val di Sole and Val di Non

The northern flank of the Brenta group is marked by the river Noce, descending from the Trentino sector of the Stelvio National Park (*see* p.289). On the way it passes through the Val di Sole and its natural extension, the Val di Non, where apples are king. This was a major route of the mule trains that once travelled between the Adriatic into Lombardy—hence all the fortified manor houses, nearly all of which are still privately owned.

Getting Around

Besides the usual buses, the Val di Non is served by a little privately run train running from Trento to Malè; call ℗ 0463 830 109 for information.

Tourist Information

Malè: Viale Marconi 7, ℗ 0463 901 280, @ 0463 901 563.
Stelvio National Park Visitors' Centre: Via 4 Novembre 4, Malè, ℗ 0463 903 046, @ 0463 903 047, *parcostelvio.tn.comitato@well.it* (*open Mon–Fri 8–12, 2–5*).
Fondo (for the Val di Non): Piazza S. Giovanni, ℗ 0463 830 133.

Val di Sole

Italy's 'Sun Valley' of soft green meadows and villages, with the lofty peaks of Monte Cevedale as a backdrop, has a name that may sound like a recent invention by the Trentino tourist board, but was first recorded back in 1071. Coming up from Madonna di Campiglio, turn left for the upper valley's most up-to-date winter sports facilities at **Marilleva**. The men here were regular slugabeds—the name *Marì levà* comes from 'Husband, get up!' In summer the main sport is whitewater canoeing down 25km of the river Noce, a wild enough adventure to make it the scene of the world canoeing championships in 1993. Many churches in the valley have charming exterior frescoes by the Baschenis family, notably La Natività di Maria at **Pellizzano**, with a beautiful *Annunciation* by Simone (1524). **Ossana**, a bit further east, was an important frontier post for the prince-bishops; its 12th-century **Castel San Michele** is currently being restored by the province. At Ossana you can follow the **Val di Peio** north into Stelvio National Park (*see* p.289); the village of **Peio** at the top of the valley has an enormous Baschenis *St Christopher* for good luck.

In the lower Val di Sole, you'll find **Malè**, the valley's chief market town and home to an ethnographical museum, the **Museo della Civiltà Solandra** (*open mid-June to mid-Sept, 10–12 and 4–7; closed Sun*) with handicrafts and agricultural and domestic implements. Malè is still an important woodworking centre. There are some fine examples in the parish church, which also has a curious chapel dedicated to S. Valentino in front, open on three sides, used during times of plague when people feared to be indoors. From Malè you can visit **Val di Rabbi**, one of the least changed valleys in the Dolomites, dotted with venerable *masi*. Like the Val di Pejo it extends into Stelvio National Park, which has a summer visitors' centre in the spa of **Bagni di Rabbi**. Just east of Malè, the 13th-century **Castello Caldès** with its frescoed rooms, old graffiti and other fittings, has recently been restored by the province, and is open for special exhibitions.

Cles and the Upper Val di Non

The wooded Val di Non, the enchanting valley running north–south along the lower course of the River Noce, is the most populous and wealthy in Trentino, in no small measure thanks to Italy's finest apples, especially Golden Delicious and 'Renetta del Canada', which look more like potatoes. Come in the spring, when its apple blossoms, emerald meadows and snow-clad mountains glow with colour.

The large artificial **lake of Santa Giustina** divides the two valleys. **Cles**, on the west bank, has been the capital of the Val di Non since AD 46 at least, when the emperor Claudius granted the city its rights stll recorded in the *tabula clesiana*. Prince-bishop Bernardo Cles was born here, in the 11th-century lakeside **Castello Cles**, which he much remodelled and decorated. The town is divided into six distinct neighbourboods called *colomelli*; the *colomello* Pés has several Renaissance buildings, especially the Palazzo Assessorile and the Pieve dell'Assunta. The older, smaller church of **San Vigilio** is coated with frescoes within, including a good *Last Supper* by a follower of Giotto, and a *Last Judgement*, with St Peter kindly taking the Elect by hand while unlocking the gates of Paradise.

Sanzeno, across the lake, is one of the Dolomites' holy vortices: in 397 St Vigil sent three missionaries, Sisinio, Martirio and Alessandro, to convert the locals. They were martyred for their trouble; the handsome parish **church** dedicated to them has 13th-century frescoes, while the town hall has a room of archaeological finds, not only from the pagans who did them in, but going back to Bronze Age Rhaetians (1300 BC). Then there's the most remarkable church in the whole of Trentino, 6km up a narrow gorge: the **Santuario di San Romedio** (*open 7.30–6*). The spot where the hermit Romedio lived as a kind of alpine St Jerome with his pet bear grew into an isolated but popular pilgrimage shrine, hanging on the cliff. The sanctuary consists of chapels in different styles stacked one atop another down the rock over the centuries, the end result somewhat resembling a dolls' house in the forest. Don't miss the 11th-century barbaric reliefs on the portal or the disarming home-made *ex votos*, or the ghastly souvenir shop.

The main road from Sanzeno leads to **Fondo**, a quiet summer resort in the upper Val di Non. On the way, stop at **Romeno** to see the frescoes on Sant'Antonio Abate telling the story of the

Hanged Man, one of the key miracles that happened along the pilgrimage road to Compostela. Fondo itself is known for the musical bells in its campanile, and more frescoes on the houses of the *centro storico*, relating to Compostela (*ex votos*, apparently, thanking St James for chasing away an epidemic); one house shows the siege of Troy. From Fondo a scenic road rises to the **Passo della Mèndola** (4472ft), with extensive views over the Adige Valley.

The Val di Non, South of Lago di Santa Giustina

South of Cles, the classic excursion is to **Lago di Tovel** (15km south), lying deep in the folds of the Brenta Dolomites. Unlike other lakes celebrated for their sapphire hue, Tovel was famous for its ruby redness at certain periods, when a rare algae, *Glendodinium sanguineum*, covered its surface. Nowadays Tovel is perhaps the only case in the world where one regrets to say that pollution has made the water turn blue. Bears are occasionally sighted in the area.

In the main valley, the area south of **Tuenno** is apple heaven; near orchard-engulfed **Tassullo** you'll find another church, **S. Vigilio**, frescoed within by the Baschenis clan. The village's landmark, the well-preserved **Castel Valèr**, stands on the old Roman road: the 130ft polygonal tower is made of granite especially brought into the area. Amid the orchards just south of Tassullo, the square Renaissance **Castel Nanno** was built as a summer residence by the Madruzzo family in the 16th century, according to legend, after a plan by Palladio.

The main road follows the east bank of the Noce (there's a bridge just north of Tassullo). Aim for **Córedo**, once more important than the farming village of 1300 souls that it is now, with a fancy bishop's palace, Venetian house and **Palazzo Nero**, named 'black' after it was burned in a peasants' revolt in 1477. It was the local seat of justice—if found guilty the culprit would be burned at the stake in the square just outside, although the frescoes inside, on the life of the French queen St Genevieve de Brabante (who was falsely accused of adultery) were meant to remind the judges to take care. Near the Palazzo Nero, the 13th-century **Castel Bragher**, surrounded by woods and orchards, is one of the best preserved in the whole of Trentino, though still privately owned. Down on the main road, there's **Taio**, a place that frowns on the movement to ban performing animal acts—it's Europe's main producer of circus whips. The nearby hamlet of Segno has a new **museum** devoted to its great man, Padre Eusebio Chino (or Kino), who left home in 1678 to preach to the Indians of Mexico and the US border states, founding churches and missions, spending much of his time in the saddle—as he is depicted in the statue outside the museum.

Prominent in the lower Val di Non, at **Vigo di Ton**, the **Castel Thun** (*gardens and other restored sections open June–Oct daily exc Mon*) was transformed in the 16th century from a military fortress into the most sumptuous palace in the province by the Thun (or Tono) family, hobnobbers with Emperors from the days of Henry IV (1190). Their palace is being restored by the Province and will soon open as a museum; the paintings in the gallery, long ignored, were recently found to be major early 17th-century works by Crespi and the Bologna school.

If you've gone all around the Brenta group and have yet to spot a bear, you have one last chance at **Spormaggiore**, on the west bank of the Noce: a large, fenced area in a natural setting has been set up as a kind of halfway retirement house for bears from zoos and circuses who couldn't survive on their own in the wild (Via Alt Spaur 82, *open summer, contributions welcome*). Further south are the impressive ruins of the **Castel Belfòrt** (1311) in a beautiful setting overlooking the Val di Non.

Marilleva ✉ 38020

★★★**Sporting Ravell**, up at Marilleva 900, ✆ 0463 757 159 (*moderate*) is devoted to fun, a complex complete with a disco, taverna and games room; it's also one of the more reasonably priced hotels in the area.

Cles ✉ 38023

Cles has a resort hotel in its ★★★**Punto Verde**, Via S. Vito 20, ✆ 0463 421 275, ✆ 0463 424 358 (*moderate*), with tennis, indoor pool, and sauna. *Open all year.* Housed in a historic building, ★**Antica Trattoria**, Via Roma 13, ✆ 0463 421 631 (*moderate*) has simple rooms and the best restaurant in Cles, serving Trentino specialities. *Closed Fri eve and Sun, part of June and July.*

Fondo ✉ 38013

Family-run and recently renovated, ★★★**Lady Maria**, Via Garibaldi 20, ✆ 0463 830 380 (*moderate*) is in the centre, not far from a little lake; a *Weinstube* and pastries and desserts baked every day on the premises are other pluses. *Closed mid-Nov–mid-Dec.*

Alto Adige/Süd Tirol

Everything has two names on the sunny side of the Alps, in the bilingual province of Alto Adige/Süd Tirol. In isolated mountain valleys people speak German and little Italian, while others still converse in Ladin (Romansch), a language that owes its origins to the days when Druso, stepson of Augustus, conquered the region in 15 BC and Emperor Tiberius sent his soldiers to crush the Celtic resistance of the mountain valleys of Switzerland and the Tyrol. Some of the soldiers stayed behind in Raetia, as the Romans called the province, and their 'Latin' descendents, the Ladini, still speak Ladin, a nearly incomprehensible linguistic fossil midway between Latin and mountain Celtic. In 590, after the fall of Rome, Rezia formed part of the duchy of Burgundy; in 901 King Ludovico, the last of the Carolingians, donated Rezia to the bishop of Sabbiona near Bressanone. Although they counted among the great peers of the Holy Roman Empire, the prince-bishops of Bressanone nevertheless had much of their authority usurped in the 13th century by the counts of Tyrol in Merano, and then by the Habsburgs after the abdication of the 'Ugly Duchess', Margaret of Tyrol, in 1363. Hence, when Napoleon alloted the Süd Tirol to Austria the region had no objection—unlike Italian Trentino, which chafed and yearned to join Venetia.

After the First World War Italy gained Trentino, and in the 1920s absorbed the lands up to the Brenner Pass as the natural frontier. Mussolini, a dedicated cultural imperialist, immediately invented Italian names for all the towns in the Alto Adige and tried to stick the language down the inhabitants' throats, until Hitler told him to lay off. Still, things were so bad that in 1939, when German citizenship was offered to anyone who didn't want to be Italian, most of the people left, leading to severe depopulation of rural areas. It was hardly an auspicious beginning, and if it weren't for the Italian vote from Trentino, the southern half of the region, separatism would have been a serious problem. Even today the Süd Tirol is 69% German-speaking, 27% Italian and 4% Ladin. In recent years Rome has done much to mollify the region, granting it a great deal of autonomy and enough economic perks to make it one of the country's wealthiest areas.

Its position at one of the great historical crossroads between north and south, its brilliant Dolomite scenery, its winter sports (Bolzano traditionally produces some of Italy's top skiers) and renowned climatic spa at Merano made the Süd Tirol a tourist destination long before the other Dolomite provinces. Although the mountains steal most of the thunder, the region is a goldmine for early medieval art, with an exceptional collection of sacred and profane frescoes , and exquisite sculpted wooden altarpieces, often with carved shutters, by masters such as Michael Pacher—a local speciality in the Renaissance. Houses with old lead windows, *Stube* (snug panelled rooms with wood stoves), *Erker* (overhanging balconies) or outer stairways have been carefully maintained through the centuries. Memories are long too—old chalet farmhouses are called *masos*, similar to the Provençal *mas*, from the Roman *mansio*. Some go back to the 14th century, and over 1200 offer inexpensive *agriturismo* lodgings.

The Alto Adige is awash in fine wines, especially whites—there are some 40 vines for every inhabitant. The most reliable labels are Herrnhofer, Bellendorf, Kehlburg, von Elzenbaum and Hofstatter; good whites to try are the light and smooth Riesling Renano, dry and snappy Gewürtztraminer, Weissburgunder (Pinot Bianco), Welschriesling (Riesling Italico), Sylvaner (with a dry, delicate perfume) and Muller-Thurgau (light and fruity).

San Michele all'Adige to Bolzano: the Wine Road

Folks on the west bank of the Adige between Trento and Bolzano have been making wine before the Romans, and this lovely Strada del Vino/Weinstrausse through the vine-carpeted hills is so well known that most of the villages along it have taken its name. The first place to see something besides vineyards, however, is **Egna/Neumarkt** on the east bank, a handsome market town founded in 1189 by the bishop of Trento, its streets lined with porticoes. Gothic architect Meister Konrad von Neumarkt built one of his finest works, the 13th–15th-century church of **Nostra Signora**, in nearby **Villa**. From here, it's a short drive up to the **Parco Naturale del Monte Corno**, a gorgeous place in early summer—botanically it's the most diverse park in the Alto Adige. Further up the Adige, **Ora/Auer** has another fine Gothic church, but there's an even better one up on the hill, 14th-century **San Daniele am Kiechlberg**, frescoed by an itinerant Lombard painter.

Cross the Adige for **Termeno sulla Strada del Vino/Tramin an der Weinstrasse**, a town that owes its fame to its blood-heating wine, Gewürtztraminer Aromatico, an aphrodisiac; try it, if you have company, at the **Cantina Hofstätter**, which claims to possess the largest wine cask in Europe. Termeno's neo-Gothic church conserves a mighty 15th-century bell tower and choir coated with elegant Renaissance frescoes by the Bolzano school. Wine paraphernalia, and items relating to Termeno's ancient carnival, are in the **Museo Locale**, Via Municipio 9 (*open Easter–Nov 1, Tues–Fri 10–12 and 4–6, Sat 10–12; closed Sun and Mon*). Just outside town, rising out of a sea of vineyards, tiny **San Giacomo in Castelaz** has extraordinary frescoes spanning the 13th–15th centuries, including some wonderful medieval monsters.

Further north, the Alto Adige's winemaking capital **Caldaro sulla Strada del Vino/ Kaltern an der Weinstrasse** overlooks Lago di Caldaro, which is warm enough for a dip from

May–September. Besides the grand old homes of the lords of the vine and their sumptuous neoclassical parish church, Caldaro has the regional **Museo Provinciale del Vino**, in Castel Ringberg (*open April–7 Nov, Tues–Sat 9.30–12 and 2–6, Sun and hols 10–12*) full of vinous lore and carved barrels, a local speciality.

Appiano sulla Strada del Vino/Eppen an der Weinstrasse, the next *comune*, has no fewer than forty castles and manor houses, many owned by wealthy abbeys further north. Occasionally the castle owners went on the offensive, most notably Federigo d'Appiano, lord of **Castel d'Appiano**, who in 1158 had the cheek to hijack a treasure the Pope was sending to the Holy Roman Emperor. Not long after, the pope and emperor obliterated his castle. The current castle was rebuilt shortly after, next to the original chapel, **Santa Caterina**, left untouched by the holy army, with its beautiful frescoes from the dawn of the 13th century, both religious and hunting scenes (*open April–1 Nov, closed Tues in July*).

Another of Appiano's castles, **Castel Moos-Schulthaus**, Via Palù 4 (1356) began as a fortified Tyrolean hunting lodge, housing not only antique furnishings but a collection of regional paintings from the first half of the 20th century (*guided tours Easter–Nov 1, Tues–Sun 10, 11, 4, 5, adm*). The *comune*'s most attractive Renaissance-era houses, half Italian and half German, are in **San Michele d'Appiano**, where the castle has walls 16ft thick. San Michele also has a far older citadel, one of the best preserved Bronze Age structures in northern Italy, with a megalithic corridor directed towards the spring equinox.

Where to Stay and Eating Out

Caldaro sulla Strada del Vino/Kaltern an der Weinstrasse ✉ 39052

No lack of places in the Alto Adige's wine HQ, including ★★★★**Kartheiner Hof**, Strada del Vino 22, ✆ 0471 963 240, 🖷 0471 963 145 (*expensive*), a stylish new hotel in the traditional style, overlooking the lake, with indoor and outdoor pools as well, and every other comfort. Central ★★★**Goldener Stern**, Via Hofer 28, ✆ 0471 963 153, 🖷 0471 964 232 (*moderate*) offers good value rooms; restaurant under separate management. *Open end-Mar–early Nov.* **Ritterhof**, Via del Vino 1, ✆ 0471 963 330 (*expensive–moderate*) offers the best dining along the Wienstrasse, with lovely views over the vineyards; it's also one of the few places in the mountains to serve fish dishes as well as game. *Closed Mon, and some of July and Aug.*

Appiano sulla Strada del Vino/Eppen an der Weinstrasse ✉ 39057

Close to Bolzano and the wine road, ★★★★**Schloss Korb**, at Missiano, ✆ 0471 636 000, 🖷 0471 636 033 (*expensive*), a fairytale 11th-century castle surrounded by vines, has 53 spacious rooms, heated outdoor and indoor pools, tennis, and a fine restaurant. *Open Easter–Nov 1.* The smaller, elegant ★★★★**Schloss Freudenstein** at San Michele, ✆ 0471 660 638, 🖷 0471 660 122, enjoys another beautiful setting and has a pool. *Open April–mid-Nov.* Also at San Michele, book a table at the award-winning **Zur Rose**, ✆ 0471 662 249 (*expensive*) for a gourmet epiphany based on Tyrolean traditions in a 12th-century house. *Closed Sun, Mon lunch and July.* A mansion houses the *osteria* **Stroblhof**, Via Piganò 25, San Michele ✆ 0471 662 250 (*moderate*), serving tasty *Schlutzkrapfen* filled with seasonal treats and other regional specialities to accompany their Pinot Nero and other wines. *Closed Mon and Nov–Mar.*

Bolzano/Bozen

Bolzano, the lively, cultured capital of Alto Adige with its high, narrow gabled houses, beer cellars and arcaded streets, is an excellent base for visiting the mountains on either side. Located on the banks of the Isarco and Talvera, which merge just downstream to form the Adige, Bolzano has been an important market town since the Middle Ages. And as of March 1998, the city has a new mascot, although one far, far older than itself: Ötzi the Ice Man.

Getting Around

Trains for Trento, Bressanone, Vipiteno, Brenner and Innsbruck, to the north; Merano and Malles/Venosta, to the northwest; and for Brunico, Dobbiaco and Lienz, to the east, all depart from the FS station, a short distance from Piazza Walther down Viale Stazione. The **bus station** is across Via Garibaldi: ✆ 1678 46047, with connections to Cortina and to nearly every town in the Alto Adige.

Tourist Information

Piazza Walther 8, ✆ 0471 307 000, ✆ 0471 980 128. For the Alto Adige/Süd Tirol region: Piazza Parrochia 11, ✆ 0471 993 808, ✆ 0471 993 899, with an extremely efficient website at *www.sudtirol.com*. Alpine information service: ✆ 0471 993 809. Another source of information on mountaineering, hiking and organized day-trips is the Club Alpino Italiano (CAI), Piazza delle Erbe 46, ✆ 0471 971 694.

Piazza Walther, the Duomo and Via dei Portici

Bolzano's cultural fusion manifests itself unexpectedly in the town's pretty parlour, **Piazza Walther**. In the centre stands a statue of one of the greatest German *minnesingers*, Walther von der Vogelweide (1170–1230) and at his feet slouch travellers from around the world munching on Big Macs from America's biggest chain, located just behind the troubadour. In front of Walther stands Bolzano's Gothic **Duomo**, with its lovely green and yellow roof and pretty tower. The big art, however, is a block behind the cathedral, in the church of the **Domenicani** (*open Mon–Sat 9.30–5.30*), now the Music Conservatory, where the chapels of San Giovanni and Santa Caterina contain lovely 14th-century Giottoesque frescoes by artists from Padua, the best medieval work in the Alto Adige.

From the Domenicani, Via Goethe leads up to jovial **Piazza delle Erbe**, Bolzano's commercial hub, where Neptune with his trident (nicknamed *Gabelwirt*, 'Mine host with fork') guards the daily fruit and vegetable market. On Via Argentieri, off Piazza delle Erbe, the 18th-century Palazzo Mercantile or merchants' centre has a lovely courtyard and hall of honour; it now houses a **Museo Mercantile** (*open Mon–Fri 10–5; adm*), where a collection of period furniture and paintings attests to Bolzano's business acumen. If you need more evidence, return to Piazza delle Erbe and stroll up the city's main street, **Via dei Portici**, lined with smart shops under its Tyrolean arcades, *Erker* and pretty stucco decorations. Via dei Portici passes the old heart of the city, **Piazza del Grano** (the former cornmarket) and ends in Piazza Municipio, where the ornate neo-baroque **Town Hall** of 1907 holds court. From here Via dei Bottai, with its beer cellars and old shops, leads to the Casa di Massimiliano (1512), the old Imperial customs house and now the new **Museo Provinciale di Scienze Naturali** (*open Tues–Sun 9–5; free*) with exhibits on glaciers and the first people to move into the valleys after they melted. From here Via Vintler leads around to Piazza della Madonna and Via dei Francescani, where the church of the **Francescani** (*open Mon–Sat 10–12 and 2.30–6*) has a pretty Gothic cloister, a 14th-century fresco of the Franciscan Doctors and a beautiful altarpiece of the *Nativity*, by woodcarver Hans Klocker (1500). The street leads back to Piazza dell Erbe.

Museo Archaeologico dell'Alto Adige: The Ice Man Cometh

On Via Museo, around the corner from Piazza delle Erbe. Open May–Sept, Tues–Sun 10–6, Thurs 10– 8; Oct–April Tues–Sun 9–5, Thurs 9–8; adm exp. Audio guides in English available for a small fee.

You might recall reading about the sensational discovery in the papers. In 1991 Erika and Hermert Simon were walking along the Similaun glacier northwest of Merano when they happened across a body. There hadn't been an accident or murder there in years. The man they found mummified in the ice had died 5300 years ago, at the start of the Copper Age.

It was the first time ever that scientists had such an ancient body in such good nick and, after years of study and analysis, Ötzi, as he's been baptised, has become the centrepiece of this new museum opened in March 1998. Videos show how he was brought in from the cold, and follow all the innumerable autopsies performed on his person. He was about 46 years old, they estimate, an experienced mountaineer who got caught in a sudden storm. He had tattoos on his torso and legs, which might have served as a kind of acupuncture map. A room reproducing the cold and humidity of the glacier was specially built to house him. And a curious, rather poignant sensation it is, peering through the window at the body of a man who could be one's grandfather, 250 generations removed.

Ötzi, in short, was a lot like us. They've made a model of what he looked like, dressed in all his gear, which is spread out in the next cases. His clothing is cunningly designed for the weather, using the few materials at hand in 3700 BC, from bearskin hat to goatskin underwear, and a mantle woven of grasses to keep off the rain; his flint dagger resembles the ones carved on statue stelae; he had a bow and arrows, and in his pouch he carried bone tools and lucky talismans. The museum's other exhibits, prehistoric to Roman, tend to pale somewhat after the Ice Man, but don't miss the statue stelae carved by his near contemporaries or the cast of the Mithraic altar of Bressanone (*see* p.282).

Museo Civico and Over the Talvera to Gries

Near here, on the corner of Vias Museo and Cassa di Risparmio, the **Museo Civico** (*open Tues–Sat 9–12, 2.30–5.30; Sun 10–1; adm*) houses Gothic altarpieces by locals masters, including more by Hans Klocker and Michael Pacher. Via Museo ends at the bridge over the Talvera, a river lined with the parks and promenades; to the right, in its own field, the stout-towered 13th-century **Castel Mareccio** no longer guards Bolzano, but hosts conventioneers. Just across the Talvera, the imposing Fascist **Monumento alla Vittoria** celebrates Italy's victory in the First World War and was purposefully placed where the Austrian monument was slated to go, had their side won; in 1978 Tyrolean nationalists attempted to blow it to smithereens. Now on Saturday morning the area hosts a peaceful but enormous market.

Corso Libertà leads through Mussolini's planned industrial suburb (1937), purposely built as a contrast to old Bolzano and everything it stood for, then ends up in **Gries**, an old health resort with two important churches—the imposing baroque **Abbazia dei Benedettini** in the main piazza, with 18th-century frescoes by Tyrolean artist Martin Knoller, and the old **parish church of Gries** (*open April–Oct, Mon–Fri 10.30–12 and 2.30–4*), housing a beautifully carved Gothic wooden altar with doors by Michael Pacher (1475) and a masterful 13th-century *Crucifix*. Bus no.10 travels back from here to the centre.

Around Bolzano

There are two beautiful paths around Bolzano. Beyond the Gries parish church, at the end of Via Knoller, begins the 1½km **Passeggiata del Guncina**, with an inn at the top for refreshments. A bit longer but more dramatic, the **Passeggiata Sant'Osvaldo** begins near the train station at Via Renico and descends along the Lungotalvera. Further upriver, **Castel Roncolo** (*open Mar–Nov, Tues–Sat 10–5*) has guarded the passage on its impregnable rock since 1237. The city gave it to Emperor Maximilian; it preserves fascinating 14th-century frescoes of knights, some of which were 'touched up' in 1508 on the emperor's orders.

Three cable cars ascend from Bolzano, the most rewarding one from Via Renon, near the station—it climbs 4006ft up the slopes of Bonzano's playground, **Mt Renon/Rittner** to **Soprabolzano/Oberbozen** (*cable car runs 7am–8pm daily*). The views are splendid, stretching across to Rosengarten, but for a truly strange sight continue from Soprabolzano on the rack railway up to **Collabo/Klobenstein**, and follow the path to the **Longomoso Pyramids**—rocks eroded to form bizarre stone drapery pierced by a dense forest of needles, some crowned with rock hats.

Where to Stay

Bolzano/Bozen ⊠ 39100

Note that in the summer you may want to base yourself higher up; the humidity in the valley can turn Bolzano into a sauna. Best here is the CIGA chain's lavish ★★★★**Parkhotel Laurin**, Via 4 Laurino, ✆ 0471 311 000, ✉ 0471 311 148 (*very expensive*) built at the turn of the century in Viennese *Jugendstil*, located in a fine old park and rose garden near the centre. It has a heated swimming pool, and the public areas are furnished with antiques clustered around black marble fireplaces; don't miss the beautiful frescoed bar and exquiste dining in the restaurant **Belle Epoque**. Also in the centre, modern ★★★★**Luna-Mondschein**, Via Pieve 15, ✆ 0471 975 642, ✉ 0471 975 577 (*expensive*) is set next to a park, with cosy rooms, parking garage, and indoor/outdoor restaurant serving Tyrolean classics.

In Piazza Walther, ★★★**Città-Stadt**, ✆ 0471 975 221, ✉ 0471 976 688 (*moderate*) is in the very heart and soul of Bolzano, and has parking. Outside the centre, the 11-room ★★★**Eberle**, Passeggiata Sant'Osvaldo 1, ✆ 0471 976 125, ✉ 0471 982 334 (*moderate*) offers guests peace and quiet, a pool, tennis, sauna and gym, in addition to cosy rooms; there's also an excellent restaurant. *Croce Bianca-Weisses Kreuz, Piazza del Grano 3, ✆ 0471 977 552, ✉ 0471 972 273 (*inexpensive*) is cheerful and welcoming; its lobby is a café that opens on to the pavement. For peace and quiet, take the Colle cable car (Italy's oldest) from the opposite bank of the Isarco (bus no.11 or a short walk from the train station) up to the refreshing breezes of Colle, where *Klaushof, Colle 14, ✆ 0471 329 999 (*inexpensive*) occupies an old farmhouse with 10 rooms, some without bath.

Eating Out

Like the language, the cuisine of Alto Adige/Süd Tirol is a bit more than half Austrian—instead of *prosciutto*, expect *speck* (smoked Tyrolean ham) on pizza. Other specialities are Wiener schnitzel, sauerkraut, goulash, *knodel* (breadcrumb dumplings in a variety of styles), *Terlaner* (wine soup) with apple, cheese, and poppy-seed strudels, Sachertorte, and rich mousse for dessert. This Bolzano cuisine, stylishly prepared according to the market, holds pride of place at **Amandè**, near the Ice Man at Viacolo Ca' de Bezzi 8 (off Via Cavour), ✆ 0471 971 278 (*expensive*). *Closed Sun.* **Da Abramo**, Piazza Gries 16, ✆ 0471 280 141 (*expensive–moderate*) offers contemporary elegance and very good Italian food; seafood is a speciality, and among their offerings are a divine risotto, turbot with rosemary, and escalopes in a white pepper sauce. *Closed Sun, some of Aug.* In the centre, **Cesare**, Via Perathoner 15, ✆ 0471 976 638 (*moderate–inexpensive*) is a fine place to tuck into fresh pasta and succulent grilled meats. The jovial 400-year-old **Cavallino Bianco/Weisses Rossel**, Via dei Bottai 6, ✆ 0471 973 267 (*inexpensive*) is still extremely popular, with an eclectic menu stretching from ham and eggs to *Bolognerschnitzel* and a very tasty onion soup. *Closed Sat eve and Sun.*

Up the cable car (or road) in Renon, **Patscheiderhof**, at Signato, ✆ 0471 365 267 (*moderate*) is the favourite of many Sunday lunchers, but the food—pure traditional homecooking—is perhaps better on other days when they aren't so rushed; tasty pasta and roast pork dishes, topped off with poppyseed cake. *Closed Tues and July.*

East of Bolzano towards Rosengarten

The two valley roads southeast of Bolzano eventually meet west of Rosengarten, one of the Dolomites' biggest celebrities, and deservedly so. The stunning road down the Valle d'Ega is the more travelled as part of the famous Great Dolomites Road.

Tourist Information

Nova Levante/Welschnofen: Lago di Carazza, ✆ 0471 613 126, ✉ 0471 613 360; *www.sudtirol.com/rosengarten*

Lavies and Nova Ponente

This route, beginning due south of Bolzano, has the merit of the unexpected: **Lavies** has nothing less than Europe's biggest ships' models, the result of a local man's obsession with naval vessals sunk in the Second World War, all housed for your delectation in the **Piccolo Museo Navale: Tragedie sui Mari**, Via Fabrio Filzi 7 (*open May–15 Nov, 4–8, closed Sun and Wed; adm*). To the east, **Nova Ponente/Deutschnofen** enjoys a fantastical setting, framed by the pinnacles of Sciliar Làtemar, and Rosengarten. Its **Museo Territoriale di Nova Ponente**, Via Castel Thurn 1 (*open Wed and Fri 3–6*) has a collection of sacred art from the region, although the best works are still in the churches: the reliefs (1425) on the altar of **SS. Ulrico and Volfango**, and beautiful frescoes from 1410 in the 12th-century church of **S. Elena**, outside Nova Ponente.

The Val d'Ega to Catinaccio/Rosengarten

From Bolzano, the main road to Rosengarten (SS241) begins at Cardara/Kardaun, just east of town, and passes through the breathtaking, narrow, deep red gorge—Mother Nature's sore throat—of the **Val d'Ega**. As the road nears the valley's main settlement and resort, **Nova Levante/Welschnofen** (the Italian rival to German Nova Ponente), the craggy peaks of the **Làtemar** group loom up to the right and the rosy pinnacles of Rosengarten soar up to the left. You can reach the slopes from here or from the Passo di Costalunga, near gorgeous aquamarine **Lake Carezza**, a popular roadside stop. For an even more spectacular, magical approach, continue along the SS241 to **Pozza di Fassa** on the eastern slopes of Rosengarten.

The sheer walls and crests of **Catinaccio/Rosengarten** (9781ft) are not only enchanting, but enchanted. The poetic German name first appears in a 13th-century Tyrolean epic: King Lauren of the Dwarves was made prisoner and dragged away from his mountain realm. Furiously Lauren put a curse on the roses that had betrayed him, that no one would ever see them again, neither by night nor by day. But he neglected to mention the dawn or the twilight, when the spellbound roses make the stony face of Rosengarten blush a deep red.

Sciliar and the Alpe di Suisi

The tangle of valleys between Rosengarten and the Val Gardena encircle the rocky mesa of the Sciliar massif (8409ft) and the **Parco Naturale dello Sciliar**, the oldest in the Alto Adige. Geologically the odd man out in the Dolomites, Sciliar is spectacularly coloured, a mélange of red and white rock against the deep green trees. From Lake Carezza, the road skirts Rosengarten's west face then descends into the seldom visited **Val di Tìres/Tierser Tal** with magnificent views; the parish church in the town of **Tìres** has good early 15th-century frescoes on the *Life of St Catherine* by the Bolzano school.

At Prato all'Isarco/Blumau, on the banks of the Isarco, the road continues around Sciliar by way of **Fiè all Sciliar/Vols am Schern**, now a popular resort town that has all but erased its infamous history as the first place in the Tyrol to hold a witchcraft trial—in 1510, under its baron Leonardo di Völs. He contributed the fine altarpiece in the parish church and remodelled his imposing 12th-century **Castel Presule**, a short drive above Fiè, giving it seven towers and a pretty loggia; it now contains a collection of Risorgimento weapons, as well as paintings from Bolzano's Ca' de Bezzi, a 19th-century rendezvous for artists and intellectuals (*tours April, May, Oct 10, 2, 3; June, Sept also at 4; July and Aug 10, 11, 3, 4, 5; adm*).

The road continues up to the major resort town of **Siusi**, with another frescoed church (the splendidly situated **S. Valentino**, 14th century) and the ruins of the Castelvecchio, the residence of Oswald von Wolkenstein (1377–1445), the well-travelled diplomat, linguist, lyric

poet and songwriter in several languages. The **Alpe di Siusi**, the local playground, is a magnificent plateau under Sciliar's jagged jawbone, the Denti di Terrarossa, noted for its sunny
skiing, world-class ski schools and endless meadows of flowers in the late spring; there are
numerous cable cars waiting to take you up. A classic but not strenuous hike from Siusi is the
4hr trek up **Monte Pez**, with an overnight stay at one of the grand dames of 19th-century
Alpine refuges, the **Rifugio Bolzano**. **Castelrotto/Kastelruth** just north of Suisi is the third
holiday centre in the area, an ancient Ladin village with a pretty historic centre.

The Great Dolomites Road: Bolzano to Cortina d'Ampezzo

The road from Bolzano through the Val d'Ega to Rosengarten and Pozza (*see* above) is the first
leg of the fabled 110km *Grande Strada delle Dolomiti*, or Great Dolomites Road, laid out
between 1895 and 1909. Buses from Bolzano or Cortina make the journey, and you should
take one—it's torture, it really is, to have to keep your eyes on this alpine Amalfi Drive. On
the other hand, your own car will allow you to linger for as long as you like at the passes and
other belvederes to drink in the views. A chauffered convertible would do nicely!

After Pozza di Fassa the road (now the SS48) continues up Trentino's Val di Fassa to **Canazei**,
the best base for the ascent of the Dolomites' mightiest peak, **Marmolada** (10,965ft). The
road from Canazei climbs past the peculiar tower of **Sassolungo** and Sella glowering on the
left, on its way to the **Passo Pordoi**, affording stupendous views of Sella and Marmolada.

From the pass the road writhes down towards **Arabba**, a ski resort dwarfed by Sella, and
Pieve di Livinallongo, below the odd-shaped **Col di Lana**, its summit blown off by an Italian
mine in the First World War. The road then climbs again, past the haunting, eroding **Castello
d'Andraz**, to the **Sasso di Stria** (Witch's Rock) and the tunnel at **Passo di Falzarego**, where
a cable car on threads ascends the vertiginous cliffs. The road then begins the descent to
Cortina, with views of the strange **Cinque Torri** (Five Towers) and vertical slopes of Tofane,
before reaching the top of the Boite valley, with beautiful views over Cortina (*see* p.244).

Where to Stay and Eating Out

Nova Levante/Welschnofen ✉ 39056

****Posta Cavallino Bianco/Weisses Roessel**, Strada Carezza 30,
✆ 0471 613 113, @ 0471 613 390 (*expensive*) has a name that recalls the
former postal relay station, though its facilities—indoor and outdoor pools,
tennis, and much more—are up to date. *Open mid-Dec–mid-April and
mid-May–mid-Oct.* ***Rosengarten**, Via Catinaccio 43, ✆ 0471 613
262, @ 0471 613 510 (*moderate*) is a pleasant place to stay, and also the
best place to eat in town, where the restaurant uses the freshest local ingredients,
herbs from the garden and home-made pasta. *Closed Mon, Tues lunch, Nov.*

Suisi/Seis ✉ 39040

***Bad Ratzes**, in a sunny meadow in the centre of Parco Naturale di Sciliar,
✆/@ 0471 706 131 (*moderate*) is a lovely place to relax in the bosom of nature; there
is also an indoor pool. *Open mid-Dec–mid-April, mid-May–mid-Nov.* Early in the 20th
century a Russian nobleman built a villa in Suisi, which was converted into a hotel

after the Bolsheviks took power: now the stylish ★★★**Schlosshotel Mirabell**, Via Laranza 1, ✆ 0471 706 134, ✆ 0471 706 249 (*moderate*) is comfortable and family-run, and equipped with an outdoor pool and sauna. *Open mid-Dec–mid April, June–mid-Oct.*

Castelrotto/Kastelruth ✉ 39040

In the heart of the village, the ★★★★**Cavalinno d'Oro**, Piazza Krausen, ✆ 0471 706 337, ✆ 0471 707 172 (*expensive–moderate*) was built in the 14th century but its large rooms with big bathrooms have been recently renovated, including two of the original *Stübe*; private ski lessons included in the room rates. *Closed Nov 10–Dec 10, and Easter.* Just south of the village ★★**Belevedere-Schönblick**, Via O. Wolkenstein 49, ✆ 0471 706 336, ✆ 0471 706 172 (*inexpensive*) is simple and friendly, with pretty views. *Open Christmas–Easter, June–mid-Oct.* Outside Castelrotto in Sant'Osvaldo, **Tschötscherhof**, ✆ 0471 706 013 (*inexpensive*) is one of the province's most charming *masi*, with *agriturismo* rooms as well as a good restaurant serving hearty dishes made out of ingredients fresh from the farm. *Closed Dec–Feb.*

Northeast of Bolzano: the Val Gardena and Val Badia

More stunning mountains loom east of Bolzano over the Val Gardena, including the mighty pinnacles of Pelmo, Civetta and Marmolada. Scores of Alpine refuges, chair lifts and cable cars, and fast buses from Bolzano to towns and funicular stations make access easy. The Val Gardena is a great place to overhear a conversation in Ladin; since 1989 it has been the official administrative language, sparking a little Ladin literary movement for the first time ever.

Tourist Information

For the **Val Gardena**: *info@val-gardena.com*.
Ortisei/Sankt Ulrich in Gröden: Via Rezia 1, ✆ 0471 796 328, ✆ 0471 796 749.
Santa Cristina: Via Chemun 25, ✆ 0471 793 046, ✆ 0471 793 198.
Selva di Val Gardena/Wölkenstein: Via Meisules 213, ✆ 0471 795 122, ✆ 0471 794 245.
Corvara: Ciasa de Comun 198, ✆ 0471 836 176, ✆ 0471 836 540.

Val Gardena/Grödnertal

Lying between the Alpe di Suisi and the jagged Odle group, the Val Gardena is off the *autostrada* northeast of Bolzano. The main valley road, the SS242, begins at **Ponte Gardena/Waidbruck**, under the 11th–16th-century **Castel Trotsburg** perched on a crag and once owned by the brother of *minnesinger* Oswald von Wolkenstein. It has a Gothic and late Renaissance décor, including a vaulted Gothic *Stübe* and a collection of castle models for mavens (*guided tours Easter–Oct at 10, 11, 2, 3 and 4; closed Mon; adm*). Just above Ponte Gardena, near Laion, **Vogelweiderhof** is one of the three disputed birthplaces of one of the first and greatest of all wandering *minnesingers*, Walther von der Vogelweide (*c.* 1170–1228), whose innovation in the art of courtly poetry was to introduce heartfelt love lyrics; patronized by emperors, he was equally well known for his 'didactic poetry' that was so critical of the pope that he has been acclaimed a proto-Protestant by some.

The capital of the Val Gardena, elegant **Ortisei/St Ulrich**, or Urijëi in Ladin, and the next two villages, **Santa Cristina** and **Selva di Val Gardena/Wölkenstein**, are all well-equipped resorts with cable cars to the Alpe di Siusi; skiers shouldn't miss the Saslonch-Ruacia piste which passes right below the 17th-century **Castel Fischburg**. Ortisei's **Museo de Gherdëina in the Cësa Ladins** at Via Rezia 83 (*open Feb–Easter, Jun, Sept Tues–Fri 3–6.30; July and Aug daily 10–12 and 3–7; adm*) has displays on the valley's history from the Stone Age to the present. Santa Cristina has lifts into the Odle group and up to the wall of spiralling, dream-like **Sassolungo** (10,434ft) to the south.

The Woodcarvers of the Val Gardena

Ortisei has specialized in wood carving for centuries, and if you're buying you'll find a wide range of works to choose from, from the artistic to cheesy alpine schlock. Farmers took up carving to while away the long winter evenings, using soft pine from the valley's slopes. In the 1640s some began to neglect their land to hike over the mountains, selling carved toys, ornaments, household furniture and implements. By 1820 300 craftsmen were working in the valley, and a school was set up in 1872 to consolidate skills and encourage trade.

Today over 3000 wood-carvers whitttle away in the Val Gardena. Ask the tourist office for their list of workshops, and stop by Ortisei's parish church and museum (*see* above) to see permanent exhibitions of their craft created over the past three centuries. If you're inspired, Ortisei's school of wood-carving holds weekly courses in July and August: contact the tourist office for details.

From the crossroads in Selva di Val Gardena you have a choice of two spectacular routes, either south over the fabulous **Passo di Sella** to Canazei in Trentino, where you can pick up the Great Dolomites Road (*see* below), or over the stunning **Passo di Gardena** down into the **Alta Badia** to the east, another beautiful valley that has retained its Ladin culture. **Corvara in Badia** and **La Villa/Stern**, one-time host of the Alpine Ski World Cup, are the main resorts. From La Villa you can take a detour into the **Valle di San Cassiano**, named for its chief settlement and site of an ornate baroque parish church, built in the 18th century when the valley had a thriving mining industry. The geology of the Dolomites, popular art and fossils—including the remains of a giant prehistoric bear—are the subjects of San Cassiano's **Pic' Museo Ladin** (*open Christmas–Easter Mon–Fri 4–7; July–Sept Mon–Sat 4–7, Sun 4.30–7.30*). Another treat in the Alta Badia is the famous **Sella Ronda**, a circuit of the entire Sella group that can be made entirely on skis, thanks to a series of refuges and lifts. To the north, the SS244 leads to San Lorenzo near Brunico, while to the south the road descends to Arabba.

Where to Stay and Eating Out

Ortisei/Sankt Ulrich in Gröden ✉ 39046

The historic ★★★★**Adler**, Via Rezia 7, ✆ 0471 796 203, @ 0471 796 210 (*very expensive–expensive*) is also the most glamorous place to indulge: in a large park, with an indoor pool and tennis courts, beauty treatments, and the best restaurant in town. *Open mid-Dec–mid-April, mid-May–Oct.* Just outside town, ★★★**La Perla**, Via Digon 1, ✆ 0471 796 421, 🖷 0471 798 198 (*expensive*) is a year-round pleasure to visit, with its park and indoor pool. *Open mid-June–mid-Oct, mid-Dec–mid-Apr.*

Selva di Valgardena/Wölkenstein in Gröden ✉ 39048

The small but very comfortable ★★★★**Alpenroyal**, Via Meisules 43, ✆ 0471 795 178, 🖷 0471 794 161 (*expensive*) is one of the few hotels in the area that is open all year, with plenty of facilities to keep its guests fit and happy—indoor pool, whirlpool baths, sauna, solarium, beauty centre and fitness room. *Open mid-Dec–mid-April, June–Oct.* ★★**Europa**, Via Nives 50, ✆ 0471 795 157, 🖷 0471 796 445 (*moderate*) is a typical little family-run mountain hotel. *Closed May, Nov.* Another choice convenient for the slopes, ★★**Freina**, Via Centro 403, ✆ 0471 795 110, 🖷 0471 794 318 (*moderate*) has 12 rooms with bath. At least half-pension is required, but the food is excellent—stop here to eat if you're just passing through.

Santa Cristina in Valgardena/Sankt Christina in Gröden ✉ 39047

★★★★**Diamant**, Via Skasa 1, ✆ 0471 796 780, 🖷 0471 793 580 (*very expensive*) has lovely mountain views, an indoor pool and sauna, and tennis courts, all in a quiet park. *Open mid-Dec–Mar, mid-June–mid-Oct.* There are several hotels up at Monte Pana, open only for the summer and winter seasons: ★★★**Cendevaves**, ✆ 0471 792 062, 🖷 0471 793 567 (*moderate*) has an indoor pool and good views.

North Towards the Brenner Pass

North of Bolzano and Ponte Gardena lies the Val Isarco/Eisacktal, the traditional 'spine' of the Süd Tirol and main highway between the Germanic world and the Mediterranean since Roman times. The modern road, known as the Kuntersweg after the merchant who began it, was drilled through the rock-bound valley in 1314 using gunpowder—the first time it was used in the west for a civil engineering project.

Tourist Information

Bressanone/Brixen: Viale Stazione 9, ✆ 0472 836 401, 🖷 0472 36067, *brixen.info@acs.it.*
Brunico/Bruneck: Via Europa 22, ✆ 0472 555 722, 🖷 0472 555 544, *bruneck@DolomitiSuperski.com.*
Vipiteno/Sterzing: Piazza Città 3, ✆ 0472 765 325, 🖷 0472 765 441.

Chiusa/Klausen and the Monastero di Sabiona

On the way up from Bolzano, the first stop north of the Val Gardena was the ancient town of **Chiusa**, its steep houses stretched out along the road. Travellers in days of yore would have to go through customs here, as they passed into the territory of the bishops of Bressanone, who kept an eye on things through their clifftop **Monastero di Sabiona**. Founded in the 4th century, this is the 'Tyrol's Cradle of Christianity'; the dramatic setting was immortalized in the detailed landscape of Albrecht Dürer's superb engraving, *The Great Fortune* (*Nemesis*), *c.* 1497. In the 5th century it was the home of a wonderful bishop named Lucano, who was denounced by Pope Celestine I for letting his congregation eat dairy products on Friday. Lucano justified himself in a way no other bishop has ever done since: he rode a bear to Rome (bear-back, one presumes) and then, in case that didn't astonish the pope enough, he took off his cloak and hung it on a sunbeam. Nearly all rebuilt in the 17th century after a fire, much of the monastery is now occupied by cloistered Benedictine nuns, but you can visit the upper-most church, **Santa Croce** (*open 7–6.30*) which has vestiges of its palaeochristian origins and curious *trompe l'œil* frescoes of landscapes and architecture painted in 1679.

Chiusa became something of an art town in the early 19th century; its **Convento dei Cappuccini**, founded in 1701 by Maria Anna, Queen of Spain, now contains the **Museo Civico** (*open late Mar–mid-Sept, Tues–Sat 10–12 and 4–7; mid-Sept–mid-Nov 9.30–12 and 3.30–6*) with Romantic landscapes and other paintings by the local school and the so-called Loreto treasure (16th–17th century) of goldwork and paintings by Flemish, Spanish and Italian workshops. Orphan sculptures from surrounding churches have found a home in the 15th-century parish church, **S. Andrea**.

Above Chiusa, a bridge conveniently crosses the Isarco for a visit to **Gudon**, the medieval 'village of seven hills' at the bottom of the quiet **Val di Funès**, enjoying lovely views of the bright white towers of the Gruppo delle Odle. Alternatively, take a side road up to the 16th-century **Castel Velturno** (*guided tours Mar–Nov at 10, 11, 2.30, 3.30, closed Mon; adm*), the elegant summer residence of the bishop of Bressanone, decorated with frescoes and wood intarsio and ceilings, all meticulously restored in the 1980s and used as a setting for art exhibits and theatre.

Bressanone/Brixen

Now a popular resort under Monte Plose, **Bressanone** is a charming ensemble of frescoed medieval buildings and arcaded streets. Capital of the region for a millennium, it was the seat of a powerful bishop who was continually at odds with the Counts of Tyrol. In 991, when the bishopic was transferred here from Sabiona, a religious city grew up in the centre of Bressanone—a northern version of the great cathedral complex in Pisa.

Unfortunately, the **Duomo** was metamorphosed into a dull baroque church in the 18th century, although the frescoes (1745–54) in the vault are Tyrolean rococo master Paul Troger's finest work. Fortunately, the remodellers never got around to the superb Romanesque **cloister**, rebuilt after a fire in 1174 and frescoed in the 1390s by followers of Michael Pacher—Leonardo da Bressanone (look for his signature scorpions of his nickname, the Maestro dello Scorpione), Giovanni, Cristoforo and Erasmo of Brunico and others (*closed between 12 and 3*), and the 11th-century **Baptistry S. Giovanni Battista**, with even earlier and rather unusual frescoes of the *Throne of Solomon* and *Seat of Wisdom* (*closed at the time of writing*). Just north of the Duomo, the parish church of **San Michele** was originally a ceme-tery chapel; rebuilt in 1503, it preserves its older campanile, while the interior was given a baroque once-over by the apprentices of the cathedral masters. Flanking San Michele, the 16th-century **Casa Pfaundler** is the handsomest palace in town.

The bishops' 13th-century palace has a princely three-storey Renaissance courtyard with terra-cotta statues in the niches, and but instead of prelates it houses the **Museo Diocesano** (*open 15 Mar–Oct 10–5; closed Sun; adm*). Here you'll find the best part of the cathedral treasure of precious artefacts and sculptures from the Middle Ages up to the 19th century, works by Michael Pacher, Lucas Cranach, Paul Troger, Giambattista Tiepolo, and a fine collection of over 10,000 *presepi* (Christmas cribs) figures.

Three kilometres north of Bressanone, the fortified, wine-making **Abbazia di Novacella** (*guided tours Easter–Oct, Mon–Sat at 10, 11, 2, 3, 4; Nov–Easter, Mon–Fri 10 and 3, Sat at 11; adm*), was founded by the Bishop of Bressanone in 1142. The abbey is a study in the evolution of architecture, with its 12th-century tower, baroque church, beautiful frescoed 14th-century cloister, and the round, crenellated 12th–16th century chapel of San Michele, all duly fortified in the late 1400s against the Ottomans—just in case they ever got this far. The one time the defences were tested, in the peasant uprising of 1525, they failed miserably. The Napoleonic deconsecration of the abbey wreaked havoc on its rich collections, but the tour still offers a small gallery of art, with a beautiful altar by Leonardo da Bressanone, and the rococo library of medieval manuscripts, although the greater part of the books ended up in Innsbruck.

Also just north of Bressanone, the **Altopiano Naz-Sciaves** is nicknamed 'Honey Plateau': planted with thousands of fruit trees, it keeps the bees busy. If you happen to be there in October, you can tuck into various treats made with stuff during the annual honey week.

Where to Stay and Eating Out

If you come between September and late November, you can join in the locals in their *Törggelen* (from the Latin *torculum*, or wine press)—going from *maso* to *maso* to try the unfermented grape juice (*Sußer*) and the new wine (*Nuie*), with roast chestnuts, speck, rye bread, and smoked salami (*Kaminwurz*), sometimes accompanied by music.

Chiusa ✉ 39043

Central, traditional ★★★**Posta**, Piazza Tinne 3, ✆ 0472 847 514, ✉ 0472 846 251 (*moderate*) has comfortable rooms as well as a summer pool in the pretty garden. In the centre of Gudon, the family-run ★★**Unterwirt**, ✆ 0472 844 000, ✉ 0472 844 065 (*moderate*) dates from 1370, with panelled rooms, a 400-year-old *Stube*, a pretty garden and homemade pasta dishes. *Closed Tues, Wed, Dec–Mar.*

Bressanone ✉ 39042

Stay in the lap of luxury at a prestigious Relais & Châteaux member, ★★★★**Dominik**, Via Terzo di Sotto 13, ✆ 0472 830 144, ✉ 0472 836 554 (*very expensive*): the spacious rooms have lovely views, and there's an indoor pool and sauna. *Open April–mid-Nov, Christmas holidays.* The restaurant, one of the best in the entire region, serves regional and Italian specialities. *Closed Tues.* Another hotel recalls a gift from the King of Portugal who, in 1550, sent an Indian elephant to Emperor Maximilian for his menagerie. En route, the pachyderm spent a week in Bressanone's post house, so impressing the locals that they had its portrait done, and there it remains to this day, on the front of the ★★★★**Elefant**, Via Rio Bianco 4, ✆ 0472 832 750, ✉ 0472 836 579 (*expensive*). Of the old Renaissance inn, only the fresco remains, but inside the ceilings and walls still have antique panelling and beautiful tile stoves. Many of the lovely rooms are furnished with antiques, though no one remembers which one the elephant slept in. There's also a pool, tennis and pleasure garden, as well as a dairy and vegetable garden that provides many of the ingredients for the Tyrolean dishes served in the restaurant. *Open Mar–Nov, Christmas; restaurant closed Mon out of season.*

By the river, little turn-of-the-century ★★★**Bel Riposo**, Via dei Vigneti 1, ✆ 0472 836 548, ✉ 0472 836 548 (*moderate*) is charming and welcoming and has a gourmet restaurant, **Zum Auenhaus**, ✆ 0472 838 344 for ultra-refined Tyrolean cuisine. *Closed Mon.* Inside the city walls the ★★**Goldene Traube**, Via Portici Minori 9, ✆ 0472 836 552, ✉ 0472 834 731 (*inexpensive*) fills up fast. The old walls are ringed with cafés; one of them, the century-old **Fink**, Via Portici Minori 4, ✆ 0472 834 883 (*moderate*) has a restaurant upstairs, serving traditional Südtirolese cooking: saddle of venison, *polenta nera* (made from buckwheat) and a wide variety of cold meats and cheeses, as well as vegetarian dishes; simpler, less pricey dishes are served downstairs in the Arkade. *Closed Tues eve, Wed, July.*

The Val Pusterìa

The Val Pusterìa, the wide and pleasant valley running east from Bressanone along the river Rienza, is dotted with typical Tyrolean villages and castles. The first, the mighty 12th-century **Castel Rodeng**, stands just east of the crossroads of the Pusteria and Isarco valleys (take the road up from Sciaves or **Rio di Pusteria**). During restorations in 1973, rare frescoes on the *Legend of Iwein* (derived from a poem by Chrétien de Troyes) were discovered on the ground floor and have been dated to around the year 1200, making them among the oldest secular pictures in Europe (*guided tours May–mid-Oct daily exc Mon at 11, 3, and 4; ✆ 0472 454 056*). If you're in the area in mid-September, take the cable car from Rio di Pusteria to the old hamlet/new ski resort of **Maranza/Meransen**, for the festival of Aubet, Cubet and Quere, three virgin daughters of the King of Burgundy, a curious cult with pre-Christian origins.

Continue up the Val Pusterìa to **San Sigismondo**, where the parish church has fine late Gothic frescoes on its exterior, and then to **Chienes**, where the Counts Künigl gave their 12th-century fortress **Casteldarne/Ehrenburg** some of the first Renaissance trimmings in the region, then baroqued the interior. They were so pleased with the result that they never remodelled it again; all the original family furnishings, tapestries and other decorations are still intact (*✆ 0747 565221; guided tours April, May, Oct Wed at 3; June–Sept Mon–Sat at 11 and 3, also at 4 in July–mid-Sept; adm*). Many churches in the Val Pusterìa contain works by the valley's 15th-century master woodcarver and painter Michael Pacher; the 13th-century parish church of **San Lorenzo di Sebato** (*closed Mon and Tues*) has his *Madonna with Grapes* on the high altar. Prominent nearby, the 11th-century convent of **Castel Badia/Sonnenburg** is now a hotel; you can visit the crypt and collection of prehistoric finds (*open daily from 10–6*).

The capital of the Pusterìa, medieval **Brunico/Bruneck** is the hub of the region. Two lovely old gates guard the town, along with a 13th-century bishop's castle at the highest point. Among the elegant shops along Via di Città, even the city pharmacy has frescoes—as does the 15th-century church **Salvatore alle Orsoline** by the gate: three beautiful painted reliefs from the same century decorate its neo-Gothic altar. Two kilometres away in Teodone, a handsome old manor houses the **Museo Provinciale degli Usi e Costumi**, Via Duca Teodone 24, devoted to traditional arts and crafts, which includes reconstructions of various mills and farm buildings (*open Easter Mon–Oct, Tues–Sat 9.30–5.30, Sun 2–6; adm*).

Brunico stands at the entrance to the heavily wooded **Val di Tures/Taufers**. The main town, **Campo Tures**, is clustered under the baronial **Castel di Tures**, guarding the entrance to the Val Aurina. Tours take in the hall of mirrors, two dozen rooms of tapestries, a chapel frescoed in 1482 by the school of Pacher and beautiful library (*Jan–Oct, Tues, Fri and Sun at 4; June–Aug 10–11, 2–4.30; adm*). Glacier alpinists come here for the **Vedrette Giganti** (or di Ríes) reached from Riva di Tures (with a waterfall), while extremists may carry on north up the narrow but dramatic Val Aurina to **Casere** and its hamlet, **Pratomagno**, with the northernmost houses in Italy.

East of Brunico, off the main Val Pusteria near Valdàora, the **Valle di Anterselva** is one of the most beautiful in the Alto Adige, growing ever narrower and narrower as it passes Lake Anterselva en route to the Parco Naturale Vedrette di Ríes, rising above a lush shawl of firs. Further east, **Monguelfo/Welsberg** was a favourite 19th-century Middle European resort (poet Hugo van Hoffmansthal spent time here) under a picture postcard 12th-century castle, rebuilt in the 1400s. In 1698 rococo painter Paul Troger was born in Monguelfo; he left three altarpieces in the parish church. From here a road turns south into the Val di Braies, where the **Lago di Braies**, fast in the Dolomites' embrace, is celebrated for its perfect stillness and intense green colour. East of Monguelfo the road continues east to Dobbiaco (*see* p.247).

Where to Stay and Eating Out

Rio di Pusterìa/Mühlbach ✉ 39037

Little Rio has a gold star on the gourmet map thanks to **Pichler**, Via Katharina Lanz 5, © 0472 849458 (*expensive*) in the heart of the village; the dining rooom, up on the first floor, provides a perfect warm and romantic setting for the finest Italian and Austrian specialities—vegetarian strudels, ravioli filled with rabbit in a *porcini* mushroom sauce, game dishes, and great cheeseboard. *Closed Mon, Tues lunch, some of June and July.* Above Rio, near the funivia station in Maranza, little ★★★**Erika**, © 0472 520 196, @ 0472 520 311 (*moderate*) is a perfect base for a sporty stay, run by an Olympic skier, with an indoor pool, tennis and other sports. *Open mid-Dec–mid-April, June–mid-Oct.* In Vàlles, 7km up the same narrow valley, the delightful ★★★**Masl**, ©/@ 0472 547 187 (*moderate–inexpensive*) has similar facilities and great food in the restaurant. *Open mid-Dec–mid-April, mid-May–mid-Oct.*

Brunico/Bruneck and Around ✉ 39031

Smack in the heart of town, ★★★**Posta**, Via Bastioni 9, © 0474 555 127, @ 0474 551 603 (*moderate*) is a traditional favourite, in the same family for 150 years. ★★★**Andreas Hofer**, Via Campo Tures 1, © 0474 551 469, @ 0474 551 283 (*moderate*) has a summer pool, gym and satellite TV, and a good restaurant. For real luxury in a large park, head up 3km to Riscone/Reischach and the ★★★★**Royal Hunter Hinterbuber**, © 0474 548 221, @ 0474 548 048 (*expensive–moderate*) with indoor and outdoor pools, tennis and other sports. *Open Christmas–Easter and June–mid-Oct.* In Ameto, a hamlet just outside of Brunico, a rural *maso* built in 1368 is the home of **Oberraut**, © 0474 559 977 (*moderate*), a cosy little hotel owned by a good chef and open to non-guests, serving homemade cheeses, pasta, and sausages; unusual Pusterìa specialities served on request. *Closed Thurs exc in season, and Jan.* In Gais, just up the Val di Tures, ***Hotel Windschar**, Via Ulrich V. Tauffers 3, © 0474 504 123, ✆ 0474 504 380 (*moderate*) is a large Tyrolean-style place in a lovely garden setting, with indoor and outdoor pools. *Open Dec–mid-April and mid-May–Nov.*

The Upper Val Isarco to the Brenner Pass

Between Bressanone and the Pass, the big news is colourful **Vipiteno/Sterzing**, a medieval company town that belonged to the Fuggers, one of Europe's greatest banking dynasties. The attraction it held for them was its mines, especially silver; although abandoned in 1979 they were lucrative enough in the Renaissance to employ 10,000 miners and for the residents to build splendid battlemented houses after a fire devastated Vipiteno in 1443. The tall **Torre di Città** was built to celebrate the reconstruction; the mines are remembered in the nearby **Museo Provinciale delle Miniere Jöchlsthurn** (*open Easter–15 Nov, Tues–Sat 10–12 and 2–5; adm*). The best houses are along Via Città Nuova; pop into the courtyard of the **Municipio** to see an impressive Mithraic altar from the 3rd century BC, with a cycle of myths carved around the main scene of Mithras sacrificing the bull. In Piazza Città, the **Museo Multscher** (*open April–Oct, Mon 2–5; Tues–Fri 10–12, 2–5; Sat 10–12; adm*) is devoted to a handful of elegant works by the 15th-century painter Hans Multscher.

Three kilometres southeast, the Counts Thurn und Taxis' magnificent 11th–14th century **Castel Tasso** has some of the best art in the province in its frescoed rooms, late Gothic decorations and a 12th-century *Stube* (*guided tours Easter–Nov 1, 9.30, 10.30, 2 and 3, closed Fri; adm*). Other excursions around Vipiteno include the scenic **Val Ridanna** to the west, with a waterfall near **Stranghe** and the **Castel Wolfsthurn** at Mareta. This castle is considered the most beautiful baroque building in the whole Tyrol—you can examine the interior while perusing the collection of stuffed deer and fish belonging to the **Museo Provinciale della Caccia e della Pesca** (*open April–Nov 1, Tues–Sat 9.30–5.30, Sun 2–6; adm*). At **Maiern**, at the top of the Val Ridanna, you can visit a mine gallery, complete with a mining demonstration (*April–Oct, Tues–Sun 9.30–4.30*); in summer (*June–Oct 12.30–2.30*) you can carry on to **San Martino Monteneve**, the highest mining town in Europe.

The main road north of Vitepeno continues to **Colle Isarco/Gossensass**, a resort and spa that was a favourite of Henrik Ibsen, with skiing and hiking on Cima Bianca and in the **Val di Fleres**, the Fuggers' silver lode; the cemetery church at Colle Isarco has a beautiful late Gothic altarpiece in the miners' chapel, **Santa Barbara**. Beyond this lies the **Brenner Pass** (4511ft), the lowest of the Alpine passes, and the route of countless invaders from the north; during the Second World War it was heavily bombed. From here it is 125km to Innsbruck.

Where to Stay and Eating Out

Vipiteno/Sterzing ✉ 39049

In the 16th century ****Aquila Nera**, Piazza Città 1, © 0472 764 064, ✆ 0472 766 522 (*expensive–moderate*) you can relax in the heart of town and take a dip in the indoor pool. A favourite place to eat, **Pretzhof**, © 0472 764 455, 8km away in Tulve (*moderate*) will fill you up on delicious traditional dishes, prepared with ingredients from the family's farm. *Closed Mon, Tues, some of June and July.*

The Upper Adige

A famous spa, a dense carpet of vineyards and enough castles for thirty games of chess follow the road up to to the Resia Pass, near the Austrian and Swiss frontiers.

Tourist Information

Merano: Corso Libertà 35, © 0473 235 223, ✉ 0473 235 524; *info@meraninfo.it*.
Naturno: Via Municipio, © 0473 87287, ✉ 0473 88270.

Merano

Just 28km up the Adige from Bolzano, Merano is an attractive town of gardens and flowers, a favourite spa since the 1830s for elderly and sedate central Europeans with respiratory complaints. Basking in a sheltered, balmy microclimate and endowed with radioactive waters, Merano enchanted Franz Kafka: 'Everlasting snow and rocky areas surrounded by storm over-look subtropical paradises, a small representation of all the continent from Scandanavia to the Riviera, from ice deserts to sweet lands in bloom.' The benefits of the waters, clean air and graded mountain walks are complemented by specific cures, such as the famous grape cure in September–October (in juice form the other months); eating two pounds of Merano grapes a day, taking care to chew them well, apparently keeps the doctor away.

Apart from possibly inflicting digestive disorders, Merano does have other attractions: along the Adige, there's the striking Liberty-style Casino and **Kursaal** topped with dancing Graces, now a Congress Centre. Two streets back, the arcaded Via dei Portici was the main street in the medieval town, and has, at No.68, the **Museo di Vestiti** (*open Mon–Fri 9.30–12.30, 2.30–6.30, Sat 9.30–1; adm*) where you can see what dedicated female followers of fashion have been wearing over the past century. The stern 15th-century Gothic **Duomo** contains International Gothic frescoes in the style of Trento's Castello di Buonconsiglio.

Via Cassa di Risparomio leads back to the little 15th-century **Castello Principesco** (*open Tues–Sat 10–5, Sun 10–1; in July and Aug also Sun 4–7; adm*), built by Archduke Sigismond and containing Gothic furnishings, arms, and swords. Opposite, you can take a chairlift up to Tirolo (*see* below) or pick up the 4km **Passeggiata Tappeiner**, the Meraners' favourite promenade, a botanical wonderland overlooking the city. At Via delle Corse 42—the next street over—the **Museo Civico** (*same hours*) has four Bronze Age statue stelae, some fine Gothic sculptures, and a *Pietà* by the school of Michael Pacher.

For centuries, the landowners of these valleys were generally left alone to govern and defend their turf, and as a result the area bristles with a large proportion of the Alto Adige's 350-plus castles. The big cheese, however, lived just above Merano in **Tirolo**, at **Castel Tirol** (*open April–Oct 10–5, closed Mon; adm*) balanced on the precipice. The castle gave its name to the region and to this day remains its symbol: it was the headquarters of the independent Counts until 1363, when Margherita di Maultasch, the 'Ugly Countess', ceded Tyrol to the Habsburgs. Adorned with a fine set of medieval monsters and frescoes, it houses different exhibitions every year. Also in Tirolo, **Castel Fontana** (*open mid-Mar–Nov, 9.30–5, closed Tues; adm*) is a rather imaginative reconstruction of a 12th-century castle, with a collection of farm instruments and memorabilia related to the poet Ezra Pound (d. 1972), who was found too crazy to stand trial for treason (he made pro-Mussolini radio broadcasts during the war) and retired here in 1958 after his release from a Washington hospital. The village facing Tirolo, **Scena**, has a round 12th-century church, **San Giorgio**, with good frescoes, and the **Castel Scena**, built in 1346 and still owned by the Counts of Meran (*guided visits Easter–Nov 1, Mon–Sat; at 10.30, 11.30, 2, 3, 4, 5; adm*) with original furnishings, frescoes and armour.

The Val Venosta

West of Merano, the Val Venosta follows the Adige towards Austria. One of the first villages, **Parcines**, was the home of Peter Mitterhofer, typewriter inventor; the **Museo della Macchina da Scrivere** at Via Stampf 2 is dedicated to the history of the machines, concentrating on Mitterhofer's prototypes (*ring ahead, © 0473 967 121*). At **Naturno**, the little church of **San Procolo** has some fresco fragments that go back to the 8th century, the oldest, in fact, in any German-speaking territory (*open Tues–Sun 9.30–12 and 2.30–5*).

A little way west on the SS38, a narrow but very scenic road digresses north up a majestic gorge into the **Val di Senales/Schnalstal**, on the western edge of the **Parco Naturale Gruppo di Tessa**, the largest park in the Alto Adige, a rocky wilderness of 10,000-foot peaks—an eyrie where the likes of Reinhold Messner, the Südtirolean master of mountain derring-do, feels perfectly at home; his 13th-century **Castel Juvale**, located at the entrance to the valley, houses his collection of artefacts from Tibet, masks from around the world, and more (*shuttle buses go up from the car park in Stava; guided tours Palm Sun–June, Sept–15 Nov 10–4; closed Wed; adm*). Up the valley, there's **Certosa/Karthaus**, a 14th-century charterhouse delightfully converted into a hamlet after it was suppressed in 1782, as well the little **Lago di Vernago**. Funivias from the top of the valley go over the mountains into Austria.

Back on the main Adige road, the 13th-century cragtop Castello di Castelbello guards the entrance in **Laces/Latsch**, a tourist centre with the only all-year skiing in this area and a collection of sacred art in the **Museo di Laces**, in a former hospital in Via Funivia (*open April–Dec Tues–Fri 2.30–5, Sat 10–12*); the prize here is a beautiful early Renaissance altar by Jörg Lederer (1524). Just southeast, **Tàrres/Tarsch** is a picturesque medieval hamlet, while on the other end of Laces the confines of Stelvio National Park (*see* below) begin at **Morter** and incorporate the entire **Val di Martello**, a wooded valley south of the Val Venosta. **Paradiso del Cevedale** (6851ft) at the top of the valley has magnificent views over the stupendous amphitheatre formed by Cevedale (12,327ft) and surrounding peaks.

In the upper valley, an hour's drive from Merano, **Sluderno/Schludrens** is sheltered enough to support orchards and even vineyards. It was long ruled by the Trapps, whose magnificent 13th–16th-century **Castel Coira** (*open late Mar–1 Nov, Tues–Sun 10–12, 2–4.30; adm*) has gloriously painted Renaissance loggias, frescoes dedicated to the greater glory of the Trapp family, and the largest private collection of armour in all Europe, with pieces going back to the 13th century. The counts' tombs fill the 16th-century church of Santa Caterina; the **Museo della Val Venosta**, in Via Merano 1 (*open April–Oct, Tues–Sun 9.30–12, 2–5*) features archaeology, art, and displays dedicated to the valley's pedlars.

Nearby, **Glorenza/Glurns** was given its city status back in 1304, but was razed to the ground in 1499 by the Swiss. Rebuilt in 1555 by Jörg Kölderer, Emperor Maximilian's architect, it stands unchanged—nothing less than the smallest walled city in Europe. One item the Swiss missed in their rampage was the church of **S. Pancrazio**, on a hill just south of Glorenza, with a *Last Judgement* of 1496 frescoed on the campanile. Two kilometres from Glorenza, **Làudes/Laatsch** is one of the best preserved medieval villages in the Alto Adige, with a striking and finely decorated church of 1408, its choir buttressed against a crag.

Both towns lie at the foot of the lush **Val Monastero/Münstertal** (SS41), 9km from Switzerland; on the way to the border, in the old frescoed village of **Tubre/Taufers**, many houses still retain their traditional exterior stairs. At the entrance to the village, the 13th-century church-hospice **S. Giovanni** was built over the ruins of a Carolingian church; the striking frescoes in the choir, painted around 1220, show the influence of Venice even here. The church in **Müstair**, just over the Swiss border, has what are generally acclaimed the finest Carolingian frescoes in all Europe.

Nearly as good, however, are those up the main valley in **Malles Venosta**, 'the town of five towers' in the chapel of **San Benedett**, built under the direct patronage of Charlemagne himself (*key at Via S. Bemedeo 31, Mon–Sat 9–11.30 and 1.30–5; adm*). Just up in **Burgusio**, the beautiful 17th-century Benedictine **Abbazia di Monte Maria** forms a gleaming white crown of towers and gables in a woodland setting; the crypt from the original church has rare, excellently preserved 12th-century frescoes of Jerusalem (*guided tours daily exc Sat pm and Sun, 15 June–15 Sept at 10, 11, 3, 4.30; Oct–May at 10.45 and 3; adm*). On the way to Austria, the road passes the romantically ruined castle of **Lichtenburg** and the artificial **Lago di Resia**, with the church spire of a submerged village poking above its surface.

South of the Val Venosta: Stelvio National Park

The SS38 at Spondigna (just before Sluderno) is one of the main roads into **Stelvio National Park**, the largest in Italy, administered by the provinces of Sondrio, Trento and Bolzano, all of which have **visitors' centres** that can tell you where to find the marked trails, alpine refuges, and the best flowers and wildlife, including chamois, marmots, eagles, and the ibex, reintroduced in 1968. As well as offering endless possibilities for climbers, the park also encompasses fifty lakes, a hundred glaciers (a tenth of the 134,620 hectares is ice) and Europe's second-highest pass, the **Passo dello Stelvio**, open June through October. In the Alto Adige section of the park **Solda/Sulden**, set in a beautiful mountain-rimmed basin, has most of the hotels and sports facilities, and year-round funivias up to the Città di Milano refuge, offering grand views over Gran Zebrù (12,635ft).

Where to Stay and Eating Out

Merano ✉ 39021

As one might expect of an old-world spa like Merano, there are a good number of luxury hotels, but not much in the lower ranges. You can sleep like a lord in a castle: near the centre, the picturesque 12th-century ★★★★**Kurhotel Castel Rundegg**, Via Scena 2, ✆ 0473 234100, 🕮 0473 237 200 (*very expensive*) has every luxury, including an indoor pool and fitness centre and a lovely park. Set among the vines above Merano, ★★★**Castello Labers**, Via Labers 25, ✆ 0473 234 484, 🖷 0473 234 146 (*expensive*), a castle-villa from the 1200s, is a little more modest, but has a pool and views too. *Open April–Nov.*

Kafka preferred the aristocratic ★★★★★**Palace**, in the heart of Merano at Via Cavour 2, ✆ 0473 211 300, 🖷 0473 234 181(*very expensive*), set in beautifully maintained grounds with a spa and beauty centre; the restaurant is considered the best in town. Another atmospheric choice, ★★★**Westend**, near the centre at Via Speckbacher 9, ✆ 0473 447 654, 🖷 0473 222 726 (*moderate*) has 22 lovely rooms in a 19th-century villa, tucked back in a garden. Near the spa, ★**Pension Tyrol**, Via 30 Aprile 8, ✆ 0473 449 719 (*inexpensive*) is quiet, in a big garden, with free parking.

Merano's restaurants are concentrated around Via dei Portici: for *typische Südtiroler* cooking try **Laubenkeller** at No. 118, ✆ 0473 237 706 (*moderate*). *Closed Thurs.* Or try **Sissi**, one of the best in town, up by the Castello Principesco on Via Galilei 44, ✆ 0473 231 062 (*expensive*), where the delicious food has a Piedmontese touch. *Closed Mon.*

Màlles Venosta/Mals im Vinschgau ✉ 39024

In a building dating back to the 16th century, ★★★**Plavina**, 3km out of the centre in Burgùsio, ✆ 0473 831 223, 🖷 0473 830 406 (*moderate*) has typical rooms with mountain views, indoor pool and sauna; the restaurant, **Moro** has been in the same family since 1665, serving seasonal dishes, *schlützkrapfen* (little ravioli) with melted butter, great roast potatoes and game in the autumn. *Closed Tues and Wed lunch.*

Solda/Sulden ✉ 39029

The oldest hotel in the valley, ★★★**Eller**, Via Principale 15, ✆ 0473 613 021, 🖷 0473 613 085 (*moderate*) has been in business in 1865, so the family knows what they're about; rooms have been recently updated. *Open mid-Nov–April, July–Sept.* Cosy ★★★**Gampen**, ✆ 0473 613 023, 🖷 0473 613 193 (*moderate*) is another of Solda's old timers, with knockout mountain views. *Open mid-Nov–April, July–mid-Sept.*

Friuli-Venezia Giulia

For many travellers, this bit of the Big Boot spilling over like a thick lumpy sock to the east is terra incognita, with a jumbly name that may ring a bell only because it often turns up on the wine list in Italian restaurants. Trieste, at the far end of Italy, evokes cloudy images of pre- and post-War intrigue, a kind of Third Man on the Mediterranean. And in between Trieste and Venice the imagination fails.

It doesn't help that the region is burdened with a history as messy as its name. In Roman days Aquileia was the most important city and became seat of the oldest patriarchate outside Rome. Its ecclesiastical and temporal authority was gradually usurped by Cividale del Friuli, the Lombard capital in the Dark Ages, and then in the Middle Ages by Ùdine, before all was snatched away by the Venetians in the 14th century. Trieste was sometimes under the doges' thumb, sometimes Venice's bitter rival under the Counts of Gorizia or the Austrians.

Napoleon threw Friuli-Venezia Giulia in with his 'Kingdom of Illyria', a piece of real estate subsequently picked up by the Austro-Hungarian Empire until 1918, when Italy inherited it along with the easternmost bit of Venice's old *terra firma* empire—all of Istria except for Fiume (modern Rijeka), an error of omission that Gabriele D'Annunzio personally went over to rectify (*see* p.220). If Italian nationalists were pleased, their Slavic counterparts were outraged. Although Istria was given a certain amount of autonomy in 1924, order was asserted only by brutal repression of the Slavic majority by Mussolini's government, especially once the Duce dictated that everyone had to speak Italian. When the Germans moved in on the scene in 1943 they gave the region a new name, Adriatische Küsterland, and in Trieste set up a extermination camp, the only one on Italian soil.

After the Second World War Istria was ceded to Yugoslavia, while Tito, whose partisans had helped to take Trieste from the Germans, angled for the big port city itself. The Allies forced him to leave, then occupied the city themselves as a neutral free port until 1954, when it was readmitted into Italy. The region's troubles were hardly over: two disastrous earthquakes in 1976 (6.5 and 6.1 on the Richter scale) killed a thousand people, levelled entire towns, and left 70,000 buildings in need of major structural repair.

Weary of being marginal, Friuli-Venezia Giulia is now creating an identity of its own, although at times it seems like putting together pieces from several different jigsaw puzzles. The population in the east speaks Slovenian, while the Carnia and Julian Alps have a sizeable German minority. Trieste has large Jewish, Greek, and Serb minorities, and in the middle, around Ùdine, you have the Friulians themselves, who, like the Ladins in the Dolomites, speak a language similar to the Swiss Rhaeto-Romansch. It's a melting pot, Italian-style, and one that is becoming spicier all the time: the reopening of Central and Eastern Europe in the 1990s means that Friuli-Venezia Giulia is no longer Italy's dead end, but an important link to its future.

Friuli-Venezia Giulia

Getting Around

Trains from Venice along the coast run roughly every two hours (journey time to Trieste two hours). **Buses** are less frequent, though Càorle can most easily be reached by direct bus from Venice. An alternative is to take the train to S. Donà di Piave and the local bus to Càorle from there. For Lignano-Sabbiadoro, take the train to Latisana, linked by bus to the coast in about 30 minutes.

Tourist Information

Càorle: Calle delle Liburniche 11, ℂ 0421 81085, @ 0421 84251.
Bibione: Viale Aurora 101, ℂ 0431 43362, @ 0431 439 997.
Portogruaro: Borgo S. Agnese 37, ℂ 0421 273 230, @ 0421 274 600.
Lignano-Sabbiadoro: Via Latisana 42, ℂ 0413 71821, @ 0431 70449.

Altino and Càorle

The SS14 from Venice passes first Marco Polo airport and then **Altino**, the modern name of the Roman city of Altinum. Once renowned for its wealth and villas, it was put to the sack by Attila the Hun—only the first of many hardships that led its inhabitants to give up and found a new city on the island of Torcello in the Venetian Lagoon. They took whatever Attila and the Lombards didn't wreck along with them, so that all that remains in the **Museo Nazionale** (*open Tues–Sun 9–2*) are mosaics, items from tombs and a few odds and ends.

The route continues over the Piave near **San Donà di Piave**, a town that had to be completely rebuilt after the First World War; it was near here that Ernest Hemingway, an ambulance driver for the Red Cross, was wounded in 1918, an experience that became the germ of *A Farewell to Arms*. From San Donà, you can make a detour to the brightly painted old fishermen's town and modern seaside resort of **Càorle**, originally Roman *Caprulae*, the port of Concordia Sagittaria. One of its landmarks is the church-lighthouse on its isthmus, and another is its cathedral, built in 1038, with a distinctive cylindrical campanile and a splendid Venetian *Pala d'Oro* (12th–14th centuries) on the altar. Wildfowl flock along the coast in the **Valle Grande** (a water valley, that is, along the inner lagoon) which preserves a relic of the primordial pine woods that once scented the shore from Grado to Ravenna. **Bibione**, east, is an even bigger resort, with a long strand of sand.

Portogruaro and Around

East of San Donà, the various *autostrade* and highways come together at **Portogruaro**, a seductive old town of porticoed streets, frescoed palazzi and sparkling canals, dreaming away under its palm trees and jauntily tilted 193ft campanile, built in the 12th century. The Duomo is a wallflower by Veneto standards, but the neighbouring 14th-century **Loggia Comunale** (now the Municipio) is one of the most striking civic buildings in the region, shaped like a mountain crested with fantail Ghibelline battlements, which lend it a curiously organic appearance. Don't miss the well (1494) in the piazza, crowned with a pair of cranes (*gru*) that gave the town its name. In Via del Seminario, the **Museo Nazionale Concordiese** (*open daily 9–7; adm*) is a church crowded with an assortment of bronzes and coins, among other finds excavated in

Concordia Sagittaria, just south of Portogruaro. This was a glass- and arrow- (*sagitta*) manufacturing Roman colony. Its Romanesque cathedral standing next to the ruins of a basilica (389) conserves part of its pavement; adjacent stands a frescoed Byzantine baptistry of 1089.

In **Summaga**, 3km west of Portogruaro, the Benedictine abbey of **Santa Maria Maggiore** (© 0421 205126) was built around a 6th-century votive chapel. The walls are covered with a fascinating cycle of 12th- and 13th-century frescoes, all recently restored; in the votive chapel, don't miss the fighting griffins and lions, chivalrous deeds, and virtues and vices. More fond old things await in **Sesto al Règhena**, 9km north of Portogruaro, a quaint medieval village with a moat in the centre, originally part of the defences of **Santa Maria in Silvis** (*open daily 8–7*), an abbey of Lombard foundation that grew to become one of the most powerful in Friuli. The current Romanesque-Byzantine basilica dates from the 11th century and has both a vestibule (with 11th-century frescoes of *St Michael*, and later ones of the *Inferno* and *Paradiso*) and an atrium with three naves. The main body of the church is frescoed as well (look for the unusual one of Christ crucified on a voluptuous pomegranate tree). Among the bas-reliefs is a beautiful 13th-century *Annunciation*, while the vast crypt contains an 8th-century Lombard-Byzantine sarcophagus of St Anastasia. Lastly, at **Fossalta di Portogruaro**, by the little church of Sant'Antonio in Vilanova, grows one of the **oldest oak trees in Europe**, 300 years old—when they signed the Magna Carta.

Lignano-Sabbiadoro

East of Concordio Sagittaria, **Latisana** was once an important port of the patriarchate, and has only one good reason to detain you: Paolo Veronese's *Baptism of Christ* (1567) in the Duomo. From Latisana a new road, the SS354, branches off to the coast: you can follow the crowds south to the Laguna di Marano and the fastest-growing resort area on the Adriatic, **Lignano-Sabbiadoro**, the 'Austrian Riviera'. Set on the tip of the peninsula, with a lovely 9km sandy beach and scores of new hotels, apartments, bungalows and campsites, Lignano-Sabbiadoro and its two adjacent resorts of **Lignano-Pineta** (the prettiest section, under the pinewoods) and smart **Lignano Riviera**, offer fun in the sun and Viennese sausages just like Mutter makes. Some of the smaller islands are dotted with *casoni*, steep thatched fisherman's cottages; some real, some recreated for visitors. Birds like Lignano too—of the 165 species that have been sighted in Italy, 141 have been seen in the Laguna di Marano.

Where to Stay and Eating Out

In the beach resorts, high season prices run from mid-June to the end of August; book ahead, especially for the first three weeks of August.

Càorle ✉ 30021

Set on its own little port, ★★★**Diplomatic**, Via Strada Nuova 19, © 0421 81087, ✆ 0421 210 089 (*inexpensive*) is comfortable and has the area's best restaurant, **Duilio**, celebrated for its succulent seafood in the *antipasti*, with the pasta, and as the main course. A charming setting, a huge wine list and reasonably priced menus are added attractions. *Closed Mon, Jan.* Immersed in pines, ★★★**Garden**, Piazza Belvedere, © 0421 210 036, ✆ 0421 210 037 (*moderate–inexpensive*) is right by the beach, and has a pool, tennis, and sauna; nearly all rooms have balconies. *Open April–Sept.* Up the Livenza river in San Giorgio di Livenza, **Al Cacciatore**, Corso Risorgimento 25, ✆ 0421 80331 (*expensive*) is a popular family-run restaurant of long standing, featuring the freshest of fish and mushrooms in season. *Closed Wed, some of Aug.*

Lignano ✉ 33054

Near the pines in shady Lignano-Pineta, ★★★★★**Greif**, Arco del Grecale 27, ✆/✉ 0431 422 261 (*very expensive*) is a large resort hotel with a pool and park, sauna and private beach. The more intimate ★★★★**Medusa Splendid**, Raggio dello Scirocco 33, ✆ 0431 422 211, ✉ 0431 422 251 (*moderate*) also has a pool, very good rooms and a garden. *Open mid-May–mid-Sept.* In Lignano Riviera, the fashionable ★★★★**Eurotel**, Calle Mendelssohn 13, ✆ 0431 428 991, ✉ 0431 428 992 (*expensive*) enjoys perhaps the most beautiful setting in the area and offers lovely rooms, a heated pool and more. *Open mid-May–mid-Sept.*

Built up in the last 25 years, Lignano-Sabbiadoro is a good place to look for self-catering bungalows as well as hotels, although none really stands out. For comfortable rooms try ★★★★**Miramar**e, Via Aquileia 47/B, ✆ 0431 71260, ✉ 0431 720051 (*expensive*), with parking and a garden as well as its own beach. *Open mid-May–Sept.* ★★★**Vittoria**, Lungomare Marin 28, ✆ 0431 71221, ✉ 0431 73292 (*moderate*), a fine older hotel, has recently had a face lift. *Open mid-May–Sept.* Good restaurants include the small but convivial **Bidin**, Via Europa 1, ✆ 0431 71988 (*expensive*), with a separate *menu degustazione* for either fish or meat. *Closed Wed.* Al Bancut, Via Friuli 32, ✆ 0431 71926 (*moderate*), in the centre of town, features fine grilled fish, traditionally prepared. *Closed Tues eve, Wed.*

Pordenone and its Province

The river Tagliamento divides Friuli into two: the fairly flat western part, *de là da aghe* (literally 'that side of the water') has a strong Venetian identity and speaks a similar dialect.

Tourist Information

Pordenone: Corso V. Emanuele II 38, ✆ 0434 21912, ✉ 0434 523 814.
Piancavallo (in season): ✆ 0434 65519 ✉ 0434 655 354.
Spilimbergo: Piazza Castello, ✆/✉ 042 72274.
San Daniele: Via Roma, ✆/✉ 0432 940 765.

Pordenone

Hemingway poked fun at it and, to be honest, there's not a lot more to say about Pordenone, provincial capital and manufacturer of Zanussi fridges and washing machines. Overlooking the Noncello, it does have a handsome if somewhat over-restored main street, Corso Vittorio Emanuele, lined with porticoes and palaces, some with frescoes from the 14th–17th centuries. The end of the Corso is closed off by the bijou **Palazzo Comunale**, where a Venetian clock tower topped by two bell-ringing Moors was superimposed on a graceful 13th-century building.

If Pordenone is known at all outside Italy, it's primarily due to the self-taught artist Giovanni Antonio de Sacchis (1483–1539), who adopted the name and whose works hang in the frescoed rooms of the **Museo Civico**, housed opposite the Palazzo Comunale in the pretty

15th-century Palazzo Ricchieri (*open Tues–Fri 9.30–12.30 and 3–6; adm*). Other paintings— Pordenone's odd masterpiece, the *Madonna della Misericordia* (1515), his unfinished high altarpiece, and frescoes—decorate the salmon-pink **Duomo**. The 236ft campanile is the town landmark, a refined tower of Romanesque brickwork of 1347. The **Museo Civico delle Scienze** in Via della Motta 16 (*open Mon–Fri 9–12 and 3–6; adm*) has a room of birds, archaeological finds, and a reconstruction of a Renaissance scientific cabinet or studiolo. The washing machine works are actually just outside Pordenone in **Porcìa**, which has a well preserved *centro storico* with a castle and an unusual 15th-century campanile.

The Pedemontana and Valcellina

If you want to escape the crowds, you can't do better than the foothills or Pedemontana on the western frontier of Friuli. Hanging over the willowy banks of the Livenza, **Sacile**, the main town in these parts, is famous for its bird festival (the *Sagra dei Osei*), held on the last Sunday in August ever since 1351. Thousands of songbirds are assembled at dawn in the main piazza, and prizes are awarded to the birds and the person who can best imitate their songs. Sacile was the 'Garden of the Serenissima' and, like many well-watered towns of the *terra firma*, has the dreamy, Venetian air to it. There are several attractive *palazzi* and a 15th-century Lombard style **Duomo**, restored after the 1976 quake; it has modern frescoes, and paintings by Francesco Bassano and Palma Giovanni in the sacristy.

Just north of Sacile, small medieval **Cáneva** huddles under the ruins of an 11th-century castle, although the castle chapel of **Santa Lucia** preserves charming frescoes. Another 10km north, **Polcenigo** on the Livenza has a Venetian core. There's a NATO air base just east, near the thousand-year-old **Castel d'Aviano**, partly rebuilt by the Venetians in 1432. Just outside the town walls, the 13th-century cemetery church of **Santa Giuliana** has Venetian-Byzantine frescoes; on the other side of Aviano near the train tracks, **San Gregorio** has a fetching 15th-century fresco cycle by Gianfrancesco da Tolmezzo.

From Aviano it's only 14km up to the Forest of Cansiglio (*see* p.232) and Monte Cavallo (7380ft), where the up and coming ski resort at **Piancavallo** recently hosted the skiing World Cup and has wide views over the plain below. Alternatively, if you've found the other Dolomites too busy, continue north into the Valcellina and the **Parco Naturale della Dolomite Friulina**. After Montereale Valcellina, the road passes through a steep, almost claustrophobic **Forra del Cellina**, like one of the valleys in Dante's *Inferno*, before reaching Lago di Barcis and the little mountain resorts of **Claut** and **Cimoláis**. Don't miss the stupendous 700ft monolithic pinnacle called the **Campanile** in the Val Montanaia.

The largest town in the region, **Maniago**, with its enormous market square, has made daggers for the Venetian army and knives and cutlery in general since the 14th century. One of the town's 250 firms specializes in antique armour, in great demand in Hollywood; the replicas are so accurate that they have to stamp each piece to keep it from being sold off to museums.

Along the River Tagliamento

East of Pordenone and not far from the wide bed of the Tagliamento, the handsome market town of **San Vito** was the birthplace of Fra Paolo Sarpi. It still has three tower houses, a porticoed Piazza del Popolo and a **Duomo** with a number of good Renaissance paintings, but the best art is in the former church of **S. Maria dei Battuti**—a cycle of 16th-century frescoes by

Pompeo Amalteo, a painter from Treviso of whom Vasari made much in his *Lives of the Artists*. Just over the big river in **Codroipo**, the **Villa Manin** (1738) (*open Tues–Sun 9–12.30, 3–6; winter 9–12 and 2–5; free*) is nothing less than the biggest villa in all Venetia, the swan song—or swan blast, rather—of Venice's *dolce vita*. When owner Ludovico Manin was elected Doge in Venice, his chief rival declared, 'A Friulian as Doge! The republic is dead.' The prediction was soon proved correct, and to add insult to injury, Napoleon parked himself at this ranch as a guest, if not a welcome one. A painting by David hangs in the room he slept in; also to see are rooms of frescoed fluff, an elegant horseshoe exedra (a secular version of Bernini's colonnade at St Peter's), the armoury, map salon, a museum of carriages and a handsome park, a great place for a picnic. From here it's 20km to Ùdine.

If you're not in a hurry, however, there's more to see along the Tagliamento. North of San Vito, **San Giorgio della Richinvelda** has more fine frescoes by Gianfrancesco da Tolmezzo (1496) in the parish church at Provesano. Further north, medieval **Spilimbergo** is a town of discreet charm and more than its share of churches—the best of these, the Gothic cathedral, has a Romanesque portal and paintings by Pordenone. On the edge of town, the pretty 12th-century 'Painted' **castle** has exterior frescoes, while in the centre there's a **mosaic school** (*open for tours by appointment, ☎ 0427 2155*), founded in 1922 to renew the great art of Aquileia; graduates have worked as far away as Japan. Off to the north of Spilimbergo, near Clauzetto, the **Grotte Verdi di Pradis** (*open daylight hours, July and Aug; sunny Sundays only other months; adm*) is uncannily green, thanks to the sun filtering through the limestone—uncanny enough to be made into a church, the 'National Temple of Speology'. Walkways follow the torrent Cosa that sculpted it up a high narrow gorge. In **Usago** a megalithic structure of cyclopean stones called the Cjadin is attributed to the Paleovenetians; in nearby **Meduno** a monolithic altar has a primitive carving of a bull.

Surrounded by fields of maize and *prosciutterie*, the most famous town in these parts is **San Daniele del Friuli**, the 'Siena of Friuli,' an ochre-tinted market town east of the Tagliamento, famous for its sweet-cured hams. Don't miss the recently restored frescoes by Pellegrino di San Daniele in the church of **Sant' Antonio Abate**: his masterpiece, painted between 1498–1522, and the finest Renaissance cycle in all Friuli. Pellegrino's real name was Martino da Ùdine, but he spent so much time in San Daniele that he became known as the town's pilgrim. To the right of the Duomo, the **Biblioteca Guarneriana**, Via Roma 1 (*open Tues–Sun 9–12*) was founded by a canon of Aquileia, Guarnerio d'Artegna (d. 1467) and has lovely medieval manuscripts in a historic library setting. But culture is only a sideline in ham-ville, especially in August during the *Aria di Festa*, when the town parties, producing hundreds of hams and bottles of wine for tasting.

Where to Stay and Eating Out

Pasiano di Pordenone ✉ 33087

Sixteen kilometres west of Pordenone, set off in a five-hectare park, ★★★★**Villa Luppis**, Via Martino 34, ☎ 0434 626 969, ● 0434 626 228 (*expensive*) was a Camaldolesi monastery in the Middle Ages, before it became a patrician's villa, before it became one of the best hotels in Friuli, its 21 rooms furnished with Louis XVI antiques. The restaurant is equally prestigious; try pasta with scampi and courgette flowers. The hotel also runs a shuttle bus to Venice, 40 minutes away.

Pordenone ✉ 33170

The elegant ★★★★**Villa Ottoboni**, Piazzetta Ottoboni 2, ✆ 0434 208 891, ✉ 0434 208 148 (*expensive*) is right near the centre, and offers fully furnished rooms; the adjacent restaurant dates from the late 15th century. For modern, comfortable rooms ★★★**Park**, Via Mazzini 43, ✆ 0434 27901, ✉ 0434 522 353 (*moderate*) is a good central choice. Dine at **Da Zelina**, in an early Renaissance palace in Piazza San Marco, ✆ 0434 27290 (*moderate*) with succulent meat dishes and pizzas in the evening (*closed Sat lunch, Mon, part of Aug*) or head out to Porcìa (4km west), to **Gildo**, Viale Marconi 17, ✆ 0434 921 212 (*expensive*) in an imposing Venetian palace in a large park. The menu is equally divided between meat and fish dishes; prices are considerably lower at lunch. *Closed Sun eve, Mon, Aug.*

Nine kilometres north of Pordenone, at San Quirino, **Antica Trattoria La Primula**, Via San Rocco 47, ✆ 0434 91005, ✉ 0434 919 280 (*expensive*) has for six generations served up the best food in the province, superb, classic and simply prepared, from the *antipasti* through the fresh seafood to the elegant desserts, served in the simple but elegant dining room. The same folks run the adjacent frescoed **Osteria Alle Nazioni**, with good food and kinder prices. *Closed Sun eve, Mon, part of Jan and July.*

Spilimbergo ✉ 33097

★★**Michielini**, Viale Barbacane 3, ✆/✉ 0427 50450 (*inexpensive*) is an old family-run hotel in the centre of town, with a good restaurant; alternatively, dine on the likes of ravioli filled with pumpkin in mushroom sauce and strudels in the castle at **La Torre**, Piazza Castello, ✆ 0427 50555 (*moderate*); anyone fond of wine will have a field day with the selection in its cellar. *Closed Sun eve and Mon.*

San Daniele del Friuli ✉ 33038

★★★**Alla Torre**, Via del Lago 1, ✆/✉ 0432 954 562 (*moderate*) is new and nice, occupying an old building in the historic centre, with a good buffet breakfast. Among the *prosciutterias*, **Antico Caffè Toran**, Via Umberto 1, ✆ 0432 957 544 (*inexpensive*) has simple meals as well as ham, cheeses and other nibbles.

Palmanova, Aquileia and Grado

In a beeline from north to south, you have a remarkable planned military town, the fascinating ruins of the Roman capital of Friuli, and the modern seaside resort—the only one in the Adriatic entirely facing south.

Getting Around

For Aquileia and Grado, take the train to Cervignano del Friuli and then a bus, or take a direct bus from Trieste. Local buses link Palmanova, Aquileia and Grado.

Tourist Information

Aquileia: Piazza Capitolo, ✆ 0431 919 491 (*summer only*); **Grado**: Viale Dante Alighieri 72, ✆ 0431 899309, ✉ 0431 899 209.

Palmanova

In the Renaissance, despite all its theories on planning, only a handful of entirely new towns were ever constructed. One that has survived, **Palmanova**, was built in 1593 by the Venetians as their eastern bulwark against the Austrians and Turks and populated by 'volunteers'. Perhaps because it was never actually needed for anything, Palmanova remains intact, a perfect example of 16th-century 'ideal' radial military planning and a geometrical *tour de force*: the star formed by its walls has nine points, while the large, somewhat eerie piazza in the heart of town, which originally contained the arsenal is a perfect hexagon. Even though most of the walls and moat are now overgrown, their stone softly moulded into serpentine hills and gullies, they are still defended by young conscripts. At the **Museo Storico**, Borgo Udine 4 (*open 10–12 and 3–6, closed Wed; adm*), ask about the torchlight tour of the walkways within the walls.

Aquileia

...the greatest city in the West

Emperor Justinian (6th century)

If Palmanova is unique in its plan, Aquileia is unique in that it was the only great Roman city in Italy to die on the vine; all the others not buried in volcanic mud have evolved into towns or cities. But Aquileia, once the proud capital of the X Legio Venetia et Histria, has dwindled from 200,000 to 3500 inhabitants, who no longer receive emperors but tend to the vineyards and tourists who flock to see the most important archaeological site in Northern Italy.

Founded as a Roman colony in 181 BC, Aquileia was renamed when eagles flew over the town while plans were being laid for Augustus' German campaign. They proved to be a good augury. Augustus himself was in and out of Aquileia and received Herod the Great here. Christianity found an early foothold in the city; the Patriarchate of Aquileia was created in 313, the very same year that Constantine the Great issued the Edict of Milan, and its patriarch was given jurisdiction that extended to the Ukraine. It didn't last; after Aquileia was sacked by Attila (452) and the Lombards (568), it lost most of its territory and the patriarch moved to a safer home in Grado, an island on the outer port of Aquileia. When Aquileia wanted the title back in the 7th century Grado refused to surrender it, and for 400 years rival patriarchs sat in Grado and in Cividale del Friuli, the Lombard capital. When they were reconciled in 1019, Aquileia's great basilica was remodelled; in 1077 the Patriarch received an added boost from Emperor Henry IV, who donated all the lands from Cadore to Istria to the Patriarchate. For Aquileia itself, though, it was the beginning of the end. Its port on the Natissa silted up, malaria chased out the population, and the patriarchate moved to Cividale, and then Ùdine. Venice took over the Patriarch's secular powers, and Aquileia was demoted to a mere archbishopric.

The Basilica

Aquileia's magnificent **basilica** (*open April–Sept 8.30–7; Oct–Mar 8.30–12.30 and 2.30–5.30*) and its lofty campanile are a landmark on the Friulian plain for miles around. It was founded and built in 313 by the first Patriarch, Theodore, but wrecked by Attila in 452; rebuilt in the same shape, it was given a Romanesque facelift by Patriarch Poppone (1020–31) and took its final form under the Venetians. One of the basilica's unique features is right out front—a loggia leads from the façade to the 9th-century 'Pagan Basilica', a kind of waiting room adjacent to the octagonal baptistry, where the pagan taint would be washed away.

When Poppone remodelled the basilica he thought Theodore's floor was a mite old-fashioned and covered it up, nicely preserving it for its rediscovery in 1909. At 837 square yards, this is nothing less than the largest **palaeochristian mosaic** in the west, a vivid and often whimsical carpet of portraits, animals and geometric patterns happily mingling with Christian and pagan scenes. On the right, the **Cappella di Sant'Ambrogio** contains the tombs of four patriarchs and a polyptych by Pellegrino da San Daniele (1503); the last chapel to the right of the altar has some of the Cathedral's oldest bits, 9th-century Lombard *plutei* and detached 4th-century frescoes. Frescoes from 1031 survive in the apse, showing Patriarch Poppone dedicating the basilica, accompanied by Emperor Conrad II and Gisela of Swabia. The tribune (1491) in between the altar steps is by the Tyrolean Bernardino da Bissone.

Set next to the left wall of the nave, the 11th-century white marble **Santo Sepolcro** is a reproduction of the Holy Sepulchre in Jerusalem. It marks the entrance to the so-called **Cripta degli Scavi** (the excavations carried out in 1917–20 around the belltower) containing more mosaics from 313, sandwiched in between Roman mosaics and others from the 8th century. The **crypt** proper under the altar is adorned with colourful 12th-century Byzantine-style frescoes (*one adm for both crypts*). The new **Museo del Patriarcato** opposite the basilica (*open April–Oct, 9.30–12.30 and 3–6; closed Mon*) contains fancy medieval reliquaries and other works from the basilica: a *Madonna del Rosario* by Giovanni Antonio Guardi and bas-reliefs of Christ with St Thomas of Canterbury, carved only a few years after his martyrdom, showing just how fast news of church politics travelled in the 1170s.

The Museo Archeologico

Open April–Sept, Tues–Sun 9.30–7, Mon 9–2; Oct–Mar, Tues–Sun 9–2; adm.

On the same road, but down to the left, a villa houses artefacts from pre-Christian Aquileia. There's a fine set of highly individualized Republican portrait busts; unlike the Greeks, who idealized themselves in marble (or perhaps were just better-looking), the Romans insisted that all their warts, cauliflower ears, and crumpled Roman noses be preserved for posterity. Tiberius, Augustus (young and old) and Trajan are among the celebrities. Among the bas-reliefs, there's a charming one of a smith with his tools; also amber and gold ornaments, glass, an enormous collection of coins, one of only two intact Roman chandeliers in the world (the other's in Alexandria) as well as a thousand and one household items that breathe life into ancient Aquileia. There's evidence of the Aquileians' lighter side: there are flies made of gold, and a wee bronze figurine of a springing cat.

The Excavations

A circular walk, beginning on the Via Sacra behind the basilica, takes in what remains of the ancient city; an unfortunate proximity to a quarrying magpie called Venice has shorn them of most of their grandeur. The Via Sacra passes **Roman houses** and **palaeochristian oratories** (some with mosaics intact), then continues up through the considerable ruins of the **harbour**, marked by cypresses: in the first century AD this was a bustling commercial port. Continue straight and bear right after the crossroads on modern Via Gemina to the **palaeochristian**

Museum (*same hours as Museo Archeologico; adm free*), with reliefs and sarcophagi, and a walkway over the undulating mossy mosaics of a huge 4th-century basilica; ancient Aquileia required not one but two enormous churches. Return by way of Via Gemina to Via Giulia Augusta (the main Cervignano-Grado road). To the right you can see the old Roman road, and, on the left, the **Forum** with its re-erected columns. Just off a fork to the right, the **Grand Mausoleum** (first century AD) was brought here from the distant suburbs. The meagre ruins of the amphitheatre, the baths, and the **Sepolcreto** (five Roman family tombs) are on Via XXIV Maggio and Via Acidino, north of the village's central Piazza Garibaldi.

Grado: Up to Your Neck in Sand

Aquileia had an inner port and an outer port, or *grado*, on the island that still bears its name. Today Grado is linked to the mainland by a causeway, and reigns as the queen of its own little lagoon. Hotels and other seaside amenities engulf the narrow alleys or *calli* of the old town, the *Castrum Gradense* and the **Duomo** (Basilica of Sant'Eufemia), seat of the 6th-century Patriarch of Nova Aquileia, as he fashioned himself. Inside, Corinthian capitals sit atop exotic marble pillars, and the 11th-century domed pulpit is carved with four Evangelists; the painted baldachin could easily be the tent of the sheik of Araby. The mosaic floor dates from the 6th century, although its scriptural adages and geometrical patterns seem austere after the garden of delights in Aquileia's basilica; note the scene in front of the altar, a map of *Castrum Gradense* and its islands. In the back glows a silver *pala* donated by the Venetians in 1372. An alley of sarcophagi separates Sant'Eufemia from its octagonal 5th-century **baptistry**, with a full-immersion font, and another, smaller basilica, the 5th-century **Santa Maria delle Grazie** with its original altar screeens and mini-theatre for the clergy behind the altar—a common feature of early Byzantine basilicas.

Grado owes its origin as a beach resort to medicine. Keen to bring tubercular children to the seaside, doctors sought a freshwater spring on the peninsula. In 1892 they duly discovered one, and Emperor Franz Josef at once included Grado on his official list of curative resorts in the Habsburg empire. A new town grew up to accommodate the nobility, who have since been replaced by athletes, models, and business people undergoing specific treatments, including the 'sand cure'—being buried up to one's neck in warm sand full of benevolent mineral salts and micro-organisms.

If the free beaches are too crowded, walk east to **Pineta**, or catch the boat to **Barbana**, an island in the lagoon with a resident Franciscan community; on the first Sunday in July, for the *Perdon de Barbana*, a colourful procession of boats sails to the monastery (*frequent daily boats in summer; Nov–May, Sat, Sun only*). There are also daily sea connections in summer to Trieste and the Istrian coast and to the fishing village of **Porto Buso**. Grado's lagoon is a major bird-watching area, and now, with the recent introduction of white horses from the Camargue in Provence, you can see them from the saddle.

Where to Stay and Eating Out

Aquileia ✉ 33051

    ★★★**Patriarchi**, Via Julia Augusta 12, ✆ 0431 919 595, ✉ 0431 919 596 (*moderate*), overlooks the excavations; all rooms are air-conditioned. The old ★**Aquila Nera**, Piazza Garibaldi 5, ✆ 0431 91045 (*inexpensive*), in the quiet main square, offers small rooms without bath. The restaurant is traditional and homely, with good gnocchi and basic meat dishes. **La Colombara**, Via S. Zilli 34, ℰ 0431 91513 (*moderate*), 2km out on the Trieste road, serves up fine cuisine, specializing in seafood prepared in various ways, accompanied by good wines from the Collio. *Closed Mon, June.*

Grado ✉ 34073

There are lots of nice hotels in Grado, but a couple that stand out, within sight of one another in the centre of the town, are the ★★★★**Antica Villa Bernt**, Via Colombo 5, ℰ 0431 82516, 📧 0431 82517 (*expensive*), a refurbished villa from the 1920s with only 22 lovely rooms, all with bath, air-conditioning, and TV (*open April–Oct*); and the ★★★★**Savoy**, Via Carducci 33, ℰ 0431 897 111, 📧 0431 83305 (*expensive*), which has a thermal pool, garden, parking and very comfortable rooms. *Open June–Oct.*

★★★**Eden**, by the beach at Via M. Polo 2, ℰ 0431 80136, 📧 0431 82087 (*moderate*) is a typical holiday hotel. *Open April–mid-Oct.* ★★★**Cristina**, Viale Martiri della Libertà 11, ℰ 0431 80989 (*inexpensive*) is similar, a bit further from the beach but in a shady garden. *Open May–Sept.* If you seek tranquillity, there's the pilgrims' hostel at the island **Convento di Barbana**, ℰ 0431 80453, with 24 single rooms; it's quite popular so book to be sure of a room.

In the winding streets around the cathedral, **All'Androna**, Calle Porta Piccola 4, ℰ 0431 80950 (*expensive*) has a daily-changing menu of fresh fish, and homemade bread and pasta. *Closed Tues out of season, Dec–Mar.* Overlooking Roman excavations, **De Toni**, Piazza Duca D'Aosta 37, ℰ 0431 80104 (*moderate*) offers fresh fish, prepared in a variety of local styles, along with a long wine list. *Closed Wed.*

Trieste

Once the main seaport of the Austro-Hungarian Empire, two world wars left Trieste a woebegone widow of the Adriatic, a grandiose neoclassical city shorn of its *raison d'être*. With the fall of the Berlin Wall, all this has changed: Trieste is now a very merry widow, courted across Central Europe and quickly regaining its old cosmopolitan lustre, something that the inhabitants accept as simply another twist in a knotted history. The streets and shops bubble with a babel of Slovene, Serbo-Croat, German, Hungarian and Czech, and cars bearing an exotic bouquet of numberplates clog up the straight, very central European 19th-century streets. Trade is picking up, too: not from tourists who once passed through on their way to points east, but from Slovenes and Hungarians flashing new-found wealth, and Austrian and Czech businessmen seeking new Mediterranean markets.

Don't come to Trieste for art or beautiful buildings: its profits have been firmly invested in banks, shipping-lines and stocks. Instead, come to sense the energy and excitement of a city shaking off decades of nostalgic sloth, and picking up from where it left off, from the vibrant days just before the First World War. Or you could just come for the breasts: plastered with naked statues, Trieste must have more perky D cups than any other city in the world.

History

Trieste's first visitors were apparently Jason and the Argonauts, who came this way on their journey home from the Danube. The Celtic port of Tergeste (from *terg*, or market) traded with the Phoenicians. The annexation of the city and its Istrian inhabitants by the Romans was violent, unlike the peaceful acquisition of the Veneto, but by the time of Augustus Tergeste was an important imperial port. From the 9th to the 13th centuries the city maintained a precarious independence under its prince-bishops, often quarrelling with Venice (and losing). After Venice's victory at Chioggia in 1382, Trieste was compelled to sign a treaty of allegiance with Leopold of Austria to keep from being submerged by the Serenissima. Rivalry with Venice only increased, especially in the salt trade, and in the mid-5th century only the personal intervention of Pope Pius II kept the Venetians from wiping the city out altogether.

Austria, always longing for a port, appeared on the scene in 1552, and, after a good deal of political instability, Charles VI granted it free port status in 1719. This initiated a golden age for Trieste: the Austrian emperors poured money into the city, especially Marie-Thérèse, who gave it a new neoclassical core. Trieste returned to Austrian rule after the fall of Napoleon in 1815, although minus free-port status. The subsequent fall in income, aggravated by heavy-handed policies from Vienna, turned the majority Italian population into ardent Irredentists ('the Unredeemed') turbulently desiring union with Italy.

The Irredentists had some interesting company. Sir Richard Burton, translator of the *Arabian Nights*, was British consul here from 1870 until his death in 1890. James Joyce, after eloping with Nora Barnacle, taught English in Trieste from 1904–15 and in 1919–20; he wrote *Dubliners* and *Portrait of the Artist as a Young Man* here. Joyce befriended and translated Ettore Schmitz, a member of the city's Jewish community, better known by his nom-de-plume Italo Svevo, 'the Italian Swabian'. And unknown to either of them, Rainer Maria Rilke was staying and working nearby at Duino.

Italian troops were welcomed in 1918, but Italian government all too soon proved to be another disappointment for Trieste. Mussolini tried to force the heterogeneous population into a cultural strait-jacket, before Hitler's Nazis went a step further, imprisoning and executing Jews and Slavs in the Risiera death camp. Another disaster came in the aftermath of the war, when Trieste found itself permanently divorced from its Istrian hinterland. Tito's Yugoslavia only gave up its last claims to Trieste itself in 1954, and the border question was not finally settled until 1975. In the mid-1960s, the city, seeking a new identity, decided to create a new role for itself as a scientific and research centre, which has paid off: Trieste now has an important institute of theoretical physics at Miramare (run by Nobel prize winner Abdus Salem) as well as departments of genetic engineering, experimental geophysics and marine biology.

Getting There

by air

Trieste's **airport**, served by daily flights from Rome and Milan, and weekly flights from London on British Airways, is at Ronchi dei Legionari, ✆ 0481 773 224, 30km to the north near Monfalcone; the airport bus departs from the main bus station in Piazzale Libertà. Alitalia: Piazza Sant'Antonio 1, ✆ 040 631 100. Most of Trieste's car hire agencies are at the airport: Avis, ✆ 0481 777 085, Hertz, ✆ 0481 777 025, Europcar, ✆ 0481 778 920.

by sea

The *Marconi* links Trieste every day except Tuesday from late May–Sept, to Grado and Lignano, Piran (Slovenia) and Umag, Porec, Rovinj and Pula (Croatia). Remember to take a passport for Slovenia and Croatia. Tickets from Piazza Unità d'Italia 6, ✆ 040 367 529 or Piazza Duca degli Abruzzi 1/a, ✆ 040 363 737. In the summer Anek runs four weekly ferries to Igoumenitsa, Patras and Corfu in Greece; for information, ✆ 040 363 242. Sem Ferries sail to Split on the Dalmatian coast once a week (Via Milano 4, ✆ 040 760 033). For more details, try the harbourmaster: Riva Tre Novembre 13, ✆ 040 366 666.

by rail

There are frequent trains to Venice, Gorizia and Ùdine, as well as to Austria, Slovenia and other destinations in Eastern Europe, from the **Stazione Centrale** on Piazza della Libertà 8.

by long-distance bus

The main **bus station** is in front of the Stazione Centrale, in Piazza della Libertà, ✆ 040 425 001. It has bus services to Venice, Treviso, Padua, Belluno, Trento, and Cortina and Sappada in the Dolomites; long-distance coaches to Milan, Mantua and Genoa; international services to Ljubljana, Rijeka, Zagreb, Athens, Istria and more.

Getting Around

Trieste's many long, straight Habsburger streets make finding one's way around relatively simple, and city **buses** are frequent. Most routes run from or by the central bus station; for information, ✆ 167 016 675. A **funicular railway** (*tranvia*) runs every 22 minutes from Piazza Oberdan to Villa Opicina above the city. **Radio taxi**, ✆ 040 307 730. Cars have been banished from the city centre and parking can be diabolical; it's best to just surrender your *macchina* to one of the garages or car parks (near Piazza della Libertà and Piazza Unità d'Italia) and get it over with.

Tourist Information

Via San Nicoló 20, ✆ 040 679 6111, 🖃 040 679 6299; also at the Stazione Centrale, ✆ 040 420 182 (ask for their Joyce itinerary). Friuli's regional tourist office is at Via G. Rossini 6, ✆ 040 363 952, 🖃 040 365 496; free phone information, ✆ 167 016 044. **British consulate**: Vicolo delle Ville 16, ✆ 040 302 884.

Along the Port to Piazza dell'Unità d'Italia

If you only have an hour or two at Trieste's train or bus station you can pop over to the **Galleria Nazionale d'Arte Antica**, Piazza della Libertà 7 (*open 9–1.30, closed Sun; adm*), with a second division collection of Italian paintings from the 15th–19th centuries, and a charming *Diana and Actaeon* by Lucas Cranach the Elder. Otherwise, take Corso Cavour into the **Borgo Teresiano**, formerly the city salt pans and now Trieste's business hub, thanks to Maria Theresa's planners, who laid out the streets with a pair of rulers, and planted them with neoclassical architecture. The Corso passes over the **Canale Grande**, an inlet with moorings for small craft; the adjacent Piazza Ponterosso is the site of the daily market. At the head of the canal stands the neo-Palladian church of **Sant'Antonio** complete with a temple front, and near it, the blue-domed Serbian Orthodox **Santo Spiridone**, an exotic orchid in this regimented Habsburg garden. Just over the canal, overlooking the sea on Riva Tre Novembre, Trieste's oldest coffee house, **Caffè Tommaseo** (1830), has recently been restored, complete with its *belle époque* fittings.

Next along the waterfront opens Trieste's whale of a heart, **Piazza dell'Unità d'Italia**, framed by weighty neoclassical piles: the hefty **Palazzo del Comune**, topped by two Moors who ring the bell over the clock, the **Palazzo del Governo** glowing in its bright skin of mosaics, and the huge brooding palace of Lloyd Triestino, now the seat of Friuli-Venezia Giulia's regional government. In the summer flowers brighten the piazza, while in winter purple cabbages hold pride of place, unless they are cowering beneath the bora, the northeast wind that whips over the Carso. In one corner, the **Fountain of the Four Continents**, built in 1750s to commemorate Trieste's new waterworks, is as graceless a doodad as you'll ever see in Italy. A good antidote is a drink at the piazza's **Caffè degli Specchi** (1839), once a famous Irredentist meeting place.

Trieste keeps its art collections a few blocks south of Piazza Unità d'Italia, around Piazza Venezia. The recently remodelled **Museo Revoltella**, Via Diaz 27 (*open 10–1 and 3–7.30, closed Tues and Sun pm; in July and Aug also open 8pm–midnight; adm*) was founded by Baron Pasquale Revoltella, one of the financiers of the Suez Canal (which was also a big boon to Trieste's port). Full of original furnishings, it contains 18th- and 19th-century paintings by Triestine artists that evoke the city's golden days, as well as modern works by Morandi, De Chirico and co. Up a block from the sea, on Largo Papa Giovanni XXIII, the **Museo Sartorio** (*open 9–1, closed Mon; adm*) housed in an 18th-century villa offers another glimpse into Triestine bourgeois life in the 19th century, along with a mix of art, including a triptych by Paolo Veneziano, a collection of drawings by Giambattista Tiepolo, and Italian ceramics.

Up the Capitoline Hill

Catch bus no.24 from the station or Piazza dell'Unità to ascend Trieste's very own Capitoline Hill, the nucleus of the Roman and medieval city. In the fifth century the Triestini raised the first of two basilicas here to their patron San Giusto, a martyr drowned during the persecution of Diocletian. An adjacent basilica was built in the 11th century, linked to the earlier church 300 years later and given an enormous campanile—hence the five asymmetrical naves of the **Basilica Cathedrale of San Giusto** (*closed 12–3*). The doorway, under a splendid Gothic rose window, is framed by the fragments of a Roman sarcophagus: six funerary busts gaze solemnly ahead like a corporate board of directors, while, embedded in the adjacent squat campanile, a Roman frieze resembles a fashion plate for armour. The interior has some beautiful mosaics, especially the early 13th-century *Christ with SS. Giusto and Servulus*, and the 11th-century gold-ground *Madonna with Archangels and Saints*, made by Venetian artists and similar to the *Virgin* in Torcello, but softer in mood. The oldest frescoes are 12th-century, while the newest were added in 1932. Buried on the right is Don Carlos, the Great Pretender of Spain's Carlist Wars, who died as an exile in Trieste in 1855.

Next to San Giusto are bits of the Roman forum and a first-century basilica, of which two columns have been re-erected. The excellent view over Trieste from here is marred by a 1933 **war memorial** by Attilo Selva, extolling the principal Fascist virtues of strength and vulgarity. The 15th-century Castello di San Giusto was begun by the Venetians during their brief tenure over in 1508–09, and finished by the Austrians. It offers more views from its ramparts and a small **Museo Civico** (*open Tues–Sun 9–1; adm*), full of armour and weapons. The Castle's Cortile delle Milizie is a favourite setting for summer concerts.

Just down the lane from the cathedral is the **Civico Museo di Storia ed Arte e Orto Lapidario** (*open Tues–Sun 9–1, Wed 9–7pm; adm*) housing intriguing finds from *Tergeste* and a famous fifth-century deer's-head silver *rhyton* or drinking vessel, imported from Greek Tarentum (modern Tàranto). The 'stone garden' contains Roman altars, stelae, a red granite Egyptian sarcophagus and the tomb of J. J. Winckelmann (1717–68), son of a poor German cobbler who became an archaeologist and the father of modern art history when he wrote his revolutionary *Reflections on the Painting and Sculpture of the Greeks* in 1755. While staying in a hotel in Trieste, he showed a fellow guest a few ancient gold coins, and was murdered for them by an eavesdropping Tuscan cook. On the way down to the city, have a look at the **Roman theatre**, built during the reign of Trajan, on the Via Teatro Romano.

More Caffès and Museums

The Grand Cafés, once the symbol of Triestine society and filled with fervent cross-cultural conversation, ideas and spies, still serve delicious cakes and pastries as well as dollops of nostalgia. Joyce was a habitué of the **Caffé Pirona**, Largo Barriera Vecchia 12, north of the castle hill and south of Piazza Goldoni (at the bottom of the 'Giant's Stair' from the Castello);

the locals claim he conceived *Ulysses* over its *pinzas* and *putizzas*. On the other side of Piazza Goldoni, at Via Cesare Battisti 18, is **Caffè San Marco**, opened in 1914 but rebuilt after it was blown up in the First World War, complete with Venetian murals that betrayed the owner's pro-Italian sentiments. According to the Triestini, the masked carnival figures in the oval over the bar portray Vittorio Emanuele and Mussolini, and you won't find a classier joint to shoot a round of pool or sit at a marble table to chug down one of the local micro-cappuccinos. One street away, on Via S. Francesco, stands the most beautiful **synagogue** in Italy, the largest in Europe, built in 1910 on ancient Syriac models.

In sombre counterpoint stands the only concentration camp in Italy to be used for mass exterminations, the **Risiera di San Sabba** at the southern extreme of the city (Ratto della Pileria 1), an old rice-husking factory that was taken over by the Nazis in September 1943 to 'process', among others, 837 Triestine Jews in its crematorium. A national monument since 1965, the building now houses a small museum (*bus no.8; open Tues–Sun, 9–1*).

In the same area the **Museo del Mare**, Via Campo Marzio 1 (*open 8.30–1.30, closed Mon and hols*) has ships' models and other salty exhibits; the **Museo Ferroviario**, in the retired train station in the Campo Marzio (*open 9–1, closed Mon*) has a display of retired locomotives. It also runs frequent summer excursions in period trains: three-hour electric train journeys around the city on the Transalpina, and steam train excursions around the region and neighbouring countries; for schedules, ✆ 040 379 4185.

Habsburgs and Karst: Excursions from Trieste

You can't go too far from Trieste without running into Slovenia. For a short jaunt, take the Opicina **Tranvia** (the funicular, built in 1902) up the cliffs from Piazza Oberdan for the fine panorama from the **Vedetta d'Opicina**. Another popular excursion is to **Miramare**, some 7km up the beach-lined **Riviera di Barcola**, jammed packed in the summer (bus 36 from Piazza Oberdan or Stazione Centrale). On the way, watch for the **Faro della Vittoria**, a lofty lighthouse and 1927 war memorial to sailors, crowned by a heavy-sinewed, big-busted Valkyrie in a majorette's costume.

Miramare: Habsburg Folly by the Sea

Open April–Sept 9–6; Oct–Mar 9–4; also Thurs, Fri, and Sat from 8.30–10.30pm in July, Aug, and early Sept; adm exp. Miramare Park open daily in summer 8–7, winter 8–4, free.

Towering up on its own little promontory overlooking the sea, the castle of Miramare hides a dark history behind its white 19th-century façade. It was built by the Habsburg Archduke Maximilian and his Belgian wife Carlotta, and visitors are greeted by a stone sphinx with a cryptic smile that seems to ask the world: why did Maximilian leave this pleasure palace and like a *dummkopf* let Napoleon III's financiers con him into becoming Mexico's puppet emperor in 1864, and why did he linger around there to face a firing squad three years later? Was he an idealist, as his apologists claim, or too much of a Habsburg to know any better?

Carlotta, after desperately trying to rally European support for her husband, went mad after his execution and survived him for another 50 years in Belgium, while Miramare acquired the ominous reputation of laying a curse on anyone who slept within its walls, after another Habsburg—the Archduke Ferdinand—stayed here on his way to assassination in Sarajevo. The

Nazis made it their headquarters in 1943; when the Americans occupied the palace in 1946, their commander insisted on sleeping out in the park in a tent. You can hear the whole sad story in the sound and light show 'Miramare's Imperial Dream' (*in Italian only, Mon, Tues and Wed at 9.30 or 10.45 pm in July, Aug and Sept, but ring © 040 679 6111 for possible performances in English*).

Inside, the palace retains its original overblown Victorian-era décor, some rather cosy rooms designed like ship cabins, a never-used throne, a historical hall (with a painting of the Argonauts, and, upstairs, 1920s furnishings brought in by the Duke of Aosta, who made this his base. Miramare's magnificent **park** was designed by Maximilian, who made a better botanist than emperor of Mexico; the gardens and coastal waters are now managed by the World Wildlife Federation and shelter the rare Stella's otter and marsh harriers.

The Carso

Most of Trieste's province is occupied by the Carso, a slender 25km ribbon of karst. Karst is pliable limestone, easily eroded by the rain into remarkable shapes—and, here, white cliffs that form Italy's most dramatic Adriatic coastline north of Monte Còrnero. Inland the karst has been buffeted by the 90mph *bora* wind into petrified waves of rock dotted with *dolinas* (swallow holes) while, underground, aeons of dripping water have formed vast caverns, subterranean lakes and rivers. Vineyards grow wherever there's room, and elsewhere the landscape is dominated by sumac, which autumn ignites into a hundred shades of scarlet. Autumn is also the season to look for farms with leafy branch signs; these are *osmizze*, a local peculiarity from the days of the Austro-Hungarian empire, which are permitted to sell wine and produce directly to the consumer.

Between Miramare and the industrial shipbuilding town of Monfalcone lies the fishing village of **Duino**, with its two castles; the ruined **Castello Vecchio** and the 15th-century **Castello Nuovo**, perched on a promontory over the sea. Castello Nuovo has long been owned by the Princes von Thurn und Taxis, who hosted D'Annunzio, Liszt, Richard Strauss, and, most famously, Rainer Maria Rilke The castle is now the seat of the United World College high school and off limits, but you can follow the beautiful, 2km **Rilke walk** along the promontory, beginning in nearby **Sistiana**, a pretty resort with a yacht harbour in its own little bay; peregrine falcons nest on the cliffs.

The Duino Elegies

When Princess Marie von Thurn und Taxis left Rilke alone in the castle that winter of 1910–11, the poet was in a restless mood. One day he received a nasty business letter, and despite the blustery winds he went for a walk along the castle bastions to sort out his thoughts before replying. In the wind and waves crashing far below he heard a voice: 'Who, if I cried, would hear me among the angelic orders?' It was the muse Rilke had been restlessly waiting for; he jotted the words down, and by the evening the first of his ten 'Duino Elegies' was finished. Another followed, but eleven years and the terrible war intervened before his 'voice' returned and he completed the Elegies.

As the expression of Rilke's very personal and prophetic vision of reality, the Elegies were notoriously as difficult to write as they are to read. Rilke felt that in the 20th century it was impossible to find adequate external symbols to express our inner lives and, like Blake, he used angels in a highly personal way. On one level, as he wrote to his Polish translator, Rilke felt a responsibility and foreboding that many Europeans of his generation dimly understood. 'Now there comes crowding over from America empty, indifferent things, pseudo-things, dummy life… The animated, experienced things that share our lives are coming to an end and cannot be replaced. We are perhaps the last to have still known such things. On us rests the responsibility of preserving, not merely their memory (that would be little and unreliable), but their human and laral worth…' Hence, in part, the Elegies.

Born in a karstic abyss in Slovenia, the **Timavo river** continues underground for 30km before reappearing by the winsome Romanesque church of **San Giovanni in Tuba**, just above Duino. The Romans were fascinated with the Timavo—Virgil mentioned it in the *Aeneid*— and their temple to Spes Augusta lies under San Giovanni; you can still see a portion of the mosaic floor from the first fifth-century church. Of the caves, the most famous, the stalactite **Grotta Gigante** near Opicina, is the easiest to visit (*bus 45, every half-hour from the Piazza Oberdan; guided tours April–Sept 9–12, 2–7; closed Mon exc in July and Aug; Oct–Mar 10–12, 2–4.30, closed Mon; adm exp*). The name for once is no exaggeration: this is the largest cavern in the world open to visitors (since 1908); its main hall could swallow the entire basilica of St Peter and is graced by a pair of record-breaking 346ft pendulum stalactites. The ceiling is so high that drops of water disintegrate before reaching the floor, forming curious leaf-shaped stalagmites. In 1996 a new path was created, past a belvedere overlooking a vertiginous sheer 360ft drop.

The Grotta Gigante is near **Monrupino** and its castle, first built by the Romans, where the people of Trieste later took shelter when the Turks raided the coast. The Romans had a second castle at Grisa, a spot now topped with the unexpected pyramid of the **Santuario de Monte Grisa**, an essay in triangular concrete modules finished in 1967. **Sgonico**, also here, has a beautiful botanical garden, the **Carsiana** (*open May–Sept, Sat and Sun*) in a sheltered karstic valley where wild Mediterranean herbs grow next to Alpine ferns, and nearly extinct blind amphibians called rosy olms hide in the rocky shelters by the pools; a path runs from Opicina to Monrupino.

South of Trieste, bus 40 from Piazza Oberdan offers an excursion to the dramatic white karstic cliffs, pierced with caves and hanging over the **Val Rosandra**, where the locals practice their rock-climbing and where you can visit the lowest alpine refuge in Europe, only a few miles from the sea. Bus 20 heads south along the coast from Trieste to **Muggia**, a higgledy piggledy Venetian fishing port at the end of Italy. The lion in its square looks very disapproving and holds a closed book—although who knows what Muggia did to offend the bosses. The pretty tri-lobed **Duomo** has a peculiar relief over the door, of God holding a grown-up Jesus on his lap; the frescoes inside date from the 13th century. The best views around are enjoyed by the Basilica di Santa Maria Assunta, a 10th-century frescoed church overlooking Muggia and the sea.

Activities

The **opera** season at Trieste's **Teatro Comunale Verdi** runs from November to March; in summer the theatre and the Sala Tripcovich in Piazza della Libertà see an **International Operetta festival** (for schedules and bookings, © 040 672 2500,

@ 040 672 2249). **Carnival** is celebrated with a Venetian flair in Muggia, with a lavish parade that's well beyond what you would expect in a small town.

Trieste ⊠ *34100*

Where to Stay
very expensive

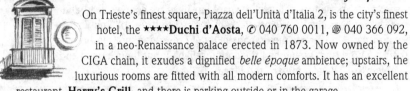

On Trieste's finest square, Piazza dell'Unità d'Italia 2, is the city's finest hotel, the ★★★★**Duchi d'Aosta**, ℭ 040 760 0011, @ 040 366 092, in a neo-Renaissance palace erected in 1873. Now owned by the CIGA chain, it exudes a dignified *belle époque* ambience; upstairs, the luxurious rooms are fitted with all modern comforts. It has an excellent restaurant, **Harry's Grill**, and there is parking outside or in the garage.

expensive

★★★**Novo Hotel Impero**, Via S. Anastasia 1, ℭ 040 364 242, @ 040 365 023, is conveniently located near the train station, a short walk from the centre (but no restaurant); some rooms are cheaper.

moderate

By the historic hill, ★★★**San Giusto**, Via C. Belli 3, ℭ 040 762 661, @ 040 7606 585, is modern, with everything you need. In a neoclassical building, ★★**Al Teatro**, Via Capo di Piazza G. Bartoli 1 (near Piazza dell'Unità), ℭ 040 366 220, @ 040 366 560, served as British headquarters after the Second World War and is a bit of a nostalgic trip back to the Trieste of yore. Near the station is the comfortable ★★★**Milano**, Via Ghega 17, ℭ 040 369 680, @ 040 369 727. If you don't like the hurly-burly of a big city, take the tram up to Opicina and the ★★★**Nuovo Hotel Daneu**, Via Nazionale 11, ℭ 040 214 241, @ 040 214 215, with a good restaurant and indoor pool.

inexpensive

There are many less expensive choices in the centre of Trieste (look around Via Roma, Via della Geppa, or Via XXX Ottobre). ★**Alabarda-Flora**, Via Valdirivo 22, ℭ 040 630 269, @ 040 639 284 is clean, comfortable, and good value. The **Youth Hostel** is idyllically but inconveniently placed overlooking the sea at Viale Miramare 331, ℭ/@ 040 224 102, 8km north of Trieste near Miramare. Take bus 36.

Around Trieste

Along the coast, at Duino (⊠ 34013) the modern ★★★**Duino Park**, near the old citadel ℭ 040 208184, @ 040 208 526 (*moderate*) has its own pool and a private piece of beach; ★★**Belvedere**, ℭ 040 299 256 (*moderate*) has a garden and views over the sea. In Muggia (⊠ 34015) ★★★**Lido**, Via Battista 22, ℭ 040 273338, @ 040 271979 (*moderate*) is modern, on the edge of town and the sea, and has a good restaurant serving local seafood.

Eating Out

Trieste is a good place to eat dumplings instead of pasta—Slovenian and Hungarian influences are strong in the kitchen. A famous first course is *jota*, a bean, potato and sauerkraut soup, or you could try *kaiserknödel* (bread dumplings with grated cheese, ham, and parsley).

For *secondo*, there's a wide variety of fish like *sardoni* (big sardines), served fried or marinated, and both tasty and inexpensive. Goulash, roast pork and *stinco* (veal knuckle) are also popular. The middle-European influence, however, is especially noticeable in the desserts: the lovely strudels, the *gnocchi di susine* (plums), or *zavate*, a warm cream pastry.

expensive

The place to partake of this *cucina Triestina* is the **Antica Trattoria Suban**, Via Comici 2, ✆ 040 54368, in the suburb of San Giovanni (and quite hard to find, so take a taxi). Founded out in the country in 1863, this wonderful old inn has since been absorbed by urban growth, though it maintains much of its old feel and its fine views over Trieste. Suban offers a famous *jota*, *sevapcici* (Slovenian grilled meat fritters), sinful desserts and good wines. Readers warn, however, that the quality depends on the presence of the regular chef; when booking ask if he's on duty, and if not, wait till he is. *Closed Mon lunch, Tues, part of Jan, Aug.* Towards Miramare, **Hosteria Bellavista**, Via Bonomea 52, ✆ 040 411 150, is a wine lover's paradise, with hundreds of bottles from around the world to go with delicate renditions of Trieste's favourites and lovely views. *Closed Sun, Mon lunch, some of Jan.*

moderate

Take a taxi into the hills for **Scabar**, way down Via dell'Istria at Erta di S. Anna 63, ✆ 040 810 368, for gourmet fish and mushroom dishes; the day's special is usually fantastic. *Closed Mon, Tues, Feb, mid-July–Aug.* Convenient to Piazza Unità d'Italia and the museums, **Città di Cherso**, Via Cadorna 6, ✆ 040 366 044, serves delicious seafood Friulian-style, topped off with heavenly desserts. *Closed Tues, some of July and Aug.*

inexpensive

Buffet da Pepi, Via Cassa di Risparmo 3, ✆ 040 366 858, was founded in 1903 and has been thriving ever since serving up Trieste's specialities. *Closed Sun, half of July.* Another old favourite, Birreria Forst, Via Galatti 11, (near Piazza Oberdan) ✆ 040 365 276, serves goulash and lots of beer. *Closed Sun.* The waiters still write the orders on the tablecloths at **Re di Coppe**, Via Geppa 11, ✆ 040 370 330, serving up a classic *jota* and boiled meats. *Closed Sat, Sun, mid-July–mid-Aug.*

Gorizia and the Collio

The frontier town of Gorizia was for centuries ruled by a powerful dynasty of counts, who were always ready to stir up trouble against Venice, with the winking approval of the Kings of Hungary. When the last count died without an heir in 1500, the city was briefly controlled by Venice before being taken over by the Habsburgs. As in Trieste, the Austrians gave Gorizia broad straight boulevards and parks and pronounced the result an 'Austrian Nice' (minus the seashore, that is).

The city saw fierce fighting in the First World War, but it was after the Second World War that Gorizia became the Mediterranean's Berlin, cut in two between Italy and Yugoslavia (now Slovenia) in such a thoughtless manner that it almost choked. Life improved in Nova Gorica and Gorizia only in 1979, when residents on either side of the barbed-wire fence were granted a 16km zone to transact their affairs freely. In 1991 Gorizia saw the first shots of the new

Balkan War, when Slovenia declared independence and the Yugoslav army was sent in to wrest back the lucrative border posts. Today, as Slovenia prospers in its independence, the town is a peculiar mix of flashy boutiques catering for cross-border traffic.

Tourist Information

Gorizia: Via Diaz 16, ✆/🖷 0481 533 870.
Gradisca d'Isonzo: Palazzo Torriani, Via M Ciotti, ✆ 0481 99217, 🖷 0481 99880.

Borgo Castello

Crowning Gorizia with its wide straight streets is its medieval core, the **Borgo Castello**, enveloped by a Venetian fortress of 1509. In the centre, the **Castle** of the Counts of Gorizia was first mentioned in 1001, but had to be completely rebuilt after its pummelling in the First World War. It now houses the **Museo del Medioevo Goriziano** (*open daily exc Mon, 9.30–1, 3–7.30; adm*) with a display dedicated to Gorizia's history, and a few antiques and paintings. Just below stands the pretty church of **Santo Spirito** (1386) and the Casa Formentini, now the **Museo Provinciale** (*open 10–8, closed Mon; adm*) featuring an exhibit on textiles, the city's old bread and butter, and local artists, especially Giuseppe Tominz, master portrait painter to the bourgeousie of Gorizia and Trieste (d. 1866), admired for getting their clothes just right. One of his best efforts is a self-portrait with his full-grown brother sitting on his lap, about to receive Giuseppe's fully laden palette on the back of his nice frock coat. There is also an altarpiece by Antonio Guardi, in which the usual saints hanging about the Madonna have, for once, better things to do than stand around and pose. Perhaps best of all are the basement rooms, dedicated to the First World War and the Isonzo front, which evoke the horror and some of the black humour of the Great War.

Modern Gorizia

Gorizia's **Duomo** is the dull result of tinkering since the 14th century, but has an altarpiece by Tominz of whom you've become a fan. Gorizia once had a prominent Jewish community that lived in a ghetto north of the cathedral. In 1943 nearly all were taken to the extermination camp in Trieste. The **synagogue** in Via Ascoli (*open Mon, Fri, Sat 4–7, Tues and Thurs 6–8, Sun 10–1, closed Wed*) was built in 1752, burned by the Nazis but rebuilt and reopened in 1984, and now houses a museum of the community and paintings by its most famous member, philosopher Carlo Michelstaedter, who tragically committed suicide at the age of twenty-three.

In 1990 Guglielmo Coronini, the last Count of Gorizia, died, and now his home, the **Villa Coronini Cronberg** (1594) on Viale XX Settembre 14, is open for tours (*Tues–Sat 10–1 and 4–8, Sun 10–12, 4–8; adm*). So far a third of the rooms are open, including the bedroom where Charles X, the last King of France, died in 1836; the impressive library; and the Count's collections—paintings by Tintoretto, Strozzi, Magnasco, Rubens, Monet, Rosalba Carriera, and of course Giuseppe Tominz; prints by Titian and Rembrandt and Japanese masters, and more. Afterwards, you can wander through the villa's English gardens.

Wine Around Gorizia

The hills around Gorizia, the **Collio**, look like a patch of Tuscany that got away. This has been Friuli's most prestigious DOC wine region since the Middle Ages, and these days is especially known for its Tocai Friulano and Ribolla Gialla. Its centre, the pleasant, leafy town of **Gradisca d'Isonzo**, straddles the blue-green river Isonzo, neat and tidy with pastel houses and little 17th-century palazzi, and the **Enoteca Regionale Serenissima**, in business since 1965, where you can taste any or all of Friuli's wines (*open 10–1, 4–11pm; closed Mon*). Medieval **Cormòns**, another major Collio wine town, was the only one in Italy to erect a statue to Emperor Maximilian. Visit its **Cantina Prodottori Vini del Collio e Isonzo**, © 0481 60579 (*closed Sun*) which produces a Vino della Pace, made from vines gathered from around the globe and sent out annually to the world's heads of state. Just north of Cormòns, San Giovanni al Natisone, Manzano and Corno di Rosazzo are the magic triangle of something a bit less glamorous, but eminently useful—chairs. Some 20 million, 80% of the national total, are cranked out annually.

Where to Stay and Eating Out

Gorizia ✉ 34170

Just north of Gorizia at San Floriano del Collio, a 17th-century manor house is now the ★★★★**Golf Hotel**, Via Oslavia 2, © 0481 884 051, ✆ 0481 884 052 (*expensive*), 15 rooms furnished with antiques and every amenity; pool, tennis and golf, too. The most attractive place to stay in town is the ★★★**Palace**, Corso d'Italia 63, © 0481 82166, ✆ 0481 31658 (*moderate*), with large modern rooms on the main street. In Borgo Castello, you can sup in medieval splendour at the **Lanterna d'Oro al Castello**, © 0481 82007 (*moderate*). The menu features Friuli specialities like *prosciutto di San Daniele*, and well-prepared dishes of venison, kid and boar. *Closed Mon*.

Cormòns ✉ 34071

The nicest place to sleep in the Collio, ★★★**Felcaro**, Via S. Giovanni 45, © 0481 60214, ✆ 0481 630 255 (*moderate*) began life as an Austrian villa and is spread out over several buildings, with a pool, tennis courts, fitness centre, and a fine restaurant, specializing in game dishes to go with its enormous wine list (*moderate*). In a charming rural setting on a hill, ★★**La Subida**, Monte 22 © 048 60531, ✆ 0481 61616 (*inexpensive*) has a handful of rooms, many sleeping up to five, with a pool, tennis and riding. The restaurant, **Il Cacciatore** (*expensive–moderate*), serves excellent regional dishes, with extensive borrowings from nearby Slovenia: the cold breast of pheasant in mushroom cream is a popular summer dish. Excellent Collio wines. *Closed Tues, Wed, Feb*. Twin chefs have put **Al Giardinetto**, Via Matteotti 54, © 0481 60257, ✆ 0481 630 704 (*expensive–moderate*) firmly on the gastronomic map with their innovative Friulian dishes—*millefoglie di polenta*, gnocchi with crinkly cabbage and game sauce. *Closed Mon eve, Tues, July*.

Dolegna del Collio ✉ 34070

Just outside Dolegena, in between Gorizia and Ùdine, the 13th-century **Castello dell'Aquila d'Oro**, Via Ruttars 11, © 0481 61255 (*very expensive–expensive*) has not only one of Italy's best wine cellars, but beautiful refined food on a menu that changes frequently with the chef's inspiration, in an ultra-refined setting, down to the last detail. An experience, *but not on Wed, Thurs, or in Aug*.

Legend states that Ùdine's castle sits on a mound erected by Hunnish warriors, who carried the soil to the site in their helmets so that their commander Attila could watch the burning of Aquileia. The story has a ring of prophecy to it, as Ùdine, granted important market concessions by the Patriarch in 1223, went on to take Aquileia's place as seat of the patriarch from 1238 to 1751. Ùdine's chief rivals were Gorizia and Cividale until 1385, when the powerful local family, the Savorgnans, took control and brought it into the Serene Republic in 1420. In the Second World War it was the last city to be liberated in Italy (May 1945).

Ùdine is a charmer, and not half as well known as it deserves to be. Its old streets are interwoven with little canals; it's also the centre of Friulian nationalism, where you're likely to hear people in the streets conversing in Friulian. Venice left its handprint on the architecture, while lagoonland's last great painter Giambattista Tiepolo brightened many of the walls, thanks to his first important patron, Patriarch Dionisio Delfino, who kept GB here with commissions between 1726 to 1730, a period when he left his early sombre palette behind and took up the brilliant colours that became his trademark.

Getting Around

Ùdine's **railway station** (with connections to Venice, Trieste and Gorizia) is on Viale Europa Unità; a private local railway links Ùdine station with Cividale (20min). The **bus station** is not far away on the other side of the same street, ☎ 0432 506941.

Tourist Information

Ùdine: Piazza 1 Maggio 7, ☎ 0432 295 972, ✉ 0432 504 743.
Cividale del Friuli: Corso Paolino d'Aquileia 10, ☎ 0432 731 461, ✉ 0432 731 398.

Piazza della Libertà and the Castello

The heart of Ùdine, Piazza della Libertà, has justifiably been called 'the most beautiful Venetian square on the *terra firma*'. Its striking, candy-striped **Loggia del Lionello**—a mini-Doge's palace—was built by a goldsmith in 1448 and faithfully reconstructed after a fire in 1876; a second loggia, the **Loggia di San Giovanni** (1533), integrates an earlier clock tower designed by Raphael's student, Giovanni da Ùdine, where the bell is rung by two Venetian-style Moors. There is the usual column topped by a Lion of St Mark (a bit of nostalgia in this case, from 1883), accompanied by statues of Hercules and Cacus (better known locally as Florean and Venturin), Peace, and Justice, the latter from the 1600s and sporting Bette Davis eyes. The **Municipio**, all in white Istrian stone, is a bravura piece of Art Deco by Raimondo D'Aronco (1910–31) that manages to blend right in with all the rest.

Palladio designed the rugged **Arco Bollari** (1556), the gateway to the sweeping portico, built in 1487 to shelter visitors to the **Castello**, once seat of the Patriarch and the Venetian governor. Rebuilt in 1517 and restored in 1990 after the earthquake, it houses the **Civici Musei** (*open 9.30–12.30, 3–6, closed Mon; adm, free Sun am*); sections include archaeology; photos, especially of Friuli; designs and prints (by Tiepolo and Dürer, among others); and a notable collection of paintings, beginning in the impressive **Salone del Parlamento**, built in 1560 by Giovanni da Udine and frescoed by Pomponio Amalteo and Giovanni Battista

Grassi, with monochromes by G.B. Tiepolo. Among the highlights are Carpaccio's *Christ with the Instruments of the Passion*, Giambattista Tiepolo (*Guardian Angel* and *Strength and Wisdom*) and a bird's-eye view of Ùdine by local boy Luca Carlefarijs (1662–1730). The castle shares the hill with *S. Maria di Castello*, a church founded in the sixth century and topped with a giant bronze archangel in the late 18th century. There are fine views over the city from here and from the adjacent 16th-century Venetian **Casa della Contadinanza**, where petitions to the Friuli parliament were processed.

Down in the City

Just east of Piazza Libertà along Via Vittorio Veneto, the oft-altered **Duomo** has a charming 14th-century lunette over the door of the *Coronation of the Virgin and Saints*, with figures so weathered they look like gingerbread. The interior, a dignified baroque symphony of grey and gold, has frescoes by Tiepolo in the first two altars on the right and in the Cappella del Sacramento. In the heavy-set campanile, the small **Museo del Duomo** is adorned with excellent 1349 frescoes of the *Funeral of St Nicolas* by Vitale da Bologna, and a 14th-century sarcophagus. Even after Tiepolo became world famous he never forgot his first patrons in Ùdine, and in 1759, when he was at the height of his powers, he returned to decorate the adjacent **Oratorio della Purità** (1680), originally a little theatre, with a masterful, partly frescoed, partly painted and recently restored *Assumption* on the ceiling and an altarpiece of the *Immaculate Conception*; the chiaroscuro frescoes on the walls are by his son Giandomenico.

Near the Duomo (down Via Calzolai) on Piazza Venerio, the austere 14th-century **San Francesco** has good 14th-century frescoes by an unknown Venetian. From here take a left on Via Savorgnana for the more ornate **San Giacomo**, with its clock tower and life-size figures gazing over the arcaded **Piazza Matteotti**, Ùdine's centuries-old market square. Note the outdoor altar on the balcony over the door of San Giacomo, used to celebrate mass on market days—as convenient for shoppers in its day as a drive-in church in a California mall.

From here, Via Sarpi leads around to join the Riva Bartolini with Palladio's **Palazzo Antonini** (now the Banca d'Italia). The Tiepolo trail, however, continues in the other direction: from the Piazza Libertà, take Via Manin through a gate to the Piazza Patriarcato and the Palazzo Arcivescovile, now the **Museo Diocesano** (*open Wed–Sun 10–12 and 3.30–6.30*), with sacred works and entire gallery of Old Testament scenes (*The Fall of the Rebel Angels, Rachel Hiding the Idols, Judgement of Solomon*) beautifully frescoed by Tiepolo—his first major commission. More recent art (Arturo Martini, Severini, Carrà, De Chirico, De Kooning, Segal, Lichtenstein, Dufy, and works by the brothers Afro, Mirko, and Dino Basaldell, natives of Ùdine) is on display in the excellent **Galleria d'Arte Moderna** (*open 9.30–12.30, 3–6, closed Mon; adm, Sun am free*), located on the northern fringes of the old town. To get there, follow Riva Bartolini to Via Palladio, then go straight on Vias Mazzini, Mantica and A.L. Moro, or take bus 2 directly from the station or Piazza 1 Maggio.

Ùdine ✉ *33100*

Where to Stay and Eating Out

★★★★**Astoria Hotel Italia**, Piazza XX Settembre 24, ✆ 0432 505 091, ✉ 0432 509 070 (*expensive*) is the *grande dame* of the city's hotels, located in the heart of town; it has air-conditioning, a garage, rooms with all the mod cons, and a fine restaurant, specializing in Venetian meat and fish dishes. Ask to have a peek in the frescoed conference room, designed by Japelli in 1833. The elegant turn-of-the-century ★★★**La' di Moret**, just north of the centre at Viale Tricesimo 276, ✆ 0432 545 096, 🖷 0432 545 096 (*moderate*) has won awards for its rooms; the restaurant, one of the best in the region, features seafood, Friuli-style. *Closed Sun eve and Mon.* Just outside the centre of Ùdine, but only five minutes' walk from the train station, ★★★**San Giorgio**, Piazzale Cella 2, ✆ 0432 505 577, 🖷 0432 506 110 (*moderate*) has modern, air-conditioned rooms. *Inexpensive* hotels include the 'Where are you going?' ★★**Quo Vadis**, Piazzale Cella 28, ✆ 0432 21091, 🖷 0432 21092 and el cheapo ★**Da Brando**, Piazzale Cella 16, ✆/🖷 0432 502 837, minus en suite baths.

The oldest restaurant in Ùdine, **Alla Vedova**, Via Travagnacco 9, ✆ 0432 470 291 (*moderate*) is quite a way from the historic centre, off the SS13 to Tarvisio; but what better way to spend an evening than at a table near the great hearth (or outdoors in the summer), dining on wild duck risotto? The house's red Refosco is famous. *Closed Sun eve, Mon.* Another historic inn, the **Vitello d'Oro** at central Via Valvason 4, ✆ 0432 508 982, 🖷 0432 508 982 (*expensive*) serves traditional specialities, with an emphasis on fish. *Closed Wed and three weeks in July.* The charming **Vecchio Stallo**, Via Viola 7, ✆ 0432 21296 (*inexpensive*) is Ùdine's best value for money; good food, and wine by the glass. *Closed Wed.*

For an exceptional meal, head 7km north of Ùdine to Tricesimo and its gourmet haven **Boschetti**, Piazza Mazzini 9, ✆ 0432 851 230 (*very expensive*), where the innovative chef bases his dishes entirely on the availability of fresh ingredients and old Friulian traditions—try pappardelle with porcini mushrooms, scallops with French beans in almond oil, or steamed salmon with vegetables, followed by exquisite desserts. *Closed Sun eve, Mon, half of Aug.*

Cividale del Friuli

Only a hop and a skip from Ùdine in the valley of the Natisone, Cividale del Friuli has an impressive pedigree. Julius Caesar founded it in 50 BC and named it after his family, *Forum Iulii*, a name condensed over the centuries into 'Friuli'. The Lombards invaded in 568, liked what they saw, and made Cividale the capital of their first duchy. The Patriarchate of Aquileia (*see* below) was moved here in 737, initiating a magnificent period, documented by the surprising works of Lombard art, and by Paulus Diaconus, the Lombard historian born in Cividale and one of the brightest beams of light we have on the 'Dark Ages' in northern Italy.

The Duomo and Archaeology Museum

The centre of Cividale is a series of squares around the old forum. In the most important, **Piazza Duomo**, you'll find the rebuilt 13th–15th-century **Palazzo Comunale**, a statue of Caesar, and the Duomo (*open 9.30–12, 3–7, until 6 in winter*), begun in 1453 and given its plain but attractive Renaissance façade by Pietro Lombardo. It contains unique treasures: the 12th-century silver altarpiece, the *Pala di Pellegrino II*, with its 25 saints and two archangels; a fine gilded equestrian monument (1617) and the Renaissance sarcophagus of Patriarch Nicolò Donato. Off the right aisle, the **Museo Cristiano** contains two masterpieces from the 8th century: the octagonal **Baptistry of Callisto** and the **Altar of Ratchis**, dating back to

749, a period when there was still considerable confusion about lion anatomy (the one on the Baptistry is part fish, part hedgehog) and exactly how hands and arms are attached to the human form. In the scene of the Magi, Mary and baby Jesus frown as if they didn't like their presents—what's a baby going to do with a pot of myrrh anyhow? (Yet compare its barbaric charms with the stuccoes in the Tempietto, below).

Next to the Duomo, the **Museo Archeologico Nazionale** (*open April–Sept 9–7, Mon 9–2; Oct–Mar 8.30–2; adm*) is housed in Palladio's Palazzo Pretorio. This vast treasure trove has Roman relics, especially the unique bronzes from Zuglio—an enormous shield with a man's portrait in the centre, of uncertain date, as well as objects found in hundreds of Lombard tombs in the 6th and 7th centuries—crosses, fibulae, swords and shield-holds (*ambone*), all that survives after the wood and leather have rotted away. The sarcophagus of the 6th-century Lombard Duke Gisulphus produced a fibula, cross and ring all wrought in gold. There are ivory pieces for a game called *ad tabulam* from a knight's tomb, the 8th-century Carolingian *Pax del Duca Orso*, adorned with an ivory crucifix in a golden frame and studded with jewels; a 1400 embroidered altar cover, a fifth-century *Evangelical of St Mark*, autographed by Lombard nobles, who thought it was written in the apostle's own hand; the Pulfero treasure of bronze axes from 2000–200 BC, discovered in 1997; and bits from the Romanesque Duomo—mermaids, monsters, and a man in a funny hat.

The Ipogeo Celtico and Tempietto Longobardo

Corso Ponte d'Aquileia descends to the Natisone (like many rivers in the area, a pretty turquoise because of the limestone) and the lofty 1442 **Ponte del Diavolo**. In the Middle Ages, it was a common folk belief that bridges were magical, and many stories grew up on how they were erected overnight by the Devil himself in the morning, in exchange for the first soul that ventured across. But Satan is a sucker in every instance; the wily Cividalesi outsmarted him by the usual ploy of sending over a cat at dawn. Just up from the bridge is the mysterious **Ipogeo Celtico** at Via Monastero 21(*the bar All'Ipogeo has the key; on Mon pick it up at the tourist office*). This dripping, creepy pit, the perfect setting for a nasty cult, may have served as a funeral chamber in the 3rd century BC, although no one's sure, because there is nothing to compare it to. Later the Romans and Lombards used it as a prison, where unfortunates would have had to look at the three monstrous, carved heads that peer out of the walls, seemingly from the dawn of time itself

Tempietto Longobardo

Follow the Natisone up to the happier **Tempietto Longobardo**, or Santa Maria in Valle (*open 9–1, 3–6.30, winter 10–1 and 3.30–5.30; adm*), the finest work of the eighth century in Italy, despite the fact that it had to be restored in the 13th century after an earthquake shattered three-quarters of its ornamentation and all of its mosaics. The stuccoes that remain, however, are a love letter from the Dark Ages, ravishing, uncanny, and perhaps even miraculous: a sextet of gently smiling saints and princesses in high relief, standing at either side of a beautiful and intricately carved window, all positioned over an even more intricately carved arch with a vine motif. Artistically, Europe wasn't to see the like again for 400 years. Under the stuccoes the carved and inlaid wooden choir dates from 1371, and there are some frescoes of the same period, replacing the mosaics; the *Adoration of the Magi* is lovely.

Cividale del Friuli ✉ 33043 — *Where to Stay and Eating Out*

The ivy-covered ***Locanda al Castello**, Via del Castello 20, ✆ 0432 733 242, ✉ 0432 700 901 (*moderate*), slightly outside the town in the suburb of Fortino, is not in a castle but a former fortified Jesuit seminary, and now offers Cividale's most atmospheric rooms, as well as a fine restaurant with views from its balcony. *Closed Nov, Feb.* Other choices are in the centre: the modern ***Roma**, Via G. Gallina, ✆ 0432 731 871, ✉ 0432 701 033 (*moderate*), without a restaurant, and the romantic **Locanda Pomo d'Oro**, in an 11th-century hostel, Piazza S. Giovanni 20, ✆/✉ 0432 734 189 (*inexpensive*).

Alla Frasca, Via di Rebeis 8a, ✆ 0432 731 270 (*moderate*) offers a charming Renaissance atmosphere to go with tasty Friulian dishes, including a *menu di funghi* that offers truffles and mushrooms with everything. *Closed Mon.* Also pleasant is **Al Fortino**, Via Carlo Alberto 46, ✆ 0432 731 217 (*moderate*), with typical Friuli fare and homemade pasta. *Closed Tues.* Behind the Duomo in Cividale **Trattoria Al Paradiso**, Via Cavour 21, ✆ 0432 732 438, is always full of locals. *Closed Mon.*

North of Ùdine: the Alpi Giulie and the Carnia

The mountainous north of Ùdine is linked to the city by a bright new *autostrada*, one of Italy's recent engineering marvels. It has yet to bring in the crowds. The valleys, especially in the eastern Julian Alps (named, of course, for Julius Caesar) are Slovene-speaking, their church towers crowned with colourful garlic domes. If the peaks lack the romance of their Dolomite neighbours, they also lack their crowds, lofty prices and resorts.

Tourist Information

Tarvisio: Via Roma 10, ✆ 0428 2135, ✉ 0428 2972; **Tolmezzo**: Piazza Centa 14, ✆/✉ 0433 44898; **Arta Terme**: Via Umberto I 15, ✆ 0433 929 290, ✉ 0433 92104; **Ravascletto**: Piazza Divisione Julia ✆ 0433 6647, ✉ 0433 66487; **Sauris** (in season): ✆ 0433 86076; **Forni di Sopra**: Via Cadore 1, ✆ 0433 886 767 ✉ 0433 886 686. For the Carnia in general: *www.carnia.org*, *apt@carnia.org*.

Towards the Julian Alps

Just off the *autostrada*, 20 minutes north of Ùdine, Gemona and Venzone were the epicentre of the '76 earthquake. Rather than move on, both were rebuilt with meticulous care, a labour of love that after 32 years is almost completed. Set in the Julian foothills, **Germona del Friuli**'s gem is a 13th-century cathedral, its façade decorated with a beautiful carved portal and a remarkable *St Christopher*, sculpted by a Nordic artist in 1331. **Venzone**, a smaller, double-walled town that began as a rest stop on the Julia Augusta road, was made a national monument in 1965. An exhibit under the painted ceiling of the loggia has astonishing before and after photographs. The Municipio had to be totally rebuilt not once, but twice, first in the 1950s after it was razed in the Second World War. Just west, **Bordano** and **Interneppo** by Lake Cavazzo are two villages always covered with butterflies—painted on the walls.

Venzone lies within the **Parco delle Prealpi Giulia**, a natural park extending to the east, with a large population of marmots, deer and ibex, which have been recently reintroduced; its centre is the Valle di Résia, just north of Venzone, where in the 6th century a wandering band of folk from Poland got stuck in its dead end and stayed; to this day they speak ancient Slav and preserve customs long forgotten in Poland itself.

The *autostrada* continues northeast into the Julian Alps, the most densely forested region in all Italy, where even the beech trees, overmolested by loggers to the south, still stand tall amid spruce, white and black pines and larches, the haunt of brown bears, lynx and eagles. The mountains around the pass at **Tarvisio** (near the Austrian and Slovenian frontiers) cradle an up-and-coming resort, **Sella Nevea**, south of Tarvisio, beyond the two pretty duck-filled lakes at the natural park in **Fusine**. You can get a ski pass here, good in the nearby resorts in Austria and Slovenia; at the time of writing, in fact, the three are pooling together as a tri-national candidate to host the 2006 Winter Olympics. One of the prettiest excursions is up to **Lago del Predil** under Monte Magante on the Slovenian border; another is to take the speedy *cabinova* up to the **Santuario del Monte Santo di Lussari**, where a Gothic Madonna has received pilgrims for centuries.

The Carnia

The Carnia mountains rise to the west, next-door neighbours and cousins to the Dolomites. **Tolmezzo**, an 18th-century producer of damasks and taffetas, is the main town and transportation hub of the mountains. Its old prosperity shows up in its stately streets and the rococo parish church with a giant archangel on the campanile. In a 16th-century palace in Piazza Garibaldi, the **Museo Carnico** (*open 9–1, 3–6 closed Mon*) has an exceptional ethnographic collection, covering mountain life from the 14th to the 19th centuries.

Beyond Tolmezzo the scenery grows increasingly delightful. **Arta Terme** to the north is a spa known since antiquity for its sulphurous waters, where Roman matrons came for beauty treatments and legionaries to soak their wounds. *Julium Carnicum*, the local Roman capital, stood at modern **Zuglio** just down the road from Arta; remains of the basilica and forum can still be seen, and finds are displayed in a smart new museum (although the finest pieces, the bronzes, are in the museum at Cividale). Further north, the district around **Paularo** is especially rich in *casolari*, traditional wooden multi-storeyed chalets that resemble walk-up barns. Northwest of Tolmezzo, the stone village of **Ravascletto** is the capital of the Valcalda and a ski resort; from **Comeglians** in the north of the valley there is a lovely scenic road up to Sappada in the Cadore (*see* p.243).

West of Tolmezzo, along the valley of the Tagliamento, **Socchieve** has one of the artistic jewels of the Carnia: the little 14th-century church of **San Martino**, with frescoes by Gianfrancesco da Tolmezzo (1493). Further west, **Ampezzo**, the second town of the Carnia, is where you can turn off on a road (only finished in 1950) that winds through the deep gorge of the Val Lumiei to **Sàuris**, now a small resort by a beautiful turquoise **lake**. Famous for its smoked hams, Sàuris (both Upper and Lower) was isolated for so long that it has preserved its medieval dialect as well as its medieval houses.

The road west up the Tagliamento crosses over the 'Pass of Death', where in 1844 volunteers from the Cadore heroically took on the Imperial army. Beyond is another typical Carnian church, with frescoes by Gianfrancesco da Tolmezzo, followed by **Forni di Sotto**, a village rebuilt after the Nazis burnt it to the ground in 1944 in reprisal for its partisan activities. They spared **Forni di Sopra**, the upper hamlet with stupendous front row views of the Eastern Dolomites. Its Romanesque church of **San Floriano** is covered with Gianfrancesco's very best frescoes, painted in in 1500, and has a striking 15th-century polyptych by Bellunello. From here the road crosses the Passo della Màuria into the Cadore (*see* pp.242–3).

Where to Stay and Eating Out

Tarvisio ✉ 33018

Nothing special here: ★★★**Valle Verde**, near the ski lifts at Via Priesnig 12, ✆ 042 82342 (*moderate*) has pretty views and a good restaurant featuring game and mushroom dishes in the autumn, open to non-guests. *Closed Mon, Nov–mid-Dec.*

Tolmezzo ✉ 33028

The place to stay and especially to eat in Tolmezzo is smack in the heart of town: ★★★**Roma**, Piazza XX Settembre 14, ✆ 043 32081, ✆ 043 343 316 (rooms *moderate*, restaurant *expensive*) where Friuli's top chef, Gianni Cosetti, holds forth, giving his clients gastronomic sweet dreams—try the traditional *toc in braide* (polenta with cheese), porcini mushroom dishes, pheasant cooked with fresh herbs and lovely desserts. *Closed Sun eve, Mon, some of June and Nov.*

Arta Terme ✉ 33022

★★★**Poldo**, Piano d'Arta, ✆ 043 392 056, ✆ 043 392 577 (*inexpensive*) enjoys a peaceful setting in the trees, with an exotic garden and lovely views down into the valley. *Open June–Oct.* Nearby, ★★**Salon**, Via Peresson 70, ✆ 043 392 003 (*inexpensive*) has more basic rooms, but an excellent restaurant, where mushrooms and fresh herbs are plentiful; stop here if you're just passing through. *Open May–Oct, restaurant closed Tues.*

Ravascletto ✉ 33020

Ravascletto is famous for its *cjarsons*, the favourite sweet and sour pasta of the Carnia: ★★★**Valcalda**, Viale Edelweiss 8, ✆ 043366120, ✆ 043366420 (*moderate*) is a good place to try it and to sleep in the able hands of a family in business for over 60 years; pretty views are a plus.

Sauris ✉ 33020

In a gorgeous setting, the traditional ★★★★**Rikhelan Haus**, Sauris di Sopra, ✆/✆ 0433 86082 (*expensive*) has kept all the best features of the past alongside modern amenities; there's an outdoor pool, but only seven rooms. *Open mid-June–mid-Oct, mid-Dec–mid-Mar.* ★★**Pa'Krhaizar**, Fraz. Lateis 5, ✆/✆ 0433 86165 (*moderate*), is a charming old house beautifully restored as an intimate hotel with an excellent restaurant. *Closed in May and Nov.*

atrium: entrance court of a Roman house or early church.

badia: *abbazia*, an abbey or abbey church.

baita: traditional wooden Alpine hut.

baldacchino: baldachin, a columned stone canopy above the altar of a church.

barchesse: wings of a Veneto villa orginally used as farm buildings, for storing grain or other supplies

basilica: a rectangular building, usually divided into three aisles by rows of columns. In Rome this was the common form for law courts and other public buildings, and Roman Christians adapted it for their early churches.

Calvary chapels: a series of outdoor chapels, usually on a hillside, that commemorate the stages of the Passion of Christ.

campanile: a bell tower.

cardo: transverse street of a Roman castrum-shaped city.

cartoon: the preliminary sketch for a fresco or tapestry.

caryatid: supporting pillar or column carved into a standing female form; male versions are called telamons.

castrum: a Roman military camp, always nearly rectangular, with straight streets and gates at the cardinal points. Later the Romans founded or refounded cities in the form, hundreds of which survive today (Verona and Padua are clear examples).

cavea: the semicircle of seats in a classical theatre.

cenacolo: fresco of the Last Supper, often on the wall of a monastery refectory.

centro storico: historic centre.

ciborium: a tabernacle; the word is often used for large, free-standing tabernacles, or in the sense of a baldacchino.

chiaroscuro: the arrangement or treatment of light and dark in a painting.

comune: commune, or commonwealth, referring to the governments of the free cities of the Middle Ages. Today it denotes any local government, form the Comune di Roma down to the smallest village.

condottiere: the leader of a band of mercenaries in late medieval and Renaissance times.

confraternity: a religious lay brotherhood, often serving as a neighbourhood mutual aid and burial society, or following some specific charitable work (Michelangelo, for example, belonged to one that cared for condemned prisoners in Rome).

cupola: a dome.

decumanus: street of a Roman castrum-shaped city parallel to the longer axis, the central, main avenue called the Decumanus Major.

Architectural, Artistic & Historical Terms

doss: hill, in Trentino.

duomo: cathedral.

erker: covered overhanging balcony, common in the Süd Tirol.

forum: the central square of a Roman town, with its most important temples and public buildings. The word means 'outside', as the original Roman Forum was outside the first city walls.

fresco: wall painting, the most important Italian medium of art since Etruscan times. It isn't easy: first the artist draws the sinopia (q.v.) on the wall. This is covered with plaster, but only a little at a time, as the paint must be on the plaster before it dries. Leonardo da Vinci's endless attempts to find clever shortcuts ensured that little of his work would survive.

Ghibellines: one of the two great medieval parties, the supporters of the Holy Roman Emperors.

gonfalon: the banner of a medieval free city; the gonfaloniere, or flag bearer was often the most important public official.

grotesques: carved or painted faces used in Etruscan and later Roman decoration; Raphael and other artist rediscovered them in the 'grotto' of Nero's Golden House in Rome.

Guelphs (see Ghibellines): the other great political faction of medieval Italy, supporters of the Pope.

intarsia: work in inlaid wood or marble.

intonaco: the stucco-like material covering the brick substructure of Palladio's villas.

malga: Alpine hut.

maso: traditional stone and wood Alpine farmhouse complexes.

monte di pietà: municipal pawn shop.

narthex: the enclosed porch of a church.

palazzo: not just a palace, but any large, important building (though the word comes from the Imperial palatium on Rome's Palatine Hill).

palio: a banner, and the horse race in which city neighbourhoods contend for it in their annual festivals.

Pantocrator: Christ 'ruler of all', a common subject for apse paintings and mosaics in areas influenced by Byzantine art.

piano: upper floor or story in a building; piano nobile, the first floor.

pieve: a parish church, especially in the north.

podestà: a mayor or governor from outside a comune, usually chosen by the emperor or overlord like Venice, although sometimes a factionalized city would itself invite a *podestà* in for a period to sort it out.

polyptych: an altarpiece composed of more than three panels.

predella: smaller paintings on panels below the main subject of a painted altarpiece.

presepio: a Christmas crib.

putti: flocks of plaster cherubs with rosy cheeks and bums that infested Baroque Italy.

quadriga: chariot pulled by four horses.

Quattrocento: the 1400s—the Italian way of referring to centuries (duecento, trecento, quattrocento, cinquecento, etc.).

rocca: a citadel.

Sacra Conversazione: Madonna enthroned with saints.

scuola: the headquarters of a confraternity or guild, usually adjacent to a church.

sinopia: the layout of a fresco (q.v.), etched by the artist on the wall before the plaster is applied. Often these are works of art in their own right.

stube: traditional Tyrolean panelled room, usually with a woodstove.

terra firma: Venice's mainland possessions.

thermae: Roman baths.

tondo: round relief, painting or terracotta.

transenna: marble screen separating the altar area from the rest of an early Christian church.

triptych: a painting, especially an altarpiece, in three sections.

trompe l'œil: art that uses perspective effects to deceive the eye—for example, to create the illusion of depth on a flat surface, or to make columns and arches painted on a wall see real.

tympanum: the semicircular space, often bearing a painting or relief, above a portal.

The fathers of modern Italian were Dante, Manzoni and television. Each played its part in creating a national language from an infinity of regional and local dialects; the Florentine Dante, the first to write in the vernacular, did much to put the Tuscan dialect into the foreground of Italian literature. Manzoni's revolutionary novel, *I Promessi Sposi*, heightened national consciousness by using an everyday language all could understand in the 19th century. Television in the last few decades has performed an even more spectacular linguistic unification; although many Italians still speak a dialect at home, school and work, their TV idols insist on proper Italian.

Italians are not especially apt at learning other languages. English lessons, however, have been the rage for years, and at most hotels and restaurants there will be someone who speaks some English. In small towns and out-of-the-way places, finding an Anglophone may prove more difficult. The words and phrases below should help you out in most situations, but the ideal way to come to Italy is with some Italian under your belt; your visit will be richer, and you're much more likely to make some Italian friends.

Pronunciation

Italian words are pronounced phonetically. Every vowel and consonant is sounded. Most consonants are the same as in English, exceptions are the c which, when followed by an 'e' or 'i', is pronounced like the English 'ch' (*cinque* thus becomes cheenquay). Italian g is also soft before 'i' or 'e' as in *giro*, or jee-roh. H is never sounded; r is trilled, like the Scottish r; z is pronounced like 'ts' or 'ds'. The consonants sc before the vowels 'i' or 'e' become like the English 'sh'; ch is pronouced like a 'k' as in Chianti; gn as 'nya' (thus *bagno* is pronounced ban-yo); while gli is pronounced like the middle of the word million (Castiglione, pronounced Ca-stil-yohn-ay).

Vowel pronunciation is as follows: a is as in English father; e when unstressed is pronounced like 'a' in fate as in *padre*, when stressed it can be the same or like the 'e' in pet (*bello*); i is like the 'i' in machine, o like 'e', has two sounds, 'o' as in hope when unstressed (*tacchino*), and usually 'o' as in rock when stressed (*morte*); u is pronounced like the 'u' in June. But beware of the Venetian accent where vowels and consonants are often slurred into a porridge of 'u's, 'v's, 'x's (pronounced 'sh') and 'z's.

The stress usually (but not always!) falls on the penultimate syllable.

Language

Useful Words and Phrases

yes/no/maybe	*sì/no/forse*	Speak slowly	*Parla lentamente*
I don't know	*Non lo so*	Could you assist me?	*Potrebbe aiutarmi?*
I don't understand	*Non capisco*	Help!	*Aiuto!*
(Italian)	(*italiano*)	Please	*Per favore*
Does someone here	*C'è qualcuno qui che*	Thanks (very much)	(*Molto*) *grazie*
speak English?	*parla inglese?*	You're welcome	*Prego*

It doesn't matter	*Non importa*	Why?	*Perché?*
All right	*Va bene*	How?	*Come?*
Excuse me	*Mi scusi*	How much?	*Quanto?*
Be careful!	*Attenzione!*	I am lost	*Mi sono smarrito*
Nothing	*Niente*	I am hungry	*Ho fame*
It is urgent!	*E urgente!*	I am thirsty	*Ho sete*
How are you?	*Come stai?* (informal)	I am sorry	*Mi dispiace*
	sta (formal)	I am tired	*Sono stanco*
Well, and you?	*Bene, e Lei?*	I am sleepy	*Ho sonno*
What is your name?	*Come si chiama, Lei?*	I am ill	*Mi sento male*
Hello	*Salve* or *ciao*	Leave me alone	*Lasciami in pace*
	(both informal)	good	*buono/bravo*
Good morning	*Buon giorno*	bad	*male/cattivo*
	(formal hello)	It's all the same	*Fa lo stesso*
Good afternoon,	*Buona sera* (also	slow	*lento/piano*
evening	formal hello)	fast	*rapido*
Good night	*Buona notte*	big	*grande*
Goodbye	*ArrivederLa* (formal)	small	*piccolo*
	Arrivederci (informal)	hot	*caldo*
What do you call	*Come si chiama*	cold	*freddo*
this in Italian?	*questo in italiano?*	up	*su*
What?	*Che cosa?*	down	*giù*
Who?	*Chi?*	here	*qui*
Where?	*Dove?*	there	*lì*
When?	*Quando?*		

Shopping, Service, Sightseeing

I would like ...	*Vorrei ...*	money	*soldi*
Where is/are?. . .	*Dov'è/Dove sono?...*	museum	*museo*
How much is it?	*Quanto via questo?*	newspaper (foreign)	*giornale* (*straniero*)
open	*aperto*	chemist	*farmacia*
closed	*chiuso*	police station	*commissariato*
cheap	*a buon mercato*	policeman	*poliziotto*
expensive	*caro*	post office	*ufficio postale*
bank	*banca*	sea	*mare*
beach	*spiaggia*	shop	*negozio*
bed	*letto*	telephone	*telefono*
church	*chiesa*	tobacco shop	*tabacchaio*
entrance	*entrata*	WC	*toilette/bagno*
exit	*uscita*	men	*Signori/Uomini*
hospital	*ospedale*	women	*Signore/Donne*

Time

What time is it?	*Che ore sono?*	today	*oggi*
month	*mese*	yesterday	*ieri*
week	*settimana*	tomorrow	*domani*
day	*giorno*	soon	*fra poco*
morning	*mattina*	later	*più tardi*
afternoon	*pomeriggio*	It is too early	*E troppo presto*
evening	*sera*	It is too late	*E troppo tardi*

Days

Monday	*lunedì*	Friday	*venerdì*
Tuesday	*martedì*	Saturday	*sabato*
Wednesday	*mercoledì*	Sunday	*domenica*
Thursday	*giovedì*		

Numbers

one	*uno/una*	twenty	*venti*
two	*due*	twenty-one	*ventuno*
three	*tre*	twenty-two	*ventidue*
four	*quattro*	thirty	*trenta*
five	*cinque*	thirty-one	*trentuno*
six	*sei*	forty	*quaranta*
seven	*sette*	fifty	*cinquanta*
eight	*otto*	sixty	*sessanta*
nine	*nove*	seventy	*settanta*
ten	*dieci*	eighty	*ottanta*
eleven	*undici*	ninety	*novanta*
twelve	*dodici*	hundred	*cento*
thirteen	*tredici*	one hundred and one	*cent'uno*
fourteen	*quattordici*	two hundred	*due cento*
fifteen	*quindici*	thousand	*mille*
sixteen	*sedici*	two thousand	*due mila*
seventeen	*diciasette*	million	*milione*
eighteen	*diciotto*	billion	*miliardo*
nineteen	*diciannove*		

Transport

airport	*aeroporto*	port station	*stazione maritimma*
bus stop	*fermata*	ship	*nave*
bus/coach	*autobus/pulmino*	automobile	*macchina*
railway station	*stazione (ferroviaria)*	taxi	*tassi*
train	*treno*	ticket	*biglietto*
train/platform	*binario*	customs	*dogana*
port	*porto*	seat (reserved)	*posto (prenotato)*

Travel Directions

I want to go to . . .	*Voglio andare a …*	When does the next train leave?	*Quando parte il prossimo treno?*
How can I get to…?	*Come posso arrivare a …?*	From where does it leave?	*Da dove parte?*
The next stop, please	*La prossima fermata, per favore*	How long does the trip take?	*Quanto tempo dura il viaggio?*
Where is … / where is it?	*Dove … /Dov'è?*	How much is the fare?	*Quant'è il biglietto?*
How far is it to …?	*Quanto siamo lontani da … ?*	Have a good trip!	*Buon viaggio!*
What is the name of this station?	*Come si chiama questa stazione?*	near	*vicino*
		far	*lontano*

left	*sinistra*	south	*sud/mezzogiorno*
right	*destra*		(the South of Italy)
straight ahead	*sempre diritto*	east	*est/oriente*
forward	*avanti*	west	*ovest/occidentale*
back	*indietro*	around the corner	*dietro l'angolo*
north	*nord/settentrionale*	crossroads	*bivio*
	(the North of Italy)	street/road	*strada*
		square	*piazza*

Driving

car hire	*noleggio macchina*	breakdown	*panna*
motorbike/scooter	*motocicletta/Vespa*	driver's licence	*patente di guida*
bicycle	*bicicletta*	driver	*guidatore*
petrol/diesel	*benzina/gasolio*	speed	*velocità*
garage	*garage*	danger	*pericolo*
This doesn't work	*Questo non*	parking	*parcheggio*
	funziona	no parking	*divieto di sosta*
mechanic	*meccanico*	narrow	*stretto*
map/town plan	*carta/pianta*	bridge	*ponte*
Where is the	*Dov'è la strada*	toll	*pedaggio*
road to . . . ?	*per. . . ?*	to slow down	*rallentare*

Italian Menu Vocabulary

Antipasti

These appetizers can include almost anything, among the most common are:

antipasto misto	mixed antipasto	*gamberi ai fagioli*	prawns with beans
bruschetta	toast with garlic and	*mozzarella*	cow or buffalo
	tomatoes	(*in carrozza*)	cheese (fried with
carciofi (*sott'olio*)	artichokes (in oil)		bread in batter)
crostini	liver pâté on toast	*olive*	olives
frutti di mare	seafood	*prosciutto*	raw ham
funghi (*trifolati*)	mushrooms (with	(*con melone*)	(with melon)
	anchovies, garlic	*salame*	cured pork
	and lemon)	*salsiccia*	sausage

Minestre e Pasta

These dishes are the principal first courses (*primi piatti*) served throughout Italy.

agnolotti	meat-filled pasta	*minestrone*	soup with meat,
cacciucco	spiced fish soup		vegetables and pasta
cappelletti	small ravioli, often	*orecchiette*	ear-shaped pasta,
	in broth		often served with
crespelle	crêpes		turnip greens
fettuccine	long strips of pasta	*panzerotti*	ravioli filled with
frittata	omelette		mozzarella,
gnocchi	potato dumplings		anchovies and egg
minestra di verdura	thick vegetable soup	*pappardelle alla*	flat pasta ribbons
		lepre	with hare sauce

pasta e fagioli	soup with beans, bacon and tomatoes	spaghetti alla carbonara	with bacon, eggs and black pepper
pastina in brodo	tiny pasta in broth	al pomodoro	with tomato sauce
penne all'arrabbiata	pasta tubes in spicy tomato sauce	al sugo/ragù	with meat sauce
		alle vongole	with clam sauce
polenta	cake or pudding of corn semolina, fried, baked or grilled	stracciatella	broth with eggs and cheese
risotto	rice cooked with	tagliatelle	flat egg noodles
(alla Milanese)	stock, saffron and wine	tortellini al pomodoro/	stuffed rings of pasta filled with meat
spaghetti all'	with tomatoes, bacon	panna/	and cheese, served
Amatriciana	and garlic, plus pecorino cheese	in brodo	with tomato sauce, cream, or in broth
		vermicelli	very thin spaghetti

Second Courses—*Carne* (Meat)

abbacchio	milk-fed lamb	lepre (in salmi)	hare (marinated in wine, herbs etc)
agnello	lamb		
anatra	duck	lombo di maiale	pork loin
animelle	sweetbreads	lumache	snails
arista	pork loin	maiale (al latte)	pork (cooked in milk)
arrosto misto	mixed roast meats	manzo	beef
bistecca alla Fiorentina	Florentine beef steak	osso buco	braised veal knuckle with herbs
bocconcini	veal mixed with ham and cheese and fried	pancetta	bacon
bollito misto	stew of boiled meats	pernice	partridge
braciola	pork chop	petto di pollo	boned chicken breast
brasato di manzo	braised beef	(alla Fiorentina/	(fried in butter/
bresaola	dried salt beef served with lemon, olive oil and parsley	Bolognese/ Sorpresa)	with ham and stuffed and deep fried)
capretto	kid	piccione	pigeon
capriolo	roe buck	pizzaiola	beef steak with tomato and oregano sauce
carne di castrato/suino	mutton/pork	pollo	chicken
carpaccio	thin slices of raw beef served like bresaola	(alla cacciatora/ alla diavola/	(with tomatoes and mushrooms cooked in
cassoeula	winter stew with pork and cabbage	al Marengo)	wine/grilled/fried with tomatoes, garlic & wine)
Cervello	brains	polpette	meatballs
(al burro nero)	(in black butter sauce)	quaglie	quails
cervo	venison	rane	frogs
cinghiale	boar	rognoni	kidneys
coniglio	rabbit	saltimbocca	veal scallop with
cotoletta	veal cutlet (fried in		prosciutto and sage,
(alla Milanese/	breadcrumbs/with		cooked in pieces of
alla Bolognese)	ham and cheese)		beef or veal, usually
fagiano	pheasant		stewed
faraona (alla creta)	guinea fowl (in earthenware pot)	stufato	beef braised in white wine with vegetables
fegato alla veneziana	liver and onions	tacchino	turkey
involtini	rolled slices of veal with filling	trippa	tripe
		vitello	veal

Pesce (Fish)

acciughe or alici	anchovies	merluzzo	cod
anguilla	eel	nasello	hake
aragosta	lobster	orata/dorata	gilthead
aringhe	herrings	ostrice	oysters
baccalà	salt cod	pesce azzuro	various small fish
bonito	small tuna	pesce S. Pietro	John Dory
branzino	sea bass	pesce spada	swordfish
calamari	squid	polipi	octopus
conchiglie	scallops	rombo	turbot
cefalo	grey mullet	sarde	sardines
cozze	mussels	seppie	cuttlefish
datteri di mare	razor (or date) mussels	sgombro	mackerel
		sogliola	sole
dentice	dentex (perch-like fish)	squadro	monkfish
		tonno	tuna
fritto misto	mixed fish fry, with squid and shrimp	triglia	red mullet (rouget)
		trota	trout
gamberetto	shrimp	trota salmonata	salmon trout
gamberi (di fiume)	prawns (crayfish)	vongole	small clams
granchio	crab	zuppa di pesce	mixed fish in sauce or stew
insalata di mare	seafood salad		
lampre	lamprey		

Contorni (Side Dishes, Vegetables)

asparagi (alla Fiorentina)	asparagus (with fried eggs)	lattuga	lettuce
		lenticchie	lentils
broccoli (calabrese, romana)	broccoli (green, spiral)	melanzane (al forno)	aubergine/eggplant (filled and baked)
carciofi (alla giudia)	artichokes (deep fried)	patate (fritte)	potatoes (fried)
		peperonata	stewed peppers, onions and tomatoes
cardi	cardoons, thistles		
carote	carrots	peperoni	sweet peppers
cavolfiore	cauliflower	piselli (al prosciutto)	peas (with ham)
cavolo	cabbage	pomodoro	tomato
ceci	chickpeas	porri	leeks
cetriolo	cucumber	radicchio	red chicory
cipolla	onion	radiche	radishes
fagioli	white beans	rapa	turnip
fagiolini	French (green) beans	sedano	celery
fave	broad beans	spinaci	spinach
finocchio	fennel	verdure	greens
funghi (porcini)	mushroom (boletus)	zucca	pumpkin
insalata	salad	zucchini	courgettes

Formaggio (Cheese)

Bel Paese	soft, white cow's cheese	fontina	rich cow's milk cheese
cascio/ casciocavallo	pale yellow, often sharp cheese	groviera	mild cheese
		Gorgonzola	soft blue cheese

Parmigiano	Parmesan cheese	*provolone*	sharp, tangy cheese;
pecorino	sharp sheep's		*dolce* is more mild
	cheese	*stracchino*	soft white cheese

Frutta (Fruit, Nuts)

albicocche	apricots	*mandorle*	almonds
ananas	pineapple	*melograna*	pomegranate
arance	oranges	*mele*	apples
banane	bananas	*melone*	melon
cachi	persimmon	*more*	blackberries
ciliege	cherries	*nespola*	medlar fruit
cocomero	watermelon	*nocciole*	hazelnuts
composta di frutta	stewed fruit	*noci*	walnuts
dattero	date	*pera*	pear
fichi	figs	*pesca*	peach
fragole (*con*	strawberries (with	*pesca noce*	nectarine
panna)	cream)	*pompelmo*	grapefruit
frutta di stagione	fruit in season	*pignoli*	pine nuts
lamponi	raspberries	*susina*	plum
macedonia di frutta	fruit salad	*prugna secca*	prune
mandarino	tangerine	*uve*	grapes

Dolci (Desserts)

Amaretti	macaroons	*panforte*	dense cake of
cannoli	crisp pastry tube		chocolate, almonds
	filled with ricotta,		and preserved fruit
	cream, chocolate or	*Saint Honoré*	meringue cake
	fruit	*semifreddo*	refrigerated cake
coppa	assorted ice cream	*sorbetto*	sorbet
crema caramella	crème caramel	*spumone*	a soft ice cream or
crostata	fruit flan		mousse
gelato (*produzione*	ice cream	*tiramisù*	mascarpone, coffee,
propria)	(homemade)		chocolate and
granita	flavoured ice,		sponge fingers
	usually lemon or	*torrone*	nougat
	coffee	*torta*	tart
Monte Bianco	chestnut pudding	*torta millefoglie*	layered custard tart
	with whipped cream	*zabaglione*	whipped eggs, sugar
Panettone	sponge cake with		and Marsala wine,
	candied fruit and		served hot
	raisins	*Zuppa Inglese*	trifle

Drinks

acqua minerale	mineral water	*latte*	milk
con/senza gas	with/without fizz	(*magro*)	(skimmed)
aranciata	orange soda	*limonata*	lemon soda
birra (*alla spina*)	beer (draught)	*sugo di frutta*	fruit juice
caffè (*freddo*)	coffee (iced)	*tè*	tea
cioccolata	hot chocolate	*vino* (*rosso, bianco,*	wine (red, white, rosé)
(*con panna*)	(with cream)	*rosato*)	

Cooking Terms, Miscellaneous

aceto (balsamico)	vinegar (balsamic)	*mostarda*	sweet mustard sauce, served with meat
affumicato	smoked		
aglio	garlic	*olio*	oil
ai ferri	grilled	*pane (tostato)*	bread (toasted)
al forno	baked	*panini*	sandwiches
alla brace	braised	*panna*	fresh cream
arrosto	roasted	*pepe*	pepper
bicchiere	glass	*peperoncini*	hot chilli peppers
burro	butter	*piatto*	plate
cacciagione	game	*prezzemolo*	parsley
conto	bill	*rosmarino*	rosemary
costoletta/cotoletta	chop	*sale*	salt
coltello	knife	*salmi*	wine marinade
cucchiaio	spoon	*salsa*	sauce
filetto	fillet	*salvia*	sage
forchetta	fork	*senape*	mustard
forno	oven	*tartufi*	truffles
fritto	fried	*tazza*	cup
ghiaccio	ice	*tavola*	table
limone	lemon	*tovagliolo*	napkin
magro	lean meat/or pasta without meat	*tramezzini*	finger sandwiches
		in umido	stewed
marmellata	jam	*uovo*	egg
miele	honey	*zucchero*	sugar

Barzini, Luigi, *The Italians* (Athenaeum, 1996). A perhaps too clever account of the Italians by an Italian journalist living in London in the 1960s, but one of the classics.

Burckhardt, Jacob, *The Civilisation of the Renaissance in Italy* (Phaidon, 1995). The classic on the subject (first published 1860), the mark against which scholars still level their poison arrows of revisionism.

Calvino, Italo, *Invisible Cities* (Harcourt Brace 1986). Provocative fantasies woven around Marco Polo and Kublai Khan that could only have been written by an Italian. Something even better is his compilation of *Italian Folktales*, a little bit Brothers Grimm and a little bit Fellini.

Dante, Aligheri, *The Divine Comedy* (trans. by Mark Musa, 1971–84, Penguin). Few poems have ever had such a mythical significance for a nation. Anyone serious about understanding Italy and the Italian world view will need more than a passing acquaintance with Dante.

Goethe, J. W., *Italian Journey* (Penguin Classics, 1992). An excellent example of a genius turned to mush by Italy; brilliant insights and big, big mistakes.

Hale, J. R., editor, *A Concise Encyclopaedia of the Italian Renaissance* (Thames & Hudson, 1981). An excellent reference guide, with concise, well written essays.

Lane, Frederic C., Venice, *A Maritime Republic* (Johns Hopkins, 1973, out of print). The most thorough history of the republic in English.

Lauritzen, Peter and Wolf, Reinhart, *Villas of the Veneto* (Pavilion, 1988). Lush pictures and light descriptions.

Levy, Michael, *Early Renaissance* (1967) and *High Renaissance* (1975), both by Penguin. Old fashioned accounts of the period, with a breathless reverence for the 1500s—and full of intriguing interpretations.

Littlewood, Ian, *A Literary Companion to Venice* (St Martin's Press, 1995). Concentrated dose of Venetian inspiration.

McCarthy, Mary, *Stones of Florence and Venice Observed* (Penguin, 1986). Brilliant evocations of Italy's two greatest art cities, with an understanding that makes many other works on the subject seem sluggish.

Morris, Jan, *Venice* (*The World of Venice* in the USA, Harcourt Brace, 1995). A beautifully written classic on the World's Most Beautiful City; also *The Venetian Empire* (Penguin, 1990).

Norwich, John Julius, *A History of Venice* (Penguin, 1983). A classic, wittily written account of the Serenissima.

Murray, Linda, *The High Renaissance* and *The Late Renaissance* and *Mannerism* (Thames & Hudson, 1983). Excellent introduction to the period.

Parks, Tim, *Italian Neighbours* (1993) *An Italian Education* (1995). Grove/Avon Books. Humorous accounts of real life in Montecchio near Verona by a scholar-novelist from Manchester married to an Italian.

Petrarch, Francesco, *The Canzoniere, or Rerum vulgarium fragmenta;* bilingual verse translation with notes and commentary by Mark Musa (Indiana University Press, 1996). Among the most influential works in western literature; Petrarch, 'the first modern man', created the archetype of the hapless lover among many other things.

Procacci, Giuliano, *History of the Italian People* (Penguin, sadly out of print). An in-depth view from the year 1000 to the present—also an introduction to the wit and subtlety of the best Italian scholarship.

Rilke, Rainer Maria *Duino Elegies* (translated by C.V. MacIntyre, University of California 1989). With helpful hints to help with the understanding.

Steer, John, *A Concise History of Venetian Painting* (Thames and Hudson, 1984). A well illustrated introduction.

Vasari, Giorgio, Lives of the Artists (Oxford World Classics, 1998). Readable, anecdotal accounts of the Renaissance greats by the father of art history, also the first professional Philistine.

Further Reading

Wittkower, Rudolf, *Art and Architecture in Italy 1600–1750* (Pelican, 1992). The classic on Italian Baroque. Also *Architectural Principles in the Age of Humanism* with lots of insights into Palladio's villas (John Wiley and Sons, 1998).

Zorzi, Alvise, *Venice: City–Republic–Empire* (Sidgwick & Jackson, 1980). Beautifully illustrated, with a large section on Venice's dealings in the Veneto and eastern Mediterranean.

Index

chemists 31
Chienes: Castel Badia/Sonnenburg,
    Casteldarne/Ehrenburg & San
    Lorenzo di Sebato 284
Chiericati, Ludovivo 188
Chioggia 23, 24, 45, 130–1
    Alberoni 130
    Corso del Popolo 130
    Duomo 130
    Granaio 130
    Malamocco 130
    murazzi 130
    Pellestrina 130
    San Domenico 130
    San Pietro in Volta 130
    Sottomarina 130
    War/Battle of 49, 73, 81, 305
Chirico, Giorgio de 59, **60**
Chiusa/Klausen 283
    Convento dei Cappuccini 282
    Monastero di Sabiona 281–2
    Santa Croce and S. Andrea 282
Christian Democrats 53
Church
    history of *see* Council of Trent;
        Crusades; Inquisition; papacy
    opening hours of churches 32–3
Cima da Conegliano (Giovanni Battista)
    57, **60**, 105, 106, 109, 111, 113,
    158, 183
Cima, Giambattista 231
Cima Grappa 173
Cima Tosa 265
Cimasappada 243
Cimoláis 297
cinema 53
Cinque Torri 278
Cisalpine Republic 50–1
Cisano 226
Cittadella 24
Civetta, Il 99
Civezzano 257
    Pieve dell'Assunta 258
Cividale del Friuli 22, 56, 258, 292,
    316, 318–20
    Duomo 318–19
    Palazzo Communale 318
    Piazza Duomo 318
Claut 297
Clement VII, Pope 50, 68
Cles 270
    Castello Cles & San Vigilio 268
Cles, Prince-Bishop Bernardo 251–2,
    254, 255, 257–8, 262, 268
climate and when to go 20, 78–9
coach travel *see* bus
Codroipo: Villa Manin 298
Codussi, Mauro 57, **60**, 90, 91, 94
    Grand Canal 100, 108, 109, 110,
    112
    Lido and Lagoon 131
Col di Lana 278
Col Rodella 261
Collabo/Klobenstein 275
Colle Isarco/Gossensass: Santa Barbara
    286

Colle Santa Lucia 247
Collio 314–15
Cologna Veneta 25, 208
Colonna, Francesco 182
Colonna, Mengozzi 186
Comeglians 321
Comelico 246
Comini, Giovanni 151
Communists 53
comuni 47, 65–6, 323
Concordia Sagittaria 45, 295
Conegliano and area 60, 231–2, 233
    Casa di Cima 231
    Duomo 231–2
    Sala dei Battuti 232
    Strada del Prosecco 232
    Via Venti Settembre 232
Congress of Vienna 51, 82
Conselve: Villa Sagredo 159
Constantine, Holy Roman Emperor 45,
    56, 98, 185
Constantinople and Byzantium 48, 79,
    80, 81
consulates 21–2
Copper Age megalthic tomb 189
Córedo: Castel Bragher & Palazzo Nero
    269
Cormòns: Cantina Prodottori Vini 315
Cornaro, Luigi (Alvise) 140, 142, 152
Corno del Doge 246
Cortina d'Ampezzo and area 22, 24,
    244–8
    excursions 246–8
Corvara in Badia 279, 280
Costa, Lorenzo 147
Costagno, Andrea del **60**
Costozza di Longare: Villas Eolia, da
    Schio and Trento Carli 193
Council of Trent 50, 58, 68–9, 74
Counter-Reformation 50
Cranach, Lucas the Elder 307
Creazzo: Villa Fedinelli Seppiej 189
Cricoli: Villa Badoer–Trissino 188
crime 20–1
Crivelli, Carlo 57, **61**, 105, 202
Crocetta del Montello 166
Crusades 47–8, 65, 66, 80
currency 11
customs 11
cycling 18, 129, 138, 179, 197

Dandolo, Doges 80, 98, 143
Dante Alighieri 110, 143, 146, 172,
    202–3
Dark Ages 46–7, 56
Dasindo 264
Depero, Furtunato **61**, 249–50
Desenzano del Garda 64, 217–18
    High Speed Monument, Santa Maria
    Maddalena & Villa Romana 217
disabled travellers 21
Dobbiaco/Toblach 246, 247, 248
Dolada, Monte 242
Dolegna del Collio 315
Dolo 35, 142

Dolomites 237–90
    Brenta 263–7
    foothills *see* North of Padua
    history 47
    map 238–9
    museums and galleries
        Alto Adige 271, 282, 284–5, 286,
        287, 288, 292–3
        Bolzano and area 273–5, 277, 280
        Cadore 242, 244, 247
        Noce valley 268, 269
        Trentino 249–50, 253–6, 261,
        262, 264
        see also Alto Adige; Bolzano;
        Cadore; Cortina d'Ampezzo; Piave
        Valley; Trentino; Trento
Donatello 49, 57, **61**, 107, 111, 151–2
Donato, Nicolò 318
Dondi, Giovanni 143, 150
Dont 247
Dorigny, Ludovico 188
Doss delle Strie 262
Drena 25
    Castello 223
drink *see* food and drink
Dro 223
Due Carrare: Castello di San Pelagio 156
Duino 310, 312
Dürer, Albrecht 67, 262, 281–2, 316

eating out *see* food and drink
Egna/Neumarkt: Nostra Signora 271
embassies 21–2
emergencies 20, 31
Emilia-Romagna
    history 51
Enoteca Regionale Serenissima 315
entry formalities 10–11
Erto 23
Este 35, 44, 45, 55, 155, 157–8
    Castello dei Carraresi 158
    Duomo 158
    Piazza Maggiore 158
    San Martino 158
    Villa de Kunkler 158
Este family 47, 161
Euganean Hills 155–9
    Abbazia di Santo Stefano 156
    museums and galleries 158
    see also Arquà Petrarca; Battaglia
    Terme; Este; Monsélice; Teolo;
    Valsanzibo
exhibitions and art festivals 125
    see also festivals; museums and
    galleries
Ezzelini 47
Ezzelino da Romano 48, 65–6, 143,
    148, 153, 157, 158, 164, 196

Fabriano, Gentile da 67
Fai della Paganella 263, 264
Falcade 260
Falconetto, Giovanni Maria **61**, 69, 150,
    152, 155, 188
Fanzolo 64, 166
    Villa Emo 164–5

San Martino di Castrozza and area 259–60
Pale di San Martino 259
San Martino Monteneve 286
San Michele all'Adige 264, 265
San Michele d'Appiano 272
San Michele island: San Michele in Isola 131
San Pietro di Cadore: Palazzo Poli-de Pol 243
San Pietro di Feletto 232
San Sigismondo 284
San Vito 165
  Duomo 297
  Santa Maria dei Battuta 297–8
San Vito di Cadore 242, 243
San Zeno di Montagna 211
San Zenone degli Ezzelini 35
Sanctuary of SS. Vittore e Corona 236
Sansovino, Jacopo (Jacopo Tatti) 58, **63**, 91
  Veneto 151, 158, 159
  Venice 99, 100, 101, 103, 130
Santa Cristina di Valgardena/Sankt Christina in Gröden 279, 280, 281
Santa Croce, Lago di 235
Santa Giustina lake 268
Santa Lucia di Piave 25
Santa, Pietro and Caterina Leopoldo della 147
Santacroce, Girolamo 155
Sant'Ambrogio di Valpolicella 210, 212
Sant'Anna d'Alfaedo 210
Santi, Andriolo de 185
Santo Stefano di Cadore 242, 243
Santorso: Villa Bonifacio Rossi 175
Santuario della Madonna della Corona 211
Santuario de Monte Grisa 311
Santuario del Monte Santo di Lussari 321
Santuario di San Romedio 268
Sanzeno 268
Saonara 61
  Giardino Storico di Villa Valmarana 140
Sappada 242, 243
Sardagna 256
Sarpi, Paolo 68–9, 72, 131
Sasso di Stria 278
Sassolungo 278, 280
Sàuris 320, 321, 322
della Scala (Scaligeri) family 196, 199, 215, 222, 225
Scamozzi, Vincenzo 58, **63**, 71, 149, 157, 179, 181, 184, 187, 192
Scarpa, Carlo 165
Scarpagnino 107
Schio: Duomo, Fabbrica Alta, Nuova Schio & San Francesco 175
Sclìliar 277
Scorzè 165
Scudelletta Gorge 192
sea
  travel 84, 306
  see also boats
  Venice's battle with 82–3, 130

Sebastiano del Piombo (Sebastiano Luciani) **63**
Second World War see under wars
Segonzano 262
Sella Nevea 321
Sella Ronda 280
Selva di Cadore 247, 248
Selva di Valgardena/Wölkenstein in Gröden 279, 280, 281
Senales 23
Sesto 246
Sesto al Règhena 56
  Santa Maria in Silvis 295
Sgonico 311
Shelley, Percy Bysshe 138–9, 158
ships see boat and ships
shopping 34–5, 326
  opening hours 32
  Venice 114–16
Sicilian Vespers 48
Sigurtà, Dr Count Carlo 207
Silvio, Giampiero 147
Sirmione 55, 214–16
  Grotte di Catullo 215
  Rocca Scaligera 214–15
  San Pietro in Mavino 215
  Santa Maria Maggiore 215
  Stablimento Termale Catulo 215
Sistiana 310
Siusi/Seis 278–9
  San Valentino 277
skiing 36, 241, 244, 270, 278, 280
Sluderno/Schludrens: Castel Coira 288
Soave 23, 25, 35
  Castle of Scaligers 193
  Enoteca del Castello 193
Socchieve: San Martino 321
Solda/Sulden 289, 290
Soprabolzano/Oberbozen 275
Sopracastello 169
Sossano 192
South of Padua 154–62
  see also Euganean Hills; Little Mesopotamia
Sovizzo: Villa Sale di San Damiano Curti 189
special-interest holidays 11–13
Speranza, Giovanni 183
Spilimbergo 296, 298, 299
Spluga della Preta 210
Spormaggiore 269
sports and activities 35–7, 117, 129
  see also skiing
Squarcione, Francesco **63**, 147, 148
Stefano da Verona 57, **63**, 201, 202
Stelvio National Park 267, 289
Strà 63
  Villa Foscari-Negrelli-Rossi 140
  Villa Nazionale/Pisani 139–40
Stranghe 286
Strozzi, Bernardo 160, 314
students and youth travel 7
Süd Tirol see Alto Adige
Summaga: Santa Maria Maggiore 295
swimming 129

Tagliamento River 297–8

Taglio di Po 162
Taio 269
Tambre 235
Tarcento 22
Tàrres/Tarsch 288
Tarvisio 25, 320, 321, 322
Tassullo: Castel Nanno, Castel Valèr & S. Vigilio 269
telephones 37
Tempietto Longobardo 319–20
tennis 36, 129
Teolo 23, 24, 155, 157
  Abbazia di Praglia 155
Termeno sulla Strada del Vino/Tramin an der Weinstrasse 271
Tesero: San Rocco 262
theatre 123
Theodore, Saint 79, 300
Thiene: Natività & Villa de Porta Colleoni 174
Tiepolo, Giambattista 55, 58, 61, 62, **63**
  Dolomites 283
  Trieste 308, 316, 317
  Veneto 159, 217
    Brenta Canal 139–40
    Monti Bérici 191, 192
    Padua 147, 148
    Vicenza 181, 184, 186, 189
  Venice 105, 106, 107, 109, 111, 113, 130, 132
Tiepolo, Giandomenico **64**, 184, 186–7, 317
Timavo river 311
time and days 37, 326–7
Tintoretto (Jacopo Robusti) 58, **64**, 101, 105, 106, 107, 114, 147, 314
Tione: San Vigilio 264
Tires 277
Tirolo 25
  Castel Fontana 288
  Castel Scena 288
  Castel Tirol 287
  San Giorgio 288
  Scena 288
Titian (Tiziano Vecellio) 58, 60, 61, 62, **64**
  Dolomites 242
  Trieste 314
  Veneto 147, 152, 200, 232
  Venice 91, 103, 105, 106, 107, 112–13
Toblino, Lake 264, 265
Toc 242
Tofana di Mezzo 244
toilets 37
Tolmezzo 320, 321, 322
Tolmezzo, Gianfrancesco da 297, 321, 322
Tominz, Giuseppe 314
Tommaso da Modena 57, **64**, 202, 228, 229, 230
Tondi di Faloria 244
Torbole 223, 224
Torcello (island of ghosts) 56, 133
  Santa Fosca & Chair of Attila 133
  Santa Maria Assunta, Cathedral of 133

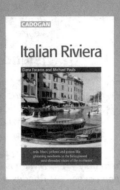
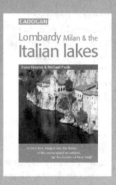

Also Available from Cadogan Guides...

Country Guides

Antarctica
Belize
Central Asia
China: The Silk Routes
Egypt
France: Southwest France;
    Dordogne, Lot & Bordeaux
France: Southwest France;
    Gascony & the Pyrenees
France: Brittany
France: The South of France
France: The Loire
Germany: Bavaria
India
India: South India
India: Goa
Ireland
Ireland: Southwest Ireland
Ireland: Northern Ireland
Italy
Italy: The Bay of Naples and Southern Italy
Italy: Lombardy, Milan and the Italian Lakes
Italy: Venetia and the Dolomites
Italy: Tuscany and Umbria
Japan
Morocco
Portugal
Portugal: The Algarve
Scotland
Scotland's Highlands and Islands
South Africa, Swaziland and Lesotho
Spain
Spain: Southern Spain
Spain: Northern Spain
Syria & Lebanon
Tunisia
Turkey
Western Turkey
Yucatán and Southern Mexico
Zimbabwe, Botswana and Namibia

City Guides

Amsterdam
Brussels, Bruges, Ghent & Antwerp
Florence, Siena, Pisa & Lucca
Italy: Three Cities—Rome, Florence & Venice
London
Manhattan
Moscow & St Petersburg
Paris
Prague
Rome
Venice

Island Guides

Caribbean and Bahamas
NE Caribbean; The Leeward Is.
SE Caribbean; The Windward Is.
Jamaica & the Caymans

Greek Islands
Crete
Mykonos, Santorini & the Cyclades
Rhodes & the Dodecanese
Corfu & the Ionian Islands

Madeira & Porto Santo
Malta
Sicily

Plus...

Southern Africa on the Wild Side
Bugs, Bites & Bowels
Travel by Cargo Ship
London Markets

Available from good bookshops or via, in the UK, **Grantham Book Services**, Isaac Newton Way, Alma Park Industrial Estate, Grantham NG31 9SD, ℡ (01476) 541 080, ✆ 541 061; and in North America from **The Globe Pequot Press**, 6, Business Park Road, Old Saybrook, Connecticut 06475-0833, ℡ (800) 243 0495, ✆ 820 2329.